CIMA Official
Learning System

PUBLISHING

Strategic Level

E3 – Enterprise Strategy

Neil Botten

ELSEVIER

AMSTERDAM   BOSTON   HEIDELBERG   LONDON   NEW YORK   OXFORD
PARIS   SAN DIEGO   SAN FRANCISCO   SINGAPORE   SYDNEY   TOKYO

CIMA Publishing is an imprint of Elsevier
The Boulevard, Langford Lane, Kidlington, Oxford, OX5 1GB
30 Corporate Drive, Suite 400, Burlington, MA 01803, USA

First edition 2008
Reprinted 2011

British Library Cataloguing in Publication Data
A catalogue record for this book is available from the British Library

Library of Congress Cataloguing in Publication Data
A catalogue record for this book is available from the Library of Congress

ISBN: 978-1-85617-782-5

For information on all CIMA publications
visit our website at www.elsevierdirect.com

Typeset by Macmillan Publishing Solutions
(www.macmillansolutions.com)

Printed and bound in China

11   12   13   14   15   7   6   5   4   3   2

Working together to grow
libraries in developing countries
www.elsevier.com | www.bookaid.org | www.sabre.org

ELSEVIER   BOOK AID International   Sabre Foundation

Contents

CONTENTS

The CIMA *Learning System*

Acknowledgements

Every effort has been made to contact the holders of copyright material, but if any here have been inadvertently overlooked the publishers will be pleased to make the necessary arrangements at the first opportunity. Neil Botten wishes to thank previous authors for their work. He also wishes to thank those whose kindness, affection and support has been beyond valuation.

How to use your CIMA *Learning System*

This *E3 Enterprise Strategy Learning System* has been devised as a resource for students attempting to pass their CIMA exams and provides:

- a detailed explanation of all syllabus areas;
- extensive 'practical' materials, including readings from relevant journals;
- generous question practice, together with full solutions;
- an exam preparation section, complete with exam standard questions and solutions.

This Learning System has been designed with the needs of home-study and distance-learning candidates in mind. Such students require very full coverage of the syllabus topics, and also the facility to undertake extensive question practice. However, the *Learning System* is also ideal for fully taught courses.

The main body of the text is divided into a number of chapters, each of which is organised on the following pattern:

- *Detailed learning outcomes* expected after your studies of the chapter are complete. You should assimilate these before beginning detailed work on the chapter, so that you can appreciate where your studies are leading.
- *Step-by-step topic coverage.* This is the heart of each chapter, containing detailed explanatory text supported where appropriate by worked examples and exercises. You should work carefully through this section, ensuring that you understand the material being explained and can tackle the examples and exercises successfully. Remember that in many cases knowledge is cumulative: if you fail to digest earlier material thoroughly, you may struggle to understand later chapters.

THE CIMA LEARNING SYSTEM

- *Readings and activities.* Most chapters are illustrated by more practical elements, such as relevant journal articles or other readings, together with comments and questions designed to stimulate discussion.
- *Question practice.* The test of how well you have learned the material is your ability to tackle exam-standard questions. Make a serious attempt at producing your own answers, but at this stage don't be too concerned about attempting the questions in exam conditions. In particular, it is more important to absorb the material thoroughly by completing a full solution than to observe the time limits that would apply in the actual exam.
- *Solutions.* Avoid the temptation merely to 'audit' the solutions provided. It is an illusion to think that this provides the same benefits as you would gain from a serious attempt of your own. However, if you are struggling to get started on a question you should read the introductory guidance provided at the beginning of the solution, and then make your own attempt before referring back to the full solution.

Having worked through the chapters you are ready to begin your final preparations for the examination. The final section of this CIMA Learning System provides you with the guidance you need. It includes the following features:

- A brief guide to revision technique.
- A note on the format of the examination. You should know what to expect when you tackle the real exam, and in particular the number of questions to attempt, which questions are compulsory and which optional, and so on.
- Guidance on how to tackle the examination itself.
- A table mapping revision questions to the syllabus learning outcomes allowing you to quickly identify questions by subject area.
- Revision questions. These are of exam standard and should be tackled in exam conditions, especially as regards the time allocation.
- Solutions to the revision questions. As before, these indicate the length and the quality of solution that would be expected of a well-prepared candidate.

If you work conscientiously through this CIMA *Learning System* according to the guidelines above you will be giving yourself an excellent chance of exam success. Good luck with your studies!

Guide to the Icons used within this Text

 Key term or definition

 Equation to learn

 Exam tip or topic likely to appear in the exam

 Exercise

 Question

 Solution

 Comment or Note

Study technique

Passing exams is partly a matter of intellectual ability, but however accomplished you are in that respect you can improve your chances significantly by the use of appropriate study and revision techniques. In this section we briefly outline some tips for effective study during the earlier stages of your approach to the exam. Later in the text we mention some techniques that you will find useful at the revision stage. Please remember that the topics that are covered in the managerial papers are examinable in P6. You may have studied and passed under an earlier syllabus than P4 and P5. You should obtain a copy of the syllabus for those Management level papers and make sure that you are familiar with the content.

Planning

To begin with, formal planning is essential to get the best return from the time you spend studying. Estimate how much time in total you are going to need for each subject that you face. Remember that you need to allow time for revision as well as for initial study of the material. The amount of notional study time for any subject is the minimum estimated time that students will need to achieve the specified learning outcomes set out earlier in this chapter. This time includes all appropriate learning activities, for example face-to-face tuition, private study, directed home study, learning in the workplace, revision time, etc. You may find it helpful to read *Learning to Learn* by Sam Malone, CIMA Publishing, ISBN: 9781856177825. If you have not done so already you should read *Pass first Time!* by Robert Harris. These book will provide you with proven study techniques. Chapter by chapter they cover the building blocks of successful learning and examination techniques.

The notional study time for Enterprise Strategy is 200 hours. Note that the standard amount of notional learning hours attributed to one full-time academic year of approximately 30 weeks is 1,200 hours.

By way of example, the notional study time might be made up as follows:

	Hours
Face-to-face study: up to	60
Personal study: up to	100
'Other' study – e.g. learning in the workplace, revision, etc.: up to	40
	200

Note that all study and learning-time recommendations should be used only as a guideline and are intended as minimum amounts. The amount of time recommended for face-to-face tuition, personal study and/or additional learning will vary according to the type of course undertaken, prior learning of the student, and the pace at which different students learn.

Now split your total time requirement over the weeks between now and the examination. This will give you an idea of how much time you need to devote to study each week. Remember to allow for holidays or other periods during which you will not be able to study (e.g. because of seasonal workloads).

With your study material before you, decide which chapters you are going to study in each week, and which weeks you will devote to revision and final question practice.

Prepare a written schedule summarising the above – and stick to it!

The amount of space allocated to a topic in the study material is not a very good guide as to how long it will take you. For example, 'Summarising and Analysing Data' has a weight of 25 per cent in the syllabus and this is the best guide as to how long you should spend on it. It occupies 45 per cent of the main body of the text because it includes many tables and charts.

It is essential to know your syllabus. As your course progresses you will become more familiar with how long it takes to cover topics in sufficient depth. Your timetable may need to be adapted to allocate enough time for the whole syllabus.

Tips for effective studying

1. Aim to find a quiet and undisturbed location for your study, and plan as far as possible to use the same period of time each day. Getting into a routine helps to avoid wasting time. Make sure that you have all the materials you need before you begin so as to minimise interruptions.

2. Store all your materials in one place, so that you do not waste time searching for items around the house. If you have to pack everything away after each study period, keep them in a box, or even a suitcase, which will not be disturbed until the next time.

3. Limit distractions. To make the most effective use of your study periods you should be able to apply total concentration, so turn off the TV, set your phones to message mode, and put up your 'do not disturb' sign.

4. Your timetable will tell you which topic to study. However, before diving in and becoming engrossed in the finer points, make sure you have an overall picture of all the areas that need to be covered by the end of that session. After an hour, allow yourself a short break and move away from your books. With experience, you will learn to assess the pace you need to work at. You should also allow enough time to read relevant articles from newspapers and journals, which will supplement your knowledge and demonstrate a wider perspective.

5. Work carefully through a chapter, making notes as you go. When you have covered a suitable amount of material, vary the pattern by attempting a practice question. Preparing an answer plan is a good habit to get into, while you are both studying and revising, and also in the examination room. It helps to impose a structure on your solutions and avoids rambling. When you have finished your attempt, make notes of any mistakes you made, or any areas that you failed to cover or covered only skimpily.

6. Make notes as you study, and discover the techniques that work best for you. Your notes may be in the form of lists, bullet points, diagrams, summaries, 'mind maps', or the written word, but remember that you will need to refer back to them at a later date, so they must be intelligible. If you are on a taught course, make sure you highlight any issues you would like to follow up with your lecturer.

7. Organise your paperwork. There are now numerous paper storage systems available to ensure that all your notes, calculations and articles can be effectively filed and easily retrieved later.

Paper E3 – Enterprise strategy

Syllabus overview

Paper E3 continues the integration of skills across functions, but concentrates on developing the knowledge and skills used in designing and implementing strategy. Strategy is developed in a context, and understanding how the organisation's external environment and stakeholders affect strategy development is important. Context and the internal capabilities of the organisation shape the generation and evaluation of strategic options. Implementing strategy involves tools and techniques associated with change management. Finally, the paper requires the application of tools to assist in the evaluation of the performance implications of a given strategy.

Syllabus structure

The syllabus comprises the following topics and study weightings:

Topics	Study Weighting
(A) Interacting with the competitive environment	20%
(B) Change management	20%
(C) Evaluation of strategic postion and strategic options	30%
(D) Implementation of strategic plans and performance evaluation	30%

Assessment strategy

There will be a written examination paper of three hours, plus 20 minutes of pre-examination question paper reading time. The examination paper will have the following sections:

Section A – 50 marks
A maximum of four compulsory questions, totalling 50 marks, all relating to a pre-seen case study and further new un-seen case material provided within the examination. (Note: The pre-seen case study is common to all three of the strategic level papers at each examination sitting (i.e. Paper E3, P3 and F3.)

Section B – 50 marks
Two questions, from a choice of three, each worth 25 marks. Short scenarios will be given, to which some or all questions relate.

Learning outcomes and syllabus content

E3 – A. Interacting with the competitive environment (20%)

Learning outcomes		Content
Lead	**Component**	**Content**
1. Evaluate the key external factors affecting an organisation's strategy. (5)	(a) Evaluate the impact and influence of the external environment on an organisation and its strategy.	• Non-market strategy and forms of corporate political activity. (A, B)
	(b) Recommend approaches to business/government relations and to relations with civil society.	• External demands for responsible business practices and ways to respond to these. (A, C)
	(c) Discuss the drivers of external demands for corporate social responsibility and the firm's response.	• Stakeholder management (stakeholders to include government and regulatory agencies, non-governmental organisations and civil society, industry associations, customers and suppliers). (C, D)
	(d) Recommend how to manage relationships with stakeholders.	• The customer portfolio: Customer analysis and behaviour, including the marketing audit and customer profitability analysis as well as customer retention and loyalty. (E)
	(e) Recommend how to interact with suppliers and customers.	• Strategic supply chain management. (E)
		• Implications of these interactions for Chartered Management Accountants and the management accounting system. (B, C, D, E)
2. Evaluate the impact of information systems on an organisation. (5)	(a) Evaluate the impact of the Internet on an organisation and its strategy.	• The impact of IT (including the Internet) on an organisation (utilising frameworks such as Porter's Five Forces, the Value Chain). (A, B)
	(b) Evaluate the strategic and competitive impact of information systems.	• Competing through exploiting information (rather than technology), e.g. use of databases to identify potential customers or market segments, and the management of data (warehousing and mining). (A, B)
		• Contemporary developments in the commercial use of the internet (e.g. Web 2.0). (A, B)

E3 – B. Change management (20%)

Lead	Learning outcomes Component	Content
1. Advise on important elements in the change process. (5)	(a) Discuss the concept of organisational change. (b) Recommend techniques to manage resistance to change.	• External and internal change triggers (e.g. environmental factors, mergers and acquisitions, re-organisation and rationalisation). (A, B) • Stage models of change. (A, B) • Problem identification as a precursor to change. (A, B) • Cultural processes of change (i.e. change within the context of the whole firm). (B)
2. Evaluate tools and methods for successfully implementing a change programme. (5)	(a) Evaluate approaches to managing change. (b) Compare and contrast continuous and discontinuous change. (c) Evaluate tools, techniques and strategies for managing the change process. (d) Evaluate the role of leadership in managing the change process.	• The importance of managing critical periods of discontinuous change. (A) • Tools, techniques and models associated with organisational change. (C, D) • Approaches, styles and strategies of change management. (C, D) • Importance of adaptation and continuous change. (A, B) • Leading change. (D)
3. Recommend change management processes in support of strategy implementation. (5)	(a) Evaluate the role of change management in the context of strategy implementation. (b) Evaluate ethical issues and their resolution in the context of organisational change.	• Change management and its role in the successful implementation of strategy. (A) • The advantages and disadvantages of different styles of management on the successful implementation of strategy. (A) • Group formation within organisation and its impact on change processes within organisations. (A) • Business ethics in general and the CIMA Code of Ethics for Professional Accountants (Parts A and B) in the context of implementation of strategic plans. (B)

E3 – C. Evaluation of strategic position and strategic options (30%)

Learning outcomes		Content
Lead	**Component**	
1. Evaluate the process of strategy development. (5)	(a) Evaluate the process of strategy formulation. (b) Evaluate strategic options. (c) Evaluate different organisational structures. (d) Discuss the role and responsibilities of directors in the strategy development process.	• Mission statements and their use in orientating the organisation's strategy. (A) • The process of strategy formulation. (A) • The identification and evaluation of strategic options. (B) • Strategic options generation (e.g. using Ansoff's product/market matrix and Porter's generic strategies). (B) • Real Options as a tool for strategic analysis. *Note: Complex numerical questions will not be set.* (B) • Scenario planning and long-range planning as tools in strategic decision-making. (B) • Game theoretic approaches to strategic planning and decision-making. *Note: Complex numerical questions will not be set.* (B) • Acquisition, divestment, rationalisation and relocations strategies and their place in the strategic plan. (B, C) • The relationship between strategy and organisational structure. (C) • The role and responsibilities of directors in making strategic decisions (including issues of due diligence, fiduciary responsibilities). (D)
2. Evaluate tools and techniques used in strategy formulation (5)	(a) Evaluate strategic analysis tools. (b) Recommend appropriate changes to the product portfolio of an organisation to support the organisation's strategic goals. (c) Produce an organisation's value chain. (d) Discuss both qualitative and quantitative techniques in the support of the strategic decision-making function.	• Audit of resources and the analysis of this for use in strategic decision-making. (A) • Forecasting and the various techniques used: trend analysis, system modelling, in-depth consultation with experts (Delphi method). (A) • Management of the product portfolio. (B) • Value chain analysis. (C) • Strategic decision-making processes. (D)

E3 – D. Implementation of strategic plans and performance evaluation (30%)

Learning outcomes

Lead	Component	Content
1. Evaluate the tools and processes of strategy implementation. (5)	(a) Recommend appropriate control measures. (b) Evaluate alternative models of performance measurement. (c) Recommend solutions to problems in performance measurement. (d) Advise managers on the development of strategies for knowledge management and information systems that support the organisation's strategic requirements. (e) Recommend changes to information systems appropriate to the organisation's strategic requirements.	• Alternative models of performance measurement (e.g. the balanced scorecard). (A, B, C) • Business unit performance and appraisal, including transfer pricing, reward systems and incentives. (B) • Project management: monitoring the implementation of plans. (B) • The implementation of lean systems across an organisation. (C) • Theories of control within organisations and types of organisational structure (e.g. matrix, divisional, network). (A, B, C) • Assessing strategic performance (i.e. the use and development of appropriate measures that are sensitive to industry characteristics and environmental factors). (B, C) • Non-financial measures and their interaction with financial ones. (Note: candidates will be expected to use both qualitative and quantitative techniques). (A, B, C) • The purpose and contents of information systems strategies, and the need for strategy complementary to the corporate and individual business strategies. (D, E) • Critical success factors: links to performance indicators and corporate strategy, and their use as a basis for defining an organisation's information needs. (A, B)

Setting the Goals of the Organisation

Setting the Goals of the Organisation

According to the rational model the first stage of strategy formulation is the setting of mission and objectives. This chapter looks at this process, the analysis of stakeholders, and the roles performed by mission and objectives, in detail.

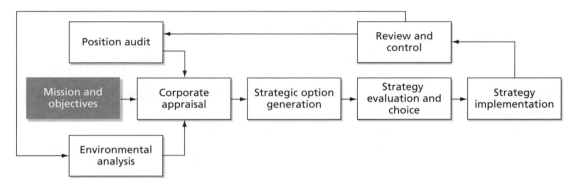

LEARNING OUTCOMES

After completing this chapter you should be able to:

▸ identify relevant stakeholders in respect of an organisation;

▸ discuss how stakeholder groups work and how they affect an organisation;

▸ recommend proactive and reactive approaches to business/government relations and to relations with civil society.

1.1 The identity of stakeholders

You will be familiar with the concept of stakeholders from your earlies studies and, it is recommended that you revise that section of the manual in addition to reading what follows.

> Stakeholders are defined by CIMA as 'Those persons and organisations that have an interest in the strategy of the organisation. Stakeholders normally include shareholders, customers, staff and the local community.' (CIMA: *Management Accounting Official Terminology*, 2005, p. 53).

As such we can consider them to be people and organisations (Figure 1.1) who have a say in:

- what you are to do,
- what resources you have,
- what you should achieve.

They are affected by, and feel they have a right to benefit or be pleased by what you do.

For a commercial organisation they include, amongst others:

Internal stakeholders	Owners/founders
	Management
	Staff
Mixed internal and external stakeholders	Trade unions
	Communities where organisation is based
External stakeholders	Bankers
	Other investors
	Governments & regulatory bodies

Figure 1.1 Stakeholders

If we consider a not-for-profit or public sector organisation this list increases quite dramatically and, in a recent exercise, over a hundred were identified for the BBC World Service. Bryson (1995) makes the point, strongly, that for a non-profit or public organisation a thorough analysis of stakeholders is essential.

It is important to remember that if an organisation tries to implement strategies which are in conflict with the interests of powerful stakeholders those strategies are highly likely to fail. This does mean, however, that if powerful stakeholders agree with what we are trying to do it will greatly improve our chances of success.

With that in mind it is important for an organisation to identify an organisations' stakeholders and their power to affect the decisions and outcomes.

Within this process (Figure 1.2) it is worth noting that stakeholder values may not be immediately apparent and it is important to distinguish between desired, stated and lived values. For instance, if we consider a Fire Brigade the desired values will be based on Fire Prevention and minimising the number of fires that start usually by a process of education. The stated values usually involve response times to fires that have already started, in fact that is how their performance is measured by the government, so a conflict exists there. The lived values are those of the firefighters themselves and usually relate to their professional skill in putting out difficult fires – again a conflict exists.

Identify stakeholders
Identify their interests, values, and concerns
Identify sources of stakeholder power
Identify what claims they can make on the organisation
Identify the most important stakeholders from the organisations
  perspective
Map the relationships between them
Identify the resultant strategic challenges.

Figure 1.2 Stages in stakeholder analysis

Much the same as in real life, when mapping stakeholders you should always consider that individuals might be members of more than one stakeholder group. For instance, an employee, who is a trade union member, may also be active in the local community.

This would place that person in three different groups – which you might consider to have completely different values. It would be silly to think that the groups did not communicate with each other and form alliances or that the same person could be treated in different ways depending on which group you choose to include them in.

1.1.1 Sources of stakeholder power

Power is the potential ability of an individual or group to exert an influence on others, to persuade them into following a particular course of action. This means that those who have power have the potential to influence behaviour, to change the course of events, to overcome resistance, and to persuade people to do things that they might not otherwise do.

Power comes from a number of sources and only some of them have anything to do with the individual's position in the organisation. Although there are many ways that sources of power may be described the following categorisation encompasses most definitions;

- *Positional power.* This arises because of an individual's position in an organisational hierarchy and is reflected in their formal authority and reputation
- *Resource power.* This arises because an individual can control, obtain or create resources or other items of value. Those items of value need not necessarily be tangible; they can be affection or a sense of belonging to a particular group. This affords the holder the ability to reward, coerce or punish those over whom the power is exercised.
- *System power.* This arises because an individual is central to a group, has political access, has high visibility, and relevance to a particular situation. This is sometimes known as network power because the individual that wields the power is 'connected' to the right people.
- *Expert power.* This arises because an individual has information, knowledge, expertise, professional credibility, and fits with the organisations requirements.
- *Personal power.* This form of power arises because an individual has, charisma, energy, attractiveness, determination, communication skills, personal reputation or the ability to confront. Quite often this will be a person who is self-effacing and is able to let others take the credit for a success. This is sometimes known as charismatic power.

It is worth remembering that;

- Power is exercised by individuals, not groups, and is invariably personalised in some way. The power will only be effective if an individual exercises it over another individual or group.
- Power is based on a system of ideas and a body of common knowledge. The leaders or other person's power is dependent upon their success in developing and convincingly communicating a clear and compelling message that embodies the core system of ideas and the new body of common knowledge. The message must be powerful and simple enough to overcome competing messages.
- Although power is exercised by individuals it is manifested through organisations, and its exercise is legitimised and constrained by the organisation's common knowledge. Some type of organisation, institution or group, is necessary for the enduring exercise of power.
- Power actions occur in a context that includes various stakeholders and audiences. Any important stakeholder group or significant body of opinion must be involved in some way.

However, a leader's power can be extended to larger groups or organisations by delegation.

- Power vacuums occur when power is not exercised or is abused which will result in the increased incidence, and cost, of conflict and other problems such as poor quality, lowered productivity, decreased adaptability to change.

Sources of power, with examples from a hospital, that stakeholders may be able to bring to bear are shown in Figure 1.3.

Type of power	Example
Expertise	Doctors, anesthetists
Control over access to resources	Hospital budget manager
Control of access to information	Records management officer
Physical strength	Porters (possibly)
Preparedness to fight/confront	Trade union representative
Charisma	Consultants
Networks or relationships	Those with membership of professional body

Figure 1.3 Sources of power

1.1.2 Stakeholder claims on an organisation

When we consider what claims stakeholders can make on an organisation we are looking at their expectations and we must consider how these can be managed.

For instance, considering the stakeholders in Figure 1.1, staff could reasonably expect a good salary, a safe working environment, security and opportunities for advancement. The community in which the organisation is based might have expectations of a local employer with a social conscience but also have expectations of opportunities for employment of the local population. Bankers and other investors would, mainly, be looking for a return on their investment. You know from your studies elsewhere that those investors may be more or less risk averse and therefore have a different view on what constitutes a respectable return on investment.

Carroll (1991) has described the responsibilities that an organisation might typically have towards stakeholders:

1. *Economic.* The firm's economic responsibility is to be profitable (e.g. the responsibility to generate an acceptable rate of return for the shareholders).
2. *Legal.* The firm's legal responsibility is to obey relevant laws that are society's codification of right and wrong (e.g. the responsibility to file audited financial reports with government agencies).
3. *Ethical.* The firm's ethical responsibility is to do what is right, just, and fair and to avoid harm (e.g. the responsibility to choose wisely between several alternative investments of the firm's resources).
4. *Discretionary.* The firm's discretionary responsibility is to be a good corporate citizen by contributing its resources to improving stakeholders quality of life (e.g. whether the company should devote some of its resources to a community in which they have a key plant).

Once the power and expectations (and therefore their likely interest) has been established we can use a power interest matrix to assist the analysis. Mendelow (1991) has proposed such a matrix (Figure 1.4).

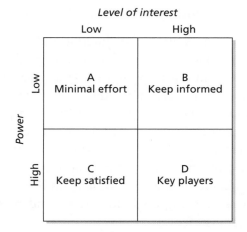

Figure 1.4 The Mendelow matrix (1991)
©Aubrey Mendelow

If the stakeholders are plotted regularly this matrix can be used to determine the potential influence of stakeholder groups. As strategies are proposed or modified by the organisation the matrix can be used to highlight possible threats (or assistance) from particular stakeholders groups.

1.1.3 Challenges and opportunities presented by stakeholder groups

When the vacuum cleaner manufacturer Dyson proposed closure of a factory and relocation abroad the completed matrix for the stakeholder groups looked like the one shown in Figure 1.5.

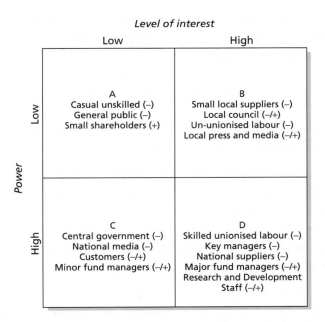

Figure 1.5 Illustration of Mendelow's matrix applied to Dyson

Scholes (1998) suggests the following strategies to deal with each quadrant:

- Box A – *direction*. This means their lack of interest and power makes them malleable. They are more likely than others to accept what they are told and follow instructions.

  Factory management should not reappoint the casual staff but rather provide limited redundancy support. There is no need to tell the small shareholders or customers.

- Box B – *education/communication*. The positively disposed groups from this quadrant may lobby others to support the strategy. Also if the strategy is presented as rational or inevitable to the dissenters, or a show of consultation gone through, this may stop them joining forces with more powerful dissenters in C and D.

  Factory management should brief all groups here on the reasonableness of the case for closure and of the provisions being made for the redundant staff. Advance notice will give each more time for adjustment.

- Box C – *intervention*. The key here is to keep the occupants satisfied to avoid them gaining interest and shifting into D. Usually this is done by reassuring them of the likely outcomes of the strategy well in advance.

  Factory managers should assure the government and suppliers that the closure will result in a more competitive firm that is able to compete worldwide. A similar message may reassure investors if it is backed up with a reassuring short-term dividend forecast.

- Box D – *participation*. These stakeholders can be major drivers of the change and major opponents of the strategy. Initially there should be education/communication to assure them that the change is necessary, followed by discussion of how to implement it.

  The factory managers should involve the unions in determining the redundancy package or redundancy policy. Key managers should be involved in deciding the basis on which early retirements should be handled and how redeployment or outplacement should be managed. Key shareholders will be consulted throughout to reassure them that costs will not be excessive.

1.1.4 Conflict between stakeholders

The objectives of the stakeholder groups will inevitably be different and may be in direct conflict. For example, the staff's desire for better pay and work conditions may conflict with the shareholders' desire for higher profits and the customers' desire for lower prices. The job of management is to develop and implement the overall strategy with these differences in mind. This can be further complicated in organisations where the employees are also shareholders!

Additionally there will be differences between the goals of members of the same internal stakeholder group. Two examples are particularly important:

1. *Differences between shareholders*. This commonly manifests itself as a polarisation between those who broadly require their income as short-term dividends and those who are happy for profits to be retained to promote capital growth.
2. *Differences between managers*. The goals of managers and the departments they lead may conflict. Consequently many strategic objectives are the outcome of a political bargaining process at boardroom level.

It is worth emphasising that individuals may be members of more than one stakeholder group at any point in time. For instance, workers in a factory may well be members of the local community or even elected local councillors. As such there may be conflicts between their interests and objectives in respect of a particular decision that the company is about to make.

1.1.5 Management of stakeholders

It is always important to consider why stakeholders might react to an initiative that the organisation has taken or proposes to take.

There are number of possible reasons why those reactions might occur:

1. Your initiative may result in economic loss to them.
2. They may view your initiative (e.g. using the application of new technology) as a potential threat to their health and safety.
3. Politicians may get involved as a way of showing their concern for their electors and the public in general (e.g. NIMBY – not in my back yard).
4. Your initiative is critical to those most directly linked to it (e.g. you are considering reviving a moth balled factory that will provide the stakeholders some new jobs).
5. Your initiative could reflect, or conflict with, the change in values or lifestyles characteristic of the stakeholder group (e.g. a risque new TV show that shows singles trying to lure away committed partners in relationships).
6. Your initiative is attractive to opportunists.
7. Your initiative becomes a lightning rod for disaffected groups.
8. Your initiative can serve as currency for exchanging support among stakeholder groups (e.g. they help Group A against your initiative in order that Group A gives them help with one of their pet issues).
9. They are suffering from pique, because you did not involve them in the decision-making process.

Wood (1994) suggests that stakes can be considered as falling into the following analytical categories:

1. *Single or multiple issue stakes.* Single-issue stakeholders are only concerned with one facet of an organisations operations whilst multiple-issue stakeholders care about many.
2. *Economic or social stakes.* Those with economic interests care about the distribution of financial or material resources (shareholders care about corporate profitability, employees about salary levels, etc.), whilst those with social interests usually have beliefs, values or concerns (corporate social responsibility, equal employment opportunity, witness protection, etc.)
3. *Concrete or symbolic stakes.* Concrete interests are related to the allocation of material resources, whilst symbolic interests are displayed in more difficult to define terms such as demands for something to be done, reassurances, gestures and goodwill.
4. *Local, national or international interests.* The boundaries of various stakeholders groups may vary from the local issue to the national agenda to an international or even global framework.

Stakeholder groups have the potential to present both opportunities and challenges to the management of an organisation. The firm could be presented with the opportunity to build harmonious, long standing, positive and productive relationships. Alternatively, if the situation is mis-managed threats could take the form of resource withdrawal or damage to reputational capital. Both can be viewed in terms of the potential for cooperation or confrontation.

These opportunities and threats should be analysed in terms of:

1. *Importance of effect.* How seriously will stakeholders interests and actions affect the company's performance?
2. *Direction of effect.* In which direction is the principal effect flowing. From the company to the stakeholder (e.g. bad smell from the plant over a residential area) or from the stakeholder to the firm (e.g. resistance to relocation of work to another site).
3. *Immediacy of effect.* At what time period – short, medium or long term – the company may be affected by stakeholder demands and action.
4. *Probability of resolution.* Whether the company has the capabilities and resources to deal with the stakeholder demands.

A number of studies have suggested broad classifications of stakeholder management strategies do Berman *et al.* (1999), for example, differentiate between instrumental and intrinsic stakeholder management models. Both models assume that firms should manage stakeholder interests proactively as it is 'good' management; to improve financial performance or because of a moral commitment to stakeholders. However, they do not provide a clear depiction of the organizational actions undertaken under the two models.

Jawahar and McLaughlin (2001) assert that firms will use different strategies to manage different stakeholder groups. Based on insights from resource dependence theory and prospect theory, they set out how a firm focuses on particular stakeholders in each stage of its organizational life cycle. The model implies that at each stage interests of different stakeholder groups will not be equally attended to, but a firm will prioritize groups that are particularly important at that stage. Jawahar and McLaughlin (2001) distinguish between reaction, defense, accommodation and pro-action strategies, but do not detail the exact behaviors typifying the implementation of these strategies.

Management will need to take the following basic decisions before deciding the approach to dealing with stakeholders;

Do they deal directly or indirectly with stakeholders? Do they take an offensive or defensive approach? Do they, accommodate, negotiate, manipulate, or resist stakeholder claims? Do they employ a combination of the above approaches or pursue a singular course of action? We shall consider this area in more detail when we look at change management in a later chapter.

At this point you should look at Question 4 in the November 2007 paper which examined this area.

1.2 Mission statements

CIMA defines a mission statement as 'Published statement, apparently the entity's fundamental objective(s). This may or may not summarise the true mission of the entity.'

The mission is defined as 'Fundamental objective(s) of an entity expressed in general terms'. (CIMA: *Management Accounting: Official Terminology,* 2005, p. 49).

The implication might be taken that the mission statement is for public consumption and only reflects what the organisation wants the public to believe its intentions are.

You will be familiar with the concept of mission statements from your earlier studies. However, in addition to revising the appropriate sections of that syllabus you should consider the following issues.

First, let us refresh our memories about the different approaches to strategy proposed by the various schools of thought. There are many ways in which the strategic management process can be described. Various authors have described the process with differing degrees of formality and this had lead to a variety of schematics that they have felt indicate a sequence in which the various stages of the process occur. Approximately 10 years ago Hamel and Heene (1994) made the point that 'After almost 40 years of development and theory building, the field of strategic management is, today more than ever, characterised by contrasting and sometimes competing paradigms.' Whittington (1993) offers definitions of four distinct approaches to strategy making.

The Classical School is thoroughly prescriptive in approach believing that both the environment and the organisation are susceptible to rigorous analysis with a planning focus on profit maximisation. Key authors are Chandler (1962), Ansoff (1965) and Porter (1980).

The Evolutionary School advocates an efficient approach believing that a Darwinian approach to development is more appropriate since the environment of the organisation is not susceptible to analysis or prediction. The objective of the organisation is survival. Key authors are Hannan and Freeman (1988) and Williamson (1967).

The Processual School focuses on internal processes believing that outcomes are arrived at by an internal political process of bargaining and learning. Objectives of the organisation are likely to be less well defined than those of the Classical School and the strategy emergent. Key authors are Cyert and March (1956), Mintzberg (1978) and Pettigrew (1973).

The Systemic School adopts a more social process feeling claiming that any strategic process needs to be more aware of the cultural environment and societies in which the organisation must operate. Key authors are Granovetter (1985) and Marris (1964).

The mission statement of an organisation sets out the broad directions that they should and will attempt to follow and summarises the reasoning and values on which it is based.

Advocates of classical, prescriptive theories of strategy, would expect an organisation to set out its mission statement and objectives for the foreseeable future based on an analysis of the environment and the firms resources. However, some of those who believe that strategies emerge, particularly those who are uncertainty based, feel that a prescriptive mission statement is a waste of time since an organisations route is rarely, successfully, chosen.

Those who favour a processual or systemic approach would expect to see mission statements being the result of consultation between the various stakeholder groups and to reflect the interests of all involved parties. They would see the purpose of the mission statement as one of communication to all stakeholders both inside and outside the organisation. The message would be about what the company stands for and the direction in which it is going.

Whilst there is no clear decision amongst theorists about the definition of a mission statement, many companies find the process of deriving one to be beneficial. BAA, for instance, have in the past, run workshops every few years with delegates from a cross section of the organisation to check if the mission statement in use accurately reflects the values and purpose of the organisation. Lynch (2003) has summarised the steps in the formulation of a mission statement which also indicates what it should contain.

1. Consideration of the *nature* of the organisations business. Typical questions include: 'What business are we in?' 'What business *should* we be in?'
2. The responses need to be considered from the customer or client perspective, rather than the organisation itself: 'We are in the business of developing books that will inform and educate our readers about strategy', *rather than* 'We are in the business of developing textbooks on strategic issues.'

3. The mission needs to reflect the basic *values and beliefs* of the organisation: We believe it is important to respect the environment and offer employment that is free from any prejudices associated with culture, race or religion.'
4. Where possible, the mission needs to reflect the element *of sustainable competitive advantage:* 'It is our aim to be a leader in this field.' This may not be possible in a diversified holding company. It may also be more appropriate to adjust this to reflect *distincitiveness* in an organisation which has no direct competitors, for example a charity.
5. The mission needs to summarise the main reasons for its choice of approach: We are a team. We must treat each other with trust and respect' would be a good example.

The published version of a mission statement should be carefully worded so as to be clearly understood since it will be read by a variety of people. They should also be plausible and not leave the organization open to ridicule.

Lynch goes on to offer the following criteria with which to judge mission statements:

1. They should be specific enough to have an impact upon the behaviour of individuals throughout the organisation.
2. They should reflect the distinctive advantages of the organisation and be based upon an objective recognition of its strengths and weaknesses.
3. They should be realistic and attainable.
4. They should be flexible enough to take account of shifts in the environment.

Examples of mission statements might include those for;
Ford Motor Company
'World leadership in automotive equipment and financial services. To improve products continually to meet customer needs so as to provide a reasonable return to owners.' www .ford.com/en/default.htm

It is worth noting that various stakeholders are addressed in the mission statement and there is a clear indication of the what the purpose of the company is
British Heart Foundation – a charity
'The aim of the British Heart Foundation is to play a leading role in the fight against heart disease so that it is no longer a major cause of disability and premature death by:

- Funding medical research into the causes, prevention, diagnosis and treatment of heart disease
- Providing support and information to heart patients and their families through British Heart Foundation Nurses, rehabilitation programmes and support groups.
- Educating the public and health professionals about heart disease prevention and treatment
- Promoting training in emergency life support skills for the public and health professionals
- Providing vital life-saving equipment to hospitals and other health providers'. www.bhf .org.uk

Again the mission addresses the purpose of the organisation and a number of the stakeholders who have an interest in what the organisation actually does.

1.3 Corporate social responsibility

Corporate social responsibility (CSR) is a key element in the management of the organisations relationships with governments and regulatory agencies, NGOs and civil society.

Building on the work of Carroll (1991) referred to earlier it has become increasingly important to consider how companies manage their business processes to have an overall positive impact on society.

At this point we can distinguish between business ethics and corporate social responsibility (CSR) which, although the two are often used interchangeably, have distinct meanings. Business ethics comprises principles and standards that govern behaviour in the world of business. Actions can be judged to be right or wrong, ethical or unethical, individuals inside or outside the organisation. These judgements will influence society's acceptance or rejection of the actions taken. CSR, however, refers to a firm's obligation to maximise its positive impacts upon stakeholders whilst minimising the negative effects. As such, ethics is just one dimension of social responsibility. The extent to which stakeholders judge that businesses meet, legal, ethical, economic and philanthropic responsibilities placed on them by their various stakeholders will determine the degree of corporate citizenship exhibited by the firm.

CSR has been defined as having four dimensions: economic, legal, ethical and philanthropic. As such society can;

- require business to discharge its economic and legal duties,
- expect business to fulfil its ethical duties,
- desire business to meet its philanthropic responsibilities.

CSR has also been defined as: '… the continuing commitment to business to behave ethically and contribute to economic development while improving the quality of life of the workforce and their families as well as of the local community and society at large' by representatives of the World Business Council for Sustainable Development. From the same source perceptions of CSR from different societies and cultures were given as 'CSR is about capacity building for sustainable livelihoods. It respects cultural differences and finds the business opportunities in building the skills of employees, the community and the government' (Ghana), 'CSR is about business giving back to society' (Philippines). In America there is more emphasis on the philanthropic approach to CSR, where companies will make charitable donations to society or its representatives. We can contrast the European approach where the emphasis is on business processes which are more socially responsible, complemented by investment in communities for reasons which are supported by good business cases. It is argued, by Mallen Baker, that the European approach is more sustainable since social responsibility becomes an integral part of the wealth creation process which should enhance the competitiveness of the business and maximise the wealth created from both the business and society. With a more philanthropic approach when times are hard and the bottom line is under pressure it becomes very easy to cut the size of the donation.

We can see that there is no one definition, or theory, of corporate social responsibility. We can consider an 'ethical conception' which is concerned with corporate self restraint, expansive public policy and corporate altruism which can be contrasted with an 'economic conception' involving fiduciary responsibility, minimalist public policy and customary ethics. In short the former is about general welfare and the latter about private wealth. The third conception that of corporate citizenship, concerned with corporate reputation, strategic philanthropy, political influence and multiple jurisdictions sits, uncomfortably, somewhere between the two.

It is certain that there will be increasing pressure on organisations to play an increasing role in the solution to social issues. This will be particularly true of those that have a global presence. This means that multinationals and NGOs will increasingly be looked to take a lead in addressing those issues where a national government or local firm has not been able, or willing, to arrive at a solution. With increasing globalisation, which we will discuss later, the power of the institutions attached to the nation state (national governments, judiciary and police for example) are declining.

The OECD principles – the *OECD Guidelines for Multinational Organisations.* This is somewhat of a misnomer since the guidelines are just a reflection of good practice and it is intended that they should be followed by all organisations regardless of size. Although the guidelines provide quite detailed prescriptions, a brief overview of the material under each heading would include;

- *General policies.* These suggest that organisations should take into account established policies in the countries in which they operate. They should contribute to the economic, social and environmental progress of the country with a view to obtaining sustainable development and encourage local capacity building. Whilst respecting human rights they should develop human capital in the country and facilitate training opportunities. The company should support and uphold good corporate governance principles and not seek to avoid within the regulatory framework of the country. They should develop self-regulatory practices amongst their management and staff and promote staff awareness of company policy. There should be no discrimination or disciplinary action taken against those who make bona fide reports on acts which contravene law or good practice. Whilst abstaining from improper political involvement they should encourage local business partners to behave appropriately.
- *Disclosure* of reliable and relevant information concerning activities, structure, financial performance and situation should be done on a timely and regular basis. The standards to which that information is compiled and published should also be reported.
- *Employment and industrial Relations* should comply with the applicable law, regulations and the prevailing labour relations and employment practices. The rights to trade union representation should be respected, those bona fide representatives of the workforce should be allowed to enter into constructive negotiations regarding conditions of employment. The company should actively contribute to the effective abolition of forced, compulsory and/or child labour. The company should observe standards of employment and industrial relations not less favourable than those observed by comparable employers in the host country.
- *Environment.* Within the framework of laws, regulations and administrative practices in the countries in which they operate companies should take due account of the need to protect the environment, public health and safety. Generally they should conduct their activities in a manner contributing to the wider goal of sustainable development. This should be done within the context of the relevant international agreements, principles, objectives and standards. A system of environmental management should be established within the country relevant to the local needs and conditions. The system should assess, and address in decision making, the foreseeable environmental, health, and safety-related impacts associated with the processes, goods and services of the enterprise over their full life cycle. The company should maintain contingency plans for preventing, mitigating, and controlling any serious environmental and health damage from their operations, including accidents and emergencies, and mechanisms for immediate reporting to the competent authorities.
- *Combating bribery.* Enterprises should not, directly or indirectly, offer, promise, give, or demand a bribe or other undue advantage to obtain or retain business or other improper advantage. Nor should enterprises be solicited or expected to render a bribe or other undue advantage.

- *Consumer interests.* Whilst dealing with consumers, enterprises should act in accordance with fair business, marketing and advertising practices and should take all reasonable steps to ensure the safety and quality of the goods and services they provide.
- *Science and Technology.* Companies should endeavour to ensure their activities are compatible with the science and technology polices and plans of the countries in which they operate and, where appropriate, contribute to the development of local and national innovative capacity. They should also, where practicable in the course of their business activities, adopt practices which ensure the transfer and rapid diffusion of technology and knowledge to the host country, with due regard to their intellectual property rights. Where relevant to their commercial objectives they should develop links with local universities, public research facilities, and should participate in cooperative research projects with local industrial and/or industrial associations.
- *Competition.* Companies should, within the framework of applicable laws and regulations, conduct their activities in a fair competitive manner and promote awareness amongst their employees of the importance of so doing.
- *Taxation.* Companies should contribute, via the taxation system, to the public finances of the host country in a timely manner. In particular, enterprises should comply with the tax laws and regulations in all countries in which they operate and should exert every effort to act in accordance with both the letter and the spirit of those laws and regulations.

When it comes to measuring or assessing an organisations performance with regard to CSR there are several common elements. A North American organisation, Kinder, Lydenberg & Domini is an independent rating service that assesses CSR using a number of parameters related to stakeholder concerns. The factors they use include: community, diversity, employee relations, environment and product. These factors are really about the management of relationships with different stakeholders. Additionally they will look at a factor they describe as negative screens. This tends to cover fairly specialised considerations such as military involvement or involvement in the generation of nuclear power.

A global survey in 2005 included a total of 20 items which better reflected the evaluation of CSR for multinational organisations. The 20 items were grouped as follows;

Internal aspects
- Written policies on non-discrimination in the workplace.
- Equal opportunities statements and implementation plans.
- Statements covering normal working hours, maximum overtime, and fair wage structures.
- Staff development, in-house education and vocational training.
- The right for freedom of association, collective bargaining, and defined complaints procedures.
- The protection of human rights within the company's own operations.

External aspects
- Policy on labour standards adopted by suppliers in developing countries.
- Policy on restrictions no the use of child labour by suppliers.
- Commitment to the protection of human rights in the company's sphere of influence.
- Inspection of suppliers' facilities for health, safety, and environmental standards.
- Commitment to the local community protection and engagement.
- Policy on responding to stakeholders including procedures for the resolution of complaints.
- Policies on fair trade, equitable trade, and end-price auditing.
- Policies on the protection of indigenous populations and their rights
- Code of ethics, including bribery and corruption policies

Accountability

- Commitment to reporting on corporate social responsibility and/or sustainable development.
- Polices and procedures for engaging a wide range of stakeholders in two way dialogue.

Citizenship

- Direct support for third party social and/or sustainable development related initiatives.
- Education programmes for the promotion of corporate citizenship.
- External campaign programmes for raising social and sustainable development issues.

This list should not be considered as static or set in stone; it is only really useful as a broad outline. Any CSR system should be a dynamic process that is part of the strategic planning process. To translate CSR into managerial action, the people concerned must first understand the norms and requirements of the social, political and legal requirements of the environments in which they operate. Those norms and requirements will change over time.

The environment and stakeholders should be assessed and appropriate issues identified and then plans put in place to deal with them. CSR is about adaption to the external environment and the organisations ability to be responsive to different needs. The three components of responsiveness: the context (environmental assessment), the actors (stakeholder assessment and management) and interests (issues management) are logically and consecutively linked.

An indication of the importance of this area is the fact that CIMA now include's corporate social accounting in their official terminology. They define it as 'Reporting of the social and environmental impact of the entity's activities upon those who are directly associated with the entity (for instance, employees, customers, suppliers) or those who are in any way affected by the activities of the entity, as well as an assessment of the cost of compliance with relevant regulations in this area.'

1.3.1 The importance of CSR

One of the central assumptions underpinning CSR is that organisations are social entities with responsibilities which are more than just the maximisation of shareholders wealth. There is also an expectation that the organisation will add value to the primary stakeholders. Those primary stakeholders will include shareholders, customers and suppliers, employees, creditors, and the public stakeholder group. The public stakeholder group can be considered to consist of the residents of the community, the natural environment, and the levels of government that provide access to the natural resources, infrastructure and other support necessary for the smooth running of business. Building better relationships with those stakeholders will, it is argued, accrue intangible assets to the organisation which can form part of the competitive advantage of the firm. One of those intangible assets is the organisations reputation and is often described as the reputational capital of the organisation. The intangible components of that reputation are trust, reliability, quality, consistency, credibility, and transparency. To that we can add the tangible elements such as investment in people, diversity and the environment. There is a widespread consensus of opinion that investing in stakeholder relations can lead to loyalty from suppliers, customers and staff. This will lead to improved staff turnover and an improved reputation. These valuable assets will lead to a positive relationship with the firm's primary stakeholders and, therefore, shareholder value and subsequent improved financial performance. Most people would rather deal with an organisation that has a 'good name' and a strong reputation.

Various studies in the late 1990s proved that those companies that invest in CSR perform well financially. The resource-based view of the firm suggests that a firm's ability to perform better than its rivals depends on the combination of human, organisational, and physical resources it is able to bring to bear on its markets. The resources that lead to competitive advantage are, invariably, the social complex and ambiguous elements such as, reputation, corporate culture, knowledge assets, and long-term relationships with their stakeholders. Therefore, by developing longer-term sustainable relationships companies are able to grow the set of value creating exchanges with those stakeholders above and beyond the relationships which would result from purely market driven transactions. These relationships will be difficult for other firms to copy and so will provide competitive advantage.

There may well be improved access to finance for the companies that follow this route as socially responsible investment is now measured by at least two indices. The Dow Jones Sustainability Index and the FTSE4Good both publicly rank major international companies according to their social and environmental performance. Socially Responsible Investment (SRI) occurs where social, environmental, ethical and corporate governance considerations are taken into account in the selection, retention and realisation of investments and the responsible use of voting rights attached to the investments. In that way SRI combines the investor's financial objectives with their concerns about CSR issues. The SRI covers not only investment by financial institutions in developing countries by way of investment funds, stocks and loans but also the investment by multinationals in their own operations in those countries.

The impact of CSR on the employees can be considerable. Not only will a company with a good reputation be able to attract and retain better people (since it will have more choice) but the motivation of those who work there is likely to be higher. Bearing in mind that a very large proportion of the value of large companies resides in their intellectual capital, innovation, learning, and creativity are very important. The technology and management skills that companies make available to poverty relief and community projects normally brings benefits in that the individuals who do the work return to the firm better rounded and developed employees. In the field they often have experiences and enjoy a level of responsibility that no internal training programme could provide.

Better risk management is likely to be possible for a company that conducts in- depth analysis of its stakeholders and the relationship it has with them. The company is more likely to become aware of changes in technology, societal and regulation changes and even market expectations if it is regularly consulting and relating to its external stakeholders.

The debate on the benefits and problems of globalisation are continuing and, those companies that are seen to be responsible are likely to improve not only their reputation but the reputation of the business community in general.

1.4   Setting strategic objectives

1.4.1   The link between mission and objectives

A mission is an open-ended statement of the firm's purposes and strategies. Strategic objectives translate the mission into strategic milestones for the business strategy to reach.

A strategic objective will possess four characteristics which set it apart from a mission statement:

- a precise formulation of the attribute sought;
- an index or measure for progress towards the attribute;

- a target to be achieved;
- a time-frame in which it is to be achieved.

Another way of putting this is to say that objectives must be SMART, i.e.

- Specific, unambiguous in what is to be achieved;
- Measurable, specified as a quantity;
- Attainable, within reach;
- Relevant appropriate to the mission of the firm;
- Time-bound, with a completion date.

Table 1.1 lists some strategic objectives.

Table 1.1 Examples of strategic objectives

Mission	Attributes	Measure
Growth	Sales volume	'000s of units
	Share of market	% of total volume
	Asset base of firm	Net assets
Quality	Customer satisfaction	Repeat purchases
	Defects	No. per '000
	Consistency	Adoption of standard procedures
Innovation	Peer group respect	Industry awards received
	Speed to market	Development time
	Successful new products	% of sales from new products
Social responsibility	Non-discrimination	Workforce composition
	Environmental pollution	Cubic metres of waste
	Safety	Notified incidents

You must expect questions requiring you to convert mission statements into objectives or to comment on the appropriateness of particular objectives for implementing the mission.

1.4.2 The goal structure

The *goal structure* is the hierarchy of objectives in the organisation. It can be visualised as the diagram in Figure 1.6. This pyramid parallels the organisation chart in Figure 1.6.

For a definition of the hierarchy of objectives look at the CIMA: *Management Acounting: Official Terminology*, 2005, p. 50.

Objectives perform five functions:

1. *Planning*. Objectives provide the framework for planning. They are the targets which the plan is supposed to reach.
2. *Responsibility*. Objectives are given to the managers of divisions, departments and operations. This communicates to them:
   (a) the activities, projects or areas they are responsible for;
   (b) the sorts of output required;
   (c) the level of outputs required.
3. *Integration*. Objectives are how senior management co-ordinate the firm. Provided that the objectives handed down are internally consistent, this should ensure *goal congruence* between managers of the various divisions of the business.

Mission statement
Translated into a small number of

**strategic
objectives**
reached by
following strategies
communicated to management
as numerous
tactical objectives
which in turn are implemented and reviewed
through setting a large number of
operational objectives
which may be communicated to managers and staff
responsible through their
individual performance targets

Figure 1.6   A goal structure

4. *Motivation.* Management will be motivated to reach their objectives in order to impress their superiors and perhaps receive bonuses. This means that the objectives set must cover all areas of the mission. For example, if the objectives emphasise purely financial outcomes, then managers will not pay much heed to issues such as social responsibility or innovation.
5. *Evaluation.* Senior management control the business by evaluating the performance of the managers responsible for each of its divisions. For example, by setting the manager a target return on investment (ROI) and monitoring it, senior management ensure that the business division makes a suitable return on its assets.

You may be familiar with these five functions (often recalled using the acronym PRIME) from your studies in budgetary control. Budget targets are a good example of operational level objectives. In this chapter, however, we are working at a higher level by considering the strategic objectives of the firm.

1.5   Critical success factors

1.5.1   Defining critical success factors

This approach first emerged as an approach for linking information systems strategy to broader commercial goals by first identifying the crucial elements of the firm's business strategy. More recently it has been appropriated by strategists in general as an alternative to the goal structure approach described above.

According to its originators, critical success factors (CSFs) are: 'the limited number of areas in which results, if they are satisfactory, will enable successful competitive perform-ance' (Rockart and Hoffman, 1992). More recently Johnson and Scholes (1997) have defined CSFs as:

… those components of strategy where the organisation must excel to outperform competition. These are underpinned by competences which ensure this success. A critical success factor analysis can be used as a basis for preparing resource plans.

CIMA defines critical success factors as 'An element of the organisational activity which is central to its future success. Critical success factors may change over time, and may include items such as product quality, employee attitudes, manufacturing flexibility and brand awareness.' (CIMA: *Management Accounting: Official Terminology*, 2005, p. 47).

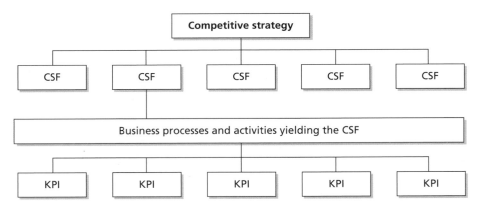

Figure 1.7   Critical success factors and key performance indicators

The attraction of the approach lies in the fact that it provides a methodology for identifying strategic goals (or CSFs) by basing them on the strengths, or *core competences,* of the firm. These are implemented through the development of key performance indicators (KPIs) for milestones in the processes delivering the CSFs (Figure 1.7).

1.5.2   Methodology of CSF analysis

According to Johnson and Scholes, this is a six-step process. We have illustrated them here using the example of a chain of fashion clothing stores.

1. Identify the critical success factors for the specific strategy. They recommend keeping the list of CSFs to six or less. The store chain might decide that these are:
   - right store locations;
   - good brand image;
   - correct and fashionable lines of stock;
   - friendly fashionable store atmosphere.
2. Identify the underpinning competences essential to gaining competitive advantage in each of the CSFs. This will involve a thorough investigation of the activities, skills and processes that deliver superior performance of each.
   Taking just one of the store's CSFs, the issue of correct stock, as an example:
   - recruit and retain buyers with acute fashion sense;
   - just-in-time purchasing arrangements with clothing manufacturers;
   - proprietary designs of fabrics and clothes;
   - close monitoring of shop sales by item to detect trends in which items are successful and which are not;
   - swift replenishment delivery service to minimise amount of stock in the system.
3. Ensure that the list of competences is sufficient to give competitive advantage.
   The store needs to consider whether improvement to the systems and processes underlying its CSFs will be sufficient to secure its place in the high street or whether more needs to be done. For example, have they considered whether they need to develop a direct ordering facility to raise profile and gain loyalty?
4. Identify performance standards which need to be achieved to outperform rivals. These are sometimes termed *key performance indicators* and will form the basis of a performance measurement and control system to implement and review the strategy.

KPIs that the clothing store chain might consider to match its key processes (listed above) include:

- staff turnover among buyers and designers;
- lead times on orders from suppliers;
- percentage of successful stock lines designed in-house;
- installation of a real-time store sales information system by the end of the year;
- establishment of 1-day order turnaround for store replenishment.

5. Ensure that competitors will not be able to imitate or better the firm's performance of each activity, otherwise it will not be the basis of a secure competitive strategy.

   Our store would compare its competences against Gap, Miss Selfridge, Next, River Island, etc. It would need to consider whether its present advantages are sustainable.

6. Monitor competitors and predict the likely impact of their moves in terms of their impact on these CSFs.

   This process is carried out principally by discussions between management, although there is a clear additional role for the special expertise of the chartered management accountant in mapping the key process, developing KPIs and monitoring them.

It is worth remembering that critical success factors are specific to an organisation at which you are looking. They should not be confused with the survival factors and success factors which relate to the industry in general and which we will consider later in Chapter 2.

1.6 Meeting the objectives of shareholders

1.6.1 Maximisation of shareholder wealth as an objective

Traditional economic theory specifies that the objective of the firm is to maximise profit. However this assumption does not accurately reflect the goals of the shareholder for a number of reasons:

1. *It is a single-period measure* (typically annual). The shareholder wants financial returns across many years.
2. *It ignores risk.* Shareholders will require higher returns if risks are higher but will be satisfied with lower returns if risks are low.
3. *It confuses profit with cash flows to the investor.* The investor wants cash flows not a figure for profit on the income statement.

It can be argued that a more appropriate version of rational shareholder objectives is either (a) maximisation of the present value of the free cash flows of the business, or (b) maximisation of the share price.

We will return to this topic later in your studies when we consider the calculations in more detail.

1.6.2 Financial and non-financial objectives

Traditionally the shareholders' objectives have been translated into financial objectives such as profit or profitability (e.g. return on capital employed or earnings per share).

These accounting measures have several drawbacks when used as strategic targets:

- *They are not useful for start-up businesses.* During their first few years many firms do not make a profit or return a positive cash flow due to the high costs of set-up and getting established in the market. For example, in its early years, Amazon.com, the on-line bookstore, had a market capitalisation of $15bn, yet did not make a profit. Profitability measures are better suited to mature businesses.
- *They are inherently short-termist.* Because profit is an annual measure it encourages management to focus on short-term returns at the expense of the long-term development of the business. Hence managers may decide to cut product development, promotion or staff development to improve profit performance at the expense of the long term.
- *They provide no control over strategic behaviour.* The profit figure is a financial summary of the effects of a year's economic activity. The competitive strategy of the firm will seek to do business in particular ways in order to make this profit. This strategy should also feature in the goal structure.
- *They can be manipulated by creative accounting.*

Some of the drawbacks of profit-based measures are addressed by value-based measures. These are discussed in Chapter 8.

Consequently the strategic targets of firms usually contain a mixture of financial and non-financial measures of performance. These ensure that:

- managers follow courses of action consistent with the competitive strategy;
- shareholders and others can form an opinion of the success of the firm's strategy even when financial results are low;
- the strategic objectives can be more easily translated into tactical and operational o bjectives for divisions and processes without an immediately discernible impact on profits (e.g. human resources, marketing, etc.).

The issue of developing balanced scorecards of financial and non-financial objectives for the purposes of control is discussed in Chapter 8.

The debate on the primacy of financial targets widens when we recognise the impact of other stakeholders and the issues of corporate social responsibility.

1.7 Objectives of not-for-profit organizations

1.7.1 The nature of not-for-profit organisations

The previous sections dealt with organisations that pursue profits as their primary objective. What about those that do not?

Examples of not-for-profit organisations (NPOs) include:

- government departments and agencies (e.g. The tax authorities);
- trade unions;
- schools;
- charities (e.g. Greenpeace, Oxfam, Red Cross, Red Crescent, Caritas);
- mutual associations (e.g. building and some life assurance societies).

Unlike privately-owned businesses their primary objectives are unlikely to be financial. Instead they are seeking to satisfy particular needs of their members or the sections of society which they have been set up to benefit.

1.7.2 Example: the Chartered Institute of Management Accountants

Objectives

The Objectives of the Institute as set out in the Royal Charter are:

- To promote and develop the science of Management Accountancy and to foster and maintain investigations and research into the best means and methods of developing and applying such science and to encourage, increase, disseminate and promote knowledge, education and training and the exchange of information and ideas in respect of all questions relating thereto or connected therewith.
- To provide a professional organisation for Management Accountants and by means of examination and other methods of assessment to test the skill and knowledge of persons desiring to enter the profession.
  Source: CIMA website www.cimaglobal.com

1.7.3 Key features of NPO objective setting

1. Possibility of multiple and contradictory objectives. Unlike firms, NPOs may not have one dominant stakeholder group. Consequently the NPO seeks to satisfy several different groups at once, without having the touchstone of one primary objective, such as profit, to adhere to. For example, CIMA seems to have the following stakeholder groups in mind:
   - its qualified membership;
   - its student membership;
   - users of the information provided by management accountants;
   - the accountancy profession generally;
   - the research community engaged in management accounting research.
   With limited funds at its disposal, which one(s) of these gets priority?
2. *Participation in setting strategic objectives.* Many NPOs are compelled by their constitutions or law to go through processes of open consultation with their members and beneficiaries before deciding on strategy. For example, the housing services division of a local authority will ensure that it has tenant relations groups and tenant representation at its meetings in the same way as schools must have some parent-governors as well as teaching and council representatives.

   CIMA consulted widely among members, employers and academics in devising its new professional examinations syllabus. The Council of CIMA is made up of members and has a committee structure made of members.

   This need for participation and consensus can make objective setting slow, introduce conflict and compromise in objective setting and lead to contradictory objectives.
3. *The providers of funding are often different from the beneficiaries of the NPO's activities.* This increases the influence of charitable donors, funding bodies or government over the objectives of the NPO. Their objectives might not, however, be the same as the beneficiaries or members.
4. *The priorities of NPOs may change more frequently.* One obvious example is the changing objectives of schools according to which political party is in office. Another is aid charity that must suddenly cease long-term health education programmes to deal with a humanitarian disaster.

SETTING THE GOALS OF THE ORGANISATION

5. *Changed role for financial objectives.* NPOs do not need to make a profit, although some will wish to make a financial surplus to allow investment or the giving of financial assistance.

CIMA does not mention finance, though we take it for granted that it does not intend running into financial deficits. This reflects the tendency for financial prudence to be a *requirement* in an NPO, rather than an objective.

6. *Increased role for personal objectives.* The nature of NPOs can lead to a lack of close scrutiny. Consequently particular individuals will pursue their own goals. For example, climbing the career ladder is a common feature of political parties and public bodies, while focusing on building up personal reputation is a feature of universities and among hospital consultants.

1.7.4 Public sector objectives

The public sector is diverse and includes:

1. *Nationalised industries:* A commercial enterprise that sells its goods on a market but which has its priorities set mainly by political rather than market conditions and reporting to government-appointed boards and government ministers rather than shareholders. They are often expected to develop a surplus (i.e. profit) from their operations to enable replacement investment.
2. *Government agency:* A service organisation such as a welfare benefits service or taxation body. Generally required to deliver an appropriate level of service to its customers (claimants or taxpayers) using the resources at its disposal.
3. *Public service organisation:* These provide a service on behalf of central or local government such as health, defence or policing. Generally no price is paid by the public for the use of these services which are instead financed from taxation.

Public sector organisations come under particular scrutiny for the following reasons:

1. *Lack of a profit motive* can lead to suggestions that they are not interested in ensuring efficient use of their resources or providing a good service to their clients.
2. *Lack of competition* means they cannot be compared to other organisations nor be subject to the disciplines of the market.
3. *Inadequate scrutiny* from shareholders means there is the danger that they will be swayed by the personal or political objectives of powerful stakeholders.
4. *Public interest* in their behaviour, usually in the form of questions from politicians or press articles, due to the desire for them to be democratically accountable.

One model for setting objectives in public sector organisations was suggested by the UK National Audit Office. It consists of evaluating performance according to three E's:

Effectiveness, That is, the extent to which it carries out its allotted tasks. For example a police force may have targets for detected crimes or a hospital for cure rates.
Efficiency: This relates to the level of service it delivers with the inputs or resources at its disposal. For example a social services office might be evaluated according to the number of cases being handled per number of staff or a tax office assessed on how quickly it processes tax returns and raises assessments.

Economy is the cost of the operation (or the surplus it generates). For example, a school might be evaluated on the cost per pupil per year.

Strategy in public sector organisations has a number of differences from that in profit-seeking organisations:

1. *Wider stakeholder involvement in deciding strategy.* Public sector organisations are democratised and hence management will be expected (sometimes under a statutory mandate) to consult with the public and employees before taking initiatives.
2. *Limited resources.* In profit-seeking organisations greater demand for services will cause a rise in revenues and hence increase the ability of the firm to extend supply. However, many public sector organisations must afford supply from a predetermined budget allocation. Consequently greater demand will cause queues and shortages such as hospital waiting lists or lack of spaces in desirable schools.
3. *Subject to changes in political priorities.* The expectations of the service, the funds available and the constraints on its operations will change as governments or policies change. These may be quite unpredictable and hence make planning difficult. Moreover many public sector organisations avoid committing to long-term strategic investments if they believe a change in political masters is likely.

1.8 Competing objectives

1.8.1 Importance of the existence of competing objectives

It has been shown that profit-seeking, not-for-profit and public sector organisations may have competing objectives arising from:

- conflicts between profit and social responsibilities;
- differences in the goals of particular managers;
- conflicts between the goals of influential stakeholder groups.

This has important implications in the following areas:

1. *Development of consistent strategies.* If the organisation does not have clear objectives, or if its objectives are in conflict with one another, then it will not be able to follow consistent courses of action. For example, a firm that seeks to satisfy objectives for short-term dividends while also pursuing long-term growth will eventually be forced to sacrifice one or other due to lack of funds.
2. *Deciding between strategic options.* Options are evaluated against the objectives of the business before management agree to devote resources. However, if one option provides a good financial return while another provides jobs in an area of high unemployment, a firm with both financial and social responsibility objectives will not be able to choose.
3. *Development of appropriate performance measures.* The more objectives an organisation has, the more control measures it will need to monitor performance towards them. If the objectives are competing there is a danger of conflicting signals or, worse, excessive focus on one at the expense of the rest. For example, a school will have many objectives such as producing good citizens, ensuring emotional development, catering for special needs, etc. However, parents and government prefer to have a single

measure to decide whether a school is performing well or badly and tend to focus on examination results. This immediately distorts behaviour in the school towards exam results at the expense of other equally worthy objectives.

1.8.2 Resolving competing objectives

There are various techniques available:

1. *Prioritisation.* Management can specify that any strategy considered must as a minimum satisfy one or more specific objectives before they are prepared to consider it.

    For example, management may set a minimum profitability threshold for any strategy (say 15 per cent return on investment). Once this is assured they turn their attention to achieving it in a more socially responsible way.

2. *Weighting and scoring.* Each objective is weighted according to its relative importance to the organisation (a high weight denoting high importance). Each strategic option is scored according to how well it satisfies the objective (a high score showing high attainment). A weighted score is calculated for each objective, they are totalled and the strategic option with the highest overall score is accepted.

3. *Creation of composite measures.* These are used for strategy implementation and control rather than for strategy formulation and choice. Approaches include the use of *balanced scorecard* measures and techniques of data envelopment analysis (DEA).

    DEA is used to assess performance of a group of branches or divisions (e.g. a objectives to achieve. Data is fed into a sophisticated computer program which identifies for each objective the best performer among the group. It calculates the comparative performance of the remaining branches against this 'best in class' branch. It can also give an overall performance metric for each branch, based on a composite index of its performance against a notional 'best in class at everything' branch.

    The above techniques are rational, mathematical ones. In their study *A Behavioral Theory of the Firm* (1963), management researchers Cyert and March identify some less obviously rational techniques by which competing objectives are resolved:

    - *Satisficing.* Here the strategy selected is the one that keeps all, or at least the most powerful, stakeholders happy. It usually emerges as a result of negotiation between the competing stakeholders.

    - *Sequential attention.* Stakeholders are kept happy by taking turns to get their objectives realised. Therefore staff may get a large pay rise every three years but, in between, pay remains static while dividends are paid.

    - *Side payments.* Where particular stakeholders' objectives cannot be addressed, they are compensated in another way. For example, a shareholder may be compensated for a low profit by a higher dividend, or a local community may have a new leisure centre built by a company whose new superstore will inevitably increase noise and traffic congestion in the area.

    - *Exercise of power.* Where management are deadlocked due to competing objectives, this is often resolved by one or more powerful figures using their power to force through their preferred option.

At this stage it will be worth going back to our earlier discussion about stakeholders and the management of stakeholders. Please remember in your answers that strategies that do not meet the approval of the most powerful stakeholders are unlikely to be successful. An organisation ignores them at its peril!

1.9 Summary

This chapter has looked at the role of mission and objectives in the strategy process. The key points to remember are:

- according to the rational view of strategy, mission and objectives are its starting point and also provide the basis for performance measurement to assist its implementation and control;
- a resource-based approach criticises this and argues that objectives should be set after the corporate appraisal in order to encourage the exploitation and development of core competences;
- the existence of stakeholders means that missions and objectives are often formulated to satisfy key stakeholder groups in addition to just shareholders;
- concerns of social responsibility and business ethics also affect the mission and objectives of the firm and may dilute the importance of shareholder wealth as a primary objective but are an increasingly important area for all organisations;
- not-for-profit organisations are a very clear example of where stakeholder power and the lack of an overriding financial objective can affect the process of strategy formulation and control;
- competing objectives arise from all these causes and management may employ a variety of rational and behavioural techniques to resolve them.

References

Ansoff, H.I. (1965) *Corporate Strategy*. Penguin.

Berman, S.L., Wicks, A.C., Kotha, S. and Jones, T.M. (1999) Does stakeholder orientation matter? The relationship between stakeholder management models and firm financial performance. *Academy of Management Journal*, 42(5): 488–506.

Bryson, J.M. (1995) *Strategic planning for Public and Nonprofit Organisations*. Jossey Bass.

Campbell, A. and Nash, L. (1992) *A Sense of Mission: Defining Direction for the Large Corporation*. London: Addison-Wesley.

Carroll, A.B. (1991) The pyramid of corporate social responsibility: Towards the moral management of organisational stakeholders. *Business Horizons*, 34(4): 39–42.

Chandler, A.D. (1962) *Strategy and Structure: Chapters in the History of the American Industrial Enterprise*. Cambridge, M.A.: MIT Press.

Cyert, R.M. and March, J.G. (1956) Organisational factors in the theory of monopoly. *Quarterly Journal of Economics*, 70(1): 44–64.

Cyert, R.M. and March, J.G. (1963) *A Behavioural Theory of the Firm*. Englewood Cliffs, N.J.: Prentice-Hall.

Friedman, M. (1963) *Capitalism and Freedom*. Chicago: University of Chicago Press.

Granovetter, M. (1985) Economic action and social structure: The problem of embedeness. *American Journal of Sociology*, 91(3): 481–501.

Hamel, G. and Heene, A. (1994) *Competence-based Competition*. London: Wiley.

Hannan, M.T. and Freeman, J. (1988) *Organisational Ecology*. Harvard University Press.

Holme and Watts, *Making good business sense,* World Business Council for sustainable Development.

Hooley, G.J., Cox, A.J. and Adams, A. (1992) Our Five Year Mission: To Boldly Go Where No Man Has Gone Before… *Journal of Marketing Management*, 8: 35–48. (Cited in *Corporate Performance Evaluation in Multinationals* (1993). London: CIMA).

Jawahar, M. and McLaughlin, G.L. (2001) Toward a descriptive stakeholder theory: An organizational life cycle approach. *Academy of Management Review*, 26(3): 397–414.

Johnson, G. and Scholes, K. (1997) *Exploring Corporate Strategy* (4th edn). Hemel Hempstead: Prentice-Hall.

Lynch, R. (2003) *Corporate Strategy*. Prentice Hall.

Marris, R. (1964) *The Economic Theory of Managerial Capitalism*. MacMillan.

Mendelow, A. (1991) 'Stakeholder Mapping', Proceedings of the 2nd International Conference on Information Systems, Cambridge, MA (Cited in Scholes, 1998).

Mintzberg, H. (1978) Patterns of Strategy Formation. *Management Science*, 24(9): 934–948.

Pettigrew, A.M. (1973) *The politics of organisational decision making*. Tavistock.

Porter, M.E. (1980) *Competitive Strategy: Techniques for Analysing industries and Firms*. Free Press & McMillan.

Rand, A. (1989) *The Virtue of Selfishness: A New Concept of Egoism (reissued)*. N.J.: New American Library.

Rawls, J. (1999) *A Theory of Justice* (revised edn). Oxford: Oxford University Press.

Rockart, J.F. and Hoffman, J.D. (1992) *Systems delivery: Evolving new strategies, Sloan Management Review*, Summer: 7–19.

Scholes, K. (1998) Stakeholder Mapping: A Practical Tool for Managers. In Ambrosini, V. (ed.) *Exploring Techniques of Analysis and Evaluation in Strategic Management*. Hemel Hempstead: Prentice-Hall International.

Sternberg, E. (1994) *Just Business: Business Ethics in Action*. London: Little, Brown.

Whittington, R. (1993) *What is Strategy and does it Matter?* London: International Thompson.

Williamson, O.E. (1967) The Economics of discretionary Behaviour. Markham.

Wood, D.J. (1994) Business and Society, Harper Collins www.mallenbaker.net/csr/CSRfiles/definition.html

Revision Questions

1

Question 1

Router plc, a mining company, has said in its mission statement that it will 'endeavour to make the maximum possible profit for its shareholders while recognising its wider responsibilities to society'.

Router plc has an opportunity to mine for gold in a remote and sparsely populated area. The mining process proposed, in this instance, means that all vegetation will be removed from the land concerned; after mining has finished, there will remain substantial lagoons full of poisonous water for at least 100 years. The mining process is a profitable one, given the current world price of gold. However, if the company were to reinstate the mined land, the process would be extremely unprofitable. The company has received permission from the government to carry out the mining. The few local residents are opposed to the mining.

Requirements

(a) Discuss the extent to which Router plc's mission statement is contradictory.

(5 marks)

(b) Explain how Router plc could establish a procedure whereby its wider responsibilities to society could be routinely considered when making strategic decisions.

(8 marks)

(c) Advise Router plc how it could deal with strategies that present a conflict of objectives.

(6 marks)

(d) Discuss the ethical dimensions of the decision to mine for gold. **(6 marks)**

(Total marks = 25)

Question 2

A publicly-funded department within a local administrative authority provides a health advisory service to its local community. This is not a hospital. Its function is purely advisory in respect of preventive medicine and focuses on good health promotion and prevention of accidents and illness.

In recent years, the funding for this service has been reduced in real terms, requiring greater levels of efficiency to be provided. The manager of the service has recognised the need to make economies. Despite receiving criticisms and complaints from the local administrative authority's elected representatives, the manager has reduced the level of service provision in an attempt to remain within budget. However, there has been no reduction in the staffing level which accounts for about 80 per cent of expenditure.

Last year, an independent public audit report criticised the management of the service. The report focused on the fact that the service overspent its budget, was considered to be inefficient in its methods of delivery, and wasted resources allocated to it. The report went on to state that according to annual performance statistics, there was a decline in the numbers of people using the service. It concluded that the service was failing to operate economically, efficiently or effectively. The result of this was that the local administrative authority reduced the funding still further and gave the manager a written warning that the whole service would be reviewed if there was not an improvement in this financial year.

The manager has responded by making further cuts to the service, but has protected the staffing levels. It is projected that the service will remain just within its budget allocation this year.

Requirement

Discuss the reasons why the service has received criticism.

Explain how the manager can improve the effectiveness and efficiency of the service while ensuring that it remains economic and within its allocated budget. **(25 marks)**

Solutions to Revision Questions

✅ Solution 1

- This question tackles the problem of a mission statement with particular reference to the social responsibility of a firm if there is a conflict between profitability and pollution.
- In part (a), note that the mission statement uses the term 'profit', a short-term measure, rather than 'shareholder wealth', the presumed economic objective of businesses. This allows you to contrast the conflict of social responsibility with profit in the short run, while using the sustainable enterprise to indicate that in the long run the interests of shareholders and society may not be in conflict.

(a) The mission statement that Router plc has published states that the firm aims to make the 'maximum possible profit'. It is quite common for objectives of this kind to be included in mission statements. In addition, the 'wider responsibilities to society' are recognised. This company objective is difficult to measure and there will be instances where the maximisation of profit on behalf of the shareholders conflicts with 'wider responsibilities to society'. The gold-mining project provides an example of such a conflict. It is expected to provide a profitable opportunity, but will result in 'substantial lagoons full of poisonous water for at least 100 years'.

In the short run this reveals a significant conflict between the interests of the shareholders and the public, particularly those living in the vicinity of the proposed mine. While it is often possible to reduce adverse environmental effects, these remedies will involve the business in costs that will reduce the profit available for distribution to the shareholders.

However, theories of the sustainable enterprise suggest that in the long run the following of socially responsible policies may safeguard shareholder wealth. Router requires that the authorities grant it operating licences and that shareholders continue to hold its shares. If it develops a reputation as a 'dirty firm', both may change their minds. This would cause a fall in both profits and share price. This would of course be a fall in shareholder wealth.

(b) There are various ways that social responsibility may be incorporated into the firm's decisions:

1. *Include costs of environmental restoration in project appraisals.* It is essential that the economic costs of a project are incorporated into the project evaluation. It is usual for a firm to include all relevant financial costs in a project evaluation, but it is also important that the effect of the investment should be considered. In this example, Router must include the cost of reinstatement in its calculations. This will result in the rejection of the project, as it does not meet the profitability criterion.

2. *Include social responsibility in the firm's mission and objectives.* It is necessary that policy decisions of this type are widely publicised within the firm to ensure that all managers are aware that the environmental factors must be incorporated into all decisions. Router has a commitment in its mission statement and there should be a written undertaking given by each manager that social issues will be taken into account.

3. *Employ outside consultants to advise on, or audit, decisions.* The appointment of a person either from within the firm or an outside consultant to monitor the position could be a useful method of implementing the environmental policy. It is possible that managers could neglect the 'wider responsibilities', especially if they are under pressure to boost the results of the company. In this situation, there may be a temptation to understate the costs by omitting the cost of coping with the 'wider responsibilities to society'. A procedure, therefore, should be introduced to ensure that the environmental effects are properly considered and this should include the regular use of outside 'experts' or impartial non-executive directors to assess the environmental effects before decisions are taken within the company.

4. *Develop a social consultation panel.* Router could convene a panel of stakeholder representatives to act as a consultative committee to discuss its decisions. In this case the inclusion of local people and environmentalists on such a panel would point up the issues mentioned in the case.

(c) It is usual for an organisation to have a number of objectives. It is common to find that the objectives conflict and a profit-maximisation objective will always be compromised by any other objective which reduces the revenue received or increases the cost of an organisation. Furthermore such conflicts may arise from the fact that organisations are led by a group of managers and therefore the conflicting personal agendas of each must be considered.

Methods of dealing with this include:

1. *Establish a hierarchy of objectives.* By prioritising objectives and scoring alternative projects against them, it becomes possible for management to choose the option with the highest weighted score. This one will best meet its overall objectives.

2. *Satisficing.* Where the conflict of objectives means that no single objective can be maximised, management may decide to adopt the course of action that is most acceptable to all by giving each stakeholder group something of what it wants. In this case perhaps to dig the mine but also provide some small amount of environmental restitution so that some of the damage is averted.

3. *Sequential attention.* This involves giving each stakeholder group's interests consideration over time, though not necessarily for every project. The effect is to keep them on board. In this case perhaps the mine will abandoned because the consequences are so great, but the next project, with lesser environmental damage, will be adopted. The environmentalists on the management team will feel that they have achieved something.

4. *Side payments.* These are compensatory payments to buy acquiescence. In this case perhaps quality housing might be provided for the labour force which would remain after the works had finished. This could be pointed to as some compensation for the environmental damage and population displacement.

(d) In an article in the August 1992 edition of *CIMA Student*, the author identified common features and issues of ethical questions:
- different perceived long- and short-term advantages and disadvantages;
- advantages to one group compared with disadvantages for another;

- issues of public responsibility and the accountant's duty as a professional;
- difficult implementation problems.

The principal ethical issues in mining are:

1. *The use of non-renewable resources.* The mining operation results in a non-replaceable asset being extracted from the mine. This deprives both present owners and future generations. It is, therefore, important to ensure that proper and equitable compensation is provided to the original owners of the resources. Moreover, the resources extracted should not be wasted or used for frivolous purposes out of consideration for future generations.

2. *The use of power in the negotiations.* The negotiations will raise a number of issues which will bring an ethical component to the negotiations. In the negotiations, it is important that the profit motive does not cause the developer to act improperly and exploit the present owner of the mining rights. Where the country is poor, it is too easy to give inadequate return for the value extracted.

3. *The environmental damage that will remain.* 'Lagoons full of poisonous water for at least 100 years' is clearly not an acceptable outcome for society. Router has an ethical responsibility to minimise the effect of this pollution. It would appear to be essential for the company to develop a plan to deal with the problem. It is likely to reduce the profitability of the project, as there are bound to be significant costs to treat the effluent, but to minimise the effect would appear to be the minimum responsibility of the company.

4. *Impacts on the quality of life of local residents.* The project must consider the effect of the mining operation on the local residents. Although they may benefit from the establishment of the mine in the area in which they live, it is likely that the pollution will also affect them. It is essential that Router explains the steps which will be introduced to minimise the effects on the local environment. This may reassure local residents that the company is adopting a responsible attitude towards the ethical aspects of the mining operation in their area.

5. *Safety of processes.* Mining is an industry noted for its poor safety record. Router must ensure that it conforms to best practice in the safety measures it follows, which may be more stringent than the legal minimums in the country of operation.

✔ Solution 2

The advisory service has been criticised for overspending its budget, inefficient delivery of services and wastage of resources. There are severe criticisms of the manager of the organisation and so it is essential that changes are implemented if the service is to continue.

It is essential that the whole method of operation is reconsidered. This will necessitate a review of its economy, efficiency and effectiveness. It is very important for revised strategy that the nature of the organisation's cost is analysed. It is stated that about 80 per cent of the total expenditure is related to the staff costs. It is therefore essential that this aspect of the problem is tackled at an early stage. The manager has obviously avoided this 'difficult' decision, as it is likely to lead to problems with the staff employed at the advisory service.

However, it is clear that major cost savings can only be achieved by tackling the area in which most of the resources are used. It appears that the manager is ineffective and is protecting the staff by not addressing the problems that arise from the high staff costs of the organisation.

At the outset, the overall aims and objectives of the service should be established. What does the local administrative authority expect from this department? Are the aims and objectives of the managers of the advisory service in line with those of authority? This is extremely important and the managers must ensure that views of all the stakeholders are known and incorporated as far as possible into the strategic planning process. Also, the managers must ensure that the methods of assessing performance are appropriate.

It is essential that the managers of the health authority service prepare a strategic plan that is focused and co-ordinated on the goals of both the health authority service and the local administrative authority. At the outset, it may be useful to initialise a zero-based budgeting exercise to establish the overall goals and the alternative courses of action that could be implemented at different levels of funding. In general terms, the economy, efficiency and effectiveness of the organisation must be reviewed.

The *economy* of the operation must be determined. It is important that the review considers if the organisation is using the minimum resources required to provide the present level of services. This might require comparisons of the costs with similar organisations in different locations. Although it is always difficult to measure the output in several companies, it is essential that these basic comparisons are undertaken. The situation faced by the advisory service is typical, as it will probably be difficult to use the number of consultations as the measure of output. The time and resources needed for each consultation may differ significantly and so perhaps a different measure should be developed.

The *efficiency* of the advisory service must be considered. The question to be asked is whether or not the resources are being used in an appropriate manner. The inputs required to achieve the outputs of the unit must be considered. This is also very subjective, as the output of an advisory service cannot be ascertained accurately. In essence, it is trying to assess the impact of the advice provided by the advisory service. This will be a difficult task, but it is essential to measure the output in relation to the input of resources.

Finally, the *effectiveness* of the advisory service must be considered. The review must establish that the outcomes are meeting the objectives of the organisation. To a large extent, the nature of the objectives that are identified at the outset will affect the extent to which the organisation is considered to be effective in reaching its objectives. This will also be problematic, as the objectives will be difficult to quantify.

Once these different aspects of the problem have been carefully thought about, it will be possible to review the different strategies that could be adopted. The effect of each strategy will have to be measured in terms of its impact on both the advisory service and the general public who will benefit from the advice that is available. Initially, it may be appropriate for a zero-based budgeting exercise to be undertaken to consider the alternative courses of action that could be undertaken with the resources that are available.

It would be advisable for the managers to undertake a benchmarking exercise to ensure that the levels of cost and service can be compared with the inputs and outputs of similar service providers. This may provide insights of 'good practice' and enable the efficiency of the advisory service to be reviewed and recommendations made to attempt to meet the expectations of both the elected representatives of the administrative authority, the independent auditor, the employees and the public who use the service.

2

Appraising the
Environment

Appraising the Environment

2

Strategy is concerned with the ability of the organisation to fit with, or cope with, its environment. This chapter continues the examination of the competitive environment of the organisation and explains the range of information sources which management may use to assess and interact with it.

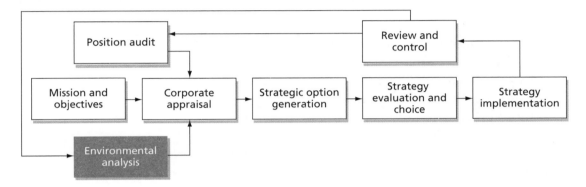

LEARNING OUTCOMES

By the end of this chapter you should be able to:

▶ evaluate the impact of regulatory regimes on strategic planning and implementation;

▶ evaluate the nature of competitive environments, distinguishing between simple and complicated competitive environments;

▶ distinguish the difference between static and dynamic competitive environments;

▶ evaluate the impact and influence of the external environment on an organisation and its strategy;

▶ explain the role and activities of pressure groups.

2.1 The importance of the business environment

2.1.1 Environmental impact assessment

According to CIMA this is:

 'A study which considers potential environmental effects during the planning phase before an investment is made or an operation started.'

CIMA: *Management Accounting: Official Terminology*, 2005, p. 48.

In the rational model this is part of the stage of environmental analysis.

2.1.2 Environmental segmentation

The environment may be thought of as all the factors outside of management control which can affect the performance of the business and the success of its strategies.

Management frequently use models to help them make sense of the environment of their organisations. These models separate the mass of factors impacting on the firm into groups, or segments, to aid closer analysis.

2.1.3 A model of the organisation in its environment

The model shown in Figure 2.1 incorporates two of the main models of environmental analysis required in the *Enterprise Strategy* syllabus:

(a) The Five Forces Model (Porter, 1980):
  - rivalry among existing firms,
  - bargaining power of buyers,
  - bargaining power of suppliers,
  - threat of new entrants,
  - threat of substitute products or services.

  Refresh your memory by looking at CIMA: *Management Accounting: Official Terminology*, 2005, p. 50.

(b) PEST analysis:
  - political/legal influences,
  - economic environment and influences,
  - social and demographic patterns and values,
  - technological forces.

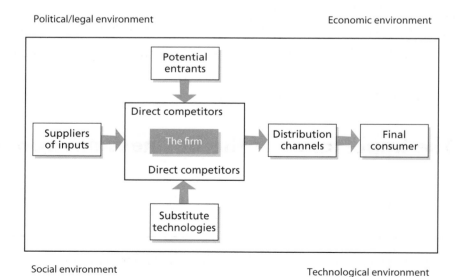

Figure 2.1 Model of the business environment

Although PEST analysis is the 'industry standard' for macroenvironmental analysis some writers prefer the greater detail provided by a PESTEL analysis. This separates legal from political and specifies ecological separately, for example,

Political:
- taxation policy,
- foreign trade regulations,
- government stability.

Economic factors:
- business cycles; GNP trends; interest rates;
- inflation; unemployment disposable income.

Sociocultural factors:
- demographics,
- income distribution,
- lifestyle changes; Attitudes to work and leisure;
- consumerism.

Technological factors:
- government spending on research,
- new discoveries/development,
- rates of obsolescence.

Ecological factors:
- protection laws,
- energy consumption issues,
- waste disposal.

Legal factors:
- monopolies legislation,
- employment law, product safety, etc.

A further elaboration by one author leads to the use of DEEPLIST: demographic, economic, environment, political, legal, informational, social and technological.

The practical point for any organisation is that it is irrelevant which acronym is used as long as the process is practised within the company and that they remain aware of the business environment and the changes that are occurring within it.

> The examiner frequently requires candidates to explore the impact of one model on another. It is not worth the risk of just learning one or two models and hoping they come up. For example, in the past the examiner has set part of a scenario question specifically on the five forces and in the next section asked candidates to discuss environmental threats and opportunities. For instance changes in the political climate may bring about changes in the competitive environment described by Porter's five forces model. Instability may disrupt supply. Deregulation, particularly of utilities, may remove monopolies and change the cost structure significantly. This was a clear reference to PEST or PESTEL.

You will be familiar with Porters Five Forces model from your earlier studies. By way of revision it is worth considering the example of a car manufacturer. It is worth remembering that the examination for E3 *Enterprise Strategy* assumes that you are familiar with the material covered in the earlier papers. For example, it will prove difficult to fully understand strategic supply chain management without a good understanding of both Porters five forces model and his value chain model (q.v. and the work of Brandenburger and Nalebuff 1996). Some of you may have studied, and passed, under an earlier version of the syllabus. I would strongly advise you to obtain a copy of the latest syllabus and ensure that you are familiar with the contents of all of the managerial pillars – they can be examined in E3!

2.1.4 Example of a car manufacturer

The detail of the Porter's model has been considered earlier in the pillar. The best way to refresh our memory and to understand how the model works is by reference to an example. Let us consider the situation of a motor manufacturer with operations based in the United Kingdom (say Ford, General Motors, Honda, Nissan or Toyota).

1. *Direct competitors.* These are the other car companies selling products in the United Kingdom. The actions of these competitors will affect prices, levels of sales, promotional expenditure and product specification. They are large and well funded and to a greater or lesser extent are trying to attract the same customers. New competitors have arrived from low-cost overseas economies (e.g. Seat, Skoda, Hyundai, Daewoo, Kia and Proton). The wave of mergers and acquisitions (Renault/Nissan, Ford/Jaguar/ Mazda/ Volvo/LandRover, General Motors/Saab, Daimler-Benz/Chrysler) and financial crises (Kia, Daewoo, BMW/Rover) increases the uncertainty in this market.

2. *Distribution channels.* Car manufacturers sell cars through two channels:
   - small firms and private motorists may buy from garage showrooms;
   - vehicle leasing companies are major volume customers which then provide cars to large and small business users.

   Both channels will seek to obtain the vehicles at low prices to increase their sales margins. Amalgamation between garage chains has significantly increased *buyer concentration* in recent years and this has put pressure on the profits of car manufacturers. As such it is an example of *buyer power*. Another trend has been the growth of 'car search' firms, which are able to provide motorists with cheaper cars through imports or special arrangements with particular dealers.

3. *Suppliers of inputs.* These affect the costs of production, quality and flexibility of the car manufacturer. The chief inputs used by car manufacturers based in the United Kingdom are labour, auto components, transportation services, information services and energy. Many car manufacturers have deliberately changed their relationships with suppliers from one based on bargaining around prices to one based on partnership. Relations with organised labour are based on openness and consultation, while supply–chain partnership agreements are formed with the component suppliers.

4. *Potential entrants.* During the 1990s UK car manufacturers faced competition in the home market from the arrival of low-price competitors from the Pacific Rim. Additionally the US Chrysler Corporation, absent since the demise of Hillman in the 1970s, reappeared with Jeep, Voyager and Neon brands imported from production bases in the United States and Austria. These entrants will increase industry supply and, through providing distribution channels and final consumers with more choice, reduce prices, cut sales volumes and raise product expectations.

5. *Substitute technologies.* These can reduce demand for the firm's product or render it obsolete altogether. As demand declines, the industry becomes oversupplied which introduces pressure on prices as each struggles to survive. Within the car industry there

has been clear switching between classes of car as motorists have reduced their demand for 'hot hatchbacks' and small saloons and embraced small sports cars, multi-purpose vehicles and estate cars. Some manufacturers were obviously wrong-footed by this trend to substitutes. Car firms will also need to keep a weather-eye on developments in rail transport and the increasing popularity of two-wheeled vehicles in metropolitan areas.

6. *Political/legal.* Many issues face the car manufacturer here, including:
   - the apparent shift in government transport policy towards public transport;
   - the Office of Fair Trading investigation into car prices and allegations of restrictive trade practices affecting car distributors;
   - European Union 'Social Chapter' regulations on maximum working hours and labour rights;
   - environmental and safety regulations affecting the design of cars and the processes by which they are made;
   - European Union free-trade policies enabling easier importing of lower-price cars to the UK from continental Europe.

7. *Economic.* Examples under this heading include:
   - UK policy on joining the European single currency and its effects on input and sale prices;
   - general health of the UK economy and its likely growth over the coming 5 years – this will affect demand for cars;
   - taxation of cars and petrol;
   - employers' contribution to employee insurance and welfare;
   - patterns of global economic development affecting target export countries.

8. *Social.* This broad heading includes:
   - attitudes to car safety and performance;
   - tastes and fashions in car colours and styling;
   - extent to which cars are still seen as a status symbol or lifestyle accessory;
   - lifestyle changes (e.g. activity sports);
   - size of families and growth of 'second families'.

9. *Technological.* This affects the product but also the demand for products:
   - technological developments affecting cars (e.g. driverless technology, navigation systems, etc.);
   - development of internet and interactive TV, opening the possibility for the manufacturer to sell direct to the final consumer;
   - increased teleconferencing and homeworking, reducing the need for private transportation.

Porter's model owes much of its success to the fact that it provides a unitary analytical framework in which to insert, in addition to some original concepts, many of the partial theories of industry analysis developed by studies of industrial economics, such as economies of scale, the degree of concentration and entry barriers. However, although clear from a theoretical point of view the model becomes increasingly difficult to apply as industries become harder to define and delimit. It is harder to define where an industry's boundaries lie and which industries should be considered suppliers and which customers and, moreover, what their cost structures are. It is increasingly difficult to define the boundaries of the telecommunications industry, or to say who the competitors are in the publishing industry. Similarly it is difficult to define the competitive dynamics of the electronic publishing industry. This was recognised by Brandenburger and Nalebuff (1996) with the introduction of the concept of the value net. This adds complements to the five forces of the Porter model. However, unlike the other five forces, which are competitive in nature, the more complements there are and the closer their relationship to the products supplied by the industry the better. For instance a conventional analysis using the five forces of the micro chip industry would suggest that Intel can gain competitive advantage by developing faster and faster products. But this is only part of the story, as is well understood by Intel. Most of us would already have more computing power than we needed but for the development of ever more power hungry applications. So Intel realises that to create a market for its faster and faster chips it must co-operate and share information with the manufacturers of computers, cell phones bandwidth and other products which will increase the demand for faster and faster chips. The complementor concept is particularly relevant in the information economy, since no one traditional industry can build it alone. Hardware needs software and the Internet needs high speed phone lines or other connections. This means that we will often find companies conducting development work with their suppliers or customers via joint ventures so that value may be captured.

It is worth remembering that although complementors are not competitors in the industry they can affect the competitiveness of the industry influencing the demand for products or services and by influencing the purchasers' choice between different suppliers. As such they are relatively powerful if there are few substitutes for the service they provide. A further example of a complementor is the firm that makes the hand-held stock taking device that is seen in supermarkets. As the employee keys in the stock they see on the shelf the information goes to the supermarket system and to the suppliers system – speeding the restocking process and benefiting both the supermarket and their supplier.

It is important to remember that Porter's model is an analytical model and it is about the strength of the forces that impact upon the industry it is not enough to just describe the forces.

For instance, you can usually recognise fierce competition because there are price wars and heavy discounting, expensive advertising and promotional efforts, litigation and expensive commitments to investment and product development. You should expect to see declining margins and ROCE for all firms other than the market leaders.

At this point you might want to look at Question 3 in the November 2006 examination. Although Porters analysis is not mentioned, a good knowledge of the model and what it means is essential for a good answer.

2.1.5 Process of understanding environment

Environmental analysis may take place in two ways:

1. *During the strategy formulation process.* This suggests that the firm has a formal and rational strategy process. The information is gathered as a preliminary to the corporate appraisal and may include special reports on particular factors affecting the present or proposed strategy.
2. *As part of a continuous process of environmental scanning.* This describes the organisation maintaining a weather-eye on its environment, watching out for emerging opportunities and threats. This will be a key part of an emergent approach to strategy, where it is recommended that as many staff as possible are involved in order to maximise the information and create greater acceptance of the need for change.

2.1.6 Evaluation of environmental segment models

The main benefits of environmental segment models are:

1. *They ensure that management consider a wide range of potential impacts when devising strategy.* There would otherwise be a danger that they would concentrate on competitors and suppliers and not see the broader forces at work.

2. *They allow division of the work of environmental analysis.* For example, one team can look at buyers, while another examines the economy and reports back to the strategy team.
3. *They provide a common language for discussion of strategy between the managers.* Most managers will know the 'Five Forces' and PEST analysis models used above.
4. *They provide insight into key strategic issues.* Some models have empirical research to back them up which may help the team identify key threats.

However, management should be aware of the dangers of segmentation models:

1. *They distort reality.* The real business environment does not fall into neat segments. This is just a structure put on it by strategy writers. Had we chosen a model with a different categorisation we might have obtained a completely different perspective. For example, combining legal with political suggests that political power works in a legal framework. If we separate legal from political we might recognise that in some of the countries we deal with the law is ignored and real political power lies with particular elite groups.
2. *They present the environment as external.* The models assume that there is an internal domain called the firm which management can control and that there is a boundary between this and the environment which they cannot control. For example, distribution channel, suppliers and customers are seen as separate and external. This is very hard to square with modern strategy theory which sees them as stakeholders and partners. Marketers would argue that customers are at the centre of the organisation, not some external force off to the right-hand side. Human resource managers would certainly not agree that staff are an input from the environment with the same status as spare parts.
3. *They may cause management to overlook networks and interdependencies.* In the example in Section 2.1.4, one car company will see another as a competitive rival. This ignores the fact that they are joint venture partners in a particular technology, that the rival owns one of the car hire firms it sells to and that they are all members of the same trade association lobbying government.
4. *They overload management.* Management cannot expect to develop a strategy to deal with all the environmental issues raised by the models. Some writers suggest that management should monitor just the small number of key factors for success and deal with those.

The fact that such segmentation models are still popular is evidence that they are a useful tool. However, management should ensure that they reflect on the assumptions underlying them and their value in practice.
In practical terms it is important to:

1. Remember that most important factors will transcend the categorisation as political, economic, societal or technological. For instance the advent of G.M. crops may be a technological issue at first sight which may offer economic benefits and is enjoying some political support. But its social acceptability is in some doubt. Remember that PEST (or which ever acronym is in use) is only an aide memoire – rigid characterisation is unnecessary and counterproductive.
2. Indicate how much and in what direction a particular theme will affect the nature of the firm's business.
3. Outlook how these themes may strengthen or weaken in the future.

2.1.7 Game theory

One of the criticisms of Porters model is that it is static and does not take account of the dynamic nature of the relationships between the firms in an industry. Just as the relationship between suppliers, the firm and buyers changes as they gain more, or less, negotiating power so does the relationship between competitors. By relegating to mediating variable links profitability only with structure, the model ignores the fact that the essence of competition is the interaction between the players in an industry and the decisions that they make in reaction to, or anticipation, of the actions of other players. There is limited consideration of the decisions to either compete or cooperate, the subsequent moves made and the role of, and reaction to, threats, promises and commitments. Over the last few years Game theory has made a contribution to this debate based on an analysis of political events and international policy using concepts from the fields of sociology and psychology.

As such Game theory offers two particularly valuable insights into the consideration of strategic management;

- *The theory facilitates the framing of the decisions made by the players in an industry.* Game theory provides a structure, a set of concepts, and a terminology, with which to describe a competitive situation faced by firms in an industry. This can be summarised as;
    1. the identity of the players,
    2. a specification of each players options,
    3. the specification of the potential payoffs from each combination of options,
    4. the sequencing of decisions using game trees.
       (You will be familiar with game trees, possibly describing them as decision trees, or Markov chains, from your studies in other pillars.)
       By providing this set of parameters, Game theory allows us to understand the structure of the competitive landscape and facilitates a systematic and rational approach to the analysis of the decisions that have been, and can be, made.
- *It can predict the outcome of competitive situations and identify strategic options for the players involved.* Game theory offers insight into situations of competition and bargaining and can predict the consequences of strategic actions and also the likely equilibrium outcomes of those situations. The technique can provide an insightful analysis of central issues of strategy that go beyond guess work. Grant (2002) claims that 'simple models, such as the Prisoners Dilemma, predict cooperative versus competitive outcomes, whereas more complex games permit the analysis of the effects of reputation, deterrence, information, and commitment – especially in the context of multiperiod games.' This is particularly important for managers where they have the option of manipulating the structure and outcome of the game by changing the payoffs to the different players.

During the 1900s, interest in the theory was awakened by its application to analyse, and provide insightful discussions, of the rivalry between Airbus and Boeing, the problems experienced by OPEC in agreeing to production cuts, auctions of airwave spectrum and the competitive impact of the 'Marlboro Monday' price cuts introduced by Philip Morris.

Cooperation

As we discussed earlier, the work of Brandenburger and Nalebuff (1996) *Co-opetition* recognises the duality of competition and cooperation that can exist in an industry. Game theory helps us to view an industry in this way and will help to explain why this occurs. Whilst the relationship between Microsoft and Google is one of competition the relationship between Microsoft and Intel is one of cooperation, since their products/services are complementary.

- A player is your competitor if buyers value your product less when they have the other players product than when they have your product alone.
- A player is a complementor if buyers value your product more when they have the other players product than when they have your product alone.

However, there isn't a simple division between those companies that are your competitors and those that are your complementors. For example, Exxon and Shell are rivals in terms of both exploration and at the forecourt where petrol is sold. But in other situations they are complementors; they cooperate in a number of joint ventures such as the Dutch gas company NAM and Infinium, a manufacturer of lubricant additives. This ties in with the idea of clusters, which is considered in more detail elsewhere as part of Porter's diamond, where competitors 'cluster' together in geographical areas of expertise – for example, the financial centres of the City of London and the software developers of Silicon Valley. Whilst those companies are competing with each other for the rewards of creating value for the customers they are also cooperating in creating an infrastructure and market to increase the overall value available to share.

Quite often competition will result in a worse aggregate result for the players than will cooperation. For example;

- Price wars between two relatively evenly matched competitors usually results in lower profits for all concerned and no change in market share. No one wins, except the customer.
- Competitive bidding such as that seen in the auction of the 3G licences in the UK. The only 'winner' was HM Treasury and this was even short sighted on their part since those companies that 'won' the auction at ridiculously high prices had insufficient capital left to develop the technology required, and make the infrastructure investment necessary to roll out the new mobile phones. The telephone companies lost out immediately and, in the longer run HM Treasury lost out on tax revenue and position of UK companies in the world league of telephony providers.

That being said, cooperating too closely will lead to prosecution under the competition legislation which exists in both the EU and the USA.

Deterrence

The equilibrium of a game, or competitive situation, can be changed by adjusting the potential payoffs and by introducing an element of deterrence. The key to the effectiveness of a deterrent is that it must be credible. The threat of dramatic price cuts by those already established in an industry in the event of a potential new entrant establishing itself may not be credible. The new entrant may believe that it would not be rational for the existing companies to reduce their profits dramatically just to keep out a new player. There must be a believable signal that the threatened action will be taken. John Lewis, a UK retailer, makes the commitment that it will 'provide a refund to any customer able to buy the same product elsewhere at a lower cost' and thus deters other high street stores from entering damaging price wars. Large manufacturing companies will often invest in 'over capacity' to deter new entrants – this has been common in the aluminium smelting industry with Alcoa attempting to prevent new entrants to the lucrative US aluminium industry. Once a company has a track record of carrying out its threats the approach of deterrence is far more effective. Gillette successfully kept *Bic* out of the US market for disposable razors by dramatically reducing its prices for disposable razors. The depth of the discounts given actually reduced Gillette's own sales of ordinary razors whilst the battle was on going.

These types of aggressive behaviour are often described as 'hard commitments', companies can also make what are known as 'soft commitments' where they signal that they will not become involved in aggressive behaviour. One example of this is the introduction of frequent flyer programmes by airlines where every airline attracts a number of Airmiles – sufficient of which can be redeemed for free flights. The airline concerned is sending out the message that they do not intend to compete on price – but are shifting the playing field to other aspects of the product offering.

According to Grant (2002) where companies compete on price hard commitments will have a negative effect on profitability and soft commitments will have a positive effect. Where they compete on output, hard commitments, that is a threat to increase capacity will have a positive effect and soft commitments the opposite.

Changing the structure of the game

By creating alliances and other agreements, companies may be able to change the structure of an industry and achieve greater profits for themselves and, possibly, their partners. It may also be the case that they are able to increase the size of the market so that all benefit, but if the intention, and the outcome, may be more self-centred and only lead to increases for themselves. Both Microsoft and Intel have changed the nature of the market in which they operate by making their technology relatively cheaply available to ensure that their technology became the industry adopted standard. Microsoft originally sold MS-DOS to IBM at a very low cost so that it would be incorporated in every PC sold. Since, at that time, IBM was a clear market leader, this helped Microsoft to dominate the market for PC operating systems. Similarly, Intel, aware that IBM was concerned about their supplier power, by virtue of the 8086 computer chip licensed the technology relatively cheaply to rivals AMD and IBM themselves. Intel had given up an effective monopoly position but had 'encouraged' IBM and AMD to not invest heavily in an alternative design of computer chip since they no longer feared the market dominance of Intel to the same extent. Since they did not have to 'fight' AMD and IBM, Intel were able to use their resources elsewhere and develop the next generations of computer chips; 286, 386, 486 and Pentium. Subsequently, when they became more aggressive over the licensing agreements that they granted, AMD developed their own design of computer chip and the two now compete aggressively.

The mathematics of Game theory

The mathematics involved in Game theory can get quite complicated, but it is unlikely that the examiner will ask any calculations that are complicated. Here are two examples of typical, simple calculations.

An example of a simultaneous game

Consider two companies who are involved in selling the same product in a market which they, collectively, dominate. The possibility exists that they can spend heavily to gain market share. (This is a similar situation to the one in which Coca Cola and Pepsi Cola find themselves.) However, the possibility exists that the increased sales from the high advertising expenditure may not offset the additional cost. Consequently, a logical conclusion for both firms would be to keep advertising expenditure at the present levels, effectively colluding, and maintain the current situation for their mutual benefit. If both firms adopt this strategy then the payoff for each is shown in the bottom right hand quadrant of the table.

Table 2.1   Payoff returns to A & B

		Competitor A	
		High advertising	**Low advertising**
Competitor B	**High advertising**	B= 10 A= 10	B = 24 A= 2
	Low advertising	B=2 A = 24	B = 18 A= 18

The danger, of course, is that knowing these likely outcomes either A or B will cheat and one will suffer significantly lower returns of 2. In the event that both cheat and spend heavily on advertising both will get a sub-optimal return of 10. According to Game theory it is highly likely that this will be the outcome since it represents a dominant strategy. *A dominant strategy* is one which outperforms all other strategies regardless of what strategy is chosen by rivals. Essentially this is what is known as the Prisoners Dilemma – it makes sense for the two companies to cooperate, but if either cheats the other company will lose out significantly. This, of course, assumes that the two companies start out equally – not often the case.

An example of a sequential game

In sequential games, the theory looks at the reactions of one player to the actions of another. The theory argues that the guiding principle is to think forwards and then to reason backwards. Consider the actions that a competitor might make based on a reasoned assumption about the competitors objectives.

If we consider two innovative companies which have to make a decision about the level of investment they will make in a new product. X has the better R&D skills but limited finance, Y has better financial resources but is not so well resourced in terms of R&D. Both companies are aware that investing heavily in R&D would bring their products to market sooner by shortening the development time, but the additional cost might not be recovered. So both the companies would prefer not to invest heavily in R&D.

As we can see from Figure 2.2 if X decides to invest heavily, having raised the finance, Y will be placed in a difficult position. Y can either invest high, in which case its return

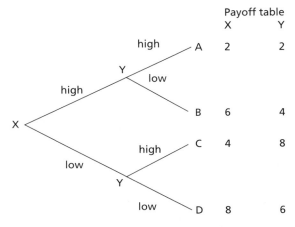

Figure 2.2   Payoff table for investment decision for X and Y

will be 2 (the same as Y's return) or it can invest low, in which case the return will be 4. However, should X decide to invest low then Y gains the upper hand and will almost certainly invest high giving outcome C which although better that the worst outcome for X still doesn't match its favoured outcome B. If the management of X can safely assume that the decision-maker at Y is aware of Game theory X should chose to invest high, knowing that Y will recognise that investing high would be a ***dominated strategy*** and would chose to invest low and outcome B will be achieved.

An evaluation of Game theory

For economists, the theory of strategy IS Game theory. Grant (2002) quotes an economist 'The essence of strategic thinking is to anticipate your competitors' moves in advance. Studying your competitors' likely reaction dramatically improves your ability to choose a strategy that will be successful.'

Arguably, the great value of Game theory is the rigour of its language in facilitating the description of the actions and reactions of the players in an industry. There is quite a strong body of mathematical application which underpins the theory – and which is outside the scope of this learning system and syllabus. However, this mathematical rigour comes at a cost. Game theory has been very useful for analysing past situations, decisions and outcomes. Similarly, it provides accurate predictions in highly stylised situations involving a few variables and very restrictive assumptions. Therefore, the applicability of the theory to the real world seems, on the face of it, to be limited. The result is described as;

'A mathematically sophisticated body of theory that suffers from unrealistic assumptions, lack of generality, and an analysis of dynamic situations through a sequence of static equilibriums. When applied to more complex (and more realistic) situations, game theory frequently results in either on equilibrium or multiple equilibriums, and outcomes that are highly sensitive to small changes in assumptions.'

Porter (1991)

In general, Game theory has done a far better job at explaining the past than of predicting the future. At this point in time, Game theory has not developed to the point where it permits us to model real business situations in a level of detail that can generate precise, or even useful, predictions.

2.1.8 Survival and success factors

At the end of an environmental analysis a company should be able to recognise the survival factors and success factors that relate to the industry in which they operate or wish to operate.

For instance;

Where there are powerful buyers with low switching costs,

- *Survival* – meeting minimum buyer requirements.
- *Success* – a strongly differentiated product, strong relationships and bonds of trust with high negotiating skills.

Where there are low barriers to entry,

- *Survival* – very difficult without success factors!
- *Success* – strongly differentiated product and low costs.

Where the industry is enjoying fast growth,

- *Survival* – technology and cash for growth.

- *Success* – advanced technology, cash for growth and superior relationships with researchers and funders.

Where the industry is mature,

- *Survival* – minimum economic scale.
- *Success* – significant scale or other cost advantage and strong buyer relationships.

2.2 Causes of environmental uncertainty

2.2.1 Components of uncertainty

CIMA defines uncertainty as:

> 'The inability to predict the outcome from an activity due to a lack of information about the required input/output relationships or about the environment within which the activity takes place.'

CIMA: *Management Accounting: Official Terminology*, 2005, p. 97.

Uncertainty can also be defined as 'the difficulty in making reliable assumptions about the future'.

Managers perception of uncertainty will be increased by two factors – complexity and dynamism.

1. *Complexity*. This is the number of variables which can impact on the firm and how difficult they are to predict or understand. Also if the relationships between the variables is complex, this will also increase uncertainty. For example, in financial markets the very large number of international banks, the wide variety of assets now available and their complex structuring have all contributed to making financial forecasting very complex.

   The car industry has an increased number of competitors and multinational business means that each manufacturer sources parts from, and sells cars in, a multitude of countries each with its own specific sets of environmental variables. This has significantly increased the complexity of its environment.

2. *Dynamism*. This is the rate of change of the business environment. Increased dynamism means that management's models of 'how things work' will become out of date much quicker. It also suggests that competitors will be able to respond more quickly to a firm's initiatives.

Examples of the factors which have increased dynamism include:

(a) *Swifter information communications*. These mean that something happening on one side of the world will have global impacts very quickly. The speed with which financial crises spread is often cited as an example.

(b) *Accelerated product life cycles*. Modern competitive strategy leads most firms to invest heavily in research and development to render rivals' products obsolete. The cumulative effect is to reduce the lifetime of all products. Management will find it very hard to predict the sales of their products or their ability to recoup investment expenditure on them.

2.2.2 Impact of uncertainty

High uncertainty affects business strategy in several ways:

1. *Reduces the planning horizon.* If a firm operates in an uncertain environment its management are unlikely to develop plans for more than a few years ahead because they accept that they will be subject to large margins of error.
2. *Encourages emergent strategies.* Some writers believe that high uncertainty brings into question the idea of planning a strategy at all. For example, Stacey (1996) suggests that formal strategy processes have failed to recognise the impact of chaos theory. The latter recognises that prediction in any open system is impossible due to the diversity of factors which may affect it. He cites long-range weather forecasting as a casualty when it was abandoned once it was recognised that a falling leaf in Brazil could eventually affect weather patterns in Europe. These writers argue for an emergent approach to strategy and therefore suggest that management should focus on creating more-flexible organisations and encouraging strategic awareness among staff.
3. *Increases information needs of the organisation.* Where the environment is no longer predictable, management will require more regular information and on a greater range of factors to make it more certain. This will increase further still if the organisation elects to adopt emergent strategy formulation because the number of recipients of such information will increase.
4. *May lead to conservative strategies.* Managers will tend to stay closer to the 'strategic recipes' that have worked in the past because they fear trying anything new due to not being able to forecast its effects. This approach is flawed because under conditions of high uncertainty there is no reason to believe that old 'recipes' will still work.

2.2.3 Has uncertainty really increased?

The modern assumption is that the business environment has become more uncertain and that more information is needed by management in order to restore certainty. Hatch (1997) observes that 'Environments do not feel uncertain, people do', and the only thing which has demonstrably increased is the amount of environmental information available to management. She ventures that perhaps the world has always been dynamic and complex but that we never fully appreciated it before.

Hatch's suggestion is deliberately far-fetched to make a point. The more environmental data we provide to managers, the more uncertain and stressed-out they may become. This gives weight to the argument, noted before, that in strategy formulation management should pay attention to only a few key success variables and ignore the rest.

Recent events leading up to and including the 'credit crunch' were, arguably, predictable but very few economists or policy analysts did so. Those who did forecast the problems of the financial system were ignored and often ridiculed. One such person was Nicholas Taleb whose books 'F*ooled by Randomness*' and '*The Black Swans*' now make interesting reading – both were published before the present problems arose.

2.3 Competitor analysis

As recently as 1998 a survey of American firms by Ram and Samir (1998) found that only 24 per cent of firms surveyed had a systematic competitor profiling system in place. East

Asian competitors had been benefiting from advanced competitor profiling systems for a decade or longer.

2.3.1 The importance of competitor analysis

Ultimately business strategy is about the commitment of the organisation's resources to courses of action which are believed likely to improve its long-term financial performance.

> CIMA: *Management Accounting: Official Terminology*, 2005, (p. 47) defines competitor analysis as: Identification and quantification of the relative strengths and weaknesses (compared with competitors or potential competitors), which could be of significance in the development of a successful competitive strategy.'

Figure 2.3 shows the impact of varying levels of competitor action on the profits of the business. These may include:

- price cuts;
- launching of a rival product;
- aggressive expansion of production which reduces the firm's market sales;
- inclusion of costly modifications to the product which the firm must also undertake.

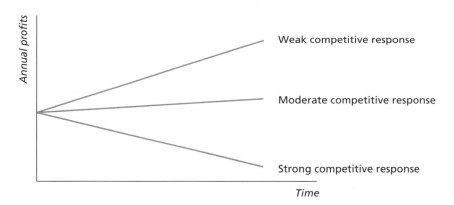

Figure 2.3 Impact of competitor responses on profit

The unit of analysis here may be a product, customer segment, geographical region or technology. The implications for management's choice of product/market strategy is clear. A suitable strategy is one which yields satisfactory financial returns after taking into account the potential responses of competitors.

According to Wilson and Gilligan (1997) competitor analysis has three roles:

1. to help management understand their competitive advantages/disadvantages relative to competitors;
2. to generate insights into competitors' past, present and potential strategies;
3. to give an informed basis for developing future strategies to sustain or establish advantages over competitors;
   To these we may add a fourth:

4. to assist with the forecasting of the returns on strategic investments for deciding between alternative strategies.

2.3.2 Levels of competitors

Kotler (1997) identifies four levels of competitors:

(a) *Brand competitors*: Firms who offer similar products to the same customers we serve and who have a similar size and structure of organisation as ourselves, for example:
- Pepsi and Coca-Cola;
- Unilever and Procter & Gamble.

(b) *Industry competitors*: Suppliers who produce similar goods but who are not necessarily the same size or structure as ourselves, or who compete in a more limited area or product range, for example:
- British Airways and Singapore Airlines;
- Unilever ice creams and Mars ice creams;
- Nestlé and Cadbury's.

(c) *Form competitors*: Suppliers whose products satisfy the same needs as ours, although they are technically quite different, for example:
- speedboats and sports cars;
- book publishers and software manufacturers.

(d) *Generic competitors*: Competitors who compete for the same income as the company, for example:
- home improvements and golf clubs;
- foreign vacations and new homes.

The extent to which these pose a threat to the firm depends on factors such as:

1. *Number of rivals and the extent of differentiation in the market.* Greater numbers of rivals increases the complexity of the industry, but because they are smaller it reduces the danger of one competitor breaking from the rest in an attempt to deliver a knockout blow. Instead each will try to carve a niche and hence increase differentiation. This makes it less likely that one can invade the market of another.
2. *Entry and mobility barriers* These are costs that the firm must pay to get admission to the industry or to the firm's particular segment of it. For example, the Levi Strauss brand has a strong presence in the market for casual clothing. It proved an insuperable impediment when the firm tried to make tailored suits.
3. *Cost structure.* If the rival has a high-cost structure this effectively denies entry to a market that contains a cost leader. For example, the high-cost structure of an exclusive department store would effectively deny it access to lower market segments.
4. *Degree of vertical integration.* Highly vertically integrated firms have considerable strength in a market. However, they are also inflexible because they are committed to buying from their own upstream supply divisions. International oilfirms have repeatedly lost out to discounting petroleum retailers able to buy supplies on the world's spot markets.

As a rule of thumb it is likely that the most significant present or potential competitors are the ones who conform most strongly to one or more of the following descriptions:

- they presently serve the same or similar customers to ourselves;
- they have a similar or cheaper distribution network;

- they are at the same stage of production as ourselves;
- they utilise a similar technology in providing their goods and services;
- they utilise similar types of management and staff skills;
- they have a similar geographical spread.

These explain the sudden arrivals of:

- retail stores in the banking services markets;
- electronic goods manufacturers in the photographic equipment market;
- household electricity providers also offering telephone services, gas and water.

Competitor analysis must, therefore, focus on two main issues; acquiring as much relevant information about competitors and subsequently predicting their behaviour.

The prediction of the competitors behaviour can be considered to have two main purposes:

1. to forecast their future strategies and how to counteract them,
2. to forecast their likely reactions to a firm's strategic decisions.

*You should distinguish carefully between entry barriers and mobility barriers. Entry barriers are fairly straightforward and refer to the situation where a new entrant tries to enter the industry. Mobility barriers are different and relate to a situation where an existing player in the industry attempts to change their competitive position. For instance, Skoda, who had a reputation for building cheap and low-quality cars, had to overcome significant mobility barriers to become recognised as a supplier of high-quality vehicles. They left one strategic group and joined another. They were only able to do this because the take-over by Volkswagen allowed them to improve their production methods and image. Even then it took them roughly 4 years to change customer's perception. Similarly, within the UK Tesco moved from a strategic group which could, at best, be described as 'pile it high and sell it cheap' to a quality supermarket. This involved a change of senior management, very expensive refurbishment and a period of more than 10 years!

2.3.3 Gathering competitor intelligence

The gathering of competitor intelligence is the subject of many books and there is at least one journal devoted, specifically, to the subject, *Competitive Intelligence Review*, John Wiley. There are professional bodies associated with the activity, The Society of Competitive Intelligence Professionals (www.scip.org) and The Canadian Institute for Competitive Intelligence (www.cici-icic.ca) and a key motivation for their existence has been to establish and enforce ethical standards in the industry.

Competitive Intelligence is not just about the gathering of information but about developing an understanding of the players in the industry. This may even involve the psychological profiling of the key decision makers in rival firms.

Grant (2002) has produced a four-stage framework for competitor analysis:

1. *Identifying the current strategy*. This can be identified from what a company says and does. More often than not what they do will be more important than what they say – their explicit statements of intent in the annual reports and at presentations to financial analysts may not be matched by the actions that represent their emergent strategy.
2. *Identifying competitor's objectives*. A knowledge of a competitors goals is an essential component of any analysis. Whether they are driven by short-term cash or profit goals or whether they have the reserves to focus on long-term objectives will result in them

exhibiting significantly differing behaviours. From this perspective it is important to recognise the goals of a parent organisation where such exists and their attitude to the performance of subsidiaries. If a company appears happy with its current level of performance then there are unlikely to be any changes to their present approach.

3. *Identifying a competitors' assumptions about the industry.* A competitors' decisions are governed by their perceptions and assumptions about industry structure and the players with whom they compete. These perceptions will often be driven by the value systems of the senior management and according to Spender (1989) these perceptions will converge over time, limiting the players in an industry to behave in a particular way, 'rationally', as time goes by. This often explains the complacency of existing players when a new entrant picks off a new segment of a market with out reaction from the incumbents.

4. *Identify the competitors' resources and capabilities.* Without a rigorous analysis of the resources that a competitor possesses there can be no realistic prediction of the seriousness of a possible challenge. It is easy to determine what they are doing but the emphasis here should be on what they are capable of doing. Ideally a company should know as much about its competitors as it knows about itself, this is, of course, unlikely to be achieved but is something for which a company should strive. We shall be considering the analysis of resources in a later chapter and can leave this section until then.

Once the information has been gathered and the analysis, used to predict competitor behaviour, conducted it must be presented in the most accessible format to those who will make the decisions on a timely basis. Thereafter the rivals should be continuously monitored for signs of activity and the industry scanned for the emergence of potential rivals.

If the technique is well developed it will become one of the firm's core competencies allowing a more confident, proactive, approach to the market place contributing to competitive advantage rather than leaving the firm to react, often defensively, to the strategic initiatives of other players in the industry.

It is worth noting that much of the information required for successful competitor analysis will be qualitative. Fleisher and Bensoussan (2002) give a full listing of the information that an organisation should gather about their competitors. The broad headings are as follows:

> Products and Services
> Marketing
> Human Resources
> Operations
> Management Profiles
> Sociopolitical
> Technology
> Organisational structure
> Competitive intelligence capacity
> Strategy
> Customer value analysis
> Financial.

An extract of a few of those categories will give an indication of the detailed qualitative nature of much of the information (Table 2.2):

Table 2.2 Detailed qualitative information for competitor analysis

Products/services	*Competitive intelligence capacity*
Number of products and services	Evidence of formal CI capacity
Diversity and breadth of product lines	Reporting relationships
Quality, embedded customer value	Profile
Projected new products/services	CEO and senior management level of support
Current market shares by product and product lines	Vulnerability
	Integration
	Data gathering and analysis assets
Marketing	
Segmentation strategies	
Branding and image	*Customer value analysis*
Probable growth vectors	Quality attributes
Advertising/promotions	Service attributes
Market research capability	Customer goals and motivations
Customer service emphasis	Customer types and numbers
Key customers	
Sociopolitical	
Government contacts	
Stakeholder reputation	
Breadth and depth of portfolio of sociopolitical assets	
Public affairs experience	
Nature of government contracts	
Connections of board members	
Issue and crisis management capability	

2.3.4 Forecasting competitors' response profiles

Kotler (1997) identifies four response profiles:

1. *The laid-back competitor.* Does not respond to competitive moves.
2. *The selective competitor.* Reacts to attacks on certain markets but not in others, or certain types of attack (e.g. to price cuts but not to promotion offensives).
3. *The tiger competitor.* Always responds aggressively to any threat, in order to send a message to all contenders that it will retaliate.
4. *The stochastic competitor.* No predictable pattern to responses. Often does not respond to moves, then on one occasion decides to retaliate.

Kotler advises management to consider the reasons why a competitor does or does not have a track record of responding. For example, the following might be reasons to think again about taking advantage of an apparently docile rival:

- they believe the market is not worth defending any more;
- they know the market is one in which it will be hard to dislodge customers;
- the management have their eyes on sequel products and so do not care if their present one is knocked out.

Cost structures are an important factor to consider:

(a) *High fixed-cost structure.* Rivals will respond more aggressively to threats to their sales volumes. This is because their high *operational gearing* means that any fall in revenues will cause drastic cuts in profits. Such costs tend to characterise:

- vertically integrated firms;
- firms employing capital-intensive production technologies;
- firms in industries with fixed supply schedules which must be maintained regardless of demand (e.g. scheduled transportation, football clubs, broadcasting).

(b) *High unit costs*. These make it impossible for the rival to effectively respond to price cuts. These are often masked by high prices based on high market positioning. Cutting prices is impossible without damaging this positioning.

(c) *High exit costs*. These are the one-off costs of leaving an unprofitable industry. Examples of exit costs include:

- dedicated assets which cannot be used elsewhere;
- costs of redundancies;
- decommissioning costs such as making former storage and workings safe;
- danger of the stigma of failure attracting rivals to attack in other parts of its business.

Where the rival cannot exit easily they are forced to stay and fight in the hope that something can be salvaged. Their response will be aggressive.

At this point you might want to look at Question 5 in the November 2006 examination which covers this topic.

2.4 Competitor accounting

2.4.1 Description

Competitor accounting is a term used by Ward (1992) to refer to the calculation of the relative costs and of competitors and their likely strategies to evaluate their potential effects on the profits of the firm.

2.4.2 Evaluation of barriers to entry

Barriers to entry include:

(a) initial capital costs,
(b) legal and patent protections,
(c) the costs and economies of scale of incumbent firms,
(d) extent of vertical integration,
(e) brand barriers,
(f) scale of investment in R&D,
(g) potential defensive action by incumbent firms (e.g. price cutting) and
(h) if economies of scale are important and the learning curve is effective.

Most barriers can be overcome by an outsider, provided that they are prepared to spend the money, for example:

- investing in the capacity, R&D, branding, etc.;
- acquiring an incumbent firm;
- riding out the losses caused by high initial costs or competitive retaliation.

You should always assume that entry barriers are low – until the evidence proves otherwise!

Competitor accounting must estimate the present value of the costs that an entrant will incur to overcome these barriers and compare this with the present value of the returns an entrant could achieve:

(a) If costs exceed revenues, then there will be no financial incentive to join and the threat of market entry is low.

(b) If revenues exceed costs, then there is a financial incentive to join. The threat of entry is higher and the incumbent firms must downgrade assessments of the market's attractiveness.

Where entry is likely, the incumbent firm may take *entry forestalling action* by increasing the entry barriers artificially:

(a) deliberate adoption of highly capital-intensive production techniques;
(b) high R&D spending to increase costs of participation;
(c) high advertising leading to strong branding and a psychological switching cost;
(d) reduction of price to reduce segment attractiveness.

Competitor accounting should compare:

(a) the present value of profits lost through undertaking these pre-emptive strategies; *with*

(b) the present value of profits lost as a consequence of market entry and advise management of whether to resist entry and even whether to invest further in the industry.

2.4.3 Estimate competitors' costs

Knowing these can help strategic decisions by giving a guide to:

(a) their likely future pricing behaviour;
(b) their response to strategic action, say price reductions, by the company;
(c) their ability to remain profitable as prices fall and therefore whether they will stay in the market or not;
(d) their potential prices in a tender or sealed bid for a contract.

Sources of data on competitors' costs include:

- from partnership agreements in a joint venture;
- physical analysis of competitors' products;
- banks and financial markets;
- ex-employees of competitors;
- generalisation from own cost base;
- industrial experts and consultants;
- physical observations (e.g. stand outside, or inside, their factory);
- published financial statements;
- competitor press releases;
- trade and financial media coverage;
- inspection of wage rates for grades of staff in the firm's area;
- availability of space for expansion on their present site;
- availability and cost of their finance;
- the characteristics of the market segment they serve;
- the work methods they employ.

This will entail the management accountant working with other experts such as production engineers, marketers, human resource specialists, etc.

2.5 The global economic environment

2.5.1 The main sources of economic impacts on the firm

The economic environment of the firm exists at two levels:

1. *The global economic environment.* The global environment contains such factors as:
   - changing patterns of global trade and economic development;
   - development of regional economic groupings;
   - international impacts on currencies and interest rates.
2. *The operational economic environment.* This relates to the immediate economic influences on the country(ies) in which the firm operates and sells. Factors here include:
   - stage of the economy in the trade cycle;
   - macroeconomic policies of domestic governments;
   - levels of interest, inflation and exchange rates.

One of the factors increasing the complexity of the firm's environment has been the increased influence of global economic forces on the economies of particular states. This has been accompanied by an increase in the influence of supranational economic bodies such as the European Union (EU) or the G8 summits of the major industrial nations. Having said that it is always worth considering economic forces at regional and local levels as well since, within a country, there will be differences from place to place in a number of factors. For instance, propensity to save, which is important to the financial services industry, changes markedly across the UK.

2.5.2 The new global economy

Earlier in the pillar you will have been referred to *Global Shift,* Peter Dicken (1998) and you should refresh your memory from your earlier studies on the following features of the global economy described in that book and also in Knox and Agnew, 1998. Dickens identifies two dynamics affecting world economic development:

- *Internationalisation.* The extension of trade across national economic boundaries. This more extensive pattern of trade does not fundamentally affect national economic and political boundaries.
- *Globalisation.* A qualitatively different process in which there is a functional integration of internationally dispersed activities.

Dicken cautions against getting swept up in the idea that globalisation of business is demolishing cultural and political boundaries between countries. Significant national differences remain. However he accepts that there has been a significant change in the extent of globalisation brought about by:

- *Extension of production chains across national boundaries.*
- *Patterns, and importance of foreign direct investment* (FDI).
- *The creation of supranational organisations* and the moves towards harmonisation of laws, taxes and even currencies.

- *Technology acting as an engine of economic transformation.*
- *The development of 'webs of enterprise' through the spreading of multinational enterprises.*
- *The impact of particular industries on transferring cultures, lifestyles and personnel across national boundaries.*

You will remember that Dicken predicts a number of challenges facing governments, organisations and individuals in the industrialised nations as a consequence of the increased growth of the globalised economy:

- Increased unemployment in the older industrialised countries, particularly among the unskilled, poorly educated or immobile.
- Widening differences in incomes and living standards within industrialised countries.
- Increased demand for flexibility in workforces, both numerically (through more extensive use of part-time workers) and functionally (through multiskilling).
- Changes in government policies towards ones aimed at removing obstacles to economic adjustment, promotion of small firms, increased harnessing of new innovative technologies and attracting foreign investment.
- Increased pressures for global governance to keep pace with the global businesses that authorities wish to regulate.

For less industrialised nations Dicken sees considerable problems with their ability to cope with worse poverty and unemployment, a point agreed with by Knox and Agnew (1998).

2.5.3 The European Union

It is worth remembering the aims of the EU, according to its website in 2000:

The ultimate goal of the European Union is 'an ever closer union among the peoples of Europe, in which decisions are taken as closely as possible to the citizen'; the objective is to promote economic and social progress which is balanced and sustainable, assert the European identity on the international scene and introduce a European citizenship for the nationals of the Member States.

Please refresh your memory on the detail, but one way to understand the detail of what it seeks to achieve is to consider its work thematically:

1. *Development of a single market.*
2. *Extension of citizens' rights.*
3. *Economic and monetary union.*
4. *Enlargement and inclusion of all countries which can be described as European in the broadest sense.*
5. *Representation of the EU in the world.*

Clearly the EU has come a long way from its simple objective in 1957 to form a European Economic Community. It is hard to resist the conclusion advanced by 'Eurosceptic' commentators that it has mutated into a super-state. Consideration of the following list of areas debated by its Economic and Social Committee reveals the scope of the modern-day EU:

- regional policy, structural funds, economic and social cohesion, cross-border and interregional co-operation;

APPRAISING THE ENVIRONMENT

- agriculture, rural development, fisheries;
- trans-European networks, transport, information society;
- spatial planning, urban issues, energy, the environment;
- social policy, public health, consumer protection, research, tourism;
- employment, economic policy, single market, industry, small and medium-sized enterprises;
- education, vocational training, culture, youth, sport, citizens' rights.

Naturally, it is up to you whether you take the view that the EU is an unnecessary, cumbersome, expensive and remote body bent on meddling in national affairs, or alternatively an essential bulwark against similar economic and political blocs elsewhere in the world and a safeguard against the carnage of the sorts of European war suffered twice in the twentieth century. Either way, the EU is a major part of the environment of most firms who will ignore its influence at their peril.

2.5.4 The North American Free Trade Agreement (NAFTA) and other trade blocs

You should similarly be aware of NAFTA and the other trade blocs which have been developed across the globe and their purpose. These include MERCOSUR originated in 1988 as a free trade pact between Argentina and Brazil and, based on its early success, was expanded in 1990 to include Paraguay and Uruguay representing a combined market of 200 million people. In the event that the Free Trade Area of the Americas is successfully formed in 2005 MERCOSUR would become a component part.

Outside of Western Europe and the Americas the only significant attempts at regional economic consolidation have been the Association of Southeast Asian Nations (ASEAN) and the Asia–Pacific Economic Cooperation (APEC).

ASEAN was formed in 1967 with the basic objectives of fostering free trade and cooperation in industrial policies. The original members, Brunei, Indonesia, Malaysia, Philippines, Singapore and Thailand were more recently joined by Laos, Mynamar and Vietnam which has slowed progress since their economies lag some way behind those of the founder states.

APEC was founded in 1990 at the suggestion of Australia and has 18 member states collectively accounting for half the world's GNP, 40 per cent of world trade and most of the growth in the world economy. Major players include China, Japan and the United States. The stated aim is to increase multilateral cooperation in view of the economic rise in the Pacific nations and the growing interdependence within the region. It has been suggested that the ultimate aim should be to form a free trade area and, at a meeting in Jakarta in 1994, a joint statement was issued formally committing APEC's industrialised members to removing trade and investment barriers by 2010 and for developing economies to do so by 2020. Despite further statements in 1997 the Brookings Institute, a respected American economic analysis unit noted that APEC 'is in danger of shrinking into irrelevance as a serious forum'. However, if it does eventually become a free trade area it will probably be the world's largest.

2.5.5 Globalisation of macroeconomic policies

Most discussions of macroeconomics assume that macroeconomic policies are undertaken by nation-states. Several features of the modern economic scene bring the role of the nation-state into question:

1. *The increased role of international capital markets.* The network of international banks has currency balances that dwarf those of the central banks of most countries. This makes concerted defence of particular exchange rates by national economies very difficult and has led to the creation of international monetary institutions to countervail the power of the international banks (e.g. G8, European Central Bank).

2. *The development of multinational businesses.* These span national boundaries and have levels of sales of turnover greater than the national incomes of all but a handful of national economies. Their ability to switch profits, investment and activity between nations has led one former UK energy minister to liken his meetings with the chief executive of an oil company to that of a country parson meeting the emperor. Some commentators see the creation of cross-national economic entities such as the EU as an attempt to strengthen the regulation of multinationals. Others see it as an attempt to remove national economic and legal differences at the behest of the multinationals.

3. *The creation of pan-national economic and political bodies.* Institutions such as the EU and the G8 summits, formed in the second half of the twentieth century, demonstrate that economic policies are being pursued in a more co-ordinated way than in the past. Furthermore pan-national organisations exist to regulate and co-ordinate industries ranging from banking and securities dealing to fibre production.

4. *The global trend to free trade.* Since the initial signatories adopted the GATT (General Agreement on Tariffs and Trade) in 1947, there has been a trend to greater openness in markets and the abolition of barriers to free trade. This culminated in the formation of the World Trade Organisation in 1994. The WTO is discussed below.

2.5.6 The World Trade Organisation

The WTO, based in Geneva, was formed in 1994 and has assumed the role formerly carried out by the GATT. Originally a treaty aimed at harmonising trade relations between its signatories, the GATT assumed the role of arbiter of trade disputes and enforcer and extender of the principles of international trade. Its role is to create a *multilateral trading system* to increase the wealth of participating nations by allowing the economic benefits of specialisation and free trade to be realised. Through successive 'rounds' of negotiation GATT has reduced tariff barriers and secured anti-dumping agreements between its year 2000 total of 130 members in agreements covering 90 per cent of world trade. In 2001 the Republic of China joined the WTO which was seen as a signal of its willingness to enter the global market economy. The WTO describes its functions as:

- a forum for trade negotiations;
- handling trade disputes;
- monitoring national trade policies;
- provision of technical assistance and training for developing countries;
- co-operating with other international organisations.

Areas of particular interest in its work are:

- protection of intellectual property through the creation of an agreement on copyrights, trademarks and industrial designs;

- provision of an 'integrated framework' to assist least-developed countries to participate and benefit from trade. This includes preferential terms of trade with more-developed nations and the provision of technical assistance and training;
- provision of a Dispute Settlement Understanding to provide a mechanism for members to resolve trade issues;
- Regulation of unfair trade practices such as tariffs, quotas, subsidies and dumping.

The worldwide wave of riots that accompanied WTO meetings in Seattle, Prague and Genoa demonstrate that the WTO is not seen universally as a force for shared prosperity. To the rioters at least it is an agent of international capitalism and of the already well-off industrialised nations, enabling them to exploit developing nations by imposing rules that guarantee them low prices for their crops and products. Environmentalists also despair at the destruction of traditional lifestyles and habitats as countries switch to producing lucrative cash crops to afford their place in the global economic order.

Possibly the environmentalists are right to be concerned. Foreign direct investment has increased dramatically in the last couple of decades. In fact it has increased 20-fold in the 25 years up to the year 2000 and, at that time was worth over $400 billion. In 1970, there were 7,000 companies operating internationally and by the year 2000 there were over 50,000. That year those companies were responsible for 30 per cent of world output and nearly 70 per cent of world trade. Of the worlds 100 largest economic actors, 29 were transnational companies and only 6 nation states had revenues larger than the top 9 transnationals. In January 2005 the largest company in the world was Wal-Mart with annual revenues of $300 billion and $103 billion in pre-tax profits. The 10 largest companies are shown in the table below.

	2004 Revenue $billion. Approx.	2004 Profit $billion. Approx.
Wal-Mart Stores (US)	295	10.3
BP (UK)	290	15.4
Exxon Mobil (US)	280	25.3
Royal Dutch/Shell (UK/Netherlands)	280	18.2
General Motors (US)	195	2.8
DaimlerChrysler (Germany)	185	3.1
Toyota Motor (Japan)	180	10.9
Ford Motor (US)	180	3.5
General Electric (US)	160	16.8
Total (France)	155	12.0

Not all large multinationals are from Western countries. In 2001 there were four developing countries represented by Hutchinson Whampoa (China), Singtel, (Singapore), Cemex (Mexico) and LG Electronics (China) By 2004 there were 30 companies from developing countries listed in the fortune 500 (a ranking of the largest companies produced annually by the Fortune business journal). This trend is expected to continue as companies from developing countries, particularly those from Asian countries, internationalise their operations.

To put these figures in context, every year The World Bank lends between $15–20 billion and the annual budget of the International Labour Office (a division of the UN) is $0.25 billion – only 1 per cent of the annual profit of Exxon Mobil. This affords those transnationals tremendous levels of power particularly at a time when the influence of national governments is in decline. In an increasingly globalised world economy the decisions of those transnational companies impact directly on government policies, human rights and other CSR concerns.

2.6 National competitive advantages

2.6.1 Background

Earlier in the pillar you will have considered the work of Michael Porter and his book The Competitive Advantage of Nations (1992) and you should refresh your memory about the questions Porter sets out to provide answers to:

1. Why do certain nations house so many successful international firms?
2. How do these firms sustain superior performance in a global market?
3. What are the implications of this for government policy and competitive strategy?

Porter concludes that entire nations do not have particular competitive advantages. Rather, he argues, it is specific industries or firms within them that seem able to use their national backgrounds to lever world-class competitive advantages.

2.6.2 Porter's Diamond

Porter's answer is that countries produce successful firms mainly because of the following four reasons but, as you will see in Section 2.6.6 there may be other factors (Figure 2.4).

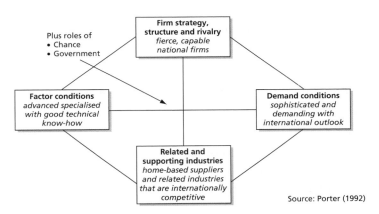

Figure 2.4 Four elements of national competitive advantage. Reprinted with the permission of The Free press, a Division of Simon & Schuster Adult Publishing Group, from The Competitive Advantage of Nations.
© Michael E. Porter 1990, 1998. All rights reserved

2.6.3 Demand conditions

The demand conditions in the home market are important for three reasons:

1. If the demand is substantial it enables the firm to obtain the economies of scale and experience effects it will need to compete globally.
2. The experience the firm gets from supplying domestic consumers will give it an information advantage in global markets, provided that:

(a) its customers are varied enough to permit segmentation into groups similar to those found in the global market as a whole;

(b) its customers are critical and demanding enough to force the firm to produce at world-class levels of quality in its chosen products;

(c) its customers are innovative in their purchasing behaviour and hence encourage the firm to develop new and sophisticated products.

3. If the maturity stage of the plc is reached quickly (say, due to rapid adoption), this will give the firm the incentive to enter export markets before others do.

2.6.4   Related and supporting industries

The internationally competitive firm must have, initially at least, enjoyed the support of world-class producers of components and related products. Moreover success in a related industry may be due to expertise accumulated elsewhere (e.g. the development of the Swiss precision engineering tools industry owes much to the requirements and growth of the country's watch industry).

2.6.5   Factor conditions

These are the basic factor endowments referred to in economic theory as the source of so-called comparative advantage. Factors may be of two sorts:

1. *Basic factors* such as raw materials, semi-skilled or unskilled labour and initial capital availability. These are largely 'natural' and not created as a matter of policy or strategy.

2. *Advanced factors* such as infrastructure (particularly digital telecommunications), levels of training and skill, R&D experience, etc.

    Porter argues that only the advanced factors are the roots of sustainable competitive success. Developing these becomes a matter for government policy.

2.6.6   Firm structure, strategy and rivalry

National cultures and competitive conditions do create distinctive business focuses. These can be influenced by:

- ownership structure;
- the attitudes and investment horizons of capital markets;
- the extent of competitive rivalry;
- the openness of the market to outside competition.

2.6.7   Other events

Porter points out that countries can produce world-class firms due to two further factors:

1. *The role of government.* Subsidies, legislation and education can impact on the other four elements of the diamond to the benefit of the industrial base of the country.

2. *The role of chance events.* Wars, civil unrest, chance factor discoveries, etc. can also change the four elements of the diamond unpredictably.

2.6.8   National competitive advantage

Successful firms from a particular country tend to have *linkages* between them; a phenomenon that Porter calls *clustering*.

Clustering allows for the development of competitive advantage for several reasons:

- transfer of expertise, for example, through staff movement and contracts;
- concentration of advanced factors (e.g. telecommunications, training, workforce);
- better supplier/customer relations within the value chain (i.e. vertical integration).

Clustering may take place in two ways:
1. common geographical location (e.g. Silicon Valley, City of London);
2. expertise in key industry (e.g. Sweden in timber, wood pulp, wood-handling machinery, particleboard furniture).

2.6.9 Losing competitive advantage

Nations may lose their competitive advantage through the erosion or deterioration of the factors which created the advantage to start with:

1. *Factor deterioration.* This occurs due to poor economic policies such as:
   - failure to maintain and improve the country's skill base;
   - lack of investment in technology and product;
   - failure to have developed beyond primary advantages when they run out.
2. *Local demand conditions.* Here local customers may fall out of step with world demands or inappropriate government policies cause a collapse or distortion of demand at home.
3. *Collapse of supporting clusters.* This is usually due to firms pursuing diversification strategies and ceasing to concentrate on their core business. The effect is that the members fail to remain world class against their more focused rivals overseas.
4. *Decline of competitive rivalry.* An excessive concentration between firms or pursuit of diversified business strategies reduces the keenness of the competition at home. This leads to shoddy products and excessive prices abroad.

2.6.10 Porter's strategic prescriptions

Porter suggests that the firm identifies its most promising strategy in the following ways:

1. Identify which clusters in the home country give a competitive advantage – either through
   (a) permitting lower costs of production than global rivals;
   (b) allowing a differentiated product.
2. If these advantages are likely to be world class, the firm should compete in global markets.
3. If these advantages are not world class, the firm should find a niche market at home or abroad where it can use its available strength.

2.6.11 Comment on Porter's Diamond

Although not as popular as his models of Five Forces, value chain and generic strategies, this model has still achieved a lot of recognition for Porter. It is not, however, without its difficulties:

1. *Companies not countries.* The industries that must succeed globally have their own management and strategies. By focusing on their country of origin Porter does not explain

why a given country produces both stars and duds in the same industry. For example, Toyota and Honda are both Japanese car makers which are a success. Nissan and Mazda are less successful and have been rescued by Renault and Ford, respectively.

2. *Ignore multinational or global corporations.* The idea that Microsoft is an American company or ICI is British seems outdated when we consider that their staff, shareholders and customers are from all over the world. Porter's model seems to apply better to firms that are exporting and less well to ones who are actually setting up outside of their home country.

3. *Ignores the target country.* Commercial success or failure will depend more on the environment in the target country than it will on the environment in the home country. Therefore it is necessary to analyse the target country too.

4. *Less applicable to services.* Porter's examples are restricted to manufacturing and closely allied industries such as banks and management consultancies. It is hard to see how his model would apply to Starbucks or McDonald's where so much of the product and staffing depends on the local economy and not a US industrial base.

2.7 Country analysis and political risk

As we have already discussed an analysis using Porter's diamond will ignore the environmental factors in the target country. It is important, therefore, that as well as conducting a PEST analysis for the home country of a company a similar analysis is conducted for any country within which a firm is currently operating or considering operating. Particular emphasis should be placed on determining any political and cultural differences.

2.7.1 Political risk

Political risk can be considered to arise at the macro or micro level. Macro political risks will affect all foreign firms in the same general way. Expropriation, the seizure of private businesses with little or no compensation to the owners would be an example as would indigenisation laws which require that national citizens hold a majority share in all enterprises. In recent years with the liberalisation of trade in Eastern Europe, the entry of China to the WTO and the negotiation of a trade agreement between Vietnam and the US macro political risk has diminished somewhat but still needs to be monitored by multinationals.

Micro political risk tends to affect selected sectors of the economy or specific foreign companies and is often driven by the dominance of those firms. These risks often take the form of industry regulation, taxes on specific types of business activity and local content laws.

Rugman and Hodgetts (2003) have produced a useful summary:

Sources of risk:
political philosophies that are changing or are in competition with each other;
changing economic conditions;
social unrest;
armed conflict or terrorism;
rising nationalism;
impending or recent political independence;
vested interests of local business people;
competing religious groups;
newly created international alliances.

Groups that can generate political risk:

current government and its various departments and agencies;

opposition groups in the government that are not in power but have political influence;

organised interest groups such as teachers, students, workers, retired persons, etc;

terrorist or anarchist groups operating in the country;

international organisations such as the World Bank or United Nations;

foreign governments that have entered into international alliances with the country or that are supporting the opposition within the country.

Effects of political risk:

expropriation of assets (with or without compensation);

indigenisation laws;

restriction of operating freedom concerning, for example, hiring policies and product manufacturing;

cancellation or revision of contracts;

damage to property and/or personnel from terrorism, riots, etc.;

loss of financial freedom such as the ability to repatriate profits;

increased taxes and other financial penalties.

When forecasting political risk whether the company does this on a formal or ad hoc basis, it is usual to focus on two areas:

1. the political system in which the company is doing business;
2. the goods/services to be produced and the operations to be carried out.

As regards the political system the major concerns would be the prospect of political up-heaval in the country, the likelihood of the government giving preference to local firms or the prospect of a government acting on a totalitarian fashion. They would also consider the strength of lobby groups within the target country. For instance, within the United States, lobby groups have considerable strength in the areas of steel, textiles, softwood timber and semiconductors and have been able to bring considerable pressure to bear on their government to bring about favourable decisions.

Products and operations also face an element of political risk. For instance where a government requires a joint venture to exist with a local partner there is both a limit to control and the risk of theft of product knowledge or technology. Where local laws do not offer patent protection this can be a significant risk. Similarly a requirement to source a fixed percentage of components locally can be a source of risk as can the governments approach to monopolies, cartels and price fixing.

2.8 Sources of environmental information

2.8.1 Environmental scanning

Although you will have considered environmental screening earlier in the pillar, it is impossible to evaluate the impact and influence of that environment unless you are completely familiar with the analysis that underpins it.

It is important to distinguish between different intensities in the use of environmental information. Environmental scanning is low-intensity gathering of information. Effectively it is keeping a 'weather-eye' on developments. Responsibility for scanning arguably rests at three levels:

1. *Line management.* In addition to their regular operational responsibilities line managers, or a designated manager, will be responsible. Given the operational concerns of these members of the team, this scanning is unlikely to extend beyond the medium term and will be limited to the technologies and products they control.
2. *Strategic planning.* Conducted by members of the strategic planning team. While their time frame of analysis will be longer than that of line managers, their lack of understanding of the operational and technologies details may mean they miss many important leads. For this reason more modern 'bottom-up' approaches to strategy may be preferable.
3. *Specialist unit.* Persons with specific responsibility for scanning. They may be called names such as 'business intelligence units'.

    Jain (1990) suggests that the following benefits arise from environmental scanning:
    - helps firm to identify and capitalise upon opportunities rather than losing out to competitors;
    - provides a base of objective qualitative information;
    - makes the firm more sensitive to the changing needs and wishes of its customers;
    - provides information to help the strategy formulation process;
    - provides intellectual stimulation for the strategists;
    - improves public image by showing that the firm is sensitive to its environment;
    - provides a continuing broad-based education for managers in general and strategists in particular.

2.8.2 Accessing environmental information

Wilson and Gilligan (1997) note that successful environmental scanning requires two elements to be present:

1. The *generation* of an up-to-date database of information.
2. The *dissemination* of this information to decision-makers.

This raises the important issue of how the knowledge of staff and managers can be effectively pooled and accessed. Possible techniques include:

- regular management meetings;
- encouragement of broader participation in the business strategy process;
- creation of an internal environmental information database for knowledge to be entered into under specified codes or headings.

2.8.3 Detailed environmental analysis

This is more focused and looks at the specific issues. It may be necessary in a number of situations:

1. In deciding on the viability of a particular product which is being considered for launch or continuation.
2. As part of an analysis of a particular business unit and its performance.
3. To assist with deciding whether to develop business divisions and products for another country.

The process of scenario planning, which we will discuss in the next chapter is often used as a means of considering the specific issues that a company needs to monitor more closely in this way.

2.8.4 Categorisation of information sources

In an excellent if now rather dated guide, Tudor (1992) provides the following categorisation of information sources:

1. *Primary sources*:
   (a) Annual reports and statements of competitors or firms in the target market or industry and those of their suppleirs.
   (b) Transcript services from newspapers, analysts and on-line data sources such as proprietary company information services.
   (c) Statistical sources such as government censuses and surveys of household expenditure, production and demographics.
   (d) Newspapers and newsletters such as the business press or industry bulletins.
   (e) Magazines and journals including the trade media, business and management journals, technical journals.
   (f) Analysis services such as Datastream and Extel.
   (g) Patents registered with the national patents office.
2. *Secondary sources*:
   (a) Directories and yearbooks covering particular industries (who's who) and ownership patterns (who owns what).
   (b) Market research reviews and reports produced by specialist research firms including Mintel, Economist Intelligence Unit, etc.
   (c) Abstracts, index journals and current awareness services. These are specialist databases (on paper, CD-Rom or on-line) which index technical articles under codes and keywords. The firm can set up a profile of keywords relevant to its industry and source the material written on it.
   (d) Government publications such as special reports of select committees on particular industries, economic forecasts and reports.
   (e) Grey literature. A generic phrase covering theses, conference reports, special research papers, maps and photographs.
3. *Computer-based information services*:
   (a) CD-Rom-based abstracts and journals.
   (b) On-line databases of professional and academic journals, newspapers and business information.
   (c) Internet resources such as:
      - homepages of rival firms;
      - economic information from national governments;
      - homepages of management consultants and professional bodies;
      - discussion groups;
      - academic papers via sources such as Google Scholar.

2.9 Summary

The key points to remember are:

- the components of the Five Forces model and the factors which influence them;
- the presence and influence of complementors;
- the fact that it is an analytical model and not merely a descriptive one;

APPRAISING THE ENVIRONMENT

- the components of PEST (institutions like the EU and WTO are examples of factors from PEST);
- the elements contributing to uncertainty (complexity and dynamism);
- the frameworks for competitor analysis;
- the threats that competitors can pose;
- factors leading to globalisation and the elements of the Porter Diamond;
- the nature of political risk;
- the main sources of environmental information.

Although specific questions on the environment may be asked, it is more frequently assessed as part of the scenario. We will find ourselves using the material from this chapter again as our knowledge of strategy builds up.

References

Brandenburger and Nalebuff (1996) *Co-opetition*, Doubleday.

Dicken, P. (1998) *Global Shift: Transforming the World Economy* (3rd edn). London: Paul Chapman.

Fleisher, C.S.F. and Bensoussan, B.E. (2002) *Strategic and Competitive Analysis*, Prentice Hall.

Gardner, H.S. (1998) *Comparative Economic Systems* (2nd edn). Fort Worth: Dryden Press.

Grant (2002) *Contemporary Strategy Analysis: Concepts, Techniques, Applications* (4th edn, Blackwell).

Hatch, M.J. (1997) *Organisation Theory: Modern, Symbolic and Postmodern Perspectives*. Oxford: Oxford University Press.

Jain, S.C. (1990) *Marketing Planning and Strategy*. Cincinnati, OH: South Western Publishing Company (cited in Wilson and Gilligan (1997), *op. cit*).

Knox, P. and Agnew, J. (1998) *The Geography of the World Economy* (3rd edn). London: Arnold.

Kotler, P. (1997) *Marketing Management: Analysis, Planning, Implementation and Control* (9th edn). Englewood Cliffs, NJ: Prentice-Hall.

Porter, M. (1991) Towards a dynamic theory of strategy. *Strategic Management Journal*, special issue 12(Winter): 95–117.

Porter, M.E. (1980) *Competitive Strategy: Techniques for Analysing Industries and Competitors*. New York: The Free Press.

Porter, M.E. (1992) 'Four elements of national competitive advantage' Figure 3.1 page 72. Reprinted with the permission of the Free Press, A Division of Simon & Schuster Adult Publishing Group from *The Competitive Advantage of Nations*. © 1990, 1998 by Michael E. Porter. All rights reserved.

Ram, S. and Samir, I.T. (1998) Competitor analysis practices of U.S. companies: an empirical investigation. *Management International Review*, 38(1): 7–23.

Rugman, A.M. and Hodgetts, R.M. (2003) *International Business* (3rd edn). Prentice-Hall.

Stacey, R.D. (1996) *Strategic Management and Organisational Dynamics* (2nd edn). London: Pitman.

Spender, J.C. (1989) *Industry recipes: The Nature and Sources of Management Judgement*. Blackwell.

Taleb, N.N. (2001) *Fooled by Randomness: The Hidden Role of Chance in Life and in the Markets*. London: Random House.

Taleb, N.N. (2007) *The Black Swan: The Impact of the Highly Improbable.* London: Random House.

Tudor, J. (1992) *Macmillan Dictionary of Business Information Sources.* Basingstoke: Macmillan.

Ward, K. (1992) *Strategic Management Accounting.* London: Cima/Butterworth-Heinemann.

Wilson, R.M.S. and Gilligan, C. (1997) *Strategic Marketing Management.* Oxford: Butterworth-Heinemann.

Revision Questions

2

❓ Question 1

A clothing company based in the United Kingdom believes that its domestic market is limited and is proposing to expand by the manufacture and sale of its products abroad. At this stage it has not identified where it will locate its manufacturing facility. The company believes that there are major advantages to be gained by setting up a factory in a country with a low-wage economy.

The company recognises the need to understand the marketing environment of the country within which it establishes its manufacturing facility. It appreciates that, besides labour, there are other local environmental issues that need to be fully considered before entering negotiations to build a factory.

Requirements
(a) Compare and contrast the environmental factors that apply in both the UK and the other country. **(15 marks)**
(b) Explain the possible cultural influences on the effectiveness of the workforce in respect of local education and training, technology, working hours and domestic amenities. **(10 marks)**

(Total marks = 25)

❓ Question 2

Michael Porter, in his book *Competitive Advantage: Creating and Sustaining Superior Performance*, suggested that a firm must assess the industry's market attractiveness by considering:

- the extent of the rivalry between existing competitors;
- the bargaining power of suppliers;
- the bargaining power of buyers;
- the threat of substitutes;
- the threat of new entrants.

Requirements

(a) If a firm wishes to monitor the bargaining power of buyers, recommend the factors that should be included in the monitoring system implemented by the firm.

(10 marks)

(b) Explain four different methods whereby a firm can reduce the threat of new entrants to an industry.
(10 marks)

(c) Explain the reasons why firms often continue to operate in an industry which is generating below normal returns in the short run.
(5 marks)

(Total marks = 25)

Solutions to Revision Questions

☑ Solution 1

- This question is very closely structured. Part (a) is obviously a reference to the four elements of PEST. You should structure your answer under these four headings and try to find more than one example of each. Note that the examiner asks you to *contrast* the factors between the United Kingdom and the low-wage economy'. It is a good idea to visualise a low-wage economy in your mind (say India or Mexico) and that will help bring ideas to mind. What is different between the two economies?

- Part (b) also has four elements:
  - local education and training;
  - technology;
  - working hours;
  - domestic amenities.

  Again you should structure your answer under these headings and find at least two examples of each.

- Be careful not to repeat yourself between sections (a) and (b).

- You are required to relate these factors in (a) and (b) to the strategy of the clothing manufacturer. In part (a) you should consider the impact of the PEST factors on it as both a manufacturer and a seller in the country. In part (b) your comments are restricted to the impact of the cultural factors on its role as a manufacturer only.

- Note how key points have been underlined to add emphasis. The marker can almost make sense of the paragraph by reading the underlined sections.

(a) Before making a decision to set up manufacturing facilities abroad, the company should consider the environmental factors which can be subdivided into the economic, the political and legal, the cultural, and the technological business environments.

  1. *Economic environment.* When appraising a foreign investment, the management needs to consider many factors.

     A particular issue is the cost of materials and of labour with an adequate level of skills. This will affect the decision on what level of technology to employ and how much expatriate management and staff to use. The experience of operating within the domestic market will mean that the management is aware of both the supply and skills of the local labour force available. However, the management may not have this information for the foreign country.

     Another economic issue will be the effect of the exchange rate regime on the costs and earning from the overseas subsidiary. Because it is freely convertible, the foreign exchange market establishes the UK exchange rate. However, the low-wage economy may have a nonconvertible currency. This will affect the ability to repatriate profits and also the costs of goods exported back to the home economy.

Other issues you might mention, given time, include the relative growth rates of the economies, inflation rates, extent to which markets are developed, extent of state involvement in the economy, attitude to free-trade and the permissibility of foreign ownership of businesses.

2. *Political and legal environment.* The political risk must be investigated before making any decision to set up a manufacturing process abroad.

   For example, the problem of remittance of profits or management fees to the parent company does not arise in the domestic situation and the ability to remit funds is a key objective of firms that invest abroad. Governments in host countries may have policies to forbid such flows, thereby forcing the firm to invest funds in developing businesses and assets in the host country.

   There may be differences in political stability. The UK political system is mature and governments are elected and bound by the rule of laws passed democratically. In some low-wage economies these democratic safeguards are not in place. This means that agreements reached to safeguard investments or give access to markets may be rescinded without warning and even assets sequestrated.

3. *Cultural environment.* The customs and values of the country are often important in determining the ultimate success of an investment. The firm knows these for its home market in the UK but to sell overseas it will have to be sure that the design of the clothing and the styles and fabrics are acceptable in the new markets. Market research and past experience should provide the company with information to forecast accurate future sales.

   The languages spoken in the foreign economy may be different from the UK and this will present communication problems for management from the UK.

4. *Technological environment.* The UK is a developed industrial nation and hence has electricity and a workforce familiar with the disciplines of factory life. These may not be present in the new economy. Management needs to investigate the foreign infrastructure. This will ensure that facilities are adequate to allow the firm to operate with a reasonable level of efficiency.

   Factors that may be considered are:
   - The availability of telecommunications within the country and the quality of connections back to the United Kingdom. This will have implications for management control.
   - The reliability of electrical power. The firm may decide it needs to provide its own generators as a primary or back-up power source.

(b) In planning the move of the manufacturing operations, it is essential that the management know about any issues which are particularly important to the workers.

1. *Education and training.* The foreign employees are likely to need training in order to work efficiently. Their level of previous experience will be vital to the success of the investment in their country. The firm may discover that in addition to the need for training in specific skills the workforce lack basic skills of numeracy and literacy which will affect their abilities to follow written job instructions and understand machine read-outs.

APPRAISING THE ENVIRONMENT

2. *Technology.* At the macro-level some low-wage economies already have substantial experience of factory working. Others are agricultural societies where the day is measured by the progress of the sun and hence notions of keeping factory hours is altogether strange.

   At a micro-level local workers may not have experience of particular technological processes such as computer-controlled machinery or computer-assisted design for clothing or laying out of jobs. This would necessitate use of expatriate workers in the short run and considerable training. Once trained, these local staff present a staff-retention problem because other firms will wish to employ them.

3. *Working hours.* Social and religious factors can sometimes differ in a foreign environment. Specific areas include the importance of the family unit, attitudes to the aged and special conditions regarding holidays and 'free time'. In particular, additional holidays may be required by groups of workers in order to allow them to perform religious rites or undertake significant social commitments. In some situations, the management may consider these demands to be excessive. However, a lack of understanding may result in problems within the workforce.

4. *Provision of local housing and amenities.* In some countries, it is expected that an employer will provide facilities for the staff. This will reduce the travelling time of the workers, but may increase the amount of capital employed in the project. It is likely that the employer who provides housing will be seen as 'caring' and this may be important for achieving acceptance within the foreign country.

   This can extend to the provision of other amenities such as clean water, health care and education for workers and their families. These enable the firm to be seen to make a contribution to the local society, safeguard future labour sources and may permit lower wage costs.

 ## Solution 2

This is a very standard revision of basic theory in part (a). Parts (b) and (c) require additional thought.

(a) The bargaining power of buyers represents a major factor in establishing the attractiveness of an industry. It is therefore important that the power of buyers is monitored in order that organisations are aware of the forces which are important in the development of a strategic plan. Factors which will influence the relative bargaining strength of the buyers include:
   - the number of different buyers and sellers in the market;
   - the relative size of both the buying and selling organisations;
   - the buyer's purchases are large in relation to the total sales of each seller, as a major customer can often dictate terms and conditions, especially if the cost structure of the seller includes a high level of fixed costs;
   - the level of profit earned by the buyers is low;
   - the product is undifferentiated;
   - the 'switching costs' are low;
   - the quality of the component purchased is not particularly important in the final product;
   - the extent to which buyers can undertake backward integration.

There will be a number of different sources of information that could be obtained to enable a firm to monitor the bargaining strength of buyers. These include:

- Details can be obtained from the financial reports of companies buying the product. The gross margins they report give an indication of the potential for their suppliers to raise prices if the buyer power could be reduced.
- The uniqueness of the technical specification of the product could be considered to reveal whether it is unique or whether several suppliers are capable of making it.
- A survey of the structure of the supply industry will reveal the number and location of alternative suppliers. Estimates can be made of their ability to supply and the costs of transport that might be involved.
- Information may be published by specialist organisations such as industry groups, and *ad hoc* reports could be commissioned.

(b) There are a number of different barriers to entry that are likely to reduce the number of potential entrants to the industry. Potential competitors can be deterred and competitive advantage retained by any of the following:

1. *Patents, licences and government/legal constraints*. It is possible for a firm to use any of these as a form of protection and to prevent new entrants to the industry. Once this type of legal barrier has been obtained by a firm, it can be of great value in retaining competitive advantage.

2. *Branding or customer loyalty (differentiation)*. Often at considerable expense, an organisation will try to establish customer loyalty which will ensure that people will buy the product in preference to other brands and substitutes that are available.

3. *Economies of scale including the learning curve*. In some industries, large-scale operations can produce the products at a lower cost than the smaller producers. This provides an example of 'overall cost leadership' which can be very significant in planning for competitive advantage.

4. *Access to cheaper factors of production*. Some firms are able to produce products at a lower cost, as they have been able to obtain materials, labour, finance or other expenses at a lower rate than their competitors.

5. *Switching costs*. The ability to change to another supplier without many costs being incurred. Incumbent firms can increase these by offering volume discounts, special delivery facilities or electronic ordering systems.

6. *Control of unique distribution channels*. If a firm can exclude other producers from distributing their products through the most effective distribution channels, then this can represent a significant entry barrier.

7. *The scale of investment needed to establish the operation*. If the amount of investment is so large that most competitors are unable to consider entering the industry, this represents a way in which potential competitors can be excluded and the existing firms have competitive advantage and possibly even a monopoly.

8. *Technological advantages that result in cost leadership*. Successful research and development often results in a firm having a process that reduces the cost of production so that competitors are unable to compete on a level playing field' This gives the firm that has invested in the R&D an important advantage over their competitors and will exclude potential entrants to the industry.

(c) There are exit barriers that result in firms remaining in an industry, even though the returns are below the normal level. When a firm realises that the probability of success is low or acknowledges that there is excess capacity in the industry, a decision to close may be appropriate. However, decisions of this kind are often postponed. This is likely to occur if the closure will result in substantial costs being incurred by the firm. These are termed exit costs. In general terms, the costs of closure are estimated to be higher than continuing the operation.

Particular costs are redundancy payments to staff or long-term supply contracts that will result in damages being due as a result of breaking the contract. In these situations, the closing may be delayed until a more appropriate time.

The ownership of assets with no resale value or assets shared with other processes could be another factor that delays the decision to close an operation. Similarly, common costs that are absorbed by a particular process may influence the decision to close down a portion or the whole of an operation.

Apart from the exit costs, a firm may decide to stay in an industry because the market has a strategic importance to the firm. For example, a commercial bank may continue to provide current (checking) accounts despite their low profitability because they are the cornerstone of a client relationship from which more valuable products can be sold.

3

Position Appraisal
and Analysis

Position Appraisal and Analysis

3

In the previous chapters we have been discussing the process by which the firm sets its strategic goals and how it analyses its environment. In this chapter we move on to discuss the process of how the firm interprets the potential impacts of the factors in its environment on its ability to reach its goals.

LEARNING OUTCOMES

By the end of this chapter you should be able to:

▸ identify an organisations value chain;

▸ evaluate the product portfolio of an organisation and recommend appropriate changes to support the organisations strategic goals;

▸ prepare a benchmarking exercise and evaluate the results;

▸ discuss how suppliers and customers influence the strategy process and recommend how to interct with them.

3.1 The SWOT analysis

3.1.1 SWOT and corporate appraisal

According to CIMA, a SWOT and a corporate appraisal are the same thing:

> *Corporate appraisal.* A critical assessment of the strengths and weaknesses, opportunities and threats (SWOT analysis) in relation to the internal and environmental factors affecting an entity in order to establish its condition prior to the preparation of the long-term plan.

CIMA: *Management Accounting: Official Terminology*, 2005, p. 47

It has also appeared in CIMA examinations as 'corporate review' and as 'position appraisal', so be prepared to understand it by different names.

Recalling the diagram of the rational approach to strategy we discussed in Chapter 1 (Figure 1.1), we can see that the corporate appraisal stands at the intersection of two other parts of the analysis: the environmental analysis and the position audit (Figure 3.1).

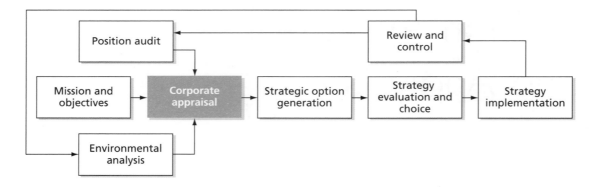

Figure 3.1 A model of a rational strategy process

We shall discuss the position audit at length later in the present chapter. Let us concentrate on the SWOT for now.

3.1.2 Purpose of a SWOT analysis

The SWOT analysis enables management to interpret the information they have gathered about their organisation and its environment in relation to how it affects the ability of the business to reach its strategic goals.

To do this, the members of the management team involved need to establish some ground rules on what the SWOT terminology means:

1. *Strengths and weaknesses are usually internal and specific to the firm.* A strength is something the firm is good at doing or a resource it can call upon to reach its goals. They are sometimes termed *distinctive competences*. A weakness is generally a resource shortage which renders the firm vulnerable to competitors.

2. *Opportunities and threats are generally external to the firm.* Opportunities and threats are strategic challenges to the firm. Because these are so often things like competitors, changing technology or imminent economic recession, most managers assume them to be solely external. However some things inside the firm can also be threats or opportunities, for example, unrest among the labour force or the discovery of a new product innovation respectively (although these are often linked to external factors such as better job offers elsewhere or a market need which the innovation can satisfy, for instance).

3.1.3 The cruciform chart

This device is reported by Argenti (1973) as one that assists managers to visualise their firm's strategic position.

'Cruciform' literally means '*cross form*'.

The example shown in Figure 3.2 was developed as part of its strategic review by a small privately owned UK regional brewery. This firm brewed its own beer at a centrally located factory operation and distributed it via its own bars (public houses or 'pubs'). The beer was 'real ale' which means that it was prized for natural and traditional qualities that distinguished it from the mass-produced beers of larger industrial brewers. The public houses had, 100 years earlier, been the main meeting place and source of entertainment for the working-class men from houses in the surrounding city streets. During the past 40 years

Strengths	Weak
Real ale brewers	Lack of economies of scale and scope
Financially independent	Limited access to capital
Local customer loyalty	Reliant on national lager brands
Own sales outlets	Poor catering in pubs
	Pubs situated in low-income inner-city areas
Opportunities	Threats
Premium home-market for bottled real ale	Tightening drink-drive laws
Increased eating-out Demand for premium bottled lager from abroad	Customer tastes moving from heavy beers to light beers and wines
Liberalisation in attitudes to having children in pubs and restaurants	Restaurant chains competing for evening custom
Legal pressures on large brewers to end anti-competitive practices	Health concerns reducing drinking of beers and spirits

Figure 3.2   A cruciform chart for a small brewery

more comfortable homes and the growth of television had reduced the popularity of the public house.

Argenti suggests that a cruciform chart should be no larger than the size of a flip-chart. The lack of space to write things forces management to put things down succinctly and to concentrate on the large, essential issues in the firm's strategic situation (the 'elephants' as he would call them) and not to get bogged down in lists of trivial detail ('the mice').

3.1.4   From SWOT to strategy

If the organisation's approach to strategy is to make itself 'fit' the environment this might be achieved by:

1. *Matching*. The firm should build on those strengths that enable it to take advantage of the opportunities in the market place. For example, the local brewer in Figure 3.2 considered:
    - marketing its beer as a bottled real ale through supermarkets and independent off-licences;
    - converting some of its pubs to restaurants;
    - arranging distribution deals with importers of bottled lagers;
    - creating children's 'fun areas' in suitable pubs.
2. *Converting*. This is a more complex process in which management question their interpretation of a factor as a threat or weakness and consider whether it can be reinterpreted or turned to its advantage (sometimes called *flipsiding the negative*). The local brewer decided to:
    - emphasise its traditional brewing methods as the reason for its relatively higher costs and prices;
    - distribute maps of the city in which most of its pubs were based and introduce a promotion based on having a 'passport' stamped by each pub the drinker visited – this emphasised how easy it was to walk to the pubs;
    - introduce a 'designated driver' scheme where the driver was given free soft drinks and coupons for alcoholic drinks which could be redeemed at a later date.
3. *Remedying*. Removing weaknesses that leave the firm exposed to threats or unable to grasp opportunities is a priority for strategic action. The regional brewer in Figure 3.2

decided to:

- set up a franchised brewing arrangement for lager with a known brand to reduce its reliance on sales of the major national brands brewed by its rivals;
- rationalise its public houses by introducing a scheme where landlords could buy their pubs from the brewery;
- adopt selective investment in developing restaurant areas inside suitably located pubs;
- institute provision of training to publicans in providing cooked food;
- increase the quality and variety of wines, spirits and mineral waters on sale.

3.1.5 The TOWS approach

Another approach to generating strategic options from a SWOT analysis was identified by Weihrich (1982).

This uses the extended matrix shown in Figure 3.3.

Method

Management insert the elements of SWOT into the outsides of the matrix in the same way as discussed in Section 3.1.3.

Strategic options are identified in the four internal quadrants

- *SO strategies* – Ways in which the business could use its strengths to take advantage of opportunities.
- *ST strategies* – Considering how to use company's strengths to avoid threats. It can be hoped that rivals with be less able to do this and hence they will suffer deteriorating relative competitive performance.
- *WO strategies* – Attempting to take advantage of opportunities by addressing weaknesses.
- *WT strategies* – Primarily defensive and seek to minimise weaknesses and avoid threats.

	Strengths (S)	Weaknesses (W)
Internal factors / **External factors**		
Opportunities (O)	SO Strategies	WO Strategies
Threats (T)	ST Strategies	WT Strategies

Figure 3.3 TOWS matrix

© Professor Heinz Weihrich Reprinted with the kind permission of the author

3.1.6 The value of SWOT

When managers first encounter SWOT analysis its simplicity often leads them to discount its value. 'Surely its not possible to understand a firm's strategic position from a single flip chart?' they ask. Of course the answer is 'no'.

The people who understand the various facets of the issues facing the firm are the managers themselves. SWOT analysis and the cruciform chart captures their knowledge about the firm's operations and about its environment and asks them to identify what these things mean for its future. The discussions surrounding which things to put on the chart, and whether or not they really count as strengths or weaknesses, is where the value of SWOT lies. It focuses attention and encourages strategic thinking.

It should always be remembered that an effective SWOT analysis can only be completed in conjunction with an environmental analysis – it is the PEST (or STEEP) analysis which will give an indication of the opportunities and threats components of the grid.

There are many critics of the technique of SWOT analysis and the majority of the criticism revolves around the temptation to complete a 'wish list' of many of the characteristics that those completing the grid would like to think the firm has. In terms of truly superior attributes, compared to the rest of the players in the industry, it is unlikely that a firm will have more than a very few actual strengths.

> You may well be asked to complete a SWOT analysis for a company represented in a scenario as part of a question. Please remember to be realistic and critical in your analysis – do not produce a wish list!

3.1.7 When should SWOT take place?

In the model shown in Figure 3.1 the SWOT takes place after the setting of mission and objectives and the conduct of the environmental analysis and position audit. Not all strategists are agreed that objectives should be set before the position of the firm is understood. There are arguments for putting SWOT elsewhere in the strategy formulation process:

1. *Putting SWOT at the start of the strategy process.* Proponents of resource-based approaches to strategy suggest that a strategy should seek to build up and strengthen the 'distinctive competences' of the firm. The SWOT analysis is the first step in understanding what these competences are. Therefore setting the objectives for a strategy comes after the SWOT analysis and should consist of indicating how the competences will be levered in the coming few years.

2. *Putting SWOT before a detailed position audit.* The management team have a good idea of the position of the business and can draft a valuable SWOT analysis without first undertaking a detailed position audit. However, once they start depending upon particular strengths or wishing to adopt certain strategies it is important that they have detailed information on whether the firm has got sufficient resources to carry it off. Therefore a detailed position audit is directed to investigate the resource areas highlighted in the SWOT and, wherever possible to quantify the detailed information gathered.

3.2 The position audit

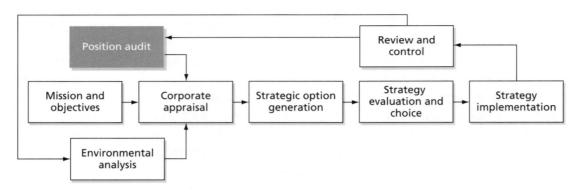

Figure 3.4

3.2.1 Definition

 Position audit is defined as:

Part of the planning process which examines the current state of the entity in respect of:

- resources of tangible and intangible assets and finance;
- products, brands and markets;
- operating systems such as production and distribution;
- internal organisation;
- current results; and
- returns to stockholders.

CIMA: *Management Accounting: Official Terminology*, 2005, p. 51

However, there are other suggested lists that can assist management in directing their attention to appropriate areas, as shown below.

3.2.2 The Ms model

This model suggests that the items in a position audit can be categorised into factors beginning with 'M':

- *Men*. The human assets of the firm such as their skills, morale and relative costs (naturally this includes both female and male genders: both are essential organisational resources).
- *Management*. The quality, expertise and experience of the top team. Is the firm well managed and does it have the skills and vision it will need to progress?
- *Money*. The financial health of the business and the support management receive from its shareholders and bank. Key factors here are likely to be current results and the availability of capital to finance investment.

- *Make-up*. The organisational structure and culture of the firm. For example, is the firm centralised or not and how willing are business unit managers and other staff to take responsibility?
- *Machinery*. This covers the physical assets of the business. For example, their flexibility and the relative costs and quality of what they produce.
- *Methods*. The processes adopted by the business. Issues here could include the extent to which activities are outsourced and whether the firm uses capital – or labour-intensive production processes. Just-in-time systems are an important business method in many markets.
- *Markets*. The firm's products and the markets it currently serves. The position audit should examine the relative quality and position of the firm's outputs and the extent to which it is exposed to threats from buyer power.
- *Materials*. This covers the relationship the firm has with its suppliers. In modern manufacturing there has been a trend towards 'partnering relationships' with suppliers, where the firm agrees not to shop around for lower prices provided that its suppliers work with it to improve quality and to reduce inventory costs. Some managers would regard reliance on a single supplier as a weakness and instead hope to see that the firm sources from a wide number of suppliers in order to enjoy better prices.
- *Management information*. This evaluates the quality and timeliness of the information available to managers (and others) and its suitability for basing their business decisions on. Factors to consider here would be whether it is suitably structured to allow managers to see the effects of their actions, its intelligibility to the user and whether it contains any environmental and competitor information. Although information technology has a very large part to play in automating the collection and dissemination of such information, remember also the value of meetings and face-to-face contact with customers.

3.2.3 Conducting the position audit

The important thing in a position audit is to ensure that it considers all facets of the organisation that may impact on its performance. In practical business situations a position audit will be carried out by a multidisciplinary team, for example, the corporate board, and will use reports developed by experts in the areas of human resources, finance, marketing and systems. A chartered management accountant will have two key roles:

1. Providing information on the costs and financial situation of the firm and forecasts of how these are likely to change through time. Increasingly this may include non-financial indicators of performance too.
2. Working with other specialists to assess the financial impacts of issues in marketing, systems, human resources, or to help develop quantitative measures of performance in these areas (e.g. quality, customer satisfaction, etc.).

In the examination room you must be prepared to conduct a position audit on a firm in a question all by yourself. The categorisation suggested above may help to ensure you consider all relevant aspects.

This chapter continues with a review of some models and techniques that are particularly useful in position audits.

3.3 Value chain analysis

3.3.1 Generating superior performance

Porter (1985) developed the concept of the value chain and value system to demonstrate how management can analyse their business in terms of how it generates 'value' for the customer and the shareholder.

According to Porter there are two routes through which a firm can generate superior competitive performance:

1. By consistently being more innovative than its rivals in finding ways to satisfy its customers. This enables it to *differentiate* its products and services and so charge a higher price for them as well as enjoy high demand.
2. By providing customers with the same quality of product or service as rivals but at a low cost to itself. This *cost leadership* strategy enables the firm to enjoy a superior margin in a market where differentiation is not possible.

Porter's approach suggests that shareholder value (by which he seems to mean long-term profits) of the firm will be higher than that of its industry rivals for two reasons:

1. Profits will be higher due to better margins being enjoyed.
2. The firm will survive longer in the industry because it will not be so subject to the five competitive forces (discussed in Chapter 2).

A full discussion of Porter's concepts of generic competitive strategies appears in Chapter 6.

3.3.2 The value chain

> 🔑 CIMA defines a value chain as: 'The sequence of business activities by which, in the perspective of the end user, value is added to the products or services produced by an entity.'

CIMA: *Management Accounting: Official Terminology*, 2005, p. 54.

Porter introduces the value chain as: '… a systematic way of examining all the activities a firm performs and how they interact … [the value chain] desegregates a firm into its strategically relevant activities in order to understand the behaviour of costs and the existing and potential sources of differentiation.'

Porter views the individual firm as a sequence of *value-creating activities* instead of as an organisation chart detailing *business functions*. He suggests the business unit of the firm can be visualised as a *business system,* using the diagram in Figure 3.5.

The business unit receives inputs into the left-hand side of its value chain, passes them through a series of activities, and passes them on to its customer. The difference between the costs of inputs and activities it performs and the revenue it earns from the sale of its outputs is *margin* (i.e. long-term profit).

Focusing on each of the nine activities enables management to see how each creates *value* that may be understood as the difference between cost and revenue. Management can then decide to improve the activity in one of two ways:

1. Enhance the capacity of the activity to differentiate the firm's output in the eyes of customers as part of a differentiation strategy.

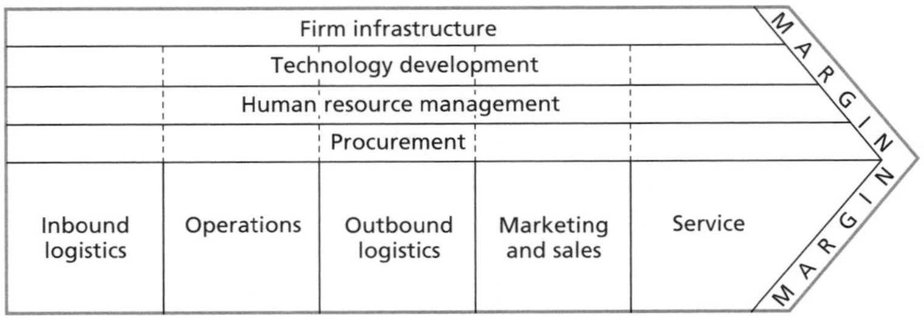

Figure 3.5 Porter's value chain. Reprinted with the permission of The Free Press, a division of Simon & Schuster Adult Publishing Group, from Competitive Advantage: Creating and Sustaining Superior Performance by Michael E. Porter. © 1985, 1998 by The Free Press. All rights reserved

2. Reduce the costs involved in conducting the activity without harming the competitive position of the final output as part of a cost leadership strategy.

3.3.3 Primary activities

1. *Inbound logistics.* Receipt and handling of inputs into the process and disseminating them within the firm, such as warehousing, inventory control and vehicle scheduling.
2. *Operations.* Transforms the inputs into final product such as machining, packaging, testing and equipment maintenance.
3. *Outbound logistics.* Collecting, storing and distributing the products to buyers. This may include finished goods warehousing, delivery vehicle operation, order processing and scheduling.
4. *Marketing and sales.* Concerned with providing customers with a means to buy and enjoy the product and inducing them to do so. Includes advertising and promotion, channel selection, sales force management and pricing policy.
5. *Service.* Post-purchase service to enhance or maintain the value of a service such as installation, maintenance, training and supply of parts and consumables.

3.3.4 Support activities

These activities support the primary activities of the business. They are normally classed as overheads because they do not have a discernible relationship to the product of the firm.

Porter disputes this. He observes that a so-called overhead like purchasing (or procurement as he calls it) is not a central function but rather is carried out by a number of departments across the firm. For example, the purchasing of raw materials will be part of inbound logistics, whereas the purchasing of advertising space will take place in marketing and sales.

By disaggregating overheads according to the primary activities that give rise to them, Porter believes that opportunities for value creation can be identified more accurately:

1. *Procurement.* Purchasing of inputs needed by the firm.
2. *Technology development.* This includes a broad range from basic product and process research, through media research to servicing procedures.
3. *Human resource management.* The recruitment, training, development, retention and discharge of staff. In some firms the creation of a set system of working and its inculcation through training is the key resource of the firm.
4. *Firm's infrastructure.* The activities of the firm which cannot be tied back to specific primary activities. These include general management, accounting and finance and legal services. You will note that in his diagram Porter does not attempt to segment this support activity according to the primary activities.

POSITION APPRAISAL AND ANALYSIS

3.3.5 Linkages within the value chain

Linkages are the relations between the activities in the value chain. Porter suggests that substantial differentiation can be gained, or costs saved, by attending to these.

For example, a car plant employing a just-in-time (JIT) production system enjoys substantial value gains by the following linkages:

- procurement from a limited number of suppliers who can supply on a JIT basis reduces the need for a goods-inward warehouse for inbound logistics;
- inbound logistics require that the sequence of components in a delivery is synchronised with the sequence which they are needed by operations to cut down on search times and errors;
- sales input orders electronically into the production management system of the factory to automatically schedule production and order inputs (so-called manufacturing resources planning systems);
- staff are recruited and trained by human resources to be multi-skilled in order to switch between jobs in a flexible manufacturing system (FMS).

3.3.6 Vertical linkages in the value system

Porter uses the concept of the *value system* to describe the position of the firm relative to the firms upstream and downstream of it. In Figure 3.6 the firm inhabits a point in the value system between suppliers value chain and the distributors value chain.

The value added by the entire system is the difference between the revenue received by the last-time buyer and the costs generated in the system. This is shared between the firms at the various stages of the value system.

Vertical linkages are the relations between the firms in the value system. A firm in the value system can:

1. Take steps to ensure it gains as much of this value as possible:
   (a) by inhabiting the highest value segments of the system through backward or forward integration;
   (b) by striking good deals with suppliers (low prices) and customers (high prices) to take as much of the available value for itself.
2. Collaborate with others in the system to increase the total value available in the chain:
   (a) by increasing the ability of the final product to generate satisfaction (reflected in the price);
   (b) by working together to reduce the total costs in the value system.

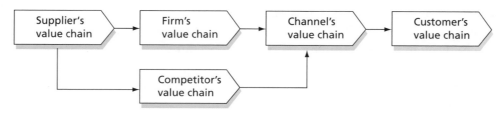

Figure 3.6 Porter's value system. Reprinted with the permission of The Free Press, a division of Simon & Schuster Adult Publishing Group, from Competitive Advantage: Creating and Sustaining Superior Performance by Micheal E. Porter. © 1985, 1998 by The Free Press. All rights reserved

For example, in a JIT manufacturing value system suppliers, transporters, manufacturers and retailers work together to eliminate stocks of components and finished products. Instead they develop a *demand-pull* system which produces and supplies the product very swiftly upon receipt of the customer's order:

- it increases satisfaction because the customer can have a customised or recent product and does not suffer long waits if the final seller is out of stock (e.g. fresh sandwiches delivered just in time at the supermarket);
- firms reduce the costs associated with high inventories.

3.3.7 Organisational implications of the value chain

The implications of the reasoning contained in the value chain and value system has exerted a significant influence on organisations.

1. *Business process re-engineering.* A technique popularised by Hammer and Champy (1995) is discussed in detail in Chapter 7.
2. *Supply chain partnerships.* The value system suggests that it is possible to increase industry profits through replacing adversarial relations between suppliers and customers with a system based on collaboration. This has led to considerable data sharing between organisations to make the value system work more smoothly. For example, collaboration in design of new products, on-line notification of stock availability or production capability. To the outside observer it is difficult to see where the value chain of one firm ends and the other's begins. This is sometimes referred to as the development of the *network organisation* or the *permeable organisation boundary* and we will come back to that in Section 3.3.11.

Supply chain management is discussed in detail in Section 3.3.12.

3.3.8 Management accounting and the value chain

The value chain ignores conventional departments and looks at activities and processes instead. It also seeks to examine the potential for reducing overheads by identifying the primary activities that cause them. Because this will necessitate a reconfiguring of cost information, the chartered management accountant is likely to be a key figure in any value chain exercise.

You should note the similarity between Porter's approach to overheads and the philosophy of *activity-based costing* (ABC). The latter also accepts that so-called overheads are not caused by factors outside management control, but rather are often generated by the way the firm carried out its activities, the diversity in its product range and the variability between the demands of its customers. Identifying what causes overheads is a first step to controlling them or rethinking what drives the firm's profitability.

The following approach pursues 'strategic cost analysis' suggested by Shank and Govindarajan (1993) which builds on the insights of ABC.

Strategic cost analysis will involve the following steps:

1. Identify the activities conducted by the business units and group them within the value chain categories.
2. Ascertain the costs generated by conducting each activity. This may necessitate identifying several sub-activities within the category of the value chain (e.g. the various

POSITION APPRAISAL AND ANALYSIS

factory processes which together make up 'operations') which may have different cost characteristics.

3. Identify opportunities for cost reduction by changing the activity or its linkages without harming its value to the customer. Alternatively, value may be enhanced, augmenting an activity and so allowing a higher price to be charged for the product.

3.3.9 A practical example

Shepherd (1998) provides a value chain analysis of a UK-based network of sandwich bars called Prêt à Manger. These replaced the processes of traditional 'made while you wait' sandwich bars by providing pre-prepared sandwiches from in-shop chillers. The chain has been very commercially successful. The value chain analysis in Figure 3.7 translates into costs and margins as shown in Figure 3.8 (figures in percentage of total costs).

The approaches adopted by Shank and Govindarajan and by Shepherd concentrate primarily on managing the costs of the operation. Activity-based approaches have moved beyond this now with the advent of activity-based management (ABM) which seeks to examine the revenue-creating potential of activities too.

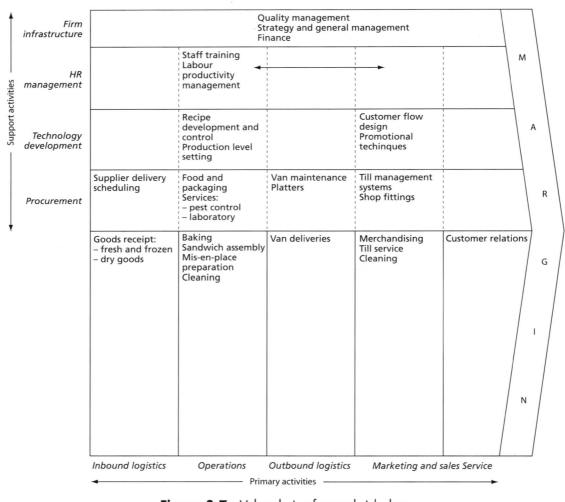

Figure 3.7 Value chain of a sandwich shop

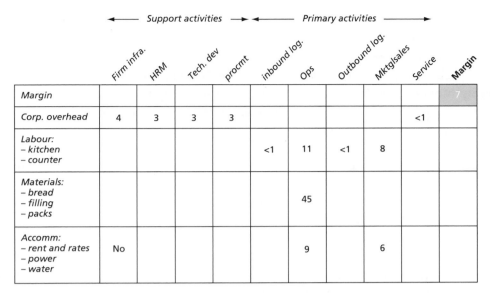

| | Support activities | | | | Primary activities | | | | | |
	Firm infra.	HRM	Tech. dev	procmt	inbound log.	Ops	Outbound log.	Mktg/sales	Service	**Margin**
Margin										7
Corp. overhead	4	3	3	3					<1	
Labour: – kitchen – counter					<1	11	<1	8		
Materials: – bread – filling – packs						45				
Accomm: – rent and rates – power – water	No					9		6		

Figure 3.8 Percentage costs by activity

3.3.10 Evaluation of value chain analysis

The impact of value chain analysis on management thinking has been profound and the model continues to be applied more than 15 years after its first formulation. Presumably it has been found useful by many. Principally these uses have been to provide:

1. *A way of analysing the firm in terms of the processes it uses to serve its customer.* By looking cross-functionally it can spot places where departmental processes, friction and self-interest reduce the quality of the service to the customer or increase costs.
2. *A way to analyse rivals.* Recognising that a rival in your industry (or incumbents of an industry you wish to enter) have a particular value chain ensures that you can take their best ideas but also improve on activities where they are incurring excessive costs.
3. *A common set of terminology for management to use in discussing operations.*
4. *A basis for other management techniques.* These are specialist techniques designed to improve the firm's operations. They include:
   - benchmarking;
   - business process re-engineering;
   - activity-based management;
   - information systems strategy;
   - analysis of transactions costs and outsourcing decisions.

   These techniques are discussed elsewhere in this text or in other subjects at Strategic Level.
5. *A way of identifying ways of generating superior competitive performance.* The value chain is Porter's solution to the task of finding ways to achieve cost leadership or differentiation. Even if management do not want to go to these extremes, the value chain is a useful place to look for ideas on how to reduce costs and/or improve customer satisfaction. We can illustrate this by some examples of how Dell seeks to gain competitive advantage;
   - *Inbound logistics.* JIT deliveries by component suppliers, decision not to take delivery of bulky items like monitors and speakers but have them delivered direct to customers via standard courier, provision of sales forecasts to non-JIT suppliers.
   - *Operations.* JIT manufacturing process, testing, loading software.

POSITION APPRAISAL AND ANALYSIS

- *Outbound logistics*. Direct delivery by courier to final customer, suppliers of sub-assemblies supply direct to customer.
- *Marketing and sales*. Telesales and website operations, provision of customer advice on specification and price, more up-to-date product specification due to no stocks-everything made to order: development of relationship with end-customer.
- *Service*. No specific mention – which is interesting because it is the area in which they are currently heavily criticised.
- *Procurement*. Encouragement of suppliers to site locally in return for guaranteed orders, creation of supplier hubs (i.e. supplier-managed distribution points) near Dell plants, payment for components only on demand, limited supplier base.
- *Technology development*. Development of website and e-service system, investment in developing server technology.

6. *A basis for developing performance measures*. Earlier we discussed the requirement that key performance indicators (KPIs) should monitor the critical success factors of the business strategy. If management choose to use the value chain to develop this strategy, they will also provide an understanding of the processes that deliver the strategy. It follows that KPIs should be based on the activities in the firm's value chain.

Like all the models in business strategy it is not 'true' in any objective sense. It is a way of 'seeing things' that may or may not yield helpful insights into how the firm works. There are some health warnings to go with it.

1. *Management may be exasperated by the complexity of the model*. The strategic management team are busy people with divisions to run. They also believe that they know how their firm works. Explaining the value chain to them will take up time and they may feel this could be spent better 'getting on with the planning'. If it is to be used it must be appropriate to the firm (it seems to be more appropriate to larger firms with physical production processes) and introduced sensitively.

2. *It cannot be easily applied to services* (but see Section 3.3.11). The value chain is conventionally illustrated by reference to firms with physical flows of product, for example motor manufacturing and retailing. Here customer service is assigned to the final two primary activities. However, in an industry like banking, education or hotels the service to the customer is of much greater central importance and is the most obvious generator of costs and revenues. Some applications present the customer as the element being passed through the primary activities (e.g. management of queues or receipt of applications or telephone calls becomes inbound logistics). This can encourage management to view the client as a factor of production to be processed. For example, an airline taking this approach would end up with their customers having the same status as their on-board meals and luggage!

3. *The value system is linear and ignores value networks* (but see Section 3.3.11). Consider Figures 3.9 and 3.10 with regard to the position of Microsoft Corporation. The phenomenal success of Microsoft has not been won through adjustments to the value system in Figure 3.8. After all, the costs of its inputs are minimal compared with its profits and most of its operating systems are installed by computer manufacturers at their own expense.

   More fundamental has been its ability to position itself, through its *Windows* operating systems, at the hub of a large number of value systems, many of which it does not participate in directly, but which could not operate without it. For example, Microsoft

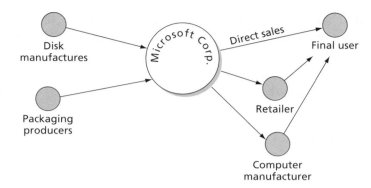

Figure 3.9 Value system diagram for Microsoft

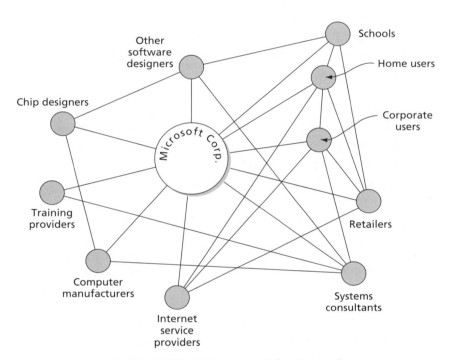

Figure 3.10 Value network for Microsoft

has no role in the value system between producers of games and educational software and schools, retailers and households. However, the need for a common operating system ensures that developers and households end up paying for *Windows* licences.

The linearity of Porter's value system might cause managers to overlook the character of the value networks around them. For a response to this criticism please see Section 3.3.11.

4. *Costs of value chain analysis may exceed benefits*. Using the chain to visualise a firm in a different way costs little more than the management time involved in getting to grips with it. However, if it is to be used properly, then hard data on the costs of the various activities, the value put on them by customers and measures of relative performance must be developed. This is likely to be an extremely expensive exercise. There are no

guarantees that it will lead to worthwhile cost reductions or revenue enhancements. The financial costs of a value chain exercise are very obvious to management in the first few years (consultants, extra accounting staff, travel, etc.) but the financial benefits will be much longer in coming. Many exercises break down due to a loss of patience or an unwillingness to undertake the restructuring it recommends.

3.3.11　Alternative value chains

As we mentioned above one of the main criticisms of the value chain, as originally described by Porter, is that it is not easily applied to service companies. With this in mind other authors have developed diagrammatic value chains which are more appropriate to other types of company. Stabell and Fjeldstad (1988) show the following alternative representations of value chains for professional services firms and network organisations. For a generic value chain for a professional services firm the support activities remain the same, but, the primary activities have been changed from those of a typical manufacturing firm and are more representative of the type of process that a management consultancy or architects practice might employ in it's work.

- *Problem acquisition and diagnosis* – Persuading clients and potential clients to bring their problems to the firm may well involve marketing activities in commercial environments or, whilst dealing with governmental agencies, by ensuring that the firm is on the preferred supplier list by making presentations.
- *Finding possible solutions* – Using the professional expertise and knowledge of the staff within the firm.
- *Choice between solutions* – Making the choice between the possible alternatives, or facilitating the choice by the client.
- *Implementing chosen solutions* – Putting in to effect the solution agreed with the client.
- *Control and feedback* – Monitoring the effect of the solution to ensure that it has actually solved the original problem.

There are a number of differences between this type of organisation and a typical manufacturing firm. There is far less division of labour in the typical service firm and, those that contribute to the solution of the problem are often expected to bring the problems into the firm in the first place. The importance of specialist human resources in this type of firm cannot be emphasised enough. The primary activities are more like a cycle than a chain. The knowledge and experience gained in the solution of one problem will frequently contribute to future problems acquired by the firm.

Stabell and Fjeldstad also address the criticism that the generic manufacturing value chain ignores value networks and produce a generic value chain for a network organisation. At this stage it is important to distinguish between network organisations and network structures. A network structure describes the linkages within a company between internal stakeholders formed to better address the customers needs. A network organisation exists to link together external, unrelated, stakeholders. A typical example would be an Internet service provider. Whilst they provide a service to those who log on they also provide a service to those who wish to supply content to be made available to those who log on. There is sometimes a difficulty in distinguishing between suppliers and customers.

For a generic value chain for a network organisation the support activities remain the same, but the primary activities have become:

- *Network promotion and contract management* – For instance our internet service provider will not only have to find subscribers for the service by giving away free discs and promoting through various consumer channels they will also need to negotiate with content providers for, preferably, exclusive content to appeal to those subscribers.
- *Service provisioning* – The day to day operation of the network, billing, minimising and handling complaints, tracking usage together with the day to day operation of the servers.
- *Infrastructure operation* – Basically keeping the network ready to service customers. The specification and management of physical resources.

Having given you two more generic value chains it is worth making the point that when you start to look at an organisation there is nothing to prevent you making modifications to the diagram to suit the situation you are considering.

For instance, if you consider the manufacture of prototypes, or made to measure clothing, an appropriate value chain is more likely to look like that of a professional services firm than a traditional manufacturer.

When you use a value chain approach to analyse an organisation do remember that the linkages between the activities are often as important as the activities themselves and can give a source of competitive advantage. If we consider the primary activity of 'operations' within a generic manufacturing value chain: attention to specifications by procurement can reduce waste (which means that human resource management have trained the buyers well) a JIT system within the inbound logistics department will minimise stock holding, good training (by human resource management) will cut down reworks in operations and technology development (together with training) have developed superior manufacturing processes.

3.3.12 Strategic supply chain management

Supply chain management is often explained with reference to Porter's value chain and value systems. According to a leading authority (Christopher, 1998):

The supply chain is the network of organisations that are involved, through upstream and downstream linkages, in the different processes and activities that produce value in the form of products and services in the hands of the ultimate consumer. (p. 15)

Note that it is different from *supply management*: the management of goods inward to the firm. Supply chain management is the entire chain leading to the end customer in which the firm concerned will be only one link.

Logistics management is most well known in its military application: the development of procurement, storage and supply lines to support battlefield troops. Both Napoleon and Hitler lost armies and eventually campaigns when their logistic chains into Russia became too long to maintain and defend. However, very similar concerns face burger bars, retail stores, car manufacturers and airlines as they attempt geographical expansion. In fact, one of the main reasons for the leading position of Toyota is the world automobile market is its management of the whole supply chain. Logistics management deals with issues such as:

- procurement management;
- materials movement and storage;

- finished inventory;
- moving of finished goods through distribution channels.

Supply chain management considers logistics but also relationships between members of the supply chain, identification of end-customer benefit and the organisational consequences of greater inter-firm integration to form 'network organisations'. According to Christopher (1998), several forces have led to a radical rethink of traditional logistics management:

1. *The customer service explosion.* Customers have come to expect service excellence and will leave any firm that does not provide it. This increasingly means reliable availability and on-time delivery of the final product. This demands that all links in the supply chain can provide the same to their downstream customers.
2. *Time compression.* Short product life cycles and rapid new product development are the norm. Thus the supply pipeline must be short to avoid slow response and lots of obsolete product and inventory.
3. *Globalisation of industry.* Many organisations operate globally and depend on a complex web of international transfers of materials, components and finished product. Many seek to use logistics to combine the benefits of the economies of scale from volume production with the potential to customise products to the needs of local markets.
4. *Organisational integration.* Classical organisation theory believed in chopping businesses up into departments and divisions. This puts barriers up to the sorts of communication and information flows that are essential to meet the fast-changing needs of customers and challenges of competition. Consequently teams are the norm, backed up by partnerships between suppliers and their customers.

Supply chain management has three themes:

1. *Responsiveness.* Firms must be able to supply their customers quickly. This has led to JIT systems.
2. *Reliability.* These deliveries must be reliable. This means that there must be transparency in the supply chain such that upstream firms can 'see the order coming' from the customer well in advance.
3. *Relationships.* Responsiveness demands that members of the supply chain develop a high degree of mutual understanding of each other's methods and trust in each other's ability to supply. This cannot be sustained if the former confrontational model of customer/supplier relations is used where each constantly looks for better deals elsewhere. Single sourcing and long-term contracts are the norm in modern supply chain management.

Supply chain management should proceed through the following stages:

1. *Create a logistics vision.* This is deciding how logistics strength can be used to deliver customer value. It will require the firm to identify which logistics activities it excels at (i.e. its core competence) and which it should contract out. For example, a national retail and wholesale newsagents found that it excelled at the shop and warehouse elements of the supply chain from publisher to reader. However, its attempts to manage a delivery company and lorry fleet were abandoned and contracted out. Trying to do it all leaves the entire supply chain only as good as its weakest link, which may not be good enough in a competitive world.
2. *Develop the logistics organisation.* Traditional organisational structures are divisionalised into separate business functions (marketing, production, sales, etc.), and each is arranged

hierarchically. This impedes information flows and, as a consequence, reduces 'pipeline transparency'. Moreover, a 'functional silo' mentality is created, which puts divisional interests before those of the organisation or the customer and leads to inventory being built up at the interfaces. This should be replaced with a 'horizontal organisation' that focuses the key processes of supply chain management on the customer.

3. *Increase integration*. The organisation and its upstream and downstream partners should be linked by information. This necessitates the following supply chain policies:

   (a) Supply base rationalisation: That is cut the number of suppliers and let each supply more of the final assemblies or components. This enables closer relationships to be built.

   (b) Supplier development programmes: Cross-functional specialists work with supplier organisations to improve quality and ensure process improvement.

   (c) Early supplier involvement in design: Let the supplier help design cost-effective components for the finished product.

   (d) Integrated information systems: Replace paper orders and instructions to suppliers with information networks. For example, by using computer-aided design (CAD), suppliers can have access to the firm's designs and so get working on designing components quicker. Similarly, electronic data interchange (EDI) is much quicker and more accurate than oral or paper orders. If these EDI orders originate from the point at which the customer orders the product, then suppliers can fine-tune their supply better.

   (e) Centralisation of inventory: The final sales point carries a minimum of inventory but instead is able to gain access to the supply chain database to specify products on a 'cook to order' basis.

4. *Manage the supply chain as a network*. This replaces the 'us and them' mentality of the conventional buyer/seller relationship with one based on collaboration and common interest. Elements of this include:

   (a) Collective strategy development: All members of the network share their strategic thinking.

   (b) Win-win thinking: An end to thinking that the only way to increase the firm's profits is to strike harder bargains with upstream and downstream partners. All partners come to believe they are better off by collaboration.

   (c) Open communication: This involves EDI links but also *open book accounting* in which cost data is shared with upstream and downstream partners to ensure that all partners are paid reasonable fees and there are no suspicions of excessive profits being enjoyed by one member of the network.

3.3.13 The lean supply chain

Not only can the 'lean concept' be applied to non-production organisations, it can also be applied to entire supply chains. Lean supply can be defined as '. . . the elimination of duplication of effort and capability in the supply chain, combined with a philosophy of continuously increasing the expectations of performance and self-imposed pressure to excel. This is achieved by recognition of mutual dependence and common interest between customer and supplier – beyond the principle of operational collaboration . . .'

Lean customer–supplier relationships are claimed to exhibit a series of characteristics, as shown in table 3.1.

The main objective of developing a lean supply chain is the complete removal of waste in order to achieve a competitive advantage. That advantage can be achieved by both the

Table 3.1 Lean supply relationships

Factor	Lean supply characteristics
Nature of competition	• Global operations – local presence • Based on contribution to product technology • Organic growth and mergers/acquisitions • Dependent on alliances/collaboration
Basis of sourcing decisions	• Early involvement of established supplier in new product development • Joint efforts in target costing/value analysis • Single sourcing • Supplier who provides greatest global benefits • Re-sourcing as a last resort
Role/mode of data/information exchange	• True transparency on costs etc. • Discussions of costs and volumes • Technical and commercial information exchanged • EDI
Management of capacity	• Kanban system • Strategic investments discussed • Synchronised capacity • Flexibility to operate with fluctuations
Delivery practice	• True JIT
Dealing with price changes	• Price reductions based on cost reduction joint efforts
Attitude to quality	• Supplier vetting becomes redundant • Mutual agreement on quality targets • Continual interaction • Kaizen • Perfect quality as the goal
Role of R&D	• Integrated between assembler and supplier • Long-term joint development • Supplier/assembler systems integration
Level of pressure	• Very high • Self-imposed

reduction of costs and the improvement of quality (whether product or service). Although, in theory, the competitive advantage should be shared between all the 'actors' in the supply chain, in reality the share of the benefits will depend on relative power as we discussed in Chapter 1

Other benefits of lean supply are claimed to be;

• Reduced inventories (and thus improved cash flow and profit);
• Shorter lead-times, and thus faster delivery to consumers;
• Fewer bottlenecks, so better utilisation of resources, and further improvements to profit;
• Fewer quality problems, so less re-work, lower costs of quality failure, and happier consumers.

Critiques of 'lean'

The following criticisms have been made of the lean supply chain approach:

1. Assuming that the lean approach does give more customers more choice, then this will probably increase the overall level of consumption. This may not be a socially desirable outcome, given the impact on the environment and the possible depletion of scarce resources.
2. The ability of lean chains to satisfy customer whims even more quickly may result in overproduction of 'throw-away' goods. This will again have serious environmental consequences.

3. Microeconomics suggests that perfect competition leads to the optimal level of efficiency in the market. As the lean supply chain consists of a series of partnerships and 'preferred supplier' relationships, it must represent a sub-optimal solution. With reduced competition comes complacency. The entry barriers created by cooperation will reduce competition and increase the levels of margin earned. This may be 'good' for the organisations concerned, but it is 'bad' for the consumer.
4. Concentrating on leanness in the supply chain may lead to 'shakeout' in the industries affected, resulting in an overall reduction in manufacturing capacity and significant job losses. While this may benefit the supply chain, it has significant economic and social consequences.
5. Over-leanness may lead to a situation where there is insufficient 'slack' in the system to take account of fluctuations in demand.
6. The cost burden involved in becoming lean may be too high for many smaller suppliers, and they may be driven away from the supply chain despite, perhaps, being the optimal suppliers.

There are also other arguments against the lean chain approach:

1. Large, powerful customers can dominate lean supply chains. Though the ideal situation is that all the actors in a supply chain share the benefits of leanness, in reality the greater share of cost savings will be taken by the most powerful organisation in the chain.
2. Most of the leanness tools concentrate on reducing cost rather than improving quality. Any resulting savings may be kept as increased margins, rather than being passed on to the customer.
3. Too much concentration on cost reduction may, in fact, worsen quality or at least increase the risk of quality failure.

3.4 Benchmarking

3.4.1 Definition

> CIMA defines benchmarking as: 'The establishment, through data gathering, of targets and comparators, through whose use relative levels of performance (and particularly areas of underperformance) can be identified. By the adoption of identified best practices it is hoped that performance will improve.'

CIMA: *Management Accounting: Official Terminology*, 2005, p. 46.

3.4.2 Purposes of benchmarking

All organisations have systems in place to help management monitor key factors such as profits and sales. However, if the financial results or market share of the firm start to deteriorate, management needs to know the reasons why. Better still, it needs advance warning to stop such falls occurring.

The problem with indicators such as profit, volume and sales is that they are of limited use in such steering of a firm, for example:

- A sales variance may indicate to what extent a fall in revenue is due to a fall in sales volume and how much to a fall in price. It does not indicate why people are less inclined to buy our product or are now only prepared to buy it at a lower price.
- A variable overhead variance may show us that factory overheads are rising. It does not tell us why we need to hold a greater stock of inventory than before.
- An analysis of our sales returns may show that products are being returned more than before. It does not tell us what is wrong with them or why people are buying a competitor's product.

The purpose of benchmarking is to help management understand how well the firm is carrying out its key activities and how its performance compares with competitors and with other organisations who carry out similar operations (see Motorola example below).

In its *Management Accounting: Official Terminology*, 2005, p. 46 CIMA describes four types of benchmarking:

1. *Internal benchmarking:* A method of comparing one operating unit or function with another within the same industry [assume it means 'firm' rather than industry].
2. *Functional benchmarking:* Internal functions are compared with those of the best external practitioners of those functions, regardless of the industry they are in.
3. *Competitive benchmarking:* Information is gathered about direct competitors, through techniques such as reverse engineering [decomposition and analysis of competitors' products].
4. *Strategic benchmarking:* A type of competitive benchmarking aimed at strategic action and organisational change.

Example: Benchmarking at Motorola

'Best practice benchmarking concentrates on manufacturing technology'

At Motorola's semiconductor plant in East Kilbride, BPB [best practice benchmarking] concentrates on manufacturing technology. Typical areas it has recently benchmarked are:

- Yield and product characteristics for a new MOS 9 silicon wafer, against Toshiba, under a technology transfer agreement.
- General wafer fabrication technology: all Motorola plants exchange benchmarking information on cycle time, scrap, yield, productivity and other key measurements. Having identified best performance, the relevant operations managers meet quarterly around the world to pass on how they do it.
- Automated assembly performance: this is benchmarked weekly against its Japanese Motorola counterpart, which in turn benchmarks against a Japanese subcontractor.
- Warehouse performance: in particular, cycle time, quality, productivity and space use against other Motorola installations.
- Purchasing performance: both against Motorola companies and friendly companies outside the group.
- Salary and benefits packages, through a Motorola-initiated exchange of data with other Scottish manufacturing companies. Source: *DTI Best Practice Benchmarking website*

Another famous example of the benefits of benchmarking was the experience of Rank Xerox. In the 1970s, such was the dominance of the firm that the phrase 'Xerox' meant 'photocopier'. A decade later and they had serious competition, notably from Canon. Something had gone wrong … but what?

Rank Xerox found that clients were switching to other providers because Rank Xerox machines were perceived as being 'always out of order'. It used benchmarking to restore its fortunes.

A reading at the end of this chapter shows how benchmarking also seeks to compare costs rather than more customer- and strategy-based issues. You will find the context surprising.

3.4.3   Stages in setting up a benchmarking programme

1. *Gain senior management commitment to the benchmarking project.* To ensure that the programme enjoys the co-operation and commitment of managers it is essential that the senior management publicly and unequivocally endorse the benchmarking programme. Senior managers should be informed of:
   - the objectives and benefits of benchmarking;
   - the likely costs of the programme;
   - the possibility that sensitive data may be revealed to outside organisations;
   - the long-term nature of a benchmarking programme and the likelihood that business improvements will take time to achieve.
2. *Decide the processes and activities to be benchmarked.* To work properly this should commence by identifying the outcomes which drive the profits, sales and costs of the business. Factors which might be considered are:
   - activities which generate the greatest costs;
   - processes which have been the subject of customer complaints;
   - processes essential to delivering the firm's competitive advantage.

   Practitioners recommend that benchmarking considers entire processes rather than individual departments.

   Rank Xerox identified a number of processes which could be measured and improved to ensure that clients enjoyed 'best in class' reliability from their machines. One of these was the quality and reliability of the service engineers.
3. *Understand the processes and develop appropriate measures.* Mapping the processes involves three sorts of activity:
   (a) *Discussion* with key stakeholders in the process. Obviously this will include the process managers but also should include the operative staff, customers and suppliers.
   (b) *Observation* of the process. The benchmarking team should be prepared to walk through the process, observing and documenting the activities and any problems they see.
   (c) *Experimental* approaches involve making adjustments to the process or trying to force it to make mistakes in order to understand how it works better.

   Rank Xerox discovered that a major source of customer frustration was the length of time that machines were out of action. Discussions with engineers revealed that a major problem was the sheer diversity of machines and parts and the difficulties in getting these parts in good time.

   In the short term, attention was focused on the processes of:
   - conducting routine preventative maintenance;
   - allocating engineers to breakdown calls;
   - inventory management of spare parts;
   - delivery of spare parts to engineers on site;
   - quality of technical back-up to engineers on site.

   The actual KPIs used by Rank Xerox remain confidential, but the following might be suggested as helpful:

- incidence of call-outs which could have been avoided by better preventative maintenance;
- length of time between receipt of service request and arrival of the engineer on site;
- length of time taken to fix the machine;
- length of time needed for parts to arrive with the engineer;
- inventory levels in the service depots (and particularly stock-outs);
- number of call-outs delayed due to need for engineer to gain assistance from colleagues.

4. *Monitor the process measurement system.* The measures will need time to bed down. There are two aspects to this:
   (a) The need for data capture systems to become reliable. For example, for operatives to learn to fill out the forms correctly.
   (b) The need to establish the reliability of the measures themselves. In new control systems it is quite common to find that some key performance indicators do not relate to the strategic outcomes very well. This is usually because management misunderstand the drivers of their business success.

   Consultants recommend that the system be operated for at least a year before its measures are taken as reliable. As the above Motorola example shows, benchmarking is not limited to numerical performance. Recognition of differences in organisational structures and staffing procedures is often a valuable outcome of the exercise.

5. *Choose appropriate organisations to benchmark against.* There are four sources of comparative data:
   (a) *Internal benchmarking*: These are other branches within the same organisation. The basis of this approach is to identify which branch conducts each measured activity the best to enable best practice to be identified and transferred to other branches.
   (b) *Competitive benchmarking*: This involves comparing performance with rival companies. This presents problems with data access and hence is usually carried out through a benchmarking centre. This will be a central authority such as an industry association or professional body. It will collect data from each participant, then supply an analysis to each firm showing its relative performance against the 'best in class' under each activity as well as its overall relative position in the industry.
   (c) *Activity (or process) benchmarking*: The firm may share operations in common with noncompetitive external organisations. For example, Rank Xerox in the USA is known to have compared several aspects of its inventory management with Texas Instruments because the latter was best in class.
   (d) *Generic benchmarking*: This is benchmarking against a conceptually similar process. It is unlikely that this will result in comparison of detailed measures but rather the observation of methods and structures. Motor manufacturers are known to have studied the pit-crews of Formula One racing teams to help them reduce the changeover times on their factory production lines. Rank Xerox studied the US mail order house L.L. Bean to see how they handled bulky items like canoes, in order to improve their own handling of photocopiers.

6. *Obtain and analyse data.* For example, John Welch, Quality Manager of Rank Xerox writes:

'We compared our distribution against 3M in Dusseldorf, Ford in Cologne, Sainsbury's regional depot in Hertfordshire, Volvo's parts distribution warehouse in Gothenburg and IBM's international warehouse and French warehouse.'

Source: DTI Best Practice Benchmarking website

7. *Discuss results with process management and staff.* Benchmarking is not supposed to be a process which pinpoints people to blame for poor organisational improvement. Rather it is an opportunity for improvement. For this reason, any instances of below-par performance should trigger detailed consideration of ways forward with the management and staff involved. Factors to watch out for here are:

   (a) Differences in the operating environment. For example, call-out time is bound to be higher in sparsely populated areas due to the need to travel greater distances.

   (b) Differences in factor endowments. Frequently the very high labour productivity of one plant is compared with the poor performance of another without considering that the former has the benefit of much greater mechanisation of processes.

   (c) Differences in product or customer mix.

   Management should have every opportunity to explain possible reasons for deviations in performance. It helps no one to set targets which are intrinsically unattainable.

8. *Develop and implement improvement programmes.* Benchmarking simply monitors relative process performance. It cannot improve it. Once the management accept that there are serious deficits in certain processes, it must look for ways to improve things. This can include:

   (a) visiting the best-in-class to see how they do things;

   (b) work study and process improvement programmes;

   (c) capital investment in R&D and better production and information processes;

   (d) product redesign;

   (e) management and staff training;

   (f) outsourcing;

   (g) organisational restructuring.

   Initiatives taken by Rank Xerox were:

   - replacement of the wide range of photocopiers with a smaller number of machines featuring greater flexibility;
   - standardisation of key components and mechanisms across the range;
   - reduction in the number of component suppliers;
   - development of an electronic messaging system to enable engineers to consult technical experts and colleagues on problems without leaving the customers site;
   - self-diagnostic systems on the machines which enable them to anticipate breakdowns and request the key operator to call for a service engineer (in the United States this extended to the machine actually making the telephone call itself);
   - creating a main board position for logistics management;
   - shortening inventory management by abolishing national level warehousing.

9. *Monitor results.* The benchmarking firm will need to monitor the success of its improvement strategies. However, by its nature benchmarking is not a one-off process. Instead it is one of continuous improvement. Once the firm has achieved best in class under a criterion, it should try to find someone better to benchmark against. Failure to keep moving forward provides an opportunity for rivals to catch up.

3.4.4 Benchmarking and performance measurement

Benchmarking may be used alongside other performance measures such as unit cost to help control an organisation. However, if benchmarking measures become part of management control information difficulties can arise:

1. *Overloads management with measures.* Despite its failings, budgetary control does have the benefit of focusing on a small number of variables. In the UK Health Service the

management team of a hospital are assessed on up to 160 measures which is dispiriting and distracting.

2. *Increases cost of control.* Benchmark measures must be monitored by measurement and turned into reports and then discussed. This needs teams of staff and additional hours of work, and office space in which to do it.

3. *Measures and not processes become the focus.* Benchmarking is supposed to highlight good practice and indicate where managers fall short of it. The next step is for managers to visit places where good practice is recorded and learn how it is done. However, very often the measures are used as a stick to beat managers with, without giving them the opportunity to learn how to improve.

The Readings section of this chapter contains an interesting article on the use of benchmarking by the UK National Health Service to identify how treatment costs vary between hospitals.

3.4.5 Evaluation of benchmarking

The main benefits of benchmarking are:

1. It helps to improve organisational performance:
   (a) increased customer satisfaction;
   (b) reduced waste and costs of poor quality;
   (c) reduced overhead through business simplification;
   (d) transmission of best practice between divisions.
2. It can assist in overcoming complacency and drive organisational change.
3. It provides a way to monitor the conduct of competitive strategy.
4. It provides advance warning of deteriorating competitive position.
5. It improves management understanding of the value-adding processes of the business.

The drawbacks of benchmarking are:

1. It increases the diversity of information which must be monitored by management. This increases the potential for information overload.
2. It may reduce managerial motivation if they are compared with a better resourced rival.
3. There is a danger that confidentiality of data will be compromised.
4. It encourages management to focus on increasing the efficiency of their existing business instead of developing new lines of business. As one writer put it: 'Benchmarking is the refuge of the manager who's afraid of the future.'
5. Successful benchmarking firms may find that they are later overloaded with requests for information from much less able firms from whom they can learn little.

3.4.6 An example of benchmarking

Possibly one of the most useful articles concerning benchmarking and the challenges associated with it is covered in the following article which was published in *Financial Management* in December 2001. The article, which was written by Deryl Northcott and Sue Llewellyn, follows together with some discussion questions that you should attempt.

Although the article is longer than the typical scenario that you will find in an examination, it gives you an opportunity to rehearse a number of important issues.

X-ray vision

Deryl Northcott & Sue Llewellyn, *Financial Management*, December 2001.

Practitioners and researchers have long been aware of the challenges involved in costing healthcare activities. There are many reasons why it is important that hospitals know the costs of the services they provide, but the costing exercise is fraught with complications and the task of the NHS cost accountant is a difficult one.

And it is not getting any easier. Since the Department of Health introduced the national reference costing exercise (NRCE) in 1998, cost accountants in English NHS trusts are required to compile cost data returns in June each year. This cost information is collected by the NHS Executive, which publishes annual indices ranking hospitals according to their relative cost efficiency.

The NRCE also produces national information on the range of costs incurred across all NHS trusts for more than 500 healthcare activities (known as healthcare resource groups or HRGs). It now seems easier than ever for a trust (or anyone else) to see whether its costs are 'normal' for any particular healthcare activity, or for its entire range of activities.

A key aim of publishing this comparative cost information is to facilitate benchmarking, highlighting cost variability so that hospital managers can identify areas where they may be able to improve cost efficiency. However, there are also other ways in which this cost information is important.

Trusts that have been highlighted as relatively inefficient, according to the NRCE results, have faced public and political scrutiny, and pressure from their purchaser/funder (i.e. the health authorities) to reduce costs or increase the level of service provided. For NHS cost accountants, the potential uses and consequences of NRCE results have increased the pressure to get the costing exercise right. But how easy is this?

A recent CIMA-funded study examined the challenges faced by NHS cost accountants who have the job of compiling consistent cost information for the NRCE. The study explored the extent to which cost variations between trusts represented real efficiency differences. For healthcare cost information to be useful for benchmarking and decision-making, cost data must be produced in a rigorous and systematic way in all NHS trusts. If it is not, then factors other than relative efficiency contribute to cost variations and the interpretation of comparative hospital cost data is a problem. Between July 1999 and October 2000, cost accountants in six English NHS acute hospital trusts were asked for their views on the causes of variability in published cost data. Finance directors (FDs) were also interviewed, adding another perspective on the problems of costing healthcare activities.

The interviews revealed that a number of issues are complicating the task of producing accurate and consistent healthcare cost information. In order to check that the views expressed in these interviews were representative of cost accountants and FDs in all NHS trusts, a questionnaire was sent to 228 NHS trusts, whose cost data had been included in the *New NHS 1999 Reference Costs*. Responses were received from 105 trusts (46 per cent). The results confirmed that many of the issues identified in interviews are widely perceived as difficulties in costing healthcare activities.

Although the Department of Health produced a new costing manual in 1999 to help NHS cost accountants compile NRCE cost data, most cost accountants felt that there was still a lot of room for inconsistent costing methods. In particular, routines for allocating indirect and overhead costs were not the same in every trust, since the guidelines prescribed only the minimum standard requirements and some trusts went well beyond this minimum.

Cost accountants and FDs found it difficult to decide the best allocation approach to use. Inevitable variations in allocation approaches also meant that HRG costs produced by trusts may not be directly comparable.

A second issue was the problem of how to construct costed care profiles. Since it is clearly impossible to measure the actual cost of every procedure that is performed in a hospital, costed care profiles are used to identify a standard cost for healthcare procedures. There are usually several procedures grouped together in any HRG code, so an HRG cost comprises a weighted average of the relevant costed care profiles.

To construct costed care profiles, any identifiable direct cost is traced to the procedure from the bottom-up (e.g. the cost of expensive drugs or prostheses), while other costs are pooled and apportioned to procedures based on the consumption of cost-driving activities (such as patient length of stay (LoS)). The more sophisticated the bottom-up costing approach used in constructing the costed care profile, the more an HRG cost can be thought of as reflecting direct cost causality rather than an arbitrary process of cost allocation.

However, variations in how costed care profiles are produced by trusts were thought to distort the way in which costs are attributed to HRGs. Trusts achieved different levels of accuracy in tracking cost-driving activities within costed care profiles. These differences were perceived as being a barrier to producing systematic and comparable cost information. HRGs are the cost objects to which hospitals' costs must be attributed. They are assumed to represent clinically similar treatments, to consume similar quantities of resources, and to incur similar costs across all trusts ('Reference costs: consultation document', Department of Health, June 1998).

Yet cost accountants and FDs noted that the make-up of HRGs may differ between trusts because of the variations in the nature and complexity of their case mix. For example, a specialist or teaching hospital may take on more complex cases than a general district hospital in the same HRG.

The time that patients spend in hospital is another crucial, yet difficult, aspect of costing HRGs. A patient's LoS in a hospital bed is usually related to the severity of their condition or the complexity of their treatment. Length of stay is seen as a key driver of patient care costs, so has a significant impact on the way in which costs are attributed to HRGs. Yet cost accountants and FDs noted that LoS varies widely between trusts, often for reasons beyond their control, such as the availability of nursing home beds for discharged patients.

Although the NRCE costing guidelines require that excessively long stays be trimmed down to an acceptable maximum for reporting purposes (so avoiding excessive LoS variation), cost accountants and FDs noted that significant variation remained in patient LoS even below the maximum trim points. There was no systematic means of accounting for such variations in costing procedures. This variety, together with variations caused by case-mix differences, mean that cost accountants have problems ensuring that their cost data is directly comparable with that produced by other trusts.

Two main problems exist over the quality of information used in the healthcare costing exercise. First, cost accountants and finance directors perceived problems with the counting and classification of patient activity, which determines the denominator in the unit HRG cost calculation. Each episode of patient care (called a finished consultant episode, or FCE) occurring in a trust must be assigned to its relevant procedure code by a specialist clinical coder.

However, it seems that there are variations in trusts' methods of determining what constitutes an FCE and working out which HRG it belongs to. Interviews revealed common concerns about inconsistent methods of collecting, coding and recording FCE data, all of which affect the reliability and quality of the patient activity data that forms the basis of the costing exercise.

Second, there is a more general problem related to the capability of trusts' information systems to collect the information needed to cost healthcare activities. Some interviewees noted that their information systems were poor, a concern echoed by respondents to the follow-up questionnaire survey.

Systems for gathering information on patient admissions, theatre information and general ledger records were all mentioned for their inability to capture and report reliable and complete information for the costing exercise. Cost accountants in NHS trusts listed many problems: activity data is inconsistent and sometimes incomplete; cost data from the general ledger is inaccurate; and measures of cost-driving activities within hospitals rely on poor information systems.

So where does this leave NHS cost accountants? While it has always been important for hospitals to generate good information about their costs for decision-making and management purposes, the NRCE imposes a new, external requirement for rigorous cost information that is standardised and comparable across trusts. The task of the cost accountant would be easier if trusts resource, monitor and work towards improving both information systems and the measurement and coding of patient activity.

Accountants also play an important role in applying appropriately the costing guidelines provided by the Department of Health. However, since it is unlikely that the challenges and inconsistencies can be fully eradicated, perhaps a more important role for NHS cost accountants will be that of assisting with the interpretation of cost information for benchmarking and management purposes.

Within trusts, managers need to be able to interpret and understand the possible reasons for the apparent cost variations reflected in NRCE results. Without a clear and informed knowledge of the limitations of the costing exercise, there is a danger that managers may make inappropriate decisions on the basis of HRG cost information This will harm all NHS stakeholders.

Discussion points

Think carefully about the following issues before reading the outline solutions:

1. What general difficulties does this article say will be encountered in comparing costs between organisations? How could they be overcome?
2. Do you think the benchmarking exercise (NRCE) addresses the right issues?
3. What problems would a manager have in participating in the NRCE, or making use of its findings?

Outline solution

1. The main difficulties seem to be:
   * different methods of attributing overheads and other costs to operations;
   * the inherent difficulties in tracing costs accurately. The approach clearly invokes ABC to calculate 'costed case profiles' and this leads to arbitrary judgements on where costs are pooled and further distorts HRGs;
   * the different circumstances of the hospitals led to different costs. These were outside the control of management (e.g. length of stay due to lack of nursing home beds);
   * poor information systems to collect the raw data.

   They could be overcome by:
   * instituting a common method of calculating costs;
   * better database management;
   * isolating controllable and uncontrollable costs and then calculating the measures on the basis of costs that can be controlled by management

2. This is a loaded question and deliberately so. It depends on your viewpoint.
   * A doctor or public authority wishing to get the greatest value from their budget will want to send patients to hospitals that can perform the operations at least cost (assuming these reference costs are also the prices charged to users). Even so, they may be concerned that the measures do not seem to record the quality of the care or success of operations.
   * Hospital managers will also wish to manage their budget and so if they discover that their operations cost more than at another hospital, then it will signal a need for investigation. However, it seems that a lot of the costs are overheads and others are affected by things beyond the manager's control. These, together with the acknowledged distortions in the costing systems, may lead them to conclude that the information is not valuable for decision-making purposes. However, they will realise that high costs will lead them to be criticised or lose referrals, and so they will wish to criticise the accuracy of the measures to avoid being wrongly held to account.
   * The patient would not agree. There seem to be no measures here directly related to their experience or the quality of the operation.

3. The main difficulties would be:
   * Affording the costs of management accounting staff to reconfigure cost information with a formula that calculates cost per procedure. Previously, the hospital would have systems for ensuring that overheads remained within budget and have considered only periodic costs of medicines and staff and tried to keep them in budget. The idea of operations and procedures as cost generators and revenue receivers is wholly different.
   * Changing the culture of hospitals to accept the importance of keeping costs low. Staff at the patient interface will prioritise the well-being of the person in front of them, and not perhaps the well-being of those invisible sick people denied a bed due to poor cost control or bad use of resources. This said, they may be right in being suspicious of initiatives to streamline care if it means discharging patients before they are ready to go home.
   * Fear that the measures will be used to penalise them or their hospital.

3.5 Gap analysis

3.5.1 Definition

> A comparison between an entity's ultimate objective (most commonly expressed in terms of demand, but may be reported in terms of profit, ROCE etc.) and the expected performance of projects both planned and under way. Differences are classified in a way which aids the understanding of performance, and which facilitates improvement.

CIMA: *Management Accounting: Official Terminology*, 2005, p. 48

3.5.2 Example of a gap analysis diagram (Figure 3.11)

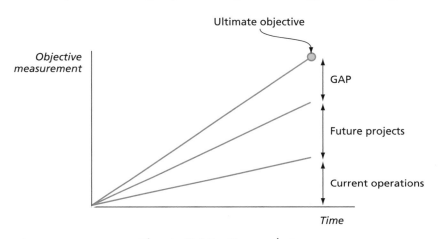

Figure 3.11 Gap analysis

3.5.3 Using gap analysis

Gap analysis has its origins in the rational planning approach to strategy. Its proponents suggest it be used as follows:

1. The firm sets its key strategic objective for some time in the future, for example:
    * a firm with profits of £250m may decide to set a target that these are to grow at 15 per cent per annum; therefore the strategic target for 5 years' time will be £503m;
    * a firm may decide that it needs to have sales of a given amount in 5 years' time.
2. The firm forecasts the likely performance of its current operations and also the likely contribution to performance of new strategic initiatives. These are separated because the strategic initiatives are subject to greater uncertainty than current operations and hence the firm's forecasts have a much wider margin of error.
3. Management assess whether there is any remaining gap between the desired objectives and the forecast level of performance of the firm. If there is a gap, then additional strategies are required.
4. The strategies which may be used to fill the remaining gap are classified as:
    (a) *Efficiency strategies*: Designed to increase profits (or throughput) by making better use of resources.

(b) *Intensive strategies*: These exploit the firm's existing products and markets further:
- market penetration to increase sales to existing markets;
- market development to find additional markets for the products;
- product development to find additional products for the firm's existing customer base.

(c) *Diversification strategies*: These aim to reduce the risks of the business or increase its growth prospects by taking it into new industries.

CIMA describes a method for understanding the origins of a sales performance gap:

Potential market demand	Existing market demand	
		Demand gap
		Distribution gap
		Product gap
		Competitive gap
		Existing sales

Demand gap:	the difference between total market potential and current demand from users.
Distribution gap:	loss of product demand due to lack of access to or utilization of distribution channels.
Product gap:	the proportion of market demand lost through product failure or deliberate product-positioning decisions.
Competitive gap:	loss in sales due to factors such as failures in pricing or promotion. CIMA: *Management Accounting: Official Terminology*, p. 45

The various strategic options available to a firm will be discussed in detail in Chapter 6.

3.5.4 Forecasts and gap analysis

Gap analysis depends on the ability of the firm to forecast performance into the future. It is valuable to consider carefully what this involves.

According to CIMA, forecasts and projections are different. A *projection* is:

 An expected future trend pattern obtained by extrapolation. It is principally concerned with quantitative factors, whereas a forecast includes judgements.

CIMA: *Management Accounting : Official Terminology*, 2005, p. 52.
Whereas a *forecast* is
A prediction of future events and their quantification for planning purposes.

CIMA: *Management Accounting: Official Terminology*, 2005, p. 48.

Although capable of quantification a forecast is not derived purely from a mathematical process. This is because of the problem of *uncertainty*. If management believe that the future is likely to be substantially different from the present, say due to the threatened arrival of a new competitor, they will not be able to rely on projecting sales volumes and prices on the basis of past data. They need to add in assumptions.

One of the reasons that gap analysis has declined in popularity, along with planning approaches to strategy in general, is because of the problem of uncertainty which makes forecasting very difficult. Many managers regard it as too fraught with inaccuracies and prefer to perceive of strategy as a process of developing core competences instead.

However, chartered management accountants still need forecasts in order to permit budgeting for profits and deciding on capital expenditure. Without forecasts it is hard to see how financial control can be exercised.

3.5.5 Four levels of uncertainty

It is possible that management are taking an artificially simple view of the problem of uncertainty by dividing situations into just two classes:

1. Those that are certain and therefore can be forecast, assessed by conventional investment appraisal techniques and budgeted for.
2. Those that are uncertain and where it is therefore pointless trying to develop forecasts or use conventional decision-making techniques.

Courtney et al. (1997) criticise this 'binary notion' of uncertainty and suggest that there are four levels of uncertainty:

1. *A clear-enough future*. Managers can develop a single forecast of the future because the business environment is tolerably stable and predictable. For example, the product is established, the factors determining demand are known and competitors behave in predictable ways.

    This appears to be the ideal environment for gap analysis.
2. *Alternative futures*. Here uncertainty about the future revolves around which of a number of possible scenarios will come about. For example, the impact on the market of the threat of a new competitor entering may resolve itself into the following three scenarios:
    (a) the market stays the same because the competitor decides not to enter;
    (b) the competitor joins as an additional new player in the market;
    (c) the competitor acquires or teams up with an existing firm in the market.

    Note that the scenarios are discrete and are essentially three different forecasts represented by the alternative lines on the gap analysis chart shown in Figure 3.12.

    In this situation management will seek to assign probabilities to each alternative future to decide on a course of action.

Courtney and colleagues suggest that management should try to form an assessment of the likelihood of each scenario, but also that they should remain alert for the appearance of any 'trigger variables' (in this case the sudden rise in the share price of a rival suggesting imminent acquisition perhaps) which suggests that one scenario rather than another is coming true.

Decision trees would be a useful tool under this form of uncertainty because it can deal with discrete outcomes.

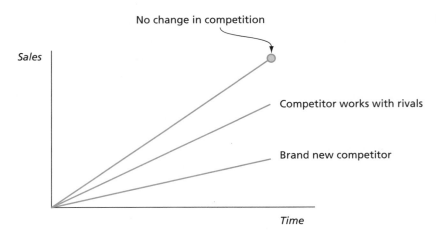

Figure 3.12   Gap analysis with alternative future scenarios

3. *A range of futures*. This is where the one desired outcome may take a wide range of values. This situation is best understood using the example of a new product launch. Actual sales will be somewhere on a continuum from the most optimistic forecast to the most pessimistic one, in accordance with the impact of a number of influences such as:

   - its price;
   - the effectiveness of advertising;
   - the response of the competitors;
   - the attitude of professional reviewers in the media.

   Unlike level 2, it is not possible to visualise two or three possible outcomes and monitor a few trigger variables for each. The actual outcome lies somewhere within a range of possibilities. Here there is substantial complexity and with it greater uncertainty. Forecasts will be very hard to derive and the absence of past data will make expected values of little value.

   Techniques which might be used to help evaluation and decision-making here usually involve modelling the relationship between independent variables and the sales volumes of the product. For example:

$$\text{Total sales volume} = F\{P_c, Y_d, R\}$$

   where F is the coefficient of function (i.e. 'sales volume is influenced by'); P_c is the competitors' prices; Y_d is the disposable income levels; and R is the enthusiasm of the professional reviews (measured on a scale of 1–10).

   Management can then see how viable the strategy is under a number of different assumptions about the likely values of the variables P_c, Y_d, and R. This may be done by:

   - What–if?' analysis – Each variable is adjusted and its impact seen. This leads management to concentrate their resources on achieving more reliable forecasts of the variables which have been revealed to have a substantial impact on the success of the strategy.
   - High–low forecasts – The strategy is evaluated with each variable set to its most favourable likely level and then its most unfavourable level. This shows the range of possible outcomes and hence the risk of the strategy.
   - Simulation – The model is run with a computer putting in random numbers for the variables and the sales volumes are monitored. This shows the impact of the interactions between the variables in more complex models. Again it helps management assess potential risk.

4. *True ambiguity.* Here the environment is virtually impossible to predict. The example cited by Courtney and colleagues is the decision by many firms during the 1990s to invest in the economies of the former USSR. The political instabilities and lack of clear laws and regulations made any form of forecasting impossible. Similar uncertainties apply to the world of internet commerce (e-commerce).

> In this situation, management proceed by analogies to try to understand how the environment is developing and to make sense of the range of data they are receiving. For example, investors building telecommunications and internet 'superhighways' often seek to make analogies with the railroad pioneers of the eighteenth and nineteenth centuries. Others make less favourable analogies with the gold-rush fever of the same historical era which left many prospectors destitute.

So, as we have previously discussed, our ability to forecast successfully is dependent not only on whether an industry is stable or unstable, often referred to as dynamic, but is also complicated by the degree of complexity that an organisation faces.

In the first case above, *a clear enough future*, the company is dealing with a simple environment where events are quite stable. This might well be a bakers or other manufacturer of relatively simple products where competition is established and well understood with limited environmental change.

In the second case, *alternative futures*, the environment is still simple but with the possible entrance of new competitors the events have become more unstable. The computer industry would fit this category, there is instability but the environment is not really complex as most of the environmental factors are reasonably well understood.

For an example of an environment which is complex we can consider a University which span a large number of technologies and are a focal point for cultural and value exchanges. They are required to interact with Government and funding institutions, professional and scientific associations, alumni, students, unions and corporations, amongst others. They must also create a large number of external linkages with a variety of stakeholders.

3.5.6   A conclusion on gap analysis

The clarification of levels of uncertainty has implications for the use of gap analysis. It would seem useful only in the level 1 situation of 'clear-enough future'. This is of course unsurprising, because this is where rational planning approaches to strategy also flourish.

Otherwise strategy formulation and implementation processes need other techniques to cope with uncertainty. One of these is increased organisational flexibility, another is the development of core competences whilst, scenario planning is a third.

3.6   Scenario planning

3.6.1   Planning scenarios

Amongst the many quotes that are used to demonstrate the examples of misjudgement that various experts have made over the years these are amongst my favourites and ought to strike a cord with you:

Computers in the future will weigh no more than 1.5 tons
Popular Mechanics, forecasting advance in science, 1949

I think there is a world market for maybe five computers
Thomas Watson, Chairman of IBM, 1943

There is no reason why anyone would want to have a computer in their home
Ken Olson, president, chairman and founder of Digital Equipment Corp, 1977

640k ought to be enough for anybody.
Bill Gates of Microsoft, 1981

Mr. Gates was talking about RAM rather than salary! Those of you who are familiar with Microsoft Office will know that it now needs megabytes of memory.

There are similar examples involving virtually every form of technology or engineering and, although it is easy to be critical with the benefit of hindsight, most have arisen because the expert concerned has misjudged the social or economic impact of the technology. As we discussed in Chapter 2 there are no really 'pure' political, economic, societal or technological factors in the environment, and a thematic approach is far better.

The reason for these errors is a failure to grasp (or to *conceptualise*) the way the world is moving. What managers need is a picture of the way the world might be in a decade or two. They can then be in a position to evaluate technologies and strategies in terms of how well they fit in with the imagined future state. This picture of the future is known as a *scenario*.

3.6.2 Constructing scenarios

Management must create a team to develop the scenarios. This will often be a special group rather than senior management themselves. Frequently, outside consultants will be used on this team to take advantage of their expert knowledge. There is no one particular way to create scenarios and many authors have offered different versions. One of the earliest, and still amongst the best, is that given by Schoemaker (1995).

Schoemaker (1995) suggests that the ten steps below be used to create scenarios:

1. Define the scope of the scenario. In this context scope means
   - time frame;
   - products considered;
   - markets considered.

   The issue is to decide what knowledge is likely to be of greatest use to the firm. Royal Dutch Shell, a pioneer of scenario planning, focuses on the factors affecting future energy usage and, because of the relatively slow movement of the oil industry, is able to develop long-term scenarios. In the 1980s, Anglo-American chose to focus on political developments in southern Africa over the next decade in order to understand the factors likely to affect its mining interests there.

   One technique of deciding what factors are potentially relevant to the business over the next 10 years is to consider which factors have influenced the past 10 years.

2. *Identify the major stakeholders*. Decide which stakeholders are likely to drive change in the future and which will have the greatest potential influence on events.

   Today, Shell would consider national governments, environmental pressure groups, its shareholders and the large energy-using industries such as transportation and power generation as major stakeholders. In the 1980s, Anglo-American considered world political groupings (such as the United Nations, European Community, World Bank,

etc.), the races and population groups in southern Africa, and the operations of political and religious organisations with an interest in southern Africa.

Clearly these actions of these stakeholders will influence the shape of the business environment to come.

3. *Identify basic trends*. Looking at the business environment today, what trends are emerging or playing-out? These could include technological, social, economic or political. Often scenario planners will consult the work of experts in this field – futurologists such as Toffler. (1973), (1980), (1990), (2006).

    The company may chose to use a Delphi technique to gather expert opinion. A panel of experts (both internal and external) is separately questioned (to reduce peer bias) through a series of interviews regarding current and future trends in their area of expertise. The results are analysed and fed back to the individuals to give them the opportunity to modify their opinion on the basis of the consensus view. After several iterations the results are statistically manipulated to give both a consensus, and any minority, views.

    Shell may believe that energy usage is influenced by patterns of national economic development (in particular economic growth), population settlement patterns, location of industry, use of transportation, size of households, types of housing and consumption patterns and lifestyles.

    Anglo-American saw trends that pointed to the development of rich groups of countries (North America, Western Europe and Japan) and consequent economic isolation of developing countries like Africa. In Africa, it saw a bleak set of trends of political turmoil, exploding population and poor food production, with natural resources being scarce at home due to exporting them for cash.

4. *Identify key uncertainties*. Uncertainties are the factors that will influence the ways things develop. Some writers call these the 'drivers for change'. The children or grandchildren of the scenario planner may be taught them as the 'turning points of history', but for the scenario planner they are merely future possibilities. They can include the outcome of particular court cases or elections, the public's attitude to things, scientific breakthroughs or outbreak of wars.

    Shell might today identify the development of the world wide web, public support of the elderly and out-of-work, the competitive battle between rail, road and air transport, the future economic development of former communist and other nations and the political will to combat 'greenhouse gases' as key issues.

    Anglo-American looked at the future of US–Soviet relations, the development of free trade in the world and the spread of Islamic fundamentalism as key issues. It deemed two uncertainties to be critical:

    - whether US–Japanese trade issues would be resolved by accommodation or by trade war – this would affect the patterns of world trade.
    - whether detente or an arms race would prevail in the US–Soviet relationship – again, this would affect world development and trade.

    This left the company with four possible paths of world development, each triggered by the alternative playing-out of the two pairs of uncertainties.

5. *Construct initial scenario themes*. Based on the alternative playing-out of the critical uncertainties, it becomes possible to envisage future worlds. These are often given bizarre names by the team, who try to fill in the detail in a narrative description of each of the future worlds. For example, an oil corporation might develop three scenarios

based on alternative assumptions on how the governments of industrial nations will respond to increased use of information technology:

- Clampdown – state decides to censor internet content and to tax the rest. This will limit the development of the internet and may allow governments to manipulate its impact on the population to their own ends.
- New medievalism – electronic commerce is allowed to destroy jobs in shops and offices, leading to a concentration of earning power into the hands of the 'knowledge workers' who understand the technology and have something to trade. The rest will be dispossessed and depend on crime to stay alive, populating decaying inner cities which have been deserted by knowledge workers who now work and shop from their homes in villages fortified against attack by the dispossessed of the inner cities.
- Soft-landing – government takes steps to ensure that education incorporates information technology to spread participation in its benefits. Generous social welfare schemes and job-sharing initiatives ensure that all members of the population gain some stake in the information society.

Each scenario would have implications for transportation patterns and the level and distribution of national income. These in turn could be used to forecast energy usage. Anglo-American ruled out the possibility that the United States would simultaneously embark on a trade war with Japan and an arms race with the Soviet Union. This left three scenarios:

(a) Industrial renaissance (detente and trade accommodation).
(b) Protracted transition (detente and trade war).
(c) Imperial twilight (arms race and trade accommodation).

It factored into each scenario the other uncertainties (e.g. spread of AIDS, religious fundamentalism, drug abuse, etc.) and forecast economic development for major country blocs under each scenario.

6. *Check for consistency and plausibility.* This is a process of re-examining the scenarios to decide whether they make sense. For example, would each of the trends work together in the way the scenario assumes (e.g. Anglo-American ruled out the possibility that the United States would allow itself to become isolated by a conflict with both Japan and USSR)? Also is the end scenario stable (Anglo-American saw the trade war as unstable and part of a protracted transition rather than a permanent end to US–Japanese trade)?

7. *Develop learning scenarios.* This is the final fleshing out of the main scenarios. This process is where senior management should become involved because in considering the broader implications of each scenario they start to see the potential impacts on their business.

For example, Shell might take each of the scenarios above and try to figure out what size of families each would point to, and from there to issues such as location of schools and need for transportation, sorts of holidays, types of home and relative energy efficiency. Anglo-American developed two scenarios for South Africa in the light of the global scenarios:

- High road – strategic alliances between countries to assist development of South Africa, sharing of political power and creation of a democratic welfare state.
- Low road – continuing circle of violence between races propelling South Africa into an economic wasteland of international isolation.

8. *Identify research needs.* This involves filling in the gaps and blind spots in the remaining scenarios to better understand:

- the forces that may bring the scenario about;
- its implications for the business.

This research will be carried out and the scenarios enriched by the findings.

9. *Develop quantitative models.* This is the development of economic models that can forecast the effects of the different elements of the scenario on the activity and profits of the business. This was discussed in the previous section.
10. *Evolve towards decision scenarios.* Against each scenario, management must now develop strategic courses of action.

In the case of Anglo-American, it took its scenarios to the stakeholders in the process of determining the future of southern Africa where perhaps it played a role in the remarkable developments in that region during the last 10 years.

Shell publishes shortened versions of their scenarios, once they are no longer commercially sensitive, and you can find them at www.shell.com (once you have got onto the web site key 'scenarios' into their search engine). You will find them an interesting read and a good example of 'real-world' practice.

3.6.3 Using scenarios in strategy formulation

Schoemaker (1997) suggests a four-step approach for using scenarios:

1. Develop scenarios to examine the external environment and identify key trends and uncertainties.
2. Conduct industry analysis and strategic formulation against each scenario to develop strategies that enable the firm to fit with each scenario. These strategies will not of course be consistent.
3. Identify the core capabilities of the business and strengthen these to withstand or benefit from each of the scenarios.
4. Adopt the appropriate strategic option as the future unfolds and the key uncertainties resolve themselves.

This exposes an interesting dilemma for management. Because they are alternatives, not all the scenarios can come true. This means that a strategic investment that appears the right thing to do under one scenario will also appear the wrong thing to do under another scenario. In other words, management are faced with committing shareholders' funds to projects in the knowledge that at least one must fail.

Management may take a variety of courses of action faced with multiple scenarios:

1. Decide which scenario is the most likely and base the strategy on that one. This would necessitate very high degrees of quality in the estimates behind the scenario, particularly of the probabilities of the key uncertainties going one way rather than another.
2. Invest to some extent against each scenario and then wait to see which one emerges as the correct one before investing further.
3. Wait and see what will happen, but have ready-made responses to each eventuality which can be deployed at short notice once the future becomes clearer
4. Avoid long-term investments based on future events and instead concentrate on developing core competences that can sustain the firm regardless of the way the industry changes over time.

For example, a car company may decide it cannot predict the future of automobiles and so it focuses on developing its brand reputation in each type of market while extending its product range and deepening its engineering skills. It may later find itself selling motorcycles, electric cars or buses using these skills.

5. Concentrate on the present business and hope the future does not happen. This is not a good idea but is nevertheless very common.

You may like to consider the link between this topic and the techniques of real options in investment appraisal, which are covered in *other areas of the strategic level papers*.

3.6.4 Advantages of scenario planning

Scenario planning rarely comes up with an accurate picture of how things will happen in the future. They are always inaccurate and will be very expensive and time consuming to create. Management also often dismiss them as 'silly stories'.

The benefits are enough to make some substantial firms use them however:

1. They provide a method of exposing the key uncertainties on which the business turns. Once these are identified the firm can:
   - seek to influence the uncertainty, for example, by political lobbying as Anglo-American did;
   - monitor the uncertainty to adapt plans if one scenario rather than another looks more likely.
2. They provide a method of focusing management on the business environment rather than just internal operations and past events:
   - management can read the scenarios;
   - management can participate in developing the scenarios.
3. They can assist decision-making under conditions of extreme uncertainty.
4. They will encourage senior management, who have been involved in the process to 'think outside the box'. There have been a number of examples of decision makers in organisations changing their assumptions about the future of the industry in which they were operating.

3.7 Foresight

Foresight is a process of developing a range of views of possible ways in which the future could develop, and understanding those ways sufficiently well to be able to decide what decisions can be made today to create the best possible future for tomorrow. Foresightedness is a combination of developing an understanding of possible futures for an organisation and acting upon that understanding in a way that will benefit to the organisation. There have been several national foresight exercises, most notably in the UK, Germany, the Netherlands, the USA and Japan, carried out at governmental level. The exercise has also been carried out by a number of large companies as part of their longer term strategic planning. This is not to say that smaller organisations cannot benefit from the process.

Within an organisational context there will be a need to look at a range of areas which may include technology but will almost certainly include demographics, economics and politics.

The foresight process can be described in the following four stages:

1. The collection, collation and summarisation of available information into a form that provides foresight knowledge. This information will be in the form of trends, expected developments, unusual events and anything that may affect the future.
2. The translation and interpretation of the knowledge gathered to produce an understanding of the implications for the future from the perspective of a particular stakeholder or group of stakeholders, such as an organisation.

3. The assimilation and evaluation of the understanding developed to arrive at a course of action for the organisation and a commitment to that action.
4. The communication of the proposed course of action, with sufficient justification, to all of the members of the organisation that need to take action to arrive at the preferred future.

Effectively, foresight is about a value chain for information, knowledge, understanding and action within an organisation.

There are a number of techniques involved in the development of foresight:

- Scenario planning – which we have discussed earlier.
- Visioning – involves the development of a desired, or possible, future state by a process of intuition. The developers will start with a systematic review of past events and the current situation, move to a detailed description of a desired future state and then identify specific ways by which that desired future can be achieved.
- Delphi surveys – this technique was developed as a specialised methodology of technology assessment to arrive at both qualitative and quantitative data. First developed by the RAND Corporation it originated as a method for gaining expert opinion by a structured communication process which minimised the effect of the personalities of the participants. This was achieved by four main characteristics; anonymity (no physical contact between participants), iteration (there are usually several rounds in the exercise), controlled feedback (the aggregated results of the previous round are circulated to participants) and a statistical presentation of the group response (average and dispersion).
- Brainstorming – involves the generation of ideas by a relatively small group assembled to think creatively about a specific area of the future. Participants are encouraged to build on each others ideas and to offer suggestions and not to criticise, or negate any idea or theme that is offered.
- Issues analysis – by looking at current issues a group will attempt to identify trends and how they may develop in the future and consider the actions that should be taken now to derive maximum benefit should they occur. The exercise will also consider the impact of unexpected events, or wild cards, on those trends.
- Opportunity mapping – the technique is designed to build on an understanding of the current environmental situation and the strengths of the organisation. By identifying possible futures that the organisation is currently in a position to exploit, or could do if certain changes were to be made, an action plan can be developed.
- Cross impact analysis – this technique involves creation of a matrix with one row (and one column) for each identified trend. The discussion of the impact of each combination is designed to develop alternative futures and lead to discussion of their attractiveness (or not) and the actions that might be taken to achieve them.

3.8 Summary

The main techniques introduced in this chapter have been:

- SWOT analysis;
- position audit, and particularly the Ms model;
- value chain
- strategic supply chain management;
- benchmarking;
- gap analysis;
- uncertainty and scenario planning.

POSITION APPRAISAL AND ANALYSIS

For each of these you should concentrate on understanding:

- the basics of the techniques;
- how they may be used in the strategy process;
- the limitations of the techniques and the circumstances when their use might not be appropriate;
- how you would apply the techniques to the scenarios in questions in your examination.

References

Argenti, J. (1973) *Systematic Corporate Planning*. Wokingham: Van Nostrand Reinhold.

Christopher, M. (1998) *Logistics and Supply Chain Management* (2nd edn). London: Financial Times/Pitman Publishing.

Courtney, H., Kirkland, J. and Viguerie, P. (1997) Strategy Under Uncertainty. *Harvard Business Review*, 75(6): 66–80.

Hammer, M. and Champy, J. (1995) *Re-engineering the Corporation*. New York: Nicholas Brealey Publishing.

Porter, M.E. (1985) *Competitive Advantage: Creating and Sustaining Superior Performance*. New York: Free Press.

Schoemaker, P.J.H. (1995) Scenario Planning: A Tool for Strategic Thinking. *Sloan Management Review*, 36(2): 25–39.

Schoemaker, P.J.H. (1997) Disciplined imagination: from scenarios to strategic options. *International Studies of Management and Organisation*, 25(2).

Shank, J.K. and Govindarajan, V. (1993) *Strategic Cost Management: The New Tool for Management Control*. New York: Free Press.

Shepherd, A. (1998) Understanding and using value chain analysis. In Ambrosini, V. (ed.) *Exploring Techniques of Analysis and Evaluation in Strategic Management*. Hemel Hempstead: Prentice-Hall International.

Stabell, C.B. and Fjeldstad (1988) Configuring value for competitive advantage: on chains, shops and networks. *Strategic Management Journal*, 19: 413–437.

Toffler, A. (1970) *Future Shock*. New York: Bantam Books.

Toffler, A. (1980) *The Third Wave*. New York: Bantam Books.

Toffler, A. (1990) *Powershift: Knowledge, Wealth and Violence at the Edge of the 21st Century*. New York: Bantam Books.

Toffler, A. (2006) *Revolutionary Wealth*. New York: Knopf.

Weihrich, H. (1982) 'The TOWS Matrix – A Tool for Situational Analysis'. *Journal of Long Range Planning*, 15(2): 54–66.

Revision Questions

Question 1

A company which manufactures and distributes industrial oils employs a team of salespeople who work directly from home and travel around different regions in the country. Each member of the sales team has his or her own geographical area to cover and they visit clients on a regular basis.

The sales team staff are each paid a basic monthly salary. Each member of the team is set an identical target for sales to be achieved in the month. A bonus payment, in addition to the basic salary, is made to any member of the team who exceeds his or her monthly sales target.

Generally, experience has been that the members of the sales team succeed in improving on their targets each month sufficiently to earn a small bonus.

However, the managers are unclear whether all the team members are achieving their maximum potential level of sales. Consequently, the managers are considering introducing a system of benchmarking to measure the performance of the sales team as a whole and its individual members.

Requirements

(a) Explain the objectives of benchmarking and how it may be used to assist the managers in evaluating operational performance. **(9 marks)**
(b) Describe how a system of benchmarking could be introduced to measure the performance of the sales team:
  (i) as a whole; **(8 marks)**
  (ii) as individuals in comparison with each other. **(8 marks)**
  (Total marks = 25)

Question 2

Analysis of the 'added value' achieved by an organisation will reveal how much has been contributed by each of its primary and support activities. The object of the analysis is to identify those activities undertaken by the organisation which contribute the most to the total value added. This is so that strategies may be established to increase their contribution still further in order to meet organisational objectives.

Requirements

Explain how value chain analysis may help a company:
  (i) to assess the value added by each of its primary and support activities; and
  (ii) to determine its priorities for strategic resource allocation. **(25 marks)**

Question 3

AL plc is a company which supplies industrial cleaning services. After it was founded, 15 years ago, AL Ltd (as it then was) achieved rapid growth and high levels of turnover. The board of directors at the time believed that its traditional scientific management style, based on Taylorian principles, was the main reason for the company's success. As the company grew, the directors found that the company had insufficient capital resources to meet the increasing levels of demand for its services. As a result, AL Ltd was floated on its domestic stock exchange and increased capital resources flowed into the business, allowing it to maintain its rate of expansion. This seemed to be further evidence of the success of the traditional management style employed.

In each of the last 3 years, however, AL plc has found that its turnover and profit have fallen below the industry average and that its market share has reduced. There is increasing concern among the shareholders about the long-term decline in turnover and profitability. The finance director of AL plc (to whom you report as management accountant) has quoted the performance of CC Ltd, a similar-sized company in the contract catering industry. While CC Ltd is not a competitor, it is often viewed as a benchmark against which AL plc can measure its own performance even though it employs a different management style which requires the consent and commitment of employees. CC Ltd has managed to increase its market share, turnover and profitability consistently over the last 5 years and the finance director has turned to you to analyse why AL plc seems to be producing continuously unsatisfactory results.

Requirements

(a) Explain to the directors of AL plc how value can be added by carrying out a programme of benchmarking. **(10 marks)**

(b) Explain how you would implement a benchmarking exercise comparing the performance of AL plc with CC Ltd. Discuss the possible implications for the style of management which should be employed by the company after carrying out such an exercise. **(15 marks)**

(Total marks = 25)

 ## Question 4

MDT Ltd is a private limited company. It was formed in 1983 by three former electricians because they liked working together and they thoght that they could make a living by making good-quality, inexpensive, electrical appliances. Each of the founders invested £10,000 as the share capital of their company in 1983 and the share capital has remained unchanged since then.

MDT Ltd manufactures small electrical appliances, such as kettles, hair dryers and irons. These are sold to wholesalers and eventually retail for around £25 each.

MDT Ltd currently employs 35 people and has a turnover of £3 million. The business normally makes a post-tax profit of between £150,000 and £200,000 and distributes half of this to the founders.

MDT Ltd had the following assets at its last year end:

	£
Freehold property*	500,000
B Plant and equipment	250,000
Cars	50,000
Stocks and debtors	250,000

*This figure represents the property's market value at 30 June 1993.

MDT Ltd had no long-term debt at the year end. It did have an overdraft of £10,000. MDT Ltd had no creditors at the year end. This was due to its policy of paying every bill as soon as it was received. The founders were reluctant to employ debt in their financing as they felt it was likely to compromise their independence.

Product research and development was managed until 1990 by Mr M, one of the founders. In that year he retired from full-time work with MDT Ltd, but continues to work part-time for 2 days a week. Mr M is still a shareholder with an equal amount of shares as the other two founders.

Mr M's replacement was a graduate electronics engineer who had previously worked for the company during vacations. Since the appointment, she had devoted most of the time of her department on developing a new product. She has now finished this and the product has performed well in initial trials. She is not a shareholder.

Product

The product has been given the name of the 'Integrator'. It is a remote-control device that can operate any remotely-controlled electrical appliance, for example, television, video, alarm system, microwave, camera. The Integrator was made in the development department and the variable cost of its manufacture was £10 per unit. The component which is unique to the Integrator is a computer chip designed by the engineer. The chip has been patented and ownership of the patent is vested in MDT Ltd.

Market prospects

MDT Ltd does not have a marketing department and so it commissioned a leading firm of consultants to study the market prospects for the Integrator in the United Kingdom. The results are very encouraging. The consultants believe that the Integrator would sell at least a million units in the first year in the United Kingdom. They believe it would retail for £50. Sales would remain at this level for 5 years and then fall to 250,000 units a year for the foreseeable future. The consultants also suggest that MDT Ltd should seek worldwide patent protection for the Integrator as it will be attractive in many other countries.

The consultants charged £50,000 for their report which is double the amount MDT Ltd would normally spend on marketing in a year. The consultants have offered to study the world market for the product for £100,000, or they would study individual countries at £10,000 each.

Future options

Following the UK marketing study, MDT Ltd felt it needed to make some plans for the future. It felt it appropriate to gain further guidance from the consultants who had the experience that MDT Ltd lacked. This further study cost £80,000 and MDT had to arrange a bank overdraft to finance it.

In the opinion of the consultants, MDT Ltd has the following choices:

- Manufacture the Integrator. In order to do this, MDT Ltd would have to invest £20 million in its manufacturing processes, working capital and launch costs to enable it to meet UK demand. To meet future world demand, the investment would need to be more substantial but the consultants cannot forecast this until they do the further marketing study.
- Sell the patents. The consultants are sure that the patent would fetch a substantial sum of money but until they seek offers they are not sure how much.
- Franchise the rights to manufacture and market the Integrator. The consultants believe that such a franchise would be eagerly sought by many companies.

Requirements

(a) Carry out a SWOT analysis for MDT Ltd. **(8 marks)**

(b) (i) to evaluate the three strategies suggested by the consultants, indicating particularly the finance, production, marketing and personnel implications of each of the strategies. **(24 marks)**

　　(ii) where necessary, to recommend and justify alternative strategies for MDT Ltd. **(10 marks)**

(c) Discuss whether or not the original objective of the founders – that of working together – is still applicable after the invention of the Integrator. **(8 marks)**

(Total marks = 50)

Question 5

Introduction

IP, a large public company, is one of the world's leading generators of electric power. The board of directors has stated that the company's corporate aim is to be the leading generator of electric power in the world, building a business which is profitable and provides long-term shareholder value. The directors have set a financial objective of increasing IP's gross operating profit percentage to 1.2 times its current level over the next 3 years. The board of directors is willing to consider undertaking environmentally-friendly as well as conventional methods of power generation. (Environmentally-friendly methods of power generation can be regarded as non-conventional.)

Financial review

The following table provides comparative financial information for IP's home and overseas operations over the last 3 years in its conventional power generation markets. (These figures exclude information related to environmentally-friendly forms of power generation.)

	Last year $m	2 years ago $m	3 years ago $m
Turnover	4,500	5,300	5,000
Gross operating profit	900	1,200	1,100
Profit before tax	720	1,100	1,000
Earnings per share	$0.525	$0.765	$0.72
Dividend per share	$0.45	$0.42	$0.40
Dividend cover	1.17	1.82	1.8
Levels of gearing (debt: equity ratio)	1.08:1	0.88:1	0.85:1

IP has managed to maintain a 20 per cent share of its home and overseas markets (in terms of power energy supplied) over this 3-year period. The expected overall annual rate of growth in the home and overseas power generation markets (in terms of units of power supplied) is 5 per cent compound. This is the actual rate at which it has grown over the last 3-year period.

IP's selling prices are expected to reduce on average by 1 per cent compound each year over the next three years in both its home and overseas markets. The company's management accountants have forecast that over the same period, the company's operating costs will increase by 2 per cent compound each year. This does not take into account any changes in the level of sales. Turnover is expected to increase over the next three years as both the home and overseas markets are expanding. Analysts working on behalf of IP have forecast a compound rate of growth in IP's turnover (in terms of units of power supplied) of 2.5 per cent each year.

The chairman has proposed a substantial reduction in dividends next year. The details of this will be made known after the strategic review which is expected to be completed in 3 months' time.

Business review

IP increased its output and operational efficiency in power generation last year, but turnover reduced by 15 per cent from two years ago. It has placed much emphasis on low-cost production and efficient working practices. In addition, IP acquired a retail gas supplier last year in order to diversify its energy provision market.

Total capital expenditure on overseas investments next year is expected to be $1 billion. The company is developing new markets overseas, particularly in respect of hydro (water-driven) electricity generation and is increasingly using other forms of fuel such as gas and oil rather than coal to generate power. IP suffered a reduction in earnings last year because of reduced turnover and lower contribution from one of its power stations in an overseas country.

The company made provisions for $100 million relating to income which had been earned, but not received, from the sale of electricity to an overseas government. The overseas government withheld payments to IP because, in its opinion, the emission levels from one of IP's power stations in the country are intolerably high. The overseas government has further accused IP of acting irresponsibly in not applying strict safety procedures in operating the power station in an attempt to reduce costs. This has been refuted by the directors who claim that they place great emphasis on health and safety and have initiated an audit programme to monitor performance and review initiatives to promote safer working practices. In addition, IP undertakes training programmes for staff, encourages health campaigns and provides opportunities for health screening of its workforce. The directors also state that they believe the emission levels to be within internationally-agreed limits.

IP is a founding member and substantial financial contributor to the International Association of Power Generators (IAPG) and has appealed to that association to assist in resolving the dispute with the overseas government. So far, the IAPG has not carried out a specific investigation of the case. It has issued general guidelines stating that its members should, as a minimum, aim to conduct their generating activities in accordance with established international standards. The overseas government has stated that this action (issuing guidelines) from the IAPG is insufficient and that IP should be made to account for the alleged high emission levels.

Environmentally friendly forms of power generation

IP undertakes considerable research into environmentally friendly forms of power genera-tion. This includes investigative research into hydro, wind, wave and solar power. IP's gross operating profits before tax from businesses established using these power sources increased by 40 per cent over the previous year to $30 million last year. Its investment in these plants was $450 million which gave a sales revenue of $130 million, an increase of 20 per cent over the previous year. (These results are not included in the information contained in the table within the financial review section.)

Turnover and operating costs of these businesses are both expected to rise by 5 per cent compound each year over the next three years. IP has committed an increase of $50 mil-lion each year in research investment in these forms of power generation over the same period.

The chairman of IP has stated that the company operates within permitted annual emis-sion limits both in its home and overseas operations. He has further stated that 60 per cent of IP's home electricity production is from 'cleaner' plant which meets international standards for environmental management. In evidence, the chairman has produced statis-tics which demonstrate that IP's plants in many overseas locations reduce dust emissions to the level of industry best practice and that newly commissioned plants are using 'state of the art' technology ensuring cleaner power generation.

Requirements

(a) Explain the diverse needs of IP's various customer types (retail, corporate and govern-ment) with regard to the supply of energy and the responsibilities these place on the board of directors. **(8 marks)**

(b) Review separately the performance of IP's conventional and environmentally friendly power-generating operations and assess whether its three-year financial objective is likely to be achieved. Assume no other changes to turnover and costs besides those stated within the scenario. Support your answer with relevant calculations. **(13 marks)**

(c) Appraise the position and the future strategic potential of IP from the perspective of a potential rational ordinary shareholder proposing to invest in the company. **(8 marks)**

(d) Discuss the ethical position of the IAPG and IP with regard to the latter's dispute with the overseas government. **(12 marks)**

(e) Propose and justify a strategy which IP should adopt to improve its market share.

(9 marks)
(Total marks = 50)

Solutions to Revision Questions

✅ Solution 1

Notice how this question is structured to test different levels of skills. Part (a) tests knowledge and uses the verb 'explain'. In other words it is asking whether you can recall the objectives of benchmarking (e.g. from Section 3.5) and if can you describe in broad terms how it is done (e.g. from Section 3.5.3). Part (b) is about application. You are asked to describe how it can be used in sales management. This requires you to decide for yourself what are the *processes* and *outcomes* required of a sales manager and of a sales team as a whole and discuss *potential measures* and uses. Also you must consider comparisons. Presumably individual salespeople are measured against one another (but watch out, they have different territories so travel distances, customer value and competition will be different). How about the sales team as a whole? Are you going to benchmark it against itself *through time*? Or are you going to find *another firm* with a similar sales team and product to benchmark against? The examiner is inviting you to talk about internal, competitive, activity and generic benchmarking here.

(a) *Definition*: Benchmarking involves the comparison of the output or processes of an organisation with that of another which is involved in the same activities for the purposes of *organisational improvement*.

It is usual to select a firm that has a good reputation for quality to ensure that the comparisons are made with an organisation that displays a good standard of performance. For this reason it is often called best practice benchmarking.

Benchmarking can be used to improve a firm's products, service, quality and internal procedures. It is sometimes difficult to obtain access to data relating to a firm in the same industry, as there are likely to be 'trade secrets' which firms may be unwilling to disclose to present or potential competitors. However, on the basis of mutual benefit, the sharing of information will enable both organisations to review their policies and practices.

The benchmarking process will involve interaction between the managers of different firms and this may act as a spur to innovation within each firm. The discussions may lead to improvements and enable the people involved to display creativity in dealing with existing and potential problems.

Discussing mutual problems will allow the managers to learn from the experience of the other organisation and it is possible that costly mistakes could be avoided. It is essential that the managers are prepared to discuss both past successes and failures if the benchmarking is to be of maximum benefit in establishing the 'best practice' within the industry.

131

In the evaluation of operational performance, benchmarking will:
- provide a basis for establishing standards of performance;
- highlight differences between the performance of the company and the other organisations;
- enable steps to be taken to improve the performance of the firm, resulting in lower costs and better quality.

(b) Benchmarking will enable the firm to assess its current policies and practices in respect of the management of the selling function.

(i) The areas of the sales department as a whole which will be affected by the introduction of a system of benchmarking are:
- *Planning*. It is important that the company's current practices are reviewed and assessed. If comparisons are to be made with similar organisations, it is essential that the present processes are understood to allow an objective view to be taken of the firm's current sales management function. An effort will need to be made to identify a firm which is prepared to share information which might be regarded as confidential by many firms. As an example, it may be important to analyse the selling costs of both firms for comparative purposes.
- *Research*. To facilitate the benchmarking process, it will be necessary to identify the activities which can be compared. In a sales department, these will include the number of calls per week, the distances covered by each salesperson, the costs relating to the sales force and the sales generated by each call. These might be useful starting points in the overall benchmarking process. It may be beneficial to the benchmarking process if the company has already undertaken an internal benchmarking of the company's present sales department before trying to compare its performance with other firms.
- *Analysis*. It is essential that the method used and the specification of the variables is established within the company before comparisons are made with the other organisations. When comparative information has been generated, it will be possible to establish performance indicators which will highlight the weaknesses and inefficiencies of the organisation. It is likely that operating costs, past sales levels, the control methods and mechanisms used and new business generated would be performance indicators that should be analysed to provide the basis on which the benchmarking can be undertaken.
- *Implementation*. The information obtained from the benchmarking exercise will be invaluable in the future in order to monitor the selling activities of the company. In addition, it will assist in making better decisions regarding sales areas, the need to target new customers in some areas, the relative costs of the selling function and the methods of remuneration that are most effective with the sales staff. Although it is likely that benchmarking will be a time-consuming process, it is possible that considerable benefits will be realised by comparing the activities of the sales force with a firm which is regarded as operating an efficient sales organisation.

(ii) Impact of benchmarking on individual salespeople would be in the following areas:
- *Planning*. As the activities of each salesperson will need to be analysed, it is essential that the co-operation of the sales personnel is obtained if the benchmarking process is to be successful. It is possible that there will be some resistance to change, especially if it is possible that their remuneration will be reduced

as a result of the exercise. It will be necessary to reassure the staff that the process will not affect them adversely.

- *Research*. It is necessary to establish performance measures in a flexible manner as it is often difficult to make direct comparisons. For example, travelling times and the size of purchases by customers are factors which are particularly significant in determining the performance of each representative. At the present time, the same targets are set for each sales area. However, by establishing criteria in a number of areas, it will be possible to be objective in assessing the performance of each individual.

- *Analysis*. It will, therefore, become possible to compare performance both within the firm and also with other firms operating in the same areas. This is likely to make comparisons more realistic and a more effective basis for determining the bonus payable.

- *Implementation*. For the firm as a whole, the benchmarking of activities of the individuals will provide a better appreciation of the factors involved in setting sales targets. The whole benchmarking process should be aimed at improving the performance of each salesperson and this will increase the performance of the whole firm. As a result of the process of benchmarking, the selling costs should be controlled more effectively and result in a better selling function in the company.

 ## Solution 2

When this question was set the examiner reported his disappointment that most candidates simply wrote all they knew (which often was not a lot) about the value chain. Let us look closely at the requirements. Although you will need to say what is meant by terms like *value* and *primary and support activities* the context is clearly the ways in which these can help management identify where value is gained or lost and, having done this, decide to which activities or linkages resources should be devoted. The examiner has made it quite clear that he is not asking you what a value chain is; he is asking you how it may be used (and perhaps whether it has any limitations).

When assessing the current position of an organisation, it is useful to consider the added value that results from the company's activities. Michael Porter developed the concept of a value chain which enables the contribution of each of the primary and support activities to be measured. The purpose of value chain analysis is to enable activities to be eliminated if they do not contribute value to the final product. By focusing on the costs and benefits of each activity, it would be possible to adapt the products to maximise benefits and minimise costs in both existing products and new products.

Initially, the managers will establish the value added to the product or service by each of the primary or support activities. The inbound logistics are concerned with the receipt of the factors of production used by the company. The costs incurred in maintaining adequate stocks of materials, an appropriately skilled workforce, suitable machinery and adequate financial resources would be assessed to ensure that excessive costs are not incurred.

Operations refers to the conversion process within the organisation, the efficiency of the labour and also consideration given to whether the technology used is appropriate. It would be necessary to consider the possibility of 'outsourcing' the production process if lower-cost alternatives can be negotiated from other producers. However, the problems associated with loss of control would need to be taken into account before an outsourcing decision was taken.

The outbound logistics will consider the distribution channels and methods used. The effectiveness of the alternative means available would be compared to ensure that the best method in terms of value for money is used. Similarly, the activities of marketing and sales and service must be analysed to establish that the needs of the company and the customer are being met by the current arrangement. This will provide a basis for evaluating the need for change if more effective methods can be devised.

The support activities include the company's infrastructure, the human resource management, technological development and procurement process. By establishing the value added by each of these activities and comparing this with the current costs, it would be possible to alter the arrangements to consider the value added against the cost implications within each activity.

Basically, by using the value chain, management is seeking to establish the source of the company's competitive advantage. It would then be appropriate to develop strategies which will build on the company's strengths and minimise the effect of any weaknesses that are identified. It is intended that value-chain analysis should establish the total value added by each activity so that the added value can be compared to the cost. This will ensure that the company's competitive advantage is retained and resources will be allocated to activities which generate the greatest added value.

 ## Solution 3

(a) It is often difficult to assess the standard of performance of an organisation and the concept of 'benchmarking' has been developed to enable the management to compare an organisation's activities with that of another organisation in a similar industry. The comparison of the organisations will highlight areas that can be improved in both organisations. This should result in increases in efficiency, customer satisfaction and, possibly, cost savings. In all these ways, the organisation can 'add value' by implementing the findings from benchmarking against another organisation.

It is usual for organisations to be selected for benchmarking which have a good reputation for quality and efficiency. By comparing and contrasting the activities of each organisation, it is possible to judge the standard achieved in both organisations. It is intended that this will provide an insight into the manner in which improvements can be introduced. It is usual to find that each organisation benefits from the benchmarking exercise and is able to improve the quality of its products. It may also be possible to improve the operating efficiency of all their activities.

The commitment and co-operation of all the staff and particularly the senior managers of the organisations are essential if the benchmarking is to be successful. As it is inevitable that most organisations will have some areas that are regarded as 'trade secrets', it is essential that the areas to be benchmarked be made clear at the outset. In this way, managers can discuss mutual problems and try to find the best way of tackling the problem.

By learning from the experience and expertise of the staff in each organisation and comparing the practices and policies that are most effective, it should be possible for both organisations to add value through the benchmarking of their operations. It must be recognised that the process may result in substantial changes being introduced into the organisation and it may take a considerable amount of time to implement the changes. It is vital that the objectives of the benchmarking exercise are clearly defined and accepted by all participants.

(b) The benchmarking exercise will need to be planned and implemented carefully to ensure that the maximum benefits are obtained from the exercise. As CC Ltd has been selected as the most suitable company for the purpose of benchmarking, it will be necessary to approach the company to find out if they are prepared to participate in a benchmarking exercise. The areas to be discussed must be agreed and then the whole process will need to be planned carefully in order to maximise the benefits. It is likely that the benchmarking will be possible, as the two companies are not in direct competition.

Planning

At the outset, a team should be selected which will undertake the benchmarking. A range of expertise would be required as it is intended that all aspects of the two companies should be compared. It therefore seems at least one manager from Operations, Marketing, Selling, Human Resources and Finance should be asked to participate in the benchmarking process.

Research

It will be necessary to identify the activities that will be compared. Agreement will have to be obtained between the two parties, as there will be some aspects of the business that the management will not wish to discuss. As the proposed benchmarking between AL plc and CC Ltd is very wide-ranging, a range of different measures will have to be discussed. Examples are:

Operations	Staff numbers
	Levels of customer complaint
Marketing	The effectiveness of different marketing methods
	Amount spent on marketing
Selling	Number of calls per week by each salesperson
	Transport costs of each salesperson
Human Resources	Staff turnover rates
	Average wage rates
Finance	Cost of new staff
	The weighted average cost of capital

Analysis

Details should be obtained on each of the factors that are considered to be important. It will be necessary to ensure that the implications of each factor are understood, as superficial comparisons could be misleading.

Although it is possible that the benchmarking will need to be carried out over a number of months, it is likely that a picture will emerge of the areas in which each company is superior to the other. Another factor that must be taken into account is that one of the companies is in the industrial cleaning industry and the other is in the contract catering industry. There are bound to be differences in the activities of the two companies and this must be considered when conclusions are drawn from the benchmarking exercise. Once a clear pattern is found, the managers of AL plc will

POSITION APPRAISAL AND ANALYSIS

need to discuss the implications of the findings. In addition, ways of improving the performance of AL plc will need to be considered.

It is possible that the process of discussion and the generation of alternative courses of action will be difficult in AL plc. If the organisation is managed in a traditional manner, the managers will not be used to offering criticisms and it is possible that they will not offer suggestions of methods in which the processes can be improved. In the past, this type of comment may have seemed to be an implicit criticism of senior managers and so it may be necessary to encourage them to participate in the bench-marking exercise. Nevertheless in order to benefit from this activity it is important that the employees are encouraged to offer suggestions and possible changes to the working methods in order to improve the efficiency and effectiveness of the organisation.

In addition, it is vital that the managers involved in benchmarking should receive the support of the senior management of the company and they should encourage innovation and suggestions of methods of improving the performance of AL plc. It is essential that the senior managers create a climate within AL plc, which will engender trust, and co-operation within the organisation. If the Taylorism style of management has become established, there may be mistrust and attitudes of self-preservation within the management team. This would not facilitate the benchmarking exercise and it may be necessary for the management style to change to ensure the long-term success of AL plc.

 Solution 4

This is the first 50 mark scenario question we have tackled in *Management Accounting – Business Strategy*. These kinds of question can seem daunting at first but there are some general policies that will help you:

1. *Read the requirements first.* This will help you to understand the areas of the syllabus that are being examined and also the skills that you are required to demonstrate. When reading the requirements, pay attention to their sequence. Is the examiner leading you through the case? For example in this question you are initially undertaking a SWOT, then you must evaluate the three proposed strategic options and make recommenda tions. Finally you consider the possibility that the three founders can still work together. There is a logic running through these requirements. You should evaluate the options according to whether MDT Ltd have the skills and resources necessary to make it a success. For example, a firm that has no experience of managing debt is about to borrow £20m. Does that seem sensible to you? Do you think a bank would lend them the money when they only have £500,000 of assets? If they did manage to arrange the money, could the three of them actually hope to manage a global marketing and exporting business without additional members on the management team?

   By using the sort of reasoning above, you are already half way to your answer.

2. *Read the scenario in whole paragraphs.* A common problem candidates have with scenarios is that they get bogged down in the detail of the case and do not see the larger issues. To avoid this, ensure that you read to the end of each paragraph before trying to take notes. This way you focus on the sense of what is being said. You can come back to pick up the detail later if you need to substantiate your reasoning and arguments.

3. *Take some time to plan your answers.* Having read the case and re-read the requirements you should try to jot down a few ideas under each requirement to get your ideas flowing. Having done this you should decide what you want to do or say under each

heading. For example, in this case you might jot down a cruciform chart and scribble a few points in each quadrant. Then you would put down the headings 'manufacture', 'sell patents' and 'franchise' and scribble some points under these. Finally 'work together?' and again a few points. A quick tidy up and you have a plan.

4. *You have planned your writing, now write your plan*! Once you have a plan you can concentrate on writing your answer. Do not depart from the plan as you write just because another idea comes into your mind. That only leads to a confused answer or loads of irrelevance. Remember, you are not trying to write the perfect and most comprehensive answer available. You are just trying to show the examiner that you have the basic ideas about the processes of strategic management.

(a) As the first step in the decision process, the management of MDT Ltd must consider the strengths, weaknesses, threats and opportunities of the firm. The SWOT analysis will provide the basis for the strategic decisions in respect of the new product.

1. *The strengths*. MDT Ltd has been extremely fortunate in developing a new product with the potential of the Integrator. Its national and worldwide sales potential and gross margin on sales of £40 per unit (£50–£10) suggests high profitability.

   Whether the graduate engineer is a strength or not depends on whether she is able to develop similar innovations in the future.

   The core business of producing electrical goods is successful but, given the potential impacts of the increased staffing and volumes from undertaking to make the Integrator, it is unlikely to confer much competitive advantage on MDT.

2. *The weaknesses*. The expansion is very large in relation to the existing business and this will demand management skills that the present directors may not have. They are very rooted in the technical skills of low-technology electrical engineering.

   The firm has inadequate capital resources to fund the expansion. It will need to take on considerable capital gearing to cope with the project which will increase its risk.

   The firm has inadequate marketing expertise to handle national, still less international, marketing of the Integrator.

   Lack of experience of the technology of electronics manufacture. Moving into the electronics business involves a higher level of technology. MDT Ltd's previous experience was in the relatively low technology area of electrical goods.

   Poor financial management skills. The paying of invoices on demand while granting customers credit is not prudent cash flow management and would lead to a cash flow crisis if the firm grew.

   No experience of international business. In addition to marketing, the firm needs to cope with exporting and foreign exchange risk.

   Lack of international patents on the Integrator. There is a danger that the innovation could be copied, particularly if the inventor decides to leave because she presently has no financial interest in the success of her invention.

   Lack of collateral to pledge as security for the debt of £20m.

3. *The opportunities*. The development of the new product creates an excellent opportunity for MDT Ltd to diversify into a new market both at home and overseas. The products controlled by the Integrator are a growing market.

4. *The threats*. High reliance on the consultants' market assessment. As the new project requires considerable investment of capital, the estimate of sales is crucial.

   Danger of larger overseas rivals copying or rivalling the Integrator.

The high level of capital gearing, and the interest upon it, will jeopardise the viability of MDT Ltd generally. For example, the interest on £20m at 10 per cent would be £2m per annum, which is ten times MDT's present profits.

(b) The proposed expansion will affect every part of MDT Ltd. Since the new product represents a major strategic decision for the business, it is important that the correct decisions are taken. Before making the final decision to develop the Integrator, MDT Ltd must consider a number of options relating to finance, production, marketing and personnel functions.

1. *Manufacture the integrator.* This strategy requires MDT Ltd to obtain funding to finance the acquisition of the machinery, working capital and land. An investment of £20m is very large for a company which has only been generating annual profits of, at most, £200,000. MDT Ltd does not have any cash reserves and so this strategy is likely to force the company to raise funds by the existing shareholders investing additional funds in the firm, issuing additional shares privately (MDT Ltd is not listed on the stock market) or borrowing debt to fund the new investment.

A rough investment appraisal can be attempted using the data provided by the consultants.

π Retail price = £50 per unit

π Variable cost = £10 per unit

π Sales = 1m units per annum for 5 years then 250,000 per annum thereafter

If we assume the following:

- cost of capital at 10 per cent;
- retail margin and distribution costs are 50 per cent of retail price;
- product life cycle is ten years and capital investment has nil scrap value;

then annual net revenue is:

$$\{0.5 \times £50\} - £10 = £15 \text{ per unit.}$$

Therefore, £15m for five years followed by £0.25m for a further 5 years.

Present value of net revenues	£m
£15m × 3.791	56.90
£0.25m × (6.145 − 3.791)	0.59
Total	57.50
Less initial investment	20.00
Net present value	37.50

The project provides a substantial return in the United Kingdom alone.

However it is unlikely that the existing shareholders will have this amount to invest in the new project and, since an issue of shares would reduce the existing shareholders' control of the firm, they are not likely to favour this course of action. This means that the expansion would have to be funded by debt which will increase the risk of MDT Ltd. This is because interest has to be paid even if the project does not generate profit. This could cause difficulties if the new project is not as successful as expected. As the founders wish to safeguard their independence and, at present, do not use long-term debt, they are unlikely to favour borrowing £20m to fund the new project.

In the past, the firm has produced a relatively low-technology range of products. It appears that the present production facilities have coped with the task, but this may not continue with the new product. This is because advanced technology is required to produce the Integrator. If the expansion is to be successful, the quality of the new product needs to be excellent. It is doubtful that MDT can achieve this and hence it might be better for MDT Ltd either to franchise the rights to another manufacturer or to sell the patents. Although both these strategies may reduce the profit generated by the new product, these may be the best courses of action for MDT Ltd.

Alternatively the firm could contract-out the manufacturing to a more experienced and possibly cheaper producer. This would also avoid some of the investment risks and leave them just the task of marketing the product.

However, the firm lacks the ability to market the product. For more than ten years the business has marketed its products through wholesalers. In addition, they do not have a marketing department, giving the impression that its expertise in marketing might be relatively limited. The question that must be answered is do the firm have the skill to tackle the launch and sale of a product which will have an expected annual retail turnover of £50m. Based on its past record, this does not seem likely. This means that, in order to launch the product successfully, marketing skills must be improved. One solution may be to hire an experienced marketing manager, who will ensure that the launch has a greater chance of success.

Additional considerations will be the large increase in staff needed to manufacture the Integrator. The workforce will become much larger and perhaps professional human resource management expertise will be called for. Also professional financial and marketing managers will need to join the team which will compromise the independence of the three founders.

The graduate engineer, who has invested a considerable amount of time and energy in developing the Integrator, may not welcome the decision to sell the patent. She may see it as a 'sell-out' and is likely to prefer the company to invest in the production facilities. The other staff are likely to favour the manufacture and sale of the product by MDT Ltd, as this would expand the manufacturing facilities and create additional jobs within the firm. They need to be reassured about the safety of their jobs.

2. *Sell the patent*. This might fit in well with the personal objectives of the founders, especially as Mr M has already retired from full-time work. The founders may prefer to avoid the risks arising from the launch of the new product and opt for the certainty of the sum negotiated for the sale of the patents.

This sum, for UK rights alone, might be as high as the £37.5m calculated above.

The value of this option would be significantly enhanced if the rights to overseas sales could also be included. In order to assess the overseas value of the patents it is recommended that the consultants undertake the assessment of worldwide potential at a cost of £100,000. The management of MDT may need to *borrow against the value of the factory* premises to afford this research.

It is also crucial that MDT Ltd secures the worldwide patent right as soon as possible. This should be done through instructing an experienced patent agent to represent them.

3. *Franchise the rights to manufacture and market the product.* This strategy will reduce the amount of capital investment required and, therefore, the risk of the venture. The existing shareholders of MDT Ltd are likely to favour the reduced commitment of resources.

However, franchise agreements normally involve the franchisor in providing central services such as marketing and technical advice to the franchisee. In this case it is doubtful that MDT Ltd has any experience to offer. The firm will also not have as much control over the quantities produced, the delivery dates and the product quality if the manufacture is franchised. The management of MDT Ltd must ensure that the manufacturing firm is not able to produce a similar computer chip. If the manufacturing firm can do this, it would result in a competitive threat to MDT Ltd. However, even if MDT Ltd manufactures the product itself, the threat of competition cannot be eliminated.

Although a franchise might enable MDT Ltd to participate in the success of the Integrator by taking a percentage of the sales revenue, it is unlikely to be purchased by manufacturers and the sale of patents seems the better route.

In conclusion, there are some doubts about the ability of a relatively small firm managing an expansion of the magnitude suggested by the consultant's report. From the information available, it would seem that the directors should either subcontract the manufacture of the product or sell the patent. Adopting either of these strategies means that MDT Ltd does not have to raise large amounts of capital to finance the manufacturing facilities.

If the patent is sold, the firm will not be involved in the marketing and sales of a new product. As wholesalers were used for the selling of the electrical appliances, MDT Ltd lacks marketing and sales experience. This is the least risky strategy, which should maintain the original objectives of the founders.

Finally, the decision about who should produce the Integrator will depend to a large extent on the attitudes and objectives of the directors. At the outset, the founders appeared to be relatively 'easy-going', but the possibility of a very successful product could change their outlook. They may want to maximise their competitive advantage by manufacturing and marketing the Integrator themselves.

The lack of manufacturing and marketing expertise indicates that the preferred strategic decision is to sell the patent. This will reduce the amount invested by MDT Ltd in the project. This means that both the company's risks and the consequences of error will be reduced.

(c) The successful launch of the product will significantly increase both the size and profitability of the firm. Although this is a most desirable situation for the firm as a whole, it is likely that the nature of the operation will change substantially. The founders might be worried by the proposed expansion as their objectives will be affected in the following ways:

1. The tasks of the directors will alter with the expansion of the business. The increased staff, larger production requirements and the need for specialised activities will have a major impact on the firm. Specialists will be required for both the marketing and financial management functions.

2. The firm will require professional managers who have the skills which the founders may not possess.

3. Employing additional staff may change the original atmosphere in which the founders 'liked working together'. It is important to note, however, that one of the

founders, Mr M, has already retired from full-time work. It is also possible that the others will be close to retirement age.

4. The new product will require considerable capital investment in both machinery and working capital. Additional finance will, therefore, be needed and it is likely to be obtained by increasing the firm's debt. This increases the risks of the business and may conflict with the objectives of the founders who are reluctant to use any debt at the present time.

 Solution 5

(a) IP generates power and supplies energy to users in its home country and abroad. At the present time, the company is mainly supplying electricity produced by conventional methods, but non-conventional methods are also being used to generate power that is considered as being environmentally friendly.

The company supplies power to governments who then distribute it to the public. However, IP also supplies power direct to the end users. This means that IP has retail and wholesale customers and also governments that distribute the power to the final users of the energy. All these customers will expect an uninterrupted supply of power. They will also be interested in receiving relatively cheap energy. However, there will be some individuals and groups that will be particularly concerned about environmental issues.

The board of directors must try to meet the expectations of these different groups of customers. It appears that the company strategy will meet its customers' expectations in the following ways:

- All customers will benefit from the expected decreases in the price charged for their power. Although the retail users will be pleased with lower selling prices, the corporate users will also benefit from the lower cost of power. This can be particularly significant in industries that use large amounts of power and the lower energy prices should improve their competitive position.

- There are some customers and pressure groups which are concerned that top priority is given to the environmental issues. There is evidence that resources are being made available to undertake research into developing alternative means of generating power that will be more 'environmentally friendly'. The power industry faces particular problems as a high proportion of the resources used are non-renewable. Fossil fuels are an example of the type of material that will eventually be exhausted and IP must take steps to seek alternatives.

- In the past, the company has focused on providing low-cost production and developing efficient, low cost working practices. It is important that the priorities be changed to ensure that the company's power stations have acceptable safety levels. This will be an issue that is particularly important to the governments of the countries in which IP operates. It is important that there is a speedy resolution to the current problem in the overseas country that is withholding the funds. This problem must be tackled to ensure that IP's reputation as a founder member of the IAPG is retained.

Although the board has a responsibility to meet the demands of the company's customers, it must also provide an acceptable return to the company's shareholders. Expenditure on additional plant will increase the capital employed. At the same time, more expensive processing, and high levels of expenditure on research and development, will reduce the company's profit. Both these factors will reduce the shareholder value that the company generates.

The board must take all these issues into account in the review of the company's strategy that is currently being undertaken. In general terms, there will be a conflict between the customers who favour cheaper sources of energy and those who are prepared to pay more for the power that they use if it is produced in an acceptable manner. The company will have to try to meet both these conflicting views.

(b) The results from the traditional operations can be summarised as follows:

	Turnover	GOP	Profit before tax
	$ m	$ m	$ m
Three years ago	5,000	1,100	1,000
Two years ago	5,300	1,200	1,100
Last year	4,500	900	720
Market share	20%	20%	20%

Although the market has been growing at a rate of 5 per cent per annum, IP's turnover last year decreased from $5,300m to $4,500m. This would suggest that the prices charged by IP have been lower than the rest of the industry. However, the selling prices charged by IP are expected to fall further over the next three years. This is an issue that should be investigated.

Two years ago, the profit reported by IP was $1,100m, but this fell to $720m last year. This represents a fall of more than 34 per cent over the year and the decreased selling prices will have contributed to this decrease in profit. However, the gross operating profit (GOP) as a percentage of sales fell from 22.64 per cent to 20 per cent over the same period. In fact, the GOP was 22 per cent three years ago. This shows that the operating expenses have been 78 per cent, 77.36 per cent and 80 per cent of turnover over the three years. This trend in operating costs and turnover should be a major concern of IP's board and it is important that the review addresses the issues that have caused this decrease in the profitability of the company.

IP's non-conventional activities have been more successful over the past two years. The GOP has increased by 40 per cent and is at a level of $30m. The turnover increased by 20 per cent over the period to $130m. It is, therefore, possible to establish that the results from non-conventional power generation are as follows:

	Turnover $m	GOP $m	GOP as % of
	$m	$m	Turnover
Three years ago	108.3	21.4	19.8%
Two years ago	130.0	30.0	23.1%

The GOP, as a percentage of turnover from non-conventional activities, has improved over the two-year period. Although these businesses have nearly met the company's financial objective of 1.2 times the GOP as a percentage of turnover, they are producing percentages that are much the same as the conventional power companies. The turnover and operating costs are expected to increase by 5 per cent compound over the next three years and so the profit from these operations will not increase significantly. The company, as a whole, therefore, appears to face a difficult future and is unlikely to meet the objectives that have been adopted by the board.

The financial projection for conventional activities in respect of the next three years will be affected by the expected reduction in selling prices by 1 per cent each year.

In addition, the sales growth will increase the turnover by 2.5 per cent per annum. The turnover figures will, therefore be:

Year 1 $4,500 × 0.99 × 1.025 = $4,566.375m
Year 2 $4,566 × 0.99 × 1.025 = $4,633.349m
Year 3 $4,633 × 0.99 × 1.025 = $4,701.337m

The question states that the operating costs will increase by 2 per cent compound each year. However, the operating costs will not increase (that is are not affected by) the change in the level of sales. Assuming, therefore, that the operating costs will increase by 2 per cent compound each year, the estimated operating costs will be $3,672 in Year 1, $3,745.44m in Year 2 and $3,820.35m in Year 3. From the table below, it is clear that the GOP will decrease each year and the GOP as a percentage of turnover is also falling.

The details are as follows:

Conventional power

	Turnover $m	Operating costs $m	GOP $m	GOP as % of Turnover
Last year	4,500.00	3,600.00	900.00	20.00
Year 1	4,566.38	3,672.00	894.38	19.59
Year 2	4,633.35	3,745.44	887.91	19.16
Year 3	4,701.34	3,820.35	880.99	18.74

Non-conventional power

	Turnover $m	Operating costs $m	GOP $m	GOP as % of Turnover
Last year	130.00	100.00	30.00	23.08
Year 1	136.50	105.00	31.50	23.08
Year 2	143.32	110.25	33.07	23.08
Year 3	150.49	115.76	34.73	23.08

Total of conventional and non-conventional power

The total GOP for the whole company was $930m last year. This is expected to fall to $925.88m in Year 1, $920.98m in Year 2 and $915.72m in Year 3. However, the board has set a financial objective of increasing the GOP to 1.2 times its current level over the next three years. Based on the projections, the income and expenditure in Year 3 will be $4,851.83 and $915.72 respectively. The GOP as a percentage of turnover will be only 18.87 per cent and this is below the target of 1.2 times the current level, which is the financial objective set by the directors.

(c) Although the company is unlikely to meet the objective in respect of the GOP, it is possible that the company can 'provide long term shareholder value'. If the capital employed can be reduced, it is possible that the return on equity could be improved.

The factors that need to be considered are the dividends to be paid to shareholders and the increase in share values that can be expected. The chairman has suggested that there will be a 'substantial reduction' in dividends next year. As this is taking place when the operating profit of the company is only decreasing marginally, it is possible that the financial markets will not view this with confidence and the share price would fall. Both the lower dividends and lower share price would not lead to an improvement in the shareholder value.

A major element in appraising the company's future strategic potential is the benefits that will be received from the investments in the non-traditional sector. It is possible that the present forecast of annual growth of only 5 per cent per annum may be conservative, as more people become concerned with the environment and also the use of non-renewable resources. At this stage, IP is developing the skills and experience of the staff in these areas and it is possible that this could give them a competitive advantage in the future. Although this is an appropriate strategy for the company, it is possible that the benefits will only be evident in the longer term. However, at the present time, the expenditure that is required will reduce the profits and increase the capital employed. This will reduce the return on capital employed and reduce the value generated for the shareholders.

The dispute with the foreign government should be resolved at the earliest opportunity, as it will not enhance the reputation of IP as a responsible energy producer. The board must act to minimise the damage that is caused by this dispute.

In general terms, the company does not appear to be in a strong position, as the future earnings are static and there are many areas of uncertainty ahead.

(d) The dispute about the level of emissions is a matter that could have serious consequences for IP. At the present time, a foreign government is holding $100m as it is alleged that the emissions are 'intolerably high' from the power station in its country. Although the cash flow is reduced by the amount that is being held and the current profit has been reduced to reflect the possible loss, the main problem is the impression that this will give of IP in respect of its dealings in foreign countries.

The company is trying to develop its markets in foreign countries and this publicity could damage the reputation of IP as a socially responsible power producer. The board does not accept the allegations of unacceptable levels of emissions. There is no scientific proof of the problem. It is clear, however, that the company is a responsible employer and has taken steps to ensure that the working conditions are safe and an audit programme has been initiated to monitor the performance of the company.

The board of IP has a duty to ensure that acceptable standards are maintained at all the generating plants. It is important that the board shows a high degree of integrity to ensure that the company avoids any adverse publicity. If there is any foundation to the accusations of the overseas government, it is essential that steps be taken to rectify the position. It is important that an investigation be undertaken to ascertain both the nature and cause of the alleged high pollution levels and unsafe practices. Scientific evidence should be obtained from an independent expert who is acceptable to both parties to the dispute. This is vital, as it is unwise for these allegations to be left unresolved, as the image of the whole company could be badly affected by the accusations.

If it is found that the emissions are at an unacceptable level, immediate steps must be taken to resolve the problem. The other power stations must also be tested to ensure that their emissions are at an acceptable level.

The IAPG could be used as the expert, but as IP has close links with the body, it is not likely that its ruling will be acceptable to the foreign government. It appears that the IAPG is compromised as it has a duty to IP as a member that provides support, but it also must provide protection to the public. However, the IAPG should be involved in the resolution of the dispute. It seems that this body has not really identified its role in this type of dispute.

IAPG must establish itself as an unbiased arbitrator in these disputes. The issue of guidelines that provide standards, that can be understood by all parties, should be addressed by the IAPG in the future. However, this would not seem to be possible immediately. The body should, therefore, provide every assistance to both parties to resolve the dispute fairly in order to meet the expectations of its members (IP), the general public and all government departments that are charged with monitoring environmental issues.

The company should review its procedures regarding the monitoring of emissions at all its power stations throughout the world. This is clearly going to be a major factor that will be faced by IP in the future. At the present time, 60 per cent of the electricity production at home is from plants that meet international standards. In addition, in many overseas locations, IP's plants are operating at emission levels which are in accordance with best practice. In addition, newly commissioned plants are using technology to ensure cleaner power generation. It appears, therefore, that IP is making efforts to improve its environmental position, but it is important that IP's position, both at home and in overseas countries, is reviewed to ensure that the likelihood of emission problems is minimised.

It is clear that the new plants are being built to meet the required standards, but it is important that the company investigates the current position and also estimates the financial implications of any changes in environmental policy within the company.

This is a matter that should be initiated immediately, as it could be very important to IP in both the short term and the longer term. The trends would indicate that this could be a vital factor that must be incorporated into all the company's strategic plans.

(e) The management of IP could use Ansoff's Growth Vector matrix to consider the different strategic options that are available to develop a strategic plan to improve its market share and management of the markets. The alternatives that are available are:

1. *Market penetration.* It is possible that sales of existing services could be expanded in IP's existing markets. The possibility of success for this strategy will depend on the strength of competitors and the opportunities for increasing the demand in the areas where IP is already operating.

2. *Market development.* Expansion by means of developing new markets for the existing products. It is clear that IP has the technology in both conventional and non-conventional power generation. This option could require large amounts of capital if it is necessary to invest in projects to develop the infrastructure. It is possible that the non-conventional sources of power would be more feasible.

   Alternatively, IP could form strategic alliances in which it will supply new technology and where it will be possible to expand businesses that are already established. It is possible that some governments will have established power supplies and they may be interested in forming strategic alliances with IP to improve the efficiency and effectiveness of the power supply in their countries.

3. *Product development.* The company is already involved in the development of non- conventional power generation. This is an area that is likely to be a major source of growth as more concern is shown about the problems associated with the use of non-renewable resources and environmental issues, such as the pollution from the use of fossil fuels. In the future, the public may demand that alternative sources of power generation are used. IP could have a major competitive advantage if it has already developed the technology and skills for non-conventional power generation.

4. *Diversification.* It is possible that there might be opportunities to diversify into both related and unrelated activities. Retail outlets that sell and maintain electrical

equipment is an example of related diversification. At the present time, the management of IP does not have the skill required to establish retail outlets but these skills would be available in most countries. The risks of this strategy are likely to be significantly large. However, a strategic plan that moved into non-power activities would represent an even greater risk to IP.

Market and product development strategies would appear to be most appropriate courses of action for IP to consider in order to improve the company's market share.

4

Strategic Aspects
of Marketing

Strategic Aspects of Marketing

4

You will be familiar with the basic concepts of marketing from your earlier studies.

The previous chapters have been concerned with analysing the environment of the organisation in terms of the objectives it has set itself and conducting a position audit to assess whether it has the resources it will need to meet its objectives. This chapter is the first of three that examine the actions a firm can take to improve its financial position. It examines the sources of a firm's revenues and profits, its products and customers.

LEARNING OUTCOMES

By the end of this chapter you should be able to:

▶ discuss how customers influence the strategy process and recommend how to interact with them;

▶ evaluate the product portfolio of an organisation and recommend appropriate changes to support the organisations strategic goals;

▶ discuss the concepts of data warehousing and data mining.

4.1 Sources of earnings

4.1.1 Earnings as an objective

In Chapter 1 we discussed the objectives of the business and recognised that among them would be financial objectives related to the earnings of shareholders.

The job of the chartered management accountant is to help ensure that management has the information it needs to assure these earnings. Therefore it seems sensible to consider what this means. Where do earnings come from?

4.1.2 Product *versus* customer views of earnings

Consider a simple business, say a shop where customers walk in to buy newspapers and chocolate. What is the source of the firm's earnings here?

There are two possible answers:

1. *The products sold are the source of the earnings*. An accountant would presumably point out that each line of stock has a price and that the earnings of the shop are determined by the number of units sold at this price. According to this view, the way to commercial success is to sell more.
2. *The customers are the source of earnings*. A marketer (a member of the *marketing* profession) might argue that the source of the earnings is the customer. They would point out that a customer who comes to the shop each morning is a better source of earnings than the customer who shops at the store only once. According to this view, commercial success depends on retaining the loyal customer and encouraging them to buy more things on each visit.

Traditionally management accounting has assigned costs and revenues to products or divisions. By assigning costs and revenues to products, customers or business divisions (or locations or technologies) Ward (1992) defines the sources of profitability in a different way. In this chapter we will consider the concept of direct product profitability and also customer account profitability (CAP).

4.1.3 Implications of the different views of earnings

The distinction is important for deciding a firm's strategy. It raises the following questions:

1. In calculating revenues and costs should we take the customer or the product as the basis of calculation?

   The answer is 'whichever provides the more useful information for the decision you wish to make'. In your examination you will be expected to understand both *product profitability* and *customer profitability* analysis.
2. In calculating profit do we calculate the profit of each individual product and customer or do we take the transaction as a whole?

   In the example of the shop we may discover that the profit on the newspapers is very small. However, without the newspapers to attract the customer into the shop it would not sell the chocolate. Therefore we should add some of the profits from the chocolate sales to the profits of the newspapers. Ignoring these associations between products is called direct product profitability (DPP) analysis, whereas including associated purchases is part of a fuller product profitability analysis (PPA).
3. In deciding whether a product or customer is profitable should we consider just this year's costs and revenues or should we consider all the earnings we may receive in the future too?

   The topic of *life cycle profitability* is critical to strategy. Commercial banks know that providing bank services to young people and small businesses is rarely profitable. However they still do it because some young people will later rely on the bank for insurance, personal loans, savings products and other more profitable services and so building brand loyalty which is vitally important. Similarly some small businesses grow up to be successful big ones.

   Understanding whether the future earnings of the product or customer are growing or not is critical to this decision.
4. When we develop new products what will determine their profitability, the volume we sell or the kind of people that we sell them to?

   Almost certainly it is the kind of people that buy it who will influence profits. Understanding the saying that 'firms do not have profitable products, only profitable customers' is one of the most important lessons a chartered management accountant can learn from a marketer.

Premium branded items like Mercedes, Rolex and Montblanc are profitable more because of the sorts of people who buy them and less because of any technical features they may have. Before developing a product it is best to consider the likely value of the people who will buy it and ensure that it is developed with their needs in mind. This is what Lexus, Tag and Parker decided to do when they started to produce their own premium brands.

4.2 Product life cycles

4.2.1 The product life cycle model

The concept of a product life can be used at the level of product offering and even then can be used at a number of levels. For instance, we could consider the product life cycle of the automobile, or the product life cycle of diesel power cars, or of leaded petrol cars or convertibles.

The model presents a generalised account of the stages through which a product passes from its initial launch until its final withdrawal from the market due to obsolescence (Figure 4.1).

The main characteristics of each stage are:

1. *Introduction stage*. This is a new product and hence will be unfamiliar to the market. The firm will need to invest considerable resources in developing and launching the product (including promotion, stock-building, staff training, etc.) without any guarantees that the product will succeed. Therefore:
   - strongly negative cash flows;
   - high risk due to product novelty;
   - single or limited product range to avoid confusing the customer;
   - few if any competitors willing to take similar risks;
   - high need to induce recognition and trial of the product;
   - very high costs per customer.
2. *Growth stage*. Rapidly increasing sales due to acceptance of the product and a 'bandwagon effect' developing as buyers copy one another. The substantial investment needed to keep up with demand depresses cash flows. The most significant feature of this stage is increasing

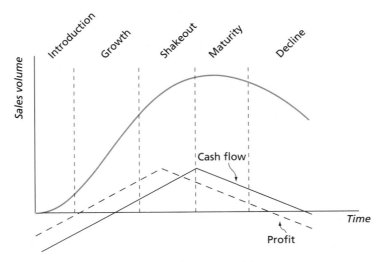

Figure 4.1 The product life cycle

complexity as rivals enter the market and the range of products widens as producers seek to attract customers from each other with novel features:

- negative cash flows;
- reducing risk due to product having achieved acceptance;
- market entry by 'copycat' or 'me-too' producers;
- growth sustained by attracting additional types of customers, sometimes through reductions in price or product features;
- marketing focus switches to seeking to differentiate the firm's product and brand in the minds of customers.

3. *Shakeout stage*. The sales growth rate turns down (i.e. becomes *ex-growth*) due to the market having become saturated. Initially there will be an imbalance between supply and demand because participants will not have forecast the downturn. This is usually resolved by a wave of product or business failures or amalgamation of businesses through takeover or merger. Briefly:
   - overcapacity creates stimulus for price-cutting;
   - number of producers reduces due to failures or industry concentration;
   - peak levels of profitability.

4. *Maturity stage*. This is where purchases settle down into a pattern of repeat or replacement purchasing. For fast-moving consumer goods (FMCGs) like canned foods, soft drinks and confectionery these may be habitual purchases. For durables such as televisions, computers, cars and furniture the frequency of repurchase will be influenced by changing technical features, fashions and wearing-out of old product. The main features will be:
   - reduction in investment in additional capacity leads to improved current cash flows;
   - gradual price decline as firms compete against one another for a larger share of a fixed-size market – during this stage buyer and supplier power (Porter) increase because of the large number of industry members to choose between;
   - firms seek to capitalise on product loyalty by launching spin-off products under the same brand name;
   - gradual fragmentation of the market as firms seek out buyer groups to monopolise with special value-added features on products (e.g. premium quality foods in addition to regular and budget lines);
   - peak profitability and least risk.

   The later phases of the mature stage are often characterised by a second wave of consolidations as some firms pursue industry rationalisation to restore profitability. This has been noticeable in recent years in industries such as oil and banking.

5. *Decline stage*. The product declines into obsolescence as technically better substitutes replace it. The existence of such substitutes will cause sharp profit reductions among producers of the product. Many firms will have already found alternative industries, while those remaining will be looking for an orderly way to exit the industry:
   - falling profitability and marginal cash flows;
   - firms seek to leave industry.

4.2.2 Using the product life cycle model

The product life cycle can be used in a number of ways:

1. *To determine appropriate strategies for the firm*. As the discussion above shows, each stage brings with it a number of strategic prescriptions.

One great strength of the product life cycle is that it encourages managers to look beyond present returns when deciding on product investment strategy.

2. *To evaluate investment in products.* Investment in products should be taken on the basis of the forecast net revenues of the product over the life of the investment asset. The stage of the product life cycle gives an indication of whether these revenues may be expected to grow or not and also the likely level of further investment needed.

3. *To develop performance measures for the product.* Traditional financial control measures are of greatest use in the mature and decline stages where the most appropriate management style is one of critical use of resources and maximisation of cash flows. During the introduction and growth stages, the factors which should be controlled are ones related to the product's market success because these will determine its future financial value.

The subject of appropriate performance measures is dealt with in greater detail in Chapter 8.

4.2.3 Problems of the product life cycle model

Wilson and Gilligan (1997) call this 'one of the best-known but least understood concepts in marketing'. This alludes to some of its limitations:

1. *Lack of clarity of which level the model works at.* The product life cycle can be used at a number of levels:
   - *Industry level*: This would consider smoking products, motor transportation or cosmetics.
   - *Product categories*: These exist within an industry. Taking the example of the industries above, it would look at generic types of product such as cigarettes, cars or perfume.
   - *Product form*: Customers may switch between different forms of the same product. Continuing the example: Low-tar cigarettes, sports cars or body sprays.
   - *Brand form*: This is the particular product made by the firm, for example, Marlboro lights, Mazda MX5, Cacharel.

     It seems quite possible for a manager to claim to have an introductory brand of a growth form in a mature category in a declining industry. This hardly helps management decide whether to invest in it or not!

2. It is not possible to forecast the precise shape or duration of a firm's life cycle from the model. Although useful as a descriptive model it has no predictive value.

3. *Firm cannot locate its position on the life cycle.* Management have only past sales data. Suppose it shows annual volume increases for the past 3 years. Does this mean the product is in the early, mid or late growth stage? Suppose the sales fell last year. Is this due to the onset of the decline stage or is it the effect of a short recession in the economy?

4. *It focuses on the* product *rather than on the* market. As discussed earlier, it is possible to argue that the customer or customer group is the proper unit of strategic analysis rather than the product. For example, a food store would form a better idea of its future profitability if it used the life cycle as shown in Table 4.1.

5. *It invites managers to assume the stages are inevitable.* There are no guarantees that a product which is presently at its introductory stage will actually achieve growth. Products such as the Ford Edsel, digital compact cassette technology and telephone hygiene services are all examples of failures.

   Similarly mature products do not necessarily stay mature or necessarily decline. Perrier water and Schlitz beer both seemed set for a long future and then suddenly

Table 4.1

Stage	Customer group	Product
Introductory	First-time shoppers, e.g. just left home	New recipe microwave meals
Growth	Young families with youngest child under 6	Fresh baked bread and morning goods. Pharmacy products
Mature	Families with youngest child over 6 years	Breakfast cereals, baked beans, soft drinks
Decline	Families with youngest child over 18	Tinned food, deep-frozen foods

declined due to management failures. Meanwhile Imperial Leather and Ivory soaps continue to be major sellers worldwide after more than 100 years.

Other products seem to return from the decline stage and become major contenders again. In soaps this occurred with the 1960s brand 'Dove', while in entertainment artist 'come-backs' are a frequent occurrence.

The role of management in marketing the products is critical to success and the shape of real-world life cycles.

6. *It invites management to consider product singly and not in conjunction with one another.* Earlier we discussed the possibility that one product is essential to attract customers in order to sell another. The product life cycle does not explicitly acknowledge such connections.

4.3 The BCG portfolio matrix

4.3.1 Levels of portfolio analysis

A portfolio means a 'collection'. In the present context it means a collection of products or businesses.

In business, portfolio analysis management seek to visualise their operations as *a collection of income-yielding assets*. This approach is based on an approach used in financial strategy and is intended to give guidance on where to invest additional funds.

1. *A product portfolio.* A business unit may provide a range of products to its customers. For example, a life assurance firm may offer a number of products such as pensions, endowments, whole life, critical illness and guaranteed income policies.
2. *A business (or corporate) portfolio.* This is the business as seen from head office. Here the strategic business units (SBUs) are being seen as a collective whole.

4.3.2 The growth-share matrix

The most well-known example of product or corporate portfolio analysis is provided by the Boston Consulting Group (BCG). There is a definition of the model in CIMA: *Management Accounting: Official Terminology*, 2005, p. 46. The BCG model requires management to plot the position of their business units (or products) against two axes:

1. *Relative market share.* This is calculated as the firm's market share against their largest rival, so a firm with a 20 per cent share of the market which has a rival with a 60 per cent share would have $0.3x \left(\frac{20}{60} = 0.3x \right)$, while the rival would calculate their relative share as $\frac{60}{20} x = 3x$.
2. *Market growth rate.* This is the annual percentage change in sales volume in the industry as a whole.

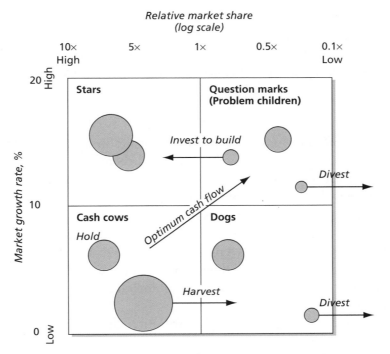

Figure 4.2 The BCG matrix

This allows the business units to be plotted on a two-dimensional space, as shown in Figure 4.2.

An additional factor is the inclusion of sales turnover in the model. The proportion of total group sales turnover accounted for each division is converted to the radius of a circle, with its centre as the coordinates of the division.

4.3.3 The importance of relative market share

High relative market share is of central importance as the key to competitive success argues the BCG. This is principally based on its earlier discovery of *experience curves*.

An experience curve is in many ways similar to a learning curve effect: the organisation becomes more efficient in producing and marketing a given product as it produces more of it. This leads to the statement that *unit cost declines and cumulative volume increases*. BCG claim this typically amounts to a 15 per cent fall in unit costs for every doubling of cumulative volume.

BCG argue that all firms in the industry face essentially the same experience curve effects. Consequently as the industry progresses the unit costs of each participant will fall. Inevitably this will lead to falling prices. The firm that survives this process will be the firm with the lowest costs which, by extension, will be the one with the highest cumulative volume.

The conclusion is that *domination of the market is essential for low costs and hence competitive success*. Hence high relative market share is sought within the BCG matrix (Figure 4.2).

High relative share therefore brings several benefits:

- the enjoyment of lower unit costs and therefore higher current margins than competitors at the same price levels;

- the ability to be a price leader – if the firm decides to cut price, others must follow to maintain their sales, but in so doing may find themselves selling at below unit cost;
- the dominance of the market means that the product will become the benchmark product – 'the real thing' against which others may be seen as pale imitations.

4.3.4 Strategies for each quadrant

1. *Question marks (problem children)*. These products are in a high growth market which means that it is early in the product life cycle and therefore has the potential to repay present investment over its life cycle. Indeed the high market growth rate means that the firm will already be investing considerable sums in it.

   The low relative market share, however, means that this business unit is unlikely to survive in the long run because it will have a lower cost competitor.

   Management must decide between investing considerably more in the product to *build* its market share or shutting it down now before it absorbs any further investment which it will never repay. Investing to build can include:
   - price reductions;
   - additional promotion and securing of distribution channels;
   - acquisition of rivals;
   - product modification.

2. *Stars*. Very competitively strong due to high relative market share, although their current results will be poor due to the need to invest considerable funds into keeping up with the market growth rate.

   The strategy here is to *hold* market share by investing sufficient to match the commitment of rivals and the requirements of the marketplace.

3. *Cash cows*. These are mature products (low growth rate) which retain a high relative market share. The mature stage means that their prospects are limited to falling prices and volumes. Therefore investment will be kept under strict review and instead the priority is to maximise the value of free cash flows through a policy of *harvesting* the product.

   Harvest means to minimise additional investment in the product to maximise the case the division is spinning off. This cash can be used to support the question mark products as well as satisfy demands for dividends and interest.

   Holding may also be used for early-mature stage products where the market may repay the extra investment.

4. *Dogs*. Dogs come into being from two directions:
   - former cash cows that have lost market share due to management's refusal to invest in them;
   - former question marks which still had a low relative share when the market reached maturity.

   In either case the BCG recommends divestment of the product or division. This can mean selling it to a rival, or shutting it down to liquidate its assets for investment in more promising business units.

   In deciding whether or not to divest a dog, the following considerations should be taken into account:
   - (a) Whether the dog still provides a positive contribution or not.
   - (b) What is the opportunity cost of the assets it uses? For example, the contribution from products that could be made using its factory or the interest on the net proceeds from liquidation of the SBU.

(c) The impact on the rest of the portfolio that would result from divesting the SBU. Is it essential to attract customers for example?

In later versions the BCG introduced the notion of a *cash dog* to accommodate another strategy of creating a niche position for a dog product based on its nostalgia value (e.g. Mini cars) or because a group of loyalist customers remain who will continue to pay high prices for the product (e.g. hand-made cigars).

4.3.5 Evaluation of the BCG matrix

The principal benefits of the BCG matrix are that it:

1. Provides a convenient way for management to visualise a diverse range of businesses or products.
2. Ensures that management perceive of the portfolio of businesses holistically, rather than assessing each unit independently. Specifically management will:
   - pay attention to cash-flow balances within the product portfolio;
   - recognise the need for question mark and star products to be developed to ultimately replace present cash cows.
3. Can be used to analyse the portfolios of rival firms:
   - to identify which products they may decide to devote resources to;
   - to spot potential areas for attack such as knocking out a crucial cash cow with an identical product.

However, the BCG matrix has been criticised on a number of accounts:

1. *The experience curve, and hence rationale of increasing relative share, is faulty.* Kay (1993) suggests that the experience curve is flawed. In some industries the high cumulative output does *cause* lower unit costs (e.g. aircraft manufacture), whereas in others (e.g. broiler chickens) the large cumulative volume is the *consequence* of low unit costs because it was these that increased the size of the market by making chickens affordable. Mistakes in estimating the effect of experience can cause serious problems to companies that price in anticipation of cost efficiencies. Texas Instruments lost market position and a lot of money in a number of industries in which it had held a strong position from overestimating the effect.

   Kay (1993) also notes that firms which are encouraged to price down their experience curve to gain share tend to treat initial capital costs as sunk costs and therefore ignore them. Failure to recover these capital costs through selling at prices related to unit costs alone never recoups this capital investment and therefore destroys shareholder wealth. Also it means that when this capital needs replacement, the firm will not be able to afford it.

2. *Problems with defining the market.* Both axes demand that management define which market the business unit is trading in so that its relative share and growth can be calculated. However this is a matter of judgement. For example, in attempting to calculate the relative market shares of rival supermarkets, the following issues will cause complications:
   - whether to include non-food items such as clothes, banking services and audio–video in the computation;
   - whether to include just the stores in the country or perhaps include ones abroad too;

- whether to separately analyse and compare mega-stores, medium-size stores and convenience stores;
- whether to include other firms who are not food retailers in the calculations;
- whether all rivals actually seek to serve the same customers, for example, does a quality food store need to compare itself with a budget chain?

3. *The axes are too simplistic.* Relative market share is supposed to denote competitive strength. However, this strength can depend on other factors too; for example:
   - strength and reputation of brand;
   - extent of vertical integration of the business;
   - level of costs;
   - quality of the product.

   Similarly industry growth rate is supposed to convey the attractiveness of the industry. This again is questionable as high-growth industries also demand a lot of investment and present significant risks.

   This would make low-growth markets more attractive to firms without capital or which were risk averse. Other factors making industries attractive could include:
   - fit with the present business of the firm;
   - similarity of customers it serves;
   - knowledge and abilities of management to operate in it.

4. *Ignores potential links between the products.* The BCG matrix focuses on just cash flow associations between products. It does not consider other potential links such as:
   - the likelihood that sales of one product will generate sales for another through *cross-selling* (both purchased at the same time) or *sell-through* (purchased at a later date).
   - the possibility that products share the same fixed costs and therefore shutting down one will make the other unprofitable too.

5. Companies are successful by following innovative strategies not 'copy cat' strategies.
   - Many authors argue that the intended strategy should be based on an innovative approach rather than 'more of the same'.
   - A number of companies make a good living by acquiring *dogs* and waiting for others to leave the market – by becoming suppliers of last resort their products will become *cash cows*.

6. Companies can be lulled into complacency
   - Since the matrix focuses on the competitive threat from the most dominant rival, there is the opportunity to be caught out by a rapidly growing competitor who will only show up when they become dominant in the market.
   - There are significant areas of strategic analysis that are not considered by the model – for instance supply side dynamics.

4.3.6 Customer portfolio analysis

The BCG matrix focuses on products as the source of a firm's revenue. With a little imagination the model can also support assessments of customer profitability.

1. *Market growth rate.* In a customer analysis this would translate into the rate of change of numbers of certain types of customer. Marketers call these groups *customer segments*.

   Customer segments* can be classified in a variety of ways termed *segmentation bases*.

   According to Jobber (2004) market segmentation is the identification of individuals or organisations with similar characteristics that have significant implications for the determination of marketing strategy. Kotler and Keller (2006) talk about the need to segment markets because marketers can better price, design and satisfy their markets.

The attributes or benefits sought by a market segment can be used to attract that segment and also to identify customer types. Once a firm or organisation knows what their customers want and need, they are better able to meet those needs. At the same time, knowing the characteristics of current customers will help to identify potential customers. Marketing efforts can be directed toward segments with the greatest likelihood of becoming customers.

For example, let us consider segmentation, and segmentation bases, in the context of the tourism market. A key step to understanding demand in a tourism context is to examine traveller markets (Godfrey and Clarke, 2000). Traveller market research reveals trends in the market that can be used for forecasting and outlines customer characteristics and motivations, which can help reduce some of the risk associated with making decisions. This is especially important since traveller markets are becoming more heterogeneous and complex, and are constantly changing (Best, 2000). Knowing the characteristics of a particular group of tourists can help tourism destinations more effectively tailor and promote their products to meet the demands of the target market. Market segmentation is one method by which a destination can better understand its visitors.

Four overriding categories that shape the needs of consumers have been identified: demographic, psychographic, behavioural patterns and geographic (Best, 2000).

Demographic characteristics, such as income, age, sex, family, life cycle, occupation and educational status, all contribute to differing sets of customer demands for a variety of products and services. Younger visitors, for example, may demand more challenging excursions than elderly people. Demographic variables are the most popular bases for distinguishing customer groups. One reason is that consumer wants, preferences and usage rates are often associated with demographics variables. Another is that demographic variables are easier to measure. However, demographics alone do not explain why customers behave the way they do (Dalrymple and Parsons, 2000).

Psychographic segmentation involves grouping people according to their lifestyle and personality characteristics (Jobber, 2004).

Psychographics examine the motives for travel behaviour. Psychographic characteristics are created by differences in values, attitudes and interests and contribute to differences in customer needs (Best, 2000). These variables primarily reflect the influence that social forces can have on the consumption process. Consumers who are demographically the same may differ significantly in their attitudes and value orientation, which may result in differing needs (Best, 2000). Psychographic segmentation is an effective method to apply because the use of tourism products is extensive among certain psychographic groups.

The third variable that can be used to segment tourism markets is ***behaviour segmentation.***

Behaviour patterns can reveal information such as how, when and how much of a product or service is used (Best, 2000). In tourism, previous trip characteristics are often examined in order to determine probable future travel patterns. Additionally, such information can help to reveal the types of activity or travel preferences of visitors.

Finally, tourist markets can be ***segmented geographically***. Such segmentations can reveal information about travellers' locations of origin and destination, and whether they are rural or urban. This is important because product usage can differ geographically (Dalrymple and Parsons, 2000). For example, tourists visiting a warmer geographical area may prefer to walk, while others visiting a colder destination may wish to stay in more sheltered, roofed accommodations.

One of the main reasons why tourism suppliers use this method is that it is easy to categorise actual customers or potential customers by the geographic area where they live and then market to them on this basis. But there are disadvantages in this type of segmentation. Customers and potential customers living in any specific geographical area may have wide differences in family incomes, ages and similar demographic factors; therefore it is often preferable to use geographical segmentation only in conjunction with one or more of other methods of segmentation.

Since the total market for tourism is huge, it is more productive and cost-effective to identify several smaller groups of people with similar attributes. The chosen segment becomes the 'target market'. The goal of target marketing is to position a business/destination within a product market so that it gains a comparative advantage. This comparative advantage is gained when the business offers products with attributes that are both unique and important to the customer.

The first step in the market segmentation process is to group customers with like traits, and then discover which demographics, lifestyle forces and usage factors set them apart from other customers (Best, 2000).

Members of a given segment (say the over 60-year olds) may require different features in a product (say a holiday or dwelling). This can help guide firms to make more appropriate and more profitable products. Moreover, a firm may identify certain customer groups as being in the ascendant while others are in decline. For example, industrialised nations have experienced a considerable rise in the buying power of these wealthy retired persons. This has led to successful development of retirement holidays, second homes and specially developed sheltered accommodation.

2. *Relative share.* One interesting concept has been firms starting to calculate their *share of a customer's total spending*. It has been suggested that part of the attraction of banking services to supermarkets is the chance to monitor what customers are spending elsewhere in order to start providing those products and services themselves (including financial services which are of course a large part of personal spending). They see this as one way to leverage the loyalty of their customers, brands and distribution chains to increase earnings in an otherwise mature food market.

*It is worth thinking about the factors that will make a particular market segment attractive;

- Broad and homogeneous – so that there is a sufficiently large market.
- Easily accessible – so that the firm can gain competitive advantage by offering a more responsive service at relatively low cost.
- Easily served through existing value chain – so that the firm can enjoy economies of scope without incurring extra costs.
- Affluent – so that there is the potential for large volume sales.
- Not price sensitive – so that there is the prospect of high margins.
- Potentially brand loyal – so that customers, once earned, can be retained.
- Have few competitors – the firm will face lower barriers to entry and there may be significant untapped demand.

With this in mind, it is important that companies new to an industry choose the 'right' market segment when they enter the market.

4.3.7 Alternative portfolio models

The criticism above that the axes on the BCG are too simplistic is addressed by the GE Business Screen Matrix. This was developed by General Electric in conjunction with the McKinsey consulting group. The axis reflecting business strength, divided into high, medium and low, covers a number of factors as shown in Figure 4.3.

For the axis indicating the business strength of the firm there are, again, more than one factor considered as shown in Figure 4.4. The axis is again split into high, medium and low.

The position of the SBU or product in the nine cell matrix will again lead to six normative strategies (rather than the three prescriptions in the BCG matrix) and, it is claimed, the analyst is offered sharper positioning options and strategic choices than with the BCG matrix.

Those normative strategies are:

- *Invest to hold*. Incremental investment in the SBU by the marginal amount necessary to offset any potential erosion due to external forces.
- *Invest to penetrate*. Increased investment with a view to increase the business strength of the SBU or product.
- *Invest to rebuild*. Investment to counter any damage done by other strategies that are no longer achieving optimal results.
- *Selective investment*. Investment in SBUs that offer a marginal return through a favorable cost/benefit ratio. Allow those with an unfavourable cost/benefit ratio to decline.
- *Low investment*. By minimising investment, pursue a harvesting strategy and release cash for other investments.
- *Divestment*. Exit the market.

As we can see this model still suffers from the criticism of offering prescriptive solutions and, as such, should only really be considered as a descriptive model. It does, however, benefit from the use of a richer set of analytical variables and allows the analyst greater flexibility. The greater flexibility arises since firstly a larger set of variables are included in each of the parameters and, secondly, because the importance of the variables can be weighted to indicate their relative importance when the position on the axes is calculated.

Absolute market size	Economic
Market potential	Technological
Market growth rate	Social
Competitive structure	Political
Financial	Environmental

Figure 4.3 Industry attractiveness factors

Size of SBU	R&D capacity
Market share	Manufacturing process
Positioning	Quality
Comparative advantages	Marketing department strengths
Brand strength	Learning capability
Human resources	

Figure 4.4 Business strength factors

STRATEGIC ASPECTS OF MARKETING

4.4 Direct product profitability

> 🔑 CIMA describes direct product profitability (DPP) as: 'Used primarily within the retail sector, DPP involves the attribution of both the purchase price and other indirect costs (for example distribution, warehousing and retailing) to each product line. Thus a net profit, as opposed to a gross profit, can be identified for each product. The cost attribution process utilises a variety of measures (for example warehousing space and transport time) to reflect the resource consumption of individual products.'

CIMA: *Management Accounting: Official Terminology*, 2005, p. 17.

4.4.1 Origins of the concept

Direct product profitability seeks to calculate the profits being made from the sale of a particular product line. It does not take into account the profits from the sale of any other associated products.

DPP was originated by consumer goods manufacturers to help them assess the profits enjoyed by the retailers stocking their products. This information may be used in two ways:

1. *To use during price bargaining sessions with buyers.* The supplier is able to confront the retailer with the amount of profit they are making from the good (and perhaps the poor margins on rival goods) and therefore reject their request for extra discounts or financial incentives to continue stocking it.
2. *To understand how to increase a retailer's willingness to stock a product.* When developing a new product, or rescuing a failing one, management will wish to ensure that it is attractive (i.e. profitable) to retailers.

   Today most retailers will calculate DPP themselves to help decide stocking policy.

4.4.2 Calculating DPP

1. *Determinants of sales revenue.* Sales revenue from stocking the product depends on:
   - the price of the product;
   - the frequency with which it is bought;
   - the amount of sales returns generated.
2. *Determinants of costs.* This is the point where DPP has yielded some of its most valuable insights. The costs to the retailer of stocking the product are:
   - the unit price charged by the supplier;
   - the costs of ordering the product;
   - inventory and storage costs;
   - the costs of transporting the product from the warehouse to the store;
   - the costs of stacking the shelves with the product;
   - wastage and breakage costs.

The DPP analysis will examine the costs generated by stocking its product. More importantly it will seek to identify what factors cause those costs in order to reduce them and increase the DPP of the product to the retailer. Typical cost drivers have been:

(a) *The size of the product.* This is a major determinant of transport, storage and display costs because large-volume items take up more space.

(b) *The uncertainty about demand.* Retailers hold stocks of product on a just-in-case basis because they do not know what demand will be.

(c) *The delivery cycle.* If deliveries are weekly, then the store will hold an average of 3.5 days' stock.

(d) *The ordering method.* Manual ordering systems are expensive and the costs of ordering are the same regardless of the volumes ordered.

Calculating these costs involves carrying out an extensive ABC analysis.

4.4.3 Improving DPP

DPP can be improved in a number of ways:

1. *Increase the final sales price of the product.* In the short run this may be done by promotion. Ultimately it necessitates the creation of products with higher customer value, for example:
   - enhanced technical benefits;
   - higher perceived quality;
   - greater convenience in use.
2. *Increase the sales volume of the product.* Once again, promotion is important. Additionally the supplier can:
   - reduce pack contents, either by making them smaller or diluting the content;
   - encourage customers to use more of the product on each occasion;
   - increase the occasions on which the product is used;
   - introduce multi-buys in order to increase household consumption.

   Frequent-use shampoos are an example of a product category introduced to increase sales volume.
3. *Reduce costs of stocking the product*:
   (a) Reduce the physical dimensions of the product. Examples have included micro-sized washing powders and tablets, CDs, and disposable diapers.
   (b) Increase the frequency of deliveries to reduce store stock levels.
   (c) Develop sales forecasts and provide stock to the stores on the basis of them. This reduces inventory and eliminates ordering by the store. One example of this is wholesale providers of fresh fruit, meat and vegetables using short-range weather forecasts to predict demand for their products. For example, a warm and dry weekend will encourage barbecues.
   (d) Provide own staff to conduct the shelf-filling and merchandising of the product.
   (e) Redesign product packaging to reduce shelf space needed.
4. *Provide incentives to retailers to stock the product*:
   (a) Supplementary payments (sometimes called 'listing allowances' or 'margin support').
   (b) Point of sale support (e.g. refrigerators, shop signs, litter bins, etc.).

Aston (1989) provides a matrix to summarise methods of improving DPP (Figure 4.5).

	Low volume	High volume
High DPP	Advertise Upgrade shelf position Stimulate movement	Advertise and promote Display to maximum effect Maintain or increase shelf stock
Low DPP	Reduce shelf allocation Limit variety Reconsider price Discontinue	Review handling methods and costs Reconsider price Downgrade shelf position Reduce advertising

Figure 4.5 Merchandising matrix

4.4.4 Evaluation of DPP

DPP is more than a technique to increase the sales volumes of existing products. It is also an important consideration in product design. There, however, are some difficulties with using it in practice:

1. It can cause management to focus on the product characteristics rather than the needs of the customer. Some DPP-engineered products struggle to deliver additional benefits to customers.
2. The costs of the DPP exercise may be greater than the loss of profit from cutting the price to retailers.
3. It overlooks the relations between products. This could lead to abandonment of a product which is an important factor in introducing customers to a product line or retailer.

4.5 The nature of a marketing audit

4.5.1 The marketing audit

A marketing audit is a particular form of position audit which focuses on the products of the firm and the relationship it has with its customers.

4.5.2 A brief description of the role of marketing

According to the Chartered Institute of Marketing: 'Marketing is the management process responsible for identifying, anticipating and satisfying customer needs efficiently and profitably.'

Modern marketing can trace its origins to an insight by Levitt (1960) that many firms take a shortsighted view of the customer which denies them many commercial opportunities and blinds them to potential threats.

According to Levitt (and all modern marketers), firms should cease to see customers simply as being the purchasers of products. Rather, *firms are in the business of satisfying needs.*

Levitt's point is that firms can only be successful if they first understand the customer's needs and in the light of this develop products which yield the benefits the customer is seeking. Levitt termed this a *marketing orientation* to distinguish it from inferior orientations.

According to Kotler (1997), the marketing orientation (or marketing concept) is built on four pillars:

1. *Target markets.* Not all customers want the same things and neither are all customers of equal value to the firm. A firm cannot hope to supply all the customers in a market. It must select groups of customers it can serve and focus on them. Look back to Section 4.3.6.
2. *Needs and benefits.* Before producing a product the firm must first understand the needs the customer seeks to satisfy and what benefits they require. This implies an important role for marketing research.
3. *Integrated marketing.* The *offering* of the firm must be integrated to portray the benefits sought by the customer. This involves appropriate combination of the *marketing mix** elements:
   - *Product*: The physical features of the offering.
   - *Price*: The terms on which the customer buys the product.
   - *Promotion*: The message conveyed and the media in which it appears.
   - *Place*: The distribution channels used.

   A second aspect of integrated marketing is the need for *internal marketing* under which the marketing function ensures that all staff in the firm are sensitised to the needs of the customer and perceive of their jobs in terms of satisfying the customers needs.

   According to Jobber (2004) the need for the extension is due to the high degree of direct contact between the firm and the customer, the highly visible nature of the service assembly process, and the simultaneity of production and consumption.

   Since services have the following qualities:
   - *Intangibility*: The features and benefits of the good will need to be represented in some other way.
   - *Inseparability*: The good can only be consumed at the point of production.
   - *Variability*: No two customer experiences are the same for the same good. As such customers are a source of variability.
   - *Perishability*: Services cannot be stored for later consumption.

   He further indicates that the extension allows a more thorough analysis of the marketing ingredients necessary for successful services marketing. Any effective marketing plan for a service, such as tourism, will need to include all of these elements.
   - *People*: Another issue for the supplier is to ensure that the service received by the customer is of the same high quality, regardless of how it is delivered. Without courteous, efficient and motivated staff, service organisations will lose customers. A survey has shown that one in six consumers have been put off making a purchase because of the way that they were treated by staff. An important marketing task, then, it is to set standards to improve the quality of service provided by employees and monitor their performance. Training is crucial so that employees understand the appropriate forms of behaviour. For example, British Airways trains its staff to identify and categorise different personality types of passengers, and to modify their behaviour accordingly. Staff need to adapt a customer-first attitude rather

---

*Note that, the services marketing mix is an extension of the traditional 4-Ps. The essential elements of product, promotion, price and place remain, but three additional variables – people, physical evidence and process – are included to produce a 7-Ps mix (Jobber, 2004).

than putting their own convenience and enjoyment before that of their customers. People are very important element in services and especially in tourism because of high customer contact with people most of the time starting from getting on the plane, being welcomed, hospitality in hotels and restaurants.

- *Physical evidence*: Physical evidence relates to the environment in which the service is delivered, and any tangible goods that facilitate the performance and communication of the service. For example, the interior of jet aircraft is pastel-coloured to promote a feeling of calmness, whereas many nightclubs are brightly coloured with a flashing light to give a sense of excitement. In tourism services physical evidence such as brochures, décor of the places such as; airport lounges, tourist offices and the general ambience of the location, are very as that important may be the only evidence which customer can rely on.
- *Process*: These are the procedures, mechanisms and flow of activities by which a service is acquired. Process decisions radically affect how a service is delivered to customers. For example, being served at the restaurant and the time that customers wait for their orders, queuing when visiting places, can have an impact on customer satisfaction levels. Providing a more effective service, shorter queues, may conflict with short-term profits as the remedy may be to employ more staff, but will contribute to long-term success by repeat business and referrals.

4. *Profitability*: Through meeting the needs of valuable customer segments better than rivals, the firm can generate superior profitability for its shareholders while at the same time improving the quality of life of the customer.

Marketing assumes a crucial *boundary-spanning role* between the organisation's internal operations and the needs of its customers (Figure 4.6).

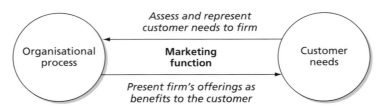

Figure 4.6 The organisational role of marketing

4.5.3 Marketing planning

Strategic marketing (or *marketing planning*) builds on the marketing orientation through assisting management to select potentially profitable target markets and then developing strategies to exploit them. An approach is shown in Figure 4.7.

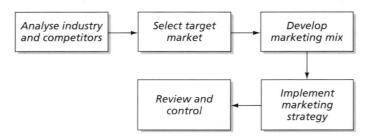

Figure 4.7 The process of strategic marketing

The stages of analysing the industry and competitors and selecting target markets are where the marketing audit comes in.

4.5.4 The content of a marketing audit

Many of the issues covered in the marketing audit are the same as the ones covered in an environmental analysis and a position audit. We have already dealt with them in earlier chapters.

4.5.5 Steps in conducting a marketing audit

Jobber (2004) suggests a five-step approach to marketing audit:

1. *Define the market.* Here management should develop a:
   - statement of the firm's purpose in terms of the benefits it seeks to deliver to its customer (or the needs it seeks to satisfy);
   - description of the products it seeks to provide and the scope (e.g. geographical range) of its coverage;
   - statement of the key characteristics of the market such as its size, growth rate and the strategies most likely to succeed in it;
   - statement of the key requirements for success in the market.
2. *Determine performance differentials.* The purpose here is to look for subsectors of the market which may provide an entry point for the firm (or, on the negative side, an entry point for a rival) or which may suggest new areas to expand into. The audit should:
   - evaluate the performance of the industry in general and any differences between the performance of competitors within it;
   - identify any differences between the products supplied, the applications to which they are put, geographical market differences or differences in the distribution channels used;
   - identify differences by customer set (or customer segment).
3. *Determine the differences in competitive programmes.* This is the first stage of competitor analysis and is really an exercise in 'getting to know your enemy'. The audit should identify and evaluate different rivals companies for their:
   - market development strategies, that is, which markets are they presently serving and which do they look minded to enter in the near future?
   - product development strategies, that is, what products do they supply at present and what additional new versions or new products may they launch in the future?
   - financing and administrative strategies and support.
   - Effectively the firm is conducting a position audit on its competitors.
4. *Profile the strategies of competitors.* This is the second stage of competitor analysis and involves deciding who are the major competitive threats and how the firm will deal with them:
   - profile each significant competitor and/or distinct type of competitive strategy;
   - compare own strategy with competitors' strategies.
5. *Determine the strategic planning structure.* This involves deciding how the strategic marketing effort is to be organised:
   - establish planning units or cells and set their goals;
   - assign staff to the product or market groups.

STRATEGIC ASPECTS OF MARKETING

Cannon's use of the term 'planning' would have been quite acceptable before the 1980s. Today we might prefer to think in terms of strategic business units, product teams and brand managers to 'manage' the process in a world where uncertainty has cast some doubt on the efficacy of planning approaches to strategy formulation and implementation.

4.6 Customer profitability analysis

4.6.1 Definitions

 CIMA defines customer profitability analysis (CPA) as: 'Analysis of the revenue streams and service costs associated with specific customers or customer groups.'

CIMA: *Management Accounting: Official Terminology*, 2005, p. 17.

Kotler (1997) defines a profitable customer as:

A person, household or company that over time yields a revenue stream that exceeds by an acceptable amount the company's cost stream of attracting, selling and servicing that customer.

4.6.2 Two views of customer profitability

Comparison of the two definitions above could suggest that they are discussing different concepts.

1. *The single-period analysis of customer profitability*. The CIMA definition suggests that CPA applies to customer groups we are presently supplying. It suggests that the management accountant should analyse the current revenues the customer is generating and compare them with the current costs of serving them. Typically this would be the flows of a single year.
2. *The life cycle analysis of customer profitability*. The Kotler definition seems to look at the value of the customer over the lifetime of the firm's association with them. His approach seems similar to an investment appraisal in which the present values of the future revenues from the customer account should exceed the present values of future costs.

Both approaches have their value and you should be prepared to answer questions on either.

4.6.3 Customer account profitability (CAP) analysis

This takes the single-period view of the value of the customer.

A UK clearing bank recently revealed that 20 per cent of its customers generated 120 per cent of its profits. Put another way, 80 per cent of its customers are unprofitable and reducing its profits by 20 per cent!

Using CAP analysis would reveal which customers this 80 per cent are (and who the 20 per cent are too). The approach would be as follows:

1. *Analyse the customer base and divide it into segments*: Marketing segmentation bases are undoubtedly valuable in other applications but they are less useful here. The basis of

segmentation for CPA should be according to factors which may have a material impact on revenues or costs. Commonly used bases include:

- *annual purchase volume* – high-activity accounts will impact on financial results most strongly;
- *average size of order* – ordering costs are related to number of orders not size of order;
- *source of order* – agents will take a commission and hence reduce revenues but also sales costs;
- *method of ordering* – personal sales calls are much more expensive than electronic ordering;
- *mix of products bought*;
- *degree of customer support needed* – answering enquiries, providing advice, training and assistance are all sources of costs;
- *payment methods used* – costs of invoicing, debtor control and advancing credit; also credit card operators will levy a merchant's fee.

Where the firm is supplying large individual accounts the analysis may be applied to individual customers. This approach is adopted in business-to-business markets and by professional services firms (e.g. accountants and lawyers) who have high-activity individual accounts.

2. *Calculate the annual revenues earned from the customer segments*: These revenues will normally be net of production costs, provided that the customer buys a standard product. If the product is customised, then this should be included in the costs as customisation can be a reason for poor profitability. Any discounts granted should be taken into account.

3. *Calculate the annual costs of serving the segments*: This will necessitate a close examination of the firm's overheads as well as its direct costs. Factors that are often examined are:
   - costs of order getting;
   - special customisation costs or rush orders;
   - promotional costs to the segment;
   - reliance on correspondence and personal enquiries;
   - number of delivery drops;
   - location of customer;
   - sales returns, warranties or refunds.

4. *Identify and retain the quality customers*: The quality customers are those who provide earnings in excess of costs. They can be the ones who are prepared to pay more for the premium service or, at the other extreme, others who demand only a rudimentary service.

5. *Eliminate or re-engineer the unprofitable customer groups*: Eliminating unprofitable customer groups means ceasing to supply them. Often this involves raising prices generally but allowing discounts to valuable clients to retain them. In the case of banks this has involved increasing the range of bank charges while simultaneously reducing the rates of interest available on small accounts.

   Re-engineering involves reducing the factors that are causing the costs. Examples have included:
   - increasing minimum order size to reduce number of orders;
   - installation of telesales or electronic ordering for small clients;
   - charging fees for services (e.g. toll lines);
   - imposition of flat charges for order handling;
   - differential prices for products according to customer.

4.6.4 Examples

An example of CAP analysis

An insurance firm was concerned about the poor profit performance of one of its types of policy. It decided to use CAP analysis. Because it had a rich source of data on each client derived from the original proposal form, it was able to conduct a complex cross-correlation between known cost drivers and demographic and other characteristics of the policyholders. The cost drivers were:

- the commission payments to financial advisers who sold the policy;
- the early surrender of the policy by the policyholder;
- changing of bank details and consequent chasing of missed premiums;
- responding to letters of inquiry.

They discovered that the policy was unprofitable when sold to recently retired persons, otherwise it was profitable. They assumed the reason was because the policyholder used their new free time to meddle with their finances and to write trivial letters. The company reduced agents' commission on the policies according to the age of the policyholder to deter them from selling it to the unprofitable segment.

This demonstrates how a modern computer system utilising a data warehouse can record a multitude of characteristics about the customers and their buying habits. Interrogation by sophisticated statistical packages can reveal clusters of buyers of differing profitability.

A further example of CAP analysis

Having recently adopted Customer Profitability Analysis the Blott Group has conducted an analysis of the cost drivers associated with their customers and the costs that can be attributed to them.

Activity – cost driver	Cost driver rate
Order processing	£350 per order
Sales representative visit	£220 per visit
Normal delivery costs	£1.50 per mile
Urgent delivery processing	500 per order
Credit collection costs	11% per annum on average debtor days

An analysis of customer data produced the following figures;

Customer	Alpha (£)	Beta (£)	Gamma (£)
Annual revenue	1,200,000	1,000,000	600,000
Operating profit contribution	90,000	120,000	80,000
Sales orders per annum	190	100	55
Sales reps. visits per annum	20	12	8
Number of normal deliveries	100	60	30
Miles per delivery	290	210	100
Urgent deliveries per annum	20	5	2
Average collection period – days	90	30	30

A calculation of the customer profitability analysis reveals the following about the customer attributable costs;

Customer	Alpha (£)	Beta (£)	Gamma (£)
Sales order processing	66,500	35,000	19,250
Sales reps. Visits	4,400	2,640	1,760
Cost of normal delivery	43,500	18,900	4,500
Cost of urgent delivery	10,000	2,500	1,000
*Credit collection costs	32,548	9,041	5,425
Total customer attributable costs	156,948	68,081	31,935

* Credit collection costs are calculated as the annual revenue $\times$ the annual interest rate $\times$ the fraction of the year debt outstanding, i.e. (annual revenue $\times$ 11%) $\times$ (average collection period/365)

Customer	Alpha (£)	Beta (£)	Gamma (£)
Operating profit contribution	90,000	120,000	80,000
Total customer attributable costs	156,948	68,081	31,935
Contribution to higher level costs	(66,948)	51,919	48,065

It can be seen from the analysis that although all of the customers make a positive contribution at the operating profit level once the cost of servicing Alpha are taken in to account they become a high 'cost to service' customer compared to the other customers. To some extent this is also true of Beta.

The exercise gives an indication of how overall profitability might be improved for the Blott Group. Efforts must be made to educate Alpha to change their buyer behaviour, reducing the dependence on sales representatives visits, paying more promptly and reducing the number of special deliveries would be a useful start.

4.6.5 Attribute costing

CAP analysis is taken a step further by Bromwich (1990), with a suggestion that management accounting should cost *product attributes*.

This approach adopts the marketing view that products are actually collections of benefits (or *attributes*) that are desired to a greater or lesser extent by different groups of buyers. Bromwich advocates that the costs of providing the attributes be calculated and compared to the revenues derived from providing them. In this way variations in customer (or product) profitability can be traced to degree of alignment of the product attributes to the needs of the customer. For example, a given customer group may be unprofitable because the firm persists in offering them a product with complicated features which they are not prepared to pay for.

This approach is more consistent with the marketing orientation than the approach to CAP described above, which seemed to take the product as a given and hence could be accused of being sales orientated.

Consider the example of personal computers (PCs). A PC has a number of potential attributes such as:

- technical performance (processing speed, size of RAM and hard disk);
- size and portability;
- ability to manage graphics and sound;
- supplied programs;
- appearance and trim;
- technical advice;
- speed of delivery;

STRATEGIC ASPECTS OF MARKETING

- installation by engineers;
- after-sales support.

These will be of varying value to different groups of buyers; for example, a household may wish to have all the attributes, whereas a commercial user might not value the technical advice or support. Someone buying the machine for office administration and document production might not value the audio and video capabilities, whereas a multimedia designer would value them very highly and so on.

The steps in an attribute costing exercise are:

1. *List separately the product benefits offered to the customers.* This will necessitate the management accountant working with marketing experts to ensure that these benefits are seen from the customer's point of view and that their role in the purchase decision process is fully understood.

2. *Decide on a set of cost categories for the product.* Bromwich recognises there are several possible approaches here:
   (a) Bromwich proposes a set of revised activity-based costing categories:
       - *product-volume related* – effectively direct cost and variable overheads;
       - *activity related* – material handling, transport, quality control and provision of site facilities;
       - *capacity related* – land and building occupancy costs, depreciation, etc.;
       - *decision related* – product design, marketing, production planning and personnel costs.
   (b) Cost the achievement of key performance indicators associated with the strategy such as:
       - on-time delivery;
       - customer awareness levels;
       - first-time resolution of technical difficulties;
       - geographic coverage of distribution channel.
   (c) Utilise the value chain and assign costs to the activities in the process. This *strategic cost analysis* approach was discussed in Chapter 3.

3. *Calculate the value of offering the product attributes.* The technique can be used in several circumstances:
   (a) to evaluate the profitability from offering the present product features to the various customer groups;
   (b) to calculate the profitability enjoyed by a rival who offers augmented features on a product that we presently do not;
   (c) to assess the desirability of augmenting our own product with additional attributes recommended by marketing or requested by customers.
   Methods of calculation include:
   (a) model the decision on paper, using assessments of the revenues and costs derived from marketing research and cost analysis studies;
   (b) experiment with the change in a limited area (e.g. shops often pilot new formats or products in a few selected areas to assess impacts on costs and revenues);
   (c) analyse firms already offering the augmented or value-engineered product.

4. *Redesign marketing offering to enhance overall profitability.* Again there are several circumstances where this may be undertaken:
   (a) to *value engineer* an existing product to restore its profitability by eliminating or streamlining the provision of attributes whose revenue contribution does not cover its costs;
   (b) to *augment* existing products with additional attributes which we forecast will generate a premium of price over costs;

(c) to *target price* new product developments by designing into the product just those attributes which are essential to ensure demand from our target customers at the target price we have set.

4.6.6 Evaluation of CAP analysis

The main benefits of the CAP approach are:

1. It takes into account non-production costs in determining profitability.

    Differences between the profitability of different groups of customers are often attributable to the costs of supporting their accounts rather than in the production costs of what they buy.

    Recognising this can help improve the firm's control over profits by:

    (a) enabling them to exclude customer accounts which are not profitable;
    (b) helping them understand the factors that are driving non-production overheads.

2. It provides a method of identifying customer groups who are of value to the firm and hence worth retaining.

    Where a customer is of high intrinsic value, this can justify additional expenditure to keep them. This insight often forms the basis of relationship marketing.

3. It provides a technique of assessing the financial value of marketing and product development expenditures.

    Many of the attributes of the product have been added as part of a marketing strategy to attract new groups of customers. Understanding whether they attract revenues sufficient to cover the costs of the strategy provides an important financial control over such expenditure. For example, the Ferrari motor company invests millions of dollars in supporting its Formula One racing team. CAP analysis would question whether the technical capability and image for performance this gives the Ferrari marque delivers sufficient additional revenues to justify the costs.

The main drawbacks are:

1. *It can encourage ill-judged product changes.* Deciding to remove a product feature based on CAP can have unintended effects if the buyer's purchasing decision is not fully understood. This is why it is essential that the process should involve experts in consumer behaviour.

    For example, a luxury car manufacturer embarked on a CAP analysis when designing its new model of one of its best-selling lines. One, now infamous, decision was to remove the spring-damper from the car's ashtrays in the view that the majority of its customers did not smoke and that the remainder left the ashtray permanently open. This overlooked the role of perception in the buying process. A buyer seeking to evaluate a car will always play with the switches and knobs, including the ashtray. Trade reviewers alighted on the cheap ashtray mechanism as evidence that the manufacturer was cutting corners on quality. The damage to the brand's image was severe.

2. *Practical calculation is extremely difficult.* Techniques of calculating the revenue benefits of an attribute or perception are very poorly developed. Similarly, assigning costs to the various activities will suffer from wide degrees of error. The financial benefits of CAP must justify the considerable costs of this exercise.

3. *It may overlook the combinations of products purchased.* Customer profitability depends on the mix of products bought. There is a danger that CAP will be used on single underperforming products and will overlook the impact on sales of other products of denying particular customers access to it.

For example, although bank accounts lose money when provided to 80 per cent of customers, they are essential if the bank is to sell its credit products, insurances and foreign exchange services.

4. *It overlooks the life cycle value of the product or customer.* The value of the customer is not restricted to their present expenditure and costs. Rather it is the total amount they will yield to the firm over the lifetime of their relationship with it.

There are two aspects to this:

(a) The costs of attracting and retaining a customer should be compared with the lifetime earnings and not just the annual earnings from the customer. Kotler (1997)cites the example of Taco Bell which sells tacos at less than $1 each. The firm has estimated that a loyal repeat customer generates up to $11,000 over their lifetime.

(b) The customer's value may increase as they move through their life cycle. Today's freeloading student may be tomorrow's high net-worth individual.

4.6.7 Life cycle customer value

The essence of life cycle evaluation is to estimate the present value of the revenues likely to arise from the customer group and compare them to the life cycle costs of attracting and maintaining them.

This process involves making complex calculations involving the following:

(a) the value of the customer account derived from its original purchases;
(b) the value of the customer account derived from each of the purchases it may undertake in the future;
(c) the probability of retaining the customer after the original purchase and in the future;
(d) the probability that the original purchaser will later buy each of the additional products;
(e) the initial costs of attracting the customer.

For example, consider the value of the following student bank account (the figures are entirely fictitious and probably unrealistic):

	£
Cost of attracting account (gift voucher and pens)	70
Net revenues from account (per annum)	
Years 0–4	(140)
Years 5–30	500
Net revenues from additional services (per annum)	
Credit card	
Years 0–4	80
Years 5–30	200
Personal insurances	
Years 0–4	20
Years 5–30	130
Home loans	
Years 0–4	0
Years 5–30	300

Assumptions:

50 per cent of students remain with their bank after 4 years;
70 per cent of students receive a credit card;
15 per cent of all bank clients also buy insurances;

10 per cent of bank clients also take home loans;
The bank has a cost of capital of 8 per cent.

Value per account attracted

	£	£
Revenues		
Bank accounts		
(140) × 2.577	(361)	
(500 × 0.5) × (8.559 − 2.577)	1,496	
		1,135
Credit cards		
(800 × 0.7) × 2.577	144	
	419	
200 × (0.7 × 0.5) × (8.559 − 2.577)		
		563
Personal insurances		
(20 × 0.15) × 2.577	8	
130 × (0.5 × 0.15) × (8.559 − 2.577)	58	
		66
Home loans		
300 × (0.5 × 0.1) × (8.559 − 2.577)		90
Total net revenues per account		1,854
Costs		
Cost of attracting account		(70)
Lifetime value per account		1,784

Although this example demonstrates the reasoning behind life cycle profitability analysis, it simplifies a number of real-world difficulties:

1. In strategic decisions firms often lack the data to know how customers will behave over their lifetime because the firm has not attracted such customers or offered such products before.
2. The analysis should factor in the impact of competitor action in the long term. This could affect retention rates, revenues and operating costs.
3. The analysis should consider the stage of the market in the product life cycle. In addition to the direct costs of attracting and servicing the customer, there will need to be capital investment (e.g. in campus branches and national advertising) to support the strategy. These might not be recouped from a declining market.
4. Environmental change should also be factored in. Changes in the economy, life expectancy or technology will impact on costs and revenues.

4.6.8 Concluding comments on customer profitability analysis

Customer profitability analysis is not a replacement for more conventional cost accounting methods. The high degrees of conjecture and the rather arbitrary allocations of costs and revenues would make it useless for operational financial control.

Its value lies in its ability to improve strategic decision-making:

1. It can provide guidance on the reasons for declining profitability of particular divisions or product lines.

2. It can assist in ensuring that product development is commercially viable by assessing the value of the customers who the product is designed for.
3. It can assist marketing strategy by calculating the value of target segments.
4. It can provide strategic control measures by relating the investments in products and promotion back to whether or not they achieve any increase in customer profitability.
5. It focuses management's attention on the value to be gained from retaining and deepening the firm's relationship with its existing customers.

4.7 Brand strategies

4.7.1 Description of a brand

A brand has three elements:

1. *A name and logo*, for example:
   - Mars;
   - Windows;
   - Coca-Cola;
   - Tommy Hilfiger;
   - Nike;
   - McDonald's.
2. *A colour scheme, packaging, livery or 'get-up'*, for example:
   - Mars is written in red edged by gold and black;
   - Coca-Cola is white on red;
   - McDonald's is yellow (gold) on red and will have the 'arches' in view.
3. *Associations*. Kotler (1997)identifies several levels of meaning in a brand:
   - *Attributes*: These are things like quality, speed, flavour, originality. For example, Coke is 'the real thing' and 'always', whereas Pepsi is 'for the new generation'.
   - *Benefits*: This is what the customer will get from being associated with the brand. Certain brands suggest wealth, others 'street credibility', etc.
   - *Values*: Brands say something about the producer's values. For example, IBM provides 'solutions for a small planet' while Volvo is associated with safety and Body Shop with softer business values.
   - *Culture*: Brands such as BMW emphasise the engineering and technical efficiency of its German origins (as do Mercedes-Benz and Audi). Alfa Romeo suggests the Italian design culture.
   - *Personality*: Good brands are like people whom you decide you like or dislike. Bacardi is the kind of person who might be lively and loud company for a night out, but not the sort you would employ as a nanny for your children.
   - *User*: The brand indicates the kind of person who should buy the product. They will be the people who respect, or wish to associate themselves with, its connotations.

4.7.2 Importance of brands to strategy

Brands may be more meaningful than products as level of analysis for strategy.

(a) *Brands may be a better unit of financial analysis*. Brands often act as an umbrella for several products or product forms. Therefore it is not possible to separate all revenues and costs out by product:

- promotion of one product (say Mars ice cream) inevitably promotes the rest of the range (chocolate bars, miniatures, drinks);
- having one product in the portfolio is essential to sales of the rest (bite-size Mars are often included in children's packed meals or given as treats. This creates later sales of the larger items in the range).

(b) *Brands have longer life cycles than products.* A product declines due to technical obsolescence. However, careful brand management can replace obsolete products with new ones to prolong the brand's life. However, brands may eventually decline if the values they represent become outmoded (e.g. Camp coffee had overtones of British colonialism), the group they appeal to declines (e.g. Senior Service cigarettes were favoured by sailors who served in the 1939–45 war, since the Royal Navy was the first military unit to be formed in the UK), or the brand becomes inextricably linked with a product (e.g. Woodbine cigarettes).

(c) *Brands are essential to determining the value of a product range.* Brands allow a premium price to be charged for a product because the association provides benefits to the customer for which they are prepared to pay.

(d) *Brands allow the firm (or firms licensing the brand) to enter unfamiliar product/market spaces more quickly and with less risk*, for example:

- Marlboro and Caterpillar clothing (based on cigarettes and earth-moving equipment);
- Gucci and Armani eyewear (based on leather goods and clothing brands).

(e) Brands dilute buyer power because they strengthen the differentiation of the product over that of the retailer. Effectively, brands act as a psychological switching cost.

(f) Brands will build barriers to entry since a new entrant will find it difficult in a market where strong brands exist.

4.7.3 Five brand strategies

Kotler (1997) identifies the following strategies:

1. *Line extensions.* Existing brand name applied to new sizes or flavours of the product or other variants, but in the same product category (e.g. Müller yoghurt launching Müllerlight yoghurt). Sometimes called *branded variants*, these are the majority of new product launches.
   - *Advantages*:
     (a) Spreads cost of brand support across more sales.
     (b) Helps stop brand becoming obsolete or knocked out by appearance of a sub-segment.
     (c) Increases survival rate of new products.
   - *Drawbacks*:
     (a) Brand loses its specific meanings (e.g. 'New Coke' was a marketing disaster).
     (b) Strong associations of brand harms sales (e.g. Easyjet only having limited success with Easycruise since the 'easy' brand is associated with value for money which is not in keeping with what most passengers want on a cruise holiday).
2. *Brand extensions.* Use existing brand to launch a product in a new category. The classic example of this was the Mars ice cream, but it is also practised with Sony's move into mobile phones from their original position in televisions and stereos.

- *Advantages*:
  - (a) Ensures recognition and early acceptance of the new product.
  - (b) Lower launch advertising coss.
  - (c) Can help strengthen the brand and increase sales of existing products.
  - (d) Can contribute to building a 'megabrand' leading to increased bargaining power with retailers.
- *Drawbacks*:
  - (a) Poor product will harm reputation of original brand.
  - (b) Brand may be inappropriate to the product (e.g. Harley Davidson ballet shoes?).
  - (c) Over-extension may lead to *brand dilution* where it loses its special place in customers' minds (e.g. the Forte brand applied to everything from Travelodges and Posthouses to Meridian and Heritage Hotels).

3. *Multibrands*. Additional brands in the same product category. For example, Kellogg's have many different breakfast cereals each with their own brand image (e.g. Cornflakes, Frosties, Rice Crispies, Special K). Similar practices exist in magazine publishing, confectionery and detergents.
   - *Advantages*:
     - (a) Able to access sub-segments with different price points or buying motives.
     - (b) Provides a barrier to entry by locking up distributors' shelf space.
     - (c) Protects major brands by setting up *flanker brands* at lower prices to fend off cut-price challenges.
   - *Drawbacks*:
     - (a) Each new brand may cannibalise the market so that no brand sells enough to gain a critical mass or economies of scale (e.g. Austin, Jaguar, MG, Morris, Rover, Wolseley and Triumph had at least three models of car each, yet all were owned by the same company).
     - (b) Increases costs of promotion and brand support.
     - (c) Brands may compete against one another and reduce prices if distributors or brand management teams are different. This reduces revenues to the producer.

4. *New brands*. A new product category is launched with a new brand because none of the existing brands is suitable. The main issues here are:
   - (a) The establishment of a new brand is very expensive and may take considerable time.
   - (b) The brand must be capable of extending if it is to be worthwhile, otherwise it is simply a product.

5. *Cobrands*. Two brands are combined in an offer. Examples have included:
   - Gold Blend coffee and After Eight mints;
   - Oral-B toothpaste with Braun electric plaque removers;
   - Sony Playstation and Tomb Raider;
   - Recording artist and record store chain.

   The advantages of this are to help the brands piggy-back on each other's reputations. The important factor is that the images of the brands should be complementary.

In practice the distinction between line extensions and brand extensions is not so clear cut in practice. For example, Sony's range of mobile telephones would not be considered as brand extensions if Sony's business was defined more broadly as 'consumer electronics'. Category definition, therefore, plays an important role and is often found to depend upon the data being used, that is A.C. Nielsen data.

4.7.4 Challenges to branding

In 1994 Marlboro had a worldwide market share of 38 per cent and was ranked the third most valuable brand in the world. The following year, on 'Marlboro Friday', Phillip Morris cut its prices by 17 per cent to win market share back from supermarket private-label and budget-line cigarettes.

This was due to two trends that have been increasingly affecting brands:

1. *Trend to generic products*. These are low-price versions of consumer goods which are either unbranded or carry the brand name of the store (a *private label*). Generally these are mature high-volume products where there is low potential for differentiation. Examples include paper towels, dried pasta, tinned fruit and sliced bread. Generally the customer is not prepared to pay for branded versions because they believe they are 'all the same anyway'. This has severely called into question the value of brands in consumer foods.

2. *Channel power*. Surveys demonstrate that customers trust particular retail chains in the same way that they trust their family doctors. This gives the retailer brand power that can dilute the power of proprietary product brands. Customers take the view that 'if Tesco (or whoever) put their name on it, then it must be okay'. At the same time the stores want to bind customers in to them, so they are keen to develop loyalty to their own-label brands that of course cannot be bought at their rival's store. The end result is a de-listing of branded goods in favour of private-label goods.

Branded goods manufacturers can adopt a number of responses to these trends:

1. *Collaborate with stores by providing private-label versions*. This ensures that the supplier does get some of the available profit and also helps absorb its fixed costs. The dangers are that they will be exposed to margin pressure from the bargaining behaviour of the stores. Also their own brands will be undermined if the public realises the generics are the same as the higher-priced brands.

   Some firms agree to produce private-label versions in return for a guarantee that the store will stock their existing and new branded products.

2. *Increase the promotion of their branded products to gain loyalty*. This takes the form of advertising, contests and other sales promotions. One tactic used for children's products is to develop collectables (mugs and toys) which require repeated purchases. Advertisements often stress nostalgia and tradition.

   Brand extension strategies can also reinforce the brand.

3. *Concentrate on developing new products which cannot be compared to generics*. Generics are always the established products, so new product types do not immediately become generics. They are also higher margin. Examples of this have included NutraGrain breakfast bars (Kellogg's), Sunny Delight (Procter & Gamble), 'I can't believe it's not butter' (Unilever).

   This strategy also features high investment and risk.

4. *Emphasise the exclusivity of their products*. Many customers assume that the generic products are actually made by the branded good manufacturer. Some brands (e.g. Kellogg's and Colgate) assure customers that this is not the case. This sharpens the exclusivity of the brand.

   For this to work the brand must have value, that is the customer must believe the brand is worth looking for.

5. *Create flanking brands.* The producer may produce a low-price brand in the same product area as its main brands to ensure it gains revenue from the price-conscious shopper without exposing itself to the generic buying power of the stores. This strategy is followed in cigarettes, biscuits, paper tissues and toiletries.

4.7.5 Financial management of brands

Putting a financial value in brands has three potential benefits for a firm:

1. *To include on the balance sheet as part of net assets.* Brands can provide a continuing source of earnings. They also represent a use of shareholders' funds. Putting them on the balance sheet will bring a number of benefits:
   (a) It will demonstrate to investors the true worth of the firm and therefore reduce the tendency to undervaluation.
   (b) It will reduce capital gearing levels (i.e. including brands as an asset would necessitate a corresponding adjustment to increase shareholders' equity).
   However, there are a number of difficulties with this suggestion which have led the accounting profession to reject the practice:
   (a) There is no clear agreement on a technique to value brands. This threatens the comparability of financial statements if firms use different methods.
   (b) Products not brands are sources of income. Maintaining a brand therefore demands continuing expenditure upon the product development to maintain the value of the asset. This sets brands apart from other assets on a balance sheet.
   (c) There is no way to predict the life expectancy of a brand. This could lead to considerable instability in net asset values (and gearing) if brands must suddenly be written off.
   (d) It will be difficult to separate the portion of a year's promotional expenditure which boosted current year sales (an expense) from the part which maintains or boosts brand value (an investment). This is the *identifiability problem.*
2. *To enable firm to use investment appraisal techniques to evaluate brand support expenditure.* Allen (1992) argues that if a brand is seen as an income-generating asset this means that expenditure upon its development and support should be treated as an investment and be required to show a positive net present value. Management should compare the present value of the income streams from the brand to the present value of the initial development costs and subsequent support costs. This income stream would be the difference between the revenues anticipated from a branded version of the good, compared with the revenue of providing it as a generic good (or perhaps providing it under an existing brand name rather than a new one).
3. *To provide a performance indicator for brand management decisions.* Brands are significant at several stages of the product life cycle:
   (a) *Introductory stage*: Applying an established brand to a new product will hasten its acceptance and reduce the risks of its failure. In markets where it is important to gain a dominant share quickly, this is critical.
   (b) *Growth stage*: Brands are a significant barrier to entry to the market against 'me-too' competitors. They are also crucial as the market shifts from product awareness to brand awareness and will have an impact on the long-term market share of the firm.

(c) *Mature stage*: Brands are part of a differentiation strategy to offset the competitive forces and boost short-run margins and long-term survival. They are also the basis for spinning-off new products.

(d) *Decline stage*: Brands are one of the assets which has an opportunity cost. An accurate valuation can help the firm decide whether to continue making the product or sell off the brand rights to recoup shareholder value.

One way of deciding the strength of brands and their likelihood of success is to value them in comparison with rival brands.

4.7.6 Valuing brands

Various approaches have been suggested. Provided that they do not need to appear in final accounts, the lack of agreement between authorities in the area should not be used as an excuse not to attempt this exercise. Management merely need to arrive at an evaluation approach that suits their needs and they can monitor brands.

1. *The aggregate cost of all R&D and marketing expenditure on the brand over a specified period of time*. This approach has two key flaws:
   (a) It is hard to identify which expenditures apply to which brands. Particularly common are R&D and promotions.
   (b) It does not assess whether the brand has been successful.
2. *Valuation based on the present value of the price premium that the brand can command over the unbranded good*. This is one of the most common approaches. However:
   (a) It is hard to identify generic equivalents for some brands.
   (b) It ignores the role of brands in giving stability of earnings. Some brands have very modest price premiums.
   (c) It overlooks the value of brands as a barrier to entry or their basis as an umbrella under which to launch new goods.
3. *Valuation at market value, for example if the brand were auctioned off*. Conceptually sensible but almost useless in practice:
   (a) Too thin a market in brands to allow accurate valuation.
   (b) The auction price would assess the value of the brand to the buyer's portfolio. This is not necessarily the same as its value to the current holder's portfolio.
4. *Valuation based on consumer-based measures such as esteem, recognition or awareness*. This does not necessarily translate into commercial value, for example do they actually buy the product or just respect it?
5. *Valuation based on future earnings potential discounted to present-day values*. Tends to include all the measures above, but it is very difficult to get a reliable forecast of future earnings and growth.

4.8 Relationship marketing

4.8.1 Factors giving rise to relationship marketing

Relationship marketing is the devoting of marketing resources to maintaining and exploiting the firm's existing customer base rather than to use the resources solely to attract new customers.

STRATEGIC ASPECTS OF MARKETING

During the 1980s relationship marketing attracted increasing attention from practitioners, consultants and academics. This was in response to a number of factors:

1. The increased willingness of buyers to switch suppliers and to break long-standing market relationships.
2. The increased costs of attracting customers such as promotional expenditures and initially low prices.
3. The strategy of increasing the breadth of products being offered by the supplier could only be justified if the customer could be retained.
4. The realisation that in mature markets the most likely source of future earnings was through retaining and increasing the value of the firm's existing customers.

4.8.2 Relationship marketing *versus* transactions marketing

Christopher et al. (1991) summarise the differences between relationship marketing and more conventional transactions marketing, as shown in Table 4.2. This has implications for the way that marketing is carried out.

4.8.3 Strategies to develop relationship marketing

1. Develop incentive schemes for the staff that encourage customer retention, for example:
   - avoid rewarding salesforce on the number of new accounts opened;
   - reward staff against customer satisfaction surveys;
   - pay group-based bonuses – customer retention is a job for everyone.
2. Reduce staff turnover to maintain loyalty of customer and ensure consistent service standards.
3. Ensure that senior management endorse the importance of customer retention in order that staff give it a priority too.
4. Adopt quality procedures which monitor and influence all aspects of the customer relationship (e.g. total quality management).

Table 4.2 Relationship marketing versus transactions marketing

Transactions marketing	Relationship marketing
A focus on single sales or transactions	A focus on customer retention and building customer loyalty
An emphasis on product features	An emphasis on product benefits that are meaningful to the customer
Short timescales	Long timescales, recognising that short-term costs may be higher, but so will long-term profits
Little emphasis on customer retention	An emphasis on high levels of customer service which are possibly tailored to the individual customer
Limited customer commitment	High customer commitment
Moderate customer contact	High customer contact, with each contact being used to gain information and build the relationship
Quality is essentially the concern of production and one else	Quality is the concern of all, and it is the failure to recognise this that creates minor mistakes which lead to major problems

5. Monitor and track customer relationship and take appropriate action:
   - regular contact with customers to assess satisfaction and loyalty;
   - ascertain reasons for loss of a customer and address causes;
   - institute service recovery procedures if there are signs that a customer is likely to defect.
6. Develop detailed information on the customer's relationship and buying habits which is available to all staff:
   - allows different staff to continue the customer relationship;
   - enables firm to draw relevant new products and services to the customer's notice;
   - enables firm to suggest better ways of meeting the customer's needs.
7. Develop strategies to increase loyalty:
   - appoint key account managers for valuable clients;
   - introduce loyalty cards;
   - develop benefits programme for the client;
   - create affinity devices (e.g. credit cards, magazines, user workshops).
8. Modern customer relationship management (CRM) systems facilitate relationship marketing by providing functions such as:
   - automated sales-management systems;
   - customer databases with analytical processing;
   - facilities to track customer spending and profitability;
   - automated message procedures to assist telesales staff or e-mail suitable marketing messages to customers.

4.8.4 A broader role for relationship marketing

According to Payne (1995) relationship marketing should extend beyond just the interface with the customer. Instead he suggests a *six markets model* whereby relationships should be built in the following markets.

1. *Customer markets.* These are the buyers of the final product and they remain the final goal of marketing activity. To be able to deliver superior customer value in increasingly competitive industries, modern relationship marketing emphasises the importance of having appropriate relations with other interfaces.
2. *Referral markets.* These are the institutions and individuals who refer the customer to us. This could include banks, agents as well as existing customers. Therefore cultivating relationships with these intermediaries is critical to getting new customers.
3. *Supplier markets.* Partnerships with suppliers must replace traditional adversarial relations if the firm is to better meet the needs of the final customer. This can include collaboration to improve quality, set up JIT arrangements or to work together in harnessing product innovations. Marketing must sell the new attitudes essential to these supplier partnerships.
4. *Recruitment markets.* To provide good service to customers, it is essential that the firm has good staff. However in a competitive market the good-calibre staff member also has a choice. Marketing should build up appropriate relationships with the stakeholders in the recruitment markets (agencies, careers advisers, head-hunters, etc.), as well as ensuring that the corporate image of the firm is appealing to would-be recruits (e.g. through the design of corporate literature and selective sponsorship).
5. *Influence markets.* These are institutions that can influence what customers will purchase. For example an aeroplane manufacturer will need to influence national governments as well as airlines of the safety of its products. Other examples include

pressure groups, brokers, analysts, consumer associations, etc. This influence of marketing often occurs under the heading of public relations.

6. *Internal markets.* This has two aspects to it.

   (a) Each internal department is the customer of some and a supplier to the rest. For the firm to operate smoothly it is important that a client service ethos pervades all departments and replaces divisional rivalries and loyalties.

   (b) Each division should interpret what it does in terms of how it serves the customer.

You may recognise this view as the third pillar of Kotler's version of the marketing concept discussed in Section 4.6. It is the job of marketing to help all divisions to adopt a marketing orientation toward both its internal and external customers.

4.9 · Data Warehousing and Data Mining

4.9.1 Data warehousing

The concept of data warehousing is aimed at addressing two sets of organisational needs:

- the requirement for an organisation – wide view of information;
- the need for the information systems department to manage organisational data in an effective and efficient way.

Data warehousing has become a significant trend in decision support.

Mattison (1996) describes the examples of the banking industry which uses data warehousing to make various financial decisions and to generate financial statements. Similarly, telecommunications firms use the approach to support integrated marketing by analysing customer information. Harnessing the value trapped in the large quantities of data held by companies has been high on the list of priorities for many companies as it is felt that it will lead to better decisions and provide a competitive advantage.

The idea of the data warehouse has been described by Devlin (1997) as a single, complete and consistent store of data obtained from a variety of sources and made available to end users in an understandable fashion that can be used in a business context. Mattison (1996) defines a data warehouse as a database that:

- is organised to serve as a neutral data storage area;
- is used by data mining and other applications;
- meets a specific set of business requirements;
- uses data that meet a predefined set of business criteria.

Effectively a data warehouse is a large relational database that collates a vast amount of data from a wide variety of sources. Inmon (1992) offers the following description:

- the data warehouse should be organised around business subjects such as customer vendor, activity and product;
- within the data warehouse the common data elements of multiple applications should be referred to in a consistent manner;
- the operational data will be continuously updated as business conditions change.

The characteristics of every data warehouse have been summarised by Brown (1995) as:

- data extraction and movement methods,
- connectivity software for client server integration,
- high performance relational data base management system.

The database will have a distinct structure, consisting of current detail data, older detail data, lightly summarised data, highly summarised data, and meta data. The majority of the data will be held at the current level of detail, reflecting the most recent events and actions, and accessible by end user analysts. The lightly summarised data will serve mid level management, whilst the highly summarised data which will be used by senior management. Meta data, effectively data about data and the environment in which it is held, serves an important role. It will describe the meaning and structure of business data, as well as the means of creation, access and use.

Devlin (1997) describes the following functions of meta data:

- a directory to help the DSS analyst locate the contents of the data warehouse;
- a guide to the mapping of data as the data are transformed from the operational environment to the data warehouse environment;
- a guide to the algorithms used for summarisation converting the current detailed data to the lightly summarised data and subsequently to the highly summarised data.

4.9.2 Evolution of data warehousing

Devlin (1997) has traced the evolution of data warehousing through four stages over the last 30 years.

1. *Prehistoric times – before the 1980s.* Prior to the early 1970s, computing was solely the preserve of the Information systems department. The invention of the PC and the relational database contributed to the emergence of end users and the wider use of data automation. The prospect of competitive advantage rather than simple cost reduction changed the emphasis of the justification for investment. By the mid 1980s support for decision making processes became a prime objective of investment.
2. *The middle ages – mid to late 1980s.* Data warehousing began to emerge in large companies with the advent of data modelling approaches and tools to satisfy strong end-user demand. The distinction between operational systems and informational systems started at this point.
3. *The data revolution – the early 1990s.* At the beginning of this decade many firms were subject to significant changes in their business environments, such as international recession, deregulation and increasing global competition. Technological advances in data modelling, databases, and applications development methods made it possible for data warehouses to be used for enterprise wide business change and rejuvenation in the search for competitive advantage.
4. *The era of information-based management.* The present situation can be described as a desire for a single information source, distributed information availability, information in a business context, automated information delivery, information quality and ownership.

Currently a data warehouse satisfies three primary purposes:

- presentation of standard reports and graphs, consolidating data from a variety of sources into a standard format,
- it supports dimensional analysis, a query and reporting format which facilitates the comparison of results across a number of different dimensions, particularly time periods.
- it enables the process of data mining – which we shall discuss shortly.

A data warehouse can be established as a primary source of all customer information allowing the analysis of all critical customer parameters.

The success of a data warehouse depends upon the use of online data retrieval, artificial intelligence and graphical user interface tools. The online data retrieval will facilitate the gathering, cleansing and storage of large volumes of data whilst on-line analytical processing (OLAP) tools will provide for the manipulation and analysis of that information. Typical of the role of artificial intelligence is the use of neural networks to learn and recognise specific patterns of behaviour and relate these to known outcomes of previously modelled and predicted behaviour. Graphical user interfaces, with the full use of multimedia, will provide an intuitive graphical tool to navigate the data warehouse and present high impact decision support information.

4.9.3 Data mining

Data mining is concerned with the discovery of new meaningful information so that decision makers can learn as much as possible from valued data assets. Using advanced information technologies, knowledge discovery in databases (KDD) can uncover veins of surprising and useful insights in a mountain of factual data. The technique searches for hidden relationships, patterns, correlations, and interdependencies in large databases that traditional information gathering techniques might overlook. Data mining uses a broad toolkit of novel methods to help to automatically solve user defined questions.

These tools include the following general types:

- Query managers and report writers, a wide variety of SQL*-based query and reporting tools.
- Spreadsheets, typically Excel and Lotus 123, performing a variety of analytical and reporting functions.
- Multidimensional databases.
- Statistical analysis tools, such as SAS* or SPSS* enable users to gather data and perform complicated statistical analysis operations such as clusters and regressions.
- Artificial intelligence methods, such as fuzzy logic and expert systems, decision trees, rule induction methods, genetic algorithms and genetic programming, neural networks (i.e. backpropagation, associative memories) and clustering techniques.
- Graphical display tools, data visualisation is used as an important ancillary aid in the development, creation, and interpretation of data driven knowledge discovery.

* SQL stands for structured query language,
* SAS is a statistical analysis software package,
* SPSS is a powerful software package used for data management and analysis.

Data mining continues to attract considerable attention in the business and scientific communities. As long ago as 1997 the Gartner Group reported that 'Data mining and artificial intelligence are the top five key technology areas that will clearly have a major impact across a wide variety of industries within the next 3–5 years.' Already many companies use computers to capture details of business transactions such as credit and debit card purchases, retail sales, warranty claims, telecommunications events amongst many others. Data mining tools will then be used to uncover useful patterns of behaviour and relationships between the data that might otherwise have gone undetected. The tools are quite sophisticated in their operations. For instance, an intelligent text mining system will extract text fragments relevant to user queries, automatically create and process a series of new queries, and assemble a new text for the analyst providing new aspects of a given theme. As a further example the technique is capable of providing solutions for the banking and credit industry in terms of credit scoring, fraud detection and customer segmentation. It can also develop proprietary bureau scores for general risk, bankruptcy, revenue and response, that are optimised for the business needs and are not available to competitors. By learning the patterns of fraud and subsequently successfully identifying fraudulent approaches credit managers and underwriters are provided with good analysis of credit scorecards leading to increased acceptances and reduced bad debt.

In section 5.5.5 we shall look at Tesco and its use of the clubcard which is relevant to this section.

4.9.4 Data mining and the Internet

The majority of applications of data mining have been to structured databases. However, the potential application to the unstructured data available on the web has, more recently, been explored. Etzioni (1996) has said that the potential is enormous and that DM tools adapted to the Internet have the potential to provide a targeted banner campaign, rich media, a storefront, a promotion or direct e-mail, since to tools are capable of anticipating a customers' needs before, during, and after running a campaign. This is achieved by reporting behavioural data about site visitors, such as who is visiting, what content they are accessing, where they come from, and why they purchase. The knowledge gained can be used to make better, automated, online decisions with the potential to uncover relationships among products 'product affinities' and between customers and products – 'market segmentation'.

It is often difficult to separate the fact from the media hype in terms the current use of data mining techniques and their application to the Internet. Numerous companies within the financial industry are using data base mining for investment purposes but many do not disclose the system used, not surprisingly. However, LBS Capital Systems have been described as using expert systems, neural nets, and genetic algorithms to manage portfolios totalling $600 million and have outperformed the broad stock market.

The US Treasury Financial Crimes Enforcement Network are using the FAIS system to identify financial transactions that might indicate money laundering activity.

Finally, a novel and increasingly important application is one based on intelligent agents which navigate the data rich environment of the Internet. These systems ask the user to specify a profile of interest and search for related information among a wide variety of public domain and proprietary sources. For example, Firefly is a personal music recommendation agent which seeks an opinion from the user of several pieces of music and then suggests other titles. www.firefly.com/. Similarly CRAYON http://crayon. net/ permits users to create their own free newspaper (supported by advertisements) NEWSHOUND www.sjmercury.com/hound/ and FARCAST http:/www.farcast.com/ automatically search for information from a wide variety of sources, including newspapers and wire services, and email the relevant documents to the users. This offers the potential for competitive intelligence and the gathering of information about competitors with similar agents.

4.9.5 Objectives and management issues of data warehousing and mining

Investment in a successful data warehouse needs, at the outset, a clear set of objectives and understanding of management requirements so that the critical success factors of the organisation can be met.

4.9.6 Issues with objectives

If the only intention is to save cost by storing data in one database then the investment is unlikely to be worthwhile. For a large company the investment in hardware, software and developmental time can run into significant sums of money. There must be a strategic initiative to improve the existing operational efficiency, to redesign operational approaches and to create new ones. As with all project justifications there is a need for intended users to be able to visualise the concrete benefits of the proposed data warehousing and mining system. Levin (1996) has suggested that some of the intended objectives might be:

- *Supports strategic decision making*. The data warehouse provides detailed and summarised data that can be subjected to the various data mining techniques to improve end user analysis capabilities and strongly support strategic decision making.
- *Supports integrated business value chain*. Data warehousing will support a single source of authoritative, consistent, accurate and timely data allowing decisions to be made throughout an integrated business value chain on the same assumptions.
- *Speeds up response time to business queries*. Data warehousing uses OLAP to enable faster responses to business queries in minutes rather than days.
- *Data quality*. A consolidated data store will eliminate the need for reconciliation of inconsistent data. Data quality is improved when the source data are initially analysed and transformed to the data warehouse.

4.9.7 Issues with management

For the data warehouse and data mining of an organisation to provide a competitive advantage there are a number of management issues which must be addressed. Those issues can be categorised under the headings of data, process and security.

Data management

Data quality depends upon the relationship between gathered facts and their intended use. Since the intention is to use the data within the warehouse for strategic decision making the quality assurance of that data is essential. Meta data has been described by Hufford (1997) as the most appropriate tool for that quality assurance and summarises five applications for it:

- *Describing data that is in the warehouse*. The meta data model helps users find and access data that is in the warehouse by describing structure and contents, such as entities, attributes and relationships.
- *Specifying what comes into and goes out of the data warehouse*. The architecture will accommodate new sources and users of data. However, in doing this it will transform and validate the data from the perspective of the users, merge it with other extracts, aggregate at various summary levels before uploading to the data warehouse.

- *Scheduling extracts based on business events schedule.* By coordinating the dates for extracts based on the schedule of business events the meta data will improve corporate awareness of subtle differences due to different source systems in response to different events.
- *Documenting and monitoring data synchronisation requirements.* Meta data will help track imported data and captured documentation using defined rules for obtaining data from a variety of unsynchronised sources. This helps users avoid misusing or misinterpreting information they have derived from the data.
- *Measuring data quality.* The meta data model verifies the appropriateness of the data to new uses proposed by users to the DSS application. It will also measure the quality of the data and produce reports on the quality of the data imported into the warehouse and its appropriateness for specific uses.

There is now an ISO standard which addresses the rules, principals and guidelines for classification, attribution, definition, naming, standardisation and registration of data elements to ensure the consistent quality of the meta data.

Process management

It must be remembered that, since the business environment is continuously changing the building of a data warehouse is an iterative process in which the organisation continues to improve and extend the contents and capabilities of the system.

Security management

A data warehouse needs special security for data relating to financial transactions, personal medical records and human resource data. Data should be encrypted as it is moved into the database and decrypted when sent out to an authorised user. Sensitive data must be partitioned and different access rights granted to users at an appropriate level. If data is encrypted when it is captured and stored this will provide security at three levels. First only authorised users will be able to access data, second there is a protection from unauthorised dumping of information into the database and third there cannot be unauthorised access during the transmission process.

4.9.8 The future of data warehousing and data mining

The pressure to gain a competitive advantage from leveraging the data assets of an organisation is increasing and means that development of both data mining and data warehousing will continue. Data warehouses will need to be more flexible and support a greater variety of data types including text, voice, image, spatial and time series data. The size of the warehouse will grow due to the proliferation of distributed data sources (such as mobile phone networks), the inclusion of more data sets including greater importing and exporting of data and information via Internet and Intranet sources. There will be a greater incidence of the use of bots and other intelligent agents (i.e. automated software which anonymously aids a user by autonomously responding, based on learned response, to certain situations.) These developments in data warehousing will lead to the creation of new model paradigms, and the increasing sophistication of existing modelling techniques, to analyse larger volumes of data faster.

STRATEGIC ASPECTS OF MARKETING

4.10 Summary

This chapter has explored the sources of a firm's present and future profits within the context of a marketing audit. Several points have emerged:

- conventional measures of product profitability need refinement if they are to be used for strategic purposes – in particular, it should be recognised that profit varies throughout the product life cycle;
- product strategy should assess product contribution according to how it fits within the firm's overall product portfolio.
- product profit assessment should incorporate the profit enjoyed by the distributor and the factors that determine this – this is direct product profitability;
- profits can also be traced to customer groups, which is important for the selection of target markets in marketing strategy;
- assessments of customer profitability differ according to whether they take a current period analysis (CAP) or a life cycle view;
- the importance of brands for companies cannot be over emphasised nor their management is critical;
- the notion of customer life cycle profitability is the departure point for relationship marketing;
- the use of databases through data warehousing and data mining has become, and will continue to be, increasingly important in the search for competitive advantage.

References

Allen, D. (1992) *The Financial Management of Brands*. London: CIMA.

Aston, M. (1989) Method Trade-offs and DPP, Focus, Institute of Logistics and Distribution Management, 8(8), cited in Christopher, M. (1997), *Logistics and Supply Chain Management* (2nd edn). London: Financial Times/Pitman Publishing.

Best, R.J. (2000) *Market-Based Management: Strategies for Growing Customer Value and Profitability* (2nd edn). New Jersey: Prentice Hall.

Bromwich, M. (1990) The Case for Strategic Management Accounting: The Role of Accounting Information for Strategy in Competitive Markets, *Accounting, Organizations and Society*, 1 (See alternatively Bromwich and Bhimani (1994) op. cit., Chapter 5).

Bromwich, M. and Bhimani, A. (1994) *Management Accounting: Pathways to Progress*. London: CIMA.

Cannon, J.T. (1968) *Business Strategy and Policy*. New York: Harcourt, Brace & World (cited in Wilson and Gilligan, 1997).

Christopher, M., Payne, A. and Ballantyne, B. (1991) *Relationship Marketing: Bringing Quality, Customer Service and Marketing Together*. Oxford: Butterworth-Heinemann.

Dalrymple, D. and Parsons, L.J. (2000) *Basic Marketing Management* (2nd edn). New York: John Wiley & Sons.

Devlin (1997) *Data Warehouse: From Architecture to Implementation*. Addison-Wesley.

Edelstein, H. (eds) *Planning and Designing the Data Warehouse*. Prentice-Hall.

Etzioni (1996) *The World Wide Web: quagmire or goldmine? Communication of the ACM*, 39(11): 65–68.

Godfrey, K. and Clarke, J. (2000) *The Tourism Development Handbook*. Printed by Martins the Printers Ltd. Berwick upon Tweed.

Hufford (1997) Meta data repositories: the key to unlocking information in data warehousing. In Narquin, R. and Edelstein, H. (eds.) *Planning and Designing the Data Warehouse*. Prentice Hall.

Inmon (1992) Data Warehouse – a perspective over time. 370/390 *Database Management*, 48. February.

Jobber, D. (2004) *Principles and Practice of Marketing* (4th edn). London, New York: McGraw Hill.

Kay, J. (1993) *Foundations of Corporate Success: How Business Strategies Add Value*. Oxford: Oxford University Press.

Kotler, P. (1997) *Marketing Management: Analysis, Planning, Implementation and Control* (9th edn). Englewood Cliffs, NJ: Prentice-Hall.

Kotler, P. and Keller, K.L. (2006) *Marketing Management* (12th edn). USA: Prentice Hall.

Levin (1996) Developing a data warehouse strategy. In Narquin, R. and Edelstein, H. (eds.) *Planning and Designing the Data Warehouse*. Prentice-Hall.

Levitt, T. (1960) Marketing Myopia. *Harvard Business Review*, 38(4): 45–46.

Mattison (1996) *Data Warehousing: Strategies, Technologies and Techniques*. New York: McGraw-Hill.

Payne, A. (ed.) (1995) *Advances in Relationship Marketing*. London: Kogan Page.

Ward, K. (1992) *Strategic Management Accounting*. Oxford: Butterworth-Heinemann.

Wilson, R.M.S. and Gilligan, C. (1997) *Strategic Marketing Management*. Oxford: Butterworth-Heinemann.

Revision Questions

Question 1

A local administrative authority allowed a supermarket development to go ahead, provided that the company concerned built an extension to the authority's sports centre on an adjoining site.

In recent years the sports centre has encountered a growth in competition from local commercial recreational organisations. Simultaneously, the authority has experienced a reduction in its central funding, and has steadily increased its charges for the use of its sports centre facilities.

In reviewing its services at the sports centre, the authority has applied the product life-cycle (PLC) model. It has identified the stage within the life-cycle at which each of its sports centre services is positioned, as follows:

- *Introductory stage*: martial arts, with little take-up as yet.
- *Growth stage*: squash-playing facilities, which have required capital investment from the authority and ongoing maintenance costs of the courts and equipment. Demand for the facilities is increasing rapidly.
- *Maturity stage*: gymnasium facilities, which require little maintenance expense and experience steady demand which generates surplus cash. Swimming, which incurs a continual increase in maintenance and water purification costs.
- *Decline stage*: badminton, with a continual reduction in demand.

Requirements

(a) Recommend how the local authority could market its sports centre services. **(8 marks)**
(b) Comment on the strategic resource allocation implications of each stage of the product life cycle when applied to the sports centre facility. You are *not* required to describe or draw the PLC model **(12 marks)**
(c) In the light of your answer to parts (a) and (b), and paying particular attention to the increasing competitive threat, recommend what services the authority should offer in the future within its sports centre. **(5 marks)**
(Total marks = 25)

Question 2

V is a company which supplies quality floor-covering materials. These materials attract a high market price and are extremely hardwearing. They have been developed mainly for use within industry rather than in homes.

STRATEGIC ASPECTS OF MARKETING

V pays its sales staff a basic salary plus a commission based on the volume of sales made. This has resulted in some of its sales staff achieving very high earnings.

M is the sales director and has become concerned recently at the number of retail shops which have been supplied with materials by V which have then returned large quantities of unsold stocks and requested a refund. These shops are mainly engaged in supplying homes rather than industrial customers.

M has turned to you, as management accountant, for advice. He thinks that an alternative method of paying the sales staff will help to overcome the problem of the material being sold to inappropriate retail outlets. In the future, he proposes that the sales staff be paid on the basis of basic salary with the addition of a commission based on repeat customer purchases.

Requirements

(a) Explain the reasons why V is experiencing demands for refunds from many retail shops, and the implications of this on the attainment of increased shareholder value.
(10 marks)

(b) Discuss how customer account profitability (CAP) analysis could be used to provide information on which to base the commission payment to the sales staff and how this change would affect their sales practices. Include consideration of repeat customer orders within your discussion. **(15 marks)**
(Total marks = 25)

 ## Question 3

Marketing has been defined as identifying customer needs and wants and finding ways to satisfy them profitably. Selling has been described as supplying existing products or services to customers, paying little regard to their particular needs and requirements. While the marketing-oriented organisation recognises the value of satisfied customers, the sales-oriented organisation tends to have little understanding of the importance of customer satisfaction. As a consequence, the organisation which focuses on sales rather than on marketing is likely to have difficulty in analysing profitability derived from its different customer groups.

Requirements

(a) Discuss the benefits which an organisation may obtain from carrying out customer account profitability analysis. **(10 marks)**

(b) Compare the management accounting information required to assess customer account profitability in a sales-oriented organisation with one which has a marketing orientation. **(15 marks)**
(Total marks = 25)

Question 4

Customer value analysis is concerned with determining the benefit required by customers in a target market segment. It analyses how customers perceive the value supplied by different competitors.

Requirements

(a) Explain the major steps to be taken by a firm in undertaking an analysis of the value its customers place on its products or services. **(10 marks)**

(b) Discuss the strengths and limitations of value chain analysis in helping a firm to seek improved customer value. **(15 marks)**

Note: You are not required to draw or describe the value chain in answering this question.

(Total marks = 25)

 # Question 5

WG plc was formed 4 years ago following the merger of two large pharmaceutical companies. Prior to the merger the two companies had been competitors: they believed that by combining forces the shareholders of each company would benefit from increased profits arising from the rationalisation of manufacturing facilities, distribution networks and concentration of resources, towards more focused research and development.

With operating outlets in Europe, Asia, the USA and Africa, WG plc regards itself as a global company. It employs approximately 50,000 people worldwide and has developed a wide portfolio of products. Its profits before tax last year increased by 20 per cent and represented approximately 35 per cent of turnover. The company declared that its earnings and dividends per share in the same period each increased by 15 per cent over the previous financial year.

All manufacturers of pharmaceutical products claim that their pricing policies need to be set at a level to achieve high profitability in order to attract funds from investors. They argue that this is necessary to meet their high research and development commitments. In recent years, WG plc and other pharmaceutical manufacturers have encountered public and governmental challenges to their high levels of profitability.

WG plc encounters strong competition from other world-class pharmaceutical manufacturers, but these are few in number. High research and development costs present a major obstacle to potential competitors tempted to enter the industry.

Mission and objectives

The directors of WG plc have defined their overall corporate mission as being to 'combat disease by developing innovative medicines and services and providing them to healthcare organisations for the treatment of patients worldwide'.

The directors have confirmed that their main objective is to sustain profitability while achieving the company's overall mission. They have also explained that WG plc aims to work towards eliminating those diseases for which the company is engaged in providing treatments. Achievement of the profitability objective is continually threatened by patents coming to the end of their lives. Patents give the sole right to make, use and sell a new product for a limited period.

Product development

A large proportion of the company's turnover in recent years has been derived from one particular drug. The patent for this drug expires next year and it is expected that its sales at that time will represent no more than 10 per cent of total turnover. Four years ago, the sales of this drug produced almost half the company's entire turnover.

STRATEGIC ASPECTS OF MARKETING

A new product, Coffstop, has now completed its rigorous development phases and is being marketed to pharmaceutical stores throughout the world by WG plc. It is in competition with a similar drug, Peffstill, produced and marketed by a direct competitor of WG plc. Medical research and opinion has concluded that Coffstop is generally more effective than Peffstill in treating the condition for which they are intended. Both drugs are available over the counter from pharmacies. The directors of WG plc are optimistic that Coffstop will become very popular because of its improved effectiveness over other market products.

The retail market price of Coffstop is £1.50 per bottle, compared with £10 per bottle of Peffstill. However, the recommended dosage of Coffstop is six times more than that for Peffstill. The bought-in costs per bottle to the retail pharmacist are £0.50 and £7.40 for Coffstop and Peffstill respectively. Initial indications to the management of WG plc are that retail pharmacists tend to prefer to stock Peffstill on the basis that it achieves 2.6 times the level of gross contribution per bottle compared with Coffstop.

It is estimated that the cost to the retailer of holding Coffstop is £0.40 per bottle and £0.80 for Peffstill. The availability of shelf space is a limiting factor for most retailers. The shelf area occupied by each bottle of Coffstop is 18 square centimetres and 60 square centimetres for each bottle of Peffstill. Early indications show that the average weekly sales volume for retail outlets stocking both products are 120 bottles of Coffstop and 20 bottles of Peffstill.

Market development

WG plc has experienced slow growth in its mature markets of Western Europe, North America and Japan. These markets contribute 80 per cent of overall turnover, but their governments have reduced expenditure on pharmaceutical products in recent years. The company has encountered a rapid sales increase in its expanding markets of Eastern Europe, South America, the Asia Pacific region, India, Africa and the Middle East. The directors of the company hold the view that increasing population growth in these markets is likely to provide substantial opportunities for the company over the next two decades.

Research and development

Almost 15 per cent of WG plc's turnover last year was spent on research and development. WG plc has the largest R&D organisation of all pharmaceutical companies worldwide.

Much research is sponsored by national governments and world health organisations. A major piece of research which has recently been undertaken relates to new treatments for malaria, as the disease is now demonstrating some resistance to existing treatments. WG plc has established a 'donation programme' for the new drug in virulent areas for the disease. This means that the company is donating batches of the drug to the health organisations in these areas. The cost of this programme is offset by the sales of the new drug in other areas of the world by making it available to people proposing to travel to the regions where malaria is widespread.

Requirements

(a) Assess the nature and importance of the market threat which WG plc would face if it failed to provide sufficient resources for product development. **(10 marks)**

(b) WG plc's main objective is to sustain profitability through developing innovative medicines and services for treating patients worldwide. The company also aims to eliminate disease.

Discuss the nature of the five competitive forces (identified by Porter) which are exerted on WG plc in satisfying both these objectives at the same time.   **(12 marks)**

(c) (i) Demonstrate whether Coffstop can provide a higher contribution to the retailer than Peffstill by using:

1. Cost – volume – profit analysis, taking account of the gross contribution per limiting factor;   **(4 marks)**
2. Direct product profitability analysis after charging holding costs   **(4 marks)**

(ii) Explain how WG plc can market Coffstop to improve its competitive position.
                                                                            (8 marks)

(d) Discuss the practical issues which the directors of WG plc would need to consider if the company entered a strategic alliance with a competitor for the joint development of future pharmaceutical products.   **(12 marks)**

(Total marks = 50)

Solutions to Revision Questions

☑ Solution 1

- You will be familiar with marketing from your earlier CIMA studies. Part (a) of this question asks you to discuss a marketing approach. This should bring to mind the need to assess customer needs and employ a marketing mix to present the sports centre as able to meet those needs. The answer will be general because you do not have enough information to start making recommendations. Instead you should state how you would go about developing a marketing plan.
- Part (b) involves making the point that investing resources in a project should be done with regard to its future likely use rather than its present use. Also you should avoid the temptation to view each leisure service separately. For example, the pool may be an important factor in attracting customers to the gym or other facilities.
- Part (c) requires that you take a deep breath and recommend something based on your analysis in (b). The key to the marks here is to justify your recommendations in a way that lets the examiner know you have applied the proper thought process to the problem.

(a) The sports centre is facing increased competition from the commercial recreational organisations and is also experiencing a reduction in the amount of resources available from the local authority. In this situation, it is important that the management of the sports centre addresses these problems if the organisation is to meet its objectives.

Initially, the needs of the users of the sports centre should be assessed. The extent to which their needs are being met is crucial in the development of a marketing plan for the centre. This is the starting point, but in developing a marketing plan, attention should be focused on the marketing mix. This includes the product which is being offered, the price at which it is being sold, the place at which the service is offered and, finally, the present promotion activities that ensure that the public are aware of the services available. It is essential that comparisons be made in each of these areas with the commercial organisations.

Assuming that the local authority is principally interested in providing a service to the citizens and that profit is not the main objective of the organisation, then the management should consider the competitive advantages of the commercial providers. It would seem appropriate to undertake a study to consider the demand for the existing and alternative activities, the prices charged by competitors and the promotions undertaken by the competition. In addition, it may be possible that opportunities to use the facilities for other purposes, such as conferences and meetings, would increase the revenues and also provide a service to the public. This is likely to be the main objective of the organisation. It would also be useful to assess the quality of the services offered, in order to ensure that existing and potential customers are satisfied with the services.

The results of the study would provide a useful starting point in the formulation of a marketing plan for the sports centre.

(b) By considering the PLC model of the different activities, a better understanding of the likely demand for the services will be obtained. This will assist in developing a marketing plan and also provide a basis for allocating the available resources to the various activities.

At the introductory stage, products will require cash to be invested to ensure that the product can grow and become a major benefit to the firm. There is clearly a greater degree of risk as many products fail at this stage. It is, therefore, important that the management estimates the extent of the demand for the martial arts activities at the sports centre. If it is considered that the demand will increase significantly in the future, then cash should be spent in acquiring the equipment and facilities that are needed to provide the sports centre with a competitive advantage over the other organisations. This means that resources should be allocated to this activity, if it is considered to be an area with future growth.

During the growth stage, it will be necessary to expand the facilities that are available in order to meet the fast-growing demand for this activity. It is essential that the management estimate the rate of growth to ensure that there are sufficient squash courts available to meet the rapidly increasing growth in demand for this facility. The construction of squash courts requires a relatively high amount of capital investment and so the expansion of these facilities will use a high proportion of the available resources. In addition, the ongoing maintenance costs will increase with the greater use of the courts and this is likely to use a high proportion of the resources that are available for the current running costs of the centre. It is, therefore, essential that the forecasts are accurate if the sports centre is to allocate its current and capital funds efficiently and effectively.

The activities which are classified as being in the maturity stage will require a relatively small amount of the resources. However, the gymnasium and swimming facilities are likely to generate the cash which will fund the activities which are in both the introductory and growth stages. The mature products will, therefore, provide the resources to invest and thus ensure the long-term survival of the sports centre.

Badminton has been identified as being in the decline stage. Although it is important that the reasons for the decline are identified, it would appear to be unwise to continue allocating a significant amount of resources to this activity. Indeed, it may be appropriate to consider withdrawing the badminton facilities and introducing another activity that may improve the competitive advantage of the sports centre. For example, could the space be released and used for a new martial arts floor or additional squash courts?

(c) At the present time, resources should be used to improve the facilities available for the services in the growth stage, namely squash. In addition, research should be undertaken to ascertain the cause of the decline in the demand for badminton. It is possible that the increased interest in squash has affected the numbers playing badminton. It is also important to assess the potential for martial arts activities which are currently at the introductory stage of the PLC.

The managers should consider the resources that are required for both the current running costs of the sports centre and the capital investment that will enable them to compete with the local commercial recreational organisations.

Fundamentally, the management of the sports centre must ascertain the needs of the public and try to provide the facilities that are required and also to ensure that all the elements of the marketing mix model are investigated. This will ensure that the organisation is geared to meeting the needs of the existing and potential users of the sports centre.

☑ Solution 2

(a) The company is selling a high-quality floor covering and is charging a premium price for its product. This means that the company has identified a demand for a superior product that will be hardwearing and it is expected that it will be used more in an industrial, rather than a domestic, situation. The problem that has been identified is that there is a higher than expected demand for refunds, as unsold stock of the floor coverings are being returned by retailers.

An analysis has shown that the unsold stock is being returned from shops that supply households rather than industrial users. This means that the sales staff has been selling to shops that are less likely to sell the floor coverings that are usually used in an industrial context. It seems that the shops have been persuaded to purchase V's floor coverings, but the end users have not shown an interest in buying the product.

The sales staff has benefited from the commission that they have received and the basis of remuneration of the sales staff is encouraging sales to be made to retail outlets that are unable to sell V's products to the end users. The cost of delivering the floor coverings to shops that will eventually return the unsold stock is wasteful of resources. Frequent returns of goods from customers could affect the company's reputation adversely and this may have a negative impact on future sales and profitability and will adversely affect future shareholder value. It is, therefore, important that the company reviews the basis on which the sales staff is remunerated.

By analysing the problems that the company is facing, it should be possible to devise a strategy that will reduce wastage and costs. This should increase the profits generated and improve the shareholder value.

(b) At the present time, the sales staff is paid a basic salary and commission that is determined in proportion to the sales. To alleviate the problems that are being experienced, the sales director is considering alternative methods of remunerating the sales staff.

Customer account profitability (CAP) would identify the profitability of the company's customers. This would be a much better basis on which to base the commission paid to the sales staff, as it would encourage them to sell the products to shops that generate the most profit for the firm and buy regularly from the company.

At the present time, only the total sales revenue is used to calculate the commission, but if CAP were used, all the costs of producing and distributing the products would be taken into account. In particular, the costs of servicing each customer or group of customers would be highlighted and this would result in a different pattern of behaviour by the sales staff. By focusing on profit rather than sales revenue, it should encourage the sales staff to sell the products to the shops that provide the best outcome for the company.

However, the sales staff is unlikely to be prepared to accept the change in the basis on which their commission is determined. At the present time, the commission earned by some sales staff is very high. M must, therefore, expect opposition to any proposals that will alter their remuneration package.

There is a problem with using CAP, as many of the costs of servicing the customer may not be controllable by the sales staff. This is likely to create problems, as the basis of the sales commission will not be easy for the sales staff to determine. It is usual for the sales staff to keep a record of the sales that they make on a daily or weekly basis. To abandon this as the basis of their commission will require considerable persuasion by M.

It is clear that the present system is deficient, and M has made a suggestion that repeat purchases are used as the basis of the additional amounts paid over the basic salary to the sales staff. This would mean that the sales staff would focus their sales effort on the shops that are selling the floor coverings. This is likely to reduce the quantities of the product that are being returned to V and would seem to be a solution to the problem. Repeat purchases indicate customer satisfaction and it is important that every effort is made to encourage loyalty among both the retailers and the end users. If regular customers are significant in determining the level of commission paid, it is possible that this would reduce the number of new customers that are obtained. The sales staff may only target existing customers under this scheme and this might make it necessary to give a large financial incentive to sales staff generating a new customer who then purchases the product regularly.

This change in the remuneration package is likely to be unacceptable to the sales staff. However, it is important that any new method of determining sales commission is understood by all of them. If it is not both understood and accepted by the sales staff, it could lead to major problems for the firm.

At this stage, it may be wise for M to discuss the problem of returns with the sales management and suggest that some of the costs incurred through the returns from shops should be borne by the sales staff. Not only would they lose the commission paid when the original sale was recorded, but some of the additional costs could be deducted from their commission if goods were returned. This would modify the behaviour of the sales staff and should alleviate the problems that M is faced with.

It is likely that this will also be unacceptable to the sales staff. It will be difficult to define the conditions under which the penalties should be charged against the sales staff's commission.

However, this is a matter that would have to be resolved and agreed after the long-term consequences of the present problems are explained to all the sales staff. It is imperative that M presents the issues clearly and that the changes to the remuneration package of the sales staff are accepted. If the company is to be successful, it is important that the sales staff is content, as they are a vital element in the success of the company.

 Solution 3

- Despite its length this scenario is a very well-structured question with several familiar concepts from previous questions, that is:
  - the five forces model;
  - the importance of the product life cycle in an innovation-led industry, and its influence on resource commitment decisions;

    – customer profitability;

    – trade-offs between social responsibility and profits.

● The final part is a little premature, but some commonsense points will get you through. We shall discuss joint venture strategies in detail later in the study system.

(a) It is usual to find that there are significant differences in the profitability generated by sales to different groups of customers or sales through different distribution channels. The profit is affected by discounts and additional service or product modifications that are required by some customers. It is important, however, that the management is aware of the contribution generated by sales to the different categories of customer, so that this information can be taken into account when developing a strategic plan or making decisions.

Customer profitability information will be used to develop a marketing strategy to ensure that the most profitable customers are retained. Knowledge of the profitability of customers will also mean that resources, especially the time of the salesforce, can be allocated in a rational manner. A knowledge of customer profitability will also be invaluable in deciding on requests from customers for additional services or product modifications. It will be possible to consider the requests in relation to the overall profitability of the customer requiring the changes.

In most businesses there is a range of selling prices charged for the same product or service. This will reflect the bargaining strength of different customers. It is important to analyse the profitability of different customer accounts in order to be aware of the effects on profits of providing both special discounts and differentiated products to meet the demands of the more powerful customers. Management should be aware of the effect of these differences on profitability, so that steps can be taken to reduce the number of customers that generate low levels of profit.

It is important that the management is aware of the contribution generated by each group of customer. This will enable the best course of action to be identified. There are often difficulties in determining the profit resulting from specific customers, but the cost information should be obtained to enable information to be available. It is likely to be very useful in the development of a firm's strategy and should be included as part of the management information system.

(b) Sales-oriented firms will concentrate on selling the products that they are able to produce while marketing-oriented organisations will strive to meet the needs of their existing and potential customers. It is likely, therefore, that sales-oriented firms will be less concerned than marketing-oriented firms with the characteristics of the buyers of their products and less likely to monitor the implications of the different market segments and distribution channels.

As sales-oriented organisations tend to concentrate on total sales and market share, it is likely that less information will be available about the customers. However, those details which influence customer profitability will be available in marketing-oriented organisations, as there will be a much greater concern with these issues. It is also possible that sales-oriented organisations will use wholesalers and middlemen to sell their products and this will mean that they will not be aware of the characteristics of the end-users. In addition, they may not be prepared to allocate resources to gather information about the profitability of customers.

In a sales-oriented organisation, the following management accounting information should be available:

● the selling price and variable cost of each product;
● the specific costs that are incurred in respect of each product;

- the costs of the sales department and the salesforce;
- the performance indicators which assess the performance of the sales team or sales area;
- information relating to the products and brands in addition to providing information which focuses on the customers.

In a marketing-oriented organisation, information relating to individual customers or groups of purchasers will be produced. It is likely, therefore, that both financial and non-financial information will be available and this will make it possible to assess the profitability of the customer's account. Although there is a wide range of information that could be available, the following is likely to be available:

- the costs of meeting the individual requirements of customers;
- the costs of processing orders, transport, administration of the debtors' accounts and stockholding associated with each group of customers;
- statistics relating to the distribution channels, size of orders, sales points and payment methods for each customer;
- service times of individual customers and customer groups;
- the frequency of purchasing by each customer;
- the level of discount that is given to each group of customers;
- the level of complaints by all customers.

Solution 4

(a) It is useful for managers who are developing a marketing plan to understand the manner in which customers perceive the products that are being sold. It has been suggested that the steps to be followed in order to establish customer value are:

- *Identify the attributes that the customers value.* Customers will appreciate different features of a product. To some people, special features or functions, quality and price will be particularly important. It is essential that the marketing management know what customers value, as this explains why the customer has purchased the product originally and is particularly important in explaining repeat purchases. These attributes should be emphasised in the marketing of the product. In addition, features that are not valued can be eliminated, especially if this reduces the cost of producing the product.
- *Assess the quantitative importance of different attributes.* It is inevitable that different customers will be interested in different attributes of each product and so it is essential to measure the relative importance of each feature or function. In addition, it is important to rank the attributes and it may be necessary to investigate any differences that are found as this may give valuable insights into the preferences of customers.
- *Assess the company's and competitors' performances on different customers' values against the rated importance.* It is necessary to try to measure the success of the company's products in terms of all the products that are available. Research should be carried out to measure the relative success of the company's products in satisfying the customers' needs.
- *Examine how customers in a segment rate a firm's performance against a major competitor on an attribute basis.* The next step is to assess the extent to which the company's products are perceived as being better than the competitors' products

within each customer segment. This is a more focused investigation, which will make it possible to devise marketing strategies based on the findings of the customer value analysis.

- *Monitor customer values over time.* Changes in taste, fashion and technology will eventually lead to changes in customer values and the company must monitor the changes as they occur.
- By using these five steps, it is possible to obtain the views of the company's customers and this information will be very useful in the preparation of the company's strategic marketing plan.

(b) It has been suggested that the value chain provides the means by which it is possible to identify ways of creating customer value. It is recognised that each firm consists of a number of different activities that create value and also generate costs. The primary activities involve the acquisition, processing, distribution and marketing of the products that are sold. The support activities, on the other hand, are needed to ensure that the primary activities function efficiently.

It is important that organisations analyse both their primary and support activities to assess the extent to which each activity adds value to the products. If it is found that any attributes that have been included to add customer value are not rated highly by the purchasers, it may be possible to eliminate the attribute and either reduce the selling price, or introduce a function or feature that does increase customer value.

Strengths

By focusing on the value chain, managers will be encouraged to focus on the cost effectiveness of their activities. This is particularly important in relation to the activities of their competitors as it can provide the basis on which the company's competitive advantage is identified. If the research shows that competitors' products are rated as having a higher level of customer value, then steps must be taken to rectify the position. Product design modifications, changes in the quality or reduced selling prices may be some of the actions needed to ensure that competitive advantage is not lost.

Weaknesses

Value chain analysis does tend to focus on the existing linkages. However, it may be important for the management to take a much broader view of the possible methods of improving customer value and this wider picture may be hampered by focusing only on the primary and support activities in terms of the typical value chain analysis process.

Conclusions

It must be appreciated that it is not easy to conduct a value chain analysis, especially in respect of competitors. It is often very time consuming and this will usually mean that it is a costly procedure. It is also likely that the information will not be readily available, especially in respect of the competition. It is unlikely that competitors will co-operate in providing this information, which will usually be of a confidential nature. In addition, much of the analysis will be subjective, as there will be differences in the perceived customer value of different individuals. It is also difficult to quantify the precise extent to which the value is affected by different strategies.

Despite these difficulties, it must be recognised that value chain analysis provides a useful method of focusing on the activities within an organisation. By focusing on the cost and benefits received from each of the activities, a clearer picture of the best course of action to achieve sustainable competitive advantage can be obtained, as it allows customer value to be balanced against the cost of the features and functions that are provided.

 ## Solution 5

(a) If WG plc is to retain its position as one of the leaders in the global pharmaceutical industry, it is important that it is able to introduce new products each year. This means that it should be possible for the company to have new products to replace existing products when the patent expires. It is, therefore, important that WG plc invests regularly in a programme of research and development (R&D) to ensure that it has new products and services which will meet both its profitability objective and its aim of developing innovative medicines and services worldwide.

The theory of the product life cycle (PLC) suggests that there are four main stages in the economic life of a product: introduction, growth, maturity and decline. The PLC model is invaluable in the development of strategic and marketing plans, as it encourages managers to consider the stage of development of each of the company's products. It is, however, acknowledged that the PLC provides only a broad picture, as it is recognised that products move through the 'life cycle' at different rates and it is often difficult to be certain about a product's precise position in the PLC.

The Boston Consulting Group developed a matrix, based on the PLC. Using the rate of market growth and relative market share, the matrix classifies products as 'dog', 'cash cow', 'star' or 'problem child'. It is likely that, at any time, companies will have products in all these categories. A product's position within the BCG matrix has implications for the cash flows of the company and it is therefore important that management monitors the position continuously. Management must recognise that products currently classified as 'cash cows' will eventually become 'dogs' and will cease to generate cash. It is essential, therefore, that steps are taken to ensure that the company is always developing new products which have the potential to become 'stars'. This makes it imperative that adequate resources are allocated to R&D in the strategic plan.

Four years ago, one of WG plc's products produced almost 50 per cent of its turnover. However, it is now expected that this will drop to about 10 per cent of turnover when the patent expires. This is an example of the effects of the PLC and the problem, which makes the company vulnerable to the competition in the dynamic environment of the pharmaceutical industry. It is essential that WG plc develops new products continuously if it is to retain its dominant position in the industry.

At the present time, almost 15 per cent of the company's turnover is being spent on R&D and it is recognised that the company has the largest department undertaking this in the industry. It is clear that the managers of WG plc have taken a decision to allocate resources to research activities to ensure that the company retains its competitive advantage.

If the company did not provide the resources to enable the research to be undertaken it is likely that the number of new products would decrease and the company would lose its dominant position in the pharmaceutical industry. Competitors would increase their sales, market share and, possibly, profits at the expense of WG plc. In addition, resources must be provided so that WG plc continues to produce and develop new and innovative medicines and services worldwide to enable the company to achieve its corporate mission and objectives.

It is clear that R&D is the source of WG plc's competitive advantage and so sufficient resources must be allocated to this activity if the company is to retain its current dominance in the pharmaceutical industry.

(b) The main objective of the company is to sustain its profitability, but another is to combat and eradicate disease worldwide. This is likely to involve the company both in allocating considerable resources to R&D and in providing subsidies so that medicines are available to patients worldwide. However, this expenditure will reduce profitability. There is, therefore, a conflict between the company's two objectives. This is really a difference between short-term profitability and the long-term performance of the company. By using resources at the present time to establish WG plc as a major pharmaceutical manufacturer worldwide, it is likely that long-term profits will increase.

Porter identified five forces that affect the current level of competition, and these can be used as a framework to consider the objectives of WG plc:

1. *The existing level of competition.* In the pharmaceutical industry, there are a few large companies that compete worldwide. Patents mean that a company will enjoy a monopoly position for a limited period, but it is always possible that a substitute will be developed which will reduce the benefits to the holder of the patent rights. However, to compete effectively, WG plc must ensure that its research activities are at least as effective as its competitors. This will require the allocation of resources to research activities and will therefore reduce the company's short-term profitability. However, a successful R&D programme will increase the probability of the company's long-term success.

2. *The threat of new entrants.* The high level of expenditure on R&D in the industry means that it is difficult for new companies to enter the market. It is possible that individuals or small companies may make innovations, but it would probably be necessary to collaborate with the major pharmaceutical companies, like WG plc, if the new product were to be marketed successfully. This means that WG plc must have funds available to develop any products that emerge from outsiders.

3. *Possible substitute products.* Although patents provide a period during which the company has the sole right to make, use and sell the product, these benefits exist only for a limited period of time. It is essential, therefore, that the company balances the possibility of exploiting its monopoly position against the consequences of this policy becoming known, especially by the public and governmental bodies that have criticised the pharmaceutical industry. After the expiry of the patent, the competition will be fiercer and the example provided in the case study shows that the sales are expected to decrease from almost 50 per cent to no more than 10 per cent of the company's turnover within a period of about five years. This is likely to have a major effect on the profitability of the company and it is essential that other products are developed continuously to provide alternatives. This emphasises the need for considerable amounts to be spent on research to ensure that replacement products are available.

4. *The negotiating power of customers.* The availability of substitutes, especially after the expiry of the patent, will mean that buyers will purchase medicines based on the perceived effectiveness of the product, the pricing policy adopted, and the success of the company's promotional activity. It is necessary, therefore, for WG plc to focus attention on marketing its products successfully. This will use resources and the 'donation programmes' may be considered part of its marketing strategy. These tactics will increase its costs, especially in the short term, but would be expected to increase the long-term profitability of the company.

5. *The negotiating power of suppliers.* This would not appear to be a significant factor for WG plc: it is a large company that can access supplies throughout the world. The importance of the R&D activity within the company means that the company needs excellent researchers who are innovative and able to provide the stream of new products that are essential for the success of the company.

The directors' decision to allocate resources to R&D expenditure is likely to ensure that the company regularly produces new products that will be sold worldwide. This will assist in retaining WG plc's position as a leading company in the pharmaceutical industry. This policy should ensure the sustained profitability of the company, and also the aim of providing 'innovative medicines and treatments' means that it is addressing both of its major objectives and trying to balance the conflicting effects on profitability and social responsibility.

Other strategies which would enable the company to provide treatments worldwide, but which would reduce its profitability, are:

1. *The allocation of resources to develop emerging markets.* It is likely that the profit immediately generated in these countries would not be significant. Additional costs would be incurred if local management was engaged in these countries and products were modified to meet local demand.

2. *Research collaboration with other companies and universities throughout the world.* Although current costs would be increased by the expenditure involved, such ventures would mean that WG plc was aware of developments taking place in all these institutions and would be able to benefit from any successful projects that result from the research undertaken.

In essence, the managers of WG plc must strike a balance between the conflicting objectives of profitability and combating disease worldwide. It is necessary to reduce the profitability of the company now in order to develop both new products and new markets. This will provide the company with the means of sustaining its profitability and also retaining its competitive advantage in terms of innovations and being a leader within this industry. If the company is successful, it will be able to allocate resources to meet the company's objective to combat disease worldwide.

(c) (i) 1. Using the space (sq. cm) as the retailers' limiting factor:

	Coffstop £	Peffstill £
Net selling price per bottle	1.50	10.00
Buying-in cost per bottle	0.50	7.40
Gross contribution per bottle	1.00	2.60
Shelf area per bottle (sq. cm)	18	60
Contribution per sq. cm	5.56p	4.33p

This shows that Coffstop generates the higher contribution per unit of limiting factor for the retailer.

2. If the direct product profitability of both products is determined, the results are:

	Coffstop £	Peffstill £
Net selling price per bottle	1.50	10.00
Buying-in cost per bottle	0.50	7.40
Gross contribution per bottle	1.00	2.60
Other direct costs per bottle	0.40	0.80
Contribution per bottle	0.60	1.80
Average sales (bottles)	120	20
Shelf area per bottle (sq. cm)	18	60
Total shelf area (sq. cm)	2,160	1,200

Direct product profitability is determined by the following calculation:

Contribution per bottle $\times$ bottles sold/Area occupied

For Coffstop: £0.60 $\times$ 120/2,160 = 3.33p

For Peffstill: £1.80 $\times$ 20/2,100 = 3.00p

Both the CVP and DPP analyses show that retailers will prefer to stock Coffstop.

(ii) The marketing strategy for Coffstop should be based on the needs of the company's customers. The factors, which should be incorporated into the marketing plan, can be summarised:

1. *Product.* The reputation of WG plc in the pharmaceutical industry should be emphasised and the branding should link Coffstop with the other products that are sold by WG plc. Any specific qualities of Coffstop that are likely to appeal to the consumers should be highlighted in the marketing strategy.

2. *Price.* Despite the difference in dosage of the two products, there is a significant difference in the selling price per bottle of the two products. Coffstop will sell at £1.50 and Peffstill will be priced at £10. This should make Coffstop more attractive to consumers as it will enable them to try the product at a lower price. It must be recognised, however, that the price of medicines may not be crucial to consumers, as the demand may be relatively inelastic. The lower price per bottle of Coffstop should appeal to the customers and provide WG plc with an advantage over its competitor's product.

3. *Place.* The product is sold 'over the counter from pharmacies' and the details of the CVP and DPP analyses should be made available to the stockists: this provides Coffstop with a major competitive advantage over Peffstill. It is possible that alternative outlets, for example supermarkets, garages, etc., may be considered, but this may not be appropriate for the product image.

4. *Promotion.* The promotional campaign should link the product to WG plc, as the company enjoys a favourable reputation as the supplier of quality products. It may be useful to target doctors and clinics to ensure that these professionals are aware of Coffstop's qualities. This would mean that the product might be prescribed or recommended for purchase to the consumers. Promotional activities could be arranged to ensure that Coffstop became well known as an effective medicine.

(d) If the company is considering entering into a strategic alliance, there will be many issues that will need to be resolved before the agreement is finalised:

1. The input of resources (i.e. physical resources, such as capital, machinery and property) will be an issue. However, intangible assets such as skill, expertise and patents are likely to be the cause of more disputes in an organisation that is based on a strategic alliance.

2. It is essential that the control and management of the venture is discussed and finalised to minimise the possibility of serious disputes during the collaboration. It may be necessary to allocate managers to the collaboration, but there will still be issues that arise in relation to the fundamental loyalty and commitment of the staff that participate in the venture. It may be necessary to share confidential and sensitive information that might prove to be difficult before trust is built up between the parties involved at both the personal and corporate levels.

3. The extent of the alliance in terms of markets and products is an area that must be discussed and agreed at the outset of the alliance, as this is an area that could result in major difficulties at a later stage. In addition, the sharing of costs and expenses between the two participants should also be agreed so that the position is clear to both parties.

4. The effect on competitors and regulatory bodies should be considered in order to avoid any legislation or regulations that will affect the alliance adversely. By recognising that there may potential problems in this area, it may be possible to minimise the impact of these factors.

5. Finally, the manner in which the outputs from the strategic alliance are shared will be a major issue. Each participant will have provided some of the inputs and it is important that an equitable and agreed method of sharing is finalised before the commencement of the strategic alliance.

It is likely that these practical issues will need to be agreed from the outset if the alliance is to be successful. However, if the firms are able to manage this effectively, the alliance should result in major benefits. The pharmaceutical industry requires large inputs of both technical expertise and resources, as R&D activities are crucial to the success of the companies.

5

Strategic
Implications of IT

Strategic Implications of IT

5

5.1 Introduction

This chapter begins by looking at the need for organisations to take a strategic approach to information technology. It then examines the different ways in which the information system, through its IT and information components, might lead the organisation towards competitive advantage. In order to get the most from this chapter, you should ensure that you are familiar with the work of Michael Porter on competition. This is covered in detail earlier in the pillar and has been revised elsewhere in this manual. This chapter also examines the need for an information systems strategy and looks at a possible model that might be used to develop such a strategy. It then considers the issues surrounding the organisation of the IT department and the choice of outsourcing as a strategy.

LEARNING OUTCOMES

After completing this chapter you should be able to:

- ▸ evaluate the impact of electronic commerce on the way business is conducted and recommend an appropriate strategy;

- ▸ evaluate the strategic and competitive benefits of IS/IT and advise on the development of appropriate strategies;

- ▸ evaluate and advise managers on the development of strategies for knowledge management, IM, IS and IT that support the organisations strategic requirements IT/IS/IM strategy;

- ▸ identify and evaluate IS/IT systems appropriate to the organisation's strategic requirements, and recommend changes where necessary.

5.2 The strategic case for IT investment

In this chapter we assess the potential of IT and the information system in strategic management by examining the different information strategies within an organisation and then how these can be applied. We will also consider the case for, and process of, developing an information systems strategy.

5.2.1 Three information strategies

Within an organisation, there is normally a requirement to have three different strategies relating to the information being used. These are:

- information technology;
- information systems;
- information management.

> Definitions: *Information technology strategy* refers to the hardware configuration that an organisation requires to transfer information. *Information systems strategy* relates to the long-term plan concerning the use of IT within the organisation. *Information management strategy* refers to the approach to managing data and information within the organisation, specifically how data and information are stored and accessed.

5.2.2 Information technology strategy

Why does an organisation need an information technology strategy? The quick answer is because the organisation needs to know what information is in place and how it will be used. However, some slightly longer answers have been produced, and various writers, including Earl (1989), have provided lists of reasons why IT strategies are required. Earl's list includes the following reasons:

- IT involves high costs. A strategy is, therefore, required to set a budget for IT and then to monitor expenditure against that budget.
- IT is critical to the success of many organisations. Where an organisation relies on IT, it must be reliable and accessible at all times. For example, if you want to purchase a computer from an Internet company, then the IT systems of that company must be available 24 hours a day, or it will lose orders.
- IT is now used as part of the commercial strategy to help obtain competitive advantage. IT can be used in many different ways to assist an organisation, perhaps by integration of IT into products or by providing enhanced information about customers. A strategy is required to ensure that this competitive advantage is achieved and maintained.
- IT is required in the economic context. In other words, IT enables other functions and activities to take place, such as using technology in specific ways. For example, without an e-mail system, an organisation could spend a lot of money on postal services. An IT strategy is needed to ensure that electronic communication systems are in place and reliable.
- IT affects all levels of management. It is, therefore, essential that hardware and software are available to access information as well as enabling managers to perform their jobs.
- IT affects the way management information is created and presented. IT is required to support the management information systems within an organisation.
- IT requires effective management to obtain maximum benefits. Poor management of IT will mean that many of the objectives listed above will not be achieved.
- IT involves many stakeholders within and outside the organisation. Stakeholders include employees, customers, government, suppliers, etc. They may all want to check that IT is being used appropriately and to the benefit of them as well as to the organisation.

The importance of these factors will vary depending on the specific organisation. However, you can see that it is important for any organisation to have an IT strategy. Despite the early date of this reference the material is still highly relevant today.

5.2.3 Information systems and information management strategies

The information systems strategy is normally decided first within an organisation, because it defines the long-term use of information within an organisation. When an organisation has set its long-term goals, then the information system strategy can be decided to show what systems are needed to support those goals.

Having decided this strategy, then the information technology strategy will be decided; this explains what physical systems will be in place to ensure that the IS strategy is met.

Finally, the information management strategy can be determined to explain how the organisation will deal with and store the information that will be collected from the different systems.

Nolan (1979) suggested a model for the evolution of information systems that became widely used by academics and practitioners. Although this model has subsequently been revised by Nolan and others, it is still worthy of discussion.

Nolan suggests that the level of evolution and expenditure in an organisation can be seen to progress through six stages as the organisation's approach to IT changes. These stages are as follows:

1. *Initiation*. The first introduction of computers for cost saving. In this stage, the computers are often 'owned' by the accountants, and this may present a barrier to future development.
2. *Contagion*. The blossoming of computer applications into other areas in a totally uncontrolled way. This stage may be chaotic, and many of the applications fail.
3. *Control*. Senior managers become concerned about the level of expenditure and lack of control. Staff are centralised, and formal IS organisations appear. Applications concentrate on saving money, rather than making money.
4. *Integration*. The controls introduced in stage 3 are slackened, in order to introduce innovation. The IS function is reorganised to allow specialists to become involved with users in the development of systems. Large expenditures are made in core systems.
5. *Data administration*. Developments are driven by the organisation's demands for information. The business recognises the value and potential of the information system. Corporate databases are created.
6. *Maturity*. Planning and organisation of the information system is incorporated into the development of the organisation. Strategy appears.

We will come back to these stages later in the chapter with an example. One of the criticisms of the evolution model is that the level of data processing expenditure is more directly affected by the changing cost of technology than by the state of the organisation. Rapid reductions in unit cost, as seen with PCs over the last 15 years, can distort the trend.

Another criticism is that organisations frequently take advantage of totally new states of technology (such as the Internet), and this can lead to a trend as shown in Figure 5.1.

As we can see from Figure 5.1 not all change is continuous but can be revolutionary as a new technological paradigm appears and eventually becomes accepted practice. Those organisations that remain with the old technology are unlikely to enjoy a competitive advantage over those that successfully adopt the new technology.

Nolan's model is, however, still useful for the following reasons:

- it provides a simple view of trends in information systems development;
- it is necessary to understand the past in order to analyse the present and predict the future;

STRATEGIC IMPLICATIONS OF IT

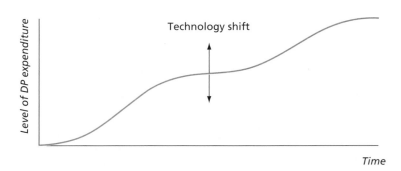

Figure 5.1 Effect of a technology shift

- it acknowledges that different stages of development require different management approaches.

It is this last point that leads us to the relevance of the model to an examination. You may come across a situation in a scenario where the organisation appears to be in one stage of evolution, while the management approach being adopted is more appropriate to a different stage. You will need to be able to recognise that and make justified recommendations as to how the appropriate changes might be brought about.

5.2.4 The applications portfolio

The importance of IT to the organisation was examined by McFarlan and McKenney (1983). They suggested that dependence on IT could be classified into a matrix (shown in Figure 5.2), based on the Boston Consulting Group (BCG) matrix which we discussed in Chapter 4.

This matrix classifies organisations into four types:

1. *Strategic*. The business depends on its information system for competitive advantage (see later in this chapter) and expects to continue to do so.
2. *Turnaround*. The business expects that the information system will become strategically important in the future.
3. *Support*. The business sees no strategic value in their information system.
4. *Factory*. The business sees the strategic significance of its information systems now, but predicts that this will disappear in the future.

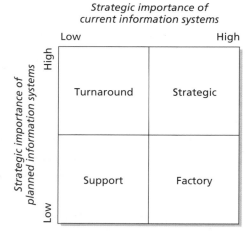

Figure 5.2 Strategic grid (McFarlan)

Although the strategic grid gives us an interesting insight into the state of information systems in 1983, its use in the modern business environment is limited. It is very difficult to believe that, given the uncertainty and rapid change in the IT environment, any organisation could be naive enough to predict that its information system will have no future strategic importance!

A development of the strategic grid that can be used is the 'applications portfolio' suggested by Peppard (1993). This looks at the strategic impact of individual applications within the organisation, and classifies them as if they were products in the BCG matrix (see Chapter 4).

Like McFarlan, Peppard suggests four classifications. This time, an organisation would use the grid to target those applications within its portfolio that have the greatest strategic potential. The four categories are as follows:

1. *Support*. These are applications that improve management effectiveness but are not critical to the business. The benefits they deliver are mainly economic. Examples include accounting systems, payroll systems, spreadsheets and legally required systems.
2. *Key operational*. These applications are critical to sustain the existing business. Such applications generally support core organisational activities. Examples include inventory control, production control and order management.
3. *Strategic*. These applications are critical to future business success (see Sections 5.3 and 5.4).
4. *High potential*. These applications are innovative, and might be of future strategic potential. Examples might include the use of the Internet, expert systems or multimedia.

5.2.5 Major investment decisions

Capital investment is normally used as an example of a tactical decision, but if the scale of the investment is large enough, such a decision can become strategic simply because of its financial impact on the business. Although individual IT investments might be relatively small, the cumulative level of investment in IT in many organisations might be a very high proportion of total business costs. This alone might make IT a critical strategic variable, as ill-advised investment may lead to the failure of the business.

5.3 Using IT to gain competitive advantage

We have discussed Michael Porter's concept of the value chain in Chapter 3, and will go on in Chapter 6 to discuss, in more detail, his idea of generic strategies. Basically, and briefly, his idea is that companies can only compete effectively in markets by one of two approaches:

- *Low cost*. Having the lowest unit production costs in the industry.
- *Differentiation*. Persuading customers that the product is better, different or unique.

These approaches can be applied in a focused or unfocussed way.

Although Porter has written mainly about business strategy, he has also looked specifically at the role of information systems in gaining a competitive advantage.

In their *Harvard Business Review* article, Porter and Millar (1985) suggest three areas where the 'information revolution' affects competition:

1. IT changes industry structure and, in doing so, alters the rules of competition;

2. IT creates competitive advantage by giving companies new ways to outperform their rivals;
3. IT spawns new businesses, often from within a company's existing operations.

5.3.1 The value chain

At this stage you should look back to Section 3.3 where we discussed the value chain in some detail. Porter and Millar stress that the information system is 'more than just computers', and suggest that the influence of the information system can be seen clearly by looking at the value chain.

This shows the direct use of IT to perform activities, but there is another issue to consider:

Every value activity has both a physical component and an information-processing component. The physical component includes all the physical tasks required to perform the activity. The information-processing component encompasses the steps required to capture, manipulate, and channel the data necessary to perform the activity.

Porter and Millar stress the importance of linking (or integrating) technologies throughout the firm. Despite the significant capital investment required, they are confident that this can bring benefits such as improved productivity, less bureaucracy, cost reduction and the opportunity to 'spawn new businesses'. They also provide a 'strategic agenda' – an action plan to exploit the information system. This agenda has five steps, as follows:

1. assess the information intensity of the industry;
2. determine the role of information technology in the industry structure;
3. identify and rank the ways in which IT might create a competitive advantage;
4. investigate how IT might spawn new businesses;
5. develop a plan for taking advantage of IT.

5.3.2 Defining competitive advantage

It is important to remember that the term 'competitive advantage' now has a very precise meaning. It is not simply about being better than your rivals.

> *Competitive advantage*: Using knowledge of the competitive forces to put the organisation in a position where it exerts more competitive force on others than they do on it.

Porter also says that the competitive forces model can be used in two ways. The following sections assume that the organisation wishes to dominate its current industry, but Porter is clear that organisations can also obtain competitive advantage by repositioning. This means identifying an industry that has weak competitive forces acting on it, and moving there. Obviously, the information system has a major role to play in the research required for this sort of strategy.

5.4 Using IT for competitive advantage

This section looks at the different ways in which IT can be used to pursue the generic strategies outlined in the previous section. It builds on the ideas put forward by Porter and Millar as shown in Figure 5.3.

Firm infrastructure	Planning models				
HR management	Automated personnel scheduling				
Technology development	Computer-aided design/electronic market research				
Procurement	Online procurement of parts				
	Automated warehouse	Flexible manufac- turing	Automated order processing	Tele- marketing Remotes sales terminals	Remote servicing Computer scheduling of repairs
	Inbound logistics	Operations	Outbound logistics	Sales and marketing	Service

Figure 5.3   Value chain from IT perspective

5.4.1   Cost leadership

As mentioned previously, cost leadership requires the organisation to achieve the lowest unit production cost in its industry.

If we consider the case of an automobile manufacturer and how it might use IT to directly reduce unit costs.

There are a number of ways in which this might be achieved, including the following:

- automating the logistics and production activities of the organisation by means of:
  - computerised stock control for raw materials and components, with systems integrated to those of suppliers, to remove administration cost;
  - computer-aided manufacturing (or automated manufacturing) in the production process, to reduce the labour content of the product;
  - using radio frequency identity devices (RFID) to track, control and manage stock;
  - computerised stock control of finished vehicles, to allow staff to locate cars more quickly thus reducing staff time;
- computer-aided design, to reduce the number of labour hours involved in the production and amendment of technical drawings and improve the productivity of designers.

5.4.2   Differentiation

In order to differentiate the product or service that is supplied, the organisation has to create an impression that the product is better, different or unique. Unlike cost leadership, the product does not have to be different, but the customer has to believe that it is. This means that an organisation can differentiate its product or service by making tangible changes to it, or by the way it communicates with the customer through marketing initiatives. The role of IT in creating a product or service that is better, different or unique depends on precisely what the product is.

For example we might consider the case of a bank trying to use IT to differentiate its services.

The use of IT as a component of financial services is a relatively new phenomenon. A bank might use IT in the following ways:

- The first automated teller machines (ATMs) gave a competitive advantage, but this was soon eroded as all banks started to provide the facility. However, enhancing the facilities provided or the number of machines might improve service levels.

- The provision of telephone- or Internet-based services can allow a tailored package to be offered to the customer, based on complex software that greatly improves the convenience level when compared with conventional high-street banking. The complexity of the relationship that develops might also create a deterrent to switching and thus increase customer loyalty.

You should remember that competitive advantage is usually a temporary phenomenon. As soon as rivals 'catch up' the advantage is eroded, and it is necessary to find new ways to compete. We shall consider, in Chapter 6, the concept of sustainability of competitive advantage.

5.4.3 Focus

In order to introduce focus into our competitive strategy we need to identify precisely what our customers need. We then segment the market and try to provide a product or service that precisely satisfies the needs of our target segment. You will remember we discussed segmentation in Chapter 4 and you should re-read Section 4.8 on relationship marketing and Section 4.9 on data mining at this point. Without the ability to mine data as effectively as some organisations currently do it would be impossible for them to practice relationship marketing as well as they do.

In some industries there are consumers who are attracted by a high IT content in the product or service; these are generally young, well-educated customers with above-average disposable incomes. If we can identify such customers, and meet their IT expectations, we can effectively provide them with a unique product that they cannot obtain elsewhere.

5.5 Using information for competitive advantage

The second aspect of competitive advantage concerns the way in which information flows support the product or service offered by the organisation.

Porter and Millar (1985) suggest that industries can be classified according to their information characteristics in a two-by-two matrix. The axes of the matrix show the following:

- The extent to which information is a component part of the product or service offered (on the x-axis).

    This is very low in a product such as cement, but very high in newspapers or financial services.
- The number of information exchanges that must take place in order for a transaction to take place (on the y-axis). This is low in fashion but high in oil refining or airlines.

Porter and Millar suggest that you can place any industry in the matrix, then determine if and how the information system is likely to be critical to the business.

5.5.1 Cost leadership

It is at first difficult to see how information can reduce the unit production cost of a product or service. We need to think more widely than the information content of the product.

In Chapter 3 we discussed the importance of supply chain management. This can only be practiced to the degree with which companies such as Dell, Toyota, Tesco and other successful multinationals do because of the advantage that they gain from their Information Systems.

In order to reduce costs we need to understand them, and the information system can be used for cost recording and analysis. We might also use information regarding the cost base of rivals to facilitate a benchmarking exercise, so we can see how to reduce our own costs to best practice levels.

5.5.2 Differentiation

The way in which we communicate with our customers is key to creating the perception of a differentiated product. In designing a communications strategy to support the product, marketing specialists will decide on the message they wish to convey to tell the market why they should buy or use the product.

For example, we could consider the case of a manufacturer of drinks trying to use information to differentiate a new drink aimed at children.

We need to consider all aspects of the way the company might communicate the features and benefits of its product to the potential customers (those who buy – possibly the parents) and consumers (those who use – probably children). All of this information is an output from the information system of the organisation, and might include the following:

- the design of the label and packaging of the product, to give messages and information regarding taste and other characteristics (such as fun, energy, etc.);
- advertising messages used in paper-based and electronic media, showing children drinking and enjoying the product;
- comparisons with rival products, for example, and advertisements showing children choosing the product in preference to rivals.

5.5.3 Focus

If we are to tailor a product to meet the specific needs of a target market segment, we first need to ensure that we know precisely what those needs are. The information system must gather and analyse data relating to customer needs, and also the extent to which those needs are satisfied by other products or services. Once we understand the needs of our target segment, a communication package must be created that convinces the target customers that their needs will be satisfied by use of our product or service. This package will contain the elements referred to in the previous section.

5.5.4 Linkages with suppliers or customers

As we saw in Chapter 3, Porter is also clear that a firm's value chain does not exist in isolation, but is part of a 'value system' that links it to the value chains of customers and suppliers. By modelling the value system of the industry, an organisation would be able to identify and assess opportunities to integrate their information system with those of customers and suppliers. Such linkages are likely to deter customers and suppliers from dealing with the organisation's rivals, thus providing a competitive advantage.

5.5.5 A composite example

The following is relevant to all of the previous three sections but should also help you to revise the material covered in both Chapters 3 and 4.

Twelve years ago Tesco, the UKs largest supermarket, and a global operator, hired a company called Dunnhumby to help with the loyalty card that Tesco operated with its customers. In every four week period nearly two thirds of UK households shop at Tesco and approximately 15 per cent of all expenditure in shops is taken by Tesco. In part that success is due to the effectiveness of the Clubcard. On behalf of Tesco Dunnhumby track the shopping habits of 13 million households in the UK. A retail analyst at Cazenove recently wrote that the advantage of Tesco was not scale, contrary to popular belief, but the Clubcard. He stated that the card gave array of tangible benefits across virtually every aspect of the business.

The purchasing behaviour of customers is used to create a picture of the kind of person the card holder actually is. Effectively the same as an observer standing at the checkout counter. Unlike a market researcher, the Clubcard records everything, doesn't forget and does it for virtually every customer rather than a 'representative' sample – it doesn't take long on this analysis either. Judgements can be made about the changing make up of the family – new babies or children have left home and can decide whether you are a good cook, time poor and make an good estimate of social class. Approximately 5 billion pieces of data are captured every week. Each separate product has its own set of attributes and these values build a composite picture of the purchasers. The information is stored in an enormous search engine that can be accessed, at a price, by more than 200 consumer goods companies such as Proctor & Gamble, Coca Cola and Unilever. The database at Dunnhumby is 40 terabytes in size and is tied into the electoral roll, the Land registry and the Office of National Statistics. Shortly after a product is new launched, or a new promotional campaign started, those companies can access information which will tell them not only the effect of the launch but who is actually buying. Brand managers can determine whether their new product is appealing to young singles, empty nesters or any other social lifestyle group. Dunnhumby claim that it is the best source that a supplier can use since no other source is so representative of the population. For £50,000 a year suppliers get access to a 10 per cent sample of the data in the system. This may seem expensive but it is the largest customer survey in the country and, increasingly, when Tesco buyers make decisions about new products they like to see the projections based on data with which they are familiar. It isn't an industry standard – but Tesco would be very pleased if it were to become so.

For Tesco the information allows better targeting of customer segments not just by knowing what they do buy but also by what they don't. An example would be meat – which very few families don't buy at some time during a month. Not all families shop exclusively at one supermarket much as Tesco's and others would like them to. By looking at the data for a particular social group Dunnhumby can identify which product categories were missing from the shopping basket – allowing Tesco to make particular offers to try to attract that group to start buying that particular category of product. This would mean that people would come into a store and would spend more each time they visited. At one store when this approach was first tested the turnover went up by 12 per cent. One of the biggest tests in this direction was wine. Although customers were buying wine in the cheaper varieties they were not buying from the more expensive end of the product range. Mining the data showed that there was insufficient variety at the top end of the range and once choice was offered sales went up significantly. It had been very noticeable that, at Christmas, shoppers were trading up to 'better' wines and these seasonal sales had been lost – until the information became available in such a user friendly form.

Dunnhumby do not use traditional social segments but group people on the basis of what they buy. One category being 'convenience' which is further subdivided into 'time poor, food rich' and 'can't cook, won't cook'. By knowing what customers want, Tesco have been able to make a number of positioning decisions such as the move into smaller format stores, Tesco Express, the launch of the Internet site, Tesco mobile phones, insurance and The Finest Food range. At one early presentation to the board of directors by Dunnhumby Lord MacLaurin the former Tesco Chairman said, "You know more about my customers after three months than I know after 10 years".

5.6   Value-added networks and extranets

> *Value-added network (VAN)*: 'A network to which services have been added, normally by a third party, over and above the basic ability to transfer data.'
> Franks (2000)

5.6.1   Description

Value-added networks are those that directly add value to the organisation's products and services. They tend to be collaborative networks that link together organisations with a common interest. Often the VAN users are all within the same industry or value system.

Examples would include the following:

- A direct link between the stores/purchasing system of a company and its suppliers (such as those used in just-in-time (JIT) systems) would enable the ordering and delivery processes and procedures to be speeded up and carried out more efficiently, thus adding value to the business.
- A customer network that enabled a company to provide a constant flow of information on customer activity to salespeople.
- American Airlines (AA) dominate the US airline booking market with their 'SABRE' reservations system. This system allows travel agents to access flight details relating to all airlines, but favours flights operated by AA and its partners. By 1988, AA made more money from SABRE than from flying planes!
- Thomson holidays operate a similar system (TOPS) for UK travel agents to book holidays.
- The Association of British Travel Agents (ABTA) operates a VAN for travel agents to access training courses from their counter-based terminals.

The key in defining a VAN is whether or not the processes and procedures handled by the network actually 'add value' to the companies' business operations. Perhaps the major difference between VANs and other communication networks is that value-added networks are normally external networks that people share and subscribe to.

5.6.2   VAN provision

The organisation that sets up the VAN is concerned to market the service to people who want access to the information and services offered by the VAN. It is through the subscription charges paid by subscribers that the VAN owners make a financial return. VANs may be provided by independent organisations, trade bodies, or a co-operative of users with a common interest.

5.6.3 Competitive advantage

In previous sections of this chapter we have looked at ways in which an individual organisation can achieve a competitive advantage over its rivals. Value-added networks are different, in that they give a mutual advantage to all subscribers over those organisations that are not VAN members.

VANs run by independent providers, in order to become profitable, have to attract the maximum number of subscribers. As more and more organisations subscribe, the competitive advantage available to subscribers is lost, and VAN membership becomes the industry norm. Like all forms of competitive advantage, VAN membership gives only a temporary benefit until rivals catch up.

5.6.4 Extranets

To some extent the term extranet has replaced that of VAN, and even the term extranet is being replaced by intronet and supranet as we shall see below.

The current competitive business climate often requires a team of separate business partners to work together to meet the diverse, complicated, demands of today's markets. This team of partners has been referred to as a 'business ecosystem'. It has been suggested that only a truly cooperative group is suited to assemble the creative ideas necessary to develop complex new products, achieve manufacturing agility, and attain a long-term customer focus. Much of this cooperation can be achieved by applying Internet technology. The fairly recent emergence of extranets may bridge the gap between Intranet and Internet applications.

An extranet can be defined as 'a collaborative network that uses Intranet technology to link businesses with their suppliers, customers, and other businesses that share common goals.' An extranet can be viewed as a part of a company's Intranet that is made accessible to other companies or that is a collaboration with other companies

Extranets can be further defined as intronets and supranets.

Intronets are extranets where external trading partners receive controlled access behind the initiator's firewall and into the initiator's Intranet. These intronets are essentially inter-organisational decision support systems where an external trading partner uses a standard browser to drill down and retrieve the desired information into the client application. In this way the user controls the usage of the system, whilst the initiator controls the system content and functionality. Typically the external party will gain access to unique information contained within the initiators Intranet. If this information is particularly up to date and useful there is the possibility of locking in the trading partner and creating a long-term dependency on the information bought.

As an example, Lucent Technologies has been the primary supplier of network and switching equipment to numerous telephone companies (telcos). Lucent developed a document management system and, as such, act as the primary engineering documents manager for many telcos and is responsible for the release, up date and maintenance of documentation as it relates to the telcos network equipment configurations – including that supplied to the telcos by other vendors, often direct competitors to Lucent. With the cooperation of the telcos Lucent opened up the database to the other vendors who can, with sufficient security clearance, now access the telco's documents within Lucent's Intranet make modifications as equipment is supplied and submit the marked up version to Lucent. Lucent has created a market where it controls the functionality of the system, sets the pricing of the information goods, and provides various levels of support to the telco vendors. Lucent has created a new market where it controls pricing for various levels of system support, training, and consultation with the other telco vendors.

Supranets, by contrast, are consortium sponsored and controlled, many to many, networks set up for the mutual benefit of all members of the consortium whose long-term objective is consortium competitiveness. They are an interorganisational network providing seamless communication services between member organisations across multiple types of applications. The typical goals of these supranets are overall consortium efficiency and reduced time to market of business to business virtual team deliverables, such as new product design.

An example of a supranet is InfoTEST International – a private consortium of several major corporations that seeks to illustrate the commercial opportunities of using Internet technology (www.infotest.com/). The InfoTEST Enhanced Product Realisation project is a case study designed to illustrate the viability of using the Internet to link consortium members via a supranet in a manufacturing environment. The consortium memders collaborate in the use of computer-aided design/manufacturing systems, electronic whiteboarding, product data exchange systems and video conferencing. Whilst all of these techniques have been used within manufacturing companies before, the EPR project creates an environment where consortium members can engage in seamless interorganisational collaborative product development as a virtual work team. One of the goals is to demonstrate that the Internet, with its non-proprietary, open standards protocol, can be used to create a virtual organisation encompassing the entire value-added supply chain, even if the consortium members are using different systems internally. The primary benefit of this supranet is a dramatic reduction in time to market for new products.

With the emergence of extranets as a strategic tool to alter the company's business to business relationships, recognising the two types of extranets and their differences becomes increasingly important. While supranets promise various efficiency improvements across a business ecosystem, the opportunity for a single dominant organisation to gain competitive advantage within their ecosystem is much greater using intronets.

5.7 Using e-commerce for competitive advantage

5.7.1 What is e-commerce?

 E-commerce is the use of electronic techniques, including the Internet, to sell products and services.

In other words, e-commerce means using some form of electronic communication media to carry out business transactions. A distinction is normally drawn between e-commerce and e-marketing; the former involves buying and selling goods, while the latter normally relates to using the Internet to promote products.

E-commerce represents a relatively new method of conducting business transactions. In addition to buying and selling or exchanging products it also facilitates the provision of services and information usually through communications networks such as the Internet, Intranet and extranet. The key drivers of e-Commerce are that it has the potential to;

- Provide a range and quality of service, meeting customer demands, assist in retaining customers and gaining competive advantage by maximising revenue.

- Improving the effectiveness of supply chains that is cost reduction.
- Improving knowledge management cost reduction and differentiation and focus.

The main potential benefits are;

- To expand the marketplace to national and international – in fact to remove borders.
- To decrease the cost of creating, distributing, storing and retrieving paper based information.
- Allowing the reduction of inventory and 'pull' supply chain management.
- Enabling customisation of products and services.
- Reducing time between payment and delivery and other administrative 'drag'.
- Improve image, service, and access to information.
- Increase productivity, flexibility and reduce transport costs.

The perceived benefits for the customer are;

- improvements to service.
- personal communications, speed (and accuracy), enhanced tracking, and (potentially) 24-hour communications.
- Reductions in price.
- Better information facilitating better feedback on quality.
- Reduction in fulfilment time.
- Flexibility of offerings allowing better fit to their needs.
- Access to a global market place.

The e-Business world can be provided with the following functions;

- electronic delivery of products, services, information and payments,
- automation of business transactions and work flow,
- reduction in service costs whilst improving the speed of delivery,
- use of online services.

The usual classifications of B2B (business to business), B2C (business to consumer) have attracted the most attention in the literature so far but C2C (consumer to consumer), C2B (consumer to business) and intraorganisational e-commerce are all growing in use and impact. A notable example of C2C is EBay the auction site which is growing a dramatic rate.

B2C, such as Amazon.com is well known but a B2B e-commerce actually generates more revenue. (In fact Amazon.com has recently launched a B2B service themselves and will now host websites for small businesses.) This is particularly noticeable in the growth of digital markets which are online business transaction platforms for buyers and sellers. These new business models include auctions, aggregators, bid systems and exchanges allowing companies to form electronic relationships with their distributors, resellers, suppliers, and other partners facilitating supply chain management. These mean that the co-ordination of order generation, order taking, and order fulfillment/distribution of products, services and information can be managed more effectively and efficiently.

Typically a digital market has the potential to offer a wide variety of supplementary services as required by trading partners;

- authenticating buyers and sellers,
- streamlining procurement workflow,
- electronic payments systems,
- risk management,

- contractual and settlement services,
- conflict resolution and legal services,
- logistical services.

A company would hope to reduce purchase prices, cycle times and transaction costs by taking advantage of the digital markets liquidity and transparency.

In the case of B2C the reduced search costs of the consumer are well recognised but there are reduced 'search' costs for the seller as well by allowing the seller to communicate more efficiently, and effectively, with potential buyers. However, more complex market dynamics are likely to result form this.

A greater degree of transparency will mean that on line retailers of commodity products will find it harder to avoid competing on price. However, few goods are truly homogeneous. On-line retailers can compensate by increasing the number of product offerings and information provided since they are not constrained by physical shelf space. The resulting increase in variety offers the possibility of customisation (or perceived customisation). Dell computer is often quoted as an example of how online ordering has allowed them to provide customised products to their buyers dramatically increasing their turnover.

If this is used in conjunction with data mining (as we discussed in Chapter 4) the prospect exists of assessing customer preferences more efficiently than physical stores or catalogue vendors. Profiling technologies allow the tracking of individual consumers, both within an online store and across different websites, to create and share customer profiles, the matching of customer identities with relevant demographic information. For example, product offerings can be customised and recommendations can be made based on a consumer's attitudes, past behaviour and demographic characteristics, or through collaborative filtering systems that offer recommendations based on the feedback and experiences of consumers with a profile of likes and dislikes similar to the targeted customer.

Merchants will attempt to differentiate themselves and to create switching costs by using superior user interfaces with which users become familiar. However, some users are known to use Amazon.com's book recommendation engine to identify potential purchases and then purchase from the lower priced Buy.com.

It is likely that price discrimination will be achieved on-line by targeted non-transferable coupons that customise discounts off a high price list or by versioning in the case of information products – whereby information (particularly) is provided at different speeds, image resolutions or with different levels of in built functionality.

There will be a shifting role for intermediaries within on-line retail markets. In bricks and mortar retailing a number of intermediaries handle the distribution of the product between the original manufacturer and the final destination. Typically we might see a wholesaler, a distributor, a retailer and sometimes a finance company to help with payment together with an insurance company to offer service guarantees. With e-commerce it has been argued that these intermediary roles will be reduced or even eliminated leading to 'disintermediation'. However, it might be better to argue that there will be new types of intermediaries resulting in 'reintermediation'. For instance, the consumer selecting a new car might select a make and model based on the experience from test drives, magazine research, and recommendations from friends. The buyer might then negotiate the price, order the vehicle, and take delivery through a car dealer, arrange finance through a bank, and purchase insurance from an insurance company. By significantly lowering the transaction and distribution costs, the Internet has allowed intermediaries such as Auto-by-Tel and Microsoft's Carpoint to offer all of the above products and services, with the exception of the physical test drive. Similarly Microsoft's Expedia and Travelocity now provide a similar, aggregated, service in travel. The most likely departures form the industry value chain are likely to be wholesalers and distributors, with on line retailers dealing more directly with manufacturers.

In conclusion, whilst intermediaries that provide physical inventory buffers are likely to be squeezed by better demand information, manufacture to order, and improvements in logistics, intermediaries that provide information based services will play increasingly important roles in retail markets.

It is certain that, potentially, the future of e-Commerce means;

- a reduction in barriers to entry
- an increase in substitution of products and services
- an increase in the power of buyers
- an increase in rivalry between competitors and in the number of competitors

5.7.2 Establishing an e-commerce strategy

Developing an Internet strategy will be similar to producing a strategy for any other area of the business. This section discusses some of the issues that must be addressed by the board of an organisation which is considering establishing an e-commerce site.

The business strategy of the organisation must be determined. Checking this is essential because the IT strategy must be seen to support the overall strategy of the company, not drive it. There is also the danger of introducing incompatible systems or offering different products which are not normally expected from the company. For example, if a bank suddenly starts selling second-hand cars, then this would not be compatible with the bank's normal operations and may even harm the bank – would you buy banking products from a second-hand car dealer?

Deciding on e-commerce may have an impact on other parts of the business. For example, setting an objective of achieving a given percentage of business through the Internet will presumably decrease percentages of business in other areas. Nike found this problem in the United States where Internet sales were seen to detract from shop sales. To try and limit the fall in shop sales, an agreement was reached with retailers that the Internet price would not be discounted.

To state the obvious, an e-commerce system will need an appropriate website to be up and running to provide the service. Given the need for security, this will require specialist assistance, either by recruitment or outsourcing the writing and monitoring of the site.

The services to be offered through e-commerce must also be determined. Decisions regarding services will have a direct impact on the writing of the website, as the authors will need to ensure that the required services can be made available.

Whichever method of writing the website is chosen, budgets must be set for this activity and agreed at board level. Similarly, charges (if any) for providing services to customers must be determined. The overall business strategy is again important. If e-commerce is to be encouraged, then some discount or other benefit can be expected to attract customers to this service.

Prior to the e-commerce service being made available, it will have to be advertised. The board will need to decide where to advertise, and how much the advertising budget will be. Possibilities will include mail-shots to existing customers and advertising on the websites of other organisations.

A full cost–benefit analysis of e-commerce may also be carried out. This will help to check the feasibility of the service by identifying specific costs and benefits and also noting which other projects cannot be undertaken because money is being spent on e-commerce this year.

One of the aims of the provision of e-commerce is to try and remain competitive. A review of competitors' online sites is advisable to help determine the content and structure of the organisation's site. This review may also help to identify other areas where competitors currently have an advantage so that the board can address this.

5.7.3 Social and technological effects of the Internet

Having established an Internet site for trading, many organisations are concerned about the social and technological effects that can arise. Some of these effects are summarised below.

Social effects will include:

- Employees (and customers) increasingly handling electronic communications, rather than making personal contact in some way. Think of buying a book online. The order is placed electronically together with the payment from your credit card. The next thing that happens is the book appears in the post (hopefully!). There has been no human contact. Similarly, within the organisation, customer queries are handled by e-mail rather than by telephone. This approach may be efficient but it can also leave staff feeling demotivated and devalued when they do not talk to any live customers.
- The location of work becoming less relevant. As long as an Internet connection to a central server is available, then a person can work from any location. Work in this context may include answering e-mails from customers, preparing and sending documents online or monitoring stock levels and placing orders direct with suppliers. Increased homeworking, for example, cuts down commuting time, and in theory allows increased productivity from fewer office distractions. However, work does become completely reliant on technology and may increase demotivation because of less human contact.
- The nature of work changing. With access to increasing amounts of customer data, for example, there is the ability to tailor contact to the customers' precise requirements. Staff within an organisation may find that they are increasingly involved in data mining to extract information on customers from a central database. This will allow individual-specific communications and offers to be made. Sales staff in particular will be involved in focusing sales efforts on specific customers rather than sending general letters to all customers.

Technological effects will include:

- Direct contact between any two people or organisations. This feature removes any requirement to have intermediary organisations to sell goods, contact customers, etc. For example, Dell sell computers direct to customers rather than using shops. This means that jobs may be lost in the retail sector, while employment in telephone call centres increases. However, this may not last long as automatic call centres are already in operation for simpler products, notably ticket bookings for Virgin Trains. The supply chain becomes shorter with fewer steps between the manufacturer and the customer.
- Electronic communication being faster and more reliable than written communications. As this becomes the standard method of communication, so some companies may need to invest in the appropriate hardware and software to provide this infrastructure.
- Communication costs with customers and suppliers decreasing. There is no additional cost of sending communications to customers or purchasers as the Internet is always

available. Previously, sending an additional letter or fax or making a telephone call resulted in additional expenditure.

In summary, you may be able to identify other technological and social effects. But, this example was specifically about a web trading site! Remember in the examination, to direct your answer to the specific comments contained in the scenario; it is important to apply knowledge to specific situations rather than provide general answers.

5.7.4 Web 2.0 and social networking

Many organisations may feel that they are using the Internet and new technology to the full. However, the current rate of change will mean more to organisations than merely setting up a website and trading on the Internet. In the twenty-first century, convergent information and computer technologies are destined to transform society. With commercial and consumer access to broadband, this technology has moved far from the uses originally conceived for it. The Internet is rewriting ways of conducting business in both the B2B and the B2C sectors.

With the Internet becoming an integral part of life, it is difficult to ignore its increased usage and convenience. The increased availability of broadband connections and computers in households across the globe has made the Internet just as feasible and practical as telephones. The Internet revolution or even evolution is transforming how, with who and when we communicate. It's allowing us to 'network with people throughout the world, 24/7, 365 days a year' (Goldsmith, 2008). It has become a standard for communication, networking, entertainment and doing business for people of all ages.

'The Internet has brought a participatory quality to any and every online pursuit' (Riegner, 2007), which has resulted in ubiquitous social or Web 2.0 sites. Tim O'Reily first created the term 'Web 2.0' in 2004 as 'the business revolution in the computer industry caused by the move to the Internet as platform, and an attempt to understand the rules for success on that new platform'. Web 2.0 isn't really a thing, it's more a description of the second generation of websites and web applications that have really changed how we use the Internet over the past few years. These include wikis, blogs, social networking sites, content sharing sites and so forth. 'The whole notion of Web 2.0 is that it connects people, versus Web 1.0, which connects documents' (Franklin, 2008).

John Seeley Brown, in his paper *Learning 2.0: The Big Picture*, introduces the notion of 'learning-to-be' where he states society is no longer learning by just being instructed by a figure of authority but by engaging in productive inquiry via participation. He further continues that in today's rapidly changing world there is a demand to extract or 'pull' tacit knowledge, whereas in the past, explicit knowledge was pushed. Proving true to his theory, society is actively pursuing tools that allow them to move away from traditional means of learning and allow them to quickly research and enhance their understanding for themselves. As a result, Web 2.0 technology grows more popular empowering people to create, distribute and share their thoughts and developments with others – in effect, providing them the opportunity to act on their creativity and introduce new ideas.

It seems that some of the predictions in the foreword of *The Cluetrain Manifesto* (Levin 1999), which talks about the beginning of 'a powerful global conversation,' in which people share information 'with blinding speed.' Are coming true.

The development of digital cameras embedded in mobile telephones is adding yet another dimension to people's ability to communicate.

These developments need to be interpreted creatively and imaginatively by organisations. For example, the impact of the Internet on book sales is not uniform. Some directories and reference books have, in effect, ceased to exist as people gain this type of reference information directly from the Internet. In some cases, the website has completely replaced the paper based version of the guide. In others it operates in tandem. Consumers now use comparison websites to seek out those products which exactly meet their requirements and their budget. Since these websites also have the facility for consumers to rank the products they have bought they become a powerful tool for the PR department of organisations. If a customer does post a critical review of one of the company's products then a swift remedy to their complaint is needed if the company is to maintain its reputation.

Whilst consumers may be happy to buy the latest blockbuster book online from Amazon. (It may be where you bought this learning system), in some cases customers will always want the ability to browse and to make a more considered purchase. There will still be the place for book shops, however a book addict is looking for a shopping *experience* and specialist shops are adapting to this, leading to trends such as coffee shops within bookshops to provide the right atmosphere and give shoppers an offline experience, the real joy of book buying. It is even more important now for companies to understand the buying decision of their customers – do they just want the utility value of the product in which case online sales will be fine – or do they want an experience, in which case a bricks and mortar offering will be better.

If you did buy this manual online you will also be aware that there are online learning products that complement it. The days of simply producing a website that contains 'additional material' are gone, consumers (and learners) are expecting exciting, interactive, material to help them study.

Of all the aspects of the technological environment, none has changed as rapidly as communications technology. Mobile phones, the Internet, cable television and media messaging mean that we can now contact pretty much anyone, pretty much anytime. 'What this means is that you are no longer the sole author of your brand. Social media involves participatory content. You need to get over your fear of that and be a participant in the dialogue yourself' (Franklin, 2008).

Social media

These types of sites represent a new mode of production and distribution for media. 'It used to be that the ability to create content and distribute it to an audience was limited to individuals and organisations that owned the production facilities and infrastructure to do so. In other words: the media, TV networks, newspapers and record companies or freelancers in these areas were often sole content generators because of their capability and tools to create media for their audiences. At present with continuous innovation in digital technology, tools are now available to allow average users become content producers. In addition, complementary products such as digital cameras, laptops and broadband access have become reasonably low in cost further supporting content creation.

Social media also facilitates the distribution of content, making it easier for content creators to reach their audience and users attain information easily. Search engines, such as Google which dominates the area, allow users to easily find information by typing in keywords related to their subject of interest. Technorati a similar, but more specialised service, to Google focuses its search engine on blogs versus the general web. As general search results are largely determined and listed by relevance, Technorati's blog search considers content most recently updated in their results. RSS (really simple syndication) technology further helps pulling content of interest which alleviates the need to regularly visit a site or blog. RSS feeds, based on subscriptions, allow users to receive regular updates from specific news sites, forums and blogs. As a result of these type of tools, social media sites driven on user generated content have become immensely popular and convenient to use.

Content on social media sites can be formed from text, images, audio or video but typically utilise a combination of these forms. For example, music and video content can be fused to produce a new outlook from the original piece of music or video resulting in a mash-up. There are many social media sites and types in existence today and with rapid innovations in technology, will continue to grow. Popular social media sites currently on offer fall into one of the following categories.

Blogs are online journals, diaries or newsletters. Presented with a casual, conversational tone of writing, they can cover any subject matter and are frequently updated with the latest entries shown first. A comment section is usually included in blogs for readers to provide feedback, suggestions or share their opinion on the subject matter. They can also be subscribed to via e-mail or some type of RSS feed updating subscribers of new content. Easy to create, service providers such as Google's Blogger or Typepad offer blogging services free of charge. Many blogs are personal in nature as people use them to describe their everyday lives, travel adventures, significant life experiences or anything else they wish to share. Businesses also use blogs to present an informal side to the business. These can be used internally or externally to build a network of people interested in the company and promote positive publicity. News sites are increasingly using blogs outside their main mode of delivery to reach a growing mobile, tech-savvy audience. There are many other types of blogs ranging from fashion and media to political in nature.

Microblogging technology is also available to those that choose to blog but would like to keep it brief. Microblogging sites such as Twitter offer this service by allowing blog entries up to 140 characters, instantly updating your friends or followers of the latest entry. In Twitter's case, the service supports mobile, instant messaging and web platforms making it easily accessible.

Podcasts are audio or video files available on the Internet for download or streaming. Uploads of music and videos can be subscribed to via podcasts enabling content owners to create a virtual audience. Apple's iTunes service offers podcasts from individual content owners and businesses such as media companies looking to broaden their audience reach. Some companies are now explaining their annual reports on podcasts – getting the message across to an audience that is time poor.

Wikis are user contributed content sites most often used for either public or private information sharing. Wikipedia, the most common public wiki site, allows people to contribute to the online encyclopedia without restrictions. Although useful, it is important to know the information contributed may not necessarily be factual. However, their use in collaborative ventures amongst project teams is reliable and useful.

Content community sites are based on the sharing of one particular type of content. Similar to social networking sites, registration and establishing a profile are necessary to begin using the service. These sites create a network amongst individuals sharing and looking for a specific type of content. Popular content community sites like YouTube and Flickr are examples of sites that focus on specific type of content. YouTube, owned by Google, provides video content sharing. The site allows users to easily upload videos to the site for others to access. Videos can be marked as favourites, linked to others and even embedded in other social media sites like blogs. Increasingly the film studios and television companies are releasing material on YouTube as a means of promoting their product and raising awareness. Flickr, owned by Yahoo, provides image content sharing. Photos can be uploaded, shared and organised directly on the site. Unlike typical photo sharing sites, Flickr allows users to easily explore photos uploaded by others. Search capabilities also make it easy to find a certain type of image or photo.

Forums provide an area for online discussion somewhat a cross between blogging and content communities. Each forum presents a specific subject area allowing for discussion via threads or strings of comments. Incorporated into other sites or stand alone, forums are monitored by an administrator who initiates discussion but then relinquishes the flow of discussion to members. Forums can be useful in gaining advice on a particular subject or engaging in debate on more serious topics. Yahoo Answers, a service akin to forums, allows users to ask a question in a forum environment and receive answers either by searching through a list of categories or having users respond. The question asked can remain active for a specified times (i.e. 4 days a week) and answer responses are then either voted by forum members as the best answer or chosen yourself.

Apart from social media sites, there is also social media technology supporting these sites. Bookmarking technology from providers such as del.icio.us allows users to reference sites and pages through an online account. Synonymous to an Internet browser's book-marks, this service allows users to make their 'favourites' mobile. Tagging or tags is another service used throughout social media sites such as social networking and content communities. Tagging are keywords applied to a specific piece of content such as images or audio making it easier to organise and search. Finally, instant messaging (IM) technology allows real-time communication between single or a group of individuals using the Internet. IM technology uses text and audio and can be incorporated into other services such as e-mail or stand alone like Skype. So popular, IM technology can replace telephone communication as it allows for cost-effective global communication either via computer-to-computer or phone-to-computer peripherals.

Social networks

As humans we have always networked but 'The major difference today is how easy it is to communicate with your network via the Web. Some research has pointed out that the maximum number of active network members is [around] 150. But that research was done before the Internet. Today, it may be possible to establish and maintain a much larger network – maybe with thousands of members – because the technology is widely available to assist in managing a network contact base, plus e-mail makes it so easy to communicate actively with a large number of network members' (Goldsmith, 2008).

Social networking, one of the most popular aspects of social media, is facilitating the way people connect and build networks via the Internet. Social networking sites are largely based on the theory of six degrees of separation by Hungarian writer Frigyes Karinthy and later updated by US psychologist Stanley Milgram. The theory proposed that anyone in the world is connected to anyone else in the world by no more than five or six acquaintances. Social networks close in on the geographical distance between acquaintances allowing people all over the world to get to know one another, in effect making the world a smaller place. A study recently undertaken by 0_2, part of Telefonica Europe, revealed that the original concept of six degrees of separation is now out of date. The research showed that each individual is usually part of three main networks; family, friendship and work. Personal interests based on hobbies, sports, music and demographics can form, on average, five additional affiliated networks. From interviews with people ranging across different age groups, the research concluded 'the growth of these shared interest networks and the influence of technology on them has reduced the degrees of separation from six to three'. Studies done by Microsoft also provide further evidence of degrees of separation changing because of technology, specifically the Internet.

The success of social networking sites has boomed, namely sites such as MySpace and Facebook. By the end of 2007, MySpace claimed 10 million plus unique users a month and Facebook 7 million. 'On 26 August 2008, Facebook reached 100 million users, a feat which Myspace claims to have achieved back in 2006' (Thayne, 2008). MarketWatch (2007) has stated global active memberships in social networking sites were expected to reach 230 million at the end of 2007. Most social networking sites are restriction-free and do not discriminate on age, gender, ethnic background and thus attract users from around the world. Despite contrary belief, they are not just used by young people but are available and cater to all sorts of people, cultures and groups. Due to wide arrays of interest, it is not uncommon for users to be active members of one, if not more, social networking sites.

But why are social networking sites so popular? First of all, social networking sites are generally free. Creating a free account is often the only thing that is required prior to becoming an active member. Once an account is created users must create a profile. Profiles can be limited to basic information such as name, age, location or include detailed information including personal, professional, social interests and/or photo(s).

With an active profile, users can begin creating their network – adding people they know or may not personally know but whom they share a common interest with. Networks can be formed on groups of people who have similar interests, beliefs, hobbies or any sort of common bond. Examples of interest driven sites can range from dating, professional, music, religious, political or fashion sites. Building a network can be done by browsing the site's user base, searching for people by name, screen name or e-mail address. It is this process of creating a network that is the underlying strategy to any social networking site.

Secondly, being part of an online network provides a sense of belonging be it with current friends or new friends. Current friends can keep in touch despite the physical distance and keep others informed of their whereabouts and activities. By updating their status, friends can see what their friends are currently doing, feeling or even wandering. Social networking sites help people who are socially inept to overcome their hesitations by replacing face-to-face interaction. Users can contact new people by poking or sending a message to become friends and not have to fear rejection. If the recipient does not poke back or reply there is no harm done, as there are still a million-some other people to befriend. Meeting new people for the first time in person can also bring on worries associated with physical appearances and proper etiquette. These fears are no longer applicable by using social networking sites. In short, you can make less of an effort to maintain friends as Thayne (2008) states.

Lastly and most importantly, the technology that social networking sites provide facilitates communication, interaction and satisfies our curiosity. These sites in a way can replace e-mail, phone and in-person contact altogether. Messaging is a basic function of most social networking sites and can be done by sending a composed e-mail or even a quick ping. Live chat is also available at some sites for immediate communication. Posting comments or messages on a friend's profile allows not only them to see what you have posted but others based on your viewing settings. Some sites are devised to allow users to comment, suggest or express their opinions on certain subject matters. User contributed sites such as Yelp provides valuable information on what restaurants, shops, places to visit, which, tied to a mobile phone and GIS offers opportunities for advertisers. These types of sites allow users to comment on their experiences and provide others with helpful reviews. An extension of this functionality is forums or blogs that are available to the public and are user contributed reviews, views or commentary on specific topics.

Niche social networking

More recently, smaller more focused social networking sites have begun to surface. These sites, outside the appeal of mass-market players such as Facebook and Myspace, can offer a more viable business model and are referred to as niche social networking sites. 'Niche social networking sites have the same tools as the major ones, but there's a desire to have a more honed group, a more specific network with whom you're interacting, so you're a little more exclusive' (Corcoran, 2007). Niche social networking sites offer users pertinent information and value to their specific interests via the ability to connect with others that share that same interest. As privacy is a growing concern for social networking site users, niche social networking sites offer an opportunity to build a network amongst a community that they purposely want to interact with and trust. This more intimate network prevents users from over exposing themselves on larger sites and helps maintain a more private online presence.

Realizing the opportunity niche social networks can offer, companies such as Ning have developed infrastructure to facilitate their growth. Ning offers a free platform for developing social networking sites loaded with general functionality typically expected from such a site – posting comments, sharing of photos and videos, building a network, etc. Using a theme of 'Create your own social network for anything', Ning's technology has resulted in the creation of over 230,000 sites from users around the world. Many of these sites have been taken up by SME's in a bid to develop an increased awareness of their products and services.

Niche social networking sites are popular because they target a community seeking specific value. They offer members information, advice and the opportunity to share their ideas and opinions on subject matter which is important to them. By focusing on the needs of a smaller community, niche social networks offer its members a more enriched experience and the opportunity to express themselves amongst a more close-knit community. Available to a wide array of interests, niche social networks can be based on business, dating, friendship or specific hobbies. As larger sites, those with a larger number of members, try to appeal to the wider public they may not offer purpose as niche social networks do.

LinkedIn, www.linkedin.com, an example of a niche social networking site, focuses on career development. The site offers the same general functionality as any other social networking site but its point of differentiation lies within its community. Professionals looking to build their business network or people looking to explore job opportunities drive LinkedIn's success. As all of LinkedIn's members have a common interest, building business contacts, the site has become a useful tool for business networking. Members start by creating a profile based on their professional history and build a CV which highlights their work experience and accomplishments. The question and answer section on the service allows members to develop expertise and to demonstrate their expertise to potential employers and clients. *The author maintains a profile on LinkedIn and is an open networker.* Then by either searching or inviting contacts to join their network, members ask colleagues, superiors and subordinates to endorse their professional qualities. As members seeking job opportunities may message those from a company of interest, these endorsements provide a point of reference ability. Members can also join groups that are of particular interest to them and stay informed of the group's activity. LinkedIn's purpose is to help professionals build their network to aid in career development and the value it offers is providing a source of people who can help achieve that.

This leads to huge challenges for companies, for example:

- Word-of-mouth on new products can grow exponentially. Viral marketing means that a weak product can be 'found out' in a matter of hours, whereas a strong product can 'stock out' in the same period. Particularly via comparison sites and 'blogs' where people write, effectively, their diary and views on anything they wish to talk about.
- On the Internet, your nearest rival is only 'one click' away. Customers are now less loyal, both to products and retailers, than they have ever been. Price comparison takes seconds, feature comparison a few seconds more.
- To combat the 'fickle' nature of online shoppers, organisations are now concentrating on creating a 'digital footprint' by means of Web 2.0 tools (blogs and wikis) and by creating online communities through social networking sites such as MySpace.

Virtual conferencing

Web conferencing as a communication service has come of age, with many companies adopting it for crucial meetings with clients, analysts and the press. It is fast becoming a key factor in cutting costs and improving operational efficiency for many organisations. They have started accepting the enormous possibilities opened by this service.

The biggest advantage of web conferencing is that it is a virtual conferencing tool that enables you to productively and cost-effectively engage in your most important business with just a phone and a web browser. Unlike audio conferencing involving only voice communication, and video conferencing, which requires considerable investments, web conferencing acts as a virtual meeting place by sharing both voice and data of any kind simultaneously to multiple users at multiple locations.

Its features include presentation sharing, document sharing, file transfer, web browser sharing and white boarding (allows users to write and draw on an unlimited number of shared pages that can be saved and printed).

Today, web conferencing has evolved from being a hi-tech tool for conducting virtual meetings to a business tool catering to different stakeholders. Some of the commonly used web conferencing applications are in sales and marketing conferences, training programmes, forecasting and reviews, software demos, software testing, product launches, global meetings and business development.

The potential of such a service was recognised by Yahoo, 'Seeing an increasing demand for alternatives to traditional in-person business meetings, Internet portal Yahoo! Inc. launched new Internet broadcasting packages that will be available through the broadband services unit of its business communications division'. The Sunnyvale, a California-based company, avoided mentioning the events of Sept 11, but said that with travel and meeting costs rising and the recent travel restrictions, it is introducing Virtual Conference services and launching an Executive Communications Center. 'Yahoo!'s solutions will allow companies to continue vital communications that were centered around large scale meetings and maintain critical and focused outreach to customers, sales forces and business partners,' said Jim Fanella, senior vice president of Yahoo!'s Business and Enterprise Services division.

It's also a step in the direction of monetizing the franchise, which Yahoo! has been working hard to do in the face of a decline in Internet advertising. It recently upgraded its other corporate offerings and recently launched two new fee-based packages at its GeoCities unit – GeoCities Pro and GeoCities Webmaster.

Yahoo! said 'The Virtual Conference solution combines audio, video, informational slides synched to presentations and a browser to view other meetings associated with the same conference; interactive tools for polling, question and answer, document sharing and audience surveys; registration, live attendance tracking and post event reporting on attendees; and archiving and hosting.'

The argument used to justify the introduction of any new technology is 'it will reduce costs'. But is this true? Certainly technology, and particularly that related to information systems, has the *potential* to reduce costs through reductions in staff levels (as we automate processes that previously were manual) or the reduction in overheads (such as office or data transport costs). However, if we try to assess the real cost impact of these technologies, quite often we find that the direct cost reductions have been more than offset by additional costs elsewhere (in support services such as administration or IT, for example).

The other problem with using technology to reduce cost is that everyone else is doing it, too!

As soon as such technology becomes the norm in our industry, someone will pass part (or all) of the cost reduction on to the customer in terms of reduced price. Others will follow suit, and soon every competitor matches the new price level, and any impact on profitability is lost.

If we cannot look to cost reductions for an increase in economic sustainability, then what about the benefits of technology? Perhaps the greatest potential impacts are in the areas of customer and employee relations:

- From the point of view of the customer, many of the benefits of technology manifest themselves in improved customer satisfaction. This should lead to improved loyalty, a higher level of business, and therefore increased profits.
- Technologies, if used wisely, should increase staff engagement. This should lead to reduced staff turnover, improved motivation levels and improved productivity. This, in turn, should result in improved profits for the organisation.

5.8 The need for information systems strategies

This section looks at the background to, and development of, strategies for the information system, information technology and information management.

5.8.1 Background

Until quite recently, most organisations regarded their IT systems and their information systems as a resource that was necessary but not strategically significant. The IT department was treated like any other collection of overheads, and the information systems allowed to evolve rather than being formally planned.

5.8.2 Why have a strategy for the IS?

Robson (1997) notes that

Despite a history of neglected planning, IS needs effective strategic planning as much as, and perhaps more than, other functional are as. Just as other functional areas do, IS consumes a portion of the organisation's finite resources. Without a clear view of value (the aim of planning) the allocation of resources is unlikely to match that value.

Many organisations now realise that the information system is a strategic resource, and should be treated as such. This often includes having a formal strategy.

The information system should have its own strategy, as part of the overall corporate strategy, for the following reasons:

- the information system is an adaptive, open system;
- the organisation exists in a dynamic environment;
- information needs are constantly changing;
- the organisation relies upon the information system in order to construct its strategic plan;
- the information system requires significant investment over a long period;
- the information system and information technology can help the organisation achieve a competitive advantage (see Sections 5.3 and 5.4).

5.8.3   Benefits of a formal strategy

The major benefits of a formal information systems strategy are the following:

- we can achieve goal congruence between the information systems objectives and the corporate objectives;
- the organisation is more likely to be able to create and sustain a competitive advantage;
- the high level of expenditure on information systems will be more focused on supporting key aspects of the business; and
- developments in IT can be exploited at the most appropriate time (which is not always when they are first available).

5.8.4   IS, IT and IM strategy

Some authors, including Earl (1989), distinguish between the components of strategy as shown in Figure 5.4. To Earl, the three components (or levels) of strategy are as follows:

1. *IS strategy*, which looks at the way in which the information systems in various parts of the organisation are organised;
2. *IT strategy*, which looks at the technology infrastructure of the systems;
3. *IM strategy*, which considers how the systems support management processes.

   In this chapter we use the term 'information systems strategy' to encompass all three of these components.

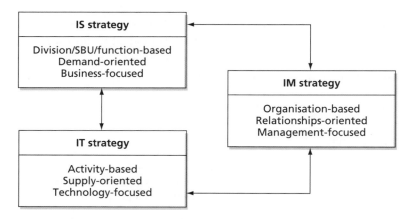

Figure 5.4   Three levels of strategy (adapted from Earl, 1989)

5.8.5   Content of IS, IT and IM strategies

It is unlikely that the IS, IT and IM strategies will remain unchanged within an organisation over any significant period of time. Strategies may need amending for various reasons including:

- change in the overall objectives of the organisation;
- development of new information technologies;
- update of existing hardware and software;
- change in the number of employees, resulting in existing systems not coping with new information requirements.

Whatever the reason for the change, it is important that some formal process is followed to ensure that the IS and business objectives remain in alignment. In the worst case scenario, the IT department may decide that some new technology is useful, and implement this. However, if it does not support the overall business objectives of the organisation, then the business may not be able to operate successfully.

A general strategy to follow when information systems require amendment is outlined below.

Initially, the business strategy of the organisation must be determined. Checking this strategy is essential, because the IT strategy must support this strategy and not drive it. Just because new IT systems may be available does not mean that they have to be used in the organisation. Also, new IT systems may not be compatible with other software or hardware used in the organisation. Additional checks will be necessary to confirm compatibility.

Within any organisation, amending part of the information strategy may have an impact on other sections. For example, if information is suddenly provided in a different format, it may no longer be accessible by other divisions or branches. Amendments to the information strategy must be checked against the business plan and individual requirements of each part of the organisation.

Having decided to amend the IS strategy in some way, a plan for developing and implementing the system will have to be developed. As well as setting out the plan in an appropriate manner (SSDAM*, etc. may be useful here) alternative hardware and software as well as development methods may need to be considered. The choice will be between development in-house or outsourcing. A full cost–benefit analysis may also be used now, or earlier in the change process, to check that the change will provide the necessary benefits to the organisation at an acceptable cost.

The Structured Systems Analysis and Design methodology (SSDAM) is an established software design methodology

Having determined the overall strategy for change, this can be implemented and systems amended. Checks may also be required to ensure that staff and customers are kept fully informed. Particularly where the change will result in some competitive advantage, advertising that the change has taken place will be essential.

The IM, IS, and IT revolution, now progressing on a global scale with the rapid advancement of computer and communications technologies, is bringing about a historic transformation of society, much like the Industrial Revolution did from the eighteenth century in the United Kingdom. The Industrial Revolution transformed the world from an agricultural society to an industrial society with the advancement of power technologies starting from the invention of the steam engine, and it revolutionised socio-economic

STRATEGIC IMPLICATIONS OF IT

activities of individuals, businesses and governments. The advancement in information system technologies, primarily the Internet, has enhanced the quality of information exchanges and revolutionised relationships between individuals, between individuals and organisations, and between individuals and society, by drastically reducing the costs and time for information distribution. This will result in the rapid transformation to a knowledge-emergent society, where the interaction of knowledge will evolve to create high added value as will discuss later in the chapter.

As we have said, any information strategy needs to be placed in the wider context of an overall Business Strategy.

In many Global organisations the business strategy shapes the information strategy and the IT strategy in turn shapes the information systems strategy, which shapes the information management strategy. Organisations should design strategies and policies that enable them to succeed within their chosen market, competitive, and regulatory environment. When devising those model strategies the Information Systems Manager (ISM) can help bring balance to strategic discussions by adhering to the model and educating others to employ this best-practice analytical approach.

Any strategy cannot be evaluated by success alone (because success is the result of both good planning and excellent execution) additional predictive, qualitative analysis is also required. The model provides a useful template for these forward-looking questions, particularly the common requirements vision document that enables strategists to test for the following three success factors:

- Predicting major areas of managerial choice, such that alternative scenarios can be created and risk factors identified.
- Understanding the degree to which business and IT decision makers agree on strategic assumptions, goals, policies and supporting investments.
- Accurately identifying the resources required to implement strategic choices far enough in advance to avoid risky programs to acquire, redeploy, or trim them. The current panicked efforts by many enterprises to restructure organisations and slash spending are evidence of failure to test for implement ability.

5.9 Collaborative strategies

Organisations that adopt a collaborative approach to the development and critical analysis of strategy will enhance their ability to allocate resources in a sophisticated way, managing risk and enhancing value delivery.

5.9.1 Business Information Strategies – Corporate Partnerships and Alliances

Alliances have been made possible, initially, by the growth in data communications. With the expansion of the Internet many more possibilities are created. There are four common types of Information Partnership (Alliance). These are:

Joint Marketing Partnerships

The first kind of alliance is where the organisations are in different market sectors sharing their information to the benefit of all. The best known examples are the SABRE and GALILEO systems where airlines, hotel chains, car hire companies and theatres have all combined to allow a single booking system to access, through data communications, the booking systems of the individual participants. Hence a customer can be offered the facility of having a complete trip being organised from one booking. In addition any information supplied is retained ready for use when booking any subsequent trip (known as a customer profile and used also by Information Agents). In 2000 the concept of the Joint Marketing Alliance has been subsumed into the concept of the macro-system and the virtual organisation.

Intra-Industry Partnerships

In this case the partners are all in the same market sector. Previously they have been in competition (and still are) but they could see cost reductions arising if they all work together. One example is the Insurance Industry where the major insurance companies have combined together to launch the IVANS system. This is a system available to insurance brokers which allows the broker to generate a single package (covering, say, house, contents, car, travel and medical insurance) for a client by searching the offerings of the different insurance companies and selecting the best offering for the client from each of the categories.

The prospective partners might have been separated by geography. With the opening of the channel tunnel there is an opening for English and French estate agents to sell properties on behalf of each other in their own countries. By establishing a data communications link both English and French properties could be available in both locations as soon as they come on the market.

Customer–Supplier Partnerships

This is the situation where a supplier and a customer join together for the benefit of both. It is seen most commonly in the car industry (where dealers are tied to manufacturers) or in the brewing industry (where pubs are tied to brewers). In the case of the car industry, the partnership deal allows the car company to offer substantial marketing advantages to the dealer. Although, from an environmental screening point (which we covered in Chapter 2) it is worth noting that the EU is trying to introduce legislation to prevent car manufacturers from having exclusive relationships with dealers allowing dealers to sell any brand of car they chose.

IT Vendor Driven Partnerships

This kind of partnership is not necessarily restricted to IT but the best example of recent time has been an IT example. It is the kind of partnership where two organisations in different disciplines (but in the same market sector) come together to create and market a new product. One example was Microsoft and IBM. The IBM PC was launched with IBM providing the hardware and Microsoft providing the software. This partnership has certainly worked to the benefit of Microsoft; now one of the largest companies in the world. IBM however has now disposed of its PC business to Lenovo a Chinese company.

5.10 Developing an information systems strategy

This section looks at different approaches that the organisation might adopt to develop a strategy for its information systems.

5.10.1   General planning models

A number of approaches could be taken to formulating an information systems strategy. One approach is to use a generalised business planning model such as those discussed in *Integrated Management* and used to structure most of the chapters in this learning system. If you decide to use such a model, remember that the thing you are planning for is the information system. If you talk about environment analysis, you are referring to the environment of the information system, not of the organisation. Similarly, if you discuss objectives you should look at the objectives of the information system, and so on.

5.10.2   The link between corporate strategy and IS strategy

Earl (1989) says:

We are trying to connect the exploitation of IT, which is in itself complex, rapidly changing, and often not well understood by managers, to development of business strategies where neither the principles nor the methods are yet agreed. Paradoxically, in seeking to bridge these two problematic and somewhat unstructured streams, the desire seems to be to find a structured methodology.

Many writers have explored the relationship between the information system and corporate strategies. It is clear that the information system should support the corporate strategy, but to what extent should it be allowed to determine it?

There are a number of ways in which the information system can influence the corporate strategy:

- developments in IT might provide the organisation with opportunities (e.g. the growth of the Internet);
- the information system will provide information to allow the corporate strategy to be formulated; and
- the organisation might decide to use IT, or the information system outputs, to pursue competitive advantage as we have seen in the earlier sections of this chapter.

Ward suggests that there is a complex relationship and complete set of inter-dependencies between the corporate strategy, the information systems strategy and the impact of information technology. This is illustrated in Figure 5.5, which shows clearly

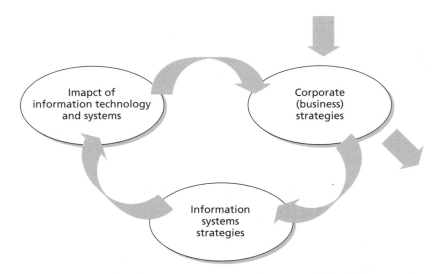

Figure 5.5   Relationships between strategies and systems (adapted from Ward (1987))

that the information systems and IT are developed as a result of the corporate strategy but also, to some extent, influence it.

5.10.3 Limitations of strategic planning models

The limitations of strategic planning models have been discussed earlier in the pillar, but it is worth noting the following main points. Whichever model is used within an organisation, there will always be some limitations. It is important to recognise these because they may have an effect on the overall reliance that can be placed on that particular model. Being aware of the limitations also helps to ensure that the model is used appropriately.

Many of the limitations will relate to the future or the assumptions within the model itself. It is extremely unlikely that the model itself will be flawed by containing incorrect formulae, etc. although this has been known to happen. This should not be the case since few organisations find themselves in a deterministic situation. As Galbraith said 'The sole purpose of economic forecasting is to make astrology look respectable'.

Some of the limitations inherent within any planning model are outlined below.

- Most models assume that the future will continue in the same way as the past. In other words, if an organisation has a specific number of branches or workers then unless the model assumes otherwise, these factors will remain unchanged. If they do change, then the results of the model will be less reliable. Changes may occur, of course, due to unforeseen circumstances. In this case the entire model will need to be re-worked to produce a new and reliable set of results.
- The model will tend to produce less accurate predictions, the further into the future it attempts to forecast. This is simply because the future is uncertain, and many changes will take place which cannot be forecasted or incorporated into the model. At this point look back to Section 3.6. Similarly, even known variables may become more inaccurate; for example, the inflation rate is known now, but forecasting this 12 or 24 months in advance will be difficult.
- The model itself may not provide information for a sufficiently long period of time. For example, some industries such as forestry work with extremely long time horizons of years rather than months. It may simply not be worth producing a model for these industries because the information provided will be effectively unreliable, given the uncertainties mentioned above.
- All models require tailoring to the specific industry before the information can be relied on. For example, there is a general rate of inflation, but it may be more appropriate to use an inflation rate specific to that particular industry. In the United Kingdom, for example, the general inflation rate is low, but the house price inflation rate is significantly higher. If a house builder is trying to forecast how much the selling prices of new houses will rise, then the specific house price inflation rate needs to be used.

5.10.4 An IS planning model

Figure 5.6 shows an adaptation of the model used by IBM to advise their customers on how to formulate a strategy for their information systems. This model has advantages over most alternatives:

- It shows clearly the relationship between the corporate strategy of the organisation and the information systems strategy. From the corporate plan we should be able to identify the information needs of the organisation, and assess how they are likely to change over the period of the strategic plan. The objective (or mission) of the information system is clearly to satisfy these changing information needs.

- It shows the component parts of the information systems strategy as three separate architectures. These are explained in more detail below, but the model shows both the order in which these architectures should be designed and the relationships between them.

The component architectures of the information system strategy, as outlined in Figure 5.6, are:

1. *Information and data architecture.* We always design and specify systems by starting with the outputs and working backwards. This is because the outputs determine the inputs and not vice versa. In designing the data and information architecture we must consider:
   - what information will be required;
   - when it will be required;
   - how it will be provided;
   - to whom it will be provided;
   - how data should be stored to provide easy access;
   - what data items should be collected and what is the most appropriate source for each item;
   - when it will be collected;
   - how the data will be collected.
2. *Applications architecture.* This considers the applications (or processes) required in order to turn the data collected into the information required, specifically:
   - what applications are required;
   - what the most logical sequence is in which those applications might be performed.
3. *IT architecture.* The IT hardware, software, peripherals and networks then become a set of tools that are used to collect data, perform applications, store data and provide information. IT is only required for these tasks if the benefits of using it clearly outweigh the costs.

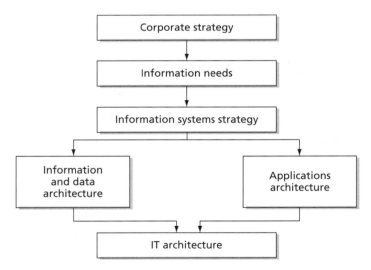

Figure 5.6 Strategic planning for the information system (adapted from Behrsin, Mason and Sharpe (1994))

5.10.5 Alternative models

You will remember from your earlier studies that Mintzberg (1994) is not a great believer in formal models and makes the point that

Search all those strategic planning diagrams – all those interconnected boxes that supposedly give you strategies – and nowhere will you find a single one that explains the creative act of synthesising ideas into strategy. Everything can be formalised except the very essence of the process itself.

In the examination you are free to use any reasonable or appropriate model of strategic planning in advising an organisation. It is not important to memorise these diagrams in order to reproduce them perfectly but you should have a clear system in your mind so that you do not waste time creating a system in the examination. Questions are more likely to require you to recommend a strategy than ask you to explain how one should be formulated. This is the real challenge, as it requires a high degree of familiarity with applying the models rather than a perfect recall of them.

5.11 The changing role of the IT department

This section looks at the changing role of the IT department and uses as a basis the first four stages of Nolan's evolution model (see Section 5.1.5). It then looks at some more recent developments in IT organisation.

5.11.1 Initiation/contagion

The earliest applications of IT in business were not thought out or planned in advance. They were a response to the technology first becoming available, and those initiating the adoption of IT were often users (most commonly in the finance department).

In this situation, sometimes still found in smaller organisations, there is no such thing as an IT department. This causes major problems for the organisation as its dependence on IT grows.

5.11.2 Control

This is the stage at which the IT department first becomes formalised. In many organisations this stage occurred in the 1960s, with the formation of a 'data processing department' or 'computer section'. This model of the IT department has a fairly rigid structure based around data preparation, data input or 'operations', and the systems development activities of analysis and programming.

The focus of this sort of structure is on operating the system, not on the way the technology supports the organisational activities.

5.11.3 Integration

It is only at the integration stage of Nolan's model that we find real dialogue between the IT specialists and the system end-users. Often the IT department staff are organised into functional teams, each of which supports a different function of the business. So, for example, the IT department might consist of a finance team, a production team and so on.

This type of structure has an obvious advantage in that it clearly supports user requirements, but it also leads to a risk that the various functional systems might not integrate into a corporate whole. In most organisations this is achieved by implementing some form of matrix structure (see the *P5 Integrated Management learning system* for details) under the control of an IT or IS director.

How an MIS department is organised in physical terms is often dictated by the organisation (functional and physical) of the company, which it serves. Examples are:

(a) *Star organisation*. This is mirrored in the retail department store. Here every store and every warehouse performs almost identical functions. Hence there is little role for local development, or even local management information, at the grass roots level. It makes sense for the MIS department to be sited at head office and for the only local user support to be of a training nature. One, or two, member(s) of staff could be specially trained as trainers and instructors.

(b) *Partially distributed organisation*. Consider, say, the vehicle manufacturer who makes family cars in one location, sports cars in another, vans in a third and heavy goods vehicles in a fourth. In this case each division is using the same computer functions (CAD, CIM, inventory control, production control, etc.) but they are using them on almost totally different data. Hence it makes sense for software to be specified and/or developed centrally but for all processing to take place locally. Each site will have its own operations centre and its own information centre but most of the large software packages will be acquired and/or generated centrally.

(c) *Fully distributed organisation*. In any virtual organisation it is inevitable that the IT function will be fully distributed. There may be a justification for common software but there is no management structure to enforce it. It may be that the component contractors in the business have their own mainframes or they may be using bureau services. Overall management, in this case, must be restricted to information sharing over some common network, such as the use of EDI over a virtual private network. Even in cohesive businesses distribution of the IT operation might be fully distributed as a result of merging a large number of wholly incompatible systems. This has been found to be a serious drawback and the emphasis today is on information integration.

5.11.4 Downsizing and rightsizing the IT department

The development of the PC and the growth of end-user computing in the 1980s led many organisations to question the need for large IT departments. There was a general feeling that the organisation was serving the IT department rather than vice versa.

This led many organisations to radically slim down their IT departments (or downsize them), which led to drastic cost reductions and widespread celebration among frustrated system users. However, there were serious consequences for the organisation as end-users began to develop their own IT solutions.

The main risks in reducing the size of the IT department are:

- the organisation might lose the ability to maintain or develop major systems that might have strategic benefit;
- the organisation will lose the knowledge of key staff, and may be unable to repair or modify existing systems;
- the controls over the information system may be relaxed, leading to increasing error and failure rates; and

- the organisation may have to incur significant costs to replace staff with external consultants in times of crisis.

What transpired was that end user computing worked well for non integrated applications such as spreadsheets and small databases (Microsoft Access for example) but not for larger databases involved in delivering consolidated accounts, customer relationship management or managing organisation wide procurement.

The consequence of these problems was that organisations began to plan their IT systems and IT departments carefully, and to determine the optimum scale of support required (rightsizing). Often this involved the provision of services to end-users through the establishment of an 'information centre'.

5.11.5 Information centres

 Information centre: A part of the IT department that is established to support end-users in developing their own information systems.

The term 'information centre' was first used by IBM in the 1970s, long before the growth in end-user computing.

Key functions provided by an information centre:

- A help desk function to try and resolve problems with the use of computer software. Support may involve the use of remote diagnostic software so help desk staff can 'see' the software on the user's computer and therefore offer advice specific to that situation.
- Advice on application development. Where an organisation allows staff to write their own computer programs, the information centre may be able to provide specific advice on application development. Not only will specific issues be resolved, but advice can be provided on how to develop programs in accordance with firm's standards.
- Staff in the centre may also try to enforce other standards including purchase of standard hardware and software, and offer advice on data processing standards for linking different applications within the organisation. Testing services may also be provided to help ensure that new programs do not damage existing programs or databases.
- Staff may be able to monitor network traffic and the number of files being stored on the network. Advice can then be provided on appropriate upgrades to the network as well as instituting automatic backup of computer systems as required.

Typically, the information centre might also provide the following services:

- evaluation of hardware and software on behalf of users, to ensure that compatibility and performance levels are acceptable;
- prototype development, where programming requires knowledge beyond the scope of the users;
- user training, or the facilitation of training courses provided by outside agencies;
- security consultancy to ensure that the system is well controlled;
- data management, for example the provision and maintenance of corporate databases or a data warehouse;

- heavy-duty IT systems, such as those centred on the corporate server; and
- maintenance.

You should be aware of the growth in outsourcing from your studies for *Organisational Management and Information Systems* and you should refresh your memory about the arguments surrounding this strategy.

5.12 Organisational knowledge management

5.12.1 Introduction

This section looks at the origins and growth of knowledge management as a strategy to achieve competitive advantage. It begins with an overview of the concept, then examines the process of introducing knowledge management into an organisation.

5.12.2 Knowledge management

CIMA defines knowledge management as 'A systematic process of finding, selecting, organising, distilling and presenting information so as to improve the comprehension of a specific area of interest. Specific activities help focus the organisation on acquiring, storing and utilizing knowledge for such things as problem solving, dynamic learning, strategic planning and decision making.'

(CIMA: *Management Accounting Official Terminology*, 2005, p. 18).

This is an area that is relatively new and very fashionable with academics, businesses and examiners. There has been considerable work in this area and Scarborough et al. (1999) have produced a useful literature review. Knowledge management strategy is also one of the fastest-growing areas of management consultancy.

Writing and research on the topic of organisational knowledge management (OKM) really only appeared for the first time in about 1993, though some of the principles can be traced as far back as the scientific management writers of the early twentieth century.

Peter Drucker claims credit for inventing the title 'knowledge work' (as compared with manual work and service work). In 1993 he characterised knowledge workers as 'those who have high levels of education and specialist skills, combined with the ability to apply these skills to identify and solve problems'.

Writings on OKM were also linked to the concept of the learning organisation, with which you will be familiar from P5 *Integrated Management,* until about 1996 when the two disciplines diverged.

To refresh your memory the 'learning organisation' is one which;

- acquires, creates and transfers knowledge
- merges new knowledge with existing knowledge
- modifies behaviour to reflect the new knowledge
- actively encourages thinking, experimentation and creativity amongst all staff
- openly rewards risk taking
- encourages and is dependent upon, absorptive capacity, knowledge creation and double loop learning.

The differences between these two approaches in their current forms are summarised in Figure 5.7.

Learing organisation	*Organisational knowledge management*
Broad focus	Specific focus
Theory-driven	Practice-driven
'Building' metaphor	'Mining' metaphor
Systems-based view of the firm	Resource-based view of the firm
Emphasis on culture management	Emphasis on IS management
Emphasis on managing tacit knowledge	Emphasis on changing tacit knowledge into explict knowledge
Strtegic/HR managers responsible	Chief knowledge officers or IS responsible

Figure 5.7   OKM and the learning organisation
Reprinted by permission of the publisher CIPD

Knowledge management requires knowledge managers who should be charged with the tasks of;

- collecting and categorising knowledge
- establishing a knowledge oriented technology infrastructure
- monitoring the use of knowledge
- encouraging the up take of available knowledge.

Even though this list is not complete one thing is missing and would be a mistake to include. Knowledge managers are not responsible for creating knowledge. To imply that they are, or that they are more knowledgeable than others in the firm would be a recipe for resentment and hostility within the company. It is this conception that leads to the comment that 'knowledge cannot be managed'. We cannot force people to share, we cannot force people to cooperate and we cannot force people to be innovative and look for new ways of working. No one can force you to acquire the knowledge and skills to pass the P6 examination – but we hope you do!

However, knowledge managers must take steps to ensure that knowledge is not lost. This is particularly true of tacit knowledge and organisations suffer significantly when tacit knowledge 'walks out the door'. For example, when London Underground conducted a voluntary redundancy programme a large number of middle aged engineers took the opportunity to leave the organisation having been with the firm for all of their careers. It only took a few months, and a few major breakdowns, to realise that these engineers were the only people who knew how to maintain, and repair, some of the electrical and signaling systems that had been installed in the Underground before those engineers had started their careers some thirty years earlier. A number had to be invited back on a consultancy basis to resolve the resulting problems. On a more serious note the US Government has recently realised that they have no serving nuclear physicists who have ever seen a live nuclear explosion. All of the current staff have only seen computer simulations which, although quite effective, are nothing like the real thing!

The transfer of tacit knowledge is an essential part of the role and apprentice systems, role play with established staff and simulations are useful techniques. It could be argued that the knowledge an employee has is only rented by the employer and is not owned. It is a feature of the nature of knowledge as an asset, that it is virtually impossible to enforce 'ownership' by the company.

The role of knowledge management never ends since, as the environment the organisation operates in changes so do the knowledge and skill requirements that the organisation must use to be successful. The situation is the same for you as an individual. Once you have passed these examinations and TOPCIMA and gained your qualification you will be required to engage in continuing professional development (CPD) to make sure that the knowledge and skills that you have are up to date.

5.12.3   What is knowledge?

Davenport and Prusak (1998) have defined knowledge as '… fluid mix of framed experience, values, contextual information, and expert insight that provides a framework for evaluating and incorporating new experiences and information. It originates in the minds of knowers. In organisations, it often becomes embedded not only in documents or repositories but also in organisational routines, practices, processes and norms.'

Individuals have different approaches to knowledge, and it is thought that they move through different stages of knowledge such as:

- know what – the knowledge of facts;
- know how – the understanding of processes;
- know why – the recognition of how the process fits with others;
- care why – the development of values to support the process.

The objective of OKM is to capture the first three of these knowledge levels and to turn them into a resource that is available to everyone in the organisation. The fourth level is more cultural, and perhaps more appropriate to organisational learning.

5.12.4   Where does knowledge come from?

Individuals acquire knowledge in a number of different ways:

- from the education process;
- from experience of performing tasks;
- from observation of others;
- from formal knowledge exchange (training/coaching);
- from informal knowledge exchange (meetings/brainstorming/anecdotes).

Knowledge can also be a development, in the mind of the knower, from information received. Davenport and Prusak (1998) suggest that information is turned into knowledge by the following means:

- *Comparison*: how does information about this situation compare with other situations we have known?
- *Consequences*: what implications does the information have for decisions and actions?
- *Connections*: how does this bit of information relate to others?
- *Conversation*: what do other people think about this information?

Knowledge can be created by:

- *Socialisation* – sharing tacit knowledge by watching other people work, brainstorming, visual thinking and systems thinking.
- *Externalisation* – by making tacit knowledge explicit by explanation, imagery and metaphor.
- *Internalisation* – using new explicit knowledge and developing new tacit knowledge from it.

5.12.5   What is the value of knowledge?

As we have discussed elsewhere knowledge is probably the closest that we can get to the ultimate source of competitive advantage and it is easy to see that what we know makes us different from others. We will come back to this in Chapter 6 when we discuss strategic resources in more detail.

Knowledge is an asset but, unlike material assets, which decrease as they are used, knowledge assets increase with use: ideas breed new ideas, and shared knowledge stays with the giver while it enriches the receiver. Like other assets knowledge requires, for its production and maintenance, the use of other assets notably money and labour. Knowledge is expensive and major consultancy companies, such as McKinsey estimate that they spend as much as 10 per cent of their annual revenues on developing and maintaining intellectual capital. Set against this must be the cost of not having knowledge or worse still having it and not using it.

You need only think of the benefits of working in a study group or with your lecturers to see that this is true.

5.13 Developing a knowledge strategy

There are five main steps in the development and implementation of a knowledge management strategy:

1. *Gaining top management support.* Like any major strategy, OKM will fail unless it has the clear support of the 'top team'. This support must be maintained throughout the lengthy development and implementation.
2. *Creating the technological infrastructure.* Hardware and software must be acquired and implemented in order for the knowledge to be communicated and stored.
3. *Creating the database structures.* 'Repositories of knowledge' that are appropriate for the organisation need to be designed and built, using advanced database management systems. These will usually consist of a network of contents pages with links to other databases where the content is held.
4. *Creating a 'sharing' culture.* All staff need to be convinced of the benefits, both to the organisation and to themselves, of sharing knowledge for the common good. This is the most difficult stage, as individuals see the ownership of knowledge as a source of power, and this is the stage most likely to cause any OKM project to fail.
5. *Populating the databases and using the knowledge.* The knowledge must be captured and recorded and individuals trained and encouraged to use it.

5.13.1 Information technology infrastructure

Many companies will provide an Organisational Management System to help knowledge workers obtain the resources they need to create knowledge, capture that knowledge within the system and finally distribute that knowledge to other workers. The system may be relatively simple, for example, provision of e-mail to share knowledge and databases to store knowledge. In other situations the system may be more complicated, involving Intranets, online access to specific Internet sites and the use of advanced data mining tools and technologies.

There are two types of knowledge which the OMS is set up to deal with: *explicit* and *tacit*.

- *Explicit knowledge* is knowledge that is already available within the organisation. This knowledge includes details of purchases and sales from the transaction processing system through to information for strategic decision making stored in the Executive Information System. This information will be available to directors and employees as required.

- *Tacit knowledge* is knowledge that is within the organisation, but it is not readily available. Tacit knowledge is normally located within the brains of employees. They may or may not know whether they have this information, but it is up to each employee to decide whether or not to share that information. Systems will be required within the organisation to help employees share this knowledge.

Having identified what knowledge is available within an organisation, that knowledge will normally then be shared. However, sharing creates its own problems, as noted below.

Sharing explicit knowledge assumes that an appropriate information system is available to share that knowledge. Sharing of information will therefore be hindered in where appropriate technology is not available or where appropriate software is not available.

The provision of appropriate technology to share knowledge will include networked computers and some form of central server. Individual members of staff can then send e-mails to each other as well as refer to documents and information on the central server.

The basic software requirements to share knowledge include an e-mail client, database or similar software to maintain the central server and appropriate search engines to locate information required by users.

Tacit knowledge is more difficult to share because it may not be clear what tacit knowledge is actually available. This knowledge may have to be released by setting up specific activities such as meetings and brainstorming sessions. This group work may well uncover knowledge that individuals do not know they have. For example, solutions may be found to problems simply because they have been discussed between a number of experts.

Many people may see the retention of knowledge actually adding to their power base within an organisation. Sharing of knowledge is therefore not an option. While this may appear to be a selfish attitude, it does prevail in many situations. It is also difficult for the organisation to do much about the problem, because by definition, no one else may know that this knowledge exists. Provision of appropriate information sharing systems may help, although other factors such as appropriate remuneration or rewards for sharing knowledge may also have to be implemented. Overall, a culture of knowledge sharing has to be developed so staff realise that there is little or no benefit to keeping knowledge to themselves.

5.13.2 Knowledge sharing systems

As knowledge creation and distribution become more important within organisations, so specific systems will be required, and developed, to help transfer that knowledge to individuals within the organisation. This section provides a brief introduction to some of those systems.

Groupware

 Groupware: A collection of tools to assist collaborative work within an organisation.

Groupware products will typically include a range of tools designed to assist communication between the members of a group, as well as to capture information that the group is working with. Groupware will typically support small groups of workers, although in some situations the products will be available on a worldwide basis. Lotus Notes is one of the more commonly-used groupware products.

Features of groupware include:

- Discussion databases where group members can ask questions and respond to discussion threads. The groupware product tracks each question and response and displays these in lists of linked items.
- Shared diaries to enable group members to book meetings with other workers quickly and efficiently.
- Task lists so each member can track the activities they are involved with, as well as allocate tasks to other group members as necessary.
- Diary pages for recording activities each day, and linking those activities to specific projects.
- Address book for storing information about group members and contacts.
- Some form of reminder utility, which may, for example, place electronic 'post it' notes on-screen as a reminder of important events during the day.

The groupware product will require appropriate hardware to run, including local and wide area networks to link group members in different physical locations.

Workflow

 Workflow is a series of tasks, which must be performed in order to achieve a specific result or outcome in an organisation.

Workflow systems will vary according to the task being undertaken. However, the basic principle is to route work or jobs through a series of tasks and employees in a specific order. For example, in an insurance company, an insurance claim may be routed from the post room, to internal assessor, external assessor, claims manager, payments department and finally central filing. As each person completes their section of the electronic paperwork, the computer system automatically forwards the information to the next person. The system therefore removes all the transferring of paper around an organisation, creating significant gains in efficiency.

Intranets

An Intranet is an information sharing system built on Internet technology. It uses a web-browser as the standard user interface, so any employee who has used the Internet will already be familiar with the screen design.

Information on an Intranet is only available within the organisation; it is therefore like an Internet but with restricted access. It can be used to share any information that employees in a specific company require.

Extranets

An Extranet is similar to an Intranet, although in this case, access is also allowed to specific third parties located outside the organisation.

Many organisations use this tool as a reason to obtain competitive advantage. For example, a computer manufacturer may allow customers to access the support database providing details of parts used in each computer along with known problems or errors with those parts. This will allow the customer to diagnose faults with their computers more quickly, and also help the manufacturer provide an additional useful service, at effectively zero cost.

STRATEGIC IMPLICATIONS OF IT

It must be remembered that the common thread in all of these knowledge sharing tools is people. Although computers are becoming ever more powerful they have not yet reached the ability which humans demonstrate for synthesising fuzzy and unstructured knowledge. Whilst computers can cope far better than the human brain with complicated but deterministic situations they are unable to deal with complex adaptive systems. Since most organisations and environments are complex adaptive systems it is unlikely that computers will completely replace humans – unless someone develops a new technology. Computers and communications systems are highly effective at the capture, ordering and distribution of highly structured knowledge even when it is changing rapidly. They are incapable, however, of providing a rich picture of, for example, the environment in which an organisation has to operate or the political situation that exists within that organisation. This is possibly one of the reasons why speech recognition software has not fulfilled its early promise. Although the machinery, can recognise the noises it cannot recognise the context or tonal pattern. Since a large, and important, part of our communication is nonverbal there is a long way to go before a machine can recognise, and infer, meaning.

With this in mind there is a need to develop hybrid systems of knowledge management whereby staff and computers work together in complementary ways. This means that with all of the tools above not only must knowledge be recorded but it must also be effectively transferred. Social networking software can be used to record the information transactions between individuals within an organisation. Once this is done the database of best practices in an organisation can be seeded with references to the contact details of individuals who have provided and used those best practices. With a sufficiently well written entry in the database this would attract the attention of those who needed further information about the particular entry and they could make the call.

5.13.3 Cultural issues

Far more important than the technology required in order to make OKM work is the change in culture that is necessary for success. Human nature is such that individuals value their knowledge, and treat it as a personal asset. 'Knowledge is power' is an oft quoted observation. This is contrary to the principles of OKM, which view knowledge as an organisational asset to be exploited for the common good (you will have studied organisational culture and the concept of power in P5 *Integrated Management* in some detail and should make sure you are fully familiar with the concepts).

Individuals also see knowledge as a source of power. Often referred to as *expert power* those things that you know make you powerful, because you can decide if and when to share that knowledge. You can also demand a price for your knowledge, not just in the form of the salary paid to you by an employer, but in terms of favours owed by colleagues and friends whom you have advised. Unless the culture of the individuals within the organisation can be changed from one of 'knowledge hoarding' to one of 'knowledge sharing', any OKM initiative will fail. It is often difficult to encourage such a culture.

The following methods can be used to encourage knowledge sharing:

- Lead from the front. A clear and obvious commitment to knowledge sharing by senior staff gives the right signals. If the bosses are not sharing their knowledge, why should anyone else?
- Invest time and money. By making significant investments, not just in the information technology infrastructure but also in the appointment of knowledge enabling positions such as Chief Knowledge Officer, the organisation demonstrates its commitment to OKM.

- Reward knowledge sharing. Make effective knowledge sharing one of the performance criteria used in the appraisal process, and link financial reward and promotion to it. You might care to think of the dilemma that arises when a firm is setting up a reward system. At your last annual appraisal you were most probably rewarded for your personal expertise rather than the fact that you had made sure that you knew no more than anyone else!.
- Buy knowledge sharers. Make a willingness to share knowledge, and a track record of sharing, criteria used when recruiting new staff.

5.13.4 Capturing knowledge

Most of the major problems with capturing the knowledge of the organisation centre on the fact that much of it resides in the memory of individuals.

Some knowledge, often called 'tacit' knowledge, is difficult or impossible to record, as it is so intangible and so difficult to put into words. This is the sort of knowledge that comes from experience. This becomes a particular problem when there are programmes of voluntary redundancy. In general, the people that take up the offer of voluntary severance are those that are close to retirement and have a wealth of knowledge or those that can easily find alternative work – and must, therefore, be good at their job. When these people leave a lot of knowledge 'walks out of the door'. In order to solve this problem, organisations create 'knowledge maps' showing who knows what. Other people needing access to the knowledge then know whom to contact, and they can talk to the knowledge holder and discuss their needs directly.

Much of the organisation's knowledge, rather than being tacit, is 'explicit'. It can be recorded in some form, either as words, diagrams, pictures, speech, film or a combination of these. In this case, the organisation must encourage knowers to commit their knowledge to electronic form so it can be stored and shared. It may even be necessary to persuade staff to get rid of all non-electronic data storage media – a paperless office! Bearing in mind that the concept of the paperless office was first proposed (and possible) over 30 years ago this is likely to continue to meet strong resistance.

5.13.5 Storing knowledge

You will already have been introduced to the concept of expert systems and are probably aware that the core of such systems is a knowledge base.

> *Knowledge base:*… the facts, rules and conditions relating to the subject matter such that expert decisions can be derived.

Creating an appropriate repository of knowledge for the organisation is like turning the information system into one big expert system. The Intranet infrastructure effectively allows all users to know anything about everything.

Since knowledge is a 'sticky' asset and grows by combining with other pieces of knowledge it is often better to store knowledge in a map rather than a model. Our minds do not work in the strict, linear, hierarchical system that we find in most dictionaries but in maps. Tony Buzan developed, and copyrighted, the concept of the MindMap and this is representative of one of the best ways to collate knowledge. With the advent of faster computers with high storage capacities these types of storage systems are now perfectly feasible.

5.13.6 The benefits of OKM

By the time you have read this far you should have a fairly good idea of the potential benefits of OKM.

Davenport and Prusak (1998) suggest the following benefits:

- higher workforce motivation levels and reductions in unproductive time leading to improvements in productivity;
- greater corporate coherence, as all staff have a clearer understanding of the organisational goals and values;
- a richer 'knowledge stock', leading to an increased ability to compete and add value;
- a stronger 'meritocracy of ideas' where people are encouraged to generate and use knowledge to improve efficiency and to innovate.

They quote Steve Jobs, one of the founders of Apple Computers, as saying

It doesn't make sense to hire smart people and then tell them what to do; we hired smart people so they could tell us what to do.

5.14 Profit impact of marketing strategy

Arguably one of the first knowledge directories was Profit impact of marketing strategy (PIMS). Developed in 1960 at General Electric to counter the problems of running a diversified corporation the PIMS model was expanded under the direction of the Harvard Business School to provide assistance to businesses outside GE. Currently managed by the Strategic Planning Institute the database possesses information on more than 1,200 product – line businesses operating in many different industries.

SPI claims that the unique database contains detailed information on thousands of strategy experiences and that this has allowed it to identify universal truths of the marketplace. These truths are said to explain the performance of any business in any time period. For instance, market share percentage, as a determinant of ROI is said to be more important for infrequently purchased products than for frequently purchased products, and more important when customers are fragmented.

The search for these universal truths of the market place or natural laws led GE to develop the GE matrix as a companion to the BCG matrix which we discussed in Chapter 4. Those not favouring a scientific approach to strategic management tend to dismiss the use of the PIMS database as an inspirational source of competitive advantage.

5.15 Executive Information Systems

An Executive Information System is a computer-based information system designed to provide senior managers access to information relevant to their management activities. With trends such as globalisation and intense competition increasing the importance of rapid and accurate decision making their use an increasing component of executive behaviour. The frequency of EIS use, and the length of time of EIS use has been shown to increase problem identification speed, decision making speed, and the extent of the analysis in decision making.

While EIS differ considerably in the number and sophistication of features, the most common feature of these systems is immediate access to a single database where all current financial and operational data can be found. In many cases the information made readily accessible was available but was difficult to access or use. Features that distinguish EIS from such systems as management information systems and decision support systems are:

- a non keyboard interface status based access to the organisational database, drill down analysis capabilities (the incremental examination of data at different levels of detail)
- rend analysis capabilities (the analysis of data across desired time intervals)
- exception reporting
- extensive graphics capabilities
- the provision of data from multiple sources
- highlighting of information that the executive has specified as critical.

In particular, whereas the emphasis with an MIS has been the storage and processing of large amounts of information, the focus of EIS is on the retrieval of specific information about the daily operational status of the company's activities as well as the specific information about competitors and the marketplace. In contrast to DSS where the emphasis is to support ad-hoc decisions as well as some routine analysis, the EIS is used to monitor and scan the environment to give the executives rapid exposure to important changes in the environment. Whilst the core of the DSS is an extensive modelling and analysis capability, the essence of the EIS is status information about the organisations performance.

5.16 Summary

This chapter began by looking at the need for organisations to take a strategic approach to information technology. It then examined the different ways in which the information system, through its IT and information components, might lead the organisation towards competitive advantage. In order to get the most from this chapter, you should ensure that you are familiar with the work of Michael Porter on competition. This has been covered elsewhere in this learning system. We have also examined the need for an information systems strategy and looked at a possible model that might be used to develop such a strategy. It then considered the issues surrounding the organisation of the IT department and the choice of outsourcing as a strategy. Finally we looked at knowledge management and how an organisation might take steps to ensure that knowledge was captured and made available to the appropriate workers in and organisation.

References

Behrsin, M., Mason, G. and Sharpe, T. (1994) *Reshaping IT for Business Flexibility*. Maidenhead: McGraw-Hill.

CCTA (1990) *Managing Facilities Management*, IT Infrastructure Library, Central Computer and Telecommunications.

Corcoran, C. (2007) For the next wave of social networking sites, bigger isn't always better. Wall street Journal, April 2007.

Davenport, T.H. and Prusak, L. (1998) *Working Knowledge*. Boston, MA: Harvard Business School Press.

Drucker, P. (1993) *Post-Capitalist Society*. Oxford: Butterworth-Heinemann.

Earl, M.J. (1989) *Management Strategies for Information Technology*. Hemel Hempstead: Prentice-Hall.

Franklin, D. (2008) Web 2.0: High Tech & High Touch, *The Internet is about more than sharing documents; it's about creating dialogue.* Credit Union Management, September 3, 2008.

Franks, R.V. (2000) *Computing Terminology*. London: CIMA Publishing.

Goldsmith, M. (2008) Interview regarding his book "*What got you here wont get you there*" reported in Business Week.

Lacity, M., Willcocks, L. and Feeny, D. (1995) IT outsourcing: maximise flexibility and control. *Harvard Business Review*, May–June: 84–93.

Levin, R. (1999) *The Cluetrain Manifesto*. Perseus Books.

McFarlan, F.W. and McKenney, J.L. (1983) *Corporate Information Systems Management*. New York: Irwin.

Mintzberg, H. (1994) Rethinking strategic planning, part 1: pitfalls and fallacies. *Long Range Planning*, 27(3): 12–21.

Nolan, R.L. (1979) Managing the crisis in data processing. *Harvard Business Review*, Mar.–Apr., 115–126.

Peppard, J. (1993) *IT Strategy for Business*. London: Pitman Publishing.

Porter, M.E. and Millar, V.E. (1985) How information gives you competitive advantage. *Harvard Business Review*, July–August, 149–160.

Porter, M.E. (1985) *Competitive Advantage: Creating and Sustaining Superior Performance*. New York: Free Press.

Reigner (2007) online source, http://newcompro.halavais.net/index.php?title=Help:Contents

Robson, W. (1994, rev. 1997) *Strategic Management and Information Systems*. London: Financial Times Management.

Scarborough, H., Swan, J. and Preston, J. (1999) *Knowledge Management – A Literature Review*. Reprinted by permission of the publisher CIPD (Chartered Institute of Personnel and Development, London).

Thayne, D. (2008) *Why is social media so popular?*, http://www.webupon.com/Social-Networks/Why-are-Social-Networking-Sites-So-Popular.239437

Ward, J. (1987) Integrating information systems into business strategies, *Long Range Planning*, 20(3): 19–29.

Revision Questions

 Question 1

HS plc is a large quoted company, which owns and maintains 42 large supermarkets in the country in which it operates. Each supermarket sells a very wide range of food and household goods to the general public.

There is a high level of competition from other supermarket groups.

HS plc has tended to be the industry leader in computerisation and has a corporate objective to offer the best computerised sales service to its customers. HS plc has introduced some computerisation in the stock and ordering systems, although there is no integrated system. Stock levels are high, being 3 days for perishable goods such as milk and up to 28 days for tinned goods. This has resulted in a high stockholding cost for the company.

HS plc is now considering an investment of over £50 million in the latest electronic point-of-sale (EPOS) systems to maintain its competitive advantage. The databases associated with the system will be able to store information relating to stock levels of each product line, cash and bankings, and even sales by individual customer. Information on HS plc's competitors indicates that they are also considering similar systems, but it will take at least two years to implement them. Because HS plc has already produced the initial feasibility study and systems specification, the company could have its system running within ten months.

The board of HS plc is meeting tomorrow to make the final decision on the investment. The managing director has indicated that he expects the investment to take place, but he would like to see a list of the benefits of the EPOS system, from both the strategic and operational viewpoints.

Requirement

Produce the report requested by the managing director that can be used at the board meeting. The report must show clearly the strategic and operational benefits of the proposed EPOS and database systems and how these relate to HS plc. **(25 marks)**

 Question 2

The board of JH Ltd has become aware that there is no IT strategy in place within the company. A decision has therefore been made to establish a working group to produce an outline IT strategy. The group members are:

Senior manager. He does not have much knowledge of IT because he has avoided IT in general as he sees it as not providing him with any benefits for his particular job. He is actually quite fearful of IT. He is very task-oriented and dislikes wasting time on non-essential work. He is very good at producing overall policy directives.

IT professional. She has an excellent knowledge of mainframe computers and enjoys being in charge of a large IT department. Her knowledge has arisen from 20 years in computing. She has tended to ignore the recent shift towards end-user computing, believing that IT is best handled by specialists. Although she has some knowledge of PCs, this is not complete. She has very little contact with the users of the information that the IT department produces. She believes that users should accept the information given and not make difficult demands on the department.

IT user – trainee accountant. He is a CIMA Stage 4 student, who has been working in various roles within the accounts function: this is his first major assignment. His agenda is to try to ensure that IT is used effectively and that all staff within the company can therefore use PC applications to support their work. He is already well read on IT matters and is now looking to advance rapidly in the company by being the IT 'champion'.

Requirements

(a) Comment on the disadvantages that could arise for JH Ltd by not having an overall IT strategy in place. **(10 marks)**

(b) Explain how the background of each individual in the working group may present barriers to the production of an IT strategy as required by the board.

Suggest how these barriers may be overcome. **(15 marks)**

(Total marks = 25)

? Question 3

Library Direct Services (LDS) is an organisation providing data to central and local government personnel. It maintains a database of:

- all laws, both statute and case law;
- reports of proceedings in central government;
- comparative data on the services provided by local government in each region of the country; and
- some comparative data on services provided in different countries.

LDS allows access to this database 24 hours a day, 365 days a year. LDS is contractually obliged to provide this information within 30 minutes of receiving a request. All requests are received by telephone or e-mail.

The existing database is accessed primarily via command line input at DOS, which the database administrators can use quickly and efficiently. Any perceived or actual decrease in the usefulness of the database will mean that the administrators are unlikely to accept the system.

Over the years, a number of small but significant modifications have been made to the original 'off-the-shelf' database software. It is essential to retain these if the database is to be used, although the programmer who made these changes has left the company and has not been replaced. Program changes are not fully documented.

LDS is now asking for tenders from database suppliers to upgrade the database to Windows functionality. This is likely to involve rewriting the database itself and implementing a new database management system. LDS needs to make a decision on which company to choose to make this change for them. For budgetary reasons, any proposed change must be completed within the next six months.

Requirement

Provide six questions that LDS can use to help evaluate potential suppliers for the systems change contract explained above.

Explain why each of these questions is relevant to the specific circumstances of LDS. **(25 marks)**

Question 4

The PPX organisation provides news and information services to a variety of clients from one central head office and eight regional offices. The information provided varies from local weather reports to details on competing companies and product developments.

The senior management of PPX consider that the current provision of information within the organisation is acceptable; there is no sign of sales decreasing in the short term so they consider that there is no need to change the overall structure of the organisation. Many managers also share this view; they have built up their own client base over the last few years, and this provides them with a significant amount of commission over and above the normal salary.

Managers in each of the eight locations have been allowed to build and maintain their own information systems. Within each location information provision is adequate, although the systems have been purchased from different suppliers to meet the requirements of that individual branch.

IT systems within PPX are fairly well integrated in terms of e-mail provision and viewing corporate information such as training manuals and suggested price lists on a corporate database located on an Intranet. The bandwidth on the WAN is currently sufficient for information transfer requirements.

Some of the major competitors of PPX have recently implemented systems to allow information to be shared across their organisations. Initial reports show that their clients are viewing this facility favourably, with additional information being available on demand in each location. A few of PPX's clients have requested a similar facility, although no clients have actually been lost due to lack of provision of information.

(a) Explain the steps necessary to implement an appropriate knowledge strategy in an organisation, discussing the specific problems that may be found in PPX regarding this implementation. **(20 marks)**

(b) Identify and explain the issues that may prevent a knowledge strategy from being implementedinanorganisation. **(5 marks)**

(Total marks = 25)

Solutions to Revision Questions

 Solution 1

Guidance

Common problems with this question include:

- Providing detailed explanation of an EPOS system, rather than looking at the benefits provided by the system. Answers would normally gain more marks by explaining the benefits of the system, the workings of an EPOS system being relatively unimportant as far as this question went.
- Not always planning the answer before writing it out in full. The level of repetition of benefits in answers can be extremely high; for example, most answers tend to mention stock control at least twice. The point being made is that having an answer plan would help eliminate the duplication and allow more time for other new and relevant benefits to be included in an answer.
- Ensuring an adequate balance between operational and strategic benefits in the answer. Most candidates will explain at least three or four operational benefits but only a minority managed to include as many strategic benefits in their answers. Although these benefits were more difficult to identify, an answer based wholly around operational benefits would score fewer marks than one with a balance of operational and strategic. The question requirement was for both benefits.

Report

To: Managing director
From: Management accountant
Date: 20 November 20XX
Subject: EPOS and database systems

1. *Introduction*
Further to your request for additional information on the proposed EPOS and database systems, I list below the benefits from both strategic and operational viewpoints.

2. *Strategic*
   2.1 *Competitive advantage.* The proposal will give us competitive advantage. Competitors are at least 2 years behind us and this will enable customer loyalty to be established well in advance of their developments.

2.2 *Future development.* The EPOS and database are in keeping with the company's corporate objective to offer the best computerised sales service. The investment will give a strategic advantage when considering future applications, particularly in respect of exploiting the marketing capability emanating from the information collected on customer preferences.

2.3 *Profitability analysis.* The development will allow overall profitability to be improved and we shall be able to focus on the products that generate the biggest margins. The system can help to establish the profitability of products and translate this into margins per square metre of floor space, so that optimum sales are achieved. This is extremely important given that gross margins are continually under pressure.

2.4 *Customer perceptions.* This investment of over £50m is at the customer-facing edge of operations. As we build further applications they will continue to enhance customer service and will be in keeping with the image customers associate with our company.

2.5 *Image perceptions.* Although very difficult to measure, we may be able to create a 'high-tech' modern image. This can appeal to customers, as mentioned above, and we have already successfully used computerisation in stock and ordering systems. We may, therefore, also be able to gain a reputation for being innovative and 'leading edge' and, as such, could gain important psychological advantages over competitors and be treated more favourably by suppliers, particularly when it comes to the further development of their systems.

3. *Operations*

3.1 *Stock levels.* The biggest operational benefit is the potential savings in stock levels. Both perishable and tinned goods stock levels are high and the proposed system will reduce these and produce consequential stockholding cost savings. As EPOS results in automatic destocking and reordering, stock levels can be managed much more effectively. This can be further enhanced by using electronic data interchange (EDI) facilities and just-in-time (JIT) practices, so that stock levels are minimised.

3.2 *Sales analyses.* Analyses of individual products by size, colour and any other attributes can be carried out so that sales are maximised. This can also be used for store layout purposes, so the most attractive and effective layout can be created using information in the database. Also, complementary products can be grouped together to bring about additional sales.

Individual customer profiles can be generated within the system that may be important for sales promotions so that they can be more effectively targeted at the right time and the right place within the supermarkets.

3.3 *Cash and bankings.* EPOS facilities assist with the quick and easy 'balancing' of tills. The bar codes on products contain price information, which is read by the bar-code reader, which automatically updates stock, sales and cash recording systems simultaneously. As this is automatic, the balancing of the tills at the end of the day is carried out much more quickly. This benefit is particularly attractive to staff as it speeds up the end-of-day routines.

3.4 *Staff savings.* There is the possibility of staff savings within the stores because of better inventory control through the EPOS system. Also, it may be possible to reduce the number of staff on counter positions if the system significantly speeds up customer throughput and improves cashiering activities.

4. *Conclusion*

It is important that an investment of this magnitude is fully considered. The advantages of the proposed EPOS and database systems are considerable and it is recommended that we go ahead with the proposals.

Signed: Management accountant

 Solution 2

Guidance

Common problems in this question tended to be:

Part (a):

- Not including appropriate comment about the IT strategy of the organisation.
- Not placing the correct emphasis on the information being provided. For example, explaining the benefits of having an IT strategy rather than explaining the disadvantages of not having an IT strategy was that the company would be falling behind its competitors.
- Explaining Earl's theory without showing how these affected the organisation.

Part (b):

- Proposing training as the only solution to the issues facing the company.
- Not showing how the barriers to implementation, such as the senior manager being fearful of IT, could be overcome.

(a) A firm's IT strategy is normally linked to the overall strategic planning and 'vision' that the firm has about the future. The disadvantages that can occur without a strategy are:

- *Costs*. Incompatible and/or aborted systems that do not integrate IT and business requirements inevitably lead to a waste of resources.
- *Automation*. Economies are not achieved because the appropriate level of automation is not in place, particularly relative to the rest of the industry.
- *Future upgrades*. Without an IT strategy it is not possible to integrate IT with the overall business plan, so future requirements are not planned and budgeted for – for example the computer capacity required at a certain point in time may not be available as appropriate provision may not have been made to acquire the equipment required at the right time.
- *Standards*. There will be no support for standards for hardware and software and so a coordinated approach will not be taken. This has obvious problems for the subsequent sharing of data, files and applications.
- *Competitive advantage*. By not developing an IT strategy, JH Ltd will be unable to gain a competitive advantage as it will not be able to offer enhanced service facilities to customers in terms of information, for example details of when products are being made and when they will be available for delivery.
- *Stability*. Without an IT strategy there is no sense of stability, and large-scale system changeovers become evident as the company lurches from one project to the next without an overall guiding framework. This has obvious repercussions in terms of training and disruption of activities.

(b) *Senior manager*. Senior managers in most organisations are not likely to be as computer-literate as younger members of the organisation. The major problem facing the senior manager, from an IT point of view, is technophobia. He has very little knowledge of IT, probably has an aversion to it (i.e. the fear of the unknown) and probably managed to survive, until now, without any such knowledge. The main human problem will be his fear of failure. As a senior manager, he may resent the fact that he does not feel in control in this area. There will be a great deal of negative emotion surrounding his perception of IT within JH Ltd. Although very good at producing overall policy directives, the senior manager will simply not be able to 'see' the IT strategy.

This inability to visualise how JH Ltd will exploit IT into the future will result in an ill thought-out strategy, probably very conservative and old-fashioned and really lacking in a strategic sense. He will base his judgements on what he knows (which is very little) and what he is told. So if the IT professional is convincing, the senior manager will go along with her suggestions rather than developing the strategy to fully match the business needs with the technology. The senior manager therefore needs to gain an understanding of IT, perhaps by attending appropriate training courses, in order to overcome this barrier.

IT professional. The problem facing the IT professional is being too close to IT and therefore not being able to 'see the wood for the trees'. Her perceptions will immediately cause her to jump to large mainframe solutions that could be far too expensive for JH Ltd in the future.

On the human side, she is comfortable with her knowledge of mainframes and will therefore steer the group in this direction rather than, say, a distributed processing or client/server approach. Also, human nature being what it is, there is a certain amount of pride in heading up a large IT department and she will not want to see her 'empire' diminished in any way. So any thoughts of end-user computing may not get a fair hearing.

Mainframe manufacturers (MM) are particularly adept at exploiting their markets, for example the FUD (fear, uncertainty, doubt) policy of one MM. Many IT professionals suffer these same emotions of fear of being left behind in a technologically obsolete watershed, uncertainty in respect of which of the MM's products are 'strategic', and doubt regarding their ability to control the situation as MMs frequently announce proprietary software version changes as a fait accompli, thereby raising upgrade issues. None of these factors are conducive to the development of a firm's IT strategy.

The IT professional would, it is hoped, be of sufficient integrity to develop an IT strategy consistent with the business requirements of JH Ltd. However, she would have a 'blinkered' approach and would tend to apply a 'more of the same' attitude of bigger mainframes, centralised networks, and rigidly enforced control of all computing by an ever-increasing number of IT staff in her department. The senior manager can ensure that the IT professional understands the aims and objectives of JH Ltd by discussing those objectives with the professional in order that the optimum strategy is developed.

IT user. The IT user will know what his current information requirements are. He will not know what he will want from an IT strategy in the future. As the IT user is professionally trained, he will have good business knowledge and also be conversant with good information management practice. He should be able to take a balanced view where IT matters are concerned.

However, he is a trainee accountant, relatively inexperienced and possibly very focused on short-term requirements. He will be looking to solve today's problems rather than developing a framework for future solutions. His approach may be too introspective as his agenda is to try to ensure that IT is used to encourage personal effectiveness. He may not be able to bring a broad enough perspective to develop an IT strategy.

The main barrier to the strategy would be suboptimisation. By concentrating on personal needs the corporate view may be lost and with it the economies of scale that shared data and information can produce. His accountancy training will ensure that the strategy is cost-effective, but he may be looking for very short-term payback and may fail to recognise the unquantifiable benefits that are frequently a feature of long-term strategic initiatives. As with the IT professional, the senior manager will need to ensure that the IT user understands the company's objectives and possible budgetary constraints.

 ## Solution 3

Guidance

Common problems with this question include:

- not providing a list of questions to ask the outsourcing company as required by the question;
- not making questions relevant to the specific circumstances of LDS itself. Many answers provided a general list of questions without regard for the case study material included with the question.

LDS will need to consider a number of factors before deciding on the selection criteria for the supplier to carry out this systems change. The types of questions that should be put to potential suppliers are as follows:

1. *Do they have the necessary skills?* The rather antiquated system being used by LDS has been changed and there is insufficient documentation. This means that a virtual rewrite is required from initial systems analysis through programming to implementation. This may compromise one of the criteria, that is the full support of the administrators may not be obtained for what is, basically, a new system. It will therefore be essential that the supplier has the necessary skills to deal with all aspects of this systems change.
2. *Are they efficient?* Suppliers need to be assessed in terms of both time and quality. LDS is working to a six-month timetable. This is the total amount of elapsed time available and this is not very long given the size of the problem. There is a natural order of analysis, design, build, test and implement, and throwing more resources at a project of this nature may just result in diminishing returns without timescales being met. Quality is equally important, as a firm can give the impression of being efficient by delivering on time, but to an inferior standard. The system change required will need a very high level of efficiency due to both the short timescales and the level of accuracy needed.
3. *Do they have the experience?* This is a specialised field. The database consists of legal information that must be accurate. There is also the requirement for 24-hour access together with a contractual service-level agreement. Therefore, the supplier should ideally have experience of similar applications requiring such a degree of accuracy and availability. Relevant experience will obviously help to speed up the systems change.
4. *Are they reliable?* Do they have a successful 'track record' of previous work or are there outstanding claims for noncompliance or non-delivery, or, worse still, consequential loss? LDS cannot afford to take risks with such an application and, given the constraints that exist on this systems change, it must satisfy itself that the supplier will achieve what it says it can deliver. Also, it will increase the confidence of LDS in the supplier if they could provide previous work of a similar nature for examination, that is LDS should ask

the supplier to provide details of similar contracts, so that the clients can be contacted to ascertain their level of satisfaction with the supplier.

5. *Is their cost reasonable?* Given the constraints of this application, it is unlikely that LDS will secure a fixed-price contract, but rather one based on 'time and materials'. There will be a very real need to ensure that the scope does not 'drift', particularly if the administrators do not like the look of the new Windows front-end. It is unlikely that this systems change will be cheap and LDS may not want to select the cheapest supplier anyway because of the factors mentioned above. With all developments of this nature, the three major aspects to be considered are time, cost and quality, and success is achieved by finding the right balance between these aspects.

6. *Are they financially stable?* The last thing LDS wants is for a supplier to go out of business part-way through the development. Although it is possible to specify an escrow agreement (whereby the program code is lodged with a third party), the sheer disruption caused in obtaining a replacement supplier would not only dramatically increase costs, but would also extend timescales to an unacceptable level. Appropriate financial analysis should therefore be carried out on the potential supplier before selection.

In conclusion, this is an ambitious project to carry out in such a timescale and potential suppliers will need to be fully evaluated over the complete range of technical, commercial and financial competencies in order to minimise the risks to LDS.

Solution 4

Guidance

The overall structure for this answer is taken from the manual. Hopefully, even if you are uncertain about a knowledge strategy within an organisation, you can still use this framework to develop a useful answer plan and answer. As regards the second part of the question, if you are short on ideas, then try to think of the general issues that will prevent the implementation of any information system; it is likely that these ideas will still be relevant for implementing a knowledge strategy.

There are five main steps to develop and implement a knowledge strategy in an organisation. All of these steps could provide difficulties for the PPX organisation.

1. *Gaining senior management approval.* Support is needed for the knowledge management policy, starting with the idea to amend the policy through to the implementation and maintenance of that policy. If support is not available, then the overall project is likely to lose direction, and may never be completed owing to lack of commitment.

   Within PPX, management support appears to be lacking. Although current information may be sufficient, management must take a strategic view regarding the development of the business, and start to make changes to maintain or enhance any competitive advantage that the organisation has. In this situation, presentations can be made to the board explaining the need for a management knowledge policy, and the potential loss of competitive position that will arise if a policy is not implemented.

2. *Creating a technological infrastructure.* PPX currently has a WAN in place that is adequate for its current systems. However, using that network for other information transfer would mean an increase in traffic that the system may not accommodate.

   The directors of PPX need to commission a feasibility study to assess the effects of any new system on the existing IT infrastructure. Recommendations concerning the use of the system in the future will be required along with the costs of any upgrade. Given that the directors do not see the need to upgrade systems at present, obtaining this study may be difficult.

3. *Creating the database structure.* The knowledge management strategy will involve establishing new databases to hold the product and marketing information required in the new system. Detailed analysis is required concerning the structure of the existing databases of each of the branches of PPX and how these can be integrated, if possible, into one central database. This review will also help to identify what additional information needs to be in the database and how to obtain this information.

   Again, given the directors' reluctance to accept any change to this system, obtaining authority for a review of the database structures will be difficult. Additional information concerning the benefits of the knowledge management system will be required to help change the directors' minds.

4. *Creating a sharing culture.* Within the existing system, staff at each branch tend to obtain and keep knowledge that they need. However, this knowledge is not shared. This may result in some duplication of information, which will be addressed in the database structure point in step 3 above. The other issue to address is the lack of sharing of information between the branches. Moving to a centralised database will mean that all staff have access to the knowledge within the organisation. However, as staff have not been used to sharing information there may be some reluctance to use the centralised system, with additional risks that secondary systems may be re-established in each branch rather than use the new database.

   Actions that the directors should consider include amending the method of remuneration to decrease the commission element and increase the basic salary. Any commission on sales could also be split between the employee obtaining the initial information and the employee actually making the sale. This will hopefully be a more equitable system, and so prevent separate information systems re-appearing. Again, director reluctance to change is an issue; if the new system can provide some benefits in terms of decreased costs or increased revenues from additional sales, then they are more likely to accept it.

5. *Populating the databases and using the knowledge.* As already noted, transferring information into the new databases could be difficult owing to different data structures being maintained at each branch.

   Using the knowledge will also be difficult at first, because of management reluctance and lack of training. Training courses will need to include not only how to use the new system, but also soft skills training on how to promote sharing of knowledge. The difficulties that are likely to be met could include:

- *Staff resistance to change.* Any change, particularly IT-related, is likely to be resisted by staff who may see their power base being eroded or working conditions changing. Staff participation will have to be encouraged to try to limit this resistance. In many organisations, having knowledge is associated with having power; staff may not want to see their knowledge shared as this implies that they have less power.
- *Lack of appropriate hardware and software.* The systems analysis phase of a project should help to identify any weaknesses in these areas. However, appropriate software or hardware may not be available for other reasons, as discussed below.
- *Providing a clear specification for the requirements of the system may be difficult where the ouputs of the system are not clear.* This may be an issue where knowledge management is a

new venture for an organisation, so the precise specification and use of the systems may not be clear.

- *Lack of sufficient budget to implement the programme.* This is a standard problem with any systems change. However, it will be particularly relevant for a knowledge management system, especially where other expenditure such as upgrading the entire WAN or LANs may involve significant costs.
- *What inputs are required for the system.* Where knowledge management is new to an organisation, then the inputs needed to provide the outputs may not be clear, either because the outputs have not be specified, or because it is not clear how to obtain the outputs.

6

Strategic Options
and their Evaluation

Strategic Options and their Evaluation

6

We can now consider the strategic options open to the firm. In Chapter 4 we reviewed strategies for particular product and customer groups. In this chapter we shall examine the general directions and methods that management may follow to build the business as a whole. Crucial to this process is taking into account the potential responses of competitors as we discussed in Chapter 2.

LEARNING OUTCOMES

By the end of this chapter you should be able to:

► Identify strategic options;

► Evaluate strategic options;

► discuss and apply both qualitative and quantitative techniques in the support of the strategic decision making function.

6.1 Three sets of strategic choices

6.1.1 Recap and overview

Returning to our rational model of strategy it can be seen that we have reached the point of strategic option generation (Figure 6.1). Applying the techniques discussed in earlier chapters will ensure that the management team has an understanding of the following strategic issues:

- the general direction that the organisation must head in and the level of performance it must exhibit to satisfy its crucial stakeholders;
- the principal threats and opportunities in its operating environment, in particular the factors impacting on its financial performance, and forecasts or scenarios for how these may develop in the future;
- arising from its position audit, an assessment of its principal strengths and weaknesses in relation to these threats and opportunities;
- an understanding of the contribution to its earnings from its portfolio of products and customer groups and how these may change in the future as their life-cycle plays out.

The next step is to decide how to develop the business in the future. This involves deciding on development strategies.

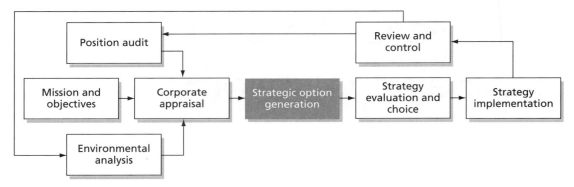

Figure 6.1 A model of a rational strategy process

6.1.2 Development strategies

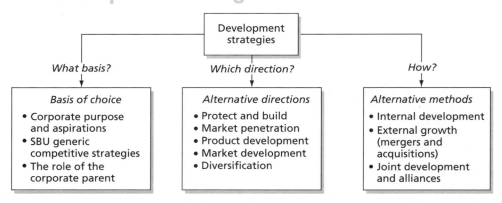

Figure 6.2 Development strategies (adapted from Johnson and Scholes, 1997)

6.1.3 Some illustrations

1. *Basis of choice.* This is sometimes called the choice of competitive strategy. Effectively it decides the business methods that the firm will use to win customers and beat rivals. Note that this will be formulated within the framework of the broader aspirations, or mission, of the business. For example:
   - Virgin Group allows business units to set their own course within a framework consistent with maintaining the corporation's image of customer friendliness, fair dealing and relative informality.
   - Disney Corporation maintains a strong central control over its business operations to ensure that the brands and characters are used consistently and that the 'magic kingdom' remains reassuring to children and parents at all times and in all contexts.
2. *Alternative directions.* This deals with the future of the product and customer portfolio of the business. It will also involve issues such as international extension of the business. For example:
   - Virgin Group remains principally focused on UK markets and its business has developed through adding additional products. Although it has extended its Megastores concept outside the United Kingdom and its airlines do attract bookings from non-UK residents, the bulk of its investment has been in the United Kingdom. For example, its operation of rail services, cinemas, financial services, mobile telephones and soft drinks are unique to the United Kingdom.

● Disney Corporation has a much more global outlook and has significant investments in many countries of the world. It has developed its business beyond film production by extending the range of products offered into toys, shops, holidays, television programming and multimedia publishing Its market segment has remained principally the same – children and parents – but its geographical scope has widened. However it has diversified somewhat through expansion into feature films (Touchstone Pictures) and film and video distribution services (Buena Vista).

3. *Alternative methods.* This considers how the firm will gain access to the products and markets it wishes to develop into. The decision may vary according to the development concerned, but the decision usually hinges upon the four considerations of investment cost, speed of access, know-how and control. For example:

● Virgin Group has utilised most methods of growth in its history. Its original record retailing business was developed using its own capital to acquire shop leases and to develop its own recordings. Similarly, Virgin Atlantic Airlines and Virgin Megastores were set up using its own resources. In contrast, its cinema chain was an acquisition from MGM and it purchased the rail franchises from the UK government. It also operates joint development partnerships. For example, its mobile telephones, drinks, financial services, railway operations and some of its holidays are actually provided by other organisations, with Virgin providing the brand, quality systems and marketing interface.

● Disney Corporation has historically preferred internal development. It owns its theme parks (or has a substantial shareholding in them), studios and video production and distribution operations. However, it uses joint development techniques also through licensing-out its images and brands to toy, confectionery and clothing manufacturers while maintaining very strict control over how they are used. Recently some of its virtual reality films (e.g. *Toy Story* and *A Bug's Life*) have been collaborative ventures with outside production companies. The latest of which, with Pixar, has recently resulted in a merger.

6.2 Porter's generic competitive strategy model

6.2.1 Three generic strategies

According to Porter (1980), 'there are three potentially successful generic strategic approaches to outperforming other firms in an industry'. He terms these:

1. *Overall cost leadership*: lowest cost producer relative to competitors.
2. *Differentiation*: creating something that is perceived industry-wide as unique for which customers will pay a premium.
3. *Focus*: serving a narrow strategic target more effectively than rivals who are competing more broadly.

Porter uses the term 'generic' to mean a *system of classification* into which we can slot the competitive strategies of real-world firms. He writes:

Successfully executing each generic strategy involves different resources, strengths, organisational arrangements and managerial style. Rarely is a firm suited for all three (p. 42).

Hence a management must dedicate themselves to *just one* of the three types of strategy to risk dilution of their competitive advantages. This is the only way that firms can outperform rivals and deliver high or satisfactory returns to shareholders.

6.2.2 Diagram of Porter's model

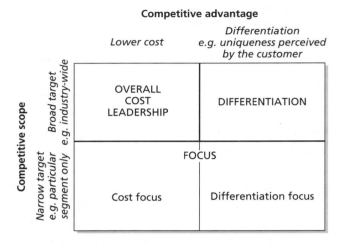

Figure 6.3 Porter's three generic strategies model. Adapted with the permission of The Free Press, a division of Simon & Schuster Adult Publishing Group from *Competitive Strategy: Techniques for Analyzing Industries and Competitors* by Michael E. Porter. © 1980, 1998 by The Free Press. All rights reserved

6.2.3 Competitive advantage

Porter's strategic prescriptions are rooted in his analysis of the impact of five competitive forces on a firm's profits. He argues that a firm must adopt a strategy that combats these forces better than the strategy developed by its rival, if it is to deliver superior shareholder value. If the firm is successful in this, its improved profitability will arise from the combination of two effects:

1. Each year it will enjoy a higher margin than its rivals operating in the same market.
2. As the product life cycle unfolds and prices start to fall during the mature stage, it will survive longer in the market than its rivals.

Adding these two together means better long-term profitability. This in turn equates to superior shareholder value, that is, higher present value of future financial returns than rivals in the same industry.

The Porter Five Forces model has been discussed earlier.

1. *Lower cost.* Achieving the industry's 'lowest delivered cost to customer' provides a number of competitive advantages to the firm:
   - reduces the impact of competitive rivalry by allowing the firm to make superior profit margins at the prevailing level of industry prices – the firm can also become the price leader because no other firm is able to undercut it;
   - reduces the impact of buyer and supplier power by giving the firm a unique cushion of profits against cost increases and price cuts – indeed, buyer and supplier power will be the forces which drive rivals from the industry;
   - low costs provide a barrier to entry against potential new entrants and hence safeguard long-term profits.

Porter recognises that cost reduction strategies are widespread due to management's adherence to the *experience curve* concept. He criticises this by pointing out that it only considers production costs, and recommends analysis of the entire *value chain* to achieve substantial cost savings.

2. *Differentiation.* This is a premium perceived value in the eyes of the buyer. This will normally result in a number of competitive advantages:
   - premium prices can be charged for the product to give better margins in the short run, while in the long run exempting the firm from the price wars of the mature stage;
   - differentiation is a barrier to entry;
   - buyer power from retailers and manufacturers may be reduced if the differentiation of the product makes it an essential element in attracting their customers;
   - the cushion of better profits reduces the impact of buyer and supplier power.

   Differentiation of the product can be achieved in terms of functionality, compatibility (to other products), richness of information provided, appearance or build quality and reliability. It is worth remembering that it is also possible to differentiate at the level of the firm. This can be done by reputation or brand, levels of support for customers (and clients) and the reach of the operating network. We can determine if a firm is successfully differentiating in that they will be able to sustain a price premium, enjoy high brand valuation and above average customer loyalty.

3. *Stuck in the middle.* Porter argues that a firm must decide whether to concentrate on differentiation or whether it wishes to be a cost leader. Failure to do so leaves the firm 'stuck in the middle' with the following results:
   - it cannot access the high-volume customers who demand low costs (or must reduce its margins to attract them which leaves it vulnerable in the long run);
   - it cannot appeal to the high-margin customers because it is also associated with cheaper offerings and customers – this will detract from its appeal and perceived quality;
   - it will have a confused corporate culture which tries to combine excellence with parsimony;
   - its management style and control systems will become contradictory. For example, a cost leader will focus on cost accounting controls, whereas a differentiator will have more interest in controlling innovation and brands. This will affect the relative power and influence of factions in the management teams and of the functions they head up. The marketing and research and development functions may predominate under a differentiation strategy. To combine both strategies will dilute control and invites conflict.
   - However, there are critics of these arguments and these have been discussed in Section 6.2.8

6.2.4 Competitive scope

Porter suggests that a firm can choose to spread its resources across the entire industry or it can focus on just one section of the industry. The latter is a focus strategy and is based on a *narrow competitive scope*. Focus has the following dimensions:

1. Buyer group: for example, try to supply all households or just one type?
2. Product: for example, make a whole range of cars or just executive limousines?

3. Geographical area: for example, supply the product throughout the country (world) or just a selected area?

4. Technology: for example, research and develop all pharmaceutical products or just anti-viral products?

To be successful in pursuing either cost leadership or differentiation the firm must be better than all its rivals. Porter recognises that there are few firms in any industry with sufficient resources to do this. The rest should follow focus strategies.

6.2.5 Focus strategies

A focus strategy (sometimes called a *niche* strategy) relies on the firm being able to address itself better to a segment of an industry than its broader scope rivals can.

Porter (1985) argues that a consequence of compromises to meet the needs of the broader market means that broad-scope players sub-optimise in one of the following two ways:

1. *Underperformance*: They do not understand or make a product which fully meets the needs of the buyer in a segment. This provides the opportunity for a smaller rival to develop a differentiation focus strategy by meeting these customers' needs better and at a premium price.

2. *Overperformance*: The broad-scope competitor is giving the segment more than it really requires and in the process is incurring extra costs. This provides the opportunity for smaller rivals to develop a cost-focus strategy by stripping the product back to its basics and providing it at a lower cost and more attractive price.

Porter warns that a focus strategy cannot be successful unless there is a substantial under-performance or overperformance. However in a given industry there is the possibility for several firms each pursuing focus strategies, provided that each pursues a different segment to focus on.

6.2.6 An illustration of Porter's model – automobiles

The world automobile industry provides an interesting example of Porter's model (Figure 6.4).

Figure 6.4 The world auto industry

6.2.7 Using Porter's model

Like the rest of Porter's models it is intended as a way to help the management team arrange and classify its thoughts. This can be useful in several ways:

1. *To help analyse the competitive position of rivals.* This will help management to avoid head-on conflict and also to spot gaps in the industry. This may involve additional data collection:
   - information or estimates of rivals' cost structures;
   - market research information on product and brand perception;
   - competitor information on their strategies.
2. *To decide on a competitive strategy for the firm.* According to Porter, commercial success demands that one of these strategies be followed.
3. *To analyse the risks of the present strategy.* Porter suggests that each generic strategy carries intrinsic risks:
   (a) *Differentiation*:
      - Brand loyalty may fail if the cost differential between it and the cost leader becomes too great. This fate has befallen branded fast-moving consumer goods firms, cars and airlines.
      - Buyer becomes more sophisticated and needs the differentiating factor less. Buyers are now more willing to buy generic computers and will also arrange their own foreign holidays rather than relying on the security offered by package tour operators.
      - Imitation reduces the differentiation of the brand. Porter argues that this is very common in mature markets. Examples would include bottled mineral water, denim jeans and motorcycles.
   (b) *Cost leadership*:
      - technological change could eliminate a low-cost base or past learning effects;
      - imitation of low-cost techniques by industry entrants;
      - product becomes out of date because firm will not invest in it;
      - domestic inflation or exchange rate changes destroy cost advantage at home and abroad.
   (c) *Focus*:
      - broad-target firm develops economies of scale which overtake the cost-focus player;
      - differences between needs or tastes in the market narrow, for example, the invention of the word processor destroyed the niche strategies of typewriter manufacturers;
      - competitors find subsegments within the focus segment and out-compete the firm;
      - segment collapses and leaves the firm with no other source of earnings.
         Clearly management must focus on these threats and develop strategies to guard against them. They must *maintain* their competitive advantages (i.e. apply resources to maintain them).

6.2.8 Limitations of Porter's model

We are still using and discussing Porter's model more than 20 years after its publication. This indicates its impact and value in the strategy process. It is an accessible model that concentrates thinking and its influence continues to be profound.

However, like all models in strategy it has its limitations and distortions. These will be illustrated in relation to the analysis of the car industry in Figure 6.4.

1. *Lack of clarity on the concept of 'industry'*. Consider Figure 6.4: it takes the definition of industry to mean cars only and ignores trucks and motorcycles. From the customer differentiation perspective this makes sense. However from the perspective of possible advantages in technology development and production costs it is less sensible. Some car firms also make trucks and motorcycles. Does its truck manufacturing and shared R&D give Mercedes-Benz cost advantages in addition to its advantages as a differentiated car company (or perhaps association with panel vans and truckers harms its image)? If we broaden the scope of Figure 6.4 to 'automotive industry', then BMW turns into a differentiation-focus player (it only makes cars and bikes) alongside Ferrari. Is this any more meaningful? What would be the impact if we were to define the industry as 'personal transportation'?

   Porter argues that competitive advantage derives from the firm's position in an industry. If we cannot decide what level of industry to consider, it is hard to see how we can use his theory. This criticism also calls into question the value of his Five Forces model. A car company conducting an environmental analysis needs to decide what industry it is in to apply that model also (cars or automotive or manufacturing or transportation?).

2. *Strategic unit not defined*. The model is set up to help the firm decide its competitive strategy against other firms in the same industry. But it is not clear whether this means the corporation as a whole or whether it is one particular business unit.

   In Figure 6.4, Seat, Audi, Bentley and Skoda each appear in separate quadrants. Yet all are part of the same company, the Volkswagen-Audi Group (VAG). This raises a number of questions:

   (a) Does each division map a matrix appropriate to the industry it is in? In this case, Seat would see itself as in fact a differentiator in the economy-car industry.

   (b) Can a corporation follow different competitive strategies in different business units? If not, then VAG is doomed.

   This again causes problems for Porter's theory because he has said that having more than one competitive strategy will dilute the firm's competitive advantage. But is he seriously suggesting that VAG will risk putting Skoda parts on a Bentley and sell it through the same outlets (or increase the costs of Skoda by mounting a large chrome grille on the front)?

This observation calls into question the value of Porter's model as a whole:

(a) If we use it at corporate level it implies that the whole group must follow a single competitive strategy. However, this generic strategy is meaningless at the level of individual products and markets. Differentiation in trucks is about reliability, economy, load capacity and manoeuvrability. This is a different differentiation from that required to be successful in executive cars and grand tourers where styling and comfort are paramount. Moreover how can the low costs of supply-chain management and assembly at a truck assembly plant in Spain be transferred to executive car production in Germany?

(b) If we use it at a business unit level (as seems inevitable) we overlook sources of competitive advantage that we (or rivals) may enjoy from being part of a larger group.

(c) Separation of business units and careful management of brands can avoid this problem for the company (a fact which Porter seems to overlook when he asserts that dilution is inevitable). However, the management accountant in particular should be wary of this situation. The management accounting controls used to minimise costs and evaluate divisional performance in a division pursuing a cost leadership strategy (say tight budgets and performance measures based on return to net assets) would be harmful if also applied to a division that was a pursuing differentiation where measured efficiency may be much lower and expenditure on promotion, development and human resources much higher.

3. *Lack of empirical evidence.* Porter's model purports to be more than a system of classification – it makes predictions that particular strategies will lead to better profitability and that a stuck-in-the-middle strategy will cause poor profits. However, the survey evidence of real firms is unconvincing and muddied by the definitional problems mentioned already.

   This is a serious issue because Porter is taking the role of the doctor, prescribing therapies and cures. Managers will invest resources, sell businesses and dismiss staff on this advice. If the evidence for his prescriptions is weak, perhaps they should think again?

4. *What's wrong with the middle ground?* Porter seems to suggest that markets can only be successfully exploited at the extremes of low-cost provision or premium provision. He suggests that the volume market is always a low-cost one.

   But people do not only live in tents or palaces, eat either rice or chocolates and travel only by bicycle or by limousine. In most markets the consumer is drawn to the middle in search of acceptable quality and an affordable price. In denying this point Porter makes use of the product lifecycle and observes that, as the mature stage progresses, the margins in the middle will get squeezed even if customers do not split into the two extreme segments he envisages.

   This opens him up to several further criticisms:

   (a) Industry life-cycles and profits tend to be driven by technological changes not competitive ones. None of his strategies can offset technological obsolescence.

   (b) All firms accept that products will become mature and will sustain their profits by launching new products.

5. *Competitive prescriptions may be misleading.* Porter's model is very abstract and many managers struggle to understand how his terms and prescriptions apply to their industry.

   (a) Differentiation strategy: Porter roots this in the customer's *perception* of the firm's position in the market. This encourages some managers to equate it with 'hype' not competence.

   - Managers may replace a sound resource-based strategy with promotion and 'hype' that is shallow and too easily seen through or imitated.

   - Managers may wrongly perceive of their rivals' strategies as likewise 'smoke and dust' and not see the resources underlying it. For example, we frequently forget that Coca-Cola's differentiation is not just about its brand image. There is also an awesome supply-chain capability in place to put their product to within 'an arm's reach of desire'.

     Porter seeks to dispel this problem by discussing the need to use the entire value chain to develop competitive advantage.

   (b) Cost leadership: this is based on the notion of the firm having lower costs and hence attracting the mass market where the economies of scale exist. There is a serious flaw in this strategy:

   - Cost leadership is not a competitive strategy because the customer is not influenced to buy a product by the nature of a firm's cost structure. They are looking at benefits and prices.

   - Therefore a cost leadership strategy must involve cutting price if it is to attract the mass end of the market.

- But if the firm needs to gain mass to get economies of scale, this implies that it is not initially a low-cost player.
  - So Porter is actually advising firms to risk sparking a price war without first having the low-cost structure it needs to survive it.

6. *It restricts the firm to its present industry.* The model does not consider how the firm might use its competitive advantages in new industries. Instead it looks only at how its resources and strategy may be developed in its existing lines of business.

Hamel and Prahalad (1994) observe that superior shareholder value is earned by 'breakthrough strategies'. These are ones that enable firms to create new markets and industries through innovative use of the firm's 'distinctive competences'. One example of this is the way Sony creates new industries and markets through leveraging its core competence of miniaturisation (e.g. personal stereos, compact discs, miniature and portable televisions).

The authors would not dispute the need to perform well in the existing market, but they criticise the excessive emphasis placed upon it by models like Porter's at the expense of genuine creativity and innovation. We will talk more of this when we come to internal development in Section 6.4.2.

6.2.9 Alternatives to Porter: the resource-based view

Porter seeks to define competitive advantage in terms of factors within a particular industry that leads to the difficulties mentioned in points 1 and 2 above. The approach also suffers from the uncertainty surrounding forecasting the threats and opportunities in particular industries.

This has led some strategists to take a *resource-based view of strategy.* This locates competitive advantage inside the firm by concentrating on the identification of the *core competences* of the firm, that is, those things which it is good at and which cannot easily be copied by rivals. Management should then look for industries to which these competences can be applied for the generation of competitive advantage or, better still, to create entirely new industries based on finding new applications for the competences of the firm.

The resource-based view of strategy was discussed earlier in the pillar and will be covered, briefly, later on.

6.3 Product-market strategies

6.3.1 The Ansoff matrix

Ansoff (1965) demonstrates the choices of strategic direction open to a firm in the form of a matrix (Figure 6.5).

6.3.2 Market penetration strategy

Firm increases its sales in its present line of business. This can be accomplished by:

- price reductions;
- increases in promotional and distribution support;
- acquisition of a rival in the same market;
- modest product refinements.

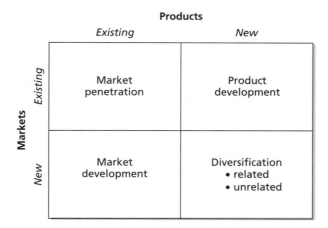

Figure 6.5 The Ansoff product–market scope matrix (adapted from Ansoff, 1965)

These strategies involve increasing the firm's investment in a product/market and so are generally only used in markets which are growing, and hence the investment may be recouped. In this respect the strategy is similar to the *invest to build* and *holding* strategy discussed by the Boston Consulting Group.

6.3.3 Product development strategy

This involves extending the product range available to the firm's existing markets. These products may be obtained by:

- investment in the research and development of additional products;
- acquisition of rights to produce someone else's product;
- buying-in the product and 'badging' it;
- joint development with owners of another product who need access to the firm's distribution channels or brands.

The critical factor to the success of this strategy is the profitability of the customer group for which the products are being developed. Also the firm's present competitive advantages in serving the market must confer on to the new good. These can include:

- customer information that allows accurate targeting;
- established distribution channels;
- a brand which can be credibly applied to the new product.

6.3.4 Market development strategies

Here the firm develops through finding another group of buyers for its products. Examples include:

- different customer segments, for example, introducing younger people to goods previously purchased mainly by adults;
- industrial buyers for a good that was previously sold only to households;
- new areas or regions of the country;
- foreign markets.

This strategy is more likely to be successful where:

- the firm has a unique product technology it can leverage in the new market;
- it benefits from economies of scale if it increases output;
- the new market is not too different from the one it has experience of;
- the buyers in the market are intrinsically profitable.

6.3.5 Diversification strategies

Here the firm is becoming involved in an entirely new industry, or a different stage in the value chain of its present industry. Ansoff distinguishes several forms of diversification:

1. *Related diversification.* Here there is some relationship, and therefore potential synergy, between the firm's existing business and the new product/market space:

   (a) *Concentric diversification* means that there is a *technological* similarity between the industries which means that the firm is able to leverage its technical know-how to gain some advantage. For example, a company that manufactures industrial adhesives might decide to diversify into adhesives to be sold via retailers. The technology would be the same but the marketing effort would need to change.

   (b) *Vertical integration* means that the firm is moving along the value system of its existing industry towards its customers *(forward vertical integration)* or towards its suppliers *(backward vertical integration)*. The benefits of this are assumed to be:

   - taking over the profit margin presently enjoyed by suppliers or distributors;
   - securing a demand for the product or a supply of key inputs;
   - better synchronisation of the value system;
   - reduction in buyer or supplier power.

     However, it also means increasing the firm's investment in the industry and hence its fixed cost base. It should also be noted that *Vertical integration* may well take the company into industries where the operating characteristics are significantly different. For instance, the oil industry can be considered, simplistically, to have three stages in the industry value chain. Those stages can be described as exploration and production, refining and, finally, marketing of petroleum and other products. The business model and the critical success factors for each of these industries are quite different and will require different types of management to be successful. They are sufficiently different to be described as *unrelated diversification.* Shell is a typical vertically integrated company.

2. *Unrelated diversification.* This is otherwise termed *conglomerate growth* because the resulting corporation is a *conglomerate,* that is, a collection of businesses without any relationship to one another. The strategic justifications advanced for this strategy are to:

   - take advantage of poorly managed companies which can then be turned around and either run at a gain to the shareholders or sold on at a profit;
   - spread the risks of the firm across a wide range of industries;
   - escape a mature or declining industry by using the positive cash flows from it to develop into new and more profitable areas of business.

   A typical conglomerate company would be Yamaha who manufacture amongst other products pianos, musical organs and motorcycles.

   There are a number of reasons why firms diversify;

   - to exploit their resources in related markets
   - to capture the benefits of synergies

- to learn from the industry into which they diversify
- to control supplies or markets – vertical integration
- to capture the value added in a different stage of the industry value system
- to spread risk
- because they have the cash to do so
- personal ambition of the board

When a company decides to diversify there will always be tradeoffs between;

- economies of scale – where the company can benefit from the overall size of the organisation and from producing particular products in large quantities. As well as higher throughput on expensive capital equipment this could result in purchasing discounts, the further spreading of overheads and optimisation through greater opportunities to specialise.
- economies of scope – where the company can benefit from being able to share resources or link activities between different products or markets. The firm could benefit from the sharing of fixed assets and overheads together with the sharing of sunk costs such as brands and distribution networks. Where there are commonalities amongst inputs purchasing discounts may also be available.
- learning by exploration – where a company may not only learn to do new things but invent new products and processes and combine them with existing ones.
- exploitation – where a company, by gaining experience, may be able to modify and improve particular processes over time.
- dependency – where a company mitigates its dependency on a particular product, customer, market or technology.
- management attention – the extent to which senior management can continue to give attention to a particular product, market or industry, understand the survival and success factors, and make appropriate strategic decisions whilst learning to do exactly the same for a new product, market or industry.
- customer responsiveness – the extent to which a company can respond quickly, and correctly, to new and challenging customer needs whilst still responding to existing customers to their satisfaction.
- overhead costs – the extent to which these will increase with the need to address a completely different market.
- competition – the extent to which competitors will react to the company's entry to an additional industry – this is particularly important in the case of vertical integration. For instance, in the case of backward integration those who were your competitors, suppliers or customers become your customers, competitors and customers respectively, as you move up the industry value system.

6.3.6   Strategic development and risk

Developing a firm beyond its present product/market space exposes it to a combination of four sorts of risks. These risks are particularly acute where diversification is concerned because of the simultaneous novelty of both product and market.

(a) *Market risk*: The firm has entered a new market where established firms already operate. The risks here are:
- not correctly understanding the culture of the market or the needs of the customer;
- high distribution costs due to lack of economies of scale;

- failure to be seen as credible by the buyers in the market due to lack of track record or brand;
- exposure to retaliation by established firms with more entrenched positions.

(b) *Product risk*: The firm is involving itself in a new production process which is already being conducted by rival firms: The risks this poses are:
- higher production costs due to lack of experience;
- initial quality problems or inferior products causing irreparable harm to reputation in the market;
- lack of established production infrastructure and supply-chain relations which will make costs higher and may limit product innovation and quality.

(c) *Operational and managerial risk*: This boils down to the danger that management will not be able to run the new business properly. This carries with it the second danger that management will also be distracted from running the original business effectively too.

(d) *Financial risk*: This relates to the share price of the business. Shareholders are generally suspicious of 'radical' departures (and particularly diversification) for the following reasons:
- the product and market risks lead to volatile returns;
- the firm may need to write off substantial new net assets if the venture fails;
- the investment needed will reduce dividend and/or necessitate new borrowing;
- a diverse and unique portfolio makes it harder to compare the firm with others in the same industry when trying to evaluate its risks and returns.

The effect will be for the share price to decline to reflect the uncertainties created by the strategy.

6.4 Alternative growth strategies

6.4.1 The expansion method matrix

This is the third element in Figure 6.2. It is the method by which the firm will gain access to the products and markets it has selected from the Ansoff matrix. Lynch (1997) presents the alternative growth strategies as shown in Figure 6.6.

Geographical location \ **Company**	*Internal development*	*External development*
Home country	Internal development	Merger Acquisition Joint venture Alliance Franchise/licence
International	Exporting Overseas office Overseas manufacture Multinational operation Global operation	Merger Acquisition Joint venture Alliance Franchise/licence Turnkey

Figure 6.6 Lynch's expansion method matrix (adapted from Lynch, 1997)

6.4.2   Internal development

Some times known as organic growth, internal development involves the firm in growing using its own resources to develop products or services, capital assets and staff, or to build market. In doing so it may well diversify away from the core business.

This approach to growth will mean that a firm will need to be adept at the management of innovation, which has been described as a core competence in its own right.

Not all firms that attempt the approach enjoy equal success. Whilst Pilkington and EMI are both innovative, Pilkington gained significant advantage from the development of the float glass process, EMI was not so successful having developed the technology for medical scanners. The product was truly innovative but the business had to be sold off at a loss since EMI was so badly wounded financially.

In contrast, Compaq and Kodak are technology followers and have seen quite different results from letting others develop the technology. Compaq was successful with the PC, whilst Kodak had limited success with its attempt to enter the instant photograph market – despite its reputation in the market for ordinary films.

For the innovative firm there will be issues about structure and management that will need to be addressed particularly if there is a core business to be managed as well. Some organisations have got around this by completely separating the innovation process from their main stream business. General Motors is just such an example; they separated their new ventures division, Saturn, and allowed very little day-to-day contact between that division and the main firm. Once new processes were developed they were migrated to the main part of the firm.

For a creative firm or business unit there will be a need to reward risk taking and independent mindedness, this will not be the case in an organisation operating in a more stable environment where cost efficiencies are more likely to be the route to success for the firm. This is just one of the paradoxes faced by a firm that wishes to be a leader in the field of innovation.

Additionally, companies will have to consider:

- the balance between the comfort of stability and the potential success of novelty
- the degree of self management versus cooperation allowed the staff
- the degree of freedom versus control in the systems used by the firm – will there actually be separate control systems for the different parts of the firm – including reward systems?
- the balance to be achieved between experience/routine and fresh view/ignorance – one of the biggest problems is to keep a fresh outlook whilst benefiting from deep and broad knowledge

Therefore for a firm to be a successful innovator there will need to be:

- Obvious senior management commitment with the provision of resources in the form of funds, equipment, training, time and the tolerance of uncertainty and failure.
- The control mechanisms need to be cultural rather than bureaucratic with project controls which allow, and encourage, procedural autonomy. At 3M's where they aim to have at least 30 per cent of turnover generated by products introduced within the previous 5 years managers are encouraged, by substantial bonuses to develop successful new products – they are expected to devote 15 per cent of their working time to doing so.
- Communication systems should be open encouraging the sharing of information, the exchange of ideas and cross functional project teams.

- A trusting atmosphere must be developed with the absence of turf wars or unhealthy conflict but healthy competition

There are two principle sources of inspiration for innovation:

- customer needs analysis – *market pull,*
- technology development analysis – *technology push.*

Market pull

Either because of new market opportunities or segments of existing markets that have been neglected there may be growth opportunities for the firm. This kind of analysis is best approached in terms of the broad customer need rather than specific market or product approaches. For instance, Canon identified a need for photocopiers which were low maintenance to be sold to relatively small businesses rather than their existing customer base which was predominately larger firms.

Whittington (1993) has indicated that the importance of market pull in successful innovation has been well proven by research but that this is a prescriptive approach to corporate strategy. As such it carries the risk that customers may be constrained in their vision by their current knowledge and experience.

Technology push

Market pull does not fully describe the way that innovation happens. Quite often innovation is born of developments, often in cooperation with their customers. Successful technology often takes time to migrate through to other industries. With this in mind companies who intend to be innovative should monitor technological change in other industries and determine the relevance of any innovations to their own firm.

There are effectively three phases of innovation. The diffusion process that usually occurs follows a typical S curve. A new technology is adopted slowly at first, the pace quickens and finally there are a few late adopters entering the market. Quite often it is not those who are first into the market with a new technology that make the most returns on their investment. Initially there are few purchasers and there may well have been heavy investment in R&D. The investors may be better served by those who are 'close seconds' into the market. The technology is still new but there are increasing numbers of adopters, making for a larger market, and the heavy R&D spend has been made by some other firm. This is supported by research described by Mansfield (1992) in the Economist. Having tracked innovations over a 30-year period he estimated that on average those who were second into a new market could manufacture the new product for two thirds of the cost and time of the first, innovative, entrant.

It is often the case that those 'close seconds' and those that follow them into a market are process innovators rather than product innovators. As a new product gains acceptance in the market place a dominant design will usually emerge. This will represent the generally accepted configuration of components that defines the look, functionality, a design characteristics most acceptable to the customer. In some cases that *defacto* standard may be imposed by regulatory bodies, as in the case of broadcasting (radio and television) and telephony. Alternatively it may arise by market power as in the case of PC operating systems where Windows tends to dominate the market.

Once this situation has been reached successful firms tend to be those that can bring about incremental (rather than revolutionary) changes in the process by which the product or service is made and/or provided. Those firms will seek to reduce costs and increase product reliability usually through larger scale operations.

A combination of the two

We described these waves of innovation earlier in terms of S curves (Figure 6.7) or envelope curves each representing a new type of technology.

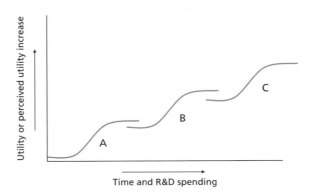

Figure 6.7 S curves or envelope curves

Figure 6.7 shows a typical set of envelope curves for the technologies relevant to a particular industry. The vertical axis is described as utility or perceived utility. Utility means usefulness or value. However, just because something is better it may not be perceived as being better. This represents an important point about product innovation for companies. They may well have produced a better product but, unless the consumers consider it to be better, it will not necessarily sell better than the old version.

Using an example from the industry that manufactures detergents, the first S curve A would represent the invention of detergents themselves. Initially a lot of money would be spent improving the ability of detergents to actually get washing clean and so the curve rises slowly but, as improvements are achieved and recognised, there will be a steep rise to the curve. Eventually as consumers recognise that the detergent is doing the best job in terms of cleanliness that it can, there is little point in spending more money developing stronger and stronger detergents.

One of the features of strong detergents is that they wash out any colour in a fabric and damage the substance of the fabric – clothes end up looking grey (rather than white) and 'scruffy'. The scruffiness is caused by the fibres of the material sticking together and the fabric looses its 'softness'.

Market research showed that the customers not only wanted their clothes to be clean but to look clean. Research then shifted to the science of chemicals called optical brighteners – chemicals which would stick to the fabric and make it reflect light, and look nice and white. The research efforts for that branch of science are shown by the envelope curve B which would be where sensible companies were spending their money. We can see that curve A has, at that point in time, started to fall away. There is no point in spending further money on developing stronger detergents – customers and users are making a judgement based on appearance and brightness of the fabric.

Similarly curve C would represent the progress of the detergent industry's efforts to deal with the problem of fabric loosing its substance and softness. A different technology would be the sensible place for companies to invest further research funds as any extra money spent on improvements in the old technology would be wasted.

Each of these examples represents a product innovation. In each case the consumer perceived an improvement in the product they purchased.

An example of a process innovation from the same industry would relate to the process for manufacturing detergents. When detergents are manufactured all of the ingredients, including the fragrance, are poured into a long rotating tube and emerge from the other end, spray dried, as finished powder. Unfortunately, when a company manufactures more than one brand of powder each will have a different fragrance. When one brand follows another down the production tube there will be a quantity of powder in between the two batches where the fragrances mix, usually with unpleasantly smelling results. This quantity of powder is wasted. By developing a chemical process whereby the fragrance could be added after the spray drying process the company no longer has any waste in the manufacturing plant. The consumers did not see any difference in the final product in their packet of detergent but the company was able to operate more efficiently. This is an example of process innovation.

If we take a closer look at a pair of the envelope curves we can consider how a discontinuity arises in an industry (Figure 6.8);

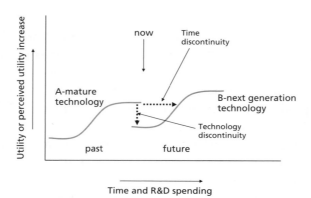

Figure 6.8 discontinuities

As we can see, in the graph, in Figure 6.8 progress along one of the curves and the utility or perceived utility is increasing as time and/or R&D spending increases then we are seeing evidence of incremental change or continuous innovation. This occurs within the boundaries of the known world. The future requirements of consumers can be met by the capabilities of the existing industry structures and technology. Continuous innovation is characterised by progressive refinements, convergent thinking and increased focus leading to increasing specialisation. Although there is a focus on continuous improvement in the literature and techniques of total quality management this will not be sufficient for the world to progress. In fact, whenever one investigates a company that has been successful over the past century in a technology intensive field it is always possible to find large leaps into major new product lines. These dramatic leaps are then followed by periods of trying to stay ahead of the competition. Although companies have become better at managing periods of incremental change there is no evidence that they have become better at managing dramatic change. There is very little perceived wisdom on when it will be necessary to shift the firms' emphasis from one technology to another. The timing for jumping from curve A to curve B in the diagram above is very important for companies and, if they get it wrong, they are unlikely to prosper or even survive. They run the risk of being very good at producing something that the market no longer wants.

Where there is a leap from one technology to another that is progress is attained by moving from curve A to curve B then this is evidence of discontinuous change. In a business sense this type of change is sufficiently major to re-invent the market place as the suppliers, competitors and customers understand it. Examples of this would include the Internet vs. the postal service and the transistor vs. the vacuum tube.

Discontinuous innovation brings about conditions that arise from fundamentally different and new knowledge in one or more dimensions of a product or service compared to what existed before. This means that we can expect products and service to have completely different attributes when this occurs. Discontinuous innovation is difficult to manage and achieve because it requires new knowledge. That new knowledge is unlikely to be found inside the existing firm and the existing way of thinking. The process is characterised by divergent or lateral thinking, by looking outside previously defined boundaries, and by discovering new knowledge related to both the technology and the potential market needs. When it occurs the knowledge boundary is, by definition, expanded.

Excess inertia will arise if early adopters of a new technology have to bear a disproportionate burden of the transient costs of moving to a new, incompatible, system – no one will be willing to take the first step. Therefore, even a much improved technology may be very slow to take hold, and the switch from the old to the new may take some time.

Discontinuous innovation does not just bring change in the simple sense, but change in a deep and systemic way that is fundamental and far reaching. Not only are products and services affected but also the infrastructure that is necessary for their use. The shift from horse to automobile for personal transport brought about a shift from urban to sub-urban communities offering new lifestyles brought about by real estate development based, in turn, upon the development of new roads. These new roads brought about new patterns of traffic movements and new forms of congestion and pollution. Not all of the outcomes of the new technology will be beneficial. The fact that we developed automobiles did make our life easier but, quite possibly; it made our life less healthy. By using our car we get less exercise, and we are subject to exhaust fumes – something which the inventors may not have considered. This law of unintended consequences will often be seen when there are complex or fundamental changes in the system. Whenever someone makes a decision to change something that is part of a complex adaptive system, such as personal transportation, the effects are often far reaching and not always beneficial. The results are often quite surprising.

There are often completely new rules of competition and whole companies, or even industries, are rendered invalid. At one point in our history there was a global infrastructure for the distribution of paraffin for lighting houses, and another for distributing ice for cooling. Both of these industries were well developed, quite sophisticated, employed many people and were profitable. Both are now long gone. At the time of writing, the computer industry and the telecommunications industry have gone through a period of dramatically discontinuous innovation. Other industries that are currently being reshaped by this phenomenon include the airline industry, the auto industry, retail, entertainment and even the previously staid world of electricity generation. It is highly unlikely that any industry or business can fully protect itself from the impact of discontinuous change.

In a stable world there would be no need for discontinuous innovation, and organisations could survive and prosper by continuous innovation alone. However, the increasing rate of change in the expectations of consumers and increasing competition, particularly on a global scale, mean that companies will, inevitably, pursue proprietary technical advances. The threat of competition from unexpected quarters, the risk of industry evolution, and the shortening of the sales cycle makes it necessary for companies to look for competitive advantage by creating discontinuities. This leads to further specialisation which, in turn, leads to further change.

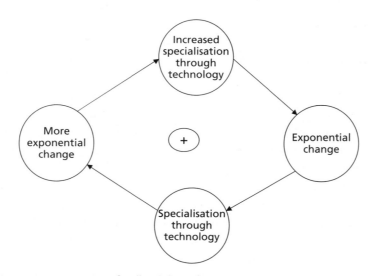

Figure 6.9 Positive feedback loop found in technology-driven markets

Figure 6.9 a positive feedback loop or reinforcing loop. Each stage of the circle contributes to the next and a never ending process is formed. In effect there is a mutual dependent learning process between the consumers and the supplying firms. As customers express what they want and require the supplier develops a product to meet that need. In doing so, they produce something that exceeds the requirement of the customer which leads them to want even more.

However a recent analysis of PIMS data shows that there is a negative correlation of product R&D to profitability. Perhaps this is the reason that many companies gain their new product knowledge through strategic alliances with companies that are more innovative. PIMS was discussed in Chapter 5.

The principal benefits of this approach are:

(a) Firm does not need to assimilate the differing personal, cultures or operating systems of another organisation.
(b) Investment can be controlled and increased, unlike acquisition when the firm must commit substantial funds in an all-or-nothing gamble.
(c) Provides development and learning opportunities to staff.
(d) Avoids the need for a goodwill premium at acquisition; instead, assets are acquired at just their market value.
(e) Demonstrates to investors the ability of management to grow their own business and create opportunities; this should improve the share price.

(f) There is no need to share proceeds of success; can build first mover advantage before competitors realise that there is a need to imitate them.

The drawbacks are:

(a) Firm will not at first enjoy the economies of scale and experience effects available to rivals.
(b) Market entry may be too slow if the industry is developing quickly.
(c) The increase in the number of firms in the industry which increases complexity and may provoke hostile responses from established firms.
(d) Firm may lack access to key resources or customers if the industry features complex long-term supply contracts.
(e) Firm has to bear all of the financial risk of product development or market entry.

It is worth noting that it is not usually the first company that enters a market that gets the advantage. Indeed they normally exit just as fast. It is rather the first company that succeeds in the market that gets the advantages and becomes the big winner. For example, Charles Stack was the first company into the online book – you may not have heard of them – Amazon.com was second and is far better known. Similarly, iTunes was not first but is strongest, Napster was first and is no more. It has been argued by Markides and Geroski (2004) that large companies are unable to create, or even compete with disruptive innovations and that they are better served by being fast second 'consolidators' of markets rather than initial stage 'colonisers'. Most radical innovation comes from dynamic young companies who, in the main, exit the market shortly after entering it. Fast second is less exciting, but strategically smarter and more practical to execute.

The power of small adaptions can be illustrated by considering, again, the Tesco Club card and its impact on the company. In the early days of loyalty cards Safeway, launched a card followed quite quickly by Tesco. Both offered a 1% discount to shoppers. Both marketing departments recognised that sales would not increase that much by virtue of the discount but that the value of the card would lie in the data which it provided. Loyalty card members would opt into a relationship with the supermarket which permitted the grocer access to their personal data in exchange for a more personalised promotional package of offers. However, the two companies approached the opportunity differently. Safeway, sought to analyse every single piece of data that came in, looking to gain information from every single transaction. They attempted to develop a better understanding of every single customer through an enormous analytical undertaking and capture all of the intricacies of the shopping experience. This enormous effort failed as it was beyond their data mining capabilities. Tesco, by contrast, consciously threw the majority of the data away and sought a few useful insights. When the knowledge gained proved useful, they slowly built on the success and kept more and more of the data, slowly adding to the complexity of their analysis and to the actions which the analysis led to. This has happened year after year and the Club card is now a potent weapon in Tesco's domination of the UK supermarket industry as we described earlier.

6.4.3 Joint development strategies

As we mentioned briefly in Chapter 2, where we discussed relationships with buyers and suppliers, firms will often collaborate with each other to jointly attack a market. This can be done under a variety of arrangements with a greater or lesser degree of formality.

It must be noted that the most extreme form of cooperation – an intent by competitors to rig markets – is illegal in most countries. There have been a number of recent, successful, prosecutions by the European Union of cartels where this has been proven such as the French firm Lafarge for their fixing of prices in the plasterboard industry.

The airline industry, entertainment industry, construction industry and banking industry have all used business alliances as a strategic approach and organisational form for managing resources for a long time. More recently, both the automotive and pharmaceutical industries have used the technique as well, particularly in the areas of R&D and production. The number of alliances between biotechnology companies increased from 152 to 375 between 1990 and 1998. According to a survey by Booz Allen and Hamilton, between 1996 and 1998, 20,000 strategic business alliances were formed and represented, collectively 21 per cent of the total revenue of the Fortune 1000. According to Naisbitt (1995), as computer, telephone, and cable TV companies come to realize that their markets will ultimately be one and the same, cross border, cross industry alliances will become the normal way of conducting business.

Alliances have the potential to create or provide the following opportunities:

- extend and compliment the core competencies of the firms involved;
- share structural costs;
- mitigate risk by spreading it amongst more firms;
- facilitate the entry into new markets on a global or regional basis;
- provide access to knowledge of another organisation;
- create new market and customer opportunities for all players concerned;
- reduce or get around barriers to entry in certain geographical or political markets;
- capitalise on significant synergies of purpose and scale;
- reduce and even destroy physical boundaries that define the traditional firm and classical industry structures;
- neutralise the strategic and operational advantages of an unaligned competitor;
- accelerate the rate of innovation and strategic renewal;

It is important to remember that these business combinations may be short lived, and indeed set up initially for a finite time period or to exploit a particular event. How they are set up and how they will be managed is an important consideration. There needs to be a perception on both sides of the agreement that there is an equality of exchange. There is evidence that alliances between unequal partners rarely work. And alliances are often cut short, the median life is 7 years and a quarter last less than 3 years. Reasons cited for termination include, cultural incompatibility (particularly with cross border alliances), mistrust or a sense of an unfair exchange.

What happens at the end of any collaboration is also an important issue. Toshiba, in its joint ventures, has a pre-alliance agreement, spelling out what each partner can expect at the end of the period of collaboration. Bleeke and Ernst (1995) found that more than 75 per cent of alliances finished with one partner being acquired by the other. This is often the intention of one of the partners, and the UK media company Emap has used this as a means of minimising its risk whilst successfully entering the mainland European market for consumer magazines.

As we can see, in all of these cooperative ventures the risk of failure is quite high but there are some ground rules which will improve the chances of success. These rules can be considered under three broad headings;

1. *The planning period prior to the alliance.* Knowledge prior to the arrangement is key to success and many failures have been attributed to a lack of clear knowledge about what the company want to achieve from the alliance and what they can expect from their intended partners.

   - There should be a clear idea of what the company wishes to achieve in the short run and what they believe the other partner(s) wish to achieve in the same time frame.

   - There should be a clear idea what competencies and capabilities all parties will bring to the partnership and what further will be needed. Is the basket of skills sufficient to achieve what is required? Ideally many partners will be lacking the skills that the company has, or they will soon evolve into capable, and direct, competitors.

   - In the longer term what can the company learn from the alliance and the partner(s)? This should be clearly established before the venture is formed and plans in place for how it will be achieved. However, as the alliance progresses it is likely that other opportunities will emerge and so this area should be constantly monitored.

   - In both the short and the long term what does the company not want the partner(s) to learn from them? Bearing in mind how many alliances end in takeover, this is an important area to consider.

   - As with any project where there is significant change communicating with staff is essential. All of those staff who are to be involved in the partnership must be kept informed of the reasons for and the objectives of the alliance. Aside from their concerns for their own future they will be better able to achieve the objectives of the alliance if they are kept fully informed.

   - The appropriate structure must be decided to ensure that the alliance is controlled but not embedded in the organisation to such an extent that problems are caused when its useful life is finished. It should be remembered that it can be finished by any of the partners and the terms and conditions for such cessation clearly understood.

2. *Learning from an alliance.* One of the most important potential gains from alliances and joint ventures is the opportunity to learn from both the experience and the partner(s) involved. Quite possibly partners will be making efforts to ensure that others do not learn from them and so this is another area that needs careful planning. A successful company will not only learn from its partners but will ensure that the knowledge gained is spread throughout its own staff.

   - There needs to be decision concerning who has the responsibility for maximising the learning from partners. Learning objectives must be clearly identified and agreed with those who have the responsibility. By making sure that those staff are sufficiently informed of the long-term goals of the organisation they will be more aware of how they might gather useful information and why there is a need to do so. Additionally, when if unexpected opportunities arise they will be better equipped to recognise them as such and capitalise upon the opportunity.

   - The machinery for the transfer of new knowledge gained from the partnership needs to be in place in the organisation. Relying on a process of diffusion is rarely effective and explicit plans should be in place to make sure that a critical mass of staff is given the new knowledge. This could be by cross disciplinary seminars, job rotation or other explicit knowledge sharing systems.

   - Introduce systems that encourage the gaining and dissemination of knowledge from the alliance. Encourage people to seek out knowledge and skills as they manage the routine of the joint venture. Appraisal systems and performance measurement systems should be modified to explicitly reward the gaining and teaching of new knowledge.

- As alliances progress they will change and these changes will present new and often unexpected opportunities to learn. Whilst the systems are being developed to monitor alliances to know when to walk away the means of identifying changes that present new learning opportunities should also be developed. These opportunities may be represented by changes in the alliance partner(s) capabilities, novel ways of working, or changes in the market that the alliance addresses. The learning goals that were originally developed may need to change as this happens.

- Recognise that other partners in the alliance will learn from the company. Whilst blocking techniques will work in the short term any partner that has taken the learning process seriously will inevitably learn what they want to from your staff. It is a fine balance between being sufficiently open to ensure that the alliance works and keeping knowledge secret to make sure that a partner does not become a strong competitor. Arguably the most important thing is to make sure that the company is a faster and more efficient learner than any of the partners with whom it chooses to enter into alliances.

- Decide early how to make sure that losses are minimised if the partner(s) leave the alliance. As with any organisation successful alliances develop unique routines which may be somewhat more dependent upon the partner(s) systems and processes than the company's. Firstly it is necessary to ensure that the company, itself, does not become dependent upon those systems and secondly they can still manage the venture if a partner walks away. This may well mean that some of the processes which are run within the alliance may need to be duplicated within the company. Although this incurs extra costs it does go some way to ensuring that the company can carry on itself and manage the new venture successfully if left to do so alone. If the purpose of the alliance is worthwhile to the company long run success may be more important than short run profits.

- Recognise that all parties to an alliance have a responsibility to develop and bring new knowledge to that alliance. Although there may be clauses in the original contract to ensure that no partner takes unfair advantage of each other there may well come a time when one or more partners are no longer making a significant contribution. At that point in time the company may choose to leave the partnership taking with it the knowledge it has gained. It may well be that the company has identified an alternative partner better able to complement its skills and make a bigger contribution. A company will only be in a position to make that kind of decision if it has taken steps to monitor the performance of its existing partners and benchmarked them against other firms with similar skill profiles.

3. *Alliance management skills.* The management of alliances and joint ventures is different to the management of an organisation or a subsidiary. Look back to Chapter 3 where we talked about alternative value chains and considered network value chains with which there are similarities. Organisations which involve themselves in alliances must have distinct structures and systems in place to manage those relationships. To treat an alliance as a subsidiary or as a completely separate third party can be a costly mistake. As we shall shortly see some organisations can be involved in a large number of alliances or joint ventures at the same time. There should be a standard approach for dealing with all of them. Internal conflict will be reduced if all alliances are managed in the same way. Additionally, since one of the potential gains from an alliance is the learning opportunities a uniform system of management should facilitate the transfer of knowledge from all alliances uniformly across all of the company and across all of the alliance teams. This will be particularly important if one group of staff involved in one alliance develop a superior routine

for gathering knowledge from their alliance partners. That routine should be transferred to other teams so that they can use and implement it as well. Well written contracts (usually called 'Heads of Agreement' in joint ventures and alliances) are essential and will govern rights, responsibilities, dispute resolution procedures, and a number of other formal considerations. Informal contracts will provide a shared understanding of the purpose and spirit of the venture but, most importantly, contracts will govern how well a alliance performs and how well a company learns from the relationship.

These cooperative ventures can arise in a number of forms.

1. *Joint venture.* The partners form a separate company in which each holds an equity stake. Usually management is provided by the parties to the agreement and is able to draw on the expertise of the parties. For example, Vodaphone uses international joint ventures to enter regional markets. In the United States it has acquired Verizon Wireless, a mobile phone operator, but has taken a local partner, retaining only 45 per cent of the equity.

   The benefits are:
   (a) Reduces risk because the firm's capital commitment is reduced to their percentage share.
   (b) Each party gains access to the competences of the other. However, to benefit from that a partner in a joint venture needs to be prepared to learn.
   (c) Avoids developing the opportunity separately and ending up in competition.
   (d) Partnership with firms in host economies allows foreign firms a route into otherwise protected markets. In some cases they are the only way into the market.

   The drawbacks are:
   (a) Disputes over operational matters such as use of trademarks, pay levels and approach to markets.
   (b) Possibility that partners will gain confidential information about each other which may be used to compete elsewhere or if the venture breaks down.
   (c) Disputes over the amount of effort being put in, the allocation of partners' costs and the division of rewards.
   (d) Lack of support from joint venture management from parent companies because neither feels they own it.
   (e) May often lead to take-over by one partner as it is a relatively low-risk method of discovering quite richly detailed information about an industry.
   Within joint ventures there are two possible structures.

   In one type all of the companies concerned will play an active role in the operation of the company formed. Each will contribute expertise as well as equity funding. For instance the National Lottery in the UK is operated by Camelot. When the initial joint venture (consortium) was formed to bid for the operating license the companies involved were; Cadbury Schweppes who had the expertise of Fast Moving Consumer Goods (in this case chocolate), DelaRue who had the experience of security printing, Racal who had the expertise in electronics and would be responsible for the sales terminals in the shops and GTech, an American company, who had the expertise of running lotteries. Together they all provided facilities and staff who brought the required knowledge with them. Each had an equity share by virtue of their financial investment and their expertise. The partnership was set up for a finite time and had the bid been unsuccessful would have been wound up.

With the alternative structure one company provides the expertise whilst the other consortium partners provide equity only. This is most common in very large projects where the investment involved is very large. One notable example, which has been fraught with problems has been the consortium of banks which lent money for the development of Eurotunnel. A lead bank would take care of all of the relationships with the Eurotunnel management and the other minority partners would only be required to respond to cash calls from the lead bank when each tranche of funding was required. A more common example would be the exploration and development of oil fields, particularly in the North Sea. The lead company, often known as the operator, would have all of the employees' necessary and appropriate skills to (hopefully) find and exploit oil reserves. By default the operator will have the largest equity share. After an initial agreement on the size of the budget the operator would be responsible for the whole of the operation and would cash call the other minority partners when each tranche of funding was required. In the case of the oil industry most minority partners would be other oil companies and would have their own geologists, engineers and other specialists but, once the initial budget was agreed, would have little say in the decisions made on the progress of the project. Their only right is one of annual audit when the operator has to 'prove' that the sums of money received have been spent on the project and not any of the other ventures in which it almost certainly be involved. At the peak of exploration in the North Sea companies like Occidental were operators of as many as twelve separate joint ventures and minority partners in a further ten. This makes for complicated relationships where a minority partner in one joint venture is an operator in another. Occasionally there were partners who did not employ oil industry specialists but they were invariably invited into consortia to satisfy license conditions of having a 'local' partner. Grand Metropolitan, a large hotel group, were such a company.

2. *Strategic alliances.* Two or more firms agree to work together to exploit common advantages. In contrast to joint ventures where the partners may be from different businesses, strategic partnerships and alliances are usually formed by firms informal agreement between management, through a legal arrangement, to a cementing of the relationship with the swapping of equity. Much will depend upon what each partner is bringing to the alliance. In some cases, notably banking and oil exploration, there will be one 'lead' or operating company who will provide all of the expertise while the other partners will only provide finance – thus spreading the risk of all concerned. They are, effectively, sleeping partners. Examples include:

   - alliances between national airlines (e.g. the 'One World Alliance') to cross-book passengers;
   - Matsushita Electrical Industrial and Hitachi, Japans two leading electronics manufacturers are jointly developing state of the art consumer electronics.
   - alliances between car manufacturers to jointly develop auto technology (e.g. the 'Prometheus' project for driverless cars).

   The benefits are similar to joint ventures but, in addition, a strategic alliance is often used to allow smaller firms to present an effective alternative to a large dominant player in the market. It is also worth noting that, in times of uncertainty, stock markets tend to prefer alliances to mergers and acquisitions. However there are some special difficulties:

   (a) Ambiguity in the alliance agreement or the breakdown of trust between partners will jeopardise the alliance.
   (b) Some informal alliances risk breaking laws against collusion and cartels.

(c) Because partners remain essentially separate, many alliances fail to achieve the integration and commitment necessary to gain significant strategic advantage. To the customer they can look and behave like a 'pantomime horse', that is stitched together, disjointed and unconvincing.

3. *Franchises.* Here the firm expands its business by granting other firms the right to use its business systems. Perhaps the most famous example of this has been McDonald's.

The firm (the *franchiser*) will provide a variety of supports to the buyer of the business package (the *franchisee*). These may include:

- management training;
- a set of procedures and instructions for supplying the product/service;
- central marketing support (e.g. inclusion in national advertising);
- inputs such as materials or products to sell on;
- technical and business consultancy;
- staff training programmes;
- preferential access to capital.

In return, the franchisee will provide:

- an initial lump sum to buy the franchise;
- a share of earnings (usually based on turnover);
- specific payments (e.g. for training).

The benefits of franchising to the franchiser include:

(a) Quicker business expansion than would be possible using its own management and financial resources which quickly builds barriers to entry to the industry.

(b) Reduced risk due to the capital having been provided by the franchisee.

(c) Retains the dynamism of local management because they run their own business.

(d) Control over the activities of the franchisees to the extent provided for in the franchise agreement.

(e) Reduced costs of control due to franchise manager being responsible for finances, assets and staffing.

The drawbacks of franchising include:

(a) Reduced profits because they must be shared with franchisee.

(b) Need to monitor franchisee to assure consistency of product service (quality, pricing, product range, sales methods).

(c) Danger that poor franchise performance will harm the parent's brand.

(d) Problem of protecting intellectual capital from being copied by franchisees who later become rivals.

Licenses are very similar to franchising in their financial aspects. However, the degree of central control and support is usually less. Licenses include:

- the right to exploit a natural resource (e.g. a logging license);
- the right to use a brand or image on a product;
- the right to produce a product using the licenser's recipes and brand names (e.g. computer manufacturers installing Windows 2000).

4. *Agency agreements.* These are usually restricted to marketing and product support arrangements. They are particularly useful in the following situations:

- where the customers like to compare a range of products and take advice (e.g. financial services, carpets, software);
- where the sales volumes are too low to justify a dedicated distribution channel (e.g. specialist holidays);
- where the sales are enhanced by social and family networks (e.g. cosmetics, children's books and toys).

The agent receives a set of samples, literature and product training. They also receive a commission from their sales that are supplied from the parent company.

Agency agreements have a number of problems:

- The danger that the product will be mis-sold by agents anxious for commissions.
- The firm fails to build a relationship with the customer, or gain data, because this would undermine the agent and make them suspicious of being cut out.
- The danger that agents will desert the firm and take the best customers with them.

6.4.4 Mergers and acquisitions

This growth method involves the firm combining with another firm. Technically a distinction can be made between mergers and acquisitions:

- under a merger the issued shares of the merger partners are annulled and replaced by shares in the new combined entity;
- under an acquisition the buyer (or predator) purchases the shares of the other (the target) and the latter ceases to exist as an independent entity.

In reality the distinction is blurred and many acquisitions are window-dressed to appear as mergers. This is because management believes that investors will look more favourably on a combination that is presented as a merger because it suggests agreement. It may also ease the problem of integrating staff by eliminating the culture of 'victor and vanquished' that may follow an acquisition.

Mergers can occur for a number of reasons:

- To solve the problems of overcapacity in an industry by reducing the numbers of competitors, achieve cost reductions and synergies, and increase power and credibility. The case of the steel industry, initially in Europe and now globally, is a point in case.
- To aggregate geographically close markets to achieve economies of scale.
- To extend the product or market offering of the combined group.
- To acquire strategic resources often in the form of intellectual capital. An example would be the acquisition of biotechnology companies by large pharmaceutical firms – effectively buying the R&D done by other firms.
- To capitalise on asset stripping or turnaround opportunities.

Most research has shown that the main beneficiaries of mergers and acquisitions have been the shareholders of the acquiring company.

There have been an increasing number of mergers and acquisitions over the past few years particularly in the service sector where the achievement of economies of scale are becoming increasingly important. During the later part of the 1990s:

- ING Bank of the Netherlands bought Belgium's Banque Bruxelles Lambert (Europe's largest ever cross border merger).
- The Finnish government announced the merger of Postipankki, the country's third largest bank with the state controlled Finnish Export Credit, a commercial lender to become the second largest bank in Scandinavia.
- The USA's sixth largest bank was created when First Union of Charlotte acquired Core States of Philadelphia in a $16.6 billion deal.
- Union Bank of Switzerland was taken over by the smaller Swiss Banking Corporation to create the world's largest asset manager.

Similarly, amongst the investment banking sector, where boundaries between the different services of investment banking, stock broking and fund management have blurred, there was a similar rush for partners and targets for acquisition:

- Morgan Stanley merged with Dean Witter, Discover,
- Merrill Lynch acquired Mercury Asset Management,
- Travellers Group acquired Salomon Brothers,
- Bankers Trust bought Alex Brown.

Managerial motivation for acquisitions

It has been suggested, somewhat cynically, that the main beneficiaries of acquisitions are the management of the acquiring firm:

- to pursue growth in the size of the firm – increase their own status, power and rewards,
- for self actualisation, making use of their talents and skills,
- to ensure their job security by diversifying risk,
- to avoid takeover.

When a firm makes an acquisition it buys 'off the shelf' a collection of tangible and intangible assets, resources and capabilities. For this approach to be successful it is important that an acquisitive firm has a clear plan for the process:

Stage 1. Development of acquisition strategy, value creation logic and target criteria. This will be followed by search, screening, identification and evaluation of target firms.
Stage 2. Development of bidding strategy, including financial evaluation and pricing of the target. Negotiation, financing and closing of the agreement.
Stage 3. Evaluation of the cultural fit and the development of an integration approach. Matching of strategy and organisational structure between acquirer and acquired.

The value creation logic may be summarised as follows:

(a) The target is undervalued by the stock market (e.g. due to poor management or recent poor results). Its share price does not reflect its earnings potential.
(b) The predator's management will be able to make a better job of running the target than its present management (i.e. increase its forecast earnings).
(c) There are potentials for increasing the earnings of the combined business that were not available to them as separate entities. These are termed *synergies*.
(d) It protects the predator from potential hostile competition which would otherwise reduce its earnings and hence the wealth of its shareholders.
(e) The target has surplus assets which can be disposed of for cash without harming its earnings or which have been overlooked by the stock market (e.g. land and buildings, brands, etc.).

For example, Tomkins a UK conglomerate acquired RHM a baking and grocery group of £935 million in 1992. Although Tomkins had no experience in the industry it believed, correctly, that it could realise value by:

- closing RHM's head office,
- introducing a more devolved management structure,
- rationalising production across a number of sites,
- divesting some of RHM's brands.

Typical target criteria (the example is from BTR, an acquisitive UK conglomerate) might be as follows:

1. predominantly definable niche businesses,
2. companies which are not making the best return on assets,
3. potential high margin businesses,
4. unlikely to be in sectors like heavy engineering, mainstream retailing and mass production businesses,
5. small enough to fit into the BTR structure.

The importance of the predetermination of criteria and sticking to them cannot be emphasised enough. Although BTR (a previously successful UK conglomerate) had actually published these criteria it acquired Hawker Siddley, an engineering company in the early 1990s for £1.55 billion in a hostile takeover. The result was far from successful and it took a number of years before BTR recovered its pre-acquisition levels of performance. The target had been too big, too complex (it was involved in a large number of joint ventures around the world – some of them with governments) and most of its markets were too large to be classified as niche markets.

Making acquisitions work

It is clear from the majority of research done on mergers and acquisitions that there are many reasons for their failure. In 1997, KMPG reported that 50 per cent of European mergers failed. One of the primary reasons, however, is the failure at the post-acquisition stage. Behavioural considerations are as important as hard nosed strategic and financial ones.

Coopers and Lybrand published the following as the major causes of success and failure (Figure 6.10):

Causes of success (%)	Causes of failure (%)
Detailed post acquisition integration plans and speed of integration (76)	Target management attitudes and cultural differences (85)
Clarity of acquisition purpose (76)	No post acquisition integration planning (80)
Good cultural fit (59)	Lack of knowledge of industry or target firm (45)
High degree of target management cooperation (47)	Poor management of target (45)
Prior knoweledge of target and its industry (41)	No prior acquisition expereince (30)

Figure 6.10 Causes of acquisition success and failure

The figures in brackets represent the number of respondents citing this cause. The post-acquisition process will depend, to a large extent, on the need for strategic capabilities to be transferred between the two companies for value to be maximised. This can range from portfolio management, preservation, symbiosis through to total absorption. An absorption approach is justified where operational resources need to be pooled and rationalised to eliminate duplication. Where there is a need for the transfer of functional skills then a more symbiotic approach will be adopted. Where the intention is to transfer general management skills the firm is more likely to take a preservation approach – a conglomerate structure.

For any of these approaches to work there has to be an atmosphere created which is conducive to the appropriate level of capability transfer. This will depend to a great extent of the culture of the two organisations. Culture was an element of your earlier studies and you are strongly advised to read that material again.

It is important to understand the financial management issues behind an acquisition or merger. Acquisitions (or mergers) are afforded:

- from cash reserves;
- by supporting a rights issue of shares to raise the cash;
- by giving new shares in return for shares in the target;
- by borrowing debt where both the principal and interest must be paid from future profits.

The price paid will be *at least* the stock market value, which is theoretically, the *discounted present value of expected future earnings* of the target. In reality a *bid premium* must be paid on top because the sellers want to participate in some of the gain otherwise going to the predator.

Therefore an acquisition usually costs more than its forecast earnings under its present management, to which must be added all the costs of legal and professional advice and any subsequent rationalisation costs. Strictly speaking this causes a *fall in shareholder value*.

Many acquisitions and mergers disappoint investors for the following reasons:

(a) Carried out by management to protect jobs and raise salaries rather than for considerations of shareholder wealth.
(b) Poor advice from professional advisers (e.g. corporate financiers) who were principally interested in their commissions and fees.
(c) Lack of 'fit' between predator and target:
   (i) different industries,
   (ii) different cultures or management styles.
(d) Failure to manage the post-acquisition phase properly.
(e) High post-acquisition costs depress profits for several years.
(f) Acquisition undertaken without considering how it fitted with competences of the firm and its longer-term strategy.
(g) Target firm was overpriced and competitively weak.

In summary we can say that benefits of a firm pursuing strategic development into a product/market space by mergers or acquisition are:

(a) firm acquires the expertise and contacts of the acquired firm;
(b) eliminates a potential rival in the market;
(c) swifter access to the industry than internal development;
(d) possibility of some risk spreading if the acquired company has businesses in unrelated areas;
(e) lower commercial risk because the target will have already established itself in the industry;
(f) possibility of acquiring assets cheaply if the target is undervalued by investors, for example, due to poor present management.

Drawbacks of acquisition-led growth are:

(a) Difficult to arrive at the correct price for the acquisition due to lack of financial information, bid fever and possibility of third parties bidding against the predator.
(b) High cost of integrating systems of work, management controls, human resource procedures and information systems.
(c) Need to rationalise operations will incur costs of redundancies, asset disposals, cancellation of leases and supplier contracts.

(d) Problems of uncontrolled staff losses and falling morale due to rationalisation programme and clashes of culture among staff from senior management down.

(e) Very high initial capital costs because the predator must compensate the target's shareholders for at least the expected present value of the profits from the target.

(f) Excessive reliance on external growth will depress the predator's share price because investors cannot assess the level of future earnings of the business without knowing what the next acquisition will be.

(g) High degrees of share price volatility fuelled by bid rumours.

(h) Failure to win a bid will leave the impression that the predator's strategy is failing.

6.5 International growth strategies

6.5.1 Types of international growth

Returning to Figure 6.6, it can be seen that Lynch refers to some specific international strategies not covered in the terms used so far. We shall look at these terms first before considering some of the specific issues surrounding international growth.

1. *Exporting strategies.* The firm sells products made at home to buyers abroad. Often this starts with the receipt of a chance order or perhaps poor sales at home force the firm to export or perish. As a strategy it has a number of advantages over other international growth strategies:
   (a) Firm can make use of any economies of scale it develops to compete in the foreign market (and home market too).
   (b) No need for any extra fixed capital investment.
   (c) Does not expose the fixed capital investments of the firm to risk.
   (d) Helps to insulate the firm from recessions in their home economy.
   The disadvantages are:
   (a) Distance from the customer means customer relationship cannot easily be developed or goods customised.
   (b) Increased working capital needed to support stocks in transit.
   (c) Firm exposed to foreign exchange risk which will affect its earnings or the competitiveness of its prices.
   (d) Firm has less information about the credit status of the customer.
       By establishing an overseas office or appointing an agent the firm can overcome some of the problems of lack of customer contact or the need for minor modifications.
2. *Overseas manufacture.* This strategy has two aspects:
   (a) Firm arranges for its products (or some parts of them) to be manufactured abroad and then imported back to its home economy.
   (b) Firm arranges for its products to be manufactured in a foreign country for sale there.
   In both cases the firm is involved in *direct foreign investment* because it is purchasing productive capital assets in the country. This brings certain advantages:
   (a) Firm can benefit from lower costs of local economy (labour, buildings and inputs).
   (b) Reduced transportation costs.
   (c) Reduced foreign exchange exposure because production costs are now incurred in the same currency with which the goods are paid for.

(d) Because it provides jobs, the firm may gain access to markets previously closed to foreign goods.

(e) Cheaper goods bolster margins in home markets.

The drawbacks are:

(a) Assets exposed to risk in the foreign economy (e.g. war, sequestration, sabotage, or collapse of the local market).

(b) Firm may have difficulty obtaining its profits due to currency controls or punitive taxation on exported dividends.

(c) Absence of an exit route if production depends on a licence, because if the firm wants to sell the factory the national government can decide who it goes to (and the price) because it is worthless without the licence.

3. *Multinational operation.* According to Dunning (1993) there are two features setting a multinational enterprise (MNE), apart from other firms with foreign trading activities:

(a) It has a deliberate policy of co-ordinating its value-adding activities across national boundaries.

(b) It internalises the cross-border trades (i.e. it does not rely on a market to carry them out but rather uses its own bureaucratic processes).

A multinational car manufacturer will have engine plants in one country, power train manufacture in a second and electrics in a third. Different countries will be assigned responsibility for assembling particular models with parts from throughout the world. Some of these will be sold in the market and the rest will be exported (and other models imported). Frequently production capacity is duplicated around the world. The advantages of this arrangement are:

(a) Firm can take maximum advantage of natural resources and lower production costs.

(b) Firm is insulated from the effects of hostile governments or trade unions in any specific country because it can always switch (or threaten to switch) output elsewhere.

(c) Firm can manage its taxation by arranging to make its profits in low-tax economies.

The main drawback is that the multinational is often viewed with suspicion by the governments of host countries because of its foreign ownership and high potential power.

4. *Global corporations.* These are essentially 'nation-less organisations' that do not owe allegiance to any 'home' economy. Typical features include:

(a) Practice of 'equidistant management' which means that senior managers do not regard a factory or customer on the other side of the world any differently from one next door.

(b) Replacement of national cultures with a single corporate culture.

(c) Development of standard procedures and products for all countries.

(d) Multiple sources of capital. The firm may be listed on several of the world exchanges to enable local participation and ownership.

(e) Encouragement of diversity in composition of management and workforce.

At present, the global corporation is more a paradigm than a reality. Within the paradigm there are substantial differences of opinion on how far the firm should adjust its practices and products to suit local conditions.

5. *Turnkey operations.* These are factories and facilities in foreign countries with which the home firm can establish production contracts. When the firm requires output it exercises the contract (i.e. it turns the key). This is sometimes termed *contract manufacturing*.

6.5.2 Issues in international growth strategies

Some management issues apply specifically to these strategies:

1. *Issues of social responsibility.* International growth strategies often involve selling to, or producing in, countries with much less developed legal protections than the firm's home country. Moreover the governments of the foreign country may practise very different policies to home governments. This raises issues such as:
   (a) Whether to take advantage of lax labour laws in setting the pay and conditions of workers.
   (b) The extent of product safety and honesty of description in advertisements.
   (c) Whether to condone the political or social exclusion of particular races or genders by not employing or promoting them.
   (d) Whether to pay private commissions to government officials in return for market access or other assistance.

2. *Development effects of involvement.* Foreign firms will have impacts on the local economy by their presence. This raises issues such as:
   (a) How far to spread the economic benefits in the country by using local staff and suppliers.
   (b) Whether to encourage economic development by training local staff in the firm's methods, management processes and technologies.
   (c) The appropriateness of the technology used and products made to the culture and development stage of the local economy.
   (d) Amount of reinvestment into the economy such as house-building, provision of amenities, support of local business start-ups, undertaking an equity stake in indigenous businesses.
   (e) How to manage withdrawal from the economy without leaving local people destitute.

3. *Cross-cultural management.* Many factors may be included under this heading:
   - differences in languages;
   - differences in the levels of respect for management and desire for participation;
   - different customs in doing business;
   - the extent of individual initiative shown;
   - different religious practices, social roles and holy days.

   These will influence the ways that business is done and may be the determinant factors for a firm in making its decision on whether to use local or expatriate management.

4. *Financial control of operations.* Management must ensure that the divisions all eventually make a contribution to shareholder wealth. There are a number of problems with exercising control across national boundaries:
   (a) The division's financial returns will be heavily dependent on the performance of the economy in which it is based. This is outside of management's control.
   (b) The returns will be in a foreign currency which must be converted back to domestic currency to evaluate it. This may be difficult if the exchange rate is volatile or subject to manipulation by the local authorities.
   (c) The profits of the division may be subject to transfer price manipulation to shift taxation or avoid restrictions of repatriating profits.

6.6 Resource-based *versus* positioning view of strategy

As you will have studied earlier in the pillar business strategy theorists disagree on the origins of competitive advantage. It is important that you are aware of their different views and, although the following section will serve to refresh your memory, it is brief and you are strongly recommended to read the section in the manual for P5. Until the 1990s most writers took the view that competitive advantage arose from the firm's position in relation to its competitors, customers and stakeholders. This is the view that we have tended to take so far and is known as the *positioning view.*

The alternative, more recent approach, known as the *resource-based view* focuses much more on the internal characteristics of the firm, claiming that competitive advantage arises from a unique asset or competence which the firm possesses.

Both approaches recognise that the firm is attempting to make 'supernormal profits' by virtue of competitive advantages. However the two sides disagree over the source and sustainability of that competitive advantage.

6.6.1 The positioning approach

Proponents of the positioning approach take the view that supernormal profits arise by virtue of:

- high market share relative to rivals;
- differentiated products;
- lower costs.

The aspects of the positioning approach that we have considered so far are:

- Stakeholder theory;
- Porter's Five forces theory;
- The BCG matrix;
- GE Business Screen;
- Ansoff product – market growth matrix

Whilst criticising the positioning approach resource based theorists argue that:

- the competitive advantage from a positioning approach is not sustainable being to easily copied;
- environments are too dynamic and unpredictable to analyse to allow positioning to be effective;
- it is easier to change the environment than it is to change the firm.

6.6.2 The resource-based view

The resources that can give a firm as competitive advantage can be considered under the following headings:

- *Assets,* things that a firm has, such as reputation, access to a particular raw material or a customer database. If these assets are rare and important they may qualify as *strategic assets.*

- *Capabilities,* things that a firm has learned to do with its assets, that is, a service orientation, or an ability to cut costs from an acquisition.
- *Competences,* a deeper seated version of capabilities, represented by a routine that has been built up over time. For example a deep understanding of a particular specialized type of technology.

Capabilities and competencies may be classified as dynamic if they are resources which will help an organisation develop or, continue to maintain, a significant advantage over their competitors. If they meet that criteria for being strategic resources they will usually be referred to as core competencies or capabilities.

Types of capability and competence:

- innovation (Sony, Tesco);
- reliability (Tesco, amazon);
- sensitivity, speed of reaction (Dell, Nokia);
- technological competences:
  – website design (Amazon),
  – site selection (Tesco),
- control (Safeway).

Barney (1991) argued that for resources to be strategic they must satisfy three criteria:

- *rare* in the industry
- *valuable* making a significant difference to the firms
  – cost or differentiation advantage
  – capacity to innovate or adapt
- *difficult to acquire, copy or imitate,* may be due to limited supply, high tacit knowledge, or high sunk costs.

Strategic resources

We can see that resources to be strategic they will need to be in limited supply, have a very high tacit knowledge content, be dependent upon a place or time and will most probably involve significant sunk costs making them difficult to imitate. Considering the usual classification of assets in a firm:

- *Physical assets*: Plant and equipment, stock, buildings, location and land are very rarely of strategic value. A very specific location may be, for instance, a café at the top of Niagara Falls may claim the falls a strategic asset.
- *Financial Assets*: Debt/equity reserves or cash may be classified as strategic in a few industries but again rarely. For a Venture Capitalist their access to significant funds may be a strategic resource but is that really due to their reputation with investors?
- *Human resources*: Knowledge, skills and expertise may possibly be classified as strategic but there is always the risk that these qualities are found in one, or at best, a few individuals in the firm. We have all seen the effect of injury on a sports team that did not have strength in depth and put all of their hopes on one star player.
- *Intellectual assets*: Databases, patents, R & D and skilled management are frequently strategic resources.
- *Reputational capital*: Goodwill, brands and relationships are often strategic resources.
- *Capabilities and competencies*: Systems and processes, successful culture of innovativeness and good team effects are often strategic resources.

You should now look back to your studies earlier in the pillar and pay particular attention to the comments of Kay (1997) and Prahalad and Hamel (1990).

6.6.3 Comments on resource-based views of strategy

RBT raises a number of issues:

1. *Conflict with conventional product/market-based views of strategy.* The notion of core competences spreads beyond the ability of the firm to compete just in particular markets and industries. Yet many of the models we have used, such as the Porter models and the product life cycle, tend to discuss particular products and markets and develop strategic prescriptions for them. This leads to two possibilities:

   (a) By using techniques which focus on products and markets individually we may develop strategies which deplete the firm's wider core competences (e.g. by deciding to withdraw from a market or to cut costs by outsourcing a crucial source of organisational learning).

   (b) Even where a firm is involved in a range of industries and has a unique core competence across them all, it is no guarantee of competitive advantage against more focused players in each market (e.g. in the 1980s IBM had a unique global architecture, reputation and ownership of proprietary technology. This did not stop it being beaten into second or third place by focused rivals in each of its sub-industries of software development, consulting, PCs and mainframe systems).

2. *Difficult to cope with a dynamic environment.* The types of competitive advantage claimed by Barney (1991) and others can only be valid whilst there is no dramatic change in the environment of the firm.

3. *Challenges the rational model of strategy.* The RBT view seems to argue that strategy should not be a process of deciding a product/market mission and competing in markets by establishing what the customer wants and exploiting the weaknesses of rivals. Instead it suggests that strategy involves deciding what makes the firm unique and building strategy on that, extending into any products or markets where it will work.

   The impacts of this are:

   (a) RBT strategy starts with the corporate appraisal not with the mission of the business. Indeed the mission must adapt to fit the most recent extension of core competence.

   (b) There is a much higher emphasis on finding an environment to match the firm rather than vice versa (management seem to be saying 'all we have is a hammer so our markets are anything that involves hitting things'). This reasoning could lead to very diverse strategies or perhaps a complete drying-up of strategic avenues (as they run out of things to hit).

   (c) Investors cannot be clear what industry they are investing in. This may increase perceived risk and hence destroy shareholder value by reducing the share price.

4. *RBT can lead to different conclusions.* The basis of RBT is the suggestion that the firm should retain any unique strategic assets it has, outsource the remainder, and focus on building up relationships with internal and external stakeholders to develop its internal knowledge to improve performance and innovation.

   Consequently it fits well with modern concepts in network organisation management such as:

   • teamworking;

   • collaboration with suppliers and customers;

- flexible working practices;
- creation of participative culture.

     However, an alternative conclusion might be that unique knowledge is too valuable to risk losing in networks that could easily be 'burgled' by rivals through enticing contract staff and suppliers/customers to defect.

     This might encourage management to deliberately keep knowledge under close control by bringing production in-house, putting staff on restrictive long-term contracts and segmenting trade secrets on a 'need-to-know' basis.

5. *Limited empirical evidence.* The resource based view is based upon economic reasoning however there is limited empirical evidence to support it. In recent research McGahan and Porter (1997) found that, overall, the choice of industry sector was more important than the firms' strategic resources in terms of the firms' profits by a factor of 19 per cent compared to 8 per cent. This research was based on work by Rumelt (1991) which had been a central plank in the resource based theory. Of particular interest is the fact that the difference in interpretation seemed, mainly, to be due to the inclusion of service sector industries in the data. If the data for the service sector was taken on its own the choice of industry sector appeared to be responsible for between 40 per cent and 65 per cent of the variance in profitability.

On balance, although the majority of strategic management theory is currently centred around the resource based view, it might be better for us to consider that there are valuable points in both of the approaches. With that in mind we need to be aware of, and be able to use, all of the tools from both schools of thought.

6.7 Divestment strategies

These strategies involve the selling off or other partition of the business. Reasons for such strategies are:

1. *To liquidate the assets in the business unit.* This is used when the prospects of the unit are poor; for example, it is a question mark or a dog in the BCG matrix. Management may decide to conserve resources by investing no further in it and, if possible, find a buyer to purchase it and so provide a cash input to the firm (or relieve it of a loss-making subsidiary).
2. *To provide a more coherent investment to investors.* Firms which are widely diversified, although low risk in themselves, do not fit easily in an investment portfolio. Consequently stripping the business back to two or three key areas makes it more acceptable to investors.
3. *To facilitate better control.* The parent company may be too widely diversified, causing difficulties in monitoring the performance of divisional managers.
4. *To avoid takeovers by removing value gaps.* A value gap is where the market value of the firm is less than its value to a predator. This usually occurs where the business has changed direction but has not yet convinced investors.

     Typical signs are where the firm has a predominantly mature business unit and has embarked on a high-growth business. The financial dynamics make sense: the low-growth business is a cash cow and can support the growth business. However, many of the firm's investors bought its shares in the anticipation of high dividends and are disappointed that these dividends are now going into capital investment. The shares fall in price which means a predator can buy a mature business and a promising growth business at a low price.

Separating the mature business from the growth business allows each to attain their appropriate share price and investor profile. The mature industry will settle at a low price/earnings ratio reflecting the low potential for capital gain, while the growth business will attain a high price/earnings ratio and consequently lower cost of capital to help its growth. If management do not divest a predator will. It is worth noting that Vodaphone, one of the largest companies in the telephone business was *spun off*, some years ago, in this way from Racal a defence electronics firm. The board of Racal recognised that the stock market would value Vodaphone differently if it was a separate firm.

5. *To enable management to focus on core competences.* The core competences of the business are the things it can do well that cannot be conducted by outside firms. It is recognised that many firms are excessively vertically integrated and management are forced to manage diverse operations that could better be bought in.

   A common example of this is in food production where many branded good manufacturers have realised that their core competence lies in brand development and that manufacturing can be bought in. By selling off their factories, the firms reduce their fixed cost base and hence attain considerable flexibility in costs as well as shifting risk partially to their suppliers.

6. *To realise cash.* The parent may be experiencing financial distress and may need to realise cash to stave of liquidation.

7. *To provide an exit route for investors.* Some business ventures are taken on as short-term investments. Selling them enables the firm to realise its investment. This occurs in two situations:

   (a) In turnaround strategies where the predator buys the troubled firm at a low price, turns it around, and sells it on at a profit. This may involve all, or part, of the original acquisition.

   (b) Where the firm has taken an equity stake in a growth venture which has now reached an established position. The division is sold off and the investment realised.

The *back to the core* aspect of this approach is indicative of the problems caused by the poor performance of conglomerates which happened because of lax anti trust and monopolies legislation.

6.7.1 Methods of divestment

1. *Sale as a going concern to another business.* This provides the seller with cash and/or equity in the buyer. It also provides an orderly transfer of business which meets the needs of staff, customers and other stakeholders.

2. *Liquidation of assets.* The division is closed and staff redeployed or made redundant. Assets are sold off at market prices. This is likely to be slow and create bad publicity due to stakeholders' interests not being met. It is also likely that the sale will not realise a significant value for the assets.

3. *Management buyout (MBO) and Management buyins (MBI).* The existing management raise the finance and buy the division. Sometimes the seller must make undertakings to assist this process such as underwriting loans or agreeing to buy or sell to the division. If an outside management team does this, it is termed a *management buy-in* (MBI).

Where the company was a public listed company this is also known as going private. These are rare. The motivations for the managers concerned can be summarised as:

- opportunity to control own business,
- long term faith in the company,
- better financial rewards,
- opportunity to develop own talents,
- absence of head office constraints,
- fear of redundancy,
- fear of new owner after anticipated acquisition.

Invariably for the divesting company this approach will be the best from the point of view of their reputational capital.

4. *Demerger.* The division is separately incorporated and obtains a listing on the financial markets. Shareholders will receive shares in the separate division pro-rata to their original holding in the combined enterprise. In the case where the parent company maintains a majority share this is known as an *equity carve-out.* This provides a vehicle for shareholders to decide which part(s) of the business they wish to hold and an exit route for their investment in the remainder.

6.8 Strategic options in the public sector

There has been considerable pressure over the past decade for the public sector to introduce 'best practice' from private firms, including strategic planning processes. There has been considerable discussion in the literature regarding the appropriateness of these processes due to the unpredictable political dimensions and relatively short-term nature of the sector. Strategic decision making within the sector is often driven more by short-term expediency rather than a longer term view of what will benefit the organisation and its users.

If we consider what strategies the public sector should be following we could summarise them as follows:

- To develop knowledge assets and competencies, effectively the organisations involved should be making every effort to get better at what it does.
- To respond to changes in Government policy. It could be argued that as different elected officers come and go, for there to be any long-term direction in the management of a country or region the public sector should be assisting in shaping policy rather than reacting to the decisions of ministers.
- To manage budgets by collecting resources from the tax payers (and others) and spending them to provide a service at an agreed, acceptable level, in a transparent and ethical manner.
- To set in place appropriate performance management systems and control measures.

Poister and Trieb (1999) observe 'strategic management in the public sector is concerned with strengthening the long term health and effectiveness of governmental units and leading them through positive change to ensure a continuing productive fit with their environments'. This should mean that management ensure that the value chains, processes and resources (staff, finance and infrastructure) are in place to allow planning, implementation and evaluation of service delivery to lead to the management of specific projects on time and within budget. Quite often they are only judged on their ability to meet their budgets.

Whilst many of the analytical tools we have discussed can be used the prescriptive models that we have so far discussed in this chapter are not so readily applicable to the public sector. This is not unexpected since, as we have described in Chapter 1 the objectives of the public sector have to be set to satisfy a far wider group of stakeholders.

Attempts to apply the Boston Matrix, which we discussed in Chapter 5, have done much to discredit the application of commercial techniques in the public sector. Prince and Puffitt (2001) make the point that, in addition to the dubious assumptions in the Boston Matrix (which we also discussed in Chapter 5), there will be political and statutory pressure to provide services even when those services may be classified by the matrix as 'dogs'.

As an alternative they describe the Maslin Multidimensional Matrix as a means of 'creative clarification' to systematically approach difficult strategic issues. The 2 × 2 matrix consists of four boxes derived from the two evaluative axes. The matrix is, unlike the Boston matrix, descriptive rather than prescriptive.

The x-axis is predefined as *Needs or wants of the client group* and needs careful consideration by the analyst. Invariably the needs of a particular group will be defined by legislation or some other rule. Their wants, however, are often more difficult to establish and satisfy and in some cases may be totally unrealistic. However those wants, no matter how unrealistic, are not irrelevant. If sufficient users desire the same outcome they may become an influential stakeholder group and sufficient pressure on politicians to achieve their end. The ranking of the defined needs will be driven by the social and political imperatives that the organisation must consider.

The y-axis *user defined dimensions* is purely user defined, according to their requirements. There are many dimensions that can be established and the political debate which will go on to establish what they are and their relative importance is an important aspect of the use of the tool. Whilst it is not possible to give a definitive list of the kinds of dimensions that can be used Prince and Puffitt (2001) offer the following as examples at the local council level:

- level of concern of elected members;
- level of concern of community;
- level of concern of national government;
- level of provision by other agencies;
- level of finance available;
- level of (non financial) resource available;
- level of staff expertise;
- level of statutory duty (mandatory or discretionary);
- level of activity currently undertaken.

It is interesting to note that a number of these dimensions; national government, elected members for example are representative of a higher authority than those conducting the analysis and that others depend on the work of other agencies who will have their own agenda and priorities. This underlines the importance of the stakeholder analysis that we discussed in Chapter 1 for strategic decision making within the public sector.

If we only take one of the were to consider only one of the dimensions form the y axis, level of provision by other agencies, our matrix might look like the one shown in Figure 6.11.

		Need	
		High	Low
Provision by other agencies	High	Targeted provision	No provision
	Low	Extensive provision	Encourage provision by others

Figure 6.11 A need and provision matrix

Since a strategic option represents a series of decisions that the organisation must make we can say that a strategic option for a public sector organisation should spell out three major components;

- a marketing strategy, and associated marketing plans;
- a service provision strategy and associated service delivery plans;
- a resource mobilisation and utilisation strategy and associated resource plans.

This division is somewhat artificial since there will always be a degree of overlap. For instance if a local authority is providing transport services for the elderly, this would not only form part of the 'place' element of the marketing plan but also part of the logistics' component of the service production plan.

Marketing strategies have been discussed in Chapter 5, but we can define the key elements of a service production strategy as follows:

- a decision about which core competencies to maintain and develop;
- a decision about which services will be provided in house and which will be outsourced;
- a decision about the procurement policy and the selection of suppliers;
- a decsion about appropriate objectives and the level of performance to be expected.

6.8.1 Innovation in the public sector

The option of internal development within the public sector will often be of considerable importance as the organisation looks for alternative provisions of services which are more effective or cost efficient. There are a number of ways in which innovation can have an impact:

- new servies;
- new target groups (customers);
- new service production processes;
- new partnership arrangements with the rest of the public sector, with the voluntary sector and with the private sector;
- new decision making processes (e-government for instance);
- new governance structures and processes;

'No change' is, invariably, not an option within the public sector but, with the potentially large list of options available, rigorous decision making will be necessary and we will discuss this is Section 6.10.

6.8.2 Joint development strategies

Bovaird and Loffler (2003) make the observation that, in practice, no public sector organisation can expect to be successful without close interaction with other agencies. Under the heading of *Joined up strategies and seamless services* they give the following examples of why public sector organisations need to work with others:

- to ensure, through their supply chain, that they have high quality inputs, of which the most important in the public sector is staff (highlighting the importance of relationships with staff training and development organisations);

- to ensure their services are well designed to meet the needs of service users and other affected stakeholders (highlighting the importance of market research organisations and co-planning with prospective service users);
- to ensure that the holistic needs of service users are met, and not just those needs in which the organisation specialises (highlighting the importance of partnership planning and delivery of 'seemless services');
- to ensure that the impact of services on the client is as high as possible (so that advice to service users, particularly that given by current or past users of the service, 'expert clients' or 'expert patients' can be valuable).

This means that there are complex interactions between and within the value chains of the various organisations within the public sector and that, ideally, these need to be cross managed carefully. The great variety of stakeholders within the public sector environment means that the political processes will be of significant importance but that the importance of those politically driven decisions will make it difficult to develop and maintain appropriate strategies.

6.9   Strategic options in the charity sector

As we have seen in Chapter 1 the stakeholder groups that have to be dealt with in the charity, not-for-profit or voluntary sector are far broader that those that influence a commercial organisation. As we did in that chapter we shall refer to these organisations as NPOs.

As with the public sector it is difficult to find a relevance for the prescriptive models which are used within the commercial sector but the analytical tools are just as relevant.

For example, you will remember the concept of a *cash cow* from the Boston matrix whereby a particular product or service produces a steady stream of cash. From the perspective of a NPO where fundraising is of vital importance and would be better described as a star!

Haberberg and Rieple (2008) have summarised the strategic options available to NPOs into three main strands:

- *Putting in place the value chain, structure and systems that allow the NPO's mission to be implemented.* To a large extent this can be considered as being very similar to the commercial sector. However the differences are likely to be in the structural and control measures that are feasible in this type of organisation. The staff, trustees and management committee will be just as political as those we encountered when we looked at public sector organisations. The volunteers in an organisation will be highly committed to its aims or at least to their interpretation of those aims. This may mean that they put their own ethos and value system before that of the organisation and, as they are volunteers it may be harder to manage them. As regards the mission it may well be that this is formulated to put the NPO 'out of business'. For example, a large cancer charity may well have a mission of 'to find a cure for all known forms of cancer'.
- *Developing a fundraising structure that allows income to be generated, in quantity, and in as regular, predictable and reliable form as possible.* There is increased pressure on NPOs as more and more organisations enter the market for funds and the public, certainly in the United Kingdom, develop donor fatigue. Parker (1998) has classified the source of funds specifically for charities as:
  1. *Has beens.* Perceived as old fashioned or out dated, although well known they are at risk of losing both sponsors and clients.

2. *Celebrity.* Well known but has not built up sufficient momentum to provide significant funds for the particular cause. Should attract new donors fairly easily but needs management support.
3. *Star.* Confusingly the equivalent of a cash cow in the Boston matrix, has a high public profile, high levels of public support and managements principal concern should be the entrance of competition to the particular sphere of operation.

- *Providing visible evidence that management of the NPO is being carried out in a transparent, professional and competent manner.* Aside from the many corporate governance issues that are surfacing within the commercial sector (and are just as likely in the NPO sector) many NPOs depend, for their fundraising efforts and volunteers, on the good will of the population at large. There is evidence that the explicit adoption of techniques of strategic planning and other 'commercial management' techniques has done much to remove the perception that the sector is managed by dedicated amateurs.

As with organisations in the Public Sector there will be similar emphasis in successful examples of these types of organisation in the planning of innovation and working in partnership with other NPOs.

6.10 Evaluation of strategy

Once an organisation has gone through the process of generating a number of strategic options to address the issues that is identified there is a need for creativity to be tempered with a rational decision making process. This must bring down the options to a coherent strategy for the firm to follow. This process must be done formally and not be on the basis of personal preference. Having said that, there will always be instances where internal politics and powerful stakeholders will get in the way of a formal rational process. We can now look at two of the most popular approaches to the formal evaluation of options.

6.10.1 The three tests

Johnson and Scholes (1997) outline three tests for assessing whether a strategic option should be undertaken.

1. *Suitability test.* This considers whether the option is the *right one given the circumstances of the firm.* The main considerations here will be:
   (a) Whether it is congruent with the firm's mission.
   (b) Whether it builds on the situation outlined in the SWOT:
      - does it build on the firm's strengths?
      - does it correct its weaknesses (or at least avoid exposing them further)?
      - does it grasp opportunities?
      - does it avoid or neutralise threats?
2. *Acceptability test.* Considers whether the strategic option will gain crucial support from the people it needs to or whether it will lead to opposition and criticism.
   One way to approach this test is to make use of stakeholder analysis as we discussed in Section 2.5 of Chapter 2:
   (a) *Shareholders*:
      - are financial returns adequate?
      - does it lead to unacceptable risks?

- does it rob them of dividend that they were expecting?
- will it cause them problems with their feelings about social responsibility?

(b) *Management*:
- will they implement it or will they start to leave the firm?
- will any of them be prepared to take on the implementation (e.g. move home, work long hours, learn a new language or technology)?

(c) *Staff*:
- will it cause strikes or greater turnover?
- will they contribute ideas and commitment in a full-blooded way?
- does it pay them enough?
- will they feel insecure and leave?

(d) *Customers*:
- will they continue to buy from us?
- is it something they want us to do?
- does it answer their complaints?

(e) *Suppliers*:
- will they be prepared to collaborate and invest to support us?
- will they continue to supply us?
- will they change their processes/products/locations as we need them to?

(f) *Local community*:
- will planning permission be granted?
- will we still enjoy its goodwill?

(g) *National government*:
- will it lead to the change in law we need?
- will it cause a clampdown or new law?
- will this raise policy or competition issues?

(h) *Pressure groups*:
- will it lead to a damaging outcry?
- does it go far enough to satisfy their complaints?

3. *Feasibility test*

This considers whether the firm will be able to carry out the strategy successfully:

(a) How reliable is the data pointing to the success of this strategy?
- sales estimates
- cost estimates
- assessments of risk
- technological projections

(b) Do we have the resources to make it successful?
- financial
- management expertise
- production capacity
- etc. (the Ms framework we discussed earlier is a good checklist for this)

(c) Does the firm have a track record of success in similar strategies or projects?

It is helpful to think of these three tests in terms of the diagram above (Figure 6.12). We can add one further test to this listing. Ideally a firm should be looking to adopt strategies which will build a long-term strategic advantage, and so we can add a test of *sustainability*. Whilst most strategies may be needed to produce short-term success the firm should be looking for opportunities to develop strategic resources which, as we said earlier, are rare

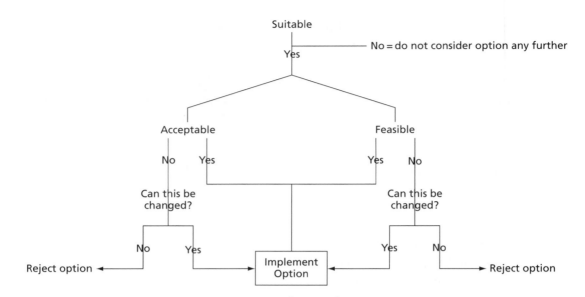

Figure 6.12 Three evaluation tests

and difficult to copy or imitate. It is likely that these will be dynamic capabilities notable the development of processes within the firm which allow it to learn.

6.10.2 RACES

Whilst the tests of strategies based on suitability, feasibility and acceptability have been described a more exacting test, Haberberg and Rieple (2008) involves the following five criteria for determining the suitability of a proposed strategic option:

1. *Resources.* Does the firm have the required resources to be able to implement the strategy successfully? The resources required could comprise physical assets, financial assets, capabilities and intellectual resources, human resources, reputational assets, relational assets and time.
2. *Acceptability.* Is the proposed strategy likely to be accepted by the principal, and by definition powerful, stakeholders? If it is not then it is unlikely to succeed.
3. *Coherence.* Are the options suitable to be implemented alongside each other and alongside the strategies that the company is already employing and does not wish to change? Any proposed strategy should not undermine established brands, values or relational contracts that are currently valued by the firm.
4. *Effectiveness.* Will the proposed strategy actually address the strategic issue or priority that has been identified? Will it work, or is it just something that someone thinks would be nice to do? Whilst the resource analysis will involve a financial analysis in terms of capability this will most probably involve an assessment of the future economic value of the decision.
5. *Sustainability.* The last test considers the likelihood that the option will build a sustainable competitive advantage in the organisation or just solve the present problem. Few options will score highly on this element of the appraisal and, in some cases, depending on the potential impact of the issue being addressed that is not important particularly where survival is at stake.

The outcome of the appraisal is rarely clear – cut and compromise will be necessary. It may well be that an option which has failed the resource component of the test offers such a significant competitive advantage that it is worth diverting resources to enact that particular option. This would not be the case if the firm were facing imminent failure. The relative importance of the five criteria will vary depending upon the situation in which the company currently finds itself.

The lack of clarity of the decision is also compounded by the lack of perfect knowledge regarding the outcome of a given strategic choice. If there were such perfect knowledge, the choice would not be strategic. Consequently, the decision maker must proceed toward the strategic outcome whilst enjoying considerable uncertainty and choose an alternative based on the best judgment applied to information at that point in time (Harrison and Pelletier, 1998).

6.10.3 Strategic *versus* tactical decisions

In our CIMA studies for Managerial Level most decisions we have learned about, and faced in exams, have had the following characteristics.

(a) the data has been given to us;
(b) the timeframe is short;
(c) we have been told that the objective is to maximise shareholder value/minimise cost;
(d) we have been fairly knowledgeable about the likelihood of success of the strategy.

Real-world strategic decisions are not like that:

(a) We have to estimate the data using forecasting techniques or sometimes mere guesswork.
(b) We are thinking ahead many years.
(c) There may be more than one objective:
  ● we wish to maximise shareholder wealth but have agreed to do so only in a specific industry;
  ● we may acknowledge social responsibilities in addition to shareholders' interests.
(d) We are dealing with uncertainty (no knowing) rather than risk (understanding probabilities).
(e) They would be hard to justify using conventional NPV or IRR approaches.
  Research indicates that management do not follow a rational approach to strategic investment appraisal:
  ● They invest in the direction of a *strategic logic*. This boils down to an acceptance that a given strategy 'makes sense' and then committing money to it.
  ● *Minimum criteria* are set up as milestones for committing further resources in the future. For example, they require that sales-related activities yield a certain level of interest before moving from pilot project to main investment.
  ● Numbers are frequently presented to *justify* investments already made rather than used as the bases for making the initial decision.
  ● Apparent failure of the investment in the early days leads to *escalating commitment* in the way a poker player with a weak hand will try to up the bids in the hope that the other players will blink and throw in their cards.

Example

An international IT/IS manufacturer agreed to invest £8 m to set up 'server farms' following an investment appraisal exercise that ranked the projects of competing dot.com firms according to their NPV, IRR and payback. It accepted the proposal with the highest score. There is no mathematical logic to this, but, as the FD said, it got the right numbers!

STRATEGIC OPTIONS AND THEIR EVALUATION

6.10.4 Towards a rational approach to strategic investment appraisal

The objective of strategic investment appraisal is to convince management that the proposed strategy will yield a positive NPV, for example:

- a telecommunications firm like Colt or Telewest installing broadband networks throughout a country based on forecasts of an on-line society;
- a corporation like Whitbread divesting its core brewing business and investing in setting up fitness and leisure clubs, coffee houses and restaurants to take advantage of changing lifestyles and enriched leisure time;
- a computer software manufacturer like Microsoft investing in the purchase of internet service providers, search engine providers and web designers, or entering joint ventures with palm-held computer makers, games machine makers and media firms, to protect themselves from the obsolescence of PC computers.

The key things to notice here are:

(a) the decisions are tinged with enormous uncertainty and conjecture;
(b) they are often defensive (protect existing level of shareholder wealth or reduce its decline) rather than offensive (designed to increase shareholder wealth).

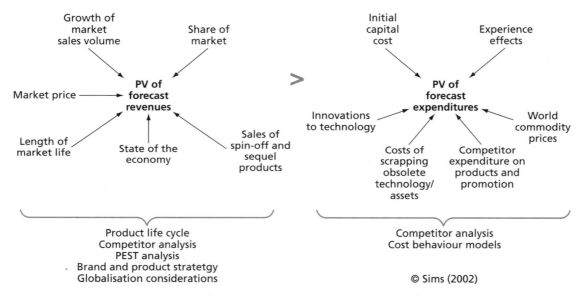

Figure 6.13 Strategic investment appraisal

Consider the diagram above (Figure 6.13):

At the heart of the model in Figure 6.12 lies familiar investment appraisal techniques. However, the diagram demonstrates that the factors that impact on the forecasts of revenues and forecasts of costs are less mathematical and more rooted in the strategic models we have been studying in this subject.

A *rational* approach to strategic investment appraisal would follow a number of steps:

1. Identify the precise scope of the project:
   - length of time over which it operates,
   - geographical scope,

- nature of service being provided,
- customer covered,
- technologies employed.

2. Gather data and opinions on all variables impacting on the revenues and costs of the project:
   - the factors outlined in Figure 6.12,
   - cost of capital for the project.
   This would inevitably involve use of the strategic models indicated.
3. Reduce the data and opinions to forecasts of revenue and costs.
4. Accept if the project shows a positive expected net present value.

There is no likelihood that a rational approach will lead automatically to correct strategic investment decisions. The problems of uncertainty are too great for that. However, it may help improve decisions. Others will argue that it will harm decisions because the options based on inspiration and creativity will be discarded!

At this point you should recognize that all of the quantitative techniques of evaluation that you have learnt so far, and are currently learning are applicable to the evaluation of strategic options and prepare yourself accordingly. There will be calculations in the examinations.

6.10.5 Real options

Real options

We have already discussed the value that organisations place on flexibility and responsiveness earlier in the study system. The evaluation of this flexibility is not particularly easy using the techniques we have discussed so far. The evaluation of strategic options using techniques such as RACES usually works on the principle that decisions and investments, once made, are irreversible. Additionally, the treatment of risk in those investment decisions was not treated as rigorously as the technique of real options permits.

Real option analysis, developed from financial theory, is proving useful in strategic decision making for those companies facing multiple risks in highly uncertain investment environments. Whilst the mathematics involved can be complicated the underlying logic is sensible and relatively straightforward.

Taking the oil industry as an example, increasingly exploration prospects have arisen in politically unstable and infrastructure poor parts of the world. The risks are numerous; price of crude, probability of success, the denial of future access, the change in tax regime, the infrastructure to remove the oil to markets are all factors that need to be considered in the investment decision. In terms of decisions made, the dcf returns looked unattractive – but the investments were still made. The important thing to remember is that none of the companies involved were actually making long-term investments in the true sense of the word. Investment in the exploration end of the oil business is a staged process. The investment in seismic investigation, is followed by exploratory drilling, and subsequently full production and the building of the infrastructure necessary to remove the oil. The process can take as long as a decade with decision points, or options, along the way. Effectively, each of these decision points gives the investing company the option to continue, wait, abandon or scale back the investment value depending on the outcome of the previous phase of the project. The flexibility that this gives is highly valuable to the companies involved, and the more uncertain the situation the more valuable that becomes. This is true of other industries as well as the oil industry where large investments are made.

We can see a similar value to the technique in the new economy is changing the way managers think about real options, and traditional pricing models are increasingly challenged to properly price the outcomes possible. The most striking modern examples of firms using real options have seen payoffs generated that do not resemble those from real options in the old economy, let alone stock options. Google's current P/E ratio cannot be justified by even the most optimistic outlooks of current projects. Clearly, technology standards ownership and lock-in effects have produced payoffs that extend beyond those that the old economy could predict. Microsoft recently sold its Xbox 360 platform at a loss, expecting to generate profits from the games to be released in the months following. That is an example of an old-economy follow-on option that is not overly difficult to model. But what about the platform as a tool for strengthening Microsoft's standards ownership in the operating system market by linking the television to the computer?

With this in mind, the use of the technique of real options to evaluate projects under increased uncertainty is becoming more popular. Over the past decade, the theory has been the subject of a growing body of literature and has gathered support across the business world in academia, consulting and the corporation. Dixit and Pindyck (1995) insist that 'the net present value rule is not sufficient. To make intelligent investment choices, managers need to consider the value of keeping their options open.' Lewent (1994) chief financial officer of Merck, suggests that all business decisions are real options, in that they confer the *right* but not the *obligation* to take some initiative in the future.

Calculating option values

If we use NPV to evaluate projects then we base our decisions on the present value of the cash flows inwards and the initial cost of the investment. These are represented by the top two boxes in Table 6.1. However, if we use real option analysis we would also take into our calculations the values of uncertainty, the duration of the option, cashflow lost by nor committing immediately and the risk-free rate of interest.

Calculating real option values for real projects is a complex operation because it will involve the modelling of uncertainty and the evaluation of a number of separate options that exist for management at the various decision points in the potential life of a project.

McKinsey have suggested that a four-stage process can be used for producing real options valuations;

Table 6.1 Components of real options valuation.

	Real options	Comments
Option value	PV of returns to the investment	The higher the NPV, the higher the option value
	Investment cost	The higher the cost, the lower the option value
	Uncertainty	The higher the uncertainty, the higher the volatility and the more valuable the option
	Duration of the option	A longer time offers greater opportunity for determining the value of potential outcomes
	Value lost over duration of option	The more cash flow that is lost to competitors that have fully committed, the lower the option value
	Risk-free interest rate	A higher interest rate increases the option value by increasing the value of deferring investment

1. Use a standard NPV approach to produce a valuation of an investment without any consideration of the inherent flexibility of the project.
2. Use scenario planning to outlook the potential futures and then model the uncertainty in the project by using event trees. So the uncertainties for a project to retrieve oil from a reservoir under the Caspian Sea in Azerbaijan would be; the likelihood of finding reserves within the exploration lease area, the amount and quality of oil to be found, the characteristics of the oil and its cost of recovery, the chances of building a pipeline across Iran or the Black Sea, the future price of crude oil and the levels of taxes imposed by the Azerbaijan government. Using different outcomes for each uncertainty the NPV would be calculated.
3. Identify the decision options that management can make at key stages of the project to convert the events tree into a decision tree. At each stage management would have the option to continue, expand, contact, defer and abandon the project.
4. The whole portfolio of options generated in that way can then be valued in a way that replicates the portfolio approach used in the Black & Scholes model that you will have studied elsewhere in your CIMA qualification.

Essentially, from the perspective of strategy it is not the underpinning mathematics that is important. More important is the concept that options for flexibility are generated at each stage of the project so that a more considered approach to the decision can be made. As Lewent (1994) stated, 'When you make an initial investment in a research project, you are paying an entry fee for the right, but you are not obligated to continue that research to a later stage.'

6.11 Summary

In this chapter we have covered the main types of strategy available to the firm:

- the firm faces three strategic choices: how it will gain competitive advantage, what product/market spaces it will develop into and what growth strategies it will use to get there;
- the main theoretical models accompanying these three decisions are the Porter three generic strategies, the Ansoff product market growth matrix and Lynch's expansion method matrix;
- particular risks are incurred by each strategy and these are deepened if acquisitions or foreign development are used;
- the traditional, prescriptive, models do not work in the public and NPO sectors
- the chartered management accountant plays a leading part in working with other business functions to undertake competitor accounting;
- in addition to products, markets and customers brands were considered as a suitable unit of strategic analysis and evaluation.

References

Allen, D. (1992) *The Financial Management of Brands*. London: CIMA.
Ansoff, H.I. (1965) *Corporate Strategy*. New York: McGraw-Hill.
Barney, J. (1991) Firm Resources and Sustained Competitive Advantage. *Journal of Management*, 17(1): 99–120.

Bleeke, J. and Ernst, D. (1995) Is your strategic alliance really a sale? *Harvard Business Review*, Jan–Feb: 97–108.

Bovaird, T. and Loffler, E. (2003) *Public Management and Governance*. London: Routledge.

Dixit and Pindyck (1995) The options approach to capital investment. *Harvard Business Review*, May–June.

Dunning, J.H. (1993) *Multinational Enterprises and the Global Economy*. Wokingham: Addison-Wesley.

Haberberg, A. and Rieple, A. (2008) *Strategic Management, Theory and Application*. Oxford, New York: Oxford University Press.

Hamel, G. and Prahalad, C.K. (1994) *Competing for the Future: Breakthrough Strategies for Seizing Control of Your Industry and Creating the Markets of Tomorrow*. Boston, MA: Harvard Business School Press.

Harrison, E.F. and Pelletier, M.A. (1998) Foundations of strategic decision effectiveness. *Management Decision*, 36(3): 147–159.

Johnson, G. and Scholes, K. (1997) *Exploring Corporate Strategy* (4th edn). Hemel Hempstead: Prentice-Hall.

Kay, J. (1997) *Foundations of Corporate Success: How Business Strategies Add Value* (2nd edn). Oxford: Oxford University Press.

Kotler, P. (1997) *Marketing Management: Analysis, Planning, Implementation and Control* (9th edn). Englewood Cliffs, NJ: Prentice-Hall.

Lewent (1994) Scientific management at Merck: An interview with CFO Judy Lewent. Harvard Business Review. Jan.–Feb.

Lynch, R. (1997) *Corporate Strategy*. London: Financial Times Management.

Markides, C.C. and Geroski, P.A. (2004) *Fast Second: How Smart Companies Bypass Radical Innovation to Enter and Dominate New Markets*. Jossey Bass: San Francisco.

McGahan, A.M. and Porter, M.E. (1997) How much does Industry matter really? *Strategic Management Journal*, 18(summer, special issue): 15–30.

Naisbitt, J. (1995) *Global Paradox*. London: Nicholas Brearley Publishing.

Parker, L. (1998) Non profit prophets: Strategy in non commercial organizations. *Australian CPA*, 68(6): 50–52.

Poister, T.H. and Trieb, G.D. (1999) Strategic Management in the public sector. *Public Productivity and Management Review*, 22(3): 308–325.

Porter, M.E. (1980) *Competitive Strategy: Techniques for Analysing Industries and Competitors*. New York: The Free Press.

Porter, M.E. (1985) *Competitive Advantage: Creating and Sustaining Superior Performance*. New York: The Free Press.

Prince, L. and Puffitt, R. (2001) In Johnson, G. and Scholes, K. (eds). *Exploring Public Sector Strategy*. London: Prentice Hall.

Prahalad, C.K. and Hamel, G. (1990) The Core Competence of the Corporation. *Harvard Business Review*, May/June.

Stalk, G., Evans, P. and Shulman, L. (1992) Competing on Capabilities. *Harvard Business Review*, March/April.

Rumelt, R.P. (1991) quoted in Kay, J. (1993) *Foundations of Corporate Success*, Oxford: Oxford University Press.

Ward, K. (1992) *Strategic Management Accounting*. London: CIMA/Butterworth-Heinemann.

Whittington, R. (1993) *What is Strategy and Does it Matter?* London: Routledge.

Wilson, R.M.S. and Gilligan, C. (1997) *Strategic Marketing Management*. Oxford: Butterworth Heinemann.

Revision Questions

? Question 1

S is a company which has traded very successfully within its domestic market for many years. It has achieved high levels of profitability in providing ground and soil sampling and testing services for a large range of clients in both the public and private sectors. This sampling is mainly undertaken to assess the suitability of former industrial land for building and public use.

In recent years, S has experienced strong competition and its Managing Director (L) has recognised that it is becoming more difficult to obtain new business from within its domestic market. Increasingly, it has been found necessary to offer more than the original basic ground and soil sampling and testing services in order to retain the loyalty of existing clients. This has necessitated a whole range of other services being offered such as testing for the presence of polluted substances in buildings, chemical analysis of water sources, geological surveys and providing for unfit land to be cleaned prior to becoming available for public use.

While these other services have been relatively successful, L is increasingly concerned about the prospects for sustaining the company's profitability because of increasing competition and saturation of the domestic market. With this in mind, L has asked you, as Management Accountant, to advise on the rationale for an overseas expansion strategy and the issues to be considered in its implementation.

Requirements

Produce a report to L which

(a) explains the business case for expansion overseas; **(10 marks)**
(b) discusses the strategic and operational issues which the directors of S should consider before making a decision on whether to implement an overseas expansion strategy.
(15 marks)
(Total marks = 25)

? Question 2

It has been stated that an industry or a market segment within an industry goes through four basic phases of development. These four phases – introduction, growth, maturity and decline – each has an implication for an organisation's development of growth and divestment strategies.

The following brief profiles relate to four commercial organisations, each of which operates in a different industry.

- *Company A*. Established in the last year and manufactures state-of-the-art door locks which replace the need for a key with computer image recognition of fingerprint patterns.
- *Company B*. A biotechnological product manufacturer established for 3 years and engaged in the rapidly expanding animal feedstuffs market.
- *Company C*. A confectionery manufacturer which has been established for many years and is now experiencing low sales growth but high market share in a long-established industry.
- *Company D*. A retailing organisation which has been very profitable but is now experiencing a loss of market share with a consequent overall reduction in turnover.

Requirements

(a) Explain:
  (i) the concept of the industry life-cycle; and
  (ii) the phase of development in which each of the industries served by the four companies is positioned. **(7 marks)**
(b) Discuss how Ansoff's product market growth vector matrix may be applied by the firms in developing their growth and divestment strategies. **(18 marks)**
(Total marks = 25)

 ## Question 3

Organisational background

SJM plc is a long-established retail organisation operating 227 supermarkets nationally. It is a listed company which has expanded over its 60-year history. The company has attained distinctive competitive advantage by stocking and selling only high-quality products. SJM plc has enjoyed profitable trading and now ranks as one of the leading retailers in the country. It has not been affected by restructuring of the retailing industry and its board is intent on maintaining the company's independence.

The board of the company has set a clear aim of achieving profitability with efficient consumption of resources, while maintaining the sale of high-quality goods and delivering a courteous and efficient service to customers. This overall aim has been incorporated within the mission statement and forms a central part of the company's promotional advertising.

Financial characteristics of the company

The following information is supplied in respect of SJM plc for the last financial year:

	£m
Turnover	2,400
Earnings attributable to ordinary shareholders	220

There were 1,200 million ordinary shares in issue at the end of the last financial year and the company's share price was £4.03.

SJM plc has established that its cost of capital is 12 per cent per annum. Over the last year, the company's share price has varied between £3.30 and £4.05.

SJM plc paid a dividend of £0.12 (12 pence) per share in the last financial year and has achieved steady dividend growth of 8.4 per cent per annum over the last 5 years.

'Out-of-town' stores

The company has recognised that its customers are increasingly using personal transport and value the convenience of 'out-of-town' locations. Out-of-town means that a store is located on a city's fringes rather than in the centre. The object of building stores in such a location is to provide customers with easier access to shopping facilities, as this is often difficult within the busy city environment. Typical of the out-of-town location is a large car-parking facility and good public transport links.

SJM plc established a plan 5 years ago to build a number of out-of-town superstores to an original design near four major cities. The first of these superstores has now been in operation for 1 year. The other superstores are in various stages of completion.

SJM plc has followed its competitors in developing out-of-town sites and is considering a partnership initiative with another retailer whose merchandise would not be a competitive threat. This would involve joint development of superstores on out-of-town sites. The only commitment to this initiative by SJM plc so far is a feasibility study of a single joint project with the other retailer. This will be completed before entering any contractual obligations.

The superstore strategy

SJM plc aims to provide a satisfactory return to its shareholders. The superstore which is already operational has achieved a high level of profitability in its first year of operation. The company has also experienced a simultaneous reduction in return obtained from other stores which it operates within the vicinity of the superstore. SJM plc is aware of growing governmental concern at the impact out-of-town developments are having on city centre retailing. These two factors have caused the company planners to pause before approving any other out-of-town developments. In addition, public transport provision has been established to service the operational superstore, but the transport providers are now objecting that there is insufficient demand to maintain frequent services as most customers travel to and from the site by car.

Superstore developments

The superstore developments are all built to a standard specification which comprises 40,000 square metres. The life of the project is 15 years. Typically, the development takes place over a 3-year period from planning stage to final commissioning. Each superstore is assumed, for investment appraisal purposes, to have a life of 12 years following completion. The cost of the first superstore development was £25 m with approximately 20 per cent being incurred in the first year. The remaining costs are split evenly over the second and third years. Included within these costs was £500,000 for architects' fees which have reduced by half in subsequent developments. The architects' fees can be assumed to fall due for payment in direct proportion to the building costs.

The superstore developments are targeted to achieve a net cash inflow of £250 per square metre per annum from the commencement of operations. Experience has shown that the first superstore has achieved this target during the first year of operation. A total reduction in net cash inflow over the same period has occurred in other SJM plc stores which trade within the surrounding areas. This has been calculated as having the effect of reducing the superstore net cash inflow by £40 per square metre per annum.

Each superstore is assumed to have a net residual value of zero. All cash flows can be assumed to occur at the end of the year to which they relate. The cash flows and discount rate are in real terms. (Taxation should be ignored.)

Requirements

(a) Prepare and comment on the financial appraisal which justified the investment in the first superstore. Assume that twelve equal annual net cash inflows commence in the first year following completion of the superstore, which takes 3 years to construct. **(8 marks)**

(b) Identify the market opportunities and threats which SJM plc will confront if it develops more out-of-town superstores. **(12 marks)**

(c) Describe and comment on the impact of the out-of-town developments by SJM plc on each of five groups of stakeholders. **(10 marks)**

(d) Discuss whether SJM plc should pursue other out-of-town developments completely on its own or jointly with the other retailer. Pay particular attention to potential planning and operational difficulties which may arise from these initiatives. **(10 marks)**

(e) Describe the contribution a management accountant may make to the planning processes of SJM plc in the areas of project feasibility, evaluation, monitoring and post audit. **(10 marks)**

(Total marks = 50)

? Question 4

C plc, a quoted chemical manufacturing company, has until recently achieved a steady increase in profitability over a number of years. It faces stern competition and the directors are concerned about the disquiet expressed by major shareholders regarding performance over the last 2 years. During this period it has consistently increased dividends, but its share price has not grown at the same rate as it did previously.

K plc, a direct competitor, is similarly experiencing a reduction in profitability. Its shareholders are diverse, with the majority being financial institutions. K plc has been criticised for under-investment and has achieved no product development over the last 2 years. Following a concerted media campaign, K plc is facing prosecution for discharging untreated pollutants into a river.

C plc is seriously considering making a bid to acquire K plc. The directors of C plc, however, are divided as to whether K plc should be closed down or permitted to continue production post-acquisition if a bid is made. In either situation, significant staff redundancies would follow.

Requirements

(a) State the strategic factors which C plc would need to consider before making a bid to acquire K plc. **(10 marks)**

(b) (i) Discuss the social and ethical implications for the managers and staff of both C plc and K plc if the acquisition goes ahead. **(8 marks)**

(ii) Discuss the environmental issues which would face the directors of C plc if it proceeds with the acquisition of K plc. **(7 marks)**

(Total marks = 25)

Question 5 The P Group

Background

The corporate history of the P Group (P) stretches back 30 years. During that time, P has developed internationally and now trades in many diverse areas. Fifteen years ago, the company launched P Airlines, which has proved to be one of its most successful business ventures. Five years ago, the company established P Rail and obtained franchises for running rail services in its home country. However, P Rail has not achieved the success that P had intended and is frequently criticised for providing services which do not run on time.

The brand

The group has a distinctive brand name which was established when P's charismatic founder and chairman launched the first business venture. The majority of citizens in its home country have heard of the brand which has over time been applied to many diverse areas of business. The chairman believes the reputation of the brand name places a burden of responsibility on P not to disappoint its customers. The chairman himself has impressed his own personality on P by pursuing personal publicity in business ventures and becoming involved in high-profile and sometimes dangerous leisure' activities.

P has achieved a reputation for entering markets which are dominated by major companies, and has been successful in taking business from some major competitors by exposing their consistently poor service and complacency.

The principal business approach which has been adopted is that of 'brand stretching' across different products and services. Each company within the group runs it own affairs but they are all encouraged to help each other resolve their particular problems in a kind of family spirit.

Key strategic factors

The chairman has stated that P is in business 'to be different' and that the P brand name should be clearly associated with this.

It is considered essential by the directors that any products or services incorporated within the brand must help to build its good reputation, provide an opportunity to add value, and yield an appropriate trade-off between risk and rewards.

The chairman considers that there are a number of key factors which have contributed to the success of P. The brand name is associated with being the consumer's champion, and has been very successful in delivering what the chairman refers to as a 'sense of excitement' in most ventures to which it has been applied. In addition, the business contacts which have been established are important and he recognises that his own personality attracts customers and venture partners. P also encourages talented staff within the group to interact with each other in order to solve problems. The management style of P is therefore seen as a major contributory factor in its corporate success. Much weight is placed on its corporate image. The chairman explains that the quality of a customer's experience when coming into contact with P is the most important item in determining its success.

Management style

The directors agree that the first priority in being able to achieve success is for P to ensure that the group employs personnel of the best quality and calibre. Their simple philosophy is that motivated staff lead to satisfied customers which results in repeat and new business and provides benefit to the shareholders.

STRATEGIC OPTIONS AND THEIR EVALUATION

P has a flat management structure with few authority levels within the hierarchy. The chairman himself is committed to providing good communication channels within and outside the group. He believes very firmly that managers within the organisation must be prepared to listen both to the customers and also the staff.

Financial performance

The business approach which has been developed is that the brand name is provided by P with a cash injection from a joint venture partner. This has generally proved to be a very successful formula, although this has not been the case with the latest venture into the domestic railway market. The directors consider that the performance of P Rail will improve following a programme to upgrade the infrastructure inherited from the previous nationalised rail network.

Comparative financial information relating to P Airlines and P Rail for the last 2 years at 31 December is as follows:

	1997 $m	1998 $m
Turnover		
Airlines	570	678
Rail	410	423
Pre-tax profit		
Airlines	60	80
Rail	30	32
Capital employed		
Airlines	750	790
Rail	530	640

Other performance indicators

The following information is provided relating to P's airline and rail businesses:

Airlines	1997	1998
Number of passengers	1.3 million	1.4 million
Passenger miles traveled	3,400 million	3,300 million
Ratio of cabin staff to passengers		
(excluding aircrew, i.e. pilots and navigators)		
Economy Class	1 to 10	1 to 12
Business and first class	1 to 4	1 to 5
Number of airline routes flown	40	44

- P Airlines sells economy, business and first-class seats to passengers. The prices reflect the level of comfort and service. For example, first-class seats cost double the price of business class seats and 10 times the price of economy seats.
- Airline passenger numbers are expected to increase by 3 per cent in the next two years in the long-distance economy-class market from which P attracts most of its customers.
- There is an increasing level of partnership emerging among airlines whereby each carries the other's passengers as well as its own on designated routes. P is engaged in such partnerships for two of its routes.
- A general survey of satisfaction among airline passengers carried out by independent representatives from the travel industry in P's home country ranks P as being within the top three for most services.

Rail	1997	1998
Number of passengers	4.3 million	4.3 million
Passenger miles travelled	150 million	150 million
Ratio of attendants to passengers		
Standard class	1 to 100	1 to 120
First class	1 to 20	1 to 25
Number of routes travelled	25	25

- P Rail sells standard and first-class seats to its passengers. The first-class seat is priced at about double that of a standard priced seat.
- An increase of 5 per cent in total rail passengers is expected over the next 4 years.
- P operates the railway services under a franchise agreement, which is due for renewal in 5 years' time.
- The government has established a Railway Regulatory Authority to monitor the quality of the services provided by the P Group and other railway franchisees, and is constantly increasing pressure on the franchisees to improve their services.
- A general survey of passenger satisfaction carried out by the Railway Regulatory Authority was highly critical of P's services with regard to its record relating to punctuality and service on its trains.

Future development

P has enjoyed considerable success in its ventures within its domestic market. However, the directors believe there is much opportunity to develop the brand name within the emerging highly-populated retail markets elsewhere in the world where currently it is relatively unknown.

Requirements

(a) Discuss the importance of the external forces which P faces in its worldwide business development. **(5 marks)**

(b) With reference to the comparative financial and other performance indicators, evaluate the performance of the P Airlines and P Rail companies. Recommend ways in which they may increase their individual contribution to the future development of the group. **(20 marks)**

(c) Advise the directors of P how their brand extension strategy may be successfully implemented in countries where the brand is relatively unknown at present.

(15 marks)

(d) Explain the main factors which have contributed to P's commercial success so far. Comment on the chairman's personal responsibilities to the group's shareholders, employees, joint venture partners and customers. **(10 marks)**

(Total marks = 50)

Solutions to Revision Questions

 Solution 1

Report
To: Managing Director **From:** Management Accountant
Re: Expansion overseas **Date:** 20 November 2001

(a) Business case for expansion overseas

The strategic process for expansion overseas is no different really from any other strategic approach. It requires the establishment of clear objectives and the reasons for the expansion must be clearly stated. In making a decision as to whether or not to pursue an overseas expansion strategy, an organisation must determine what opportunities such a move will provide and also needs to assess the costs of its implementation. In addition, the continued costs of maintaining the strategy must be determined and compared with an objective assessment of the continued benefits which are expected to accrue.

An overseas expansion strategy really means treating the world as one market and the provision of a single source of supply of goods or services. The ever-shrinking world in terms of communication and transport and the explosion of information through the Internet has meant that, in many countries, there is a similarity in lifestyle.

Many organisations have achieved benefits from increased levels of customer demand and overseas expansion has created much commonality in expectations in respect of style and quality across different continents. This is clearly illustrated by the success of such brand names as *McDonalds* and *Starbucks*.

Trading links and international alliances have been established where they did not previously exist. This is one major consequence of improved communications.

There are clear reasons why companies may adopt an overseas expansion policy given the environmental background explained above. In addition to the fear of being left behind, organisations may see that their domestic market is saturated and therefore the only opportunity for expansion is overseas if competitive advantage is no longer sustainable in the home market. This is the case which is relevant to S.

More efficient economic sourcing of resources overseas results in increased sustainable competitive advantage and benefits from increased economies of scale. This, in turn, leads to increased value added for the organisation's stakeholders, particularly its owners.

(b) Strategic and operational issues in considering whether or not to implement an overseas strategy

If S is to develop an overseas expansion strategy, it needs to recognise that there will be a series of appropriate steps in the planning and implementation process which should be followed. It may be appropriate for S to recognise that it should pursue an experimental small scale expansion overseas first before becoming too heavily committed to the strategy. This is recommended due to S's lack of experience in overseas markets.

The question arises in terms of strategic development as to whether S should take over an existing organisation in a foreign country or apply a more steady organic growth pattern. Although a take-over would give instant market access, it needs to be financed and managed. It may be more prudent at this stage to consider organic growth particularly given the advice above to expand on a small scale at first. S would be able to retain more control over an organic form of development rather than by applying an acquisition strategy.

The remainder of this report concentrates on the strategic and operational considerations of implementing an overseas expansion strategy under the headings of demand and competition, resources, technical issues and finance.

Demand and competition

S much be clearly aware of the demand potential in any overseas market which it enters. This means that the selection of the market must be carefully thought about and situated in a location where there is high level of demand for S's services. In addition, S must consider the level of competition in the overseas location which is being considered. The industry in which S is engaged is specialist by nature and therefore the directors must be clear about who its competitors are overseas. Do S's home competitors have overseas subsidiaries or partners?

In addition, S must be able to satisfy the diverse demands for its services in overseas locations. This may be a restriction or an opportunity depending on the level of regulation in the overseas country. Environmental regulations clearly differ between countries and therefore S must determine whether it possesses the technical expertise and ability to satisfy the local demand.

It is also likely that there will be variations in local demand. Will the soil and ground services supplied in the home country satisfy the demands in other countries? This may mean that S must provide a local variation in its service, although this is less likely given the nature of analytical techniques which will apply to samples of soil and water, polluted environments and methods applied to land cleansing.

Resources

S will need to be aware of the local infrastructure and methods of working in the overseas locations. It may not be able to rely on subcontractors to carry out analysis or provide materials for its own experiments. The employment of local staff may prove problematic and there may be cultural issues within S which need to be addressed. The assessment of skill levels of overseas staff would need to be determined and whether quality standards can realistically be maintained. The whole issue of the orgnisational structure for developing overseas would need to be addressed. This will be determined by the type of investment strategy which is finally determined.

Technical issues

S may need to transfer its own technology overseas and must consider what levels of investment may be necessary to do this. Alternatively, what levels of technology are available in its overseas location and how up to date is it? Will S need to train local staff, will it take samples and analyse them in its home country location or establish analytical facilities overseas? If it brings samples back to its home country for analysis, what might the implications in respect of customs and import regulations? Alternatively, establishing facilities overseas will be an expensive alternative.

Finance

In addition to issues relating to currency volatility, S must clearly consider the financing of the whole expansion programme. From where may sources of finance be obtained? What are the regulations relating to import tariffs, taxes and repatriation of profits which must be adhered to? Will there be any support from an overseas government for S to become established?

In conclusion, this report poses many questions and issues for consideration. The first step is to consider the rationale and objectives of the investment overseas. After that, consideration needs to be given to the method of entry into the overseas market. Will it be by foreign direct investment, exporting (services) or by licence to an overseas company? Would S be better advised to establish a strategic partnership with an overseas contractor in the first instance?

Signed: Management Accountant.

 Solution 2

- The candidate is presented with four companies, each operating in a different industry. Each industry is at a different stage in its life-cycle. The question requires an assessment of each of the industries to determine the stage of its life-cycle that has been reached. The candidate is further required to explain how Ansoff's product-market growth vector matrix may be applied by each of the firms in determining its growth and divestment strategies.
- The question relates to the *Appraising the Environment* section of the syllabus.

(a) (i) The concept of the Industry Life Cycle assumes that there are distinct stages in the industry's actual life. Most industries go through these stages, and the emphasis placed by the management of the firms within the industry in respect of their strategic development changes as each stage of the life-cycle is reached.

The stages of industrial development are classified into different phases: introductory, growth, maturity and decline.

The introductory phase is characterised by firms trying to develop an interest in new products or services. The embryonic stage at the very beginning of the industry's life is sometimes identified separately within the introductory phase. Competition is attracted into the industry as it grows. The aim is to exploit opportunities for potential development. Customers within the industry become satisfied by its products or services and the rate of innovation slows down. This leads to slower growth resulting in the maturity phase being reached. New competitors may still enter the market at this stage and competition for market share is likely to increase. This results in a greater degree of fragmentation and ultimately the industry begins to decline.

(ii) The industries in which each of the companies (referred to in the question) are competing appear to be in the following phases of development:
- *Company A*: New state-of-the-art door locks which recognise fingerprints – new introductory phase in an ancient industry.
- *Company B*: Rapidly expanding biotechnological company – growth phase.
- *Company C*: Confectionery manufacturer with low growth but high market share – mature phase.
- *Company D*: Retailing organisation now losing market share and turnover – decline phase for the company but not necessarily for the industry.

(b) Application of Ansoff's product-market growth vector matrix.

It is necessary to link this matrix with the four phases of the product life cycle, that is, introduction, growth, maturity and decline.

Company A is in the introductory phase of a segment of the industry which is being revolutionised by the form of door lock being developed. The industry itself is ancient, but the novel use of fingerprint technology in this way is very new. Company A must develop interest in the product in the commercial and domestic household markets. Its early customers will experiment with the product and A will need to keep innovating as competitors enter the market. It is important that A achieves rapid market penetration; it will need to have sufficient capacity to satisfy large-scale demand. The danger of not being able to do this is that competitors will take market share away from A and the company itself may become a victim of predatory action.

Losses may be sustained by A initially, but it must generate sufficient resources to keep up with demand. This will involve ensuring that there are sufficient development resources to enable production to be increased as necessary and for increased development of the product to take place. This in turn will result in increased diversity of products. Growth strategies will be mainly concerned with satisfying market demand, and keeping competitors at bay, by improving the product. In due course, as the market becomes more mature, A may be able to develop innovative uses for the product.

Company B is engaged in the rapidly expanding animal feedstuffs market. There will be an increasing number of competitors attracted to the market owing to the prediction of the likely return of abnormal profits. The customer base is expanding, and therefore it is important that B improves the quality and reliability of the product. This necessitates the extension of its R&D function, which may result in expansion of the company's facilities. It is important that B undertakes product development before its competitors take the initiative. There may be a need for B to divest itself of parts of the organisation which are not providing an appropriate amount of contribution in order to devote more resources into the development of this market. It will be necessary to sustain marketing expenditure, especially if prices begin to fall due to the introduction of increasing levels of competition.

The basic strategies to be pursued are a combination of market penetration and product development in order to maintain and improve its share of an expanding market. The emphasis is on product development, however, as the growth strategy is limited to agriculture.

Company C is experiencing the mature phase of its product life cycle with customers becoming satisfied with the products on offer. Growth is slowing down and the market itself is mature. Most customers are aware of the products, and little innovation or trials of new products are being undertaken. The main growth strategies which may be applied by C are market penetration and market development. Market penetration will have limited success, as it already holds a high level of market share. This may be achieved through price reductions and special offers, but these will only be successful in the short term. Market development is more likely to be successful, in attempting to sell current products within new markets. This may include penetration of overseas markets or introduction of mass-marketing techniques or brand-switching strategies.

Research and development will be low in respect of the portfolio currently being manufactured as the product and brand of confectionery are well known. There is little scope for growth in these product areas in a mature market. It is necessary for C to look to grow by developing new products altogether and introducing cash cows to supplement its mature cash cows. This means that research and development needs to be concentrated on different products. Some products may need to be divested from the range as they reduce in profitability and enter the decline phase of the product life cycle.

Company D is finding it increasingly difficult to compete for market share. Its turnover is declining and its marketing strategy is becoming well worn. D is clearly in decline, although the industrial environment may not be. As such, D may be subject to predatory action. D is retailing products which are well known and customers may well be more discerning in terms of price. There is little innovation and the presentation methods applied by the company are predictable. It needs to reduce costs and this may be best achieved by applying a divestment strategy. As a retailing organisation, D must consider the contribution provided by each of its outlets. It must also assess the potential for turnaround in each of those outlets. It may be that specific products sold within the stores are not attracting customers, in which case the appropriate strategy is likely to be divestment of those products from the range and their replacement with more profitable items.

If price competition exists, D may adopt a very risky strategy of withdrawing from the market altogether and diversifying into another industrial sector. It could alternatively seek to make an acquisition of a competitor which has improved market positioning in an attempt to improve its own image. Both of these strategies have serious risks attached to them. The safer course is to look towards reducing costs internally and improving its overall market image by reviewing its product profitability. This would involve a combination of market penetration for some products and product development strategies replacing those which are no longer performing for D.

Different growth and divestment strategies need to be applied in alternative situations and the most appropriate strategy in one industry will not be the same in another.

✅ Solution 3

- Another scenario question.
- This question requires you to consider the business environment throughout parts (b) and (c), yet it starts with a simple investment appraisal. One comment you could make about the appraisal is that it ignores all this environmental material (including competitors) and hence may not be reliable.
- A lot of this question is about brainstorming SWOT material and understanding the perspectives of the stakeholders. Notice how much of the syllabus it covers.

(a) The superstore achieved its target in the first year of operation and this means that a net cash flow of (£250 − £40) = £210 per square metre was generated. As the area of the superstore is 40,000 square metres, the annual cash inflow for the years 4–15 is estimated at £8.4m. The cash outflows during the construction phase were expected to be:

	£m
Year 1 20% of 25	5
Year 2 50% of (25 − 5)	10
Year 3 50% of (25 − 5)	10

Using a discount rate of 12 per cent, the net present value of this project is:

Year	Cash flow £m	Discount rate 12%	Discounted cash flow £m
1	(5.0)	0.893	(4.47)
2	(10.0)	0.797	(7.97)
3	(10.0)	0.712	(7.12)
4–15	8.4	4.409	37.04
			17.48

This calculation indicates that the first superstore was a sound investment as there was a positive NPV of £17.48m when a discount factor of 12 per cent was used. Even if the rate of discount increases to 20 per cent, the net present value will still be positive at £4.68m.

The calculation is as follows:

Year	Cash flow £m	Discount rate 20%	Discounted cash flow £m
1	(5.0)	0.833	(4.17)
2	(10.0)	0.694	(6.94)
3	(10.0)	0.579	(5.79)
4–15	8.4	2.569	21.58
			4.68

By means of extrapolation, it can be shown that the IRR of this project is more than 23 per cent and this calculation confirms the viability of the project.

However, this calculation does not appear to consider the potential for increased competition. The original investment appraisal was subsequently proved wrong by the reduction in contribution per square metre due to competitors fighting back. As the strategy rolls out across the country, this retaliation (and copycatting) will become more intense. Additionally the appraisal ignores the potential for cost reductions in operations due to economies of scale in purchasing and the use of larger units and the possible experience effects available in building and running the new-format stores.

(b) The move to the 'out-of-town' locations will provide SJM plc with both opportunities and threats. The most significant opportunity is that the new location is likely to attract additional customers who will find the superstore convenient. At the present time, some competitors have already moved to out-of-town sites and so SJM plc is responding to this change in order to retain its competitive advantage. It is possible that the move to the suburbs will increase the competition in these areas, with the result that some of the smaller stores will be forced to cease trading. Although this will reduce the total number of stores in the area, it will probably be beneficial to SJM plc as it should increase the market share of the company.

Since the new superstores will increase the volume of SJM's purchases, this should improve its bargaining strength with suppliers. The greater purchasing power will make it possible for SJM plc to obtain better terms from suppliers in the form of lower prices, better delivery arrangements or improved credit terms. As these factors are likely to improve both SJM's profitability and the service offered to customers, the company's share price and market value should also improve. In addition, the expansion of the number of stores and the increased market share should raise the profile of SJM plc at both the local and national levels.

The threats which SJM plc must consider are the reactions of existing competitors, the possibility of new entrants to the industry and government policy about this out-of-town type of development. It is likely that existing and potential competitors will react to the opening of the new SJM superstores by offering their own improved products and services to the public. The competition may also retaliate by starting a price war, which could reduce the profit margins throughout the whole industry.

Concerns have been expressed about the impact of out-of-town stores on retailing in city centres and this may cause the authorities to restrict the number of sites which are available for superstores. This would represent a major threat to the expansion of SJM plc. A decrease in the public transport available for customers travelling to suburban sites could cause another problem. If SJM plc is forced to subsidise the cost of transport to its superstores, this would further reduce the profitability of its new developments.

(c) The suburban developments are likely to affect the following of SJM plc's stakeholders:

1. *Shareholders.* From the experience gained after the opening of the first superstore, it is expected that both the company's profitability and growth will improve. This will have a direct effect on the shareholders who can expect the dividend growth of 8.4 per cent per annum to continue. Improvements can also be expected in the important financial ratios which are currently a dividend yield of 2.98 per cent ($12/403 \times 100$), an earnings yield of 4.54 per cent ($18.3/403 \times 100$) and a p/e ratio which is 22 ($403/18.3$). Although these ratios show a strong financial position for SJM plc, the shareholders are likely to receive an even better result if the expansion plans are as successful as they appear to be after the opening of the first superstore.

2. *Employees and management.* Many employees will be forced to travel to the superstores and this may prove inconvenient. However, the success of the new stores will create employment and make the jobs of the existing staff more secure. The expansion should also provide additional promotion opportunities for the existing staff in the new businesses.

3. *Customers.* For people living in the vicinity of the superstore it will reduce the need to travel to the city centre, and even for the people who live at a distance from the superstore it will be possible to obtain convenient parking in the relatively rural environment. The ability to shop in only one location is another benefit to customers.

4. *Suppliers.* Although the out-of-town stores may increase the suppliers' delivery costs, they should benefit from the additional sales.

5. *Government and the general public.* If SJM plc's new investments prove to be successful, employment will be created and work-seekers will benefit, but there could be an adverse effect on employment opportunities in the city centres. There is concern about the environmental effects of the new buildings, new roads and the use of resources to transport shoppers to the out-of-town locations. This may not represent the best use of the available resources.

(d) The return on the investment in the first superstore was expected to be significantly higher than the cost of equity capital. If it is expected that the other sites will also generate a similar income and that the initial capital costs will be reduced as a result of the 50 per cent decrease of architects' fees, then it is obvious that the net present value of subsequent projects will improve.

Although the success of the first superstore should give confidence to the management of SJM plc, there are other factors which need to be considered when assessing the overall risk of the venture. For example, it may become difficult to find suitable sites. In addition, each project is likely to have its own different problems and risks.

By undertaking the project on their own, the management of SJM plc will retain control over the superstores. This means that the company will receive all the benefits, but also carry all the risks of the project. The opportunity to open the superstores jointly with the other retailer will need to be assessed carefully. Although it is likely to reduce the risks involved, the terms of the cooperation agreement will influence the final decision. Although collaboration will mean that greater numbers of customers are attracted to the site, there are bound to be some difficulties with both the planning and the operation of the enterprise.

In terms of planning, it will be necessary to ensure that the aims and objectives of the two organisations are similar and that there are no major differences in the strategy adopted by each firm. The sharing of services, facilities and security arrangements could lead to economies of scale, but there could also be difficulties and conflict.

Marketing policies that relate to customers, pricing and promotion would have to be acceptable to both parties. The policy adopted towards suppliers could be another source of conflict and it would be wise to ensure that the two firms adopt similar policies.

The staff policy of each organisation would need to be carefully considered. This is because the staff of each organisation would be working closely together and differences in remuneration and conditons could cause operational difficulties.

Overall, the decision to proceed alone or in collaboration with another retailer will depend on the costs and benefits of the alternative courses of action.

(e) The prime purpose of a management accountant is to provide information so that the organisation can be managed more efficiently and effectively. The management accountant could also contribute to the preliminary investigations, which would include the overall assessment of the feasibility of the project. At a later stage, a more detailed evaluation of the project will be undertaken. The project will also need to be monitored and controlled, during both the investment phase and when it is operating. Finally, a post-completion audit usually requires the experience and skills of a management accountant.

The management accountant will participate in the overall assessment of the basic forecasts and estimates that are produced in the initial stages of the project. This is termed project feasibility. Awareness of the factors which will have the greatest impact on the viability of the project will be the most important aspect of the accountant's contribution.

Knowledge of evaluation techniques and the use of these methods to evaluate the alternative courses of action will be extremely important for reaching a final decision. It is particularly important that the management accountant assesses the likelihood of the organisation reaching the forecasts of the cash flows. These are often extremely difficult to estimate in an environment which is constantly changing. Another area which will require the skills and experience of the management accountant is the incorporation of risk into the project evaluation.

Monitoring during both the implementation phase of the project and in the initial stages will be extremely important. A check will need to be made to ensure that there is no major overspending or wastage of resources. In addition, regular reports will need to be produced to provide information regarding the level of expenditure, the degree of completion and the final costs that are expected when the project is complete.

The management accountant will also be involved in assessing the extent to which the original plan has been achieved. In order to provide guidance for future projects, a post-audit should be carried out at specified times after the completion of the project.

Solution 4

- Another wide-ranging question. It is included here as a basic acquisition question but it also recalls earlier topics of social responsibility and stakeholders. In part (a) the term 'strategic' should bring to mind issues of impact on future earnings and also ability of the firm to afford it. Note that the market has all the signs of maturity and C plc is propping up its shares with higher dividends. This may suggest that shareholders do not support a growth strategy and hence the availability of cash may be limited. Would a share exchange with those of K plc be better or would this risk dilution?
- For part (b) (ii) the solution below interprets this to mean just the natural environment. It would also have been acceptable to bring in other parts of PEST, such as the demand for chemicals, overseas competition, etc.

(a) Despite an increase in dividends, the rate of increase in the share price of C plc has decreased. This is an indication that the investing public are concerned about the future earning capacity of the company and the disquiet of the major shareholders also reflects these concerns. It seems likely that the 'stern competition' is responsible for this situation.

One of the ways of achieving growth and, possibly, boosting earnings may be to acquire another firm. Management is considering acquiring K plc, which will mean that the combined businesses will have a much greater production capacity if the K plc plant is not closed. The crucial issue will be what C plc can do with the additional facilities and whether it is possible to benefit from the acquisition. Competition in the industry will be reduced by the acquisition of one of the companies and savings are likely to result from the rationalisations and the economies of scale which should occur.

However, management must be aware of the effect on the management and staff of both companies involved in the acquisition. Although it is usual for acquisitions to be justified on the basis of the synergy which results from the combination of the organisations, there is often doubt regarding the extent of these benefits. This is particularly noticeable in markets in which there is excess capacity. It is also generally recognised that the management of the combined business poses a difficulty which reduces the synergistic effects of the acquisition.

The cost of the acquisition will be very important in determining its ultimate success. It is possible that during the acquisition, another company may bid for K plc and this may raise the price to a level which makes it difficult for C plc to ensure the acquisition is financially successful. C plc's expected cost of capital will be a major influence in determining the result of the acquisition.

(b) (i) It is likely that fewer employees will be needed in the combined business. In particular, the providers of specialist expertise may be particularly vulnerable as duplication of this type of activity may not be required. It is likely, therefore, that a significant number of redundancies will occur. This will create a feeling of insecurity among staff. It is important that all staff are informed of the policy in respect of redundancies. This will be particularly important in the acquired company, especially if the bid is hostile. The rationalisation process will create uncertainty within both firms and it is important for the motivation of employees that the issue is handled with openness and honesty.

Changes in employees' working conditions within the combined firm is an important issue. If it is not handled well, it is likely that the overall synergy of the acquisition will be adversely affected. Uncertainty about employment will be a problem for the staff and a clear statement on the rationale for the acquisition and the employment policies to be adopted would appear essential. Remuneration, training programmes and assistance in finding alternative employment are topics which should be discussed to improve staff morale within the firm. It will demonstrate the attitude of the directors to the staff redundancies.

It is important that employee motivation is retained if the acquisition is to reach its potential. Management must, therefore, handle the social and ethical implications of the acquisition sensitively, especially in respect of the staff redundancies which appear to be inevitable.

(ii) After acquiring K plc, some environmental issues will need to be tackled by management. The pollution problem, in particular, will have to be addressed. It is clear that the matter of the untreated pollutants should be investigated immediately so that the level of pollution is brought under control. As a priority, the company should seek to establish acceptable levels of effluent pollution and the firm would be wise to participate in establishing these standards.

At the same time, steps will have to be taken to reduce the adverse publicity that may arise through the prosecution pending against K plc. It would seem to be necessary for the company to adopt and publicise an environmental policy within the community to ensure that the negative effects of the pollution problem are minimised.

It is likely that considerable expenditure will be needed to rectify the position. The continued success of the firm may depend on the way in which the pollution problem is handled. The projected success of the combined businesses will determine the amount of expenditure that might be incurred to reduce the pollution problems.

✓ Solution 5

(a) Successful businesses must establish and sustain competitive advantage. The P Group has developed and 'now trades in many diverse areas'. This means that the company is likely to face many external forces which will make it difficult for P Group to meet its objectives, which are to ensure that their customers are not disappointed with the products and services offered by them.

Porter's Five Forces model provides a useful method of considering the different forces which the P Group faces in the development of its business.

Industry rivalry

The P Group will be trying to enter markets in which their competitors are already established and have knowledge of the markets. To try and compete effectively in the markets will be difficult. In this respect, the P Group will need to appoint excellent managers who will be able to ensure that the objectives of the company are achieved. Although the chairman has a strong personality, it will be difficult for him to have an impact on the management in all the different countries.

Power of the buyers

It will be essential that the managers have knowledge of the customer' needs and also information of the conditions in the different markets. This information will be essential if the company is to compete successfully in many sectors. The conditions in the market place, including the political, legal and social environments, will differ and if the company is to succeed, the strategy adopted must consider all these factors. At the present time, the buyers may benefit from the entry of the P Group, as it is likely that the existing suppliers are 'complacent', but this position could change and this could then represent a threat to the P Group.

Power of the suppliers

It must be established that the suppliers are available who can provide the materials and resources needed by the group. The quality and reliability of the suppliers could be a major issue and the managers must be convinced that supplies of materials, services and adequately trained labour, especially managers, can be obtained.

Substitutes

The tastes and lifestyle of consumers are likely to be different in the different businesses in which the P Group is involved. It is essential that the product sold or the services provided are adapted to meet these requirements. For example, the chairman's view of a 'sense of excitement', may be perceived in a different way by different people. It will be necessary for these differences to be taken into account in developing the strategic and marketing plans of the company. It is essential that the P Group offers value for money (VFM) and satisfies the needs of the customer if it is to prosper.

Entry barriers

The operating and business conditions will differ in each industry and information must be obtained which will enable the P Group to function effectively. If the management can introduce ventures that are innovative and 'exciting', it is possible that the P Group is actually creating entry barriers to the industry.

The intention of challenging major companies especially if they have become complacent will mean that each project should be planned and monitored carefully. It is likely that each venture will need considerable amounts of resources and it is therefore essential that the external forces be evaluated before any decisions are made. It is clear that attention must be given to these five forces, as they are extremely important to the P Group's future success.

(b) During 1998, the turnover of the Airlines business increased by 19 per cent. The turnover of the Rail business, however, only increased by 3 per cent. In addition, there were significant differences in the performance of these two divisions in the P Group.

Airlines	*1997*	*1998*
Profit as percentage turnover	10.5%	11.8%
Return on capital employed	8.0%	10.1%
Turnover/capital employed	76.0%	85.8%

Rail	*1997*	*1998*
Profit as percentage turnover	7.3%	7.6%
Return on capital employed	5.7%	5.0%
Turnover/capital employed	77.4%	66.1%

Although there has been no significant change in any of these ratios, some of the trends may become significant in the future. The Airlines division showed an increase in profitability and the ROCE improved by over 2 per cent. However, the ROCE of the Rail division declined and this must be a matter of concern to the management of the P Group.

The airlines division

The management of the airline should review the division's current strategy to ensure that the company is able to cope with the competition and problems faced by companies competing in this volatile industry which is subject to the effect of changes in the international environment. A review of the company's selling prices and operating costs should be initiated as it is important that these aspects of the business are monitored carefully.

Although the number of passengers, passenger miles travelled and the number of routes flown have increased, it is possible that the management of the P Group should consider investing additional funds to ensure that the positive trends continue. Especially as the number of passengers in the long-distance economy-class market is expected to increase by 3 per cent in the next 2 years, the P Group should take steps to ensure that they benefit from this growth in the total market.

It may be appropriate to improve the ratio of cabin staff to passengers in both the economy and business classes to ensure that customers are given good service. At the present time, surveys show that the P Group has a good reputation and steps should be taken to ensure that this competitive advantage is not lost, particularly by reducing the service provided to passengers.

It is possible that price competition may become more evident as competitors try to gain market share from the P Group. It will be essential for the airline to respond to these challenges, especially in the economy class as these travellers will be conscious of the price charged.

A review of all the routes and alliances should be undertaken to be sure that the P Group is operating efficiently and effectively. It is possible that expanding into too many routes could be detrimental to the overall success of the business. It would seem appropriate that the P Group should investigate the profitability of each route and focus on the routes that are most profitable. Similarly, the benefits of the alliances with other airlines should be considered, as the P Group may gain significantly from these.

The rail division

The profitability of the division is static and it is essential that the management review their strategic options. It is possible that ways could be devised which would enable the management to increase fares, decrease operating costs and reduce the capital employed. In particular, the operating problems, which are causing a loss of customer confidence, must be rectified as this could have a bad effect on all the divisions of the P Group. It is possible that the decrease in customer attendants is affecting the customer' perception of the services offered by the P Group, but punctuality is likely to be more significant in the Rail division.

The number of passengers and the passenger miles travelled have decreased and this is a problem, which should be investigated to ascertain the causes. The turnover to capital employed ratio has fallen significantly and some solutions to this problem must be obtained if the company is to meet its objectives. It appears that the capital employed is increasing without a corresponding improvement in the turnover. This might only be a transitional stage, but the management of the P Group must be sure that this ratio will improve soon. It is likely, however, that further investment may be required to improve the performance of the P Group. The return on this investment may be relatively long term.

Although the total market is expected to grow by 5 per cent over the next 4 years, it is possible that the P Group may not attract a high proportion of the increased trade if the opinion regarding the service does not improve.

The threat of the Regulator is another problem that the management of the P Group must address. The possible loss of the franchise would represent a major setback for the company. The passenger survey indicated that the P Group was not providing a good service to the rail users. It is, therefore, important that steps are taken to ensure that both punctuality and services provided improve. The decreased number of customer attendants might be partly responsible for the dissatisfaction and this is an issue that should be investigated immediately.

(c) As the brand name is very well known and recognised, it is possible to use this strong brand name to enter new markets. Launching a new product under a strong existing brand will mean that the product will be recognised immediately. This will mean that fewer resources need to be allocated to the launch and this would be a major competitive advantage to the P Group as they will be able to launch their products using less promotional expenditure than competitors who have a less well-known brand name.

The use of a brand extension strategy will make it easier for the P Group to enter new markets. It will be possible to diversify into both new products and markets and success may be achieved more quickly. The danger is that the brand name could suffer if the development is not successful and this could damage the whole of the P Group's reputation. It will be essential that the management ascertain that the brand name is recognised in the country if it is being considered as a target for investment. In any case, a campaign of 'brand awareness' should be arranged to ensure that the company gains this competitive advantage.

The extent to which the company can expand will be limited by the availability of resources. Extensive plans to enter new markets will mean that financial, physical and human resources will be needed to launch the product successfully. It is likely the P Group has access to these resources, but it is important that the entry into the new markets is planned efficiently. Market research regarding the product quality, price and distribution methods should be undertaken. However, it is also essential that marketing research be initiated to assess the success of the marketing approach and the possible effect of the emphasis that is currently placed on the chairman and his activities which are designed to bring the company to the attention of the media.

It is very important that the managers consider the implications of the culture in all countries to which the P Group intends to expand. This could be a major factor that determines the success of the overseas investments and is an issue that should be evaluated during the evaluation phase of the investment process. The particular areas that should be considered are the products to be promoted and the effects of the methods used to raise brand awareness. The airline industry is regulated closely in many countries and this is an issue that needs to be given attention.

Financial resources

Additional capital will have to be obtained and this may mean that the company must borrow funds in order to expand its operations into countries where it is relatively unknown at the present time. This will increase the debt burden and the consequences of the increased borrowing must be evaluated.

Physical resources

The entry into new markets will result in additional fixed assets and working capital in each country. This may increase the investment significantly and increases the company's risks as a result of foreign investment.

Human resources

The expansion will mean that additional management skills will be needed to manage the new businesses. It is possible that managers will be able to deal with the extended markets. However, the senior managers must be sure that these skills are available either within the company or that trained managers can be recruited.

It is possible that entry into the new areas could be achieved more effectively by means of collaborative and joint ventures. This should enable the company to exploit its brand name and this would provide it with significant advantage over its competitors. It would be possible to combine with companies that have knowledge of these markets and this would enable the company to expand and grow without increasing the business risk. In addition, it would reduce the amount of resources, especially management skills, that would be needed.

(d) The personality and charisma of the chairman is clearly an important factor in the success of the P Group. His dominant personality and activities which generate 'personal publicity' keep the activities of the group in the public eye. However, the company will need to achieve the expectations of their customers if the P Group is to be a successful business. Other key strategic factors are:
- the association of the brand with good value for consumers;
- the development within the company of a culture which enables employees to interact successfully;
- the emphasis that is placed on the development of a positive corporate image;

- the focus on ensuring that the staff are motivated and it is expected that this will benefit the customers and create customer loyalty;
- the concern of the chairman to be exciting and also the relaxed management style of the management may contribute to the motivation of the company's employees.

The chairman dominates the company and must, therefore, consider the effect on the principal stakeholders. The shareholders, the participants in any management buyout and the company's joint venture partners will expect dividends and capital growth on their investments.

The board must ensure that these stakeholders are satisfied. The company's employees will identify with the chairman and so he must ensure that they are treated fairly and are given opportunities to develop their talents and skills. This will benefit each employee and also the company.

The customers will be aware of the mission of the company and the public activities of the chairman but the management need to ensure that the quality of the products and services offered to the customers meet their expectations.

By taking these steps to keep his image in the media spotlight, the chairman makes it necessary for him to deliver a performance that satisfies the company's stakeholders. It is important that each group is convinced that he is able to meet their expectations. This means that the chairman of the P Group bears a much greater responsibility than the chairmen of similar-sized companies.

7

Organisational
Impacts of
Business Strategy

Organisational Impacts of Business Strategy

7

The last chapter considered the various strategies available to the business from the point of view of their impact on the firm's environment and, in particular, its competitors. However, strategic change has implications for the internal structure and operations of the business. This chapter will examine these latter implications.

LEARNING OUTCOMES

After completing this chapter you should be able to:

► evaluate the importance of process innovation and re-engineering;

► discuss the role and responsibility of directors in the strategy development process;

► discuss the role of change management in a strategic context;

► understand the implications for Chartered Management Accountants and the management accounting system.

7.1 Overview: leading issues in business organization

7.1.1 Definition of the organisation

 According to Buchanan and Huczynski (1997): 'Organisations are social arrangements for achieving controlled performance of collective goals.'

7.1.2 Issues raised

The importance of considering organisational issues in developing and implementing business strategy can be seen in terms of the definition above:

1. Organisations are arrangements developed to serve the organisation's goals. These 'arrangements' include:
   - the organisation's structure;
   - the assets it controls;

351

- the rules and processes it uses;
- the role of managerial authority and the level at which it operates.

A change in business strategy may change these goals. This suggests that some business strategies may necessitate changes to the organisational arrangements noted above. We shall discuss factors such as:

- organisational restructuring, delayering and empowerment;
- outsourcing of business operations to outside firms;
- formation of closer relations with suppliers based on trust rather than adversarial relations;
- business process re-engineering (BPR);
- network (or virtual) organisations.

Also, rapid change brings into question whether any given structure can meet the strategic needs of the business. This will lead us to look at more modern theories of organisational dynamics.

2. *Organisations are social arrangements.* This means that they involve people. This brings to mind issues concerned with motivation, political behaviour and the problems of changing people's attitudes and behaviour. To this we can add that people are occasionally fallible and suffer from bounded rationality.

3. *Organisations have controls.* These are the management processes which ensure that things go right. However, if the goals change and the organisation's structure changes, then so must the controls. Strategic initiatives will influence all of these.

4. *Organisations are also complex adaptive systems.* They will not react to the same stimuli in the same way each time. They have ability to learn, or adapt to their environment.

7.1.3 Implications for the chartered management accountant

One of the main functions of the chartered management accountant is to provide control in the organisation through techniques such as budgetary control, investment appraisal, performance evaluation and internal audit. Strategic initiatives will influence all of the following:

(a) The responsibility centres used to ascribe costs and revenues for the purposes of budgeting and reporting will change.

(b) Many of the processes will change. As one example, the flexible organisation will rely far less on waiting for decisions to be taken at the corporate centre and instead require them to be taken lower down.

(c) Strategic management will shift from the corporate centre to business units and work teams. This will change the recipients of management information and also its content.

(d) In organisations where flexible teamwork is introduced the management accountant will also be required to be a part of a team.

(e) Effective control may necessitate control over external suppliers and also over providers of outsourced services.

(f) Elements of the finance function itself may be outsourced.

The challenge for chartered management accountants of the twenty-first century will be to facilitate innovation and organisational flexibility by moving beyond the rigid numerical and financial control systems developed in the early twentieth century. However, they must also ensure that management still exert adequate control over the organisation to ensure that corporate objectives are reached. This will be a recurring theme in the remainder of this text.

7.2 Organisational Theory

7.2.1 Background knowledge

It is important at this stage that you are aware of the existing theories concerning organisational structure. A more comprehensive coverage can be found in the recommended texts for the earlier papers in your studies in this pillar. You should be able to distinguish between, and understand the benefits and drawbacks of:

- simple organisation,
- functional organisation,
- multi-divisional structure,
- holding company structure,
- matrix organisation structures.

You should also take the time to revise the classical model of organisations as described by Fayol, Weber and Taylor in earlier papers.

The influence of the classical model is evident in much of conventional management accounting systems:

(a) Concepts used in budgetary control such as standard times, outputs and costs imply that output and methods do not significantly change through time (and have their origins in the terminology and work study methods of Taylor's 'scientific management').

(b) Responsibility centres are clear examples of the principle of segregating tasks and specialising roles which, it is inferred, do not overlap or change through time.

(c) The system assumes that senior managers must control the organisation by setting targets in a top–down fashion and then scrutinising performance by comparing it with budgets.

(d) Emphasis on maximising the efficiency of fixed assets such as machinery by use of profitability-based measures, with profit expressed as a return on fixed capital investment (e.g. ROI).

(e) The emphasis on financial performance places the short-run interests of shareholders as the primary goal of the business.

(f) The system serves to constrain the decision latitude of management within close boundaries.

(g) There is little or no environmental information.

The adequacy of the classical view of organisations was called into question by the contingency approaches to organisations and you should revise the contingency theory of organisations from earlier in the pillar as well.

You will remember that Lynch (1997) explains that contingency theory implies that organisational structure will vary according to nine variables:

- age;
- size;
- environment;
- extent of centralisation/decentralisation of power;
- overall work to be undertaken;
- technical content of the work;
- degree of task diversity;
- culture;
- leadership.

7.3 Contemporary approaches to organization

7.3.1 Need for alternatives to the classical model

A central theme in this text has been the suggestion that the business environment has become increasingly uncertain due to the combined pressures of increased complexity and increased dynamism. Some of the effects of this have been:

(a) The breakdown in long-term planning, corporate-led approaches to strategy formulation in favour of business strategy formulation based on the identification of core competences.
(b) The increased power of stakeholder groups inside and outside the organisation which has diluted the power of managers to take decisions with the interests of only shareholders in mind.
(c) The much greater need for innovation in product and service design.
(d) The need for more management information on both product and customer profitability to take strategic choices.
(e) The greater emphasis on external information.
(f) The greater need for organisational flexibility.

Increasingly these forces cannot be managed within the classical model of the organisation. The emergence of new organisational forms has implications for the roles and procedures of management accounting because, as has been shown, it too is rooted in classical organisation theory.

7.3.2 Kanter: innovation, empowerment and change

Kanter (1984) conducted a survey of over 115 change situations in corporations in the United States and noted two styles of thinking:

1. *Integrative thinking.* This embraces change and sees problems as wholes by eliminating conflict between divisions to ensure that multiple perspectives will be taken into account. Innovation flourishes in such organisations.
2. *Segmentalism.* These organisations are concerned with compartmentalising problems and hiving them off for specialists to deal with. They minimise communication and rely heavily on R&D to solve problems. They find it hard to innovate and see change as a threat to the compartments and segments within the firm.

Organisations that are change-orientated will have a large number of integrative mechanisms encouraging fluidity of boundaries, the free flow of ideas, and the empowerment of people to act on new information (p. 32).

She sees this based on 'participating teams' and suggests five elements that executive management should encourage:

1. *A culture of pride*: Highlight achievements and spread innovations from one division to another.
2. *Enlargement of access to power tools for innovative problem-solving*: Such as by allowing teams access to research funds and time to develop ideas.
3. *Improvement of lateral communication*: Bring departments together and encourage cross-functional teams.
4. *Reduction of unnecessary layers of hierarchy*: 'Push decisional authority downward' and share information and intelligence about internal and external affairs.
5. *Increased, and earlier, information about company plans*: Give people at a lower level a chance to influence change through problem-solving groups.

Several of the themes started by Kanter have been very influential, notably empowerment, delayering and teamworking. Her criticisms of segmentation are also similar to the comments of the resource-based strategists we studied in P5 *Integrated Management*.

Kanter also offers ten principles to stifle innovation:

1. Regard any new idea from below with suspicion.
2. Insist that people who need your approval first go through several other levels of management.
3. Get departments/individuals to challenge each others proposals.
4. Express criticism freely, without praise, instil job insecurity.
5. Treat identification of problems as a sign of failure.
6. Control everything carefully and frequently.
7. Make decisions in secret and spring them on people.
8. Do not hand out information to managers freely.
9. Get your lower managers to implement your threatening decisions.
10. Above all, never forget that you, the higher ups, already know everything important about the business.

And we shall revisit this in Chapter 9 when we look more closely at strategic change.

7.3.3 Hope and Hope: competition in the third wave

Hope and Hope (1997) build on the forecast of the influential work of Toffler (1980) that the major dynamic affecting world economies in the coming years is a third wave of technological change, the 'information wave'. This will have an effect on society which is every bit as fundamental as the two earlier waves, the 'agricultural wave' which swept away mediaeval society and the 'industrial wave' which created cities and a capitalism based on ownership of physical productive assets.

The third wave will create an 'information society'. This has several implications:

(a) An increase in the importance of the service sector as the source of new jobs and outputs.
(b) Changed forms of trading relationships as information systems enable firms to replace direct ownership and management of productive assets with network arrangements with suppliers and customers.

(c) Increase in the importance of the global market for products as tastes become interchangeable and unified around a common global technology (as an example: think of the cultural impact of the PC and the common roles, activities and terminology it has brought about).

(d) Increased importance of 'knowledge workers' who can offer their services globally using digital communications technology.

(e) Increased importance of organisational knowledge as the crucial strategic resource.

Hope and Hope outline ten key management issues for the third wave, shown in Table 7.1.

You should recognise issue 5 from our earlier discussion of customer profitability. The rest will be addressed in the remainder of this text.

7.3.4 Impact of chaos and complexity

Stacey (1996) casts doubt on the ability of any organisational structure, traditional or 'third wave' to cope with the complexities and uncertainties of the modern commercial environment.

Stacey draws on the insights of *chaos theory*, an approach to natural sciences popularised by Gleick (1988). According to chaos theory much of the science since Newton is a *little bit wrong* and therefore a *little bit misleading* because it assumes a predictability in the systems of the natural world which does not exist. Yet despite its potential for destructive chaos, the natural world somehow adopts sustainable patterns of activity through time. Stacey sees clear parallels between this situation of 'order amongst chaos' and the problems facing the strategic management of businesses when the quasi-mechanistic organisational system breaks down under the impact of greater environmental complexity.

Stacey's ideas are thought-provoking and it is worth looking at them more closely. Let us start with chaos theory.

Anyone who has lain awake listening to a dripping tap will testify that the drips do not occur as a pattern of evenly spaced drops; rather they hear a pattern of steady drips interspersed with random pauses and sudden rushes. Similar patterns have been illustrated with other deterministic systems such as waterwheels, pendulums, oscillators and population ecology. The conclusion reached was that no system ever adopts an exact equilibrium pattern of behaviour and this, together with the fact that it never repeats itself exactly, makes it impossible to predict how it will behave in the future.

The most famous casualty of this realisation was long-range weather forecasting. All weather forecasts are a *little bit wrong*, as we all know, and this is rightly put down to the *complexity* of the variables affecting weather and we soon learn to revise our plans as the day unfolds. However, long-range forecasts were *hopelessly wrong* because the effect of minute changes in the system (the example usually cited is of a butterfly beating its wings or a leaf falling on one side of the world contributing to a hurricane some time later on the other side) made them predict the opposite sort of weather to that which actually transpired.

Chaos theory terms this *bounded instability far from equilibrium*. This is visualised in Figure 7.1.

This points to a kind of order emerging from chaos. Despite the doubts that chaos theory casts on the possibility of stable equilibrium, this is not the same thing as saying that there are no patterns in the behaviour of systems. Put simply, just because we cannot

Table 7.1 Hope and Hope's key management issues for the 'information wave'

1. *Strategy – pursue renewal not retrenchment*
   Cease to focus on downsizing
   Learn to think 'outside the box' and be innovative
   Trust and empower management teams to think and act strategically
   Develop core competences and avoid rigidities
   Create alliances and economic webs with suppliers and customers to lever economic value
2. *Customer value – match competences to customers*
   Value propositions are of three sorts:
   • Product leadership (technical content and speed to market)
   • Operational excellence (low-cost, high-quality, service)
   • Customer intimacy (customisation, relationships)
   Select, pursue and retain customers that can match the value proposition put forward by the firm
3. *Knowledge management – leverage knowledge for competitive advantage*
   Three sources of knowledge assets:
   • Human capital and competences of staff
   • Internally stored data and information system capability
   • Market and externally related such as customer loyalty, brands and network relationships
   Management must retain and leverage this knowledge to gain competitive advantage
4. *Business organisation – organise around networks and processes*
   Move from hierarchies to networks and emphasise processes and teams
   Recognise the organisation as a social structure (i.e. not as a machine) and keep people informed and motivated
5. *Market focus – find and keep strategic, profitable and loyal customers*
   Cease to pursue volumes to increase profits
   Identify the worthwhile and profitable customers
   Firm's capital is relationship with the customer
6. *Management accounting – manage the business, not the numbers*
   Know how to analyse product, customer and service profitability
   Use accounting to help improve processes
   Move to more relevant accounting systems
7. *Measurement and control – strike a new balance between control and empowerment*
   Avoid the tendency for budgets to constrain innovation and flexibility
   Strike a new balance between control and empowerment
   Implement a new strategic measurement system
8. *Shareholder value – measure intellectual assets*
   Equity prices depend on future returns
   These returns depend on human and not physical assets now
   Develop measures of human capital for appraisal and reporting
9. *Productivity – encourage and reward value-creating work*
   Move beyond seeing productivity as return to fixed capital assets
   Create right culture, recruit right staff, provide information, empower and allow them to share in the benefits
10. *Transformation – adopt the third-wave model*
    Recognise the failings of the second-wave model:
    • emphasis on productivity of physical capital
    • seeing staff as costs to be minimised
    • rigid command and control styles of management
    • profit through cost-cutting and volume increases
    Manage change to third-wave model
    Query the value of 'second-wave' management education

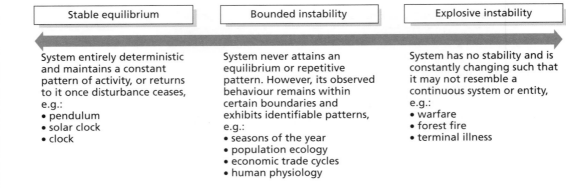

Figure 7.1 Three types of instability

forecast tomorrow's weather does not mean to say that we cannot recognise that there are seasons in the year. This is because there are *regularities* in systems even though there may not be repeated equilibrium patterns.

So what has all this to do with *Management Accounting – Business Strategy?*

Example of chaos

A month after the destruction of the World Trade Center in New York by terrorists aboard hijacked airliners on 11 September 2001, the financial controller of a leading aerospace supplier spoke to the author about the pressure he was under to revise budgets downward. He explained that he needed to factor-in the following:

- reduced wear and tear on planes due to cuts in international schedules;
- the possibility that several clients would go broke as a result of falling volumes and increased security;
- the potential that the situation might worsen with further attacks, military resolution by the United States and international boycott of the United States if response was too strong.

As the conversation progressed it was clear that he, like the rest of the world, had no idea what the next 12 months would bring, although he was keen to make parallels with the situation when conflict followed the invasion of Kuwait by Iraq in 1990. In other words his budget would be a complete fiction but would reassure investors and enable the management to make staffing and production decisions. His firm, along with the rest of the world, had moved from a feeling of bounded instability to one of explosive instability. However, he and his colleagues still sought to impose control systems based on stable equilibrium.

Various techniques of management accountancy and of business strategy seem rooted in the 'stable equilibrium' model of understanding organisations and their environments, that is in the science of the seventeenth century. The conclusion we are being invited to draw is that this is a *little bit wrong* and that any management techniques based on this understanding will be a *little bit misleading*.

Worse, if the complexity of the organisation and its environment increases, this understanding and these systems will become *deeply wrong and misleading*.

Crichton (1991) provides a best-selling fictional account of the breakdown of an organisational system from the impact of unanticipated complexity in *Jurassic Park*, a theme continued in his subsequent book *Swarm*. Closer to our daily work are the following symptoms:

(a) Escalation, or breakdown, of rules and procedures in the organisation as staff continually take more and more short-cuts to carry out their work.

(b) Increasing costs of management control such as improved management information systems, additional performance measurement systems, extra supervisory staff, introduction of performance appraisal systems and performance-related pay schemes and greater attention to human resource management.

(c) Perpetual restructuring and organisational change in a vain search for a model that works.

(d) Abandonment of strategic plans, programmes, annual budgets or departmental budgets due to 'unforeseen contingencies'.

(e) Increasing resort to ad hoc organisational solutions to problems such as special project teams, trouble shooters, 'skunk works' and off-budget spending.

(f) Increased use of outside expertise and resources to make up for perceived deficiencies inside the organisation, for example outsourcing projects, buying-in new ideas, using of consultants.

Under the conventional model these are examples of dysfunction and are seen as things to be tightened up. From the chaos theory perspective they are the inevitable outcome from an over-engineered organisation facing the challenges posed by the breakdown of its own systems and increased complexity.

Stacey sets out to describe a process by which organisations can develop the qualities of bounded instability observed in other chaotic systems and hence remain viable during periods of extreme complexity.

7.3.5 Stacey's concept of 'Extraordinary Management'

Stacey builds on the insights of chaos theory by making a distinction between two forms of management:

1. *Ordinary Management.* This form of management has the following features:
   (a) A *legitimate* organisational system consisting of hierarchy, bureaucracy and officially approved ideology.
   (b) An emphasis on team-building, consensus and conformity among managers.
   (c) Progressive, incremental change using a rational approach to strategy.
   (d) Control is predominantly 'negative feedback control', that is it consists merely in stamping out any deviations from the standard patterns of behaviour and from the targets of the plan that the firm is following.

   He argues that this approach requires high degrees of certainty in the business environment and close agreement among managers.

2. *Extraordinary Management*:
   (a) A spontaneous system of self-organisation through a 'shadow system' of political networks and contacts within the organisation, often operating against the official bureaucracy and involving bargaining and personal power.
   (b) A process of organisational learning from which innovative and creative new directions emerge.
   (c) Builds on the 'tacit knowledge' (i.e. unconscious or unexpressed knowledge) of the group members which manifests itself as awareness skill or know-how in particular situations rather than being communicated in instructions or plans.
   (d) Flourishes when the organisation is near the edge of disintegration and deeply-held beliefs are being questioned.
   (e) Features irrational decision processes which relies on gaining the commitment of the team rather than demonstrating attainment of particular organisational goals.

Both forms of management will need to exist together. However, although operational matters and staff will be controlled within the 'Ordinary Management' system, Stacey suggests that strategic management and organisational development will often take place within the shadow system of 'Extraordinary Management'. Moreover the latter is the essential 'self-organisation' which will allow the firm to remain within a state of 'Bounded Instability' rather than degenerating into 'Exploding Instability' or becoming out of step with its environment by attempting to adhere to the unattainable state of 'Stable Equilibrium'.

Stacey suggests that deliberate attempts to install a 'Shadow System' through increasing organisational flexibility (e.g. Kanter's notions of empowerment and removal of bureaucracy) runs two dangers:

1. It will undermine the hierarchy and therefore the short-term control of the organisation.
2. It removes the tension between the manager's wish for flexibility and the control structures of the organisation that often gives the impetus to the Shadow System and encourages creativity.

Instead Stacey suggests seven *intervention steps* to favour the development of creative networks in the organisation:

1. *Develop new perspectives on control.* The established hierarchy of managerial control will form the cornerstones of the informal organisation too because they hold the essential resources. Top management must learn to rely on the power of this hierarchy and its ability to network, rather than strategic planning or formal project teams, to control the creative process.
2. *Design the use of power.* Power should not be centralised, otherwise it tends to create a control culture that inhibits creativity and learning. Neither should it be evenly spread about because it encourages anarchy and little organised learning. Power should be spread about unequally and be able to shift to where it is needed (e.g. by assigning budgets to managers rather than departments), to encourage networks to be built up to attract resources.
3. *Establish self-organising groups.* This can be encouraged by regular 'issue meetings', provided that the meetings are not seen as an excuse for not taking the initiative and instigating contact outside the meetings. Stacey suggests they work better if they:
   - have freedom to operate;
   - discover their own challenges, goals and objectives;
   - have a membership drawn from a number of different functions, business units and hierarchical levels.
4. *Develop multiple cultures.* These will encourage creativity by ensuring multiple perspectives. They can be developed by discouraging standardised training programmes, broader recruitment, use of outsiders and in the construction of the project teams.
5. *Present challenges and take risks.* Senior executives should challenge lower managers but also allow themselves to be challenged. A good forum for this is 'breakout weekends'.
6. *Improve group learning skills.* Senior management must overcome corporate role-playing and other blocks to innovation and group learning. This again is best accomplished by example and by regular group meetings.
7. *Create resource slack.* Senior management must ensure that there are sufficient resources to allow innovation. These include budget, space and also management time. Stacey is critical of the delayering exercises that strip away middle management staff to the extent that those which remain are overloaded and have no time or energy for innovation. This runs counter to any idea of 'lowest cost producer' in the industry.

In emphasising the need for organisational learning, Stacey is emphasising the work of Senge (1990) on the need for organisational learning. Other authors (Kelly, 1994) have said that organisations, and even the economy, are best described by a biological metaphor than a mechanical one implying that the strict hierarchical structures that we are used to are wrong.

7.3.6 Future developments in management practice

In a CIMA-sponsored research project, Ezzamel *et al.* (1995) present a useful summary of the likely changes to the management of organisations which they term *New Wave Management* (Table 7.2).

Table 7.2 New Wave Management

The past relied upon	Future emphasis will be to
Rules, regulation and supervision, for example, a span of control	Flexibly appreciate contingency and ambiguity
Hierarchical control and a clear chain of command	Effectively develop human resources
Discipline imposed by management	Facilitate employee self-discipline
A mechanistic and directive approach to problem-solving	Problem-solving through participation
Single-function specialists and individualism or independence	Create multi-functional teams through mutual dependence
Job descriptions with defined tasks and responsibilities	Continuously review a fluid series of renegotiated assignments

7.3.7 Summary and comment

The authors cited above all seem to be pointing to the need for a change to the methods of managing organisations. Common themes are:

(a) need for greater use of teams within the organisation;
(b) empowerment and delegation of responsibility to lower level managers and teams;
(c) creation of new 'network' relations with suppliers, customers and other firms;
(d) increased importance of the knowledge worker;
(e) need for new systems of management information and control to back up the changes.

These themes are very common in management literature from the 1990s and will form the focus of our remaining discussion.

However, it is important not to focus on the emerging industries and ignore the need to control the established 'second-wave' sector. The emphasis of these writers is upon encouraging innovation and flexibility at the strategic level. The operational level of the business will still need to be controlled. As the contingency approach suggests, management needs to adopt the most *appropriate* structure and processes for the business they are running and the functions and decisions they seek to control.

This leads to the following observations:

(a) Not all firms need the innovation and flexibility implied by 'new wave' management writers. For example, it is hard to see it applying to mature industries like quarrying and brick manufacture in the same way as it applies to banks and retailers.

(b) Not all divisions of the business need the same control features. Innovation may be something that takes place at the level of middle management. Perhaps at the factory or operational level it is possible to retain command and control styles.

(c) Key stakeholders such as staff and shareholders may retain a suspicion about these new management philosophies. Moving too fast may leave them behind and jeopardise the short-run survival of the firm.

(d) Little practical progress has been made in these directions. The research by Ezzamel et al. (1995) concluded that most changes were driven by a short-run pressure for better financial results and theories of empowerment were often a smokescreen for large redundancy programmes with 'the command and control style organisation [seeming] to live on beneath the surface of the new wave management methods'.

7.4 The network organisation

7.4.1 An overview of network organisations

Externally, network organisations are organisations that rely on relationships with other organisations in order to carry out their work. You will have studied network organisations earlier in the pillar.

> At this stage you should revisit you work on the topic from that study material and read again the discussion on generic value chains for network organisations in Chapter 3. Since this form of organisation is becoming increasingly common it is likely to be examined at this level as well.

It is of particular importance that you be aware of the issues posed by network organisations:

1. How do firms decide which activities and assets to 'buy-in' and which to own and operate directly?
2. Why have network organisations become so important in recent years?
3. How can management develop systems to control operations in a network organisation?

7.5 Business process re-engineering

7.5.1 Origins of the concept

CIMA defines business process re-engineering (BPR) as:

> 'The selection of areas of business activity in which repeatable and repeated sets of activities are undertaken, and the development of improved understanding of how they operate and of the scope for radical redesign with a view to creating and delivering better customer value.'

CIMA: *Management Accounting: Official Terminology*, 2005, p. 46.

The concept of BPR developed from a research programme run from 1984 to 1989 at the Massachusetts Institute of Technology (MIT). This research demonstrated that managers were using information technology and information systems (IT/IS) to transform the way in which businesses worked, rather than simply automating their existing operations.

This became the theme of an article by Hammer (1990) entitled 'Re-engineering Work: Don't Automate, Obliterate'. This article ushered in a wave of management interest in a technique variously termed 'business process re-engineering' or 'business process redesign'.

7.5.2   An example of BPR

BPR can be thought of as attempting to secure business improvements to quality, cost and speed through a root-and-branch redesign of the way a business operates. It involves redesigning jobs, organisational structures and control systems on the basis of value-creating processes rather than business functions and departments. A commonly cited example is of re-engineering credit sales at IBM:

The IBM salesforce formerly manually recorded at client meetings the details of the firm they wished to lease equipment to. This was passed to their credit division who decided whether the client was creditworthy. Following approval, the application was passed to corporate finance division to allocate funds. The legal department issued the salesmen with the legal documentation for the prospective customer to sign. The salesmen complained that during the three weeks this took, the customer had often cooled off or found another supplier.

Research revealed that only about five minutes were actually spent processing the application. The rest of the time the documents were resting in in-trays awaiting attention.

Today the IBM salesforce have laptop computers into which they input the client details. This links via a cellular phone to the credit-scoring systems at headquarters and also to the corporate finance database. It also prints out the legal agreement. It takes about three minutes.

7.5.3   Hammer's principles of re-engineering

The IBM credit example illustrates several of Hammer's seven principles:

1. *Organise around outcomes not tasks.* Tasks are the present jobs of departments and individuals that may have developed in a bygone era and have failed to adapt to take advantage of new methods of working. Outcomes are what the process is supposed to deliver. BPR should work backwards from the desired outcome (in the case of IBM the swift approval of credit and the closing of the sale), focus on finding the most efficient and effective way to deliver the desired outcome and then redesign the organisational structure and tasks to deliver it.

2. *Have those who use the output of the process perform the process.* This is effectively both empowerment of the end-user and an encouragement for them to use the technology. The end-user (in this case the IBM salesman) is the point of contact with the customer and the best placed person to input the data and read the results. Hammer wishes to avoid the errors and time lags involved in using centralised data-processing systems (in IT/IS circles this is the mantra of 'driving the system down to the end-user').

3. *Subsume information-processing work into the real work that produces the information.* BPR generally increases on-line access to corporate databases. In the IBM case this is

symbolised by the salesforce having its own laptops with a capability for on-line analytical processing (OLAP).

4. *Treat geographically-dispersed resources as though they were centralised.* This establishes the case for establishing a corporate database of information which is uploaded from the dispersed divisions and agents (the individual salesmen) but which is also available to them. This combines a central control over information protocols with empowerment and support of end-users.

5. *Link parallel activities instead of integrating tasks.* Integrating tasks means creating larger jobs and bigger departments. These are inherently less flexible and will be slower because they will process the tasks sequentially rather than simultaneously. IT/IS has the ability to allow parallel processing of information.

   For example, manufacturing design of a complex product like a car involves many different designers such as body stylists, electronics, power-train, interior design and structural engineers. Behind them are the process engineers who must develop the body presses and tools to enable production of the finished design. In an integrated task system the body stylists must finish their work before the rest can start and the process engineers must wait until the whole car is complete. Using a common database enables each to work in parallel, with access to the most recent iteration of the car design on-screen. They can substantially complete their work in parallel and make last-minute amendments as necessary. This reduces costs and greatly speeds up product development and reduces 'time to market'.

6. *Put the decision point where the work is performed and build control into the process.* Acting on the information is again the preserve of the end-user. The salesman will decide whether to offer credit and on what terms. To avoid the salesman boosting their commissions by granting cheap credit to risky customers, the control over this process might be the abolition of commission-based payments, data fields which must be completed, on-line credit checking to reputable agencies, inability of salesman to override the programme if it rejects an application.

7. *Capture information once and at the source.* The transcribing of information from one form to another (say by keying-in from an application form) is a major source of delay and costs. Consequently BPR favours electronic data interchange whereby the originally input data serves as the file for the transaction.

7.5.4 Stages in a BPR exercise

Davenport (1993) suggests a five-stage approach to BPR:

1. *Identify the process for innovation.* The processes where BPR is commonly applied are:
   (a) The process of production or operations.
   (b) The ordering cycle (i.e. the interface with customers and suppliers).
2. *Identify the change levers.* These are the forces making change necessary and possible. Typically these will be:
   - developments in information needs;
   - competition;
   - innovation in information systems and technology;
   - changes in the culture and management of the firm.
3. *Develop the process vision.* Build a vision of how the process of the business should be, for example,

- what should the speed of service be?
- what role will there be for suppliers and customers?
- what amount of staffing will be involved?

4. *Understand the existing processes.* Document the existing processes of the organisation and the reasons for why things are done a certain way. Particularly crucial here will be:
   - the way data is captured;
   - the interfaces between the firm and outsiders;
   - the interfaces within the organisation;
   - the points at which the process is delayed for lack of information by the person performing it.

   The existing process is then critically analysed to spot the opportunities for IT/IS to increase efficiency.

5. *Design and prototype the new process.* The proposed new system is developed and tried out in a limited area (e.g. in just one branch).

7.5.5 Using BPR to enhance customer responsiveness and financial performance

Hauser and Eisele (1995) observe that BPR is predominantly intended to increase the ability of the firm to meet the needs of its customers. To deploy it effectively, management must identify outcomes most likely to generate superior customer value. The BPR exercise should be focused on delivering these.

There are two sets of factors to consider:

1. The features or attributes of the firm's own service that are most valued by the customer. They term these key buying factors (KBFs).
2. The features of its rivals' performance which are valued by customers or benchmark measures of its rivals' relative performance.

Converting the potential improvements in market share from the BPR exercise into sales revenues gives one half of the information necessary to conduct an investment appraisal.

BPR may also reduce costs through streamlining or eliminating activities. Hauser and Eisele suggest that activity-based costing techniques will enable management to incorporate these financial benefits into the evaluation of BPR.

The present value of these benefits can be calculated and compared with the investment costs in the technology and human resources necessary for the BPR exercise.

7.5.6 Comparison of BPR and other strategic management techniques

At this point in your studies these various management theories and new techniques may be blurring into one. You are not alone, because the boundaries are not clear. Each new theory is developed by people with a vested interest in promoting it. They will claim that:

- it supersedes what has gone before;
- it is much better;
- it solves many management problems;
- it is entirely unique.

Remember, if they convince people they will enhance their academic reputation and earn fortunes from publishing and consultancy. They would say that wouldn't they? Here is a simple way to understand where BPR fits in.

1. BPR draws on the insights of Porter's value chain by viewing the organisation as a set of value-generating processes rather than as a segmented structure of departments and divisions. Techniques such as activity-based costing and activity-based management can support this too.
2. BPR can support the marketing orientation to the extent that it re-engineers the business on the basis of the benefits sought by the customer.
3. BPR can be assisted by benchmarking. Management may direct BPR to those processes where relative performance is poor. Also benchmarking is a useful technique for measuring the improvements yielded by the BPR programme.
4. BPR has a role in furthering the network organisation. If it can be shown that outside suppliers can deliver certain benefits better than having the process managed in-house, then the conclusion should be to extend the network.
5. BPR also brings into focus the relationship of the firm with its suppliers. It is pointless reengineering the firm to provide streamlined performance for it to be held back by the inefficiencies of its suppliers and partners.

7.5.7 Dangers of BPR

1. *Often used as the pretext for staff reductions.* For example, Ezzamel et al. (1995) concluded that much of the impetus for organisational change came from the cost-cutting potential of IT and less from considerations of business effectiveness. Some writers (e.g. Willmott, 1995) present BPR as merely an excuse for senior management to assert their power over middle management and staff through increasing workload and cutting headcount. If true, this makes BPR entirely opposed to many of the modern 'trust-based' approaches to management.
2. *Conflicts with human resource based approaches to business improvement.* Several of the 'new wave' management approaches such as teamworking, total quality management, empowerment, etc., emphasise the value of unlocking human potential to make the firm more responsive and innovative. BPR advocated empowering the end-user and making them more flexible which is quite consistent with this. However, it does not appear to accept that staff should determine the structures in which they work, nor that these structures should adapt through time. Instead BRP envisages a group of specialists imposing their understanding on the business and designing a better process. The result will be that staff are still constrained within a new framework of operation that they did not design.
3. *Overlooks the impact on human resources.* Willmott (1995) notes that writers on BPR overlook the enormous implications of a BPR exercise for the staff involved and attributes the breakdown of many BPR exercises to this. These changes will involve learning new patterns of work, the breakup of traditional workgroups, the loss of enriching parts of the job and redundancies. The firm will incur visible costs such as training and redundancies, but also less visible ones such as the loss of goodwill and uncontrolled staff losses.
4. *Increases stress of staff.* A common outcome of BPR has been the reduction in staff numbers at middle and line management levels. The result has been the overload of the staff remaining. This reduces effectiveness.

5. *Focuses on business efficiency not business effectiveness.* One effect of BPR has been the 'hollowed-out business'. Hamel and Prahalad (1993)regard this as the loss of key competitive assets, the knowledge and creativity of middle management. They accuse BPR (and benchmarking) of focusing too much on improving existing business rather than developing new and better lines of business.

6. *May destroy existing controls within the organisation.* Management control is exerted in a variety of ways. You will be familiar with the *internal controls* such as segregation of duties, management supervision, quality of personnel and the accounting procedures used. BPR threatens these by combining tasks, stripping away levels of management and allowing the firm to use lower grade staff.

7.5.8 BPR and PI

One of the examiners for E3 *Enterprise Strategy* offers the following thoughts and observations on the birth and development of Business Process Re-engineering (BPR) and its 'twin' Process Innovation (PI).

Birth

Business Process Re-engineering (BPR) seems to have been invented in 1990, with the publication of two papers on the subject – one by Michael Hammer and the other by Thomas Davenport and James Short. The birth was further celebrated by the publication of the two leading books on the subject, both in 1993, also by Hammer (with Champy) and Davenport (this time writing alone). I say 'seems' because neither paper actually uses the term Business Process Re-engineering. Both papers (and the books that followed them) mention both business processes and re-engineering, but tend to avoid linking the phrases together. It seems that the 'full' term only became popular only in the mid-90s as a 'catch-all' for a number of differing approaches, including those of Hammer and Davenport.

Childhood

The three major BPR proponents (Hammer, Champy and Davenport) have all worked for the consulting firm CSC Index, so a high degree of similarity between their works is only to be expected. Despite this, there are subtle differences between the approaches taken in the two key (1993) texts, both in the degree to which they appear to change the organisation's processes, and in the role that they perceive for IT.

While both BPR and PI are seen as essentially 'radical' and 'fundamental' in their impact on the organisation, BPR tends rapidly to become operational and incremental in its implementation. Although Hammer's widely quoted definition of re-engineering hints at the overall objective being a step-change in performance levels, this is seen as resulting from a huge volume of relatively small, kaizen-style, incremental process improvements. Davenport, on the other hand, is keen to remind us at every opportunity that each individual PI exercise should be based on a 'process vision', and that we should be looking for a whole new way of performing each process. The end result is that BPR is often seen as tending towards 'doing things better', whereas PI has a much higher chance of resulting in the organisation 'doing better things'.

The second difference between BPR and PI is the role of Information Technology (IT). Hammer sees IT primarily as an enabler or implementation tool – IT is seen as a way of performing processes better, faster or more cheaply. Davenport, however, sees the relationship between IT and PI as more complex, and working in both directions. IT, in Davenport's view, is not just an enabler but also a change trigger. Processes often have to change because of an IT-based innovation.

All grown up

Very soon, Hammer had become one of the most famous (and wealthy) business gurus around. Davenport's profile was a little lower, but he was highly respected, both in the consultancy world and academia.

By 1994, BPR accounted for a large proportion of consultancy funds being spent world-wide, and thousands of young MBAs were employed as BPR consultants. Indeed, a 1995 article by Grint and Willcocks cites evidence that the take-up rate of BPR among major US and UK organisations was up to 70 per cent. It was very clear that many, if not most, managers saw BPR as the hot tool of the mid-90s.

The enthusiasm of the business community for BPR was more than matched by that of the academics. Peppard (1996) lists 144 citations that include both theoretical and empirical studies of BPR. The distinctions between the works of Hammer and Davenport had become less marked, and it appeared that BPR had 'come of age'.

Middle age

Towards the end of the 90s, BPR seemed to be starting to show its age. While some of the academic studies cited by Peppard are enthusiastic in their support of Hammer, others are scathing in their criticism, mainly on the grounds that BPR contains nothing new. A number of academics were starting to see BPR as a case of 'the Emperor's new clothes'. Indeed, BPR has been widely criticised for drawing too heavily on the work of the scientific management writers (Frederick Taylor, or even Adam Smith), the human relations school (Mayo), and the many Tavistock Institute writers.

In business, too, BPR was beginning to come unstuck. According to Bashein et al. (1994), 70 per cent of all BPR projects fail, the major reasons for failure including; a lack of senior management commitment, unrealistic expectations, unsound financial conditions, and animosity towards and by IT and HR specialists. Was the end in sight for BPR?

Death?

Like so many consultant-driven 'management fads', BPR was soon to be superseded by 'the next big thing', albeit difficult to choose a successor from 'knowledge management', 'enterprise resource planning' or 'e-commerce'. However, elements of BPR are still relevant to 21st century business. As managers, we can all take a 'visionary' view of the fairly ordinary processes around us, and be continually on the lookout for new and better ways of doing things. BPR has been criticised for being little more than common sense, but the irony is that common sense hardly ever goes out of fashion.

But is it management accounting?

As management accountants, our key remit is to inform our colleagues, in order to allow them to make their decisions on a timely basis and to improve those parts of the organisation for which they are responsible. If we are to do this, we need to gather data about the way processes are performed, and try to identify how those processes can be improved. Whether we call this re-engineering, innovation, kaizen or just common sense, it's still our job.

7.6 New patterns of employment

7.6.1 The flexible firm

> You will have studied the concept of flexible firms earlier in the pillar. At this stage you should revisit you work on the topic from that study material. Since this form of organisation is becoming increasingly common it is likely to be examined at this level as well.

A recurring theme in 'new management' and in strategy is the need for the organisation to be flexible.

This has arisen for four reasons:

1. *The need to be competitive*: through better use of assets.
2. *The need to be adaptive*: through being able to respond quickly to the need for change in highly turbulent business conditions.
3. *The impacts of new technologies*: which have changed the products demanded, the nature of competitors, the ways of working and the possibilities for organisational structures.
4. *The development of new organisational structures*: these network-form organisations feature loose and fluid workgroups and the breakdown of permanent structures.

Atkinson (1984) identifies the implications of this for human resources as the requirement for three forms of flexibility:

1. *Functional flexibility*: employees can respond quickly to changes tasks through *multi-skilling*.
2. *Numerical flexibility*: the numbers of employees can be increased and reduced with the volume of demand for their services.
3. *Financial flexibility*: the ability of pay levels to reflect the external costs of labour and also the financial position of the business.

7.6.2 The virtual organisation

It has been suggested that, by 2010, 50 per cent of the UK population will be self-employed or working as contract staff, and that the majority of these will be based in their own homes or in 'telecottages'.

> Telecottage: An independent facility where freelance workers can rent a workstation or 'IT den' in order to telecommute (as in 'cottage industry').

This model of the organisation as a collection of independent self-employed staff is not as strange as it may seem. Charles Handy (1991) has proposed a 'shamrock' structure for organisations of the future in which the organisation only employs 'essential' core staff to perform essential core work, with the remainder of the activities being outsourced or performed by self-employed contract staff. Other writers refer to this structure as a 'virtual' organisation, as the organisation only gives the appearance of existing.

For the virtual organisation to be an effective component of, or substitute for, physical forms of human resource location, new forms of management are needed. The idea of virtual organisations is becoming closer to reality by virtue of broadband connections and the resulting faster Internet. However the main barrier still remains the societal factors within organisations. The current situation is that most firms have yet to come to terms with staffing as a concept rather than a physical actuality (Robson, 1994, rev. 1997).

One variant of virtual organisations comes from the open source movement – made popular by software developers of products like Linux.

Open source harnesses the power of mass collaboration and to find new ideas. It is increasingly becoming the mainstream way that businesses are generating value and reach optimal decisions. For instance, Proctor & Gamble are using their online InnoCentive network to harness the ideas and expertise of over 90,000 scientists around the world to resolve difficult research challenges.

When it came to innovation, the company originally had a closed business model. As the world's largest consumer brands company, they filed thousands of patents, yet used only 10 per cent of them.

However, analysts complained that P&G's research and development (R&D) expenses were higher as a percentage of sales than those of their rivals. In 2000, P&G's share price began to plummet, losing more than half it's value between January and May 2000.

After a careful analysis of the situation, P&G realised their poor performance was because they were not developing enough new brands, and the only way to develop new brands was to be more open.

In 2001, P&G underwent a dramatic transformation. They adopted open innovation and an open business model. The goal was to look outside P&G's corporate walls to find new products, technology, packaging, design, processes and business models.

P&G has a network of Technology Entrepreneurs who search the world for good ideas.

The company focuses on certain countries for specific solutions. For example, Europe is the birthplace of the chemical industry, and remains the prime source for innovation in that industry. However, P&G will often find technology that is from one industrial domain and apply it to another category in which they compete.

The *Connect and develop* initiative is enabling faster, more cost-efficient, consumer-driven innovation on core brands. Under the new business model, anyone with a good idea can approach P&G to take their innovation to market. Some of the products that have emerged from the *Connect and develop* initiative include: Olay Regenerist (from a company called Sederma in France); The Swiffer Duster (found in Japan) and Mr Clean Magic Eraser (also found in Japan).

And instead of protectively sitting on the 90 per cent of patents that went unused, P&G looks to find partners to license and develop them. While C + D is primarily concerned with bringing things into P&G, the new open innovation business model is about inbound and outbound ideas.

P&G has 36,000 patents and over 60,000 trademarks globally. It has a vast technology portfolio in chemistry, materials and biosciences, as well as know-how in IT, manufacturing and consumer research. In 2003 the CEO of P&G announced a vision for the company that 50% of the innovation for the company would come from outside.

Collaboration is a key element of P&G's growth strategy and a key element of an open business model.

7.6.3 Implications of flexibility for management accounting

Flexible human resource management strategies pose the following issues for management accounting:

1. *Potential breakdown in management control.* A major form of control in an organisation is the collective skill and social culture of the staff cohort. By working together, groups are able to develop patterns of work and shared knowledge. These can be more effective than rules and procedures in ensuring the attainment of work goals. They are also more flexible, particularly in situations of crisis. Replacing permanent teams with an ever-changing group of workers will lose this form of *clan control*. It may need to be replaced by additional layers of *bureaucratic control*.
2. *Need for additional performance-measurement systems.* It was noted above that staff flexibility often requires the institution of payment by results systems. To operate these fairly there will need to be performance-measurement systems that can track the outputs of individual teams. Moreover these teams will need such information to monitor their performance in order to control it.
3. *Greater participation in the business decision process.* Where the rewards to staff are related to business performance and justified by concepts of participation, it will inevitably follow that these staff will seek to influence the performance of the business and monitor the decisions of senior management. This may result in management accounting information being directed to and used by staff below the level of senior management.
4. *Revision to budgetary control systems.* Conventional budgetary control treats human resources as a cost which is divided into two classes: direct labour which is used in proportion to production and indirect and overhead labour which is effectively a fixed cost. More flexible human resource strategies will lead to less labour being a fixed cost. Furthermore the costs of the labour will be harder to forecast because pay rates will differ according to market conditions and whether it is permanent or contract staff that are being used.

    Flexible labour arrangements will also make it difficult to assign labour costs to particular departments or products because labour will be switching between them.
5. *Changes in the employment of management accountants.* Management accountants will be subject to the same human resource strategies. Consequently the management accounting function may be staffed by a mixture of permanent and contract staff. Key functions may be outsourced and the individual accountant may need to exhibit greater flexibility in their skills and the tasks they undertake.

7.6.4 A critical perspective on flexible organisations

Much discussion suggests that flexible organisations are both inevitable and ultimately desirable. Concern has, however, been voiced about the flexible organisation due to its apparent similarity to the exploitative practices of nineteenth century capitalism.

According to a writer of the times (Marx 1954, from Marx, 1867), the nineteenth century factory owner's possession of the means of production gave them the upper hand in any negotiations with individual workers. The latter were frequently hired by the day, paid by piecework and lacked any job security, old-age benefits and even safe conditions of work. Others depended on 'outwork' arrangements, such as sewing and lace-making at home. An 'iron law' ensured that wages rarely rose above subsistence level. Factory owners (capitalists) were forced by commercial competition and falling prices to exploit workers further to extract their customary profit (or *surplus value*).

The development of the factory system enabled trades unions to organise in the workplace and to influence the political system. Together these led to legal protections for workers and the creation of the welfare state.

Many of the theories that lead to a belief in the flexible organisation have the effect of justifying a return to the systems of the nineteenth century.

7.6.5 The changing social role of the management accountant

The changing nature of the organisation casts the role of the chartered management accountant in an interesting light.

According to one writer (Puxty, 1993), the role of management accounting and management accounting theory has always been to facilitate and justify the control of the majority of the organisation, the workforce, on behalf of the interests of the minority (the owners and senior management). It is worth exploring this concept a little further.

At the beginning of the twentieth century the function of management accountancy was to enable control of the factory process. The use of standard labour times and the close supervision of performance through departmental budgets were symptomatic of this. Techniques were predominantly numerical, which had the effect of dehumanising the organisation by imposing the processes of a machine and reducing staff to the status of inputs. The purpose was to maximise the return on the assets provided by the factory owners.

In Chapter 1 we reviewed the role of stakeholders and the growing acceptance that businesses have social responsibilities. At the same time, management theory begins to speak in terms of unlocking the potential of staff by treating them as assets and knowledge workers. A theme in the present chapter has been to see organisations as more like organisms than like machines, adapting and interacting with their environments. Hope and Hope (1997) and others call upon management accounting to adapt to this by making greater use of non-financial measures, to encourage teams and to work at the interfaces of the networks between the organisation and its stakeholders.

The flexible organisation requires what of the management accountant? On the one hand it may be a continuation of the broadening network of the organisation to include casual and contract workers, and emphasising broader participation in both decisions and rewards. Alternatively it could be a return to the exploitation of classic capitalism.

It is not possible to say which way things will go at present. However, as we shall see in the next section, changes in the philosophy of management carries with it important implications for the work of the chartered management accountant.

7.7 Implications for management accounting

The implications for 'classic' management accounting of new management thinking has been integrated throughout the present chapter. Here a summary of the main themes is presented.

7.7.1   Three emergent themes

In their research, Ezzamel et al. (1995) discovered several important findings about the value of traditional management accounting:

(a) It has ceased to fit with or support the new organisational fluidity desired by managers.
(b) Costing information was becoming irrelevant as managers disputed the idea that any costs could be regarded as fixed. They were not prepared to risk running their business on arbitrary cost allocations.
(c) Increased payment by results for divisional managers has led to much greater scrutiny of the basis of cost allocation.
(d) Changes in management accounting practices are seen as critical to broader organisational change.

They identify three themes which impact on the design and use of management accounting systems:

1. Increased empowerment and accountability.
2. Changes to the basis of motivation and remuneration.
3. The need for management accounting to respond to the challenges.

7.7.2   Empowerment and accountability

The principal findings here are:

(a) *Need to control opportunism*: because middle management is now more able to take decisions than before, management accounting must control these to avoid these powers being used to benefit managers at the expense of the customer or organisation as a whole.
(b) *New forms of control*: detailed top-down supervision of teams and groups is too slow and expensive. New control mechanisms based on group responsibility and trust must be developed.
(c) *Increased use of electronic information systems*: the development in IT enables closer supervision to be conducted by techniques such as enterprise resources management systems which can capture a wide range of data from numerous teams and divisions at little cost.
(d) *Information must be directed to the shop floor too*: management accounting provides information for decision-taking. Empowerment means that decisions are taken at all levels in the organisation, not just at board level, and so information must be more widely available.

They identify three challenges for management accounting in this area:

1. *Defining new responsibility centres that criss-cross functions*. Traditional responsibility centres have been based on departments and technical processes. Modern management takes a process view in which the unit of analysis is a customer group, product or brand. Management accounting has to change to make these the basis for cost and revenue allocation.
2. *How to identify boundaries between teams such that each can become a unit for management surveillance*. Although overlapping and permeable teams may generate knowledge and mutual support, it is the job of the management accountant to avoid opportunistic

decisions by the teams and to ensure that value is generated by monitoring costs and revenues. Hence the management accountant must introduce some structure into this internal environment.

3. How to measure team performance while retaining individual responsibility and entrepreneurship. This is discussed separately below.

7.7.3 Motivation and remuneration

This tension between individual motivation and team performance is widely recognised as being at the heart of modern management thinking. Many of the factors leading to creativity come from the individual's own initiative and hope of personal benefit. However, refinement and implementation of the ideas is a team effort. How are management to avoid subsuming the creative individual within the team, and hence not reward their merit? How can they avoid the team spirit being destroyed, as one individual is rewarded more than the rest?

The researchers found no evidence of a resolution of this problem despite some awareness of its existence on the part of management.

7.7.4 Implications for management accounting

The increased power of information systems have led to two main developments in management accounting practice:

(a) A significant reduction in clerical level management accounting personnel due to centralisation of the management accounting information and returns.
(b) Increase in the timeliness and detail of management accounting information.

The authors note that this process has been hampered by fear of the loss of valuable information. They also express concern that the increased use of computerised management accounting systems will be at odds with the organisation's need for the richness and complexity of human relationships and interactions within a management information system (MIS).

7.7.5 Manage the business, not the numbers

Hope and Hope (1997) suggest that the key challenges for management accounting are:

1. *Switch from vertical reporting to horizontal reporting.* Management accounting must abandon the traditional role of monitoring divisional activity and reporting to senior management. Instead it must help teams co-ordinate their efforts by providing horizontal information. This can include:
   (a) Customer-based calculations of profits and revenues.
   (b) Calculations of product profitability.
2. *Switch from cost control to developing cost-reduction processes.* In a competitive market, maintaining a given standard cost is not good enough. Instead the processes of the firm should be examined and the costs systematically reduced. This involves techniques such as:
   (a) Value chain analysis and process improvement.
   (b) Benchmarking.
   (c) Activity-based costing.

3. *Strike a new balance between empowerment and control.* Budgets are regarded as a straitjacket on innovation and business improvement for three reasons:

(a) They mirror and reinforce the divisional structure of the organisation.

(b) They encourage self-centred, budget-constrained behaviour among management.

(c) They reinforce the top-down control regimes of mechanistic organisations.

However the researchers do not advocate disposing of control altogether, because in the short run costs must be controlled and in the longer term the strategy of the firm must be delivered. Instead they advocate two forms of control system:

(a) The creation of a cultural control system based on a belief system backed up by appropriate incentivisation.

(b) The development of a *balanced scorecard* of financial and non-financial measures monitoring and informing staff on the performance of critical business processes.

The topic of balanced scorecards and alternative management accounting control systems is covered in Chapter 8.

7.8   Summary

In this chapter we have reviewed the main theories supporting the view that hierarchical, classically-organised firms will not be able to cope with or generate the sorts of strategic change required for survival in the twenty-first century.

- The main sources of these changes are the need for dynamism and empowerment (Kanter), the impact of third-wave technology (Hope and Hope), and the recognition that orthodox management structures cannot deal with chaos and complexity (Stacey).
- The implications are that organisations will become 'network' organisations through outsourcing and forming alliances. Moreover, internally there will be the breakdown in traditional divisionalisation.
- These trends will be enhanced by the impact of information technology and consequent business process re-engineering, and the shift towards flexible organisations and virtual workforces.
- For the management accountant this will bring the challenge of ensuring control in less hierarchical systems, and the need to provide performance measures and decision-making information for a wider range of activities and to a lower-level empowered work team.

References

Armstrong, M. (1992) *Human Resource Management: Strategy and Action*. London: Kogan Page.

Atkinson, J. (1984) Manpower Strategies for the Flexible Organisation. *Personnel Management*, August.

Bashein, B.J., Markus, M.L. and Riley, P. (1994) Preconditions for BPR success, and how to prevent failures. *Information Systems Management*, 11(2): 7–13.

Buchanan, D. and Huczynski, A. (1997) *Organisational Behaviour: An Introductory Text* (3rd edn). Hemel Hempstead: Prentice-Hall.

Crichton, M. (1991) *Jurassic Park*. New York: Random House.

Davenport, T.H. (1993) *Process Innovation: Re-engineering Work Through Information Technology*. Boston, MA: Harvard Business School Press.

ORGANISATIONAL IMPACTS OF BUSINESS STRATEGY

Davenport, T.H. and Short, J.E. (1990) The new industrial engineering: information technology and business process redesign. *Sloan Management Review*, Summer: 11–27.

Ezzamel, M., Green, C., Lilley, S. and Willmott, H. (1995) *Changing Managers and Managing Change*. London: CIMA.

Franks, R.V. (2000) *Computing Terminology*. London: CIMA.

Ghoshal, S. and Bartlett, C.A. (1997) *The Individualised Corporation*. London: Random House.

Gleick, J. (1988) *Chaos: The Making of a New Science*. London: Heinemann.

Grint, K. and Willcocks, L. (1995) BPR in theory and practice: business paradise regained? *New Technology, Work and Employment*, 10(2): 99–109.

Hagel, J. and Armstrong, A.G. (1997) *Net Gain: Expanding Markets Through Virtual Communities*. Boston, MA: Harvard Business School Press.

Hammer, M. (1990) Re-engineering work: don't automate, obliterate. *Harvard Business Review*, July-August: 104–112.

Hammer, M. and Champy, J. (1993) *Re-engineering the corporation – a manifesto for business revolution*. London: Nicholas Brealey Publishing Ltd.

Hamel, G. and Prahalad, C.K. (1993) *Competing for the Future: Breakthrough Strategies for Seizing Control of Your Industry and Creating the Markets of Tomorrow*. Boston, MA: Harvard Business School Press.

Hammer, M. (1990) Re-engineering Work: Don't Automate, Obliterate. *Harvard Business Review*, July/August.

Handy, C. (1989) *The Age of Unreason*. London: Business Books.

Hauser, C. and Eisele, R. (1995) A concept for the market-orientated evaluation of business processes. In Burke, G. and Peppard, J. (eds.) *Examining Business Process Re-engineering: Current Perspectives and Research Directions*. London: Kogan Page.

Hope, J. and Hope, T. (1997) *Competing in the Third Wave: The Ten Key Management Issues of the Information Age*. Boston, MA: Harvard Business School Press.

Kanter, R.M. (1984) *The Change Masters: Corporate Entrepreneurs at Work*. London: George Allen and Unwin.

Kelly, K. (1994) *Out of Control: The New Biology of Machines*. Boston: 4th Estate.

Lynch, R. (1997) *Corporate Strategy*. London: FT/Prentice-Hall.

Malone, T.W., Yates, J. and Benjamin, R.I. (1987) Electronic markets and electronic hierarchies. *Communications of the ACM*, 36(6): 484–497.

Marx, K. (1954) *Capital* (Vol. 1). London: Lawrence and Wishart. (original dated 1867).

Miles, R.E. and Snow, C.C. (1978) *Organisation Strategy, Structure and Process*. New York: McGraw-Hill.

Mullins, L.J. (1993) *Management and Organisational Behaviour*. London: Pitman Publishing.

Nirmalya, K. (1996) The Power of Trust in Manufacturer-Retailer Relationships. *Harvard Business Review*, November/December.

Ouchi, W.G. (1980) Markets, Bureaucracies and Clans. *Administrative Science Quarterly*, 25: 129–141.

Peppard, J. (1996) Broadening visions of business process re-engineering. *Omega*, 24(3).

Puxty, A.G. (1993) *The Social and Organisational Context of Management Accounting*. London: Academic Press.

Robson, W. (1994, rev. 1997) Strategic Management and Information Systems, Financial Times Management, London.

Senge, P.M. (1990) *The Fifth Discipline: The Art and Practice of the Learning Organisation*. New York: Doubleday.

Stacey, R.D. (1996) *Strategic Management and Organisational Dynamics* (2nd edn). London: Pitman.

Toffler, A. (1980) *The Third Wave*. London: Pan Books. Cited by Hope and Hope (1997), *op. cit.*

Williamson, O.E. (1964) *The Economics of Discretionary Behaviour*. Englewood Cliffs, NJ: Prentice-Hall.

Williamson, O.E. (1981) The Economics of Organisation: The Transactions Cost Approach. *American Journal of Sociology*, 87(3): 548–577.

This is the most readable account produced by Williamson of his theory. A more complete formulation appears in his book. The Economic Institutions of Capitalism (1995) although his written style in the latter is often rather opaque.

Willmott, H. (1995) Will the turkeys vote for christmas? The re-engineering of human resources. In Burke, G. and Peppard, J. (eds.) *Examining Business Process Re-engineering: Current Perspectives and Research Directions*. London: Kogan Page.

ORGANISATIONAL IMPACTS OF BUSINESS STRATEGY

Readings

7

Beyond budgeting: building a new management model for the information age

Jeremy Hope and Robin Fraser, *Management Accounting*, January 1999

Early in 1998 CAM-I Europe initiated a new research project known as the Beyond Budgeting Round Table (BBRT). Now with 33 members this has developed into an exciting and leading-edge review of how to manage large businesses in the information age. This article describes the work of the project over its first year and the challenges that still lie ahead. There have been three stages so far:

1. Building a convincing case for abandoning budgeting by identifying and visiting companies that have done so (and writing case studies that describe their experiences).
2. Using these cases to build and refine a general or 'emerging' model for managing without budgets and developing a 'diagnostic' that enables a company to position itself against this model.
3. Preparing a list of 'lessons learnt' that will help us to better understand the important issues of implementation.

In 1999, the BBRT programme will be examining in much more depth the components of the steering mechanisms to be used in place of budgeting, and developing guidelines for implementing them.

Why budgets must go

Few executives need convincing that the competitive environment has changed markedly over the past 20 years and that firms need to be more responsive and agile in meeting the needs of their customers. But just when many firms seemed to be raising their game to meet this challenge (with improved quality, better service and measures of customer satisfaction) a new and more crucial competitive contest has been thrust upon them – the battle for talented managers and important shareholders. Both issues are, of course, connected. Those executives with the most imaginative strategic ideas and the freedom and capability to act are exactly what astute shareholders look for when placing their bets on the future. The point is that unless firms are attractive to both managers and shareholders they face a grim prospect – for in today's increasingly global market they will fall prey to those companies with higher market capitalisations. In other words they will lose their identity and their freedom.

Such a prospect should make every senior management team reconsider its management principles and practices, but what has all this got to do with budgeting? 'Everything' is our reply.

Take the issue of attracting the best people. In a recent McKinsey survey the top three reasons why managers chose one firm over another were 'values and culture' (58%), 'freedom and autonomy' (56%) and 'exciting challenge' (51%). Budgets are well known for reinforcing the command and control culture, constraining freedom and autonomy, and stifling the very challenges that excite prospective managers. So in the battle for management talent, budgets have a lot to answer for.

What are the issues that concern shareholders? For sure it's not just the numbers on the current balance sheet. Shareholders are taking a view on a firm's ability to generate high and growing future cashflows and these are most likely to flow from intangible assets. Strong brands, excellent processes (e.g. innovation, speed, quality and productivity) and especially the firm's ability to create strategic options and form flexible partnerships outside the firm are the issues that drive the share price. And this takes us back to attracting and keeping the best people. Not only were budgets never designed to manage intangible assets, they undermine their growth potential by directing management attention exclusively to the (short-term) financial numbers, thus ignoring the key drivers of shareholder value. Command and control goes with budgets like strawberries with cream.

To change the culture successfully you must deal with the budget and vice versa. The two are inseparable.

So if existing budgeting systems have such crucial weaknesses, why do we still rely on them? The answer lies in their history and their unchallenged position in the top division of accepted management practices. This is not to suggest that accountants don't try to improve them. They do. Zero-base budgeting and activity-based budgeting represent valiant efforts to update the process, but they only deal with part of the picture and are both time-consuming and complicated to manage.

Some companies are re-engineering their budgeting processes to make them faster and cheaper, but such an approach also fails the test, as they leave the behavioural weaknesses in place.

Let's face it, budgets are the biggest roadblock (both systemic and mental) to the future. It's now time to abandon them and develop alternative and much more effective management processes.

Our progress so far

Though many books and articles refer to firms that deride budgets (Jack Welch at GE called them 'the bane of corporate America' and Bob Lutz at Chrysler called them 'tools of repression'), we have not been able to identify many companies that have actually abandoned them. Those that have, with one or two exceptions, are in Scandinavia. Svenska Handelsbanken abandoned budgeting over 20 years ago and has since maintained its position as Scandinavia's most profitable bank, with the lowest costs of any bank in Europe. More recent converts include Volvo (one of Europe's most profitable car manufacturers), IKEA (the world's largest furniture manufacturer and retailer), SKF (the world leader in rollerbearings), Borealis (one of Europe's largest petrochemical companies), KF (Sweden's largest retailer), Schlumberger (one of the world's largest oil services companies) and Boots (one of the UK's most profitable large retailers).

All these firms are now managing successfully (in whole or in part) without budgets. Others, including Ericsson (one of Europe's most successful companies in recent years), are also on the way.

Small though the sample might be, the experience of these firms can tell us a great deal about how to manage businesses in the information age. We would list six important conclusions from our research study so far:

1. *Budgets are barriers*. Budgeting is a barrier to competitive success in the information age. Abandoning it is entirely feasible, the alternatives are better, and it is not particularly difficult to achieve.
2. *Ten principles and practices*. Just dismantling the budgeting system will not be effective unless the changes in management principles and practices are seen as an integrated approach with as much emphasis on the 'soft' cultural issues (such as empowerment) as on the 'hard' process issues (such as management reporting).
3. *New steering mechanisms*. Alternative steering mechanisms can be used to manage the business more effectively. For example, management information and control is improved with better anticipatory techniques (such as rolling forecasts) leading to more effective control and better decisions.
4. *Organisational levels*. The management model can vary according to the needs and complexity of a business and between different levels within an organisation (e.g. group head office, business units and responsibility centres).
5. *Building the new model*. The organisation, culture and values are important. They take time to develop and should be appropriate to the competitive pressures of the business. For example, decentralisation, process-teams, and knowledge management systems need to be considered.
6. *Implementation*. Careful thought needs to be given to implementation. This issue will occupy much of our attention in 1999.

Budgets are barriers

We have not found any difficulty convincing people that budgets are barriers to change. They are well aware of their weaknesses. The problem is convincing them that there is a viable alternative. Few managers relish change and uncertainty and tackling the budgeting problem raises many such issues. Loosening control, giving front-line people decision-making authority, and trusting people to act in the best interests of the firm are not easy changes to contemplate.

But it is interesting to note the reaction of managers once budgets have disappeared from the landscape. They invariably wonder why they wasted so much time for so long, how they missed so many profit-making opportunities, and how they consistently failed to respond quickly enough to customers. It is only with hindsight that the real barriers become clearly visible. Not one of more than 50 managers we interviewed at all organisational levels would wish to return to traditional budgeting – a clear endorsement for a successful programme of management change.

The ten principles and practices

From our research we are able to discern some common threads [see end of the article for the ten principles and practices]. This is not to say that all firms are approaching the problem in the same way. Nor are they adopting the same solutions. It largely depends on the competitive pressures, their existing management philosophy, their experience of management change, and their state of readiness. If command and control and empowerment and trust were the left and right extremes along a continuum (see Figure 1), then senior executives are trying to move from left to right at a speed and with support tools and

ORGANISATIONAL IMPACTS OF BUSINESS STRATEGY

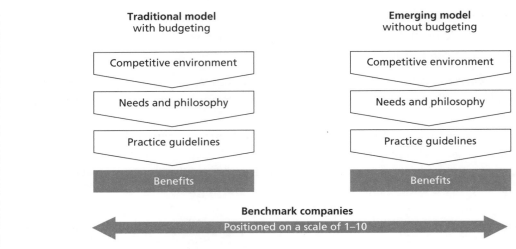

Figure 1 Where are you today?

processes that suit them. Some use the latest management techniques such as value- and activity-based management, the balanced scorecard, and process management to support the changes, while others rely more on the capabilities of their people supported by open information, rolling forecasts and regular strategic reviews. The destination is the same, however. They are all aiming to devolve more power and responsibility to front-line people yet develop an information system that enables senior managers to evaluate results and trends, and react quickly if needed.

New steering mechanisms

The new management model means, first and foremost, breaking away from the annual cycle of preparing, negotiating and then relying on budgets to drive managerial perform-ance. Such a slow, rigid and often highly 'political' process is a major handicap in today's fast changing competitive environment. Managers are given responsibility for achieving targets, are accountable for results, and can take decisions concerning income, expenditure and business improvements that help them to achieve their targets. Budgets, with their tendency to focus on expense lines and other micro targets that were set months earlier, are no longer a part of this picture. The objective within the budgeting process was to keep on track, whereas the objective in the new model is to support a continuous cycle of strategic reviews (see Figure 2). Thus there is typically a series of interlocking (short, medium and long-term) management review cycles that reflect the pace of change in a particular busi-ness or market sector. These reviews will examine targets, strategies, action plans, forecasts and management reports. Comparisons might also be made against competitors and past-year performance. These reviews will be broad-brush in scope and concentrate on the key drivers of business performance. The new emphasis is on looking ahead and being in a position to take advantage of new opportunities and counter potential threats by using an advanced information system to make decisions early. Speed of action and good decisions are the result.

Organisational levels

No management model is appropriate to every business or in some cases different parts of the same business. Size, complexity and competitive pressures all determine the needs of

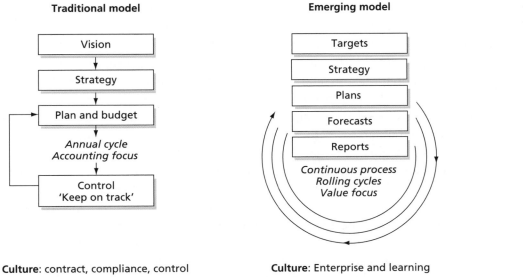

Figure 2   New steering mechanisms

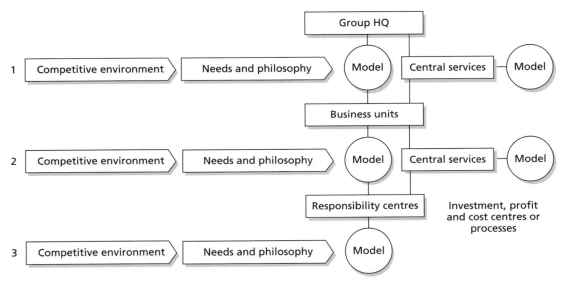

Figure 3   Models are appropriate to business needs and organisational level

a firm's management philosophy and model (see Figure 3). However, diversity and flexibility should be seen as strengths rather than weaknesses. The key objective in designing a successful architecture is to create the freedom to act and strategic capability. Both are essential but one is stillborn without the other.

In other words, managers should be able to evaluate strategic alternatives and take tactical decisions that are appropriate to their own part of the business yet ensure that these are consistent with group policy and direction. Budgets clog up these vital arteries and encourage rigid planning and incremental thinking. By removing the budgeting system, a firm has a much better chance of building strategic capabilities and flexible organisations.

How do the new steering mechanisms work across organisational levels? Let's consider how three key people would manage in this new model: the group chief executive, the manager of a business unit and the manager of a cost or support services centre.

The group CEO. In the new model the annual budgeting cycle with its months of planning, negotiation and eternal meetings has now been consigned to the corporate dustbin. Instead the group CEO sets the strategic vision and direction, decides which markets and businesses the group wishes to be in and sets targets that reflect a competitive return to shareholders over the medium to long-term. If the group wants to be 'world class' the CEO will set a target that doubles shareholder value every 3–4 years; if it is less ambitious then such a target will be lower. Whatever the outcome, such targets will drive the strategy and planning processes of the operating businesses. These will comprise a combination of income growth, process improvements and profit/cashflow/return-on-capital targets for the next cycle. A group targeting shareholder value is increasingly likely to focus on 'economic profit' (profit after tax less the cost of both debt and equity capital). Each management review cycle will review these plans and, if necessary, targets will be reset. Major investments and resource requirements will be discussed, evaluated and approved with due care being taken to co-ordinate plans across processes and business units. On a monthly basis reports are received from business units that show progress towards target and actions that have been taken to change course should this have been necessary. Thus the group CEO is freed from the mire of the budgeting swamp and now has time to focus on the big issues and challenge senior managers to think radically and to set ambitious targets.

What about controls? By eliminating the budgeting system managers are far from being deprived of vital control information. With a fast open accounting system, supported by a range of key performance indicators, rolling forecasts, and project and activity-based information (if appropriate), managers benefit from a much richer seam of information that improves decision-making. But what managers really need is not so much good control systems as effective controls. There is a world of difference. Control systems mean compliance with rules and regulations. Effective controls mean knowing what's going on and only interfering when absolutely necessary. Giving frontline managers the freedom and support to act effectively, receiving fast information that is not filtered and 'treated' by middle management, and then managing by exception, offers a far more effective system of controls over business operations. By monitoring the key business value drivers, and especially the leading indicators that tell us something about future performance, we are in a much stronger position to take action before potential problems translate into negative numbers.

The business unit manager. The business unit manager is given the responsibility and accountability for achieving the agreed targets. Planning becomes a continuous process in which strategic alternatives are evaluated and those that provide the greatest long-term value are chosen. Much thought will have gone into selecting the key value drivers that will determine competitive success and the measurement system will track these indicators on a regular basis. Taken together, these represent the firm's early warning system that the financial numbers are likely to move up or down.

Rolling forecasts provide the primary information framework for decision-making. The strength of such forecasts will benefit from a variety of (financial and non-financial) performance indicators. Instead of the monthly board meeting asking questions of financial performance against budget, new questions will be asked about which parts of the business (including product lines, customer segments, individual customers, and processes) are creating value and which aren't. Strategic questions will be considered in the light of competitive circumstances. Should we outsource underperforming processes? Should we enter or exit certain market segments? Should we increase customer satisfaction? Should we raise or lower prices? The outcome of these and many other alternative decisions will be tested within the forecasting model, and decisions taken that maximise business value. There will also be a sharp eye on competitive performance using either an internal or an external league table of benchmark businesses (or a combination of both).

In the emerging model business unit managers are trusted to make good strategic decisions and 'get on with the job'. They are judged not on line-by-line cost management but on overall performance. However, the unambitious manager need not apply. With few supervisors to help explain poor performance it is a much more demanding role.

The cost centre or support services manager. Managing cost centres is no different from managing any other business unit, with the exception that customers are internal rather than external. Thus the cycles of targets, strategies, plans and decisions equally apply but perhaps at a different pace. Much rests on the firm's ability to simulate market realities. Either functional support people such as accountants, lawyers, human resource and marketing specialists are managed directly within customer-focused process teams or they subject themselves or their functional entities indirectly to market forces. This often involves an 'internal market' in which support services negotiate periodic service contracts with operating units and charge their services accordingly with prices benchmarked against external competitors. Customers then exert downward pressure on prices. Elements of support that are 'core' to the business, such as a 'strategic' IT network, 'pure' research, and elements of tax and accounting, are managed in a similar way with 'head office' being the internal customer.

The management review cycles will focus on trends and moving averages. Provided these are within the parameters set in the medium-term plan then no further action is needed. But if this is not the case then either group or business unit managers will trigger an investigation. This might result in a 'step change' in costs or even in a decision to outsource the service. Activity-based approaches to managing costs can also be useful, particularly where indirect services are a significant cost and workloads vary. Few support services really know which of their activities add value, but with internal customers now ready to answer the question, sustainable cost reductions through eliminating unnecessary costs become possible.

Building the new model

The rationale for abandoning budgets is that they act as barriers to managing effectively when fast response, innovative strategies, good service, high quality, and other similar competitive factors determine success or failure. But implementing new management processes to replace the budgeting system is not the complete answer. They need to be reinforced by changes in management structure and style together with attention to recognition and reward systems (see Figure 4).

Budgets are the glue that holds the hierarchy together. Thus managing without budgets means to a greater or lesser degree dismantling the hierarchy and devolving authority and responsibility to the front line. The crucial issues are decentralisation and rewards.

- *Decentralisation.* The principal feature of the new management model is that it is highly decentralised. Devolution includes not just authority to spend but also strategic thinking, target-setting, and responsibility and accountability for performance. These are the

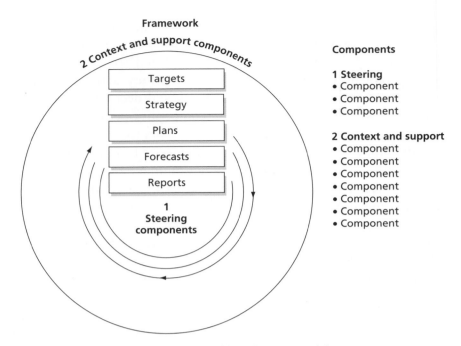

Figure 4 Building the new model

crucial issues that determine the success or failure of most management change programmes and managing without budgets is no exception. As we noted earlier, they are also key to attracting and keeping the best managers. 'Running your own business' best sums up the new approach, but creating 'businessmen' from line managers is not easy – they need lots of support, including education, training, IT networks, and continuous coaching. Indeed looser, leaner, more flexible organisations are harder to manage. For a start there are fewer middle managers to deal with problems.

Devolution of authority is hard for some senior managers to take so responsibilities need to be made clear. If it works well then managers will take quicker decisions thus improving customer response, adopt more ambitious targets, accept ownership of targets, and over time will become more capable business people.

- *Reward systems.* There has been a lot of debate over the years concerning the role of financial incentives in achieving desirable targets. Does a financial incentive make a salesperson try harder or become more effective? And can you relate extra revenue or profit to a marginal activity or piece of work? These are difficult questions to which there is no clear answer. Many successful firms are moving to a system of rewards that is linked to team/business unit/company wide performance. Rewards based on group profits and share performance are becoming increasingly common. But there is a distinct difference between providing attractive incentives that are designed to motivate people and providing some extra financial reward for team or group performance. As far as motivation is concerned, beating the competition or one's peers is a far more powerful weapon.

This is the force that drives managerial performance at Handelsbanken where all targets, rewards and performance measures are geared to beating the competition, both inside the bank (e.g. branch to branch comparisons) and outside the bank (e.g. bank to bank comparisons). And there is a long-term employee profit sharing scheme that focuses everyone's attention on always being at the top of the league.

Implementation and lessons learnt

Dismantling the budgeting process is a radical step in any company and not everyone will be comfortable with the changes. In some companies we noted that a few managers continued to use budgets for their own estimating purposes even though they were told that senior managers would take no notice of the numbers! Success depends on obtaining 'buy in' from influential people across the organisation, and particularly from senior management. The accounting community must also be persuaded and their future roles explained – a problem that a few companies felt they could have handled more effectively than they did.

In common with any other major change programme, the full fruits of abandoning budgeting take time to emerge. There are, however, many 'early wins' such as the savings in management time that happen within the first annual cycle.

But the longer-term benefits of more radical thinking, faster decision-making, and the acceptance of more responsibility at the front line depend on a number of factors such as senior managers 'walking the talk' of the new management model and thus building confidence at all levels. In all the cases we examined there was a gradual process of devolution. Typically decisions concerning capital investments, improvement projects, strategic initiatives, and effective process changes, were all taken in incremental steps, and all were accompanied by extensive support and education programmes that provided the tools needed to do the job effectively.

The formation of teams and networks occurred in a different way. In no case did we find a formal restructuring involving job losses. Instead we observed the emergence of informal teams and networks across the organisation. Bank branches at Handelsbanken became closely knit teams constantly reviewing strategy and progress. Branches of a similar size became teams where ideas were exchanged. Plant managers at Borealis formed teams, again sharing knowledge of markets, customers and suppliers.

Changing reward systems was also taken a step at a time with the reference levels moving up from small teams to large teams, divisions and business units and finally on to a company wide basis.

But perhaps the most significant change concerns the formulation and management of strategy. By encouraging managers to challenge orthodox thinking, helping them to evaluate alternative courses of action, and giving them the capability to act, senior executives are accepting a fundamental shift in organisational power and responsibility.

Aims of the research in 1999

In 1998, the BBRT has identified the key principles on which the emerging model for managing without budgets is based. This is the foundation for our work in 1999, when the scope and objectives of the research will be:

- *Framework.* To create an overall framework for the emerging model, with particular emphasis on the steering mechanisms required for managing without budgeting.
- *Components.* Targets, strategy, plans, forecasts and reports.
  - To understand in some detail how the new steering components should work at different levels in the organisation (e.g. group, business unit, responsibility centre and central services) and how they should be integrated.
  - To visit companies that are world leaders in the use of particular components to learn best practice and also how they handle conflicts with budgeting.

ORGANISATIONAL IMPACTS OF BUSINESS STRATEGY

- *Implementation.* A three-stage approach:
  - To develop an overall strategy for implementing the emerging model by stages, including (a) planning and selling-in, (b) introducing the steering components and removing budgeting, and (c) evolving the full emerging model over time.
  - To assist member companies with implementation, if requested, provided that they are willing to share their experience with the BBRT.
- *The model.* To enrich our understanding of the emerging model and develop the company diagnostic further from the learning we gain from cases in different regions and industries, and about particular components.

While the CAM-I research programme is only completing its first phase it is already apparent that companies can gain substantial benefits from managing without budgets. But this means not only abandoning budgets but also reinforcing these changes by adopting the most appropriate management structure and style and this is determined by business needs and organisational complexity. The next phase of our project will examine the crucial issues of implementing the model. We hope to provide a progress report on the 1999 BBRT later in the year.

Managing without budgets. The ten principles and practices

1. *Target setting* – Set targets to maximise long-term value and beat the competition, not the budget.
2. *Strategy* – Devolve strategy to the front line and make it a continuous and open process, not a top–down annual event.
3. *Growth and improvement* – Challenge people to think radically, not incrementally.
4. *Resource management* – Manage resources on the basis of value creation over the lifetime of an investment, not on the basis of short-term (budget) allocation.
5. *Co-ordination* – Achieve co-ordination by managing cause-and-effect relationships across business units and responsibility centres (such as processes), not by using departmental budgets.
6. *Cost management* – Challenge all costs on the basis of whether they add value, not whether they should be increased or decreased compared with last year.
7. *Forecasting* – Use rolling forecasts for managing strategy and making decisions, not merely for 'keeping on track'.
8. *Measurement and control* – Use a few key leading and lagging indicators to monitor performance, not a mass of detailed (historical) reports.
9. *Rewards* – Base rewards on company and unit-level competitive performance, not personal financial targets.
10. *Delegation* – Give managers the responsibility and freedom to act, don't micro-manage them.

Management accounting change in the UK

John Burns, Mahmoud Ezzamel and Robert Scapens, *Management Accounting,* **March 1999**

Since 1995, academics from across Europe have been investigating the issue of management accounting change. Researchers from 14 European universities have, in particular, investigated changes in management accounting systems, the adoption of 'modern' accounting techniques and the changing role of management accountants.

In April, the Euro-network of researchers will gather in a conference to discuss their findings. In addition, practitioners from organisations at the leading edge of management accounting change will attend part of the conference to share their personal experience of implementing change.

The conference promises to be a boost to facilitating further collaboration between researchers and practitioners of management accounting and its change.

The UK contribution to this European programme of research has been undertaken by the current authors, all based at the Manchester School of Accounting and Finance. Our study of management accounting change in the UK, funded by CIMA and the Economic and Social Research Council (R000236095), was conducted between 1995–98.

This article summarises key findings of the UK project. There is discussion of the changing nature of management accounting practice in the UK and the changing role of management accountants. Also, there is discussion of a framework which provides useful insight to managers considering, or in the throes of, implementing management accounting change. Finally we describe some implications of our research findings.

Background to the study

The UK research project was initially motivated by claims that management accounting had not changed for more than 60 years, despite substantial changes in production and information technologies and the organisational environment (see Johnson and Kaplan, 1987).

Various surveys of management accounting practice suggested that traditional management accounting systems and techniques continued to be used and that 'modern' techniques, such as activity-based costing (ABC) and strategic management accounting, were not being used as widely as might have been expected.

This led to the basic research question: why have accounting practices and accounting systems in particular been slow to change despite the rapidly changing technological and organisational environment in recent years?

However, as our project began it became increasingly clear that considerable change has taken place. But it is primarily change in the way management accounting is used, rather than change in management accounting systems and techniques per se.

Furthermore, such changes are often part of wider changes in processes of management. This has implications both for the nature of management accounting and for the role of management accountants in business, both of which are now discussed further.

The changing nature of management accounting in the UK

In general terms, various factors, both internal and external to organisations, appear to have been important in motivating change. There are general economic factors, including the globalisation of markets and increasing competition, which have led to an increasing emphasis on the customer and markets.

There has also been significant technological change, both in information systems and methods of production, with the increasing use of enterprise resource planning systems, such as SAP and Baan, particularly in large companies.

In addition, there have been organisational changes following from an increasing emphasis on core competencies, downsizing, outsourcing and so on, as well as changes in management structure, including delayering and team-working.

It is in this broader context that management accounting change has been taking place. For example, advances in information technology, and especially database systems, have major implications for management accounting. Information is now widely dispersed around the organisation, and managers have direct, real-time access, rather than relying on accountants to provide it.

This has given rise to a 'decentering' of accounting knowledge, with managers (or their subordinates) performing tasks previously in the accountant's domain; such as preparing budgets, analyzing performance and calculating variances [see also Scapens *et al.*, 1996].

Such change has been reinforced by a focus on forecasts, rather than budgets [see also Hope and Fraser, 1999 – reproduced earlier in these Readings]. Whereas budgeting was traditionally an accounting task, 'rolling forecasts' and 'forecasts to the year end' have to be prepared by the managers themselves. This gives them greater ownership of the information and means they need to understand the accounting system. However, it does not necessarily imply that they are unduly concerned about performance purely in financial terms.

UK managers today are more 'commercially orientated'. This does not mean that profits are unimportant, but they are put into a broader context and attention is given to the underlying factors which generate profits in the longer term.

Such a commercial orientation usually emphasises the 'key performance indicators' which measure the fundamental characteristics of the business associated with long-term profitability. These key performance indicators are usually driven by strategic considerations, and may be expressed in non-financial terms (see Burns *et al.*, 1996, 1997).

This growing emphasis on non-financial measures implies a recognition that financial information gives only a partial picture – a snapshot which may not indicate longer-term profitability.

There are two possible ways forward. Additional elements could be included in the management accounts to give a fuller picture – for example using ABC and other new techniques.

Alternatively, the partial nature of financial information can be accepted, and the management accounts kept relatively simple, but interpreted in the broader context.

It is this alternative approach which was observed in our research. As such, there is change in the form of management accounting, but not significant change in the techniques being used.

The changing role of a management accountant

The question of changing roles of management accountants has been publicised considerably during the last few years (e.g. see Matthews, 1998).

Based on our observations, a key role for management accountants today is to place financial numbers into a broader context and relate them to key non-financial measures. The management accountant integrates the different perceptions of the business indicated by the financial and non-financial measures, and integrates managers' understandings of their operating performance, the financial results and the strategic directions of the business.

This raises important questions for the education and training of management accountants. Not only do management accountants need to be experts in financial matters, but they also require a broad-based understanding of their businesses and an ability to work closely with other members of the management team.

Thus it is important to develop not only management accountants' financial knowledge, but also their broader personal skills and commercial capabilities. In some businesses such accountants are changing their job titles, becoming 'business analysts' instead of 'corporate controllers'.

In one case study, a multinational pharmaceuticals organisation, we observed considerable change in the role of management accountants. Despite a significant reduction in the size of the finance function during the early 1990s, the number of management accountants actually grew in size and now spend much of their time working alongside and advising the process managers.

Such accountants require a broad understanding of the business and an ability to interpret financial information in a strategic context. Such people were described within this organisation as 'hybrid accountants', combining financial knowledge with commercial awareness.

Significantly, despite the change in the management accountants' role in this organisation, the management accounting systems have remained largely unchanged and were described by one senior accountant as 'antiquated'.

A framework for making sense of change

The broad view of the changing nature of management accounting and the role of management accountants presented thus far is insufficient to understand the processes of change in individual companies. It provides the context for such change, but does not explain why change is easier in some organisations than in others.

Our research sought to understand organisation-specific processes of change through longitudinal case studies. As such, our analysis was informed by a theoretical framework which helped us 'make sense of' our observations (for further detail of this framework, see Burns and Scapens, 1999).

Development of the framework began by exploring the way in which 'order' is achieved in complex organisations, through rules, routines and 'common ways of thinking and doing'. Common ways of thinking and doing are the taken-for-granted, unquestioned assumptions which are shared by groups of individuals and are the basis for their understanding of their own actions and the actions of others. As such they give meaning to everyday activity in an organisation. In the academic literature, such taken-for-granted assumptions are referred to as institutions.

Accounting practices are a routine feature of many businesses and as such can become taken-for granted (i.e. institutionalised). The notions of rules, routines and institutions in the context of accounting can be illustrated through the example of budgeting.

In most organisations there will be rules concerning the production of budgets. These may be specified in a manual, or simply passed from person to person. As rules become implemented, routines will emerge through the remembering and repeating of past behaviour.

Although there will be a close association between rules and routines, routines will evolve as they are used. And so rules and routines are not necessarily identical.

Although budgets may be used in a routine manner, there is an important distinction between routines and institutions. Routines continue through the repeating of past actions, whereas institutions become separate from their historical context. Budgeting becomes an institution when budgets are simply 'the way things are done' – in other words, the use of budgets is taken for granted.

An assumption that budgets are used would be incapable of challenge, as it is a fundamental (and embedded) characteristic of the organisation. At least, it will not be challenged by the members of the group who share this assumption. This is what Hope and Fraser (1999) imply when they discuss budgeting as culturally embedded 'barriers to change'.

Such assumptions may not be shared by all members of an organisation. Furthermore, it is not being argued that budgeting is necessarily institutionalised. The above illustrates what it would mean if budgeting is an institution. In all organisations there will be institutions, but the extent to which they comprise accounting rules and routines has to be determined in each individual case.

Institutions will influence accounting change over time as they underpin the rules and routines which, in turn, are enacted day by day. Although institutions may create inertia in the change process, they will also shape the nature of the change. Thus, it is necessary to understand institutions, particularly institutional differences, when managing processes of change.

One of our case studies (see below) illustrates how accounting change which challenges the existing routines and institutions within an organisation is likely to be a source of conflict and resistance, whereas change which conforms to existing taken-for-granted assumptions within a particular organisational setting is less likely to be resisted.

Case study CHEM

This case concerns 'CHEM', a small chemicals manufacturer. In the years since it was established (1977) its production has become locked into a small number of long-term contracts for multinational customers, which they call 'captive products'. Although very profitable, these contracts carry substantial risk – they involve specialised plant and may not be renewed by the customer. In the late 1980s two major contracts terminated without renewal. This created a severe cashflow crisis. As a result, the board agreed a strategy of moving to a 50:50 split between captive products and products aimed at a wider market – 'multi-client products'. Importantly, the company's product development department (PDD) had the task of developing such multi-client products.

Within CHEM there were shared assumptions about the nature of the business and of the importance of efficiencies, yields and contribution. Shift leaders – and many operators – knew the contributions (sales less materials costs) of individual products, and there was a widespread commercial awareness and a 'results orientation'. The results orientation was grounded in shared assumptions that products had to earn contributions, and was underpinned by various routines (e.g. regular reports and daily conversations about contributions). The crisis of the 1980s reinforced the focus on contributions and 'results'.

However, by 1993 it was becoming clear to the managing director (MD) that such assumptions and a results orientation had not penetrated PDD. PDD was internally focused on the processes of chemical research, which were characterised as very slow and painstaking. PDD's taken-for-granted assumptions concerned chemistry rather than what such chemistry might contribute towards business earnings. The MD feared that this absence of a results orientation would mean that new (multi-client) products would not be ready when existing contracts for captive products ended.

Consequently, a new system of accountability was introduced for PDD. This comprised time sheets for individual research projects and a prioritisation of new products to be brought to market by agreed dates. The MD worked closely with the chief chemist (CC), who headed PDD, to develop new reports and reporting procedures. To introduce the new system of accountability the MD used the power of his position to convince fellow board members and other senior staff that the change imposed on PDD was legitimate and 'desirable'. In fact, the CC accepted the legitimacy of the new form of accountability and claimed that he welcomed the introduction of a system which was consistent with procedures used elsewhere in the company.

However, the CC acted as a buffer between the concerns of the MD and the other staff of PDD. The new systems had little impact on the individual members of PDD and did not change their ways of thinking about chemical processes, nor instil a results-orientation. Rather, the new procedures become a focus of conflict between the CC and the marketing director (MkD). It was the MkD who was driving the search for new products and developing markets for them. The speed at which new products come to the market was a constant source of friction between the CC and the MkD – with Marketing blaming PDD and PDD blaming Marketing.

However, as the more senior and powerful person (being a shareholder as well as a director), it was the MkD who tended to prevail in these conflicts. This frustrated the CC and his department. The new accounting reports for PDD were eventually abandoned (in early 1996) as offering little benefit to either PDD or the rest of the company. There had actually been little change in the routines and institutions within PDD, and eventually much of the chemical research function was passed to a newly acquired subsidiary.

Furthermore, it can be difficult for existing taken-for-granted assumptions to be 'unlearned'. In such circumstances processes of organisational politics and power can be very important in shaping responses to programmes of change.

However, in order to understand the processes through which resistance emerges, and the way in which conflicts are resolved, it is essential to explore the institutionalised features of organisational activity and, in the case of management accounting change, to explore the extent to which existing accounting practices are part of the taken-for-granted assumptions within an organisation and the challenges which new accounting practices pose against the existing routines and institutions.

Implications

Returning to our original research question, it is clear that there has been significant management accounting change in the UK during the last decade. But it is in the way that management accounting is used, and not necessarily in the introduction of new systems or techniques. This explains why surveys of management accounting practices, investigating the use of specific techniques, have continued to conclude that there has been little change.

The framework described above indicates further reasons for the continued use of existing management accounting systems. It suggests that stability and change are not mutually exclusive – some form of stability may be necessary to cope with change. Thus, retaining existing management accounting systems may be desirable in circumstances of organisational and management change. They provide the means of making sense of organisational activities, even when those activities are themselves changing.

Furthermore, there is a recognition that management accounts cannot provide all the information needed for managing a business, and need to be supplemented with non-financial information. This explains why many companies retain their relatively simple (old) management accounting systems, which they interpret in the context of other (non-financial) information, rather than introducing new accounting techniques.

To understand processes of management accounting change in specific organisations requires in-depth knowledge of the organisation's rules, routines and institutions. Even then it may be impossible to predict the outcome of a particular change, as that will depend on the complex processes through which organisational conflicts are resolved.

But it may be possible to identify potential areas of conflict and possible sources of resistance. Such knowledge will help those involved in the process of change to cope with the uncertainties and difficulties of change. The days of 'quick fix solutions' are well and truly gone!

The CHEM case illustrates the usefulness of the above framework in understanding processes of change in specific organisations, and the importance of unravelling the taken-for-granted assumptions in an organisation.

This research also has implications for both management accounting practitioners and their professional organisations, principally CIMA. At the general level, the changing nature of contemporary management accounting has important implications for the education and training of management accountants.

Not only do management accountants need to be experts in financial matters, but they also need a broad-based understanding of their businesses and an ability to work closely with other members of the management team. Thus there is a need to develop their broader personal skills and commercial capabilities, as well as their financial knowledge.

References

Burns, J. and Scapens, R. (1999) 'Conceptualising Management Accounting Change: An Institutional Framework'. Working paper available from the authors.

Burns, J., Scapens, R. and Turley, S. (1996) Some Further Thoughts on the Changing Practice of Management Accounting. *Management Accounting*, October: 58–60.

Burns, J., Scapens, R. and Turley, S. (1997) The Crunch for Numbers. *Accountancy*, May: 112–113.

Hope, J. and Fraser, R. (1999) Beyond Budgeting: Building a New Management Model for the Information Age. *Management Accounting*, January: 16–21.

Johnson, H.T. and Kaplan, R.S. (1987) *Relevance Lost: The Rise and Fall of Management Accounting*. Boston, MA: Harvard Business School Press.

Matthews, S. (1998) The Changing Role of the Management Accountant: and its Implications for Qualification Development. *Management Accounting*, September, 68–69.

Scapens, R., Turley, S., Burns, J., Joseph, N., Lewis, L. and Southworth, S. (1996) *External Reporting and Management Decisions – A Study of their Interrelationship in UK Firms*. London: CIMA.

Revision Questions

 Question 1

Business process re-engineering (BPR) has been promoted as a major management technique, but is also criticised as little more than cost reduction.

Requirements
(a) Briefly explain business process re-engineering. **(6 marks)**
(b) Explain the contribution the management accountant should make to the planning and implementation of a business process re-engineering programme. **(9 marks)**
(c) Explain the main advantages and criticisms of business process re-engineering programmes. **(10 marks)**
(Total marks = 25)

 Question 2

In both the public and private sectors, very large organisations provide broadly similar services on a national basis through a large number of local supply centres (units).

Public-sector examples include schools, hospitals, libraries and a wide range of local authority services.

Private-sector examples include banks, hotel groups, supermarkets and other shops in common ownership.

The public sector has traditionally taken a bureaucratic approach to the management of these geographically separate units.

Recently there have been a number of changes, both in the UK and elsewhere, attempting to reduce central bureaucratic control of local units by devolving more power to local units.

Requirements
(a) Explain how the problem of managing the provision of local services in the public sector differs from that in the private sector. Include an explanation of how the various problems have led to differing control systems. **(13 marks)**
(b) Explain the case for devolving more power to local units in the public sector, and the control problems that can arise.
Note: This part of the question may be answered by describing briefly an example of a new system of local management in the public sector, the case for its introduction, and the problems that have arisen. You are not limited to UK examples, provided it

is clear what you are describing. Possible UK examples include local management in schools, the establishment of National Health Service trusts and general practitioner fund-holdersinthe National Health Service.

(12 marks)
(Total marks = 25)

? Question 3

(a) It has been said that management accounting has traditionally been concerned with providing information for decision-making and controlling costs. It has often been criticised for not providing sufficient relevant information to management because it tends to impose general techniques as solutions in situations which demand custom-designed (directly applicable) methods and specific information.

Requirement
Discuss the validity of this criticism of management accounting. **(13 marks)**

(b) To be relevant to the needs of the organisation, management accounting systems need to be designed to accommodate its specific requirements, taking account of the circumstances of its particular business environment. One such circumstance may be the change in traditional working patterns. For example, it can no longer be assumed that all employees will be located on the organisation's premises in carrying out their duties. Some are likely to provide their services from remote locations.

Requirements
Compare the approach to providing relevant management accounting information for strategic decision-making purposes in:

(i) a manufacturing organisation which employs staff on site, with
(ii) a service organisation which employs contractors.

The contractors mainly work from home to provide technical solutions for customers engaged in large-scale building projects. **(12 marks)**
(Total marks = 25)

? Question 4

Maxima plc: background information
Maxima plc is a multinational telecommunications company. Its head office is in London. It is organised as a divisionalised company with divisions in three areas – the European Union (EU), the Pacific Rim, and North America (this includes Canada and the USA).

Internal computer department
Maxima plc has an internal computer department (ICD) which owns various appliances. ICD defines an appliance as any personal computer, terminal, printer or fax. It currently has 60,000 appliances. ICD supplies the appliances to all users in Maxima plc. The users are not allowed to have appliances supplied by anyone other than ICD. ICD is also responsible for servicing the appliances.

The geographical distribution of the appliances is as follows: 60 per cent of the appliances are in the EU, 30 per cent in the Pacific Rim and 10 per cent in North America. Maxima plc spent £90 million on ICD in the year ended 30 April 1994.

Funds used by ICD to purchase its appliances are provided exclusively by Maxima plc. ICD's remit from the board of Maxima plc is to recover its costs. It does this by taking its annual operating and capital costs and dividing this by the number of appliances in use. This calculation produces an annual charge per appliance which is then invoiced to the user of each appliance.

ICD's operating costs are staff, occupation of premises, installation of appliances and depreciation (all appliances are depreciated on a straight-line basis over 5 years).

The analysis of cost in a year is typically:

	%	
Staff	45	Staff costs include the cost of travel and subsistence.
Premises	15	
Installation	9	As the appliances are very reliable, very little is spent on spares.
Depreciation	20	What is spent on spares is included under installation.
Finance costs	11	
Total	100	

ICD's finance costs consist of a charge made by Maxima plc at its opportunity cost of capital (currently 12.5 per cent) to reflect the cost of its investment in ICD. The finance cost levied by Maxima plc on ICD in the year ended 30 April 1994 amounted to £10m.

Corporate review

Maxima plc has recently conducted a corporate review. One finding was that Maxima plc has too complicated a structure. It wishes to achieve an improved organisation structure having fewer levels of management. As part of the corporate review, Maxima plc also carried out a SWOT analysis. One outcome of this was that ICD has been designated a strength, a weakness and an opportunity.

This was for the following reasons:

- *Strength.* ICD is regarded by Maxima plc as being a part of its 'portfolio of expertise'. This is because ICD uses the same sort of skills which Maxima plc sells to its customers. The fact that such skills are within Maxima plc is regarded as a strength. As ICD is an internal department it is felt that is more responsive to the needs of Maxima plc's users than an external provider of services would be.
- *Weakness.* A major weakness is that it is difficult for the board of Maxima plc to assess the performance of ICD because of the charging system used by ICD. As ICD is a part of Maxima plc, it has been criticised for being insular, particularly as the charging system does not expose ICD to competition. A further weakness is that ICD requires significant investment from Maxima plc which starves other projects.
- *Opportunity.* One opportunity was identified in the course of the corporate review. This was that ICD would be sold to a third party who would contract to provide the services which were ICD's responsibility. Maxima plc would receive a capital injection from the sale. Two companies have indicated an interest in buying ICD. Preliminary indications are that each could supply and service each terminal for around £1,000 a year.

The board of Maxima plc has a policy of not being willing to sanction management buyouts as it believes that the inevitable conflicts of interest make it very difficult to ascertain what is the best outcome for the shareholders.

Conditions of sale of ICD

If ICD is sold, it would be under the following conditions:

- The buyer must acquire all of ICD's appliances, at a price to be agreed.
- The agreement would give the buyer exclusive rights to supply and service appliances to Maxima plc for the next 5 years. Subject to satisfactory performance over the first five years, the buyer would have the right to renew the agreement at a price to be negotiated at that time.
- The buyer would be required to respect the commercial confidentiality of Maxima plc.
- The buyer's performance in carrying out the agreement would be subject to regular 'benchmarking', with financial penalties for poor performance.
- The buyer would not be able to assign any of the rights under this agreement to a third party without the consent of Maxima plc.

Requirements

(a) Comment on the value and purpose of the SWOT analysis in the process of corporate review. **(6 marks)**

(b) Explain what other charging systems ICD could adopt for supplying Maxima plc. Discuss how your proposals would affect the remit under which ICD currently operates. **(12 marks)**

(c) Discuss the financial and strategic case for selling ICD. **(11 marks)**

(d) Discuss the considerations which a buyer is likely to take into account when constructing its bid price. **(13 marks)**

(e) Suggest, and briefly justify, alternative strategies which Maxima plc could implement in ICD in order to increase its competitiveness, and to identify more clearly its performance. **(8 marks)**

(Total marks = 50)

Solutions to Revision Questions

✔️ Solution 1

(a) *Explanation.* The essence of business process re-engineering (BPR) is encouraging employees to ask fundamental questions about the way outcomes are achieved in an organisation.

Although the term may have implications for cost-cutting and staff reductions, it is far more than this, often involving changes in organisation structures and job and process designs. BPR recognises that adding value in an organisation is not just about doing the same things at a lower cost. It is all about having a fresh approach as to how business is undertaken. The focus is more on business processes (how it is done), rather than on the activity content (what is done). BPR is then the radical redesign of an organisation's processes in order to achieve significant improvements in current and future performances. It should not be viewed as a one-off 'quick fix' for current poor performance, but rather as a continuous process of performance review.

(b) *Contribution to planning.* BPR programmes involve alternative ways of managing business processes and are likely to require different kinds of information, or information being provided in different ways.

Because BPR is fundamentally a customer-focused concept, managers' information requirements will probably change. Emphasis will move towards establishing best practices, that is benchmarking, in order to be competitive and the management accountant can help ensure that managers receive the appropriate control information. It is also possible that existing costing systems may have to be reviewed as an aid to decision-making, possibly reviewing the benefits of an activity-based costing (ABC) approach to overhead costs.

The management accountant will have overall responsibility for the organisation's information systems, probably being driven by the need to support the financial accounting records. The management accountant is in the ideal position to assist operational managers in reviewing their core activities and processes, and then determining the decision support systems required.

Contribution to implementation. The implementation of a BPR programme is likely to require a change in emphasis from the finance function. Although transaction processing will always be important (e.g. customer ordering, purchasing and payroll), far greater emphasis is likely to be needed in providing managers with relevant information for decision-making and control.

Operating managers may, in the past, have viewed the accounting system in a rather passive way, for example in routine budgetary control reports. However, with a renewed emphasis on customer needs and profitability, it is likely that a far broader range of information will be needed if BPR is to be successfully implemented.

Managers could reasonably expect that a significant amount of this information will be organised by the management accountant. Emphasis should be on providing information in a user-friendly way. One possibility would be providing managers with access to a database, linked to the financial accounting system, with training provided in an attempt to streamline the paper flows through the organisation. As no organisation can afford to remain static, the management accountant can assist managers by regularly reviewing their needs and the reporting systems in use.

(c) *Advantages of BPR.* There are a number of advantages claimed for BPR including:
- it is useful in providing an organisation with cost advantages over competitors, and with improved customer service;
- because significant, rather than incremental, changes in working practices are sought, an approach is encouraged which is more strategic than operational;
- it helps to reduce organisational complexity by focusing on core processes and driving out unnecessary or uneconomic activities;
- it offers an alternative perspective on formulating strategy based upon operating processes, rather than on products and markets (e.g. are we in the tram business or the transport business?); and
- it helps to link together the functional areas of an organisation by focusing on processes that cut across the value chain from inputs of materials and services to creating customer satisfaction.

Criticisms of BPR

It is often seen as being simply a review of existing tasks (can they be done better?), rather than concentrating on reducing the number of tasks necessary for effectiveness. In other words, there is a danger of squeezing cost savings out of established processes, rather than asking broader strategic questions.

It may be viewed by senior management as being a 'quick fix' to organisational problems. For example, one-off cost-saving activities, typically by sacking employees, may be sought, rather than making structural changes. This lowers morale and is likely to leave the organisation too lean to take advantage of any upturn in business. The problem is that BPR may be perceived by employees as merely a cost-cutting exercise by senior management, rather than an attempt to improve the longer-term competitive position and job prospects.

BPR will often mean a delegation of decision-making further down the organisation in an attempt to make quicker and better decisions at the customer interface, and it is not easy to change employee attitudes and behaviour. Another potential problem is that, after the initial enthusiasm, senior management may lose their commitment to programmes that have been implemented.

✓ Solution 2

(a) When the public sector has had to provide local services, its prime concern has been to match provision with need. This need is present as a demand, but is not usually associated with a market price and therefore a full-blown market, perhaps because the demand is for a public good, or market failure means that any price would not be adequate to generate adequate demand.

In the absence of a market, the prime indication of demand in the public sector has either been through some form of indicator: population served, percentage of population requiring services, presence of percentage of special needs, extent of known need; or has been via some form of political pressure; or both. These indicators have been used to assist in the distribution of resources via a bureaucratic mechanism. Control has been centralised, and requests for additional resources have been assessed via political systems operating at a district, regional or national level.

The allocation system that has evolved has been very largely based on top-down allocation of a central resource, though there has always been some local contribution to the budgeting process in terms of bids. Various systems are used to assist with allocations, including formulae of one sort or another, bidding processes (e.g. for capital expenditure), and pure politics. The control system has been almost entirely based on controlling inputs, though data are kept on the indicators used in the allocation process. The problems of this system are the lack of cost control at local levels, the slow response of the system to felt needs and the general control of the systems by experts who are only distantly accountable to the users of the services.

This approach contrasts markedly with the private sector, which has in the main used a profit-centre approach. It is usually possible to establish market demand and a market price for goods provided by the private sector, and organisations are established and controlled on the basis of demand for them in a particular area. Where such market prices are not available (e.g. where a firm has different manufacturing and marketing divisions and goods and services are passed between divisions), a market or quasi-market transfer price is often established. The use of market prices and clearly visible demand means that control can be on the basis of a single profit measure and thus cost control and user responsiveness is better than in the public sector.

(b) An example of devolving power to local units in the public sector is the introduction of internal markets in the UK National Health Service (NHS).

Until recently, the NHS has operated as a centrally-planned system with resources allocated centrally to various levels in the system. The introduction of internal markets had aimed to produce local accountability, with some general practitioners (GPs) holding budgets with which they can purchase health care for their patients at hospitals of their choice. In turn, hospitals have had to price out their services and offer them to GPs. GPs have been able to select health care for patients based on price and on length of waiting lists. The reason this has been done is to provide a market price where one would not otherwise exist, and thus introduce the benefits of private sector control to the public sector. This system is still not fully operational and so it is difficult to judge the overall effects of a fully working system. There are some general effects on control which are appearing, and generally support the case for this devolution of power via the market mechanism:

- there is now a greater awareness of cost in hospitals and by GPs;
- there is a general striving to calculate costs more accurately than was previously the case, especially as massive differences in calculated cost existed between hospitals for similar procedures;
- there has been a large rise in the number of managers needed to control the system, though there has been debate about whether this rise is justified or cost effective;

- there is some competition developing between health service hospitals and to some extent with private-sector hospitals;
- there seems to be a gradual change in the philosophy of management.

The long-term effects of this system are unclear. There are already problems such as the closing of wards when money to perform operations runs out. Some of the problems could be due to only partial implementation of the system. The government has, however, not fully abandoned control to the internal market and continues to collect and publish other statistics (e.g. length of waiting lists). These and other funding controls are additional control mechanisms on the NHS, which retains multiple performance measurement control and may weaken the impact of the internal market mechanism. Alternatively, it could be that the internal market mechanism may not be able to cope with the multiple objectives of the health service (e.g. breadth of care, prevention, accident and emergency provision).

 # Solution 3

- The traditional approach to management accounting is examined within this question. The candidate is required to assess the relevance of management accounting information and the validity of the criticism it has received in recent years. A short scenario is also presented and the candidate is asked to undertake a comparison of the provision of management accounting information in two different situations.
- This question is concerned with the syllabus section *Position Appraisal and Analysis*.

(a) Johnson and Kaplan strongly criticised traditional management accounting in *Relevance Lost*, first published in 1987. Their criticism was that management accounting tended to focus on techniques which are out of date and not meaningful as an aid to management in the late twentieth century. They perceived that traditional methods of overhead recovery were insensitive to modern processes and consequently developed the concept of activity-based costing.

Management accounting has also been criticised for being little more than a ragbag of unconnected techniques which tend to be backward-looking and do not focus on the strategic development of an organisation. The techniques employed are often not relevant to the particular organisation as they apply assumptions which are too simplistic and cannot be related to the specific situation. Examples of this include the simplified and largely unreal assumptions underlying cost, volume and profit analysis and the concentration of effort in pursuing standard costing techniques which have little relevance to most organisations, such as the calculation of fixed overhead volume capacity and efficiency variances. The techniques applied in management accounting also have been criticised for being insufficiently flexible to cater for the strategic requirements of management as they are too focused on cost control which, by its nature, is backward-looking.

In recent years there has been a move towards management accounting providing more relevant information for strategic decision-making. Examples of this have been the developments of activity-based management, customer account profitability and direct product profitability. In terms of control, the development of zero-based budgeting has also been established.

Strategic management accounting is focused on the provision of information to assist the organisation in its strategic development, and places emphasis on non-financial, as well as financial, information. This involves a strategic view being taken of management accounting information and integrating it with information supplied by other functions of the organisation. The provision of a comprehensive management information system and the need to focus on improving the quality of information provided in order to compete more successfully have been driving forces behind this development.

The dynamic business environment has forced changes in the provision of management information. Such developments as world class manufacturing, business process re-engineering, outsourcing, home working and the constant requirement to improve quality and reduce overheads, have affected the provision of management accounting information. There is a much greater need now to provide information on how product and service delivery affects overall market share and to predict the response of competitors in order to compete more effectively.

Moreover, it has become much more important that the management accounting function develops generic techniques and adapts them to its organisation's unique environment by applying contingency theory. Thus the generic techniques themselves may appear in different forms. For example, strategic variance analysis may be employed to analyse the variance from a strategic programme target, as well as being applied within the more limited confines of an operational programme. The strategic variance may be broken down into planning and operational components and these are likely to be unique to the specific organisation. This, in turn, should guide decision-making in determining future corrective action if the variance which is computed is adverse.

(b) There are some consistencies in the provision of management accounting information to both types of organisation. Management of both are interested in overall profitability, contribution per product or service, cost, the impact of overheads (which should be less in the service contractor organisation), market share, quality of output and added value. The monitoring and reporting of quality output may be similar in both organisations in certain respects, for example regarding whether deadlines have been met. Some techniques may be consistently applied in both organisations, such as benchmarking the performance of one operative with another.

The nature of both organisations is very different, with the first concentrating its activities on the one site and the second being fragmented in its service provision. There is no major change in the provision of information for the two organisations. The changes will manifest themselves in the way the information is obtained and delivered. Each organisation will need to gather costs, and so cost centres may be formally established in the site-based company. The fragmented company may regard each operative as a cost centre or allocate its costs to each job that the operative works on. This implies the need for close monitoring of their activities, which is easily accomplished through computer-logging procedures.

The staff in the fragmented organisation are contracted to it, rather than being employees in the traditional sense. They are engaged in professionally orientated activities in solving problems. Performance appraisal of employees may be more easily measured in the organisation which is concentrated on one site. The contracted operatives in the fragmented organisation are likely to encounter unique problems and, therefore, performance appraisal systems, including measures of profitability, may need to recognise the diverse constraints which they face. More emphasis may need to be placed on following up inconsistencies in performance between the contracted operatives in the fragmented organisation. The management accounting system will provide only raw information. The system will not necessarily be able to differentiate between varying operating conditions experienced by different contracting operatives. This raw information should be analysed by technical experts before conclusions are reached on it. The opportunity for liaison between the technical experts and the contracted operative may not easily be facilitated, particularly if they are located in different countries. Control will be more difficult to maintain in the fragmented organisation but standardised reports on activities may still be established. These must take account of peculiar environmental circumstances affecting the contracted operative, hence more use may be made of planning and operational variance analysis. This should provide more information for future strategic development through improved forecasting and control as more experience is gained. There will be a need for forward projection of expected outcomes and both organisations should carefully analyse this. It is not relevant that, in the fragmented organisation, the contracted operatives are off site. This should not affect the ability of the organisation to project future profitability on customer contracts.

Overall market share may be more predictable in the site-based, rather than the fragmented, organisation. This is because of the nature of the business rather than the managerial arrangements relating to the location of operatives and contractors. Nevertheless this presents more of a challenge to the management accounting function in the fragmented organisation in establishing the extent of the overall market. Heavier reliance may need to be placed on databases and external agencies to provide market share information.

The management accounting systems employed in both organisations need to be specifically related to each operating situation. The working relationships will be different in each, and therefore the control mechanisms employed to monitor output will vary in each organisation. It is clear that an open system needs to be established in each organisation in order to provide information for strategic management purposes. The provision of feedback within such a system must be capable of reflecting changing environmental circumstances. This may be more difficult to achieve in the second type of organisation.

✓ Solution 4

- This scenario involves several topics from throughout the syllabus including SWOT, strategic selection and outsourcing. Running through the question is the issue of where the firm's core competences lie and the impact on its ability to sustain these in the event of the outsourcing going ahead.

(a) A major benefit of a corporate review is that it forces the management to consider the strategic position of the organisation. If managers are working under pressure, it is possible for the corporate review to be neglected. This situation can be avoided by the top management requiring regular corporate reviews which will consider the internal and external situation of the organisation. The SWOT analysis is an important part of the corporate review process. In particular, the SWOT analysis forces the management to consider the strengths, weaknesses, opportunities and threats facing the organisation.

It is likely that many of the circumstances will change over a period of time and this means that a SWOT analysis should be carried out regularly. The SWOT analysis will provide the managers with a chance to discuss the different aspects of the business. The process will act as a forum in which crucial issues can be discussed. This is likely to lead to a better understanding of the environment in which the company operates and should increase the possibility of the ultimate success of the organisation. Most organisations operate in environments which change constantly. It is, therefore, important that the managers review the strategic position continually and by addressing the different aspects of the SWOT analysis, the managers will cover many of the issues facing Maxima plc.

(b) At the present time, an annual charge is made for each appliance. The charge is determined by dividing the total costs of the operation by the number of appliances. This means that the same amount is charged for each appliance in spite of differences in cost. It seems inappropriate to charge the same amount for different appliances as they are likely to have different capital costs, require different levels of service and some machines are likely to cost significantly more to service and repair. In addition, the cost of travelling to the different factories within a country may differ.

Other charging systems which could be used by ICD are:

- a lump sum based on the total cost of the operation could be charged to Maxima plc;
- a different cost could be calculated for each type of appliance based on the capital cost, the cost of installation, the expected life of the appliance, and maintenance costs;
- the managers of Maxima plc could be given the right to negotiate the rental charge with ICD;
- the market price of renting similar appliances could be charged to Maxima plc, and managers could purchase from outside organisations if better conditions can be negotiated.

The lump sum is similar to the current arrangement. However, this arrangement would result in ICD being regarded as a department of Maxima plc. This approach will not encourage the management of ICD to strive to reduce the operational cost of the division. As Maxima plc's managers are unable to use alternative suppliers, the charging of a total cost to Maxima plc for the services of ICD will tend to blur the inefficiencies that might occur within ICD or the excessive use of appliances by the managers of Maxima plc.

A separate charge for each type of appliance will focus more attention on the level of charges that are being levied on the 'captive users'. It will be possible to make comparisons of the prices and conditions charged with those charged by independent suppliers. This would mean that the efficiency of the service of ICD and the costs could be compared.

If the managers are expected to negotiate the prices, it can lead to an excessive amount of their time being taken up by the negotiation process. The manager's time might be better spent in managing the organisation and it is also possible that the negotiated prices might reflect the negotiating skills and relative power of individual managers. This might result in a price which is not equitable and which does not contribute to the establishment of a sound planning and control system for the firm. However, if the managers can hire appliances from outside suppliers, this could lead to the market prices being used in the negotiations. The use of market prices will also highlight the relative efficiency of ICD.

The most radical change would be to convert ICD into a profit or investment centre which charges market prices to Maxima plc. This would mean that the management of ICD would be expected to meet the needs of the users of the appliances and the profitability of ICD would provide an indication of the effectiveness and efficiency of the operation. Particularly, if the managers of Maxima plc were able to use alternative suppliers, it should act as a spur to ICD. Facing competition would ensure that the users within Maxima plc were treated as customers and dissatisfaction could be measured by the extent to which outside suppliers were used.

(c) ICD provides a service to Maxima plc, but it could be provided by an outside firm that purchases ICD as a company. Maxima plc uses 60,000 appliances and this means that £1,500 per annum is charged for supplying the servicing of each appliance. It is estimated that the purchaser will be able to supply these services at about £1,000 per annum. This will result in an annual saving of about £500 for each appliance, amounting to £30m per annum. The sale of ICD is, therefore, likely to result in an annual cost saving and there will also be a substantial inflow of cash to Maxima plc if ICD is sold.

It would be advantageous for the management of Maxima plc to assist in the choice of the company to purchase ICD. The two companies will continue to work together in the future and so the ability to choose the company is important. The new company will introduce new ideas and expertise to Maxima plc and this could be a benefit to them. However, Maxima plc must consider some disadvantages of the sale. It is likely that ICD will no longer be part of the 'portfolio of expertise' and the management of Maxima plc must be certain that the new company will provide an adequate service. The conditions of sale must be closely scrutinised to ensure that the cost, purchaser's rights and the regular 'benchmarking' of ICD's service is included in the agreement. However, it is inevitable that Maxima plc will lose some degree of control if ICD is sold to an outside firm. It is important that the negotiations ensure that the effect of this loss of control is minimised.

Other disadvantages that may arise include the possibility of redundancies if the purchaser combines some of the operations of ICD with other businesses. It is also possible that there will be problems in the transitional period.

(d) The expected 'stream of earnings' will be the crucial factor in valuing ICD. The purchaser will estimate the profit which is expected to be generated by supplying and servicing the machines to Maxima plc. Any other business which will be generated as a result of owning ICD must be included in the estimates of future earnings. It could be difficult to estimate the future cash flows, but the purchaser will have a degree of certainty from the 5-year contract with Maxima plc. In addition, the choice of the appropriate discount rate is another important factor. Maxima plc's cost of capital is 12.5 per cent, but it is not necessarily the cost of capital of the purchaser.

Although the value of the assets owned by ICD must be considered in establishing the value of ICD, it is really the current market value of the machines which would provide a minimum value in the negotiation of the purchase price. It is possible for the sum negotiated to be either higher or lower than the break-up value of the company, as the price will be based primarily on the returns expected by the purchaser.

The finance costs are 11 per cent and this amounts in £10m per annum. This means that the total annual cost of ICD are £90.9m. Currently, the costs of ICD are therefore:

	%	£m
Staff	45	41.0
Premises	15	13.5
Installation	9	8.2
Depreciation	20	18.2
Finance costs	11	10.0
	100	90.9

The expected charge to Maxima plc for the supply and servicing of the 60,000 appliances will be in the region of £60m. It will therefore be necessary for the purchasing company to generate additional profit from business with companies other than Maxima plc. Alternatively, the new company will have to reduce costs significantly if it is to generate sufficient profit to justify the purchase of ICD. It may be possible to combine the two firms and reduce total cost significantly. This would be particularly relevant if the acquiring firm has spare capacity at the present time. This is an important factor in determining the bid price of the company and it is possible that the acquiring firm will pay an amount which is lower than the book value of the assets.

On the basis of the current cost of £90m and the revenue from Maxima plc being £60m, there is an annual deficit of £30m. It is clear that the firm will have to consider this in deciding on the amount to pay for ICD. However, the buyer will be influenced by the availability of spare capacity and its overall objectives, especially in respect of the firm's marketing strategy.

It is possible that the firm that purchases ICD may have other objectives and this could affect the bid price. As an example, the acquisition may be seen as part of a marketing strategy to prevent competitors obtaining ICD's expertise and market share or the firm may wish to gain a hold over Maxima plc which might be a major strength in the future.

(e) There are a number of alternative strategies which could be implemented in ICD such as:

- The charging system could be changed. This is likely to lead to a charge which is linked to the appliance supplied and the service provided and it will be possible to compare the charge to the prices quoted by other suppliers.

- The purchase and servicing of the appliances could be separated. This would enable local suppliers to service the appliances. Maxima plc could benefit from the bulk purchasing of the appliances, but the servicing could be done by local firms and this may be cost effective.

- The managers could be allowed to use other suppliers. The possibility of using competitors would enable the users to be more aware of the market price and level of service that is available. It is intended to prompt ICD to provide a better service to Maxima plc.

- ICD could be changed into a profit or investment centre. It is possible that the change would motivate ICD's management to produce a service that is acceptable to the users at a competitive price. Profit will provide a performance measure to judge their efficiency.

- Outside 'benchmarks' could be used to monitor the performance of ICD against other organisations. This would provide the management with a measure to assess the performance of ICD. It would be possible to include factors other than profit and profitability in the assessment of ICD's performance.

8

Implementing and Controlling Plans

Implementing and Controlling Plans

8

Implementation and control of business strategies builds upon the material from your earlier studies and also the material that you will be covering in other strategic level papers. However, there are several key additions:

- A much greater emphasis on controlling business processes such as customer care and quality in addition to costs and resource utilisation.
- The possibility that the organisation must monitor its commitments to stakeholders beyond the shareholders leads to a concern with the performance measurement of non-profit-related processes.
- Control of a strategy is much more long term than operational control of a particular business. It often involves monitoring the processes that will lead to a desired outcome rather than the outcomes themselves.
- It is very important that you re-read the two articles at the end of Chapter 7 they are very relevant to this Chapter as well!

LEARNING OUTCOMES

By the end of this chapter you should be able to:

▸ evaluate and recommend appropriate control measures;

▸ prepare and evaluate multidimensional models of performance measurement;

▸ identify problems in performance measurement and recommend solutions.

8.1 Theories of control

8.1.1 Introduction

You will have looked at control theory elsewhere in your studies. The discussions in this chapter do presume your understanding of concepts from control theory.

This section will act as a refresher but is not intended as a substitute for revising the material relevant to those papers.

8.1.2 The link between decision-making and control

Control is often thought of in the terms suggested by Robin Roslender as being 'a process of ensuring that which was supposed to happen actually happens'. However, Berry et al. (1995) point out that in order for management control to be effective it must combine two elements:

1. *Regulating the process of formulating purpose*. This would involve the strategic decision-making process.
2. *Regulating the process of purpose achievement*. This covers implementation of the decided course of action.

In plain language, control involves both deciding what we want to do and also ensuring that we do it.

8.1.3 Performance measurement and control

Hopwood (1974) identifies three forms of control at work in an organisation:

1. *Administrative controls*. These involve the setting up of performance measurement systems and comparing the outputs of processes with targets set by management. Accounting controls are an example of this, alongside staff performance management systems and quality systems.

   One drawback of administrative controls is that they can be mechanistic. This means that they stem from a view of the organisation that sees it as a machine with staff being inputs or cogs. This can lead to demotivating and dehumanising control regimes and also makes the organisation very resistant to change.
2. *Social controls*. These are developed by social interaction and the sharing of common perspectives. In a hospital or school the major means of control is through the use of skilled staff that all share the same professional values. These are very powerful in ensuring that a doctor or nurse is caring for their patient. Modern management innovations such as quality circles and team-working utilise this form of control.
3. *Self-control*. These are where the individual modifies their own behaviour. Clearly the possession of advanced skills and knowledge will influence this, but it can also be harnessed with a suitable system of incentives. For example, giving a manager a target to reach, accompanied by promises of rewards if it is reached, will ensure that the manager uses their self-control to reach it.

Your syllabus takes the view that the management accountant's role in implementing and controlling plans is principally through performance measurement. However, Hopwood's comments should help us to remember two things:

(a) Management accounting systems are not the only control devices at work in the organisation. Performance measurement systems should try to fit within the other social and administrative control systems. Also sometimes the process may be controlled perfectly well by other means and therefore the accountant may be better employed elsewhere.
(b) Some modern management accounting control techniques are utilising the other forms of control. For example, the development of performance-related payment systems is a very good example of self-control systems, while reporting to teams and paying team-based bonuses is part of social control.

8.1.4   A simple example of control

In 1966 Pauline set up a business providing secretarial services to offices in the immediate locale of her small rented suite of city centre offices. She used £300 borrowed from her mother. On her retirement over 25 years later the business had grown into a successful medium-sized jobbing printing company with typesetting and artwork facilities in-house and had relocated to its own factory. Shrewd acquisitions of other firms, new capital equipment and the incorporation of several new technologies enabled the business to remain profitable despite office automation having destroyed the market for secretarial services. Pauline had continued the day-to-day management of the firm. This involved keeping an eye on cash flows and debtors, pricing and quoting for jobs, expediting jobs through the works and ensuring that the quality of the printed work met the expectations of the customers, all of whom she knew personally. Staff performance was monitored by Pauline's habit of walking around the works during the day and berating staff that did not seem to be working hard enough. At its sale the business regularly achieved a net return on its capital assets in excess of 35 per cent.

A year after its purchase by new management the firm reported the first losses in its history. Customers were ignored, staff made numerous errors on jobs and costs rose as quality fell and wastage rose. Borrowing heavily from the banks in a vain attempt to turn the business around eventually led to its compulsory liquidation. The company went into receivership with debts of around £500,000, 2 years after its sale by Pauline.

The main cause was a complete loss of control over the processes of the business once Pauline had retired. Pauline, among many other things, had been a very effective management control system.

8.1.5   A complex example of control

Johnson and Kaplan (1987) recount the story of three cousins who in 1903 bought the assets of the family explosives company, E.I. Du Pont de Nemours Powder Company and established the Du Pont Powder Company. The cousins financed the deal by redeeming shares in the old company with bonds providing a fixed rate of interest equal to the annual profits of the former firm. Further acquisitions followed, leading to the creation of several 'businesses within a business', with different departments handling different products or aspects of operations such as sales, distribution and manufacture. They established a centralised accounting system requiring accountants in each division to submit returns each month. Because it produced so many different products, and in view of the need to meet its interest liabilities, the cousins decided on return on investment (ROI) as the single performance measure. They had to make enough income to cover the interest on the assets they had issued debt to buy.

Du Pont developed the set of financial ratios, shown in Figure 8.1. The extreme right-hand boxes show the main *value drivers* of the business, the factors that generate the costs and utilise the capital of the business. The accountants at Du Pont developed operational control systems to monitor these. Perhaps most famously they developed a system of cost apportionment which calculated factory cost of sales by calculating standard labour times for each process and allocating labour costs and overheads to each product using this as a cost driver. This approach is still used and taught today as *standard costing*.

The next stage in Du Pont's development was to become *multidivisional*, as it opened factories across the United States and the rest of the world and diversified the firm's product range beyond explosives and into plastics, synthetic fibres and paints. Controlling

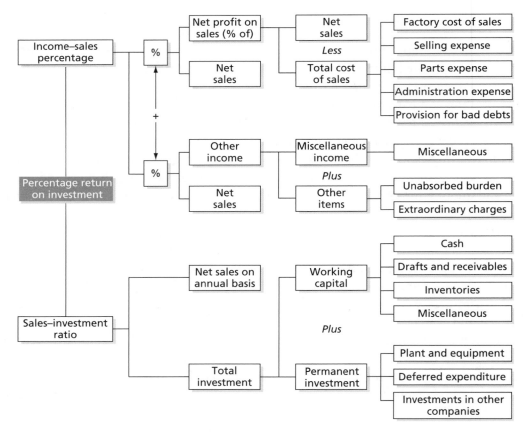

Figure 8.1 Du Pont's pyramid of financial ratios

a much larger and more diverse business overwhelmed the central administrative functions. To cope with this, greater autonomy was granted to the business divisions to run their businesses while the corporate centre looked after developing the business. However, the business divisions were still controlled through central offices monitoring of the crucial divisional performance measure, ROI. Each division set the financial ratios depicted in Figure 8.1 to ensure that it would reach the ROI monitored by the corporate centre of Du Pont.

8.1.6 Management by remote control

The contrasts between the performance systems in the simple example of Pauline's business and the more complex example of Du Pont are:

1. The larger the business the more that control by the corporate centre becomes mechanistic – that is, based on numerical measures of performance. This is because the face-to-face controls exerted by Pauline cannot be translated to a much larger and geographically dispersed business (unless we were to clone Pauline!).
2. In the larger organisation the controls are all tailored to an overriding corporate objective. In the case of Du Pont, this is the percentage ROI. This requires that the measures be congruent.
3. The corporate centre of the organisation seems to operate principally as a control box for the rest of the organisation. Provided that it can set the right targets, and monitor them, it will leave the business decisions to departmental and divisional managers.

The American management accounting academic Professor Robert Kaplan has termed this approach to corporate direction and governance 'management by remote control'.

8.1.7 Control in unitary and multidivisional organisations

(a) A unitary organisation (sometimes called a *U-form organisation*) is one with a single location and usually a single product range. Pauline's firm in the example above was an example of this.

(b) A multidivisional organisation (*M-form*) has several different operating units, possibly in different locations, and will therefore be exposed to diverse operating environments and may have different processes of production and different products. Du Pont became multidivisional once they moved away from producing solely explosives and into making paints, etc.

Figure 8.2 demonstrates the control systems at work in multidivisional organisations.

(a) At divisional level a set of managerial and operational controls operate. These ensure that the division does its work properly. Typically these will include:
- departmental budgets;
- production planning systems;
- staff appraisals;
- financial and processing controls (e.g. debtor control, bookkeeping, etc.).

(b) At the corporate centre a higher level of strategic controls will be at work. These aim to ensure that the divisions play their part in realising the goals of the corporation as a whole. These include:
- measures of financial performance (e.g. return on assets, profit, cash flow);
- strategic planning systems;
- human resource controls such as regular meetings among divisional managers and selection and development of managers with appropriate skills and attitudes.

The example of the Du Pont pyramid in Figure 8.1 shows an early system that integrated both levels of control. The expenses and efficiency measures at the right-hand side of the diagram could be controlled by departmental managers within the division and be monitored

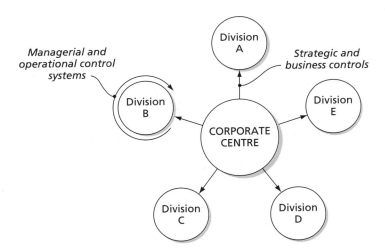

Figure 8.2 Types of control in multidivisional organisations

through a budgetary control system by the division's management. These in turn enabled the division's management to control the return on net assets of the division. Corporate centre in Du Pont merely had to monitor the return on assets of each of its divisions to ensure that the corporation as a whole gave a satisfactory return to its stockholders.

8.2 The functions of performance measurement

Neely (1998) captures this nicely by specifying 'Four CPs of Measurement'. These are the reasons why we measure performance:

1. *Check position.* Measures allow management to understand how well the business is performing at present. This can include factors such as:
   - attainment of present service goals (e.g. on-time deliveries, quality);
   - costs versus revenues;
   - relative position (e.g. benchmarking).
     This is vital if management are to detect problems and undertake remedial action.
2. *Communicate position.* This ensures that stakeholders are aware of how the business is performing. It can include:
   - financial reporting;
   - returns to regulators;
   - reports to customers (e.g. many utilities and transport firms will emphasise how well they are meeting customer needs).
     This builds up stakeholder support and establishes the legitimacy of the organisation's activities.
3. *Confirm priorities.* You may recall the earlier discussion about critical success factors and key performance indicators. Setting targets for particular aspects of the business communicates that these things are important. We also know that managers will focus on them because their ability to reach the targets will be part of senior management's assessment of their personal competence. Furthermore the measures can focus resources to where they are needed.
4. *Compel progress.* Measures can do this in several ways:
   (a) Measurement communicates priorities. Managers will always seek to 'do what is inspected' first before considering 'doing what is expected'. By setting a measure for something, management know it will be achieved.
   (b) Measurement may be linked to reward. This may be formal as part of a bonus scheme, or less formal in terms of better career progression for successful managers.
   (c) Measures make progress explicit. If the goals of the business are not being reached, it is often the missing of certain key measures that forces management to act.

8.3 Conventional profit-related measures of business performance

8.3.1 Justification of profit-related measures

The conventional assumption about organisations is that they should seek to maximise profits because this yields the greatest benefit to their owners. Consequently, profit-based measures are used at two levels:

1. In summary form they are monitored by investors using the final published accounts of the business.

   Consequently, to ensure the investors are not disappointed.

2. They are used to evaluate and control the performance of business divisions and product lines.

8.3.2 Profit-based performance measures

These measures are used to monitor the contribution to total profits made by particular products or divisions. They do not take into account issues of profitability because they do not include the assets used to create the profit.

The principal measures used are:

(a) *Sales margin*, calculated as:

Sales revenue − Variable cost

It is used to consider the return on a given product and can show the effect of changing the selling price or substituting a different-priced direct input. It can also be used to take decisions on whether to continue making or selling a given product.

(b) *Controllable profit*, calculated as:

Sales revenue − (Division variable costs
    + Divisionally separable controllable fixed costs)

This is always a divisional performance measure (i.e. is monitored by the corporate centre as a way to control business divisions). It uses the principle of *controllability* that managers shall only be evaluated against performance targets that they can influence. For example, allocated head office costs will be excluded because a divisional manager cannot control head office spending.

(c) *Contribution margin*, calculated as:

Sales revenue − (Divisional variable costs
    + Divisionally separable controllable and
      non-controllable fixed costs)

The measure indicates how much a division contributes to overhead recovery. It is not helpful for the operational decisions of divisional managers or for evaluation of divisions, because it breaches the principle of controllability. The non-controllable costs are 'sunk' and result from the decisions of top management.

(d) *Net profit*. Perhaps the least useful because it is hostage to head office decisions on overhead allocation, central charges and transfer prices.

Profit-based measures suffer from a number of problems:

(a) *They ignore the amount of capital assets used by the division.* No account is taken of the invested capital being used to generate the profit. For example, a £10 m profit from a division with assets of £100 m suggests a 10 per cent return on investment that may be acceptable. A similar profit on assets of £1bn would be only 1 per cent, and that is unlikely to be acceptable to shareholders.

(b) *They cause excessive capital investment.* Because assets are not accounted for, managers may reduce staff (an expense) and substitute capital in its place to increase measured performance.

(c) *It is a single period measure.* Profit is a single year's revenues minus a single year's costs. Businesses often need to make losses in the short run to build up a market share or develop new products in order to make big profits in subsequent years. Therefore long-run profit maximisation may not be assured by rigid adherence to short-term profit measures.

8.3.3 Importance of considering the capital base

The net assets of the business belong to the shareholder. They represent capital tied up in the business. These assets have the following *opportunity costs*:

1. *The earnings they could yield if the division was better managed.* This demonstrates that performance measures are frequently used to evaluate the performance of divisional managers relative to each other. For example, the manager of a division producing a low return on investment (ROI) may be replaced because a similar division elsewhere has demonstrated a higher ROI.

2. *The returns that could be enjoyed if the assets were used to make a different product.* This can be used to justify changing the product range. For example, if a chain of stores discovers that a better ROI is generated by stores selling youth fashion than by those selling formal business suits, it will undertake a store conversion programme to sell more youth fashion.

3. *The proceeds from liquidation of the assets.* Assume that assets are valued at realisable value. Net assets represent the amount of cash which may be yielded if the assets were sold. Assume that profits are 3 per cent of the net assets. A shareholder might take the view that they should be sold and that the money would be better invested in a risk-free account.

This last point introduces to the concept of *shareholder wealth maximisation*.

8.3.4 Shareholder wealth

Modern financial management asserts that the goal of business is to increase the wealth of the shareholder.

Rappaport (1998) defines shareholder wealth (or *shareholder value* as he calls it) as:

$$\text{Shareholder value} = \text{Corporate value} - \text{Debt}$$

where corporate value is the present value of cash flows from its activities over the forecast period plus any residual cash flows following the end of that period such as from disposal of assets.

You will recognise Rappaport's formulation from your studies in investment appraisal. He is saying that shareholder value is the net present value (NPV) of all the projects in which the firm has invested (less any debt liabilities).

Therefore to increase shareholder value, managers must at all times be using the assets at their disposal in activities that yield a positive NPV over the forecast period, for example

- the factory manager must ensure that the product line they are making yields a cash flow across its life cycle sufficient to yield an NPV on the funds invested in the factory;

- the research and development team must ensure that the cash flows obtained from selling the new drug they develop must provide a positive NPV against the money they have invested in developing it;
- the advertising manager must make sure that the increased revenues (net of production and distribution costs) from higher sales of the product must provide an NPV against the money ploughed into the advertising campaign.

To calculate an NPV it is necessary to apply a *discount rate* to the cash flows of each year to express them in present value terms. The sum of the present values of the net revenues must exceed the sum of the present values of the investments for a positive NPV to result (or in Rappaport's terms, shareholder value).

Therefore for shareholder value to increase it is necessary that the manager obtains a rate of return on the assets they control that exceeds the opportunity costs of the funds invested in those assets. This is sometimes called an *economic profit*. It is a residual income measure and is calculated as follows;

$$\text{Economic profit} = \text{Net operating profit after tax} - \text{Fixed assets}$$
$$+ \text{Net current assets} \times \text{Weighted average cost of capital}$$

In summary, it offers a number of advantages over alternatives:

- it provides the correct incentives for capital allocation, unlike return on capital employed, which can lead to under-capitalisation, and earnings, which can lead to over-capitalisation;
- it does not encourage actions to flatter short-term results at the expense of long-term performance, for example actions such as cutting research and development;
- it shows a good correlation (a coefficient of 0.44) with historical share prices, thus providing managers with a proxy for share price which they can influence (although more complex measures such as cash flow return on investment can provide a higher correlation);
- it lends itself to use as an annual performance measure, linked to executive pay, unlike some cash flow measures. Positive economic profit implies that value creation for share-holders and can be used to reward managers accordingly.

8.3.5 Return on investment and residual income

ROI was developed, as we have seen, by Du Pont. In the 1950s General Electric developed an alternative measure called residual income (RI).

1. ROI, calculated as:

$$\frac{\text{Division profits before interest and tax}}{\text{Capital employed}}$$

This measure may also be termed return on capital employed (ROCE) and return on net assets (RONA).

2. RI calculated as:

$$\text{Earnings before interest and tax} - (\text{Invested capital} - \text{Imputed rate})$$

The imputed charge can be adjusted for the degree of risk the business unit is subject to. For example, a division in an industry with a history of sharp profit volatility would have a higher imputed rate.

Example

Assume that a division has net assets of £200m and earnings of £15m. The rate of interest available at the bank is 8 per cent.

The ROI of the division will be 7.5 per cent (i.e. 15/200).

If the rate available for bank deposits is 8 per cent, then the shareholders lose wealth by investing in the firm (i.e. they get an income of £15m, whereas the bank would have yielded £16m).

Residual income approaches the same point in a different way. Using the same example the RI will be calculated as:

$$£15m - (£200m \times 0.08) = £1m$$

The residual income shows how much better off (or in this case worse off) the investor is as a consequence of investing in the business rather than the bank.

The above example shows the principle of economic income (or increasing shareholder wealth) clearly:

- Under ROI the impact on shareholder wealth is the difference between the rate of return obtained on the funds by the firm compared to the rate available externally, that is, £200m × (0.08 − 0.075) = (£1m).
- Under RI it is the actual return minus the opportunity cost of the capital, i.e. £15m − (£200m × 0.08) = (£1m).

Therefore, to ensure the corporation maximises shareholder wealth, the corporate centre must ensure that each division returns a rate of profit on the assets it uses which is at least as great as the corporation's cost of capital.

Earlier in your studies you will have learned how to calculate the appropriate imputed rate for these projects when you study the cost of capital. Here we have been concerned with the economic principles underlying shareholder wealth.

8.3.6 Comparison of ROI with RI

Before looking at shareholder wealth in more detail, let us compare the two most popular methods of divisional performance evaluation.

Both methods bring the capital base of the division into consideration and hence are superior to simple measures of divisional profit.

The main benefits of ROI compared to RI are:

1. *It enables comparison of divisions of different sizes.* ROI provides a rate, whereas RI is expressed as an amount. Consequently a large division will have a higher RI than a small one. This does not help corporate management compare management.
2. *It is widely used and understood.* Despite both having been developed at the same time (by Du Pont's accountants of course, as if you couldn't have guessed!), ROI is far more widely used than RI.
3. *It approximates to other measures monitored by investors.* Return on capital employed and earnings per share (EPS) are closely monitored. Each follows the same rationale as ROI by having a measure of profit divided by a figure representing investment.

Provided that no debt borrowing to finance assets takes place between the years, a rise in ROI will lead to an increase in EPS.

The drawbacks of ROI compared to RI are:

1. *ROI may lead managers to ignore profitable investment opportunities.* Assume a manager's division presently enjoys a return of £35m on assets of £250m, an ROI of 14 per cent.

A project requiring investment of £100m but yielding a profit of £10m is being considered. Capital can be borrowed at 7 per cent. The manager will reject the project because its ROI of 10 per cent is less than the division's present 14 per cent and if accepted will reduce it to 12.9 per cent. However, the project yields an increase in shareholder wealth of £3m per year: (10% − 7%) × £100m.

Residual income encourages the manager to undertake any project which increases earnings after the imputed cost of capital. In the example above, provided that the imputed charge to the division was less than 10 per cent the manager would undertake the project.

2. *Managers may take on a project where returns do not cover the costs of capital, provided that they have a higher ROI than presently enjoyed.* Suppose in the example above the original earnings of the division had been £15m and the cost of capital had been 12 per cent. Undertaking the investment would increase ROI from 6 per cent to 7.1 per cent and hence be acceptable to the manager despite its reducing shareholder wealth by £2m per year: (12% − 10%) × £100m.

3. RI is more flexible as it allows use of adjusted imputed rates to reflect the risks of the division.

8.3.7 Common problems of profit-based measures

There are a number of difficulties with using either ROI or RI for divisional control:

1. *They encourage divisional managers to deplete capital assets.* Managers will be encouraged to reduce the assets of the business in order to increase ROI or RI. For example, this may involve:
   (a) Contracting out processes involving capital-intensive investment.
   (b) Prematurely scrapping assets if they fall into temporary disuse.
   (c) Failing to keep capital base up to date through avoiding replacement investment.
2. *They are distorted by the conventions surrounding financial reporting.* There are numerous distortions:
   (a) Differing bases of asset valuation between divisions distorts comparisons and decision-making.
   (b) The treatment of training and promotion investments as expenses means that they reduce profits and hence are avoided in the short run.
3. *The financial returns and investment costs of a division will vary according to its geographical location and type of business.* For example, an office equipment manufacturer might discover that:
   - the service division has a higher ROI/RI due to its lower level of capital assets than the production division;
   - ROI/RI of service branches in the north are higher than those in the south because premises prices are more expensive in the south.

     This may lead to dysfunctional decisions about rebalancing the business portfolio. Management might consider selling off manufacturing in the hope that the capital released could be reinvested at higher rates of profit in the service division. There are several dysfunctions likely:
   - they may already have adequate service coverage, so additional branches yield no extra profit;

- they have destroyed the portfolio of the business because without manufacturing they would have nothing to service;
- presumably the service branches would all be in the north!

4. *Depreciation effect makes divisions with older assets appear to produce a better financial performance than one with new assets.* If followed through to its conclusion, this would lead management to shut down the newest divisions.

5. *The measures are not appropriate for divisions in the early stages of the product life cycle* (Ward's point discussed above). This leads to:

   (a) Failure to invest in new products or processes because it will reduce current-year earnings.

   (b) The encouragement of investment in old products where earnings can be raised temporarily despite lack of long-term future.

   (c) *They do not allow the corporate centre to shape the strategy and behaviour of the division without additional measures of performance.* This is one of the problems of the 'financial control' style identified by Goold and Campbell and discussed in Section 8.5.

   (d) *The measures are entirely* backward looking. Decisions on investment, divestment and evaluation of managerial performance should focus on the value that can be created in the future. ROI/RI look at what earnings have been in the previous year. This may not be a reliable guide to future earnings, particularly in growth or late maturity stage industries.

The issue of appropriate performance measures for the product life cycle is discussed later.

8.4 Value-based management approaches

8.4.1 Background to value-based management

Value-based management (VBM) may be seen as a way to control the corporation more closely in accordance with the interests of shareholders than is possible using conventional profit-based techniques. Cornelius and Davies (1997) define it as:

...a methodology that involves managing all aspects of the business in accordance with the desire to create and maximise the wealth of shareholders.

The impetus for the adoption of VBM (sometimes called shareholder value analysis: SVA) comes from several directions:

1. *Growing concern about the divorce of ownership from control.* Shareholders in a corporation have limited opportunities to control the directors they appoint and the management teams beneath them. This means that the management team are insulated from the need to keep shareholder concerns at the centre of their decisions. Consequently management may follow strategies and award themselves bonuses without regard to their impact on shareholder wealth.

2. *Adoption of VBM techniques by investment analysts.* Investment analysts make their money by being able to spot companies whose true values and prospects are different from the way they are seen by investors as a whole. Once spotted, the analysts can advise their clients to buy the undervalued ones and to sell the others. This exerts a strong influence on share prices and has led to takeovers and boardroom shake-ups.

Naturally management want to avoid this by running their businesses on VBM lines in future.

3. *Emergence of aggressive shareholders.* Various 'active value' funds have emerged that specialise in spotting firms with ineffective management and buying shares in them. The fund harasses the management by drawing attention to their shortcomings in order to provoke changes at board level or a takeover. This enables the fund to realise a capital gain as the share price rises.

4. *Problems assessing the impact of new management techniques.* This book has introduced many of the new techniques of management such as business process re-engineering, quality, relationship management, etc. Because they are new, long term and utilise staff and training they are very hard to assess using conventional investment appraisal techniques or to control using simple measures of profit or profitability. Yet management still need to ensure that they contribute to shareholder value creation.

5. *Marketing efforts of management consultants.* Most professional consultancies (including large accounting firms) have their own set of proprietary shareholder value metrics to sell to clients. They have drawn attention to the problems of ROCE and other metrics and have impelled boards to find better measures.

8.4.2 Drivers of shareholder value

Rappaport (1998) states that shareholder value is arrived at by the following formula:

$$\text{Business value} = \text{Present value (PV) of free cash flow from operations plus}$$
$$\text{value of marketable securities}$$

In other words:

- the amount of cash it is generating which could potentially become dividend and will be the basis of the market capitalisation of the business;
- the securities or investments held by the company which could be disposed of for cash without affecting its operations.

The corporation's overall value is arrived at by the following calculation:

$$\text{Shareholder value} = \text{Business value} - \text{Debt value}$$

To increase shareholder value, the management should increase business value or reduce debt.

Rappaport outlines *seven value drivers* that he demonstrates affect shareholder value. The arrows show the way they need to move to improve shareholder value.

1. *Sales growth rate* (↑): The percentage annual growth rate in sales revenues during the planning period. Obviously, higher sales growth (assuming they are profitable sales) will boost free cash flow.

2. *Operating profit margin* (↑): The percentage of sales revenue that turns into profits.

3. *Cash income tax rate* (↓): Any reduction in this rate improves shareholder value because it concerns the profit for shareholders rather than giving it away to the government.

4. *Incremental fixed capital investment rate* ($\downarrow$): If the growth of the business demands substantial amounts of new capital assets this will deplete free cash flows and hence shareholder value.

5. *Investment in working capital rate* ($\downarrow$): By the same logic, a business that needs to invest heavily in stocks or debtors to support its growth will produce lower free cash flows than one that does not.

6. *Planning period* ($\uparrow$): If the firm can forecast growth over a longer period, then it will be able to discount a longer stream of free cash flows and hence have a higher business value.

7. *Cost of capital* ($\downarrow$): This will be the rate used to discount the future free cash flows. If it is lower, it follows that the present value of the forecast flows will be higher and so business value will be higher.

These seven drivers must become the objectives of managerial control mechanisms in the firm if it wishes to improve shareholder value.

Example

The following example is derived from Davies et al. (2000):

SVA plc	
Sales last year (year 0)	£100m
Sales growth rate	10%
Operating profit margin	20%
Cash tax rate	35%
Incremental fixed capital investment rate	15%
Working capital investment rate	5%
Planning period	3 years
Cost of capital	10%
Marketable securities	£5m
Balance sheet debt	£50m

Assume that after year 3 the operating profit remains constant with no sale growth (and hence no additional capital investment).
The following forecast can be derived:

			£000	
Year	0	1	2	3
Sales	100,000	110,000	121,000	133,100
Operating profit @ 20%		22,000	24,200	26,620
Cash tax payable @ 35%		(7,700)	(8,470)	(9,317)
Operating profits after tax		14,300	15,730)	17,303
Less incremental fixed capital @ 15% of sales growth		(1,500)	(1,650)	(1,815)
Less investment in work capital @ 5% of sales growth		(500)	(550)	(605)
Operating free cash flow		12,300	13,530	14,883

The present value of this free cash flow can be found as:

Year	Free cash flow	Discount factor @ 10%	PV
1	12,300	0.909	11,181
2	13,530	0.826	11,176
3	14,883	0.751	11,177
PV of free cash			33,534

To the present value of free cash flows from years 1–3 must be added the value of the operating profits in perpetuity year 4 onwards:

$$\frac{17,303}{0.1} \times 0.751 = 129,954$$

where 0.751 is the discount factor for 3 years @ 10% (annuity valuation assumes cash received at start of year).

Therefore:

	£000
Total value of operations (33,534 + 129,954)	163,488
Marketable securities	5,000
Business value	168,488
Less debt	(50,000)
Shareholder value	118,488

whereas if the sales growth rate had been 15 per cent the value would become:

	0	1	2	3	4–n
Sales	100,000	115,000	132,250	152,088	
Profit		23,000	26,450	30,418	
Tax		(8,050)	(9,258)	(10,646)	
Profit after Tax		14,950	17,192	19,772	
Fixed incremental cap		(2,250)	(2,588)	(2,978)	
Incremental working capital		(750)	(863)	(992)	
Free cash flow		11,950	13,741	15,802	

Total free cash flow:

Year		Free cash flow	Discount	PV
1		11,950	0.909	10,863
2		13,741	0.826	11,350
3		15,802	0.751	11,867
4–n	$\frac{19,772}{0.1}$	197,720	0.751	148,488
				£182,568

Giving:

	£000
Total value of operations	182,568
Marketable securities	5,000
Business value	187,568
Less debt	(50,000)
Shareholder value	£137,568

You may like to substitute in alternative values for the value drivers and note the impact on the business value (or you can take Rappaport's word for it if you prefer).

8.4.3 Areas covered by VBM

VBM must be integrated into six management areas:

1. *Strategy selection*. Shareholder value maximisation must be the primary objective of strategy. This is particularly important in the case of evaluating one-off investments

such as acquisitions or projects. Specific management techniques such as business process re-engineering, relationship marketing or growth should also be evaluated against the drivers of shareholder value to assess whether they will improve returns.

2. *Resource allocation.* Funds should be allocated to strategies and divisions that will create shareholder value. This means that requests for funding by divisions should demonstrate how they impact on the drivers of shareholder value.

3. *Target-setting and performance measurement.* A rise in the share price will increase shareholder value. However, management cannot determine share prices, they can only influence them by their economic performance. The rest depends on market sentiment and investor perception. Management need a set of performance measures (or *metrics*) that act as lead indicators to movements in the share price. These should then be set as targets for divisional managers to reach.

4. *Managerial reward schemes.* Managerial rewards should be linked to the drivers of shareholder value and realisation of these should be a significant portion of managerial pay. This will bring the motivations of management back into line with the interests of the shareholder.

5. *Value realisation.* The market must incorporate the merits of management decisions into the share price before the value is realised. Therefore, explaining and publicising the decisions and their rationale is important.

6. *Implementation.* Adopting VBM necessitates a change in the culture of the business as the interests of the shareholder take centre stage and performance evaluation systems change. The concept must be explained and driven down into the organisation with all other targets and evaluation systems brought into line with it. However, management should not focus solely on the VBM metric and ignore the business process measures that give rise to it. For example, customer satisfaction, quality, product awareness or innovation may be quite consistent with satisfying a VBM metric.

8.4.4 Economic value added and market value added

These concepts were developed by consultants Stern Stewart, and economic value added (EVA) is copyrighted by them.

The principles are fairly straightforward. Shareholder value is the increase in the wealth of the shareholder as a consequence of investing in the firm's shares. Stern Stewart propose two measures for shareholder value:

1. *Market value added* (MVA): This is an *external measure* of how much better off the shareholders are as a consequence of management's performance.

2. *Economic value added* (EVA): This is an *internal* managerial performance measure which monitors whether managers of divisions are increasing shareholder value (measured as MVA) or not.

Figure 8.3 indicates the philosophy behind the MVA metric.

In Figure 8.3 the market capitalisation rises by £200 m and the capital invested rises by only £150 m. It follows that the wealth of shareholders has increased by £50 m.

The use of the base year is significant. MVA seeks to reflect the decisions of the present management team. Although some texts advocate going back to the founding year of the business to calculate MVA, this seems pointless and is probably impossible due to lack of suitable data. VBM is a technique to help investors form a view on the performance of *present* management (not past management) and their ability to generate future earnings.

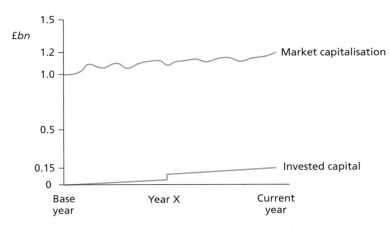

Figure 8.3 *Market value added*

More usually the MVA is tracked for the period that the present management have been in office, or perhaps across the period of a major business decision such as an acquisition. For example, an acquisition may have taken place in Year X in Figure 8.3.

MVA is calculated by the formula:

> Rise in market capitalisation during the period
>   − Increase in capital invested during the period

EVA is calculated by the formula:

> Adjusted profits after tax* − (Adjusted invested capital
>   × Weighted average cost of capital)
> *Stern Stewart term this NOPAT (net operating profit after tax)

The two measures are intended to correspond, with MVA being the external measure monitored by investors and EVA being the internal performance measure which will lead to a satisfactory MVA.

You will probably recognise EVA as essentially the same as residual income (RI).

Stern Stewart assert that ensuring that all projects and divisions are able to demonstrate a positive EVA, then the effect will be an increase in shareholder wealth measured as MVA.

The relationship between EVA and MVA is complex. It is best understood one step at a time:

1. The market capitalisation of the business is roughly equivalent to the expected present value (PV) of its free cash flows.
2. MVA is therefore equivalent to the increase in the NPV of free cash flows over the period minus the increase in the capital invested.
3. Free cash flows are cash profit less the cost of financing the capital needed to generate the profit.
4. The cost of capital is the cost of servicing the capital used by the firm. It provides for interest to debt holders and also dividends to shareholders.
5. Therefore to *maintain* or *increase* shareholder value (the NPV of the corporation's free cash flows) management must ensure that each division yields returns in excess of its cost of capital. To *increase* shareholder value requires that the firm either undertakes a greater number of projects with returns in excess of the cost of capital and/or that the EVA of existing operations be increased.

6. Therefore by ensuring that all divisions and projects can show EVA, the corporation can ensure that MVA remains steady or rising.

Some texts suggest that MVA and EVA are the same. This is not correct. MVA assumes the investment markets set the share price of the firm such that its market capitalisation equals the discounted present value of all the future earnings of the corporation. EVA is an annual measure that includes only one year's earning. Stern Stewart is simply saying that in order for MVA to increase, divisions must provide EVA. Put another way, *MVA is the present value of all future EVAs.*

However, the MVA and EVA calculations require 173 adjustments (at the last count) to standard financial statements. These adjustments affect the measures of income and the measures of capital.

Some of these can be seen in Table 8.1.

To understand these adjustments it is important to realise that EVA/MVA are essentially *backward-looking* measures. The analyst is effectively saying to management, 'over the past 10 years you have had an extra £150m of funds. Do your current free cash flows cover the opportunity costs of this extra investment such that I can feel confident that your investments increase shareholder wealth?'

Where capital has been invested from retained earnings or new issues of equity the balance sheet will record this. However, retained profits are declared after the deduction of a series of expenses and also non-cash adjustments that, if seen in a different light, look like investments:

1. Investments in intangibles such as advertising, R&D and perhaps training are treated as expenses in conventional financial accounting. They are reinstated as assets in the adjusted capital employed to reflect the fact that its discretionary expenditures by management. The money would otherwise have been used to pay dividend or reduce debt. The profit figure is increased by the amount of expenditure on such intangibles during the year.
2. Reversal of capital expenditures written-off over the period such as through depreciation and goodwill by adding them back to assets. This is because when the assets were purchased (or a company acquired during takeover) the funds used could otherwise have been given to back to shareholders. Because it represents all the funds used, the original purchase price is the relevant figure.
3. Add back increases in particular reserves such as deferred taxation warranties and bad debts. These owe more to prudence concepts than business performance and by being excessively prudent the management appear to reduce the capital base of the firm and understate the cash invested by shareholders. Moreover the increase in such reserves for the year reduces recorded profits.

Table 8.1 Some adjustments to MVA and EVA calculations

Adjustment to net profit	Adjustment to capital employed
Add net capitalised intangibles	Add net book value of intangibles
Add goodwill written off and depreciation	Add cumulative goodwill written off and cumulative depreciation
Add increase in deferred tax provision and in 'other reserves' such as warranty reserves and LIFO reserves	Add deferred tax reserve and 'other reserves' such as warranty reserves and LIFO reserves
Interest on debt added back to profit	Debt added to net assets as part of capital employed

4. Treating debt as an asset is unusual to say the least (the same approach is adopted with leases and other off-balance sheet financing). By adding it back into capital employed, the analyst avoids any distortion to EVA resulting from the effect of capital gearing. Otherwise a firm could raise EVA simply by replacing equity with debt. The interest is added back into profit, not just to complete the double entry but also to avoid the cost of capital on assets paid for with debt being set against earnings twice – once when interest is deducted from profit and again as part of the EVA calculation.

8.4.5 Critique of EVA/MVA

1. The conceptual basis of the adjustments seems sometimes quite arbitrary. For example, continuing advertising can be viewed as an annual expense of business just as much as it can be seen as an investment. The same is true of routine training. This leads to the next point.
2. It suffers from the need to make adjustments to final accounts to arrive at the capital invested figure. These are apparently arbitrary and there is much latitude for window dressing of the financial statements.
3. It limits measures of earnings to the current period and does not consider forecast profits. For example, a division at the early stage of the product life cycle will have a low EVA compared to a mature one.

    It is true that Stern Stewart suggest that investment appraisal should use the present value of future cash flows and set these against the opportunity cost of the capital used. However, they do not appear to suggest the same for divisional performance evaluation.
4. It is affected by the absolute size of the firm and so cannot compare firms. In the example above, if the firm had started with a market capitalisation of £100 m, which increased to £300 m following an investment of £150 m, this would be more impressive and encouraging than a similar increase in value in a firm with an initial capitalisation of £1bn.
5. MVA does not necessarily track the EVA in the way suggested. General market sentiment will have a considerable impact on share price.
6. The technique may be no more than a self-fulfilling prophecy. If sufficient investors are brought to believe that MVA is a relevant way to look at investment, then it is no surprise that firms who publicise that they have adopted EVA measures will enjoy a share price rise and hence a rise in MVA. Publicising its use of EVA may have as much influence on MVA as actually implementing EVA.
7. It seems to overlook the increase in the shareholders' wealth from the dividends they have received during the period. If two firms have generated the same MVA over a 10-year period, presumably the one with a generous dividend policy will have been a better investment than one that paid no dividend.

8.4.6 Total shareholder return (TSR)

This is the total percentage return to shareholders over a period and includes both share price appreciation and dividend yield. It is calculated by the formula:

$$\frac{\text{Division per share} + (\text{Share price at period end} - \text{Original share price})}{\text{Share price at the start of the period}} \times 100$$

A simple example is a share priced at £1 at the start of the period and £1.20 at the end. Also a 10p dividend is declared at the period end:

$$\text{TSR} = \frac{10 + (120 - 100)}{100} \times 100 = 30\%$$

Of this 30 per cent, 10 per cent is dividend yield and 20 per cent is share price appreciation. This measure can be compared with

(a) The risk-adjusted discount rate for investment in the company's shares. For example, the business above may suffer considerable risks due to its line of business, its capital structure or the volatility of its share price. Investors may require an annual return of 35 per cent to compensate for this risk compared with investing in a risk-free asset. If this is the case, the firm's TSR of 30 per cent indicates a destruction of shareholder value.
(b) The TSR of similar companies.
(c) The TSR of previous years.
   The technique can be adapted to cope with complications such as:
   • dividends are declared mid-year as well as end of period;
   • TSR is calculated over a number of years.

Dividends are assumed to be reinvested at the firm's WACC until the end of the period.
Unlike EVA/MVA, this measure is immune to allegations of creative accounting. It is also very simple and cheap to calculate.
The main problems of TSR are:

(a) It is not a measure of wealth creation because it ignores the amount of capital that the investor may have put into the firm during the period.
(b) It is affected by market sentiment. For example, TSR will always rise if share prices generally rise. This does not indicate the success of the firm's management.

8.4.7 Linking VBM to business strategy

The main drivers of shareholder value suggested by Rappaport can also be detected in the formula for Economic Value Added®. It is not implied here that the developers of EVA® owe a debt to Rappaport or vice versa, but merely that there are similarities of approach that it helps understanding to notice.

EVA® = Net operating profit after tax − (Adjusted capital × Imputer rate of interest)

Table 8.2 summarises the factors that can increase the EVA® measure of shareholder value.
As we have seen, the EVA® ignores future forecast earnings. Other approaches to VBM take future earnings into consideration on the grounds that the perceptions investors hold of future earnings will influence the share price and hence market value added (MVA). Therefore we can add to the drivers above:

Market expectations of future earnings	Investor understanding of firm's strategy	Length of time horizon of strategy
	Investor trust in ability of firm to deliver its strategy	Quality of strategic forecasts
	Number of years over which earnings are forecast	Past experience of firm's ability to implement strategy
	Size of forecast earnings	Extent of investor understanding of strategy
		Achievement and publication of KPIs
		Quality of investor relations

Table 8.2

Element of EVA®	Main drivers	Implications for strategy
Increased revenues	Higher sales volumes Higher prices Greater cross-selling Customer profitability	Market penetration Branding and differentiation Build patent and other barriers Capture early life-cycle by innovation Relationship marketing Improved functionality and quality of product

Reduced operating costs	More effective purchasing of
	    inputs
	Increased productivity
	Cheap locations
	Reduced waste and scrap
		Target costing of products
		Clearer identification and management
		    of cost drivers (e.g. ABC/ABM)
		Cost reduction programme
		Outsourcing
		Gain scale economies
		Captive access to materials/markets by
		    vertical integration
		Change business location

Reduced tax	Tax rates Forms of expenditure	Tax planning Transfer profits to low tax areas Increase tax effectiveness of funding

Reduce invested assets
(fixed capital + working
capital)
	Ownership v. contracted-in
	    use of assets
	Technology employed
	Amount of discretionary
	    expenditure
	Inventory levels
	Debtor/credit control
		Outsourcing high investment processes
		Utilise JIT production and purchasing
		Improve supply chain management
		Working capital management

Reduce imputed rate	Perceived risk Funding sources Capital structure Share price Credit rating	Consistent delivery of shareholder value Reduced earnings volatility Project financing to isolate risks Reduce exposure to commercial and operating risk

8.4.8 Driving down responsibility for value creation

For a performance measure to implement and control a business strategy it must have impact on the sorts of decisions taken by managers. Ehrbar (1998) describes the introduction of EVA at Briggs and Stratton, the world's largest manufacturer of petrol lawnmower engines. The example is reformulated here using the levels of control suggested by Anthony (1965) to demonstrate how a performance metric can deliver a strategy.

- *Strategic control level*: Management recognised that diversification into alternative lines of business such as electric lawnmower engines and alternative uses for petrol engines such as outboards for boats would destroy shareholder value. This is because the earnings were unlikely to provide a long-term premium over the costs of the capital involved in developing the motors, tooling up and training the factory and promotion. They took the strategic decision to stay with their core business.

- *Tactical control level*: Having decided to stay in petrol lawnmower engines the management of Briggs and Stratton set about improving the returns it generated. One concern was a factory with poor productivity and in need of substantial upgrading and investment. The production managers considered the amount of funds it would take to turn the factory around and the likely returns the factory could earn. They decided that the investment would have a negative EVA (indeed the factory was already producing negative EVA). They sold the factory to Harley Davidson Motorcycles and used the funds they gained to improve alternative factories.
- *Operational control level*: To remain competitive and deliver EVA in the lawnmower engine market Briggs and Stratton needed to make improvements to quality and operating efficiency. To accomplish this they harnessed the workforce's involvement by setting EVA targets (with bonuses) for each process on the factory floor. It was explained to workers how they could affect the drivers of EVA and they were left to their own devices on achieving improvements. Table 8.3 gives an example.

Table 8.3 EVA measures for operative staff

Revenues	• Improve quality of engines to increase perceived value and price • Increase throughput to ensure demand is met
Costs	• Increase productivity • Reduce wastage and scrap • Better manning levels • Improve quality to reduce warranty claims and repair costs
Capital employed	• Better inventory management • Avoidance of unnecessary mechanisation or capital expenditure • Preventative maintenance to lengthen life of capital assets (because EVA does not depreciate or write off capital assets so replacement assets are recorded as increases in capital employed)
Imputed rate	• Reduce industrial disruption • Adopt safe systems of work to reduce potential employer's liability investers hold of future earnings will influence the share price and hence market value added (MVA)

An excellent set of readings in this area is provided in *Scarlett* (1997).

Table 8.4 Characteristics of different strategic styles

Style	Key features	Advantages	Dangers	Examples
Strategic planning	'Masterplanner' Top-down highly prescribed Detailed controls	Co-ordination	Centre out of touch Divisions become tactically orientated	BOC Cadbury Lex Public sector pre-1990
Financial control	'Shareholder/banker' Financial targets Control of investment Bottom-up	Responsiveness	Loses direction Centre does not add value	BTR Hanson Tarmac
Strategic control	'Strategic shaper' Strategic and financial targets Bottom-up Less detailed controls	Centre/divisions are complementary Ability to co-ordinate Motivation	Too much bargaining Culture change needed New bureaucracies	ICI Courtaulds Public sector post-1990

8.5 The role of the corporate centre in control

8.5.1 Influencing how financial returns are made

Regardless of whether we use a profit, profitability or VBM measure of business performance, one key problem remains. Financial performance measures alone are too blunt an instrument to implement detailed competitive strategies.

Financial measures of performance act as benchmarks to ensure that the business meets its ultimate goal of improving the economic welfare of its owners. Financial measures alone do not guide managers into particular paths of business. They are *measures of ends not means.*

Business strategy suggests that senior management at the corporate centre will have decided to make profits in particular businesses and in particular ways. These fine details of the means of business strategy cannot be implemented and controlled by financial measures alone.

8.5.2 Strategies and styles

Goold and Campbell (1987) investigated the way in which the corporate centre of multidivisional firms influenced the development of business strategy. They identified three strategic styles:

1. *Strategic planning.* Corporate centre substantially involved in the planning processes of each SBU and maintain strict control through top-down planning. The major element of control is the strategic planning process.
2. *Financial control.* Strategic decisions are taken by the divisions. Corporate centre sets *financial targets* for each division (e.g. return on assets and profit/contribution). Here control depends primarily on financial controls such as budgets.
3. *Strategic control.* Divisions are allowed to pursue their own business strategies within a framework of *financial and non-financial* group objectives and corporate goals laid down by the corporate centre.

Goold and Campbell found that the differences between the three styles affected the way corporations approached a number of strategic control issues.

1. *Organisational structure and the co-ordination of overlaps between divisions*
   - *Financial control companies* push strategy decisions to divisions and avoid any overlaps between divisions (e.g. common assets and projects, inter-trading) in order to keep them as pure profit centres.
   - *Strategic control companies* also push strategy decisions to divisions but allow corporate centre to check that collective strategic opportunities have not been missed.
   - *Strategic planning companies* make profit centres responsible but also encourage comments, advice and co-ordination between them.
2. *The planning process* (i.e. the strategy process)
   - *Strategic planning companies* engage in a time-consuming two-way dialogue between corporate centre and each division. Sets long-term strategies and often the short-term strategies to implement them within an overall corporate view.
   - *Strategic control companies* have similar dialogues but mainly to allow corporate centre to challenge and audit the quality of divisional management, thinking rather than impose a corporate view.

- *Financial control companies* do not have formal long-term strategies but rather discussions centre on annual budget approval.

3. *Themes, thrusts and suggestions*

   In *strategic control and financial control companies* corporate centre avoids taking the lead in developing strategies. In strategic planning companies it is proactive.

4. *Resource allocation and portfolio design*
   - *Strategic planning companies* allocate resources according to its view of the group's need to secure competitive advantage in certain areas and divisions.
   - *Strategic control companies* also allocate according to long-term strategic considerations but centre does not promote the case for such spending instead leaves it to divisions.
   - *Financial control companies* allocate the funds requested by divisions, provided that it is convinced of the competence of management. However corporate centre will take the lead in the acquisition or disposal of businesses or major assets.

5. *Objective setting*
   - *Strategic planning companies* expect objectives to arise from the planning process and objectives tend to be long term.
   - *Strategic control companies* have a similar process to strategic planning companies although with a greater emphasis on the use of objectives for control purposes.
   - *Financial control firms* restrict this to the annual budget targets.

6. *Performance monitoring*

   All firms monitor performance. However financial control firms have frequent (e.g. monthly) budget reviews. The others only meet if there have been major departures from plan.

7. *Sanctions and incentives*
   - *Financial control companies* base managerial rewards and progression on the meeting of budget targets.
   - *Strategic control companies* also reward performance but trade-offs between sometimes vague targets causes ambiguity.
   - *Strategic planning companies* operate very flexible controls and are not 'target constrained'.

Table 8.4 summarises the various characteristics of different strategic styles.

8.6   Management accounting and performance measurement

8.6.1   Role of management accounting in implementing and controlling strategies

Management accounting systems can be thought of as influencing the behaviour of organisations in two ways:

1. Through the influence of the information they provide on management decisions.
2. Through the influence of the control measures they set up on managerial behaviour.

Traditionally management accounting has been modelled on the approach developed at Du Pont. That is, it has focused on calculating and providing management information based on resource utilisation, costs, volumes and profit.

8.6.2 Problems of conventional management accounting

Kaplan and Cooper (1998) suggest that cost systems (by which they mean cost accounting, that is management information systems about costs) must fulfil three primary functions:

- Valuation of inventory and measurement of the cost of goods sold for financial reporting purposes.
- Estimation of the costs of activities, products, services and customers for the purposes of pricing and also decision-making about whether they are profitable and whether to continue supplying them.
- Providing feedback to managers and operators about process efficiency.

Conventional performance management aspects of management accounting such as budgets and standard costing have taken care of the financial reporting and process efficiency roles of management accounting. However these conventional systems suffer from a number of defects:

1. *Do not recognise increased importance of fixed costs.* Conventional process costing belongs to an era where direct labour was the main cost of production and hence allocating the small amount of overheads to products using direct labour gave an acceptable approximation of unit cost. Today's mechanised manufacturing means that fixed costs account for up to 85 per cent of costs in manufacturing and hence allocating these according to a minor input, direct labour, invites serious inaccuracies in cost estimation.

2. *Misunderstand cost drivers.* Conventional costing works from the assumption that production volumes are the main driver of the firm's costs and that these are best approximated by the volume of a direct input (usually labour). However this assumes that the firm is making continuous or long runs of a single product and that fixed costs are not affected by production decisions. In a modern production environment firms often compete by providing a wide diversity of products, with many products specially tailored to the customer's specification. The persistent need to stop the process to reset machines and the high costs of work scheduling create slack time and extra costs independently of production volumes. Here diversity and set-ups are as much a cost driver as volume, yet conventional management accounting overlooks them and hence misleads management on the true costs of a given product or customer.

3. *Are more concerned with cost assignment than with cost attribution.* This important distinction is made in Kaplan and Atkinson (1998). Assignment (or allocation) of costs is 'the process of assigning a resource cost to a department or a product where a direct measure does not exist for the quantity of the resource consumed by the department or product' (p. 64). Attribution, on the other hand, is 'the process of assigning a cost that is unambiguously associated with a particular cost object to that cost object' (p. 63). Conventional cost accounting is too easily satisfied with the arbitrary assignment of costs to products for the purpose of financial reporting and overlooks the more important question of determining what is causing the costs.

    The effects of these shortcomings in conventional cost accounting are:
    (a) they lead management to misunderstand the true costs and profits from particular products or customers because they attribute costs wrongly;
    (b) they focus managers' attention on improving the efficiency of particular processes in order to reduce costs, when in fact these processes are of limited significance to the firm other than the fact that they attract substantial overheads.

8.6.3 Integrated cost systems

Kaplan and Cooper (1998) suggest that cost accounting has moved through four stages, with the final stage being the one to which management should aspire. These Stage 4 systems have been made possible by two developments:

(a) The advancement of information systems to a level where enterprise-wide systems (EWS) of performance management can be installed to replace the primitive paper-based systems of conventional management accounting. By EWS, Kaplan and Cooper seem to mean the enterprise resource planning/management systems of the sort sold by SAP, Baan, Oracle, etc.
(b) Advances in management accounting techniques, most notably the development of activity-based management (ABM) approaches and also the development of balanced scorecards for performance evaluation.

Stage 1 systems

These are wholly inadequate systems even for financial reporting where there are no accurate algorithms for allocating costs to products and hence large and uncontrolled variances occur.

Stage 2 systems

The features of these systems are:

- they are adequate for meeting financial reporting requirements such as inventory valuation;
- they collect costs by responsibility centres and not by activities and business processes;
- they report highly distorted product costs;
- they feature non-existent or highly distorted customer costs;
- they provide feedback to managers and employees that is too late, too aggregated and too financial for taking decisions on running their business.

These Stage 2 systems are the conventional cost accounting systems we discussed above. They fail to fulfil two of the roles of management accounting systems outlined earlier, that is:

- Estimation of the costs of activities, products, services and customers for the purposes of pricing and also decision-making about whether they are profitable and whether to continue supplying them.
- Providing feedback to managers and operators about process efficiency.

Either management must do without such information, to the detriment of their business, or must develop their own private information systems to make up for the failures of the official management accounting information system. This latter problem is discussed at length in Johnson and Kaplan (1987).

Stage 3 systems

These are disjointed systems where additional management accounting information is collected and distributed alongside the conventional system. The main elements are:

- A well-functioning traditional system using conventional methods of allocation of costs to goods and preparing monthly reports and financial statements.

- One or more activity-based cost systems taking data from the 'official' financial system as well as other sources to measure accurately the costs of activities, processes, products, services, customers and organisational units.
- Operational feedback systems providing operators and all front-line employees with timely accurate information both financial and non-financial on the efficiency, quality and cycle time of business processes.

Stage 4 systems

- Accounting system is managed by an enterprise-wide computerised system.
- Costs are attributed to the activities that cause them using an ABC approach and hence more accurate measures of the profitability of products, customers, divisions and actors can be derived.
- The same data is reprocessed to enable financial reports to be generated by automatically stripping out any cost allocations, etc., that conflict with the conventions of financial reporting.
- Performance measures for the costs and revenue driving activities are collected both for the purposes of ascertaining costs and also to feed back to managers and operators for the purposes of process control.

8.6.4 Activity-based management (ABM)

Activity-based management (ABM) is described thus:

> … the entire set of actions that can be taken, on a better informed basis, with activity-based cost information. With ABM the organisation accomplishes its outcomes with fewer demands on organisational resources; that is, the organisation can achieve the same outcomes (e.g. revenues) at a lower cost (lower spending on organisational resources) (Kaplan and Cooper, 1998, p. 137).

Activity-based costing (ABC) (Figure 8.4) is believed to better meet the needs of the modern manufacturing business. Modern production processes have several key differences from the processes for which standard costing was developed:

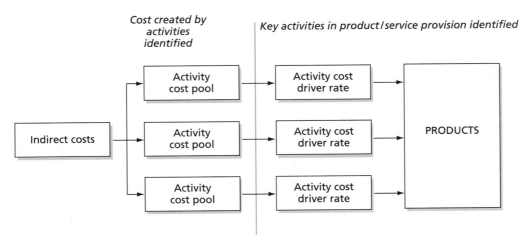

Figure 8.4 Activity-based costing approach

(a) Products are less standardised. Instead, shorter runs of products are made, often customised to meet the specification of particular customers. Techniques such as lean manufacturing have reduced batch sizes, while modern marketing often requires a wider diversity of products.

(b) Customers are also of varying profitability according to the service they demand and the amount they buy. You will recall this from our earlier discussion of customer account profitability analysis.

The stages in designing an ABC system are as follows:

1. *Identify major activities in the organisation*:
   (a) This involves a trade-off between excessive decomposition and excessive aggregation of activities. Trying to allocate costs too finely to activities will be an expensive process and may not yield much benefit. Research suggests that 20–30 activities is the norm.
   (b) The process is carried out by an *activity analysis* involving inspection of plans of floor layout, observation of processes and activities and payroll analysis and interview to ascertain what staff do.
   (c) Activities can be classified according to a hierarchical method:
      (i) *Unit level activities.* These are performed each time a unit is produced. Include direct inputs and energy.
      (ii) *Batch-related activities.* These are such things as machine set-ups, scheduling of work and purchase order generation. They are increased by the decision to produce small batches.
      (iii) *Product-sustaining activities.* Activities which must be carried out to enable the firm to still be in a position to supply a particular product, but which do not vary with actual output. They include product R&D and enhancement, staff training in making or selling the product and promotion expenditure. These costs increase if the number of product lines available rises.
      (iv) *Facility-sustaining activities.* These are costs which enable the facility to stay in existence and are not assigned to products. They include administration, insurance, heating, lighting and cleaning.
2. *Create a cost pool (or cost centre) for each activity.* Assign the costs of the business to the cost centres as appropriate. 'Accuracy' here is not as important as under conventional systems unless the data is to be used for stock valuation.
3. *Determine the cost driver for each major activity.* A cost driver is an activity that relates closely to the cost centre and the production of a good or service. Examples include:
   - purchase orders processed;
   - number of customer orders processed;
   - number of set-ups;
   - number of inspections.
   These will be customised to suit the particular firm.
4. *Assign the costs of activities to products according to the products demand for activities.* Calculate the costs of each product. This requires data on the costs drivers to be collected for each product which will increase the cost of the costing system.

This description seems to suggest that ABC is merely another form of cost allocation for absorption costing, with the only difference being that activities rather than direct labour time are used as the basis for allocating the costs. This was certainly how it was

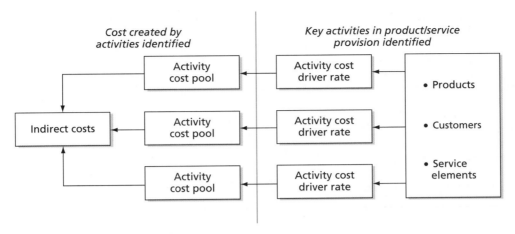

Figure 8.5 Activity-based management approach

used in practice and it led to widespread disillusionment with ABC. Its relaunch under the banner of ABM seeks to put this right. Instead of seeing the indirect costs as 'given by God', an appropriate use of ABC will help to identify the activities that cause them. For example indirect costs such as machine set-ups, ordering of inputs, quality inspections and staff training may be caused by characteristics of products such as run length or diversity of product range. This can provide insights into the causes of costs and the true profitability of product ranges.

Consider Figure 8.5. As you can see, this is ABC with the arrows reversed. The process is *cost attribution*; finding out the causes of indirect costs (ABC became cost assignment: allocating costs to products by absorption).

By recognising that particular products (or customers or provision of services) require special activities to be undertaken, the management accountant can track back the true cost of performing that activity, not only in terms of the direct costs it causes but also the indirect costs. Management can then assess whether it is really still profitable to perform it.

Example: Shoe maker

A UK-based shoe manufacturer employed a sales director who used to win orders from retail clients by promising them shoes with a 'twist', such as a special leather fob, extra lace holes or a different grade of leather. Direct costs were roughly unchanged by this. However, as the years went by and more 'twists' were promised, the amount of staff in production planning increased (along with their desks and company cars), additional management account-ants were employed to cope with the longer list of budget items each month, inventory rose to ensure that fobs, laces and leather were available (and a storeman was taken on too). Oddly enough, production volumes stayed the same but the profits of even standard lines of shoes fell as they were forced to absorb greater indirect costs.

ABM takes this ABC information and uses it to increase the economic performance of the business at two levels:

1. *Operational ABM* takes the demand for the firm's activities as given (e.g. the variety of products offered to cus-tomers; the features of the product or service; the number of markets served, etc.) and attempts to meet these demands with fewer organisational resources. This involves improving the efficiency of the key cost-driving activities. Techniques such as benchmarking, business process re-engineering and total quality manage-ment are all potentially helpful here, as are more traditional cost reduction exercises. Sometimes this involves making a simple distinction between two forms of activity:
    (a) *Value-added activities* are those which are perceived as useful by the customer purchasing the product.

(b) *Non-value-added activities* are opportunities for cost reduction without affecting the value to the customer. These might include:
- storage;
- inspections;
- moving of raw materials.

2. *Strategic ABM*: considers organisational effectiveness rather than efficiency by trying to change the demand for the organisation's resources. This may involve ceasing the supply of those products or customers revealed to be unprofitable by ABC and concentrating on the more profitable lines of business. The sorts of issues within strategic ABM are:
- product mix and pricing;
- customer relationships;
- supplier selection and relationships;
- product design and development.

8.7 Multidimensional performance measurement

8.7.1 The performance measurement manifesto

Eccles (1991) calls for a move away from reliance on financial data as the only indicators of business performance and the inclusion instead of non-financial measures to reinforce competitive strategies.

Eccles' argument can be summarised as follows:

(a) Managers have tracked non-financial measures such as quality, market share, etc., for many years but these measures have not been given their appropriate status in corporate information and bonus systems dominated by financial measures.

(b) Grafting additional non-financial measures on top of the financial reporting system achieves little because they often conflict and consequently the financial measures again take priority.

(c) Financial measures are *lagging indicators* of performance because they show the outcomes of past investment and strategic decisions and often discourage further strategic investments.

(d) Focusing on and rewarding achievement of financial measures alone causes managers to adopt short-termist behaviour to improve their financial performance (e.g. arbitrary cost cutting and under-investment) to the detriment of the long-run development of the firm.

(e) Modern competitive strategies based on quality and customer satisfaction, together with the development of benchmarking initiatives and the improvement in computer power to record and transmit multiple measures, has led to the potential for a revolution in performance measurement.

Eccles indicates five 'areas of activity' necessary for satisfactory performance measurement systems to be developed:

1. *Development of a new information architecture.* This must begin with identifying the data that management needs to pursue the company's strategy. This information must be reduced to *metrics* (i.e. performance measures).

   Capture of financial data is well established. However, the systems for data on innovation, customer service, quality or whatever are not. This is the second part of developing the information architecture and will be an evolutionary process as the firm experiments with alternative measures and becomes better at measuring these hitherto ignored aspects of its operations.

2. *Determining the necessary hardware, software and telecommunications technology.* Eccles suggests this be accomplished by a steering committee. Factors to consider here include the nature of the data and also to whom it will be made available.

3. *Align the information system with the company's incentives system.* The tradition of paying managers on the basis of financial performance (e.g. hitting budget targets) is well established. Eccles advocates a similar system for non-financial metrics but warns against mechanistic use of such formulae because they will need to change rapidly and must not be the subject of distortion by self-interested managers. Instead Eccles suggests linking rewards to performance but letting managers determine subordinates' rewards on the basis of the measures but also with regard to qualitative factors too.

4. *Draw on outside resources.* In developing the measures, outside bodies are important:
   - they may be able to help derive the measures or provide data; for example industry groups provide useful benchmarking information;
   - they may be the people who need to accept the measures; for example investors will need to be weaned off their reliance on financial measures alone and to respect and monitor some of the non-financial measures too.

   Gaining the support of these external bodies will help to ensure that the measures are taken seriously inside the firm too.

5. *Design a process to ensure that the other four activities occur.* This requires the firm to identify a person responsible for carrying out the process and appointing a group to carry the process through in their divisions and departments.

8.7.2 Suggested approach to developing a performance measurement system

The following methodology can be used to develop appropriate internal measures for the activities of the business or process:

1. *Identify the key ouputs required from the activity:*
   (a) This is often stated verbally in terms of what the various users and other stake-holders require.
   (b) It may be incorporated into a mission statement for the business unit or division.

2. *Identify the key processes in providing the outputs.* Effective control focuses on the inputs and processes as well as the eventual outputs. This will be accomplished by:
   (a) Discussions with management and staff involved in providing the service.
   (b) Observation and 'walkthrough' of the process.
   (c) Investigation into instances of service breakdown.
   (d) Examination of background to decisions and structures of authorisation.

3. *Identify the interfaces of the activity with other parts of the firm or with others in the value network.* These are the outside persons or other processes that the service provider relies on to do their work. This will include suppliers, customers and co-workers in other processes. The quality of this interface may have an impact on the service quality, for example:
   - how good is the relationship;
   - how timely are the information exchanges;
   - is the relationship managed and reviewed periodically.

4. *Develop performance indicators for the key processes.*
5. *Identify data sources for measures.* These will obviously vary enormously according to what is being measured. Many will not be readily quantifiable. The following may be useful to guide your thoughts:
    (a) Physical input/output, for example:
       - staff/customer ratios;
       - time to output measures;
       - space to staff/customer ratios;
       - chargeable time to slack time ratios.
    (b) Attitudinal, for example:
       - customer satisfaction surveys;
       - client retention, repeat business and client turnover rates;
       - staff turnover and attitude measures;
       - peer group ratings;
       - expert ratings;
       - market standing ratings.
    (c) Compliance. These measure whether the systems are being adhered to, for example:
       - achievement of key deadlines (delivery, keeping appointments, answering phones, processing orders);
       - attendance on necessary training courses;
       - accuracy of documentation and fullness of its completion;
       - data security;
       - review of process of decision-taking.
    (d) Competence, for example:
       - quality and training of staff in key positions;
       - appropriateness of capital equipment and information available;
       - abilities of management in controlling the service.
       These are likely to lead to subjective scoring by the assessor.
    (e) Comparators. Performance measures may be used:
        (i) through time to look for improvement or deterioration (time-series);
        (ii) across firms or divisions to look for best practice and poor practice (cross-sectional).
       Suitable comparators are important in both uses (e.g. through benchmarking).
6. *Develop reporting system.* This will depend on the management style and systems being used. A management that believed in empowerment of staff would wish to have this information targeted at the work teams and departments.
    Several issues will intrude in this stage:
    - the need to develop appropriate reporting media. Increasingly this will be electronic, such as enterprise information systems (EISs);
    - the need to instruct end-users in how to interpret the data.
7. *Review effectiveness of the control system.* Initial control systems will have faults. Therefore it would be prudent to:
    - pilot the system on a limited scale before a 'big bang' introduction;
    - record the improvements to key performance indicators through time;
    - review the adequacy of the system as the work of the firm changes.

8.7.3 Measures to ensure the organisation is innovating and developing

Although innovation can be crudely measured by the number of successful new products being launched, this does not really determine the degree of the organisational learning.

Innovation and improvement come from the individual and collective learning of staff. This leads to a need for measures of the processes and outputs of learning, often called *intellectual capital.*

One approach is that of Skandia, a Swedish Insurance Company. Management there see the market value of the business being dependent on both its physical and intellectual capital. They present this in the form of the tree diagram shown in Figure 8.6.

The three forms of intellectual capital – human, organisational and customer – are vital to increasing the value of the business above the book value of its physical assets, represented by financial capital.

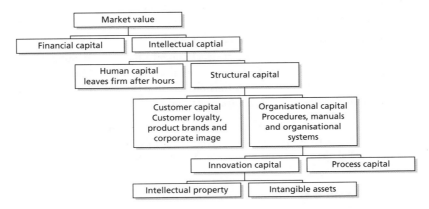

Figure 8.6   Skandia's scheme for valuing intangible assets (Source: Mouritsen (1988))

One approach suggested for valuing intellectual capital is to subtract the net assets of the business from its market value. This, even if accepted, is a summary measure and does not help management monitor the processes of developing the capital.

Mouritsen (1998) suggests a better approach to Skandia's scheme in Table 8.5.

8.7.4 The six-dimensional performance matrix

This is a model developed by Fitzgerald et al. (1991), initially to describe performance measures in service industries. It combines both financial and non-financial measures.

It identifies *six generic performance measures* which, the reports suggests, are used in varying degrees in the service industries studied (Table 8.6).

The model is sometimes termed the *results and determinants framework* because its authors recognised that two of the sets of measures, *financial performance* and *competitiveness*, were actually summary measures of the end results of business processes. These business processes were more effectively monitored by the remaining four measures.

The search covered a wide range of service industries and inevitably the measures discovered varied widely. However, Table 8.7 illustrates some of the measures found.

Table 8.5 A template for measuring intellectual capital

	Statistics	**Internal key ratios**	**Effect ratios**
Employees	Length of employment Formal education and training Expenses for education and training	Share of employees with a personal development plan Number of training days per employee Expenses for training and education per employee	Employee satisfaction Employee turnover ratio Human resource accounting Value added per employee
Customers	Distribution of revenues by markets and products Marketing expenses	Number of customers per employee Marketing expenses per £ of revenue Administration expenses per £ of marketing expense	Customer satisfaction Share of customers with long relationships
Technology	IT investments Share of internal to external IT customers	PCs per employee Computer expenses per employee	IT qualifications IT licence
Processes	Expenses per process Distribution of staff on processes Investments in R&D and infrastructure	Throughput time Product-development time Time to organisationally and administratively fit new Organisational units	Errors Waiting time Quality Company reputation

Reprinted from *Management Accounting Research*, Vol. 9, No. 4, 'Driving growth: economic value added versus intellectual capital', pp. 461–482, © 1998 by permission of the publisher Academic Press/Elsevier Science. This scheme provides process measures that link the assets of the business to the key critical success factors for its strategy.

Table 8.6 The six-dimensional performance matrix

	Dimensions of performance	**Types of measures**
Results	Competitiveness	Relative market share and position Sales growth Measures of the customer base
	Financial performance	Profitability Liquidity Capital structure Market ratios
Determinants	Quality of service	Reliability Responsiveness Aesthetics/appearance Cleanliness/tidiness Comfort Friendliness Communication Courtesy Competence Access Availability Security
	Flexibility	Volume flexibility Delivery speed flexibility Specification flexibility

Table 8.6 (Continued)

Dimensions of performance	Types of measures
Resource utilisation	Productivity Efficiency
Innovation	Performance of the innovation process Performance of individual innovations

Table 8.7 Examples of generic measures

Generic measure	Type	Measure
Financial	Profitability	Profit Value of work-in-progress Return on net assets
	Liquidity	Debtor days Creditor days Total working capital
	Capital structure	Debt/equity Long-term to short-term debt
	Market ratios	Price/earnings Return on capital employed
Competitiveness	Customer-focused	Repeat business Number of customers
	Competitor-focused	Relative market share Competitors' prices and product ranges
Service quality	Access	Walking distance Ease of finding way about
	Appearance	Appearance of staff Appearance and taste of foods Look of buildings
	Availability	Product availability Range of products Equipment availability
	Cleanliness/tidiness	Of staff Of premises Of goods
	Comfort	Congestion Seating comfort Atmosphere Ambience
	Communication	Intelligibility of information Clarity of signposting Clarity of staff – customer interaction
	Competence	Staff skill Expertise Knowledge Thoroughness
	Courtesy	Politeness Respect Propriety of staff towards customers

Table 8.7 (Continued)

Generic measure	Type	Measure
	Friendliness	Helpfulness of staff Attentiveness
	Reliability	Product reliability Punctuality Dependability of service and staff
	Responsiveness	Delivery speed Response times Number of phone lines Average time of phone call
	Security	Physical security Product safety Personal security
Flexibility	Volume	Number of orders/customers lost due to failure to meet demand Percentage of service availability Mix of staff availability (e.g. full v. part time) Amount of slack in schedule for rush jobs
	Delivery speed	Customer waiting time Frequency of service Orders lost due to late delivery Customer/enquiry/job throughput time
	Specification	Number of different products/services delivered Skill mix of staff Level of investment in staff training and recruitment Customer order lost due to failure to accommodate specification Customer satisfaction with range and flexibility
Resource utilisation	Human resources	Labour hours Percentage of slack or transit time Skill level of work performed by grade of staff
	Premises	Percentage of area used to serve customers Occupancy loading
	Direct inputs	Input/output ratios Cost per unit
Innovation	Cost	Average development cost per service Development cost of individual service Percentage of turnover spent developing new services/products/processes
	Effectiveness	How many new services developed per annum Five new services that are successful
	Speed	Concept to service launch time Concept to prototype launch time Prototype to launch time Time to adopt new concept from outside the firm

8.7.5 The balanced scorecard (BSC)

This technique was developed by Kaplan and Norton (1992, 1996) for combining financial control measures with non-financial control measures (Figure 8.7).

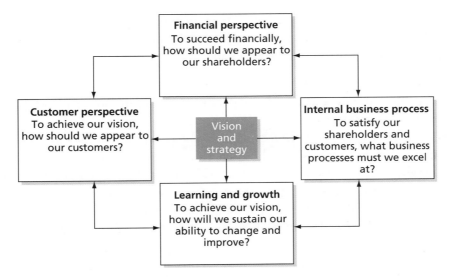

Figure 8.7 The balanced scorecard (adapted from Kaplan and Norton, 1996)

They present BSC as a technique for implementing the mission and objectives of the business strategy in a way that will bring action and enable effective monitoring and control:

> The Balanced Scorecard translates mission and strategy into objectives and measures into four different perspectives [and] provides a framework, a language, to communicate mission and strategy; it uses measurement to inform employees about the drivers of current and future success. By articulating the outcomes the organisation desires and the drivers of those outcomes, senior executives hope to channel the energies, the abilities, and the specific knowledge of people throughout the organisation toward achieving long-term goals. [It] should be used as a communication, informing, and learning system, *not* as a controlling system.

(Kaplan and Norton, 1996, p. 25)

Neely (1998) outlines the scorecard shown in Figure 8.8 for a pet food manufacturer.

Figure 8.8 An example of a balanced scorecard (From measuring Business Performance, 1998, Weekly. Reprinted by permission of Profile Books Ltd.)

Many of the critics of Kaplan and Norton's work tend to presume that the BSC is supposed to replace all other performance measurement systems in the business. This is not the view of Kaplan and Norton, who state explicitly:

1. *The four perspectives are a template, not a straitjacket.* They recognise that many firms may wish to incorporate additional perspectives such as an employee perspective or an environmental perspective.

2. *The BSC is not the only performance measurement system a firm may use.* They are keen to emphasise that subsystems may be used to measure costs or environmental impact without having them integrated into the BSC. The BSC should be reserved for the measures critical to communicating the firm's strategy in order to correct the short-termist tendencies of the existing operational measures being used.

3. *The BSC may be developed at strategic business unit (SBU) level or at corporate level.* In some divisionalised organisations the BSC may be specific to the division and there may be no need to integrate it into a corporate scorecard. Other corporations take a top-down approach by developing a corporate scorecard and then requiring SBUs to fall in line and develop a divisional BSC that will integrate with it. Presumably this decision will depend on the degree of relatedness between the divisions of the corporation.

4. *Financial measures remain important despite the BSC.* Improvements in the measures of customer, business processes and organisational learning perspectives will not immediately translate into financial improvements. Investors will still require good short-term financial results too and therefore management should continue to receive and monitor these.

5. *The BSC can support both market-based and competence-based approaches to strategy.* Although the use of a customer perspective reflects the authors' own market-based approach to strategy, they claim that it can be adapted to support strategies based on the acquisition and development of core competences. It is a strategy implementation device, not a strategy formulation device.

6. *The measures in the BSC are mutually consistent and reinforcing.* The authors are keen to present the BSC as more than a collection of disparate financial and non-financial indicators. Instead it monitors a set of cause-and-effect relationships that lead to better financial returns. This is accomplished by ensuring that a *vertical vector* runs through the four BSC perspectives, as demonstrated in Figure 8.9.

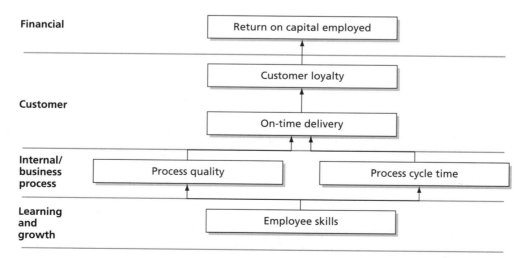

Figure 8.9 Vertical vector relationship between balanced scorecard measures (Source: Adapted from Kaplan and Norton (1996), p. 31)

Early 1990s   Mid 1990s   2000

BSC as measuring device to report on non-financial business processes and actions of managers

BSC development helps middle and line managers better understand how their processes contribute to corporate goals

BSC is a method of driving strategic change by translating strategic vision in targets for middle managers

Figure 8.10   Development of thinking about BSC

Figure 8.11   The strategy focused organisation (Adapted from: Kaplan and Norton (2001))

Kaplan and Norton (2001) recognise that their understanding of the value of the BSC has developed as it has gone along since 1990 and as firms have found additional roles for it. Roughly this has been in three phases (Figure 8.10).

Currently the authors present BSC in the way shown in Figure 8.11.

Kaplan and Norton envisage the BSC being used to improve strategic performance in several ways:

(a) The process of developing activity measures will make individuals and divisions more aware of how their work fits in with the strategy of the business.

(b) Individuals and divisions should receive regular reports of their performance against the BSC measures relevant to their area of work. This will help them moderate their own performance.

(c) Senior management should receive regular information on the organisation's overall accomplishments against BSC measures to ensure that strategy is being followed.

(d) Outside stakeholders may also have access to BSC measures to help them form a more full impression of the organisation's value. For example, there may be a special version for investors or for customers.

The large volume of data-gathering manipulation and reporting caused by the BSC inevitably means that it must be 'mechanised', that is, put into a computerised form. For this reason, Kaplan and others have developed proprietary database packages for creating balanced scorecards. The manner of information display is usually graphical, involving readily understandable graphics such as dials, pie charts and graphs. This is sometimes referred to as a *tableau de bord* (literally 'dashboard') to reflect its similarity to the information read-outs available to the pilot of an aeroplane.

The steps in the process of developing a BSC are:

1. Identify the key outcomes critical to the success of the organisation.
2. Identify the processes that lead to these outcomes.
3. Develop key performance indicators for these processes (these are sometimes termed *metrics*).
4. Develop reliable data capture and measurement systems.
5. Develop a mechanism for reporting these to the relevant managers and staff.
6. Enact improvement programmes to ensure that performance improves.

8.7.6 What does a BSC look like?

Despite the apparent role of IT in creating and supporting a BSC, many firms without such technology claim to have a BSC. This suggests that the term is often used to describe situations of multiple performance measures or greater or lesser degrees of integration, for example:

- an organisation has notice-boards on the wall that record financial measures but also staff attendance, customer satisfaction, productivity;
- staff are reviewed periodically against both financial and non-financial targets.

It is hard to resist the conclusion that many BSCs are simply legacy performance measurement systems with a flashy new name and an academic background to justify them.

The key to a true BSC seems to lie in the extent to which measure are:

- integrated and congruent with corporate goals;
- monitored and reported systematically;
- accorded proper attention by management and staff.

Increasingly balanced scorecards are being used in areas other than commercial organisations. For instance, they have started to be used in Health Services where medical professionals have seen them as a possibility to replace the financial responsibility accounting system with their view of activities. They wanted to use scorecards as a structure for dialogue and communication. The concept 'balanced' was regarded as a balance between four perspectives, implying that patients, employees and processes were as important as finances. The resulting balanced scorecards, designed by professionals, were considered effective control mechanisms in their health care organisation reducing the goal incongruence between parties and reducing the ambiguities of performance evaluation.

8.7.7 Benefits and drawbacks of BSC

The main benefits are:

(a) Avoids management reliance on short-termist or incomplete financially-based measures.
(b) Can assist in 'driving down' the corporate strategy to divisions and functions:
    - by forcing them to develop success measures for their function related to corporate goals;
    - by providing them with control information to modify their behaviour.
(c) Can assist stakeholders in evaluating the firm if measures are communicated externally.

Drawbacks of BSC:

(a) Does not lead to a single aggregate summary control. The popularity of measures such as ROI has been because they conveniently summarise 'how things are going'.

(b) No clear relation between the BSC and shareholder value. This point is discussed in more detail below.

(c) Measures may give conflicting signals and confuse management. For example, if customer satisfaction is falling together with the financial indicators, do management sacrifice one or the other?

(d) Involves substantial shifts in corporate culture to implement:

   (i) the need to shift to understanding the business as a set of processes rather than departments;

   (ii) need for a system of identifying value-adding as well as cost-adding activities;

   (iii) potential subjugation of short-term financial measures to longer-term strategic measures;

   (iv) a change to the role of performance measures from a command and control approach based on responsibility to an information provision approach.

8.7.8 Summary of issues in using the BSC

1. *Problems in gaining management commitment to the BSC*:
   (a) Kaplan has suggested that managers prefer to retain solely financial measures *because they are so inaccurate* that they can hide behind them.
   (b) BSC measures do not appear to link to year-end profit and hence are resisted as 'not relevant' and too expensive to implement.

2. *Deciding who should develop the measures*:
   (a) Needs to be done by someone with an understanding of the business processes concerned rather than by, say, a management accountant on their own.
   (b) Performance measurements may be unreliable if developed by the functional division (e.g. marketing, human resource management, etc.) due to their lack of experience in developing performance measures or the temptation for them to measure the things they know they do well rather than the things that link to competitive performance.
   (c) Internal departments (e.g. management accounting) will be suspected of 'checking up' on the division rather than acting as a consultant and resisted. Consequently many firms prefer to use consultants to develop the measures for them which will be costly and may suffer from the consultant's lack of knowledge of the business and its processes.

3. *Avoiding measuring just the things that can easily be measured*. Often this is the consequence of a lack of understanding of which business processes actually add value in the present operations. BSC measures for future performance need to be developed within a strategic plan or vision to make sense of what the organisation is trying to achieve from the strategy and what steps or milestones must be undertaken and reached on the road to this strategy.

4. *Problem of ensuring measures are congruent*. Although Kaplan and Norton assert that the measures will be congruent there are a number of problems in accepting this. For example, in Figure 8.9 they show a number of customer and process variables leading to return on capital employed. However, elsewhere they comment that these sorts of process measures often do not lead to immediate profit improvement. If management cannot know in advance the processes that actually enhance profit in the long term,

how can this congruence be assured? Piercy (1997) provides a useful example of just how hard this can be:

British Airways did a massive amount of expensive and sophisticated hard-nosed market research into the requirements of the short-haul air traveller, and what influenced airline choice. This led to the BA strategy of courtesy and sympathy and 'putting people first', with some considerable success. Even then they made a mistake with the critical business traveller market – they *believed* that the business traveller was mainly influenced by factors of timely arrival, availability of phones and faxes and other 'rational' factors. The glamorous and sophisticated British Airways lost substantial market share to a small airline called British Midland because of the 'sausage factor'. The 'rational' business traveller wanted a free breakfast sausage and would change airlines to get it. (pp. 47–48)

The point of this excerpt is to demonstrate that it is very hard to be certain that the things we are measuring (phones and faxes, say) are actually related to long-term profits.

Failure to have congruent measures will present management with conflicting measures of performance and the inevitable compromises of trading one off against another.

8.7.9 The performance pyramid

Developed by McNair et al. (1990), this model draws attention to the principle that performance measures should be appropriate for the interests and levels of management who receive them (Figure 8.12). Financial and economic measures are likely to be of importance chiefly to the heads of business divisions and the main board. Lower levels in the management will be controlling processes and hence will need non-financial measures such as quantities and times.

The work of Fitzgerald et al. (1991) and Kaplan and Norton (1996) can be seen as methodologies for linking non-financial measures to strategic and financial measures with the intention of ensuring that the strategy is properly implemented.

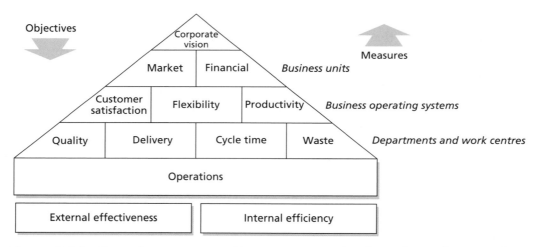

Figure 8.12 The performance pyramid (From 'Do Financial and Non-financial measures have to agree?' by McNair, Lynch and Cross, Management Accounting US, November 1990. Reprinted by permission of IMA, Montvale, NJ.) www.imanet.org

8.7.10 Control systems and the product life cycle

Ward (1992) suggests that the control systems and measures used should vary according to the stage of the product life cycle that the business or division has reached. These are shown in Figure 8.13.

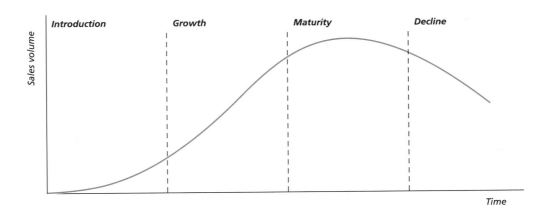

Stage	Introduction	Growth	Maturity	Decline
Characteristics of stage	High business risk Negative cash flows	High risk Neutral cash flow	Medium risk Positive cash flow	Low risk Neutral cash flow (at best)
Information needs	Information on dynamic and changing environment Potential market size and buyer value	Market growth Market share Effectiveness of marketing effort Competitor information and effectiveness of their marketing	Competitors' costs Identify limiting factor	Rate of decline When to exit Realisable asset values
Critical success factors	Time to develop and launch	Growth in share Sustainable competitive advantage	Contribution per unit of limiting factor Customer retention rates	None
Financial control measures	Evaluate using DCF of life-cycle cash flows Control using physical measures and update DCF analysis	DCF evaluation of marketing expenditures Specific marketing objectives Market share	ROI Profit margin Operating cash flow Holding of market share	Free cash flow compared with opportunity costs of assets used

Figure 8.13   Performance measures for stages of the product life cycle (adapted from Ward, 1992)

Ward introduces several issues into our discussion of financial control within a strategic context:

1. *Financial control does not always involve financial measures.* Financial control effectively means ensuring that the funds being put into a product or division will produce a satisfactory return. The *lead indicators* of commercial success (i.e. the ones that tell us how the future is likely to unfold) are often non-financial. Consider the following measures:
   - target customers recall the advertisement and view the product favourably;
   - high initial trial of the product;
   - high percentage of first-time customers return to buy more later;
   - high percentage of retail outlets have agreed to stock the product;
   - competitor's rival product proved unpopular with customers. These give us reason to believe that current and future investment in the product is likely to produce a satisfactory return.

2. *Financial measures can sometimes give the wrong recommendations.* Contrast the profitability of the products in the early stages of their life cycle with those in the later stages. Early life cycle products have negative cash flows and hence low or negative profit. Divisions with such products would exhibit low profitability. Conventional financial logic would be to abandon the products and/or shut the division. This ignores the future earnings potential of the product. To avoid this, Ward recommends that products be evaluated using life cycle earnings rather than current earnings if the product is early in its life cycle.

3. *External measures are also important.* Many of Ward's measures concern actors outside the firm itself. Notably these are customers and competitors. This recalls our earlier discussion about competitor accounting and the fact that competitors, their costs and prices, can be a major influence on the financial returns to a business.

4. *Financial measures are a more important managerial control in late life cycle markets.* Ward distinguishes between *financial evaluation* and *managerial control*. Financial evaluation involves deciding whether to commit funds to a project or whether to invest further. Ward advocates the use of DCF techniques by management to maintain financial control over such investments.

Managerial control on the other hand involves setting measures and targets for managers to reach, such as a given profit or return on assets. In early life cycle markets the estimates used to justify investment in new products or technologies are subject to high uncertainty and therefore wide margins of error. This makes them unsuitable for use as a managerial control measure because so many factors outside of the manager's control can impact on whether the target is reached.

Penalising a manager for poor financial returns or sales during the growth stage following a completely unanticipated entry into the market by a rival is neither equitable nor motivating. Furthermore, it is not actually control because the reason for the poor results is bad forecasting or competitive strategy. Merely sacking the hapless manager does not bring it under control.

8.8 Stakeholder measures

8.8.1 Background

In Chapter 1 we discussed the increased importance of stakeholder groups beyond the traditional dominance of shareholders. Several points may be recalled:

(a) Stakeholders have the ability to assist or disrupt a firm's strategies. This makes it necessary to consider their interests and to keep them informed.
(b) Many firms seek to incorporate stakeholders into their strategies through the use of mission statements.
(c) Meeting the needs of stakeholders may be essential to maintaining the legitimacy and sustainability of the business.
(d) The importance of stakeholder groups varies from business to business and can be revealed by techniques such as stakeholder mapping.

Crockatt (1992) has suggested that firms should develop performance measurement systems for planning and monitoring, in order to ensure that the needs of these stakeholders are met. Some examples are shown in Table 8.8. Let us consider these and others a little further.

8.8.2 Measuring customer attitudes

In competitive markets the customers' satisfaction will impact directly on market share, prices and therefore financial returns. There are two complementary ways of approaching the development of customer measures:

(a) Identify the key processes that determine the quality of the products and services the customer receives. This is a *process measure*.

Table 8.8 Sample stakeholder expectations and related measures

Stakeholder	Expectation	Measure
Employees	Good working conditions	Morale index
Shareholders	Improved shareholder value	Stock price and dividends
		Return on equity minus cost of equity
Government	Conformance to environmental regulations	Percentage of products in conformance
Customers	Product quality throughout product life	Warranty cost
	Dealer support	Number of profitable dealers

Reprinted from 'Revitalising Executive Information Systems' by F. Crockatt, *Sloan Management Review*, Summer 1992, by permission. © 1992 Tribune Media Services, Inc. All rights reserved. Reprinted with permission.

(b) Assess customers' actual feelings about the firm and its service. This is sometimes termed the *customer perspective* and measures *outputs*.

Figure 8.14 shows the customer satisfaction drivers of BT, a global telecommunications company. The performance measurement system would combine both process and customer perception measures. For example, the performance of the business processes of account management, repair, etc., could be monitored by weekly reports from operatives, inventory levels, etc., and be aggregated to provide an aggregate quality of service indicator. Benchmarking could also be used. Image and price perception might be subject to some internal measures such as actual price comparisons with rival operators and measures of advertising reach. However, external measures of customer perception is likely to be more important. Customer loyalty would be measured both as a customer perspective ('how likely are you to switch') and internally (number of customers who do switch – the 'churn rate').

Developing suitable customer measures can involve the following activities:

(a) *Walkthroughs*. Management reconstruct the progress of the typical customer through the firm and identify the key incidents in the client relationship for which targets should be set and performance monitored and improved. Neely (1998) suggests the following for a fast-food restaurant. On customer arrival:

- queuing;
- greeting;
- ordering;

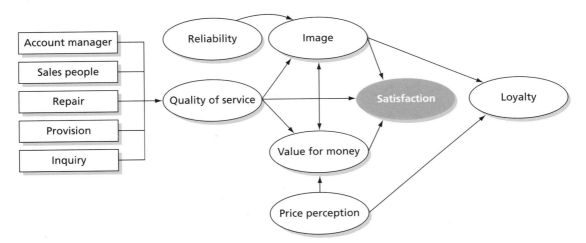

Figure 8.14 The drivers of customer satisfaction at BT (Source: From Measuring Business Performance, A Neely, Books, 1998. Reprinted by permission of Profile Books Ltd.)

- receiving food;
- finding a seat;
- consuming the food;
- disposal of the waste;
- leaving the restaurant.

Similar approaches have been used by car dealers, airlines, hotels and bank branches.

(b) *Customer reflection.* Customers can be asked to reflect on the stages in a recent purchase and the critical factors that influenced them.

(c) *Observation.* An actual customer can be tracked through a purchase. In some cases *mystery shoppers* can be used, where members of management or professional researchers pose as customers.

Naturally management will conduct a similar analysis on the service of industry rivals.

Once management have noted the critical performance issues in the customer relationship, they will seek to 'go behind them' to identify and monitor the business processes that give rise to them. This aspect of *internal business process measurement* will be discussed later.

8.8.3 Supplier relationship monitoring

The partnership with suppliers can be monitored at two levels:

(a) *The operational level*: This will focus on the supplier's conduct under the terms of the contract.

(b) *The attitudinal level*: This examines the degree of collaboration and trust that has been built up between the firm and its supplier. Clearly this has implications for the potential for collaboration.

Rover, a UK car manufacturer, provided a template to its suppliers (Table 8.9) and made it clear that they would be monitored and their contracts renewed on the basis of it. These are sometimes called *vendor ratings*.

Table 8.9 Rover Group supplier performance report: example calculation

Quality performance	A Actual Perf,	B Score awarded	C Demerit applied	D Weighting	E Weighting factor	F Actual score	G Max. score	H Demerits
Delivered quality (PPM)	1,068	1	n/a	Critical	×3	3	9	n/a
Delivered quality (incidents)	84	0	n/a	Significant	×1	0	3	n/a
Warranty category (1/PPM)	4	3	n/a	Critical	×3	9	9	n/a
Critical action	A	n/a	0%	n/a	n/a	n/a	n/a	0%
Problem resolution (quality)	C	n/a	25%	n/a	n/a	n/a	n/a	25%
Management systems certification	ISO 9001	2	n/a	Significant	×1	2	3	n/a
Subtotals						14	24	25%

Calculation quality rating = ((weighted score/maximum score) × 100%) − All demerits
= ((14/24) × 100) − 25
= [58.3] − [25]
= 33%

From *Measuring Business Performance*, A. Neely, 1998. Reprinted by permission of Profile Books Ltd.

Neely (1998) observes that the measures used to track supplier performance will change according to the degree of dependence on the supplier (Figure 8.15).

The Rover scorecard in Table 8.9 is designed to assess leveraged goods (i.e. goods which are specially made for Rover such that it is dependent on the supplier in the short run).

Category of good being supplied		Appropriate performance measure
Product/process critical		Quality of relationship (how good a customer are we?)
Leveraged goods	Increasing dependence	Supplier assessment: quality, dependability, speed and flexibility
Commodity goods		Total acquisition cost

Figure 8.15 Impact of dependence on supplier performance. From measuring Business Performance, A. Neely, 1998. Reprinted by permission of Profile Books Ltd.

Monitoring quality of relationship will be an *attitudinal measure*, that is it will depend largely on the psychological state of the parties more than on objective factors.

8.9 Additional control mechanisms

8.9.1 Criticisms of conventional budgeting

In Chapter 7 we reviewed the work of Hope and Hope (1997), which called for the creation of new methods of management accounting to help organisations to compete in the 'third wave'. Tony Hope has subsequently worked with Robin Fraser to suggest some alternatives to conventional budgetary control. This work has made use of the insights of the *beyond budgeting round table* (BBRT) (Hope and Fraser, 1998).

The basic argument is that conventional budgeting is at odds with modern management approaches:

- conventional budgeting remains based on the 'second wave' of industry where physical resource use was vital for competitive success and organisations were largely 'M-form', that is, multidivisional with no real attempts to get divisions to work together;
- it therefore fails to support competitive strategy in the 'third wave' based on innovation, service, quality, speed and knowledge-sharing;
- it tends to undervalue or ignore the 'intellectual capital' vital for these competitive advantages and constituting between 60 per cent and 96 per cent of the firm's market value;
- the 'second wave' approach to budgeting emphasises the top-down 'command and control' patterns of 'M-form' organisations – this conflicts with the philosophy of team working and collaboration behind today's N-form (network form) organisations;
- it endangers development of trust between managers, workers, partners and customers because it forces management to 'operate by the numbers' in times of difficulty which usually causes arbitrary cost reductions and declining morale;
- it reduces the value of *process-based* management approaches (such as total quality management, business process re-engineering, balanced scorecard and just-in-time) because it is rooted in responsibility centres which are constructed on functional lines;
- it maintains top-down control where modern competitive strategy requires empowerment of the front-line management.

The alternative approach suggests that SBU managers are asked for stretch targets but, instead of the usual conflict between ambitious stretch targets and monthly variance reports a sympathetic hearing is given when those targets are not meet. There is no micro management of tight financial targets but a broader basket of both strategic and financial targets is cascaded down the organisation underpinned by clear action plans that build ownership and commitment at every level. Monthly reports will consist of a balanced scorecard of graphs and trends covering the usual broader category of information. Comparisons are made to previous periods and, whenever possible, to competitors. A quarterly analysis and forecast will be aggregated for strategic and treasury purposes but is not part of the measurement of the SBU manager. The approach is particularly relevant to those organisations operating in a dynamic and competitive business environment – but must involve the coordination of the whole organisation. In that way any unexpected performance characteristics can be capitalised upon or remedied by revision of the action plans – this is made possible by the transparency of the measurement process. Not surprisingly many companies have found it difficult to implement this type of model – the traditional approach is safer and involves less trust and openness. Successful implementation of the new model can take years rather than months and needs constant reinforcement, particularly of core values. Such words as openness, trust, integrity, cooperation, loyalty and ownership define its values. Although these words often appear in mission statements they are much rarer in practice. It is very difficult for managers who are used to negotiating and achieving their 'safe' numbers, but who are poor at 'walking the talk' of the firm's core values, to accept or even support the implementation of such an approach. This is particularly true when they find themselves loosing out as the company changes its performance appraisal system to place the emphasis on values over numbers.

In today's world, SBU managers need to make fast decisions to counter competitive threats and take new opportunities as they arise. There is no time for approval procedures and management meetings. They need the self-confidence to act and the right tools and information to improve their chances of success. None of this is new, but so many companies attempt to implement this type of business model without appreciating the hidden barriers that lie in wait within the budgeting, performance measurement and reward systems.

There are five common threads to the approach;

1. Eradicate incremental thinking. Train managers to expect goals that demand 'stretch'. Encourage them to aim for them knowing that getting most of the way will bring a far better result, for them and the company, than the old incremental approach (i.e. 'x% better than last year'). Most importantly ensure that they know that senior managers will not punish them for failing to reach the full target. The performance review system will take into account all the circumstances as they occurred through the year.
2. Constantly improve shareholder value by encouraging managers to act like owners. Managers in the new model know that better trained and satisfied employees lead to more satisfied and loyal customers that lead to sustainable increases in free cash flows and thus happier shareholders. A scorecard that balances these perspectives will help them make the right improvement decisions and improve their own managerial capabilities.
3. Demanding targets drive radical improvements. Stretching targets (typically contained within the balanced scorecard) will drive radical thinking. This must result in real action plans that spell out the changes to processes, and the timescales and responsibilities for implementing them. Only when managers set their own targets and plan the changes needed to achieve them will real ownership and commitment be built. Moreover, only by tracking the results of these action plans does real feedback and learning take place.

Contrast this with numerical variances that tell managers nothing about what to do differently in the future.

4. Performance targets should be relative to other SBUs and external factors. Real success does not come through beating a rigid set of numbers that were set six or nine months previously and that are now irrelevant. It comes from beating one's contemporaries in other parts of the business and beating the external competition. Performance-based league tables (constantly available on-line) are a continuous spur to better performance. But it is essential that managers know not only what their contemporaries have achieved but how they have achieved it.

5. A major part of the performance bonus should be based on company-wide results. Setting and achieving stretch targets is tough in any business – managers need all the support they can get and this is more likely to be forthcoming if all managers share in a bonus pool that is based on share price or performance against a basket of competitors, and is long-term. Thus resource and knowledge sharing is encouraged rather than protected within 'islands of knowledge' – a common feature of the old model.

8.9.2 Alternative structures and mechanisms

Figure 8.16 shows that the modern 'knowledge-based' organisation will depend on teamwork between staff within the SBUs and also considerable communication between SBUs in networks. The job of senior executives is to motivate the SBU managers by setting *stretch targets* (i.e. strategic targets) and middle managers work between the divisions to integrate activities of the SBUs.

Hope and Fraser cite the examples of several firms who have adopted this model and consequently have abandoned or modified budgeting. These include Ikea, Volvo, 3M and Shell.

According to the BBRT findings, these firms use three 'alternative steering' mechanisms instead:

1. *Rolling quarterly plans to allow cash forecasting.* Unlike conventional budgets which are detailed, these plans bring responsibility with them and tend to be 'fixed in stone'. They are prepared quickly and will be updated as necessary.

2. *Calculation of strategic milestone targets for measurement and control.* Month-to-month variances are abandoned in favour of aggressive strategic targets (*stretch targets*) and relative

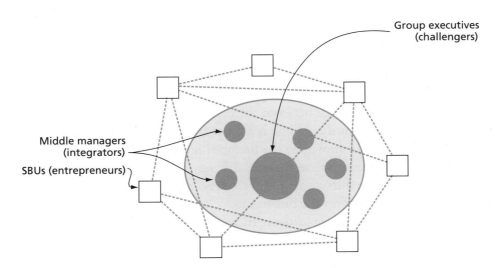

Figure 8.16 The modern N-form organization

performance measures (divisional and external comparisons). These often involve the use of a BSC.

3. *Cost management through a culture of thrift.* Staff are urged to consider value-adding and value-preserving activities, backed up by an organisation-wide rewards system. This is often backed up by activity-based management and benchmarking exercises.

   This cost management is exercised by work-based teams who meet periodically, rather like quality circles, to consider ways to improve service and to reduce costs.

8.9.3 Relationship with performance measurement

These BBRT approaches are significant for two reasons:

(a) They draw our attention to the importance of non-numerical control systems. The role of social groups, proper management and appropriate incentive systems is emphasised. It would not be appropriate to dump the mechanistic systems of departmental accounting and standard costing merely to replace them with an equally mechanistic BSC, performance pyramid or result/determinants matrix.

(b) There remains, however, a continuing need for the information provided by numerical performance measures. However, the context of these measures has changed from one of top-down control to one of facilitation and information.

8.10 Multinational industries

8.10.1 Issues in control of multinational operations

In Chapter 6 we discussed multinational development as a potential growth strategy for the firm. A multinational enterprise (MNE) has been defined as 'an enterprise that engages in foreign direct investment (FDI) and owns and controls value-adding activities in more than one country' (Dunning, 1993, p. 3).

Control in multinational companies is more complicated than other situations of multidivisional control due to the following factors:

(a) *Differing economic conditions of the different countries.* These differences can include the use of different currencies and exchange rate regimes, reduced reliance on the market mechanism, experience of different growth rates and stages in the business cycle, inflation, and different taxation regimes.

   These make performance evaluation extremely difficult. For example, evaluation of a subsidiary means being able to compare it with a similar subsidiary elsewhere. The lack of a clear rate of exchange between the currencies due to non-convertibility of one or more of them is one hurdle. If one is a growth economy and one is mature then, as the product life cycle has shown us, the financial returns will be very different.

(b) *Differing legal frameworks.* These include differences in employment law, regulations limiting overseas ownership and product safety, and minimum specifications. They will impose different costs on the businesses.

(c) *Different culture and trading conditions.* Factors to consider here include differences in the extent of authority of management, customs in trade, cultural symbolism and the impact of promotional campaigns, levels of literacy and numeracy, and expectations of quality and social responsibility.

Control by the corporate centres will require that the divisions comply with these host-economy differences. Obviously, the day-to-day compliance will be the responsibility of management in the host country. However, the corporate centre may wish to ensure compliance by receiving regular reports or performance indicators. Furthermore, the different local practices will have an impact on efficiency and financial performance.

8.10.2 Transfer pricing in multinationals

One of the important aspects of management accounting in multinational firm's is that of transfer pricing and you should revise the material you studied elsewhere for this topic. Transfer prices may be set with the following objectives in mind:

- *Minimisation of import duties.* If import duties are levied on the price of the import (rather than, say, on its volume-specific composition), then a low transfer price will reduce the import duties of the group as a whole if its goods enter a high-import-duty economy.
- *Management of direct taxation.* By being aware of the respective governments legislation concerning domestic tax neutrality, withholding taxes the firm may plan effectively to minimise their global tax charge.
- *Management of indirect taxation.* Most countries have indirect tax regimes involving a value-added tax. This requires that the firm effectively pays the tax on its purchases (input tax) and then recoups the taxes in the price of its sales (output tax). In competitive markets it may be hard to pass on the indirect tax to the price of the good and so its input tax will not be wholly recovered. To avoid this, it may transfer some goods to itself at very low prices which can then be sold on at high prices to recover the indirect tax paid on other lines of product.
- *Repatriation of profits in kind.* Where a country operates currency controls it may be difficult (or of low worth) for the MNE to repatriate profits in local currency, yet it is unable to exchange its local currency profits for a world currency. In this situation, the firm seeks to export product (either manufactured by itself or purchased with the local currency) at a low price for sale at home to gain the revenue in its home currency. This can likewise avoid local restrictions on the amount of dividend that can be declared or repatriated.
- *To win host-country approval.* To avoid accusations of overcharging locals for product or of exporting unfair amounts of value from the country, the MNE may set a transfer price that seems fair to the authorities.
- *To disguise profitability of a subsidiary.* The MNE may deliberately declare low profits in an operating country to prevent local businesses setting up in competition.
- *To enable penetration pricing.* The MNE may allow an operating subsidiary to receive inputs at low prices in order that these may be passed on in the local market as low final good prices. This will help the MNE to destroy local competitors without the subsidiary's low profits provoking the authorities to accuse it of tax avoidance.

8.10.3 Research evidence on multinational transfer prices

Research funded by CIMA involved questioning 51 UK and non-UK MNEs in a diverse range of businesses about their use of transfer prices (Elliott, 1998).

1. *The objectives of transfer pricing policies.* Elliott asked respondents to identify the three most important considerations affecting their transfer pricing decisions. The following emerged:
   - maximisation of global profit (31 per cent of the population cited this);
   - simplicity and ease of use (29 per cent);
   - aggressiveness of taxation authority (25 per cent);
   - market penetration (25 per cent);
   - stability of transfer price over time (25 per cent).
2. *Methods of establishing transfer prices.* Among UK-based groups, cost-plus was preferred by 39 per cent and CUP (comparable uncontrolled price) by 35 per cent. Among non-UK groups, cost-plus (32 per cent) and resale-minus (28 per cent) were the most popular.

8.10.4 Implications for strategic management of MNEs

There are several implications:

1. *Loss of controllability principle if country divisions are subject to central transfer prices and charges.* The controllability principle holds that managerial performance should be evaluated only against metrics that the manager can influence. If this metric is influenced by factors beyond the manager's control, several consequences follow:
   - the manager may become demotivated which will cause a decline in divisional performance;
   - managers may spend time trying to 'work the numbers' rather than running the business;
   - control is lost because the performance measures do not track all the organisational processes (say cost- and revenue-generating activities) but only those within the control of the manager. For example, overhead-creating activities, the costs of which are simply imposed on the manager, are not controlled by anyone.

   Arbitrary setting of transfer prices and charges, whether by the MNE to avoid tax or by governments to retrieve tax, put the revenues and costs of the division beyond the control of the MNE's management.
2. *Reduced ability to respond competitively to local market challenges.* The research by Elliott demonstrates that transfer prices are sometimes used to allow market penetration. This can arise in two ways:
   - the transfer price of supplies from an operating country are set at a level similar to the penetration price charged for external sales in the operating country;
   - the transfer prices of supplies to the operating country are set at a low level to enable the division to return a profit on a penetration price in that country.

   Clearly the threat that these prices may at a later date be deemed unfair or not arm's-length will restrict the ability of the firm to charge such penetration prices.
3. *Reduced profitability compared to other MNEs.* Several MNEs have complained that by not being able to manage their tax affairs favourably they are forced to charge higher prices, or forgo investments and put themselves at a disadvantage compared to other competitor MNEs whose governments allow their home MNEs more latitude.
4. *Transfer prices can affect organisational structure and ownership.* In Chapter 7 we discussed the work of Williamson, and in particular his statement that economic exchanges can be co-ordinated by either markets or hierarchies. The MNE is essentially a hierarchy solution because the firm seeks to co-ordinate resources throughout the world by owning

the production processes, instead of relying on buying-in the same goods and services from the market. Presumably this is because governance costs are less than transactions costs. To be consistent with the logic of the hierarchy, transfer prices should function as no more than an administrative mechanism (in the same way as a hotel issues meal tickets to guests to identify who may demand breakfast and to record the number of breakfasts served). However, this would leave all the profits being made at the point of final sale, which might not be tax-effective. It would also mean that the MNE could not apply financial control mechanisms (such as return on investment) to its divisions, because only the final selling division would have any revenues. Finally, it would be unacceptable to the host countries of supplying divisions because they could not levy any taxation.

However, introducing transfer prices that represent market values effectively reintroduces the market into the MNE and, with it, transactions costs. Where a division is setting its prices with reference to the prices available on an external market, it does inevitably raise the question of why the division is owned by the MNE in the first place. Why does it not simply buy in the good or service, pay the transaction costs, but save itself the extra layer of governance costs?

If setting a market-based transfer price reveals that it would be cheaper to buy an input than to make it (or that it would be more profitable to sell it externally than to pass it on for further processing), then this has done the shareholder a favour. What happens if the transfer price is incorrect, though? Artificially low transfer prices might encourage an MNE to continue making products that could be bought cheaper on the market. Artificially high transfer prices would encourage outsourcing.

5. *The threat of imposed transfer prices conflicts with strategic management logic.* Eccles (1985) suggests that the process for setting transfer prices should depend on two sets of considerations: the extent of vertical integration in the business, and the extent of diversification between divisions (Figure 8.17).

Where diversification is high there may be little synergistic relationship between divisions, and therefore each division should set prices according to its own *competitive* needs. For example, during the time that Hanson Group plc owned quarries, brickmakers and housebuilders, each was still allowed to set its own commercial transfer prices because there was little vertical integration; the majority of each division's business lay outside the group and so transfer prices were market prices.

Diversification

	Low	High
High (Vertical integration)	Co-operative MANDATED FULL COST	Collaborative MANDATED OR MARKET-BASED
Low (Vertical integration)	Collective NO TRANSFER PRICING	Competitive EXCHANGE AUTONOMY

Figure 8.17 Manager's analytical plane (adapted from Eccles, 1985)

However, if there is strong integration, as there is between the shipping and refining divisions of an oil company then, despite the high degree of diversification between ships and cracking towers, it is desirable that prices be set *collaboratively*, otherwise what point is there in the oil company owning both?

Where there is very little diversification or integration, such as between identical branches of the same business, then transfer prices should be set collaboratively (for example, they may agree on a daily rate for staff transferred from one branch to another to cope with absences) or no transfer price should exist at all because the firm is not truly multidivisional. However, if the vertical integration is high, such as exists between the component-supplying divisions and the assembly divisions of a multinational car manufacturer, then negotiation should take place to arrive at a price that assists co-operation. Eccles suggests that this will be at full cost to ensure that resources are allocated correctly and costs are adequately recovered.

8.10.5 Broader control over subsidiaries in MNEs

There is a need for the MNE to control its activities to avoid censure from shareholders and other stakeholders in other countries. Although the development of performance measures for 'social responsibility' are common ways of doing this, they are rarely enough on their own. It is too easy for managers to 'fiddle the numbers'. Many MNEs seek to implement this by requiring managers to sign statements of undertaking to abide by the principles of social responsibility. This makes it a matter of personal honour for the manager to abide by the principles.

A CIMA research report, *Corporate Performance Evaluation in Multinationals* (1993), found that MNEs exhibited the following control techniques:

- the corporate mission statement was a major control device because it enabled corporate centre to set the agenda for the country divisions;
- the mission always involved shareholder wealth as well as other goals;
- divisional performance measures incorporated this corporate mission but also went beyond it to suit the circumstances of the particular business processes and country of operations;
- UK and US multinationals put greater emphasis on profit-based measures than did German or Japanese MNEs. The latter incorporated more market-based and strategic targets.

8.11 Summary

This chapter has reviewed control, and specifically performance measurement. Several themes have emerged:

- The distinction between strategic, managerial and operational control (Anthony, 1965) demonstrates the need for goal congruence, that is the strategy will be implemented only if targets are set at both managerial and operational levels.
- Traditional cost-, revenue- and profit-based targets are not adequate for strategic control because of the need for financial control to transmit strategy (Goold and Campbell, 1987) and the need to tailor performance measures to the product life cycle (Ward, 1992).
- Financial performance measures based on profitability, such as return on investment, are being challenged by measures seeking to assure shareholder value.

- Financial measures are under attack from two groups: those who believe that firms should develop measures of interest to other stakeholders and which protect the natural environment of the firm; and those who desire to measure the processes that generate shareholder value and not just the financial outcomes.
- Alternative measurement systems stress a balance between financial measures, customer measures and business process measures. These include the results/determinants matrix (Fitzgerald et al., 1991), the performance pyramid (McNair et al., 1990) and the balanced scorecard (Kaplan and Norton, 1992).

References

Anthony, R.N. (1965) *Planning and Control Systems: A Framework for Analysis*. Division of Research, Harvard Graduate School of Business. Boston, MA: Harvard Business School Press.

Bennett, M. and James, P. (1996) Environment-related performance measurement in business. In Baynes, P. and Tilley, I. (eds.) *Contemporary Issues in Performance Measurement*. London: Greenwich University Press.

Berry, A.J., Broadbent, J. and Otley, D. (1995) The domain of organisational Control. In Berry, A.J., Broadbent, J. and Otley, D. (eds.) *Management Control: Theories, Issues and Practices*. Basingstoke: Macmillan.

Broadbent, J.M. (1999) *Measuring Business Peformance*. London: CIMA.

CIMA (1993) *Corporate Peformance Evaluation in Multinationals*. London: CIMA.

Cornelius, I. and Davies, M. (1997) *Shareholder Value*. London: FT Financial Publishing.

Crockatt, F. (1992) Revitalising Executive Information Systems. *Sloan Management Review*, summer. Cited in Broadbent (1999).

Davies, M., Arnold, G., Cornelius, I. and Walmsley, S. (2000) *Managing for Shareholder Value*. London: Informa.

Drury, C. (2000) *Management and Cost Accounting* (5th edn). London: Thompson Learning.

Dunning, J.H. (1993) *Multinational Enterprises and the Global Economy*. Wokingham: Addison-Wesley.

Eccles, R.J. (1985) *The Transfer Pricing Problem*. Aldershot: Lexington.

Eccles, R.J. (1991) The Performance Measurement Manifesto. *Harvard Business Review*, January–February, reprinted in *Harvard Business Review on Measuring Corporate Peformance* (1998) Boston, MA: Harvard Business School Press.

Ehrbar, A. (1998) *EVA: The Real Key to Creating Wealth*. New York: John Wiley.

Elliott, J. (1998) *International Transfer Pricing*. London: CIMA.

Fitzgerald, L., Johnston, R., Brignall, S., Silvestro, R. and Voss, C. (1991) *Peformance Measures in Service Businesses*. London: CIMA.

Goldratt, E.M. and Cox, J. (1984) *The Goal*. London: Gower.

Goold, M. and Campbell, A. (1987) *Strategies and Styles: The Role of the Centre in Managing Diversified Corporations*. Oxford: Basil Blackwell.

Gray, R., Bebbington, J. and Walters, D. (1993) *Accounting for the Environment*. London: ACCA/Paul Chapman.

Hope, J. and Fraser, R. (1998) Managing performance in the new organisational model. *Management Accounting*, June.

Hope, J. and Hope, T. (1997) *Competing in the Third Wave: The Ten Key Management Issues of the Information Age*. Boston, MA: Harvard Business School Press.

Hopwood, A.G. (1974) *Accounting and Human Behaviour*. Englewood Cliffs, NJ: Prentice-Hall.

Johnson, H.T. and Kaplan, R.S. (1987) *Relevance Lost: The Rise and Fall of Management Accounting*. Boston, MA: Harvard Business School Press.

Johnson, T. and Jakeman, M. (1997) *The Customer Challenge: The Inside Story of a Remarkable Transformation in Customer Service*. London: Pitman. Cited in Neely (1998).

Kaplan, R.S. and Atkinson, A.A. (1998) *Advanced Management Accounting* (3rd edn). Upper Saddle River, NJ: Prentice-Hall International.

Kaplan, R.S. and Cooper, R. (1998) *Cost & Effect: Using Integrated Cost Systems to Drive Profitability and Performance*. Boston, MA: Harvard Business School Press.

Kaplan, R.S. and Norton, D.P. (1992) The balanced scorecard – measures that drive performance. *Harvard Business Review*, January–February, 71–79.

Kaplan, R.S. and Norton, D.P. (1996) *The Balanced Scorecard*. Boston, MA: Harvard Business School Press.

Kaplan, R.S. and Norton, D.P. (2001) *The Strategy Focused Organisation*. Boston, MA: Harvard Business School Press.

McNair, C.J., Lynch, R.L. and Cross, K.F. (1990) Do financial and non-financial measures have to agree? *Management Accounting* (US), November.

Mouritsen, J. (1988) Driving Growth: Economic Value Added versus Intellectual Capital. *Management Accounting Research*, 9.

Neely, A. (1998) *Measuring Business Performance*. London: Economist Books.

OECD (1995) *Transfer Pricing Guidelines for Multinational Enterprises and Tax Administrations*. Paris: OECD.

Piercy, N.F. (1997) *Market-led Strategic Change*. Oxford: Butterworth-Heinemann.

Rappaport, A. (1998) *Creating Shareholder Value* (revised edition). New York: Free Press.

Scarlett, B. (ed.) (1997) *Value Based Management*. London: CIMA.

Society of Management Accountants of Canada (1997) *Measuring and Managing Shareholder Value Creation*, Management Accounting Guideline No. 44. Cited in Broadbent (1999).

Ward, K. (1992) *Strategic Management Accounting*. Oxford: Butterworth-Heinemann.

Revision Questions

? Question 1

The depletion of scarce natural resources in production processes is increasingly being recognised by governments, environmentalists and industry. It has been stated that the availability of natural resources needs to be considered alongside capital and production capacities in assessing limiting factors in the global economy. Chartered management accountants have a major contribution to make towards the improvement of industrial practices so as to reduce environmental damage and depletion of scarce natural resources. This may be achieved by extending their traditional techniques into environmental cost reporting and control or providing information and control systems which integrate economic and environmental criteria.

Requirement
Discuss how the chartered management accountant can provide information for the purposes of managing the utilisation of scarce natural resources. **(25 marks)**

? Question 2

In recent years there has been a considerable extension of management accounting into the public sector (e.g. hospitals and schools).

At the same time that management accounting was being introduced into these areas, many governments were specifying objectives for the public services, for example: *hospitals* – 'to improve the standard of patient care'; *schools* – 'to improve the quality of education'.

Governments have also laid stress on the efficient use of resources in these areas.

Requirements
(a) Comment on the above objectives and assess the contribution that management accounting can make towards their achievement in the public sector. **(15 marks)**
(b) Explain how activity-based costing could be used in the public-sector, non-manufacturing environments. **(10 marks)**
(Total marks = 25)

? Question 3

The choice of organisational goals is one of the more difficult parts of the strategic planning process. It is often blandly stated that a company's objective should be 'profit maximisation'. Although this is an important assumption of economic analysis, it is not usually appropriate in the management of business organisations.

Requirements

(a) Suggest three alternative organisational objectives that could be used instead of 'profit maximisation'. Explain the implications of the adoption of each of the suggested objectives. **(15 marks)**

(b) Discuss the implications of 'short-termism' for a firm which delegates responsibility to managers in its operations in several countries around the world. **(10 marks)**

(Total marks = 25)

? Question 4

PK Ltd is jointly owned by two UK-based conglomerates which manufacture mainly electrical products. In its own right, PK Ltd is regarded as a world leader in the installation and maintenance of railway transport signalling systems. The company is based in Europe, where most of its manufacturing units are located, but it has established other plants and marketing facilities in the USA, Latin America, Asia and Australia.

Activities of the company

The company specialises in the supply of railway signalling and control systems and employs over 15,000 staff worldwide. In addition to these systems, PK Ltd also supplies advanced electronic equipment for safety signalling applications which can be added to systems which have already been installed. Passenger information systems are also manufactured and supplied by the company, which uses advanced technology to provide full displays on railway platforms and stations.

Over the last two decades, PK Ltd has experienced increasing competition within its European and North American markets.

Recent international activities

In addition to carrying out major signalling work for the Channel Tunnel rail link between the UK and mainland Europe, PK Ltd has recently equipped a high-speed rail line in Asia with electronic equipment. Within Europe, the company succeeded in winning the tender to build, equip, operate and maintain a rail link between a major Scandinavian city and its airport.

Research and development

The chief executive of PK Ltd has stated that the market-oriented approach of the company requires that it should maintain and develop its position as leader in 'state of the art' technology. This is facilitated by a large established research and development unit which aims to improve product reliability and develop advanced computer software solutions in its business activities, all at lower cost, without compromising quality.

The reduction of life cycle costs and environmental damage, while at the same time pursuing technical developments, have been stated by the chief executive as key objectives of the company.

Financial position of PK Ltd

The latest report and accounting statements declared that the financial year just ended produced results which were 'disappointing'. The chief executive indicated that the company had experienced difficult trading conditions and encountered strengthening international competition. While turnover increased, operating profit after tax and overall orders were lower than in the previous year. At the year end, the number of orders in the order book was 8 per cent below the level achieved at the previous year end.

Abridged comparative accounting information for the last and previous financial year is as follows:

	Last year	Previous year
	£000	£000
Value of orders	3,750	4,600
Turnover	4,400	3,900
Operating profit after taxation	310	320
Shareholders' equity	935	850

PK Ltd had achieved on average a 20 per cent growth in turnover and a 10 per cent increase in operating profit after taxation over the preceding 5-year period until the last financial year. The chairman of one of the parent holding companies has expressed his concern regarding PK Ltd's results in the last financial year. In response, the chief executive of PK Ltd has outlined his company's strategy of international acquisition and joint ventures as a means of returning to sustained growth and profitability.

Proposed acquisition

A number of acquisitions and joint venture arrangements have been considered by the board of PK Ltd, aimed at increasing the company's profile outside Europe. In particular, the acquisition of a small South African electronics component manufacturer (RA Ltd) is being actively pursued. If acquired, RA Ltd will provide the basis for PK Ltd to increase its range of products in what is considered to be an expanding market with high growth potential.

This acquisition would enable advantage to be taken of the opportunities for development in South Africa. In addition, RA Ltd would provide a base for further market penetration of other African countries. RA Ltd is unquoted and owned by a diverse group of shareholders, with family interests in the company controlling 40 per cent of the voting shares.

PK Ltd considers that RA Ltd is under-capitalised. It is currently achieving a 2 per cent return on turnover after interest and tax, despite working at full capacity. RA Ltd employs 2,000 people, who possess mixed abilities and skills. Mostly, however, the employees are unskilled or at best very poorly trained. As many as 25 per cent of RA Ltd's products are returned by customers because of faults and this proportion has steadily increased over recent years.

The directors of PK Ltd are mindful that the South African currency (the Rand) is continuing to depreciate in value compared with the English currency (pound sterling). The Rand has continually fallen in value compared with the pound over a long period and currently stands at an exchange rate of 7.6 Rand to £1, whereas a year ago the exchange rate was 6 Rand to £1.

Requirements

(a) Explain the difficulties with which the parent companies may be confronted in assessing PK Ltd's performance. **(10 marks)**

(b) Recommend and justify what financial and non-financial measures may be applied to assess the performance of PK Ltd. **(10 marks)**

(c) Discuss the strategic objectives and market opportunities available to PK Ltd which will be created by its acquisition of RA Ltd. **(10 marks)**

(d) Discuss the managerial, cultural and financial considerations that PK Ltd will need to examine before undertaking the acquisition of RA Ltd. **(15 marks)**

(e) Explain the difficulties that PK Ltd may encounter in objectively assessing the performance of RA Ltd post-acquisition. **(5 marks)**

(Total marks = 50)

Question 5

Company development

The headquarters of the S Group (S) is located in K, a country which has experienced rapid economic growth in recent years.

S itself has been established for over 100 years. Two brothers first started trading in K and developed the group, which is now a highly profitable international conglomerate company. Its diverse business activities range from capital goods manufacture, through materials handling to operation of airlines and banking. Some of its activities involve the transfer of partly completed goods between manufacturing and assembly plants located in different countries. The group operates a divisionalised structure.

Economic circumstances

Over the last 3 years the region of the world in which K is located has been subject to serious economic difficulties. K itself has not been affected as much as some of its neighbours, owing to the fact that its independent currency is pegged to the US dollar.

There has been much activity and intervention by the monetary authorities in K to protect the value of the currency, and this has proved to be largely successful, despite the intense pressure exerted by foreign speculators. Nevertheless, the effects of the regional economic difficulties are being felt. This is exemplified by the recent emergence of unemployment after a period of 30 years of full employment and a dramatic fall in property prices.

Organisational economic objectives

Fifty-five per cent of S's holding company shares are held within the families of the original founders. The remaining 45 per cent of the shares are mainly held by international banks and other financial institutions located all over the world. These institutional shareholders maintain constant pressure on the directors to improve earnings per share and increase dividend payments. The directors have stated that their main objective is to increase shareholder value. In satisfying the requirements of the shareholders, the directors are conscious of the need for improved efficiency in the group's operations. Consequently, the holding company's board of directors carefully scrutinises the activities of the constituent subsidiary companies within the group.

Divisional performance measurement

S has always applied a traditional form of measurement to assess the performance of the group's subsidiaries. It uses return on capital employed (ROCE) and defines this as:

$$\frac{\text{Profit before interest and tax}}{\text{Average capital employed}} \times 100$$

(The capital employed value is the average of that shown at the beginning and end of the year.)

The performance of the divisional managers is strictly monitored on this basis and their remuneration increases if they achieve growth in their ROCE, which is measured annually. Inevitably, the divisional managers strive to improve their performance as measured by this method.

The Agricultural Equipment division

The Agricultural Equipment (AE) division, which is not located in K, assembles components into a single product. It receives the components from other subsidiaries in the group which are situated in other countries. The group as a whole has been able to benefit from economies of scale, as a result of other subsidiary divisions, which have long experience in manufacturing, supplying AE. Following assembly, AE ships the product to various customers throughout the world. The geographical location of the country in which AE is situated enables the product to be easily exported, but the division is subject to high levels of corporation tax.

The transfer prices of the components transferred to AE are set centrally by group head office located in K. The divisional manager of AE has no influence over them at all. The group head office may vary the transfer prices during the financial year.

Comparative results for the AE division over the last 2 years (translated into K's currency) are as follows:

	Last year K$m	Previous year K$m	K$m	K$m
Sales		800		750
Components transferred	600		400	
Assembly costs	100		75	
		(700)		(475)
Gross profit		100		275
AE Division Head Office (all fixed)		(75)		(75)
Net profit before interest and tax		25		200
Average capital employed		2,020		2,000

Selling prices over the 2 years remained stable.

It may be assumed that the variable costs of the supplying division, relating to the transferred components, were neutral in respect of AE division's profitability over the 2 years.

The budgeted and actual selling price per unit was K$50,000 in each of the 2 years. The budgeted production and sales level for each year was 18,000 units. It can be assumed that there were no opening and closing stocks of finished goods or work in progress in either of the years.

The budgeted cost per unit for each of the last 2 years was as follows:

	Last year K$	Previous year K$
Assembly	6,000	5,000
Components transferred	35,000	25,000
	41,000	30,000

It can be assumed that there was no change in the currency exchange rate between the AE division's host country and K$ in the last 2 years. There have been discussions at S Group headquarters regarding the deteriorating performance of AE and there is growing pressure to close it down. The AE divisional manager believes there is little that he can do in the circumstances, as he only controls a small proportion of the total costs of the division.

Potential for growth in AE division

Despite the reduced profitability in the last financial year, the divisional manager of AE believes there is potential for growth. He has put forward plans to group headquarters to take over a competitor company in the country in which the division is situated. This would result in an increase for the division in world wide market share and provide the capacity to increase the range of agricultural equipment supplied in accordance with the divisional manager's perception of demand. To do this AE will need to obtain funds which will be secured against group assets.

Requirements

(a) State the sources from which the board of directors of S may obtain information relating to the group's business environment and how it might use that information for strategic management purposes. Explain how the board of directors might assure itself of the quality of that information for strategic management purposes. (You are not required to consider the ecological environment in answering this question.) **(12 marks)**

(b) Making use of the information contained in the case, produce a critical appraisal of the method applied by S Group's directors to assess the performance of the AE division. **(16 marks)**

(c) Discuss the factors that should be taken into consideration by the directors of S in deciding whether the strategic development proposals put forward by AE's divisional manager should be pursued. **(10 marks)**

(d) Assume that the AE division makes the acquisition as proposed by its divisional manager. Recommend how S Group's directors should improve the methods of measuring the performance of the AE division in order to assess its contribution to the group's strategic requirement to increase shareholder value. **(12 marks)**

(Total marks = 50)

 Question 6

It has been said that 'the Balanced Scorecard translates mission and strategy into objectives and measures, organised into four perspectives: financial, customer, internal business process and finally learning and growth'. Kaplan and Norton developed the Balanced Scorecard as a means of combining financial control measures with non-financial measures.

Requirement

Critically evaluate the usefulness of the Balanced Scorecard in assisting organisations, both profit-motivated and not-for-profit, to achieve improvements in their operational performance. **(25 marks)**

Solutions to Revision Questions

✅ Solution 1

This question involves stating the case for, and techniques of, environmental accounting.

The chartered management accountant has contact with a large proportion of an organisation's senior management and therefore is able to influence the discussions that occur and also the decisions that are taken. As a contributor to the decision-making process, it is possible for him/her to make a contribution in respect of environmental issues and to ensure that the management are aware of the importance of the social and ethical responsibility of organisations.

Concern about the depletion of natural resources is a major issue facing the world. Decision-makers must be made aware of any activities which contribute to the problem and it is important that they are aware of their responsibilities to society. The problems relating to the depletion of natural resources should be placed on the agenda when the mission statement is being drawn up. If this matter is included in the overall goals and objectives of the organisation, these problems will be considered when both the strategic and the operational decisions are discussed.

Although discussion at the planning stage is essential, it is important that the chartered management accountant provides information on a regular basis to report on the extent of the implementation of the policies adopted by the organisation regarding its social responsibility obligations. In preparing routine reports, it should be appropriate to include details of:

- the amount consumed of natural resources which are being depleted;
- statistics of emissions and environmental damage that has occurred;
- the costs incurred in replenishing the natural resources used.

If the organisation is involved in the use of timber, mining operations or polluting activities, it is important that managers are aware of the social implications of these activities. The increase in legislation that deals with the social responsibilities may pose a threat to the survival of the firm, and steps should be taken to adopt a more responsible approach. It may be necessary to allocate resources to research and development activities to reduce the exposure of the organisation to these risks.

Alternatively, it may be sensible to take steps to reduce the firm's involvement in socially unacceptable practices by increasing the price of the particular products to enable additional resources to be allocated to the search for a remedy. This, however, is a decision which is liable to be resisted by managers who are more interested in short-term

473

performance. It will, therefore, be necessary for the chartered management accountant to play a role in distributing information which will focus on the implications of the misuse of scarce natural resources.

It may be helpful to establish a committee to review the issues and to:

- obtain information about the attitudes of the organisation's stakeholders to the scarce natural resources issue;
- distribute details of the extent of the problem within the organisation;
- determine the likely effect of ignoring the problem, particularly the possible effects of punitive legislation that could be introduced;
- decide on the most appropriate methods of highlighting the issues on a regular basis through including details in the monthly performance reports;
- prepare ad hoc reports which deal with specific aspects of the problem and to emphasise the social responsibility of the organisation in respect of the use of renewable and non-renewable resources.

The chartered management accountant has an important role to play in drawing attention to the issues involved in environmental accounting, and has much to contribute by providing relevant information to enable the firm to manage its scarce resources. As it is important that a firm sustains its activities, managerial attention must be focused on activities which deplete natural resources within the organisation and the industry as a whole. The effects of a sound environmental policy must be considered in making decisions, particularly regarding price, quality criteria and the monitoring of performance. The chartered management accountant usually has access to other managers and is, therefore, in a position to ensure that environmental issues are always considered when decisions are taken within the organisation. However, it is important that the senior management support the approach adopted in respect of environmental issues.

Specifically, reports could be produced by the chartered management accountant which focus attention on issues such as the extent of emissions, the quantity and value of raw materials that are consumed and also provide details of progress towards improving the anti-pollution technology within the organisation. It would be appropriate if the accounting reports showed the costs related to environmental issues as a separate item, so that all managers are aware of the costs involved. During the preparation of the annual budget, targets should be established and standards set to enable the progress to be measured in reducing the ecologically damaging processes and practices.

In essence, the chartered management accountant should provide information to enable the management of the firm to take a forward-looking approach to a problem which is often ignored in the search for short-term profitability.

 ## Solution 2

This question has a public-sector context which may be unfamiliar to you. However, it is included here to help provide you with practice in describing the evaluation and control of non-financial processes.

(a) Management accountants in the public sector can play an important role in providing advice and guidance to the people who are responsible for making decisions in non-profit organisations. The introduction of management accounting techniques within hospitals and schools has meant that the managers are now required to give more attention to the areas of economy, efficiency and effectiveness in the allocation and use of resources. Techniques and approaches previously used in the private sector have been applied more widely in local and central government.

Management accountants are expected to assist with decisions which allocate resources and to prepare budgets which can be used for planning and control purposes. Accountants should provide guidance to the managers of non-profit organisations, where a high proportion of their costs are fixed and it is, therefore, especially important for public-sector organisations to be assisted with decision-making.

The inability to measure the output from schools and hospitals is the main problem that is faced by this type of organisation. The establishment of objectives provides the management accountants with a benchmark against which the success of decisions can be judged. The objectives that are quoted in the question are far too general and will, therefore, not provide a means of judging the economy, efficiency and effectiveness of the organisations.

The first step that should be taken by the management accountants is to state the organisational objectives in a manner which makes it possible to measure the degree to which patient care and quality of education is being achieved. Thereafter, it is necessary to develop performance indicators to measure the degree to which the objectives are being met.

In addition, it is necessary for management accountants to develop a system for recording the information which will be used to assess the performance of the organisation. This will make it possible to control the amount of resources that are used in the organisation. This information will provide a basis for measuring the economy within the organisation. It will also allow a system of budgetary control to be established. This makes it possible to investigate any differences which arise after the budgets have been prepared.

The establishment of budgets and the measurement of output will also enable the accountants to measure the relationship between the inputs and outputs. This will provide a measure of efficiency.

The concept of value-for-money audits has been developed to assess the performance of organisations. By assessing the extent to which the objectives of the organisation are achieved, the effectiveness can be judged.

The management accountants will be required to introduce the managers in the public sector to techniques which will enable them to take decisions, plan and control the organisation and to measure the extent to which the plans are achieved.

(b) Activity-based costing (ABC) tackles the problems which arise from the need to allocate indirect expenses to units of output. High levels of indirect cost are experienced in service organisations. Most public-sector organisations use relatively little material and labour tends to be regarded as fixed. This results in the bulk of the expenditure being classified as overhead costs which are often fixed in the short run. In this type of situation, ABC is particularly useful to management accountants in the public sector.

By using cost drivers, it is possible to establish the expected and actual cost of the different activities which occur within a department or unit. It is possible to determine the cost of these individual operations rather than the final cost of a product or service. This makes it unnecessary to decide on a basis of allocation for each item of expense and the arbitrary allocations of overhead expenses can often be avoided.

The introduction of ABC provides a more direct method of establishing the cost of a product, and it is likely that this additional and improved information will allow managers to plan and control an organisation more effectively. The current emphasis on the need for the efficient use of resources creates a demand for useful information. This will inevitably lead to increased recognition of the value of accountants within public-sector organisations.

This question brought together objective setting and ABC in the context of the public sector. Although it was a relatively straightforward question, it seemed that candidates preferred the other questions on the paper and so only a few people tackled it.

Solution 3

(a) Although it is possible to establish many different objectives, the most common would be:
- achieving a satisfactory long-term level of profitability;
- achieving a level of growth in terms of either sales or total assets;
- achieving an acceptable market share.

Adopting any of these criteria means that the management will not be seeking to exploit every opportunity to increase the profits of the company. In essence, the management will be taking a longer perspective. This means that the managers will adopt strategies which will lead to sustainable benefits.

'Satisficing' is the usual term which describes aiming for a level of output which is acceptable to the stakeholders. This would appear to be a much more realistic criterion for managers, but it is difficult to establish a satisfactory level of profitability. It is suggested that the goal will be set by the board of directors and external directors will be particularly useful in establishing a satisfactory goal.

It is considered essential that growth is the objective of a firm. It is accepted that the other firms in the industry will grow and so it is essential to aim for growth if the firm is not to be overtaken by competitors. The growth rate may be specified in terms of either sales or total assets and in many cases, the objectives will include both. The management will need to consider different means of achieving growth and, in a mature market, it may be necessary to consider diversification, especially by means of acquisitions.

Many firms specify objectives in terms of market share. There is a link between market share and profitability, but it is possible that the increased market share can only be achieved by spending large amounts on promotional activities. In these cases, the goal of an acceptable market share may be achieved but the profitability may be adversely affected. It therefore would seem that both market share and profitability should be included in the aims of the firm.

(b) When individual managers are given responsibility and authority to make decisions, objectives are established to monitor performance. It is intended that each manager will act to attain the agreed objectives. However, it is possible that the managers will focus attention on achieving the immediate goals without considering the implications in the longer term. This is known as 'short-termism' and it is important that the top management are aware of this problem in both the process of establishing objectives and monitoring performance.

As an example, a manager may reduce the amount spent on advertising and maintenance of plant in order to reduce expenses in a time when profits are falling below the levels set in the budget. Although the reduced expenditure will boost profits, the effect on the business in the future may be significant. Concentrating on the short term is likely to be more common when managers' remuneration is related to attaining the objectives of the department for which they are responsible.

It is therefore important that the issue of 'short-termism' be taken into consideration in both the design and use of a system of control within an organisation.

✓ Solution 4

- This question has performance evaluation at its core. Note that the examiner is combining several complications here:
  - the problem of cross-national transfer charging;
  - currency differences (particularly the falling Rand);
  - the need for considerable R&D and restructuring;
  - the fact that the firms are in different stages of their product life cycles.
- There is also plenty of opportunity to brainstorm a PEST analysis.
- (a) PK Ltd has a number of different manufacturing plants and marketing operations in different parts of the world. When assessing the performance of the different units, the parent company's accountants will need to recognise that:
  - it is difficult to compare the performance of subsidiaries which operate in different countries;
  - there are problems in comparing PK Ltd's performance with other firms in the same industry.

Comparisons between subsidiaries

When assessing the performance of each subsidiary, it is essential to take into account the differences in each environment. Significant differences between countries include the strength of the competitors, the cost of producing the equipment that is sold by PK Ltd, and the demand for the products. When comparing the performance of manufacturing and marketing operations in each country, these three factors must be carefully considered.

Other factors which should be considered are the productivity of the workers, the level of wastage and spoilage in the manufacturing process, delivery times, and the sales generated by each salesperson. In addition, factors such as the inflation rate and changes in the exchange rate in each country will have to be considered, as adjustments will have to be made to incorporate these factors into the assessment process. This will ensure that each subsidiary is treated equitably.

When comparing the performance of a firm's subsidiaries, an issue which should be considered is the behavioural factors which influence the managers' decisions. It is possible for a manager to focus on the short-term aspects of performance. This can result in a less than favourable outcome in the longer term and it is important that the senior managers take this into account in judging the performance of individual subsidiaries. Expenditure on research and development (R&D) is an example of an additional cost

IMPLEMENTING AND CONTROLLING PLANS

which will reduce a subsidiary's short-term profit but which is essential for the long-term success of the company.

Comparisons between companies within the same industry

The accounting policies adopted by each company must be investigated before valid conclusions can be made about the relative performance of the companies. For example, the basis of valuation of the assets may have a crucial effect on the return on capital employed.

As PK Ltd manufactures and sells very specialised products it may be difficult to find firms which will be valid for comparative purposes. Although it is possible to compare any two firms in terms of profitability and the effective use of financial resources, there are usually significant differences between different industries and it is therefore desirable to select firms which produce and sell similar products. This will ensure that any comparisons are meaningful.

It is important that an attempt is made to assess the long-term market potential of the organisation. The expenditure on R&D will be an important aspect of this assessment. This information is not readily available and it is extremely difficult to make predictions about the success of the company in the future.

In broad terms, the extent of the delegation of decision-making to the subsidiaries will provide the managers of each unit with autonomy. However, it is still essential that the company's top management retains control, and an important aspect of this control is exercised through the financial reports which assess the performance of each unit. It is a relatively difficult task for management to do this as the company, PK Ltd, operates in an industry which uses advanced technology. This may make it difficult to compare the quality of the products, the effectiveness of the R&D activities and the standard of after-sales service provided. In addition, the strategy adopted by the different firms makes comparisons difficult. Aspects such as pricing policy, marketing and distribution policies and the concern with the long-term effect of decisions may be possible to determine from a close study of the firm's activities. However, if this type of information is not available, it makes comparisons with the performance of PK Ltd difficult.

(b) In order to assess the performance of PK Ltd, attention will have to be given to a number of different areas. In addition, it is essential that the effect on short-term performance and long-term success is incorporated into the performance-measurement criteria selected. Both financial and non-financial aspects of the business must be judged and compared either with industry standards or with other acceptable criteria.

Financial measures which will provide an insight into the performance of a company include:

- return on capital employed;
- other profitability ratios such as return on sales and gross profit percentage;
- the costs involved in the marketing of the products as this activity could be subcontracted to specialised units;
- the amount spent on R&D activities which will focus attention on the importance placed on the long-term success of the firm as opposed to concentrating on short-term goals such as profitability;
- customer account profitability, which may be particularly important in assessing the effect of offering different products or terms to different customers – in addition, PK Ltd should monitor contract costs which may differ significantly;

- employee costs in the different countries;
- the size of the company's order book which will provide information regarding the future level of activity within the company.

The non-financial measures that are relevant to PK Ltd are:

- the quality of the products measured by the number of customer complaints – this is particularly important in an industry which supplies safety equipment, and information must be maintained on the safety records of railways that use PK Ltd's signalling and control systems;
- the number of new products developed annually which will provide a view of the firm's potential;
- the number of major orders lost to competitors which will indicate the extent of the competition within each market;
- an assessment of the environmental awareness within the firm which is important in ensuring that the company is implementing socially responsible attitudes to environmental issues.

(c) In the latest report and accounting statements, the results of PK Ltd were described as 'disappointing'. Despite an increase in turnover, the value of orders has decreased by 18 per cent and the operating profit after taxation by 3 per cent. This contrasts with a 20 per cent growth in turnover and a 10 per cent increase in operating profit after taxation over the past 5 years.

Although it is unlikely that the acquisition of RA Ltd may have a beneficial effect on the current position, it is expected that it will improve the return to investors longer term. It is unlikely, however, to solve all the problems faced by PK Ltd.

The acquisition of RA Ltd will mean that PK Ltd will be able to expand its activities into both the South African market and the other African countries, as it will be possible to use the facilities acquired in South Africa as a base for the penetration of the other markets. It is possible that PK Ltd's technology and experience will mean that it has a competitive advantage over other firms in the African markets. However, PK Ltd is likely to face competition from other firms which operate in the specialised markets of transport signalling systems. PK Ltd will be able to compete effectively by having production facilities in South Africa, especially if the other firms do not have a local manufacturing base.

The acquisition of RA Ltd will provide additional products which could be introduced into all the markets in which PK Ltd operates.

Initially, it will be necessary for PK Ltd to introduce measures which will improve the performance of RA Ltd, as it is currently generating only a 2 per cent return on turnover. There are a number of problems which have to be addressed if the acquisition is to be successful. These include the improvement of the firm's product quality and the efficiency of the labour force. However, the poor performance of RA Ltd may mean that PK Ltd will be able to acquire the company at a relatively low price. It is possible, however, that the family and other shareholders will have unrealistic expectations. PK Ltd should make a realistic offer to acquire the subsidiary, as it is important that the acquisition is made without protracted negotiations. Although it is possible that both firms will benefit from the acquisition, it will be difficult to manage the change effectively.

(d) The successful acquisition and integration of the subsidiary into the company will require the management of PK Ltd to address a number of different issues.

At the present time, RA Ltd has a poor-quality product, which is produced by a badly-trained, unskilled labour force. When the change in ownership takes place it is important that PK Ltd's management is aware of all the possible problems that might occur at RA Ltd. Effective communications should be established with both the management and staff of RA Ltd. This will help to reduce any difficulties.

It is likely that the current shareholders and the workforce will be suspicious of the foreign acquiring company. There will possibly be great concern about job security within the company. From the outset, it is important that PK Ltd provides a clear statement of the motives for acquiring the new subsidiary, and the potential for growth and success should be emphasised. If possible, guarantees should be given to the South African workforce, and the labour policies of the new owners carefully explained.

The future role of the family that owns 40 per cent of the voting shares is another important issue to be addressed by the management of the acquiring company. It is possible that this family group may be able to create a feeling of confidence within the company to reduce staff mistrust and suspicion. This is particularly important as RA Ltd is not performing well.

There are likely to be significant cultural differences between the two countries and PK Ltd should recognise the possible consequences of any important differences in attitudes and working conditions. As PK Ltd has subsidiaries in many countries around the world, this knowledge and experience should be used to ensure that the takeover of RA Ltd is achieved with the minimum of difficulty.

The shortage of finance in RA Ltd is an issue which must be addressed by PK Ltd. It is possible that PK Ltd does not have surplus funds available to be transferred to the newly-acquired subsidiary, but it is essential that the finance is provided if the company is to expand and reach the potential that motivated the company to acquire RA Ltd. It is important, therefore, that PK Ltd is fully aware of the regulations regarding the repatriation of funds to head office. This is the fundamental reason that firms embark on foreign acquisitions, and it is important that the mechanism to transfer the cash is fully understood as it is sometimes difficult to make the arrangements for these transactions.

Although it is likely that a foreign acquisition is more difficult to manage successfully than a domestic takeover, it would appear that the purchase of RA Ltd provides the company with a number of opportunities which should improve its present position.

(e) It is important to give special attention to the measurement of performance of overseas subsidiaries. In the initial stages, it is often difficult to make these comparisons. This is because the organisation will be affected by the change in ownership and senior management. In addition, it is clear that major changes will be required within RA Ltd and the transitional stage may be particularly difficult. It may, therefore, not be easy to measure the effect of the changes that are introduced.

When assessing the performance of the acquired company, it will be important to consider the culture within the firm. Since both profitability and product quality have been poor, significant changes will be needed. It is, therefore, possible that the improvement in performance will not be immediate. The transitional stage could be relatively long. It is difficult to alter the culture of a firm, particularly if there are staff changes which create insecurity. Improving quality and introducing new technology can be very difficult and it is important that the timescale of the performance assessment be clearly established.

To assess a strategic decision, such as an acquisition, the criteria used should be based on the goals and objectives of the whole organisation. In the case of RA Ltd, it is important that measures of profitability and quality be devised. It is possible that RA Ltd has not used the same criteria in assessing performance and so a change in the culture of the firm may be needed. It is possible that the management of the new subsidiary will need to focus attention on different factors which were not emphasised in the past.

☑ Solution 5

- This compulsory question comprises a short case study which relates to an international conglomerate organisation. It requires consideration of strategic development issues which affect the overall business. It specifically requires an explanation of the sources of information which may be used for planning purposes, and an explanation of how its quality may be assured. In addition, it examines the measurement of divisional financial performance and requires an assessment of the problems this may generate. It includes consideration of issues concerning international transfer pricing and analysis of a strategic development proposal. Finally, the question requires recommendations as to how the division's contribution towards increasing shareholder value may be measured.

- The question incorporates all sections of the syllabus.

(a) S has a clear need for good-quality information on which to base its planning and control activities. This needs to be at various levels. It requires strategic information relating to market share, potential business environmental changes and the activities of competitors, as well as detailed information on the performance of the various businesses within the group. This means that the group requires access to detailed databases. It will be appropriate to develop an internal database, as well as obtaining access to data from external sources. Both financial and non-financial information should be gathered by S.

Sources of information

The sources of internal data will mainly come from the group's own business activities. Information will be generated on sales, costs, market share and customer account profitability. The breakdown of contribution and direct product-profitability analysis will be ascertainable from the internal information obtained. In addition, capital budgeting and post-audit activities will provide the group with long-term decision-making information. All this must be fed into the internal database and, therefore, appropriately robust hardware and software – which is capable of handling increased volumes and a variety of information – needs to be acquired.

External data will come from various sources, including market analysis reports. Subscription to industrial organisations specialising in the preparation of this type of information – such as PIMS, banks and other financial institutions, as well as government statistical reports – will be useful. Specific external research may be carried out by institutions of higher education and S could be well served if it sponsored a chair within a university. The object of this would be the pursuit of research into specific aspects of an industry, such as strategic marketing management. The external sources should also be used to confirm information gathered from internal sources (and vice versa), thus providing some measure of confidence in the data which has been assembled.

Use of the information

Gathering the information is only one part of the activity in which S must be engaged. It is important to use the information effectively for strategic planning and control purposes. This involves co-ordination of the information so that it can be presented as a complete view of the business environment, rather than a fragmented mix. Information needs to be gathered to carry out a position audit which requires the review of the group's existing activities and the degree of success achieved by its current strategies. In order to achieve its organisational objectives, senior management of S must ensure that strategies are developed which are suitable, feasible and acceptable. The information which is gathered must focus on permitting senior management to discriminate between potential alternative strategies and make an informed selection of the one which is most appropriate.

S should establish an effective strategic-planning function whose role is to gather information and involve the divisional managers in the presentation to the group's directors. It is essential that there is good liaison between the strategic-planning function and the divisions, otherwise an image of the former operating without reference to the real environment will be fostered. The use of models – for example simulation, financial planning, strategic marketing and scenario planning – will be essential to the strategic-planning function in carrying out its planning activities.

Quality of the information

The quality of the information supplied must be verified, and this implies that its validity and accuracy must be checked. The strategy which is developed must be based on information which is of good quality, and reliability. Errors contained within the information will lead to inappropriate strategic decisions being made. It is first necessary to determine the purpose of collecting the information and its intended use. This will clarify the level and detail of information required. Confidence in the information gathered will be generated through the use of appropriate statistical significance testing and the application of such techniques as sensitivity analysis and certainty equivalents. This will provide information which has been thoroughly tested and takes account of business environmental conditions.

This analysis is part of the role of the strategic-planning function and therefore it must employ a variety of specialist skills. Specialists in the particular functional areas – such as marketing, accountancy and finance, law and human-resource management – must be involved in this task, as well as personnel who have gathered specific experience of particular industries. These staff are of huge importance as they will understand the way in which the particular business environment operates and are likely to know, or be able to anticipate, competitor activity. The development of information sources over time will also reveal their reliability through experience. Comparisons of information acquired from various sources will act as a check on accuracy. This may be developed by the employment of external analysts.

(b) *Critique of ROCE.* The ROCE calculation is an historical measure and does not reflect future potential for the division. Learning from past performance can only have relevance if it influences future behaviour. ROCE may act as a disincentive for the divisional manager to invest, and this is exemplified by the mere 1 per cent increase in capital employed over the year. It is acknowledged that this level of investment should be viewed in terms of how recently the capital employed has been upgraded, and this information is not supplied. However, it appears to be a very small increase. The calculation of ROCE may be manipulated to improve the divisional results which is a major drawback of its application. For example, potential manipulation by managers may be hidden if only the overall ROCE is considered. The decomposition of ROCE into the component parts of return on sales and sales to capital employed reveals the level of increase or decrease in asset turnover if comparisons are made over time. As far as the AE division is concerned, asset turnover has remained constant over the 2 years for which information has been provided. This enables management attention to be directed to the returns achieved on sales.

Any performance measure which is based on percentages, such as ROCE, may lead to goal incongruence. The divisional manager is motivated to improve the percentage return for his or her division. This may result in a narrow focus of attention which disregards the wider perspective of the organisation as a whole. A divisional manager may succeed in increasing his or her division's ROCE by disposing of assets which provide a return which is less than the current level of divisional ROCE. However, this may adversely affect the organisation as a whole if the asset which the divisional manager discarded provides a return which is greater than the organisation's weighted average cost of capital.

Similarly, the divisional manager may improve divisional performance by increasing the numerator or decreasing the denominator in the ROCE calculation. This may be achieved by rejecting new projects, despite their achieving a return which is greater than the organisation's weighted average cost of capital. This is because their inclusion would reduce the divisional ROCE.

The numerator in the equation is relatively easily calculated, but the denominator (or divisor) may prove more complex and open to debate. This is likely to result in it being regarded as a suspect measure which can only be valid as long as all parties are agreed on its method of calculation.

Comparisons between divisions may also be distorted if the difference in the capital base and the incremental returns of one compared with the other, and the application of inconsistent depreciation policies, are not considered.

These general criticisms apply to ROCE as a measure of performance. They demonstrate a lack of forward-looking perspective if ROCE is used as a measure. Although ROCE is a popular method of assessing performance, it is in essence a backward-looking measure. It considers historical performance and does not take into account future opportunities. Previous results of divisions may not be a good guide to future potential profitability. The AE division is a good example, as its historical results do not reflect the opportunities for increased market share following the acquisition.

There is no detail contained in the case to assess how applicable these criticisms are to the AE division, but they are clearly issues which the S Group's directors should address in determining how they will measure performance. The use of economic

IMPLEMENTING AND CONTROLLING PLANS

value added as a measure of performance may overcome the problems highlighted which apply to the use of ROCE.

A further problem is that ROCE, on its own, may be misleading as it might not reveal the circumstances behind a division's performance. This is the case with the AE division which, on the face of it, appears to have experienced a deterioration in performance. In fact, more detailed inspection reveals that last year its overall performance improved on the previous year.

This may be illustrated by the following analysis.
Comparison of ROCE:

$$\text{Last year: } \frac{\text{K\$25 m}}{\text{K\$2,020 m}} = 1.24\%$$

$$\text{Previous year: } \frac{\text{K\$200 m}}{\text{K\$2,000 m}} = 10\%$$

This reveals a reduction in ROCE of 87.6 per cent. Other information contained in the case may be analysed in order to form a judgement on the actual performance of the AE division. AE suffered a 64 per cent reduction in gross profit from K\$275m to K\$100m in the 2 years. With AE's head office costs remaining constant, this resulted in a serious reduction in net profit before interest and tax of 87.5 per cent. Average capital employed increased slightly, by 1 per cent. The actual sales volumes were 16,000 last year and 15,000 in the previous year. The sales for the division increased by 6.67 per cent over the year but are still 11.11 per cent below budgeted levels. This, however, is an improvement on the previous year where the actual sales fell short of the budgeted volumes by 16.67 per cent.

The assembly costs incurred by the division increased by 33.33 per cent. This is surprising, given that production and sales volumes only increased by 6.67 per cent and that costs remained stable. The divisional manager needs to consider why assembly costs increased by so much. It may be that the AE division staff did not work efficiently in the last year. This is particularly surprising given that the budgeted increase in assembly costs between the 2 years was only 20 per cent, which in itself is questionable given that costs over the period remained stable.

Transfer prices

There was a large rise in component transfer costs between the 2 years. On the basis of the transfer price for the previous year, the transfer costs last year should only have been about K\$427m, reflecting the rise in production and sales. However, they rose to K\$600m, which is an increase of 50 per cent – far outweighing the actual increase in production. This compared with a budgeted increase in transfer costs per unit of 40 per cent.

It is difficult to justify how transferred component costs can have risen by 50 per cent when sales and production only rose by about 7 per cent. In divisional performance terms this raises a number of important issues. Are the supplying divisions transferring at full cost, which may have the effect of perpetuating their own inefficiencies and adversely affecting the performance of the AE division? What scrutiny is taking place on the transferring division's costs?

The after-tax cash flows of the AE division must also be considered by the directors. This particularly affects the transfer pricing policy of the group. Transfer prices are controlled by S Group's headquarters without any reference to the receiving (and presumably supplying) divisional management. The group as a whole has a responsibility to satisfy its overall objectives. It is under constant pressure to improve earnings per share and satisfy shareholders' demands for an improvement in their return. The fact that the AE division is located in a country which applies a high level of corporation tax is an influence for S to reduce the burden of taxation by deflating the division's reported profits. It is assumed that this is carried out by applying legal transfer prices, although they do seem to have increased dramatically over the last year as far as the AE division is concerned.

If the transfer prices are set centrally and are not established on an arm's-length basis, then their impact on AE division's results must be assessed. The transferred charges amounted to 77 per cent of AE's overall costs last year and, therefore, are significant as far as the results of the division are concerned.

Contribution

The gross contribution per unit was K$9,000 and K$20,000 for last year and the previous year respectively. This resulted in a contribution volume variance of K$18m for last year and K$60m for the previous year. (This is calculated by deducting the budgeted sales from the actual sales and multiplying by the budgeted contribution per unit.)

The contribution volume variance reveals paradoxically that the performance in the previous year was much worse than last year. The apparent improvement in performance last year was due to the budgeted sales shortfall being reduced and the lower level of budgeted contribution arising from the increase in transfer costs.

Overall divisional performance

The performance of the division was better last year than the previous year in terms of the improvement in the contribution volume variance. However, some caution should be attached to this, as the contribution volume variance may be regarded as a rather artificial measure in the context of AE, given that 86 per cent of the direct divisional costs are outside the control of the divisional manager.

It is necessary for the board of directors to consider AE division's contribution to the group's overall objectives. The contribution of the division to the improvement in shareholder value cannot be realistically assessed by the sole use of ROCE as a performance measure. It is necessary for the group to replace this short-term, historically-based, measure of performance with an approach which appraises opportunities for potential long-term development.

Conclusion

It is clear that ROCE on its own cannot be used effectively by S Group as a measure of the true performance of the AE division. It is necessary to analyse the results and go behind the constituent components of the calculation in order to come to a conclusion about the true performance of the division. In the case of the AE division, the performance last year improved on the previous year, bearing in mind that the divisional manager is being evaluated on results which include a significant amount of costs which are outside his control.

(c) *Introduction.* The main issue for consideration by the directors of S should be how AE fits into the overall strategic plan for the group. It is clear that AE's divisional manager is seeking to secure the best advantage for the division and this must be considered in the light of the best opportunities for S as a whole. The board of S must try and ensure that there is goal congruence and that AE's divisional manager does not jeopardise possible optimisation for the group in his quest to achieve the best for his division.

It is necessary for S to allow divisional managers to promote alternative strategies outside the formal planning period. This is exactly what AE's divisional manager is doing and he believes that there is a serious opportunity to increase the market share of the division. To that extent, the board of S must give serious consideration to the proposals, especially as the division is under some threat of closure due to circumstances which are mostly beyond its control. The overall objective of the board of S is to increase the earnings for the shareholders and any opportunity to achieve this must be scrutinised in detail.

Increase in market share

The proposals hinge on an increase in market share. The board of S may have some scepticism regarding AE's ability to achieve this, given that it has failed to meet its turnover targets over the last 2 years. Is the AE division capable of actually pursuing this development? Does it have the skills and managerial resources to successfully implement the take-over plan? Any takeover involves rapidly increasing capacity, which must be managed. This implies the need to overcome potential cultural and operational difficulties which may not be within the ability of the current management of the division, given its present level of resources. However, there is a more important issue regarding the potential benefit of the plan to S overall and this needs to be analysed carefully.

If the development proposal fits within S's strategic objectives, then the managerial issues may be considered separately and accommodated. The management of the division may be enhanced to overcome the practical difficulties with which the operation may be confronted. Of immediate importance would be the strategy to be used in successfully achieving the takeover.

Future strategic development

The board needs to be satisfied on the improvement in market share and the strength of the competition within the industrial sector concerned. It should recognise that AE is profitable, despite the onerous transfer-pricing policies. How more profitable might AE be after the takeover? What is the quality of the marketing research which has been undertaken? How accurate are the estimates of revenues and costs? How much will the takeover itself cost, and from where might S obtain the resources? Does it jeopardise other operations of the group? What is the opportunity cost of employing these funds in this way? Are there any opportunities for using other funds to develop the business post-takeover, such as government subsidies in third-world nations?

The board must also consider the potential future direction for the division. What opportunities might the takeover provide in future? Could other markets be developed and penetrated further? What timescales should be established for this development?

The key issue is whether the board of S believes that the market-development opportunities for AE outweigh the alternative use of project development funds and whether they fit within the overall strategic plan for the group.

(d) *Introduction*. It is clear from the analysis in part (b) that the measures which need to be applied should focus on the future potential for the division as well as the historical consideration of ROCE. This latter measure may be employed to assess the extent to which the planning gap has been closed so far. However, it is necessary to assess how much still needs to be done to completely close the gap. It can be assumed that the directors of the S Group are satisfied that the acquisition accords with the overall strategic plan for the conglomerate as a whole, given that it has been allowed to proceed. The measures applied by the group need to reflect how far the performance of the AE division has contributed towards the achievement of the objectives of the organisation.

This implies the need for consideration of the long-term prospects for the division. The directors of the group must satisfy the requirements of the shareholders, which may imply some conflicts as many of these will look for short-term returns. The strategy which has been approved for the AE division is long term in its nature and seeks to achieve an improvement in shareholder value.

Shareholder value analysis

The main assumption of shareholder value analysis is that a business is worth the net present value of its future cash flows. These cash flows must be discounted at an appropriate cost of capital. It applies one specific concept of company valuation and assumes that it will remain a going concern. This analysis enables strategic planning to take place in order to secure improved shareholder value in the future. By its nature it is focused on the long term and seeks to provide benefit for all the organisation's stakeholders, not just the shareholders.

It is essential that the directors of S Group focus their attention on those issues which affect shareholder value. The main issues which need to be addressed are: the potential increase in sales growth and profitability margin, investments in fixed assets and working capital to sustain the sales growth, the overall cost of financing the acquisition, and the effects of the rate of corporation tax on the AE division.

Taking these in turn, the sales growth and margin may be measured by the rate of growth in market share and the extrapolated increase in profitability. This may be achieved by simple regression analysis. How far has the AE divisional manager's expectations of sales growth and increase in range of products been realised? Is there a pattern to the trend and what is the likely impact of environmental forces which may affect this?

Regarding fixed asset and working capital provision, the directors of S Group must assess whether the future investment will facilitate the required growth in demand and profitability. This implies the need to assess whether the estimates used in undertaking the original NPV calculation are still valid. This may be achieved through the use of sensitivity analysis. More important, how might the investment in fixed assets and working capital need to change in the future in order to facilitate the required level of return?

Allied to this is an evaluation of the cost of capital. The directors of S Group must assess whether the cost of capital is minimised, and consider the need to provide funds in order to meet the future fixed and working capital requirements. The group is now committed to the acquisition and, therefore, it is important that the project is supported. Improvement in shareholder value is determined, to some extent, by the success of the venture. The S Group must pursue its assessment of the cost of funding the project and revise any projected net present values accordingly. More important, the activities of the AE division need to be reviewed to assess what needs to be done at the divisional level to achieve the overall objectives of the strategy.

Projected ROCE

A 'future-based' ROCE calculation, as distinct from one which is historically based, as referred to in part (b), could be undertaken by using the projected profits and capital employed values in the future years. This overcomes the historical perspective of merely assessing past ROCE, and provides a benchmark for the future. This activity should have been undertaken in assessing the viability of the acquisition. It is appropriate now to review how the estimated levels of ROCE are likely to change as more information becomes available.

Economic value added

The adoption of an historical ROCE as the sole measure of performance is clearly in question and an alternative approach would be to reward performance based on economic value added. As it stands, the notional cost of capital charge would need to be very low to compensate for the impact of the transfer charges. A notional interest rate of 1 per cent would result in a small economic value added of K$4.8m last year. An alternative approach is to apply a notional charge which more accurately reflects the cost of capital (say 10 per cent) to the overall profit, excluding the transfer priced items. Taking the last 2 years as an example, this would reveal the following:

	Last year K$m	Previous year K$m
Sales	800	750
Total divisional costs	(175)	(150)
Divisional profit	625	600
Notional interest charge at 10% of capital employed	(202)	(200)
Economic Value Added	423	400

(The variable costs of the supplying division for components transferred have been ignored, as the scenario states that these had a neutral effect on AE's profitability over the 2 years.)

This appears to be a fairer reflection of the actual performance of the AE division over the period. This may now be projected in terms of the economic value added which is expected in the future, taking account of the anticipated changes in capital employed and the future cost of finance.

Conclusion

Shareholder value analysis relates to a long-term planning horizon. The essential issue is that the directors must try to measure the incremental value which may be obtained from the acquisition. Provided that the incremental value is in excess of the cost of capital, then shareholder value will be added and the directors' main objectives for the organisation achieved. Performance measures not only need to reflect historical analysis of the AE division but, critically, to indicate what the projected future outturn is expected to be. Only then can strategic planning be implemented, to exploit any potential or to initiate corrective action.

☑ Solution 6

The Balanced Scorecard (BSC) was developed largely as a result of the perception that traditional financial measures of performance alone were insufficient in terms of providing control. Organisations need other measures of performance besides those of a financial nature to assess how far they are progressing towards the achievement of their strategic objectives. Johnson and Kaplan (1987) criticised the general management accounting control model in their book *Relevance Lost*. They claimed that the management accounting information systems were too focused on the procedures and cycles of the financial control system. The information itself was too late, too aggregated and too distorted to be relevant for management planning and control and decision-making purposes. This, in turn, led managers to concentrate too heavily on unimportant issues, to be too focused on the short term and to make decisions on unsatisfactory information, because the very simplicity of the systems led to inaccurate product and service costs.

The 'third wave' of business enterprise requires businesses to use knowledge and information as vital resources for gaining competitive advantage. This, in turn, requires the development and improvement of the organisation's intellectual property maintained by its staff. This means that management accounting control information must provide arange of meaningful information for management purposes in order to ensure that shareholder value is increased. In addition, management control information must move away from the directive form of control approach, which characterised systems in the twentieth century.

The BSC is an approach to addressing these challenges. It is not concerned with identifying an organisation's mission and strategy, but with operational control in order to determine if the corporate strategy is being achieved.

The four perspectives from which the BSC develops are financial, customer, internal business process and learning and growth.

Financial perspective

The BSC needs to retain a financial perspective in order to assess whether the organisation's strategy and its implementation are achieving the desired improvements in profitability or cost reduction. The traditional forms of financial measures include such items as ROCE in the profit motivated sector and economic value added in both profit and not-for-profit oriented organisations.

It is inevitable that financial perspectives will still form a vital control measure in both profit motivated and not for profit organisations. Overall, financial performance must still be measured and improvements achieved in order to maintain the confidence of the owners of the organisation. In the profit-motivated organisation, the shareholders must be satisfied with their return in order for them to remain loyal. In the not-for-profit organisation, it is essential that high levels of effectiveness are achieved with an economic use of resources thus permitting funds to be used for other purposes in order to add value to society.

Financial measures cannot help guide an organisation in its quest to add future value on their own. Financial measures are a historical record, but do not provide information on how long term capability and relationships with customers or clients and suppliers can be developed.

Customer perspective

The BSC identifies such items as customer satisfaction, customer retention, market share, customer account profitability and new customers won within this section. It is concerned with identifying in which market segments the organisation is engaged and how they may be measured.

It is important for all organisations to recognise the need to target specific customer groups. It is essential that profit motivated organisations obtain feedback from customers in respect of their product or service delivery. What is it that customers like and dislike about the product or service? How does this impact on the corporate image or reputation?

The not for profit organisation also provides services to its clients or members. Such organisations have an obligation to provide appropriate levels of service and will be measured against established targets. There is a danger that only the tangible items may be measured. For example, how can a measure be taken of an employee's charisma? The BSC provides a mechanism for reviewing levels of customer satisfaction. However, it does not address the overall problem of 'what gets measured gets attention'.

Internal business process perspective

The internal business process perspective measures relate to the efficiency and linkages within the internal value chain. The organisation must assess how it goes about delivering its products and services and what impacts these have on creating value for its customers. These in turn generate financial returns to the profit-orientated organisation and improvements in levels of service effectiveness in the not-for-profit sector. Both sectors need to review their levels of innovation, operational methods and after sales service or follow up.

This perspective is clearly linked with the customer perspective for both types of organisation. It is concerned with increasing efficiency and achieving improved effectiveness of internal processes focused on improved product or service delivery. In essence, it provides a mechanism for an organisation to address how it will achieve improvements in customer value, through reviewing its internal processes. The promise of improved customer and client satisfaction can only be achieved by inspection and development of internal processes. This perspective of the BSC is similar to a car manufacturer's situation. Suppose the driver, who is the manufacturer's customer, is looking for improved performance. The customer perspective will identify this and it is the internal business process perspective which will result in alterations to the engine to deliver the customer's requirements. The BSC provides for this vital form of internal analysis and applies equally to the profit-motivated and not-for-profit sectors.

Learning and growth perspective

The customer and internal process perspectives may show gaps between what the organisation is currently able to achieve and what is required in the long term by customers. The learning and growth perspective is concerned with identifying how these gaps may be closed. These may include employee-based measures and recognition of specific skills which may be required in the future. This perspective facilitates consideration of how these skills will be achieved or developed.

Both profit-orientated and not-for-profit organisations will be concerned to ensure that they learn from past mistakes. The learning and growth perspective will in theory measure how much internal processes have improved over time. This, in turn, enables the internal processes to be improved leading to improved customer or client satisfaction.

In theory, the BSC provides an appropriate mechanism to achieve overall improvement in shareholder value or effectiveness within the not-for-profit sector. However, there are some critical issues which need to be considered. There is no summary control measure, but a conglomeration of various diverse measures. The measures themselves may not always be consistent with each other and might give out conflicting signals to management. For example, an internal process measure may reveal that resources are being heavily used in the provision of a minority service in the not-for-profit sector. It is assumed at the moment that the recipient of the service is satisfied. The signal given is that the resources may be used in an alternative way, but that would mean closing the service. The service's client would therefore lose his or her customer satisfaction if the service were closed down. Thus, conflicting signals are being given by two of the BSC's measures.

The BSC requires commitment from senior management and often demands a change in corporate culture for it to be successfully implemented. This may involve the need to recognise the organisation as a bundle of inter-related processes rather than independent departments. In addition, staff will need to recognise the need to add value as well as cost and to think in terms of long rather than short-term development.

9

Change
Management

Change Management

This chapter deals with change management. Students should note there are many links to earlier chapters and aspects of the syllabus. This is unsurprising: change is an aspect of management that critically affects all functions of an organisation. You are encouraged to identify these linkages when studying this topic.

LEARNING OUTCOMES

By completing this chapter, including the readings and questions you should be assisted to:

- Explain the process of organisational development
- Discuss how and why resistance to change develops within organisations
- Evaluate various means of introducing change
- Evaluate change processes within an organisation.

9.1 Introduction

Any strategic change thought to be necessary in the organisation will involve changing the behaviour of people – not the easiest thing to do! It is worth remembering that you cannot change someones' mind – you can only present a convincing argument so that they change their own mind.

However, change in organisations is necessary, not least, because it will prevent an organisation becoming complacent – but change for the sake of it is an unnecessary cause of stress. As long ago as 1970 Toffler argued that the rate of change in society was out of control and that people could no longer cope with the resulting stress. Over 30 years later things have certainly not slowed down. Much of the change that we find in organisations is necessary due to changes in the environment in which they operate, as we discussed in Chapter 2.

When contemplating a change programme within an organisation, it has to be remembered that change is potentially dangerous for the organisation. Whilst an organisation is focusing on changing the way it operates, it may well be distracted from its core activities and everyday operations and customers may suffer accordingly.

One quotation often attributed to Albert Einstein of 'there is only one constant in this universe, and that constant is . . . change' establishes the background against which this chapter is set. Certainly we live in a fast changing world and organisational survival is dependant upon the anticipation and management of change.

Accepting that there is an inevitability of change it seems somewhat futile to bemoan what is a fact of life. Change must therefore be recognised as normal, be planned for and form part of the normal processes of management. Sometimes decisions can be made from 'on high' and passed 'down' for others to implement. This can be a mistake as it implies all knowledge falls in the domain of the senior hierarchy. If we are not careful, change management becomes synonymous with project management. This amounts to a 'task then achieve' approach performed as quickly as possible so we can get on with our 'real' work and get back to 'normal'. Real change management provides an organisation with an enduring legacy: much needed competitive advantage. It is a philosophy that permeates an organisational culture; a way of thinking and acting that is endemic and wholly shared.

Ideas and theories dealt with earlier in your studies are helpful in this context. For instance, McGregor's Theory Y people are innovative maybe even initiators of change (change agents). Under Maslow's hierarchy of need employees get promoted within the organisational hierarchy changing their needs along with cognitive perceptions and emotional feelings over time. People's own agendas for change, including pride, were the basis of the Japanese revolution in quality in manufacturing, and for quality circles and kaizen: the process of ongoing improvement. (These examples illustrate the breadth of thinking that can be applied to the subject of change.)

The questions arising from the challenge of competition and the difference between symptoms, causes and core problems include:

- what to change
- what to change to
- how to change
- how to avoid failure in the change process. (Goldratt, 1992)

This chapter attempts to explore some of these questions but first considers in more detail the 'triggers' to organisational change both externally and internally.

9.2 External change triggers

Change is often necessary because of external developments. It is clear that there are a number of external factors with which organisations must come to terms. These include the implications of a global market place, a wider recognition of environmental issues, health awareness and demographic change (Paton and McCalman, 2007). Ultimately these factors become triggers for change.

When considering these external triggers a distinction is drawn between the general (indirect-action) environment and the task (direct-action) environment of organisations; changes in both sectors need to be monitored and responded to. The 'far' or 'general' environment of an organisation can usually be categorised under a 'PESTLE' framework:

- Political implications of a new government.
- Economic changes such as exchange rates, level of macro-economic activity and global competition.

- Social or demographic changes such as levels of education and changing values/ expectations.
- Technological changes such as inventions and developments, in both products and processes.
- Legal implications of likely government policies.
- Environment implications of legislation, agreements of widely held values.

Clearly these factors are usually beyond the influence of a single organisation. The organisation however would do well to anticipate and respond to these developments as they translate directly as either a threat that must be overcome or an opportunity to be grasped.

The 'near' or 'task' environment covers all stakeholders who can influence, and be influenced by the organisation's direct actions. By now you should be fully familiar with the thinking of economist Michael Porter, a further framework devised by him is helpful in this context, and contains five dimensions:

- *Buyer power.* Single or few customers have more power over the organisation.
- *Supplier power.* Single or few single suppliers have more power over the organisation.
- *Threat of substitutes.* Could the product provided be threatened by buyers choosing to satisfy their need or want by turning to alternative substitute products? (For example, if the postal service is seen as expensive, inefficient or inconvenient the use of e-mail might be seen as a substitute means of conveying messages in writing.)
- *Barriers to entering your market.* If the difficulties and costs are high it is unlikely that new competitors will confront your organisation.
- *The degree of inter-firm rivalry.* How competitive is this rivalry? Does it lead to price wars and the need for expensive advertising?

Changes may be initiated by the organisation in order to influence this 'near' environment or at least respond to it.

 ## Exercise 9.1

Identify one example of a way in which an organisation might influence each of the five factors in this near environment.

 ## Solution

- *Buyer power.* Develop new markets for a product and try to extend the customer base.
- *Supplier power.* Seek out new sources of raw material or 'buy out' your supplier to ensure continuity of supply and price stability.
- *Threat of substitutes.* Develop customer awareness of the benefits of the product not achieved through substitute products. (Based on the postal service example cited earlier an advertising campaign with the strap line 'there is nothing like receiving a real letter', or 'a real letter means you really care', etc.)
- *Barriers to entering your market.* Try to gain economies of scale in production that will mean that cost savings can be passed on to customers. New entrants will not be unlikely as a consequence to compete on cost.
- *The degree of inter-firm rivalry.* Try to get agreement with your major competitors as to the level of advertising both engage in. The more spent on advertising within the industry the greater the drain on total profits, etc.

CHANGE MANAGEMENT

9.3 Internal change triggers

Internal triggers for change in a rational organisation may be the continuing search for efficiency. Alternatively they might arise as a result of:

- a new leader within the organizations
- benchmarking exercises against external organisation
- senior management dissatisfaction with the status quo
- employee-management conflict.

Within the organisation, the systems approach emphasises the importance of the inter-relationships between the key internal subsystems, namely:

- tasks
- technology
- people
- structure
- management.

It follows that change in response to internal triggers might adjust these subsystems.

Inevitably different thinkers conceptualise change approaches in differently. Ridgeway and Wallace (1996) for instance distinguishes hard and soft issues:

- Hard issues focus on changes to strategy, structures, systems, productivity, performance, etc. The emphasis is more on technical change.
- Soft issues approaches to change by comparison focus on culture, leadership style, behaviour, competencies, attitudes, and motivation. The emphasis here is more people orientated and time scales less definite. Organisational development (OD) is often classified in this way.

9.3.1 Organisational development (OD)

It is difficult to provide a concise explanation of OD as it covers a wide range of activities into the social processes of an organisation. Such approaches are described as 'interventionist' and are focused at developing individuals and groups (Mullins, 2005). Some of the main objectives of OD include:

- Increasing the level of trust among organisational members;
- Allowing problems to be confronted and solved by the people involved rather than being ignored;
- Enhancing openness of communication between and within groups;
- Increasing the level of individual and group responsibility for problem solving and improvement.

Mullins (2005) describes the aim of OD as improved organisational performance, with the major topics associated with organisational development and the management of change being:

- Organisational culture
- Organisational climate
- Employee commitment
- Organisational conflict
- Management Development.

Some of the most well-known and widespread uses of the approach arose in the US aerospace industry. During the space programme many specialists from a wide variety of backgrounds had to work together. Frequently these people found it difficult to collaborate efficiently and OD consultants developed techniques such as T-groups (therapy groups) and confrontation meetings to deal with problems. Essentially, these meetings involved small unstructured groups within which participants are encouraged to explore their own feelings and relationships with others: successful groups will then move on to determine more effective ways of working together.

A key feature of OD is usually the involvement of an independent 'third party' as facilitator for the change. He or she will act as a catalyst by acting as a change agent, helping members of the organisation to diagnose the underlying problems, resolve conflicts, and implement effective change. As part of the initial diagnosis, this third party will often carry out some initial survey of existing attitudes, which will be fed back to all parties involved in the change process.

The types of skills and qualities such an OD consultant would require include the following:

- Sympathy with the underlying OD approach values, which stress openness in communication and interpersonal relations.
- Extensive knowledge of behavioural science theories and practices.
- Data collection and analysis skills.
- The ability to guide and facilitate small groups in general, and particular types of groups such as T-groups and confrontation meetings.
- Team development skills to assist in building effective teams to implement changes.

Rather than using the term 'OD consultant' there is a body of literature that prefers the term 'change agent'.

9.3.2 The change agent

Potentially a change agent could be brought in as an external party (e.g. by appointing from outside a senior member of staff or employing a consultant) or a current member of staff (an internal change agent). Although the change agent is key to the change process, precise roles can vary enormously. Senior and Fleming (2006) identified their usefulness as helping the organisation:

- Define the problem.
- Examine what causes the problem and diagnose how this can be overcome.
- To arrive at alternative solutions.
- Implementation solutions.
- Transmit the learning process that allows the organisation to deal with change on an ongoing basis by itself in the future.

Certain skills and attributes are demanded of a change agent, and Buchanan and Boddy best captured these in their text *The Expertise of the Change Agent: Public Performance and Backstage Activity* (a text presently sadly out of print). These key competences were identified as:

Goals

- Sensitivity to changes in key personnel, top management perceptions and market conditions, and to the way in which these impact the goals of the project in hand.
- Clarity in specifying goals, in defining the achievable.
- Flexibility in responding to changes outside the control of the project manager, perhaps requiring major shifts in project goals and management style, and risk taking.

Roles

- Team building activities to bring together key stakeholders and establish effective working groups, and clearly to define and delegate respective responsibilities.
- Networking skills in establishing and maintaining appropriate contacts within and outside the organisation.

- Tolerance of ambiguity, to be able to function comfortably, patiently and effectively in an uncertain environment.

Communication

- Communication skills to transmit effectively to colleagues and subordinates the need for changes in project goals and in individual tasks and responsibilities.
- Interpersonal skills, across the range, including selection, listening, collection appropriate information, identifying the concerns of others and managing meetings.
- Personal enthusiasm in expressing plans and ideas.
- Stimulating motivation and commitment in others involved.

Negotiation

- Selling plans and ideas to others by creating a desirable and challenging vision of the future.
- Negotiating with key players for resources, or for changes in procedures, and to resolve conflict.

Managing Up

- Political awareness, in identifying potential coalitions, and in balancing conflicting goals and perceptions.
- Influencing skills, to gain commitment to project plans and ideas from potential sceptics and resisters.
- Helicopter perspective, to stand back from the immediate project and take a broader view of priorities.

 ## Exercise 9.2

Based on your own experience of change think about a change agent you have encountered. Did he or she display (or fail to display) these qualities and what were the consequences?

In the following extract Natalie Copper (2007) makes the point that change agents (or champions) who need the support of the workforce to make top-down change 'work'.

Winston Churchill once famously said: 'Never think that a small band of determined people can't change the world. Indeed it is the only thing that ever has.'

Yet as we look at organisational change, it always seems to be heralded as a major initiative, driven from the top by some champion with the express aim of making the organisation more effective, competitive, less vulnerable, quicker to respond, more product focused, more customer focused – the list is endless.

Chief executives have made their names by being change champions, but all the publicity overlooks a fundamental fact. None of the great and good could have done it without the support and commitment of a myriad of people throughout the organisation, not least those in HR who often, but not always, have more of a finger on the pulse than those at the top.

No organisation is perfect and it's easy to point out the faults. It is important that any change makes it better . . . .

Source: Cooper, N. (2007) How to. . . lead change from within. *Personnel Today*, 13th March.

9.4 Parameters for successful change

According to Richard Daft (1998) there are several key parameters that need to be observed if change is to be successful:

Ideas and the need for change. Ideas are generally not seriously considered unless there is a perceived need for change. A perceived need for change occurs when managers see a gap between actual performance and desired performance in the organisation. This can be difficult where the internal culture is strong or where interests are best served by internal stability.

Adoption. Adoption occurs when decision-makers choose to go ahead with a proposed idea. Key managers and employees need to be in agreement to support the change. For a major organisational change, such as an acquisition, the decision might require the signing of a legal document by the board of directors. For a small change, adoption might occur with informal approval by a middle manager.

Resources. Change does not happen on its own, it requires resources not least time in designing, planning and then implementing and reinforcing change. Most innovations go beyond ordinary budget allocations and require special funding. Other changes are very often described as self-funding either directly after implementation (e.g. a staff reduction programme) or after a period of years (such as a change of location of head office to a more rural location).

Implementation. Implementation occurs when an organisation begins to make plans to use a new idea, technique, or system. This can often be done through existing systems such as the capital spending approval system or the departmental or divisional budgeting process. Materials and equipment have to be acquired, and workers may have to be trained to use the idea. Alternatively task teams of interdisciplinary experts are assembled to define the project and drive it forward. Many writers argue for idea champions or change agents. This of course can militate against involvement and participation.

9.5 Types of change

The nature of change can be categorised in various ways. It might for instance be seen as either 'incremental', 'step' or 'transformational'. Alternatively, it could be categorised as either planned or emergent. All these aspects are discussed in this section.

9.5.1 Planned or emergent change

One common categorisation used in describing the nature of change is planned or emergent.

- *Planned.* Organisational change is seen as a process of moving from one fixed state to another through a series of pre-planned steps. As such this approach is entirely consistent with a number of theories and ideas including Daft's key parameters (above). Plans are constructed on the assumption that organisations operate in stable and/or predictable environments (which may not be the case nowadays). The emphasis is upon preplanned, rational and systematic, centrally driven, change. Contemporary criticisms centre on issues of employee commitment and the rigidity of the approach.

- *Emergent.* The popularity of alternative viewpoints including the emergent view arose as the planned approach was challenged as inappropriate given a background of often chaotic environments. The emergent approach is based on a more recent view whereby change is seen as continuous, possibly unpredictable and a process of constant adjustment to the environment. Emergent change approaches coincided with flatter organisational structures, demands for increased participation and an open systems approach. Emergent change emphasises a bottom up approach where managers need to facilitate rather than make the change, making sure employees are receptive to changes and suitably skilled. Emergent approaches assume that organisations operate in unstable and/or unpredictable environments over which they exercise very little control. Change is therefore open ended and on going, and approaches emphasise employee flexibility, cultural adjustment or development, and structural adaptation. Clearly emergent change relies on genuine consultation, good communication, and high levels of co-operation. It also implies a loss of managerial power and more trust in the individual worker which culturally not all organisations might find acceptable.

9.5.2 Incremental change

Incremental change has often comprised changes in response to trends in the environment such as sales growth or more commonly technological improvements. Usually incremental change attempts to match organisational performance with the external environment, and gap analysis feeds back to corrective action. Where the need for change is ignored, organisational decline generally follows.

IBM perceived a strong need for structural change after the company incurred operating losses for two consecutive years. This was not successful and IBM used several Chief Executive Officers as it struggled to align itself against the new environment of PCs and local area networks, instead of mainframe computers that it had specialised in.

Although not radical, even 'incremental' change may have its problems. Daft (1998) described several features of this kind of change:

- Continuous progression rather than a 'frame breaking burst'.
- Maintains equilibrium rather than reaching a new equilibrium.
- Affects only one organisational part rather than transforming an entire organisation.
- Effected through the normal structure rather than creating a new structure.
- Involves improved technology rather than breakthrough technology.
- Involves product improvement rather than a new product creating new markets.

9.5.3 Step change

'Step change' involves a situation where the trend line for a particular factor stops becoming smooth and there is a significant and unexpected jump in direction upwards or downwards. The September 11 2001 tragedy in the USA had a longer-term negative influence on world trade, with dented business confidence and prominent sectors such as airlines took many years to adjust. Other examples include significant natural disasters, such as flooding, severe hurricanes or a tsunami which will have destablising effects long after occurring.

There have been other significant step-changes such as political coups and environmental disasters that have changed the environment within which organisations must work in forever. As step change is impossible or at least difficult to spot in advance, strategic planning has moved from trend analysis towards scenario planning.

Johnson, Scholes and Whittingham (2005) describe scenarios as 'detailed and plausible views of how the business environment of an organisation might develop in the future based on groupings of key environmental influences and drivers of change about which there is a high level of uncertainty'. Far from predicting the unpredictable the process offers various logically consistent futures that an organisation might face so that they might not be totally unprepared in the future.

9.5.4 Transformational change

Johnson, Scholes and Whittingham (2005) described a further change type: transformational change. Here radical change is involved and the organisation acts in a way that is currently outside of its existing paradigm (way of thinking). Clearly this involves a huge cultural shift for this change to be successfully brought about. Unless there is a clearly understood reason for such change (e.g. a crisis of organisational survival) there is likely to be significant employee resistance to such a change.

9.6 Responses to change

9.6.1 Attitudes to change

If change is inevitable then resistance can be predicted. Key questions arise as to how and why resistance to change develops within organisations. Torrington and Weightman (1994) helpfully distinguish four broad types of change experience:

- imposition, initiated by someone else normally from 'on high' or externally,
- adaptation, changes in attitude or behaviour at the behest of others,
- growth, responses to opportunities normally with favourable consequences, and
- creativity, where individuals are the instigator and are in control.

It follows that imposition meets with resistance, adaptation meets with uncertainty, growth meets with delight and creativity meets with excitement. Management therefore needs skills in:

- Overcoming resistance, or trying alternative change methods.
- Winning over the uncertain.
- Encouraging favourable responses from colleagues and subordinates that will engender an air of expectation and excitement.

There is a spectrum of possible reactions to the objectives of a change programme:

- Enthusiastic co-operation and support, acceptance, or co-operation under pressure from management.
- Passive resignation – indifference, apathy, loss of interest, minimal contribution.
- Passive resistance – regressive behaviour, non-learning behaviour.
- Active resistance – protests, working to rule, minimal work, slowing down, personal withdrawal, committing errors intentionally, sabotage.

Virtually all attempts to introduce organisational change will encounter some resistance, which, in some cases, may be severe. Resistance is not surprising, since change can be threatening, and if a person's role in the organisation is challenged, defensive reactions are to be expected. The main reasons for resistance can be summarised as including:

- Incomplete understanding of the nature of the change and/or the reasons for it
- Individuals believing the results of the change threaten their own personal interests and ambitions
- Differing assessments of the costs and benefits of the change to the organisation
- Lack of trust in those initiating the change and their motives.

These reasons for resistance can be understood more fully by considering change at the level of the individual, then of the small group within the organisation. Some individuals have a low tolerance for personal change and are, therefore, particularly likely to resist. In part, this low tolerance may be a function of personality. Alternatively, in many cases it is a reflection of the individual's past experiences and socialisation within the organisation, particularly in the case of long-serving employees or managers. It must be remembered that resistance will often be a reflection of genuine and direct conflicts of interest, which are highlighted by the many 'downsizing' decisions being taken by large organisations involving job losses or moves from fulltime to part-time employment status.

Resistance by members of work groups or informal groups, as opposed to isolated individuals, is likely to pose even more problems for the management of change. Group resistance may be generated by the fact that the proposed changes violate important group norms, or indeed the continued existence of the group. A further possibility is that rivalries and conflicts between groups generate resistance to changes because they are perceived to challenge the existing balance of power.

9.6.2 Overcoming resistance to change

The reasons for resistance may simply be due to a lack of understanding, and the solution lies in better communication. However, if there are deeper reasons for resistance, a more complex approach will be required. Managers need to adopt a flexible approach to managing change that recognises the key contingent factors in each situation.

There are numerous sources of resistance, including cultural or belief barriers, group solidarity, rejection of outsiders, conformity to past norms, conflict, the distribution of authority, structural divisions, technology, managerial philosophy and managerial style. Resistance can be frustrating for managers, but moderate resistance to change can be good for an organisation as it provides a barrier to frivolous changes or 'change for the sake of change'.

A frequent cause of resistance is the way the proposed change is introduced. Managers need to recognise the different forms of resistance:

- Ignorance – 'I don't have enough data to decide.'
- Delayed judgement – 'I will wait and see how it goes before I decide.'
- Defensive stances – 'Other solutions are better, I don't think this will work.'
- Deprivation – 'It cannot be allowed to proceed. It will be far too costly for the firm.'
- Anxiety – 'I know I won't be able to operate the new system.'
- Alienation – 'This will mean separating me from my people and my division.'
- Experienced rejection – 'Here we go again. We tried this once before and it failed.'
- Loss of power – 'It means giving up control over budgets.'
- Default – 'I am just not interested in computers.'
- Erroneous logic – 'It didn't work in Kansas, so it won't work in Kandy.'

The list of 'political' games people can play in resisting change is endless. Undermining, circulating malicious rumours, ridiculing the change agent, questioning the motives of managers, and blaming the initiators for any small organisational shortcomings are all familiar tactics.

Resistance might be best met with face-to-face confrontation. Usually it indicates that the objectives or the sources of pressure for change have not been explained. Rumours begin to circulate, and, unless the resistance is seen as constructive and confronted in an open way, the pain and hurt may continue for years. As in all situations of conflict, it is best to hear out the complaints, let the anger surface and then try to build on calmer behaviour.

Kotter and Schlesinger (1979) identified six main methods of dealing with resistance:

- Education and communication.
- Participation and involvement.
- Facilitation and support.
- Negotiation and agreement.
- Manipulation and co-optation.
- Explicit and implicit coercion.

The final two methods raise ethical and legal problems as well as involving considerable risk of making the situation worse. These six approaches are not mutually exclusive and managers may find it effective to use a combination of them. The most appropriate approach in each instance will depend on a variety of factors, including the goals of the change programme and the likely reactions of the people involved. One of the problems of choosing the 'right' approach is that people will not always openly admit the *real* reasons why they oppose changes. In particular, those reasons relating to self-interest are likely to be disguised as technical objections, arguing that the proposed system will not work. Attempts to deal with these technical objections will not get to the root cause of the resistance to change. Only in a climate in which individuals feel free to discuss their objections and fears openly will it be possible for managers to deal with the underlying reasons for resistance.

 ## Exercise 9.3

Review Kotter and Schlesinger's listing and identify the conditions under which each of these methods might 'work'.

 ## Solution

There is no right or wrong answer, and your thinking is likely to be as valid so long as it is based on commonsense and your own experience.

- *Education and communication.* This is useful when the basic problem is a lack of information about the need for, or the nature of, the planned change. If people can be persuaded about the change they will be more likely to help with its implementation, but this approach can be very time consuming and will not work by itself if there are other reasons than misunderstanding for resisting the change. One of the principal aspects of successful change management centres on the need to talk. Open management, consultation and participation are fundamental to the effective implementation of change. Owning the problem and being part of the solution are fundamental. No major change will come about unless an organisation's managers plan what needs to be done, when things must be done, by whom and what resources should be acquired and used in order to achieve the objectives. This strategy – and its implications must be spelt out. Also these implications must be communicated to, agreed upon and supported by the organisation's managers. Communication is often described as the lubricant of change. Implementation is about capturing hearts and minds not merely writing a policy statement and pinning it on the office wall.

- *Participation and involvement.* This increases the probability that people will be committed to implementing the change and, if their views are taken into account, this may enhance the effectiveness of the change programme. This method is particularly appropriate when the individuals initiating the change do not have all the necessary information to design a change programme and when the people affected by the change have considerable power to resist it. However, as is the case with education and communication, this approach to dealing with resistance to change can be time consuming, particularly if it results in the design of an inappropriate change programme.

- *Facilitation and support.* This involves the use of techniques such as training, counselling and group discussions designed to reduce fear and anxiety. This is particularly appropriate where the principal reason for resistance is based on insecurity and adjustment problems. Some changes do of course really threaten employee aspirations and job security; in these cases facilitation and support may help but it will not address the fundamental cause of resistance.

- *Negotiation and agreement.* This may be necessary where a group clearly stands to lose out in some way because of the change, particularly if this group has considerable power to resist the change. If applied effectively this method of dealing with resistance to change may help to avoid major problems. The disadvantages are that it can be expensive and also it can encourage other groups to negotiate to 'buy' their compliance.

- *Manipulation and co-optation.* Manipulation is an approach that relies on presenting partial or misleading information to the people resisting the change. Co-optation involves identifying key individuals resisting changes and 'buying them off' by giving them positions of authority to help implement the changes. Although this may be a quick and relatively inexpensive approach, it will probably result in future problems if the people involved realise they have been manipulated.

- *Explicit and implicit coercion.* This involves the use of force, or the threat of force, to enforce the implementation of change. This type of approach may be necessary if the parties involved are operating from fixed positions and there are fundamental disagreements over objectives and/or methods.

Inevitably people feel vulnerable during periods of organisational change. It is part of a manager's job to ensure that people focus on the 'right' issues arising from change. For instance, employees may believe that the most effective way to protect their future employment is to be more conscientious, more loyal, work longer hours, etc. All this may be true but the real goal is to justify ones existence through adding value. To manage change it seems sensible to:

- anticipate where apparent threats are coming from and plan to overcome those problems
- sell the benefits of change through good communication
- consider the resource, staff and training requirements of the change
- consider best/optimum time and method of change
- plan and control the change process.

'Look to get those with authority face-to-face with the reality of the situation and seek out the key influencers, who are not necessarily the bosses,' argues Hollington (Simon Hollington, founder of Values Based Leadership, a leadership development consultancy). 'Change needs to have momentum behind it or it will wither on the vine of today's pressures.'

Remember that you see the world, and therefore the need to change, in your way, just as others see it in their way – including perhaps the need for continuity. It might be that the organisation is not ready for it, or that the way you are pushing for change is not working.

Try changing your tactic and aim to sit down with those who object to find out why you are not getting your message across.

Take time to really listen to them because these 'naysayers' are potentially your best allies. First, because they'll let you know where you've gone wrong, and second, because if you change their minds, they will bring plenty of others with them when they switch sides.

If you only do 5 things:
- Know the organisation and the key influencers
- Start with the small things that make a difference such as making it easy for people to get their expenses back
- Get out there and really listen
- Don't take a rebuff as a personal insult
- Don't wait for permission

Source: Cooper, N. (2007) How to . . . lead change from within. Personnel Today, 13th March.

9.6.3 Managerial barriers

Managers themselves can create barriers to beneficial change by the way the change is conceived, designed and implemented. Management can make mistakes by not thinking through their objectives, the resources available and the options they are competent to undertake. Crucially, the issue of who leads the change is seldom thought through. Daft (1998) described several factors and these are used as framework to discuss this issue.

Excessive focus on costs. Management may possess the mind-set that costs are all-important and may fail to appreciate the importance of a change that is not focused on costs (for example, a change to increase employee motivation or customer satisfaction). In most managerial situations a presentation of an idea that costs more than current practice is unlikely to be accepted unless the future returns are considerable.

Failure to highlight benefits. Any significant change will produce both positive and negative reactions. Education may be needed to help managers perceive more positive than negative aspects of the change.

Lack of co-ordination and co-operation. Organisational fragmentation and conflict often result from the lack of co-ordination for change implementation. Moreover, in the case of new technology, the old and new systems may not be compatible. At the operational level, real progress is painstakingly slow and deliberate as the minute detail of how the present systems work (or do not work) is not known. This is the problem with many business process re-engineering projects, as assumptions about how things currently work are made without proper thought. Taken with uncertainty, managerial actions tend to be about saving face and their own department's reputation is protected at the expense of co-operation with others.

Uncertainty avoidance. At the individual level, managers fear the uncertainty associated with change. Constant communication is needed horizontally so that the team knows what is going on and understand how it impacts on their work. An atmosphere of fear 'we've just got to have this in by . . . 'or 'we've got to get this right first time' leads to a culture of blame and negativity and the excessively defensive process of 'protecting one's own back' and a reluctance to take risks.

Fear of loss. This is of course related to the above. Managers may fear not only the loss of power and status but also even their jobs, especially if implementation is not careful and incremental.

Some of the above can be reduced or eliminated by a conscious strategic process to manage change through processes found in organisational development.

9.7 Change: approaches and ideas

9.7.1 Change through entrepreneurship

Rosabeth Moss Kanter, a Harvard professor, rose to prominence with the text 'The Change Masters: Corporate Entrepreneurs at Work' where she stressed the need for 'an American renaissance'. She complained about the 'quiet suffocation of the entrepreneurial spirit' in what she called 'segmentalist companies' (functionally-organised firms) particularly the indifference of management to employee innovations. To counteract this trend she produced various cases to show where and how change could be implemented. In common with the 'excellence school' (that included most prominently Peters and Waterman) she emphasised employee involvement and empowerment, together with a discussion of the managerial skills needed to change culture and strategy. In this context she described the 'integrative' approach to problems as 'moving beyond conventional wisdom', using 'ideas from unconnected sources'.

Kanter's offered prescriptions for encouraging organisational creativity as follows:

- Develop an acceptance of change.
- Encourage new ideas at all levels of the organisation.
- Permit more interaction between individuals and groups.
- Tolerate failure, as experimentation requires trying out new ideas, not all of which will work.
- Offer recognition and rewards for creative behaviour.

These prescriptions will be difficult to implement in a traditional, bureaucratic, role culture. Attempts at managing a change in culture may in these circumstances have to go side by side with attempts to improve innovation and creativity. In 'The Change Masters', Kanter neatly summarised some typical managerial behaviours and policies that will effectively stifle innovative efforts (Table 6.1).

 ## Exercise 9.4

Review Kanter's ten rules and try to invert them to provide a checklist of how entrepreneurship can be encouraged.

Table 9.1 Rules for stifling innovation

Regard any new idea from below with suspicion-because it is new and because it is from below

Insist that people who need your approval to act first go through several other levels of management to get their signatures

Ask departments or individuals to challenge and criticise each other's proposals (That saves you the job of deciding; you just pick the survivor)

Express your criticisms freely, and withhold your praise (That keeps people on their toes.) Let them know they can be fired at any time

Treat identification of problems as signs of failure, to discourage people from letting you know when something in their area isn't working

Control everything carefully. Make sure that people count anything that can be counted, frequently

Make decisions to reorganise or change policies in secret, and then spring them on people unexpectedly (That also keeps people on their toes)

Make sure that requests for information are fully justified, and make sure that it is not given out to managers freely (You do not want data to fall into the wrong hands)

Assign to lower-level managers, in the name of delegation and participation, responsibility for figuring how to cut back, lay off, move people around, or otherwise implement threatening decisions you have made. And get them to do it quickly

And above all, never forget that you, the higher ups; already know everything important about this business

Source: Kanter (1983)

9.7.2 A staged approach to change

A useful way of looking at successful change was proposed by Kurt Lewin (1975) over half a century ago. He suggested a three-step or stage model of change as follows:

- Unfreezing, which involves finding ways of making the need for change so obvious that most people can readily understand it and accept it.
- Changing behaviour patterns in such a way that the new attitudes, values and behaviour are internalised as part of employees' new ways of thinking.
- Refreezing, whereby supporting mechanisms are introduced to ensure the new behaviour patterns are maintained.

In terms of unfreezing, managers often use the threat of external competition to ensure employees are jolted out of complacency with the present, and promises of a more rosy future make change more acceptable. In this environment, change processes can take place, and usually an attempt is made to go for insider solutions (to avoid the 'not invented here' syndrome). These also need to show quick positive results to ensure the change process is not stalled, so that other more difficult items can be scheduled-in. Overcoming resistance is a key feature. Refreezing has its dangers in creating a new status quo.

This process model whereby organisations would attempt to Unfreeze-Change-Refreeze forms the basis of most planned approaches to change.

9.7.3 Identifying forces for and against change

Lewin (1975) also created a concept of the 'force-fields' within a workplace organisation, whereby there are driving forces pushing for change and restraining forces striving to maintain the status quo. By recognising the driving forces and using them to good advantage whilst minimising the restraining forces, change is possible. Lewin described the process

CHANGE MANAGEMENT

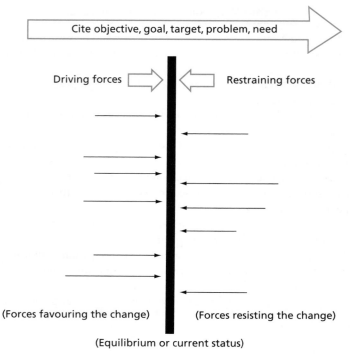

Figure 9.1 Force field analysis

of depicting these as a 'force field analysis' (Figure 9.1). A force field analysis can be constructed by taking a single sheet of paper and following a series of stages:

- Write at the head of the paper on the left hand side 'existing state'.
- Write at the head of the paper on the right hand side 'desired state' (this is the desired change).
- List forces working for the change down the left hand side of the page.
- Put a right facing arrowhead on each force and extend the line dependent upon the relative strength of the force.
- List forces working against the change down the right hand side of the page.
- Put a left facing arrowhead on each force and extend the line dependent upon the relative strength of the force.
- An equilibrium is reach where the forces meet. The challenge for the manager is to bring about movement to the desired state.

9.7.4 Constant change

As we discussed earlier, Tom Peters developed his idea of constant change in his text Thriving on Chaos (1987) in which he declared that the 'modest-sized semi-autonomous, mainly self-managing team should be the basic building-block of organisations'. Peters believed that only organisations that embraced constant change would succeed. This was the best way of improving service and getting close to the customer. (One problem with these 'best practice' approaches advocated by Peters is that a 'one best way' tendency dominates. Samples upon which studies are carried are usually small, and American, and the practical guidance managers need is generally lacking.)

Tom Peters and others regard change as the only constant. Just changing for the sake of it forces people into reviewing and evaluating what they have been doing. In some multinational and global enterprises, executives are rotated every 2 years or so to both prevent them from building up local power bases and to encourage existing cultural recipes for success to challenged.

9.7.5   Change through 'balancing'

Beer and Nohria's (2000) starting point is that a large proportion of all change initiatives fail in the USA. The reason is that the rush to change involves managers immersing themselves in detail and losing focus resulting in mess. Every organisational change conforms to a variant of either:

- *Theory E change strategies.* These are based on measures where shareholder value is the main concern. Change usually involves incentives, layoffs, downsizing, and restructuring.
- *Theory O change strategies.* A 'soft' approach to change, possibly cultural adjustment or enhancing human capability through individual and organisational learning. This involves changing, obtaining feedback, reflecting, and making further changes. Theory companies have a strong, commitment-based psychological contract with their employees.

The difficulty is that Theory E organisations ignore the feelings and attitudes of their employees, so they lose commitment and the creativity needed for sustained competitive advantage. Alternatively Theory O organisations fail to take 'tough' decisions. Beer and Nohria propose that instead of using only one theory or sequencing both theories, organisations should implement both Theory E and Theory O simultaneously and try to balance the associated tensions.

9.7.6   Change through organisational learning

Peter Senge (1992) has been one of the leading advocates of organisations developing the capacity and culture to become what he terms 'learning organisations'; these are the ones that continually expand their ability to shape their future. He explains this as follows:

The roots of the quality movement lie in assumptions about people, organisations and management that have one unifying theme: to make continual learning a way of organisational life, especially improving the performance of the organisation as a total system. This can only be achieved by breaking with the traditional authoritarian, command and control hierarchy where the top thinks and the local acts, to merge thinking and acting at all levels.

(Senge, 1992, p. 31)

Royal Dutch/Shell is quoted as probably the first global corporation to appreciate and implement the benefits of institutionalising learning as the most effective approach to strategic planning. However, many Japanese firms have long recognised the benefits of institutionalising learning around quality improvement teams and associated issues.

Senge's learning organisation concept demands critical awareness of ones own faults and the necessity of change.

According to Senge, there are five core competencies involved in building learning organisations:

- Building a shared vision to ensure that people are focused around a common sense of purpose.
- Personal mastery of learning by individuals who are continually finding out how to create more of what matters to them.
- Working with mental models for people to challenge their unconscious assumptions, and to appreciate how alternative actions could work.
- Team learning. A learning organisation requires individuals to come together and act as teams. Therefore, personal mastery of learning has to be accompanied by team learning so that it can be practised when groups of people have to confront controversial issues and make difficult decisions. Such team learning skills do not come naturally, and this probably explains the poor results of some attempts to use the Japanese practice of quality circles in Western organisations.

- Systems thinking which emphasises the importance of understanding interrelationships, and connections rather than breaking problems down into discrete parts and acting in isolation.

A learning organisation is one that learns from its external environment and adapts accordingly. For such an organisation change becomes natural and on going.

9.8 Critical periods of organisational change

It is important to manage critical periods of change throughout the life of an organisation. Organisations are not static over time: they combine both dynamic and stabilising tendencies. Some will adapt to changes but remain essentially the same size, others will decline and perhaps go out of existence or get taken over, while others grow and develop into larger organisations. Those which grow may do so simply because they have found an economical niche that provides opportunities for growth, or because their managers have consciously pursued policies to achieve growth.

Some owners and/or managers of organisations may actively resist growth because of its perceived problems, such as the difficulty of retaining control or the need to borrow capital. However, there are also potential benefits from growth that will be attractive to others: these might include increased equity, higher salaries, greater security, prestige power, and so on. Although we have already considered both growth and decline from a strategic perspective, it will be worth refreshing our memory of the main characteristics of these periods of development as we look at their change aspects.

9.8.1 Growth by acquisition

There are both positive and negative aspects to growth by acquisition. The growth of large UK organisations has been achieved mainly through external growth, acquisitions or mergers, probably more so than any other industrialised economy. The main reasons for growth through acquisition is that it provides:

- A swift means of expansion for organisations currently in mature markets.
- Opportunities for growth without necessarily attracting attention under government competition policy (e.g. investigation by the Competition Commission in the UK).
- More speedy growth than is usually achievable by internal expansion.
- A way of minimising risk of an aggressive takeover bid by another organisation.
- A means of acquiring a more balanced product portfolio for an organisation.
- Opportunities for 'asset stripping' when the shares of the acquired company are believed to be undervalued. This enables parts of the business to be sold off at a profit after the takeover.

Unfortunately, research suggests that external growth through acquisition strategies often fail to achieve the expected benefits. Although mergers and takeovers may appear to be attractive ways to grow and diversify, the benefits of such activities are not always easy to achieve, as Thompson (2005) made clear:

Many acquisitions and mergers lead to disappointing results: profitability is reduced; synergy does not emerge. It is difficult to predict success or failure in advance as issues of both strategy creation and implementation are involved. Changes in corporate strategy are generally more unpredictable and risky than those which concentrate on improving competitive and functional strategies.

The original 'excellence' studies by Tom Peters and Robert Waterman (1982), suggested that successful companies confined themselves to what they are good at ('stick to the knitting'). The difficulties involved in attempting to lever benefits following diversification into unfamiliar areas perhaps reinforce this point.

The need to merge very different organisational cultures can be a hidden dimension that is often overlooked following acquisition or organisational merger.

Peter Drucker (1982) suggested that there are five basic rules or guidelines that must be followed if acquisitions are to be successful:

- *Contribution* the acquiring company must identify exactly what contribution it can make to the acquired company and this must be more than just money.
- *Common core* the companies involved should have some common core of unity in markets, production operations or technology.
- *Value* the company making the acquisition should value the products, services and customers of the other company.
- *Management cover* it is important that there is some top management cover available in case key senior managers in the acquired company choose to, or are required to, leave after the acquisition.
- *Linkage* within a year of the acquisition managers should have been promoted across the boundaries of the two previously separate companies.

External growth need not rely exclusively on acquisitions or mergers as it can also be based on franchising or licensing. The fast food chain McDonalds operates globally and has experienced tremendous growth over a sustained period, in part due to the use of franchised restaurants.

9.8.2 Growth by organic means

If organisations pursue a strategy of internal growth this will typically be achieved organically by reinvesting profits and building on existing strengths. Economists as well as managers are interested in organisational growth, and some have put forward what is known as the 'S-curve hypothesis'. This suggests that firms will typically have short formative periods, followed by periods of rapid growth, before these tail off into greater stability. The thinking behind this approach is that when an owner first sets up a business there will be an initial period when the firm has to establish itself in the market place. It may then be able to demonstrate some competitive market advantage, which permits the owner to plough back substantial profits to exploit the opportunity. The injection of capital from these profits provides a platform for rapid growth, which will eventually tail off because of loss of competitive advantage and/or profit taking by the owner.

The S-curve thinking is interesting to organisation theorists because it suggests that there are a number of different stages of growth, raising different managerial problems. Therefore, a number of writers studying problems of organisation and management have put forward stage models of growth to explain the internal process and problems of growth.

The simplest models of organisational growth take the concept of a 'product life cycle' from marketing and apply it to stages of an organisation's development. Thus there is likely to be an initial stage of establishing the organisation, followed by growth, stability, and eventually decline. This is illustrated in Figure 9.2.

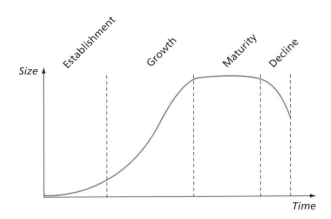

Figure 9.2 The organisational life cycle

Initially, an entrepreneur acts as a catalyst and product champion during the birth and early youth stages of organisational development. As the organisation progresses to early maturity, the entrepreneur will be supplemented or replaced by professional managers. These people are good at running an established business and achieving further growth using their expertise in strategy, organisation and finance.

The danger however is that the successful organisation becomes unwieldy or complacent in the maturity stage and the managers become overly bureaucratic. The departments and divisions within the firm become major barriers to effective communication and problem solving, and the use of fixed rules results in risk aversion and lack of innovation. Stagnation leads to decline. Reversing this decline will probably only be achieved through transformational change.

The organisational life cycle approach is useful but largely descriptive. In order to analyse why these things happen, some explanation is required of the dynamics within the organisation. One such understanding is provided by Larry Greiner (1972), and cited in many texts. Greiner put forward a stage model of growth, arguing that the underlying dynamic in each stage is evolutionary growth that eventually creates a situation of revolutionary crisis, when the organisation's existing ways of doing things are no longer efficient and effective. Thus organisations inevitable experience periods of both evolution and revolution. The implication of this thinking is that change is unavoidable, even predictable and today's solutions become problems in the future. If managers can establish ways of overcoming each crisis there will be a platform for further growth. Failure to deal with a particular crisis will result in decline or demise. Greiner's stages of growth and the crises involved are illustrated in Figure 9.3. A rapidly growing organisation will have a steep line of growth and relatively short periods between crises. Slow growth will produce a flatter line, and consequently longer periods between crises.

The first phase of growth is achieved by some creative idea, product or service that enables the organisation to become established in the market place. This is essentially the first part of both the S-curve hypothesis and the organisational life cycle. Eventually, however, a crisis occurs when the entrepreneur's informal and personal approach to managing the business simply cannot cope with its increased size: this is the crisis of leadership.

If the organisation and the entrepreneur can adopt more formal systems of management, there will be a basis for further growth through direction. This period of growth will

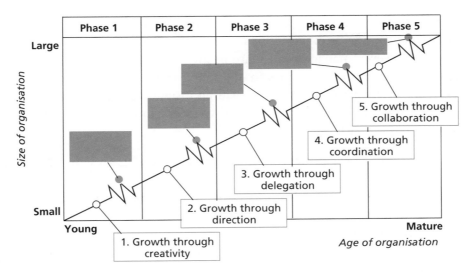

Figure 9.3 The five stages of growth

last for a considerable period if the organisation is growing slowly, but will be short-lived for the rapidly growing organisation. In both cases a crisis situation will eventually arise, because the organisation has reached a size where the slowness and costs of making decisions in a centralised way through the formal hierarchy are proving to be major stumbling blocks: there is a crisis of autonomy.

Only if ways are found of operating in a more decentralised way will the crisis of autonomy be overcome. Decentralisation will involve the owner and senior managers delegating powers of decision-making to members of the organisation closer to the customers or production processes than they are. There will almost certainly be reluctance to do this, because of the perceived risks involved, but it is essential, if the crisis is to be solved, to permit growth through delegation.

Delegation should permit quicker and more effective decision making. In this way further growth can be achieved, and the organisation is very likely to achieve some of this by diversifying into new areas of business. The next crisis will be when senior managers start to fear that they are losing control over the highly decentralised and diversified organisation. They have to find a solution that does not involve reverting to their earlier directive methods.

The solution to the crisis of control usually involves the implementation of more sophisticated management accounting information systems to permit effective monitoring of decisions without the need to intervene in actually making them all. Other actions may be to introduce product groups and formal planning procedures to improve co-ordination. These actions will facilitate growth through coordination in phase 4.

The final crisis identified by Greiner is one of red tape. This occurs when the procedures and systems introduced in earlier phases of growth start to become obstacles to its continuation. By this time the organisation will be very large, and is likely to be operating on a divisional basis, with some important functions and activities provided by a central headquarters. The tension between divisions and headquarters may eventually result in a mutual lack of trust and harmful internal conflicts. Ways have to be found to encourage collaboration and trust to overcome this crisis if the organisation is to proceed to phase 5, the final one in the model: in reality there may be other phases after this but they will only be relevant to the very largest organisations operating on a global scale.

Knowledge of the processes outlined above should help managers to anticipate problems they are likely to encounter as organisations grow, and to be aware of key variables at each stage of growth. However, managers must also be aware of the limitations of the models.

The organisational life cycle approach does not explain the underlying process of growth, and is not particularly helpful in providing insights into the points at which transitions from one stage to the next take place. Greiner's model is more precise in these respects, but still has limitations:

- It implies consistent, linear growth when in practice varying growth rates are likely at each stage.
- It is vague about how exactly to measure size, and this means it is difficult to predict when crises are likely to happen in particular instances.
- It does not explicitly deal with organisational decline.
- It might give the impression that growth is the normal state of affairs for all organisations, when it clearly is not.

Despite these limitations, models of growth, such as the one put forward by Greiner, do provide managers with some useful general insights into this complex process.

9.8.3 Alternatives to growth

Growth is not inevitable and many organisations may make a deliberate choice not to pursue such a policy. The strategic alternatives to growth include:

- Ignoring growth potential and attempting to maintain existing levels of operation.
- Specialisation of the business, and building a future on distinct organisational competences.
- Innovation of products and markets.
- Divestment strategies whereby parts of the business are closed or sold, usually as part of an attempt to consolidate or re-position the business.
- Reduction in geographical scope/product range.

9.8.4 Unbundling, downsizing and rightsizing

One consequence of many acquisitions and mergers is significant programmes of redundancy at all levels in the acquired company. Post-acquisition rationalisations are sometimes referred to as 'rightsizing'. 'Downsizing' conversely occurs without company acquisition normally in response to adverse financial situations arising. Spinning-off operations (unbundling) involves selling parts of an organisation that no longer 'fit' strategically even if they have potential. An example was ICI spinning off its pharmaceutical business as Zeneca (which incidentally soon outperformed ICI financially).

9.8.5 Managing decline

Throughout the early 1990s, because of the depressed state of their national economies, many managers in Europe and the USA were more concerned with the problems of managing decline rather than growth. The problems of managing decline pose particular dilemmas. It places in sharp perspective the ethical dimensions involved in many aspects of management when decisions affecting the workforce, its pay, conditions and employment security are items on the agenda. Slatter (1984) suggested a number of factors that individually, or in various combinations, contribute to organisational decline (Table 9.2 below).

When attempting to manage a situation in which the organisation needs to recover from a depressed situation, the strategic priorities will centre on:

- reducing costs to improve efficiency, and
- improving competitiveness in order to increase revenue.

Initially, when an organisation encounters problems, and revenue and/or profits starts to decline, the typical management reaction is to assume the situation is a temporary one requiring nothing more fundamental than cost cutting. Costs can be reduced anywhere in the supply chain, but the most obvious and usual starting point is to reduce labour costs. At first, this may simply involve altering working patterns to eliminate overtime or, as is increasingly the case, to replace full-time with part-time jobs. If this does not produce sufficient savings, the next step is likely to be voluntary or compulsory redundancies. The danger is that if the cuts are too severe there will be reductions in the quality of the product and services to customers; the impact on employee morale will also make it difficult to achieve the workforce commitment discussed in the previous chapter. Problems of employee morale will be particularly severe if there is a series of cost reduction exercises over a prolonged period. These will result in a loss of trust in management and an escalation in conflicts and levels of political activity. In the present economic climate, it is likely that these conditions will be at the forefront of managers minds for the next few years.

Table 9.2 Contributors to organisational decline

Inadequate financial control, particularly when the management accounting systems are poorly designed, and/or senior managers do not use management accounting information, and/or methods of overhead allocation distort costs

Poor management, typified by factors such as an overly autocratic chief executive, neglect of the organisation's core business and a weak board of directors

Competitive weaknesses due to products in decline and heavy emphasis on price competition

High cost structures, which may be the result of many factors, such as inability to take advantage of economies of scale or operating inefficiencies

Changes in market demand that the organisation has not anticipated and cannot respond to

Adverse movements in commodity prices can be significant in certain industries

Lack of marketing effort can cause decline; when it is a major contributory factor it is usually related to weaknesses in the senior marketing staff, and associated with other fundamental problems such as price and product competition

Too many big projects involving major capital expenditure

Unwise acquisitions, such as buying organisations which themselves have a weak competitive position, or paying too much for them. However, the most common problem is poor management of the organisation once it has been acquired

Poor financial policies, particularly overtrading and/or inappropriate financial sources

Overtrading, so that sales grow at a faster rate than the organisation is able to finance from its cash flow and borrowings

Source: Slatter (1984)

Exercise 9.5

What other measures could be considered by an organisation in such a position?

 ## Solution

- attempting to generate additional revenue through more effective marketing
- improving purchasing policies and procedures
- redesigning the product or service to reduce production costs
- contracting out services that are not considered essential to the core business
- changes to reduce duplication, improving financial control systems and so on.

The difficulty is that certain types of cost-saving measures, such as improving factory layout, might require some initial expenditure, which is not possible if the organisation is already experiencing declining revenues.

Managers may then have to consider more fundamental strategic change alternatives in order to face a decline, including:

- Complete retrenchment, doing the same as before but cutting costs drastically.
- Turnaround, whereby the organisation will attempt to reposition itself for competitive advantage. Most commentators believe that replacement of the existing top management team is a precondition for the successful implementation of such a turnaround strategy. Slatter analysed the main strategies for corporate turnaround and recovery and related them to the initial causes of decline (Figure 9.4).

Figure 9.4 Causes of decline and generic strategies
Source: Slatter 1984

- Divestment involving the external sale of part of the organisation or the internal closure of units, as part of a rationalisation programme.
- Liquidation of the business by selling it to one or more buyers; this entails an admission of failure by the senior managers, and the fear of loss of face may mean that this alternative is not considered seriously until there are no others available.

All four strategies associated with decline (retrenchment, turnaround, divestment and liquidation) require managers to make difficult decisions, which may have adverse effects on all of the organisation's stakeholders, particularly its employees. These issues are at the heart of business ethics and social responsibility, themes that have been highlighted throughout this study system. Previous chapters have stressed the importance of employee commitment for competitive success and the implementation of approaches such as TQM. Large-scale redundancy programmes harm this process, but managers sometimes have to balance the negative effects on staff against economic realities. This requires them to take into account the relative importance of factors such as effectiveness, effort, loyalty, experience and efficiency.

Management faces many difficulties when deciding that employee numbers have to be reduced. There is always the claim that with earlier action decline could have been halted so as to avoid redundancy. Additionally, employees and their representatives often claim that such action is merely short-term cost-cutting to show better profits. In the UK, such action on cutting costs has led to complex and network forms of organisation.

9.8.6 Making ethical decisions

Although management has the power to make tough, sometimes unpleasant decisions, the pressure to act honestly, caringly and ethically should be uppermost. An organisation that treats its employees poorly may damage its public image permanently. The importance of managing change carefully is particularly so under conditions of organisational decline. Senior management must exercise their judgement in deciding whether the cause of decline is temporary or more lasting. The conclusions they draw will impact on the way human resourcing is adjusted and potentially how shedding staff is handled.

If the situation is thought to be temporary, management will have to make a judgement on the level of workforce that needs to be reduced. If redundancies are unavoidable then the extent should be carefully gauged:

- if too many core employees are made redundant, continuity of operation may be difficult
- if too few are dismissed then the cost savings may not be enough and a second round of dismissals becomes necessary. Further calls for redundancy affect morale more deeply each time, reflect poorly on management and performance suffers disproportionately.

If there is no way of telling whether the downturn is permanent or not temporary layoffs and leave of absence may be possible. In one firm, employers were granted two separate leaves of absence. The first was an open leave, the second educational leave. In both cases, employees applied for the leave and were interviewed and selected according to how important their re-employment would be to the firm. Those selected were then paid an allowance and had a contract to return to the firm when given a certain period of notice, which varied with the type of leave given. In this way the psychological contract was not permanently damaged and several employees welcomed in particular the idea of a return to full-time study with a guarantee of re-employment on full wages.

Where the downturn is felt to be permanent, a different approach is needed but this need not imply actions that are uncaring or disrespectful of the individual employees affected. As part of a US government plan to save the Chrysler motor company, Chief Executive Lee Iacocca was faced with the inevitability of shutting plants. Iacocca decided to soften the blow through a series of associated plans designed to get the employees into self-employment or into other forms of work. Some employees reskilled and moved to jobs in other parts of the Chrysler group, but the majority found employment elsewhere locally.

The term 'outplacement' has come to be used to describe the urgent and genuine efforts of management to place redundant employees in other economically active positions. Some consultants have become expert in revising curricula vitae of staff and 'selling' them to a network of contacts. While the term 'redundant' is often tarnished nowadays many organisations go through severe cost-cutting exercises and many excellent staff can become redundant through no fault of their own.

9.9   The context and style of change

There are no simple universal prescriptions for the successful management of change. Each case requires careful analysis and implementation. Sometimes it may be appropriate to force changes through regardless of resistance, but the inherent danger of this approach is that people will return to the old ways of working once the pressure for change is relaxed. In managing change a number of styles are evident, for instance:

- *The participative style.* Extensive delegation of tasks to teams and groups, this requires time, trust and support.
- *The interventionist style.* Limited delegation of some aspects of the change whilst retaining overall direction.
- *The autocratic style.* No delegation – direction is centrally driven.
- *The educational style.* Facts are presented to staff and a rationale made for the change before change gets under way (a 'tell and sell' approach).

Exercise 9.6

Under what conditions might the autocratic style be appropriate?

Solution

In periods of extreme crisis where solutions are demanded quickly and decisively. The major difficulty here is potentially a lack of workforce buy-in and potential resistance.

It is worth remembering that whenever a manager or other leader attempts to change the behaviour of others they are, to some extent, exercising power over those other people. We can classify those types of power and the tools that can be used as follows;

Power of resources:
- bribery,
- offering support,
- disciplinary action,
- firing and redundancies.

Power of processes:
- coalition building,
- involving resistors,
- task forces,
- restructuring,
- changing roles, responsibilities and relationships.

Power of meaning:
- diffusing dissatisfaction,
- informing/persuading,
- cheerleading,
- symbolic action:
  - moving locus of power,
  - changing job titles.

Although there is no one success formula when implementing change and convincing different stakeholder groups of the 'best' way forward, all will involve the exercise of power in one form or another. The following diagram shows a hierarchy of methods that can be used to convince stakeholder groups to accept the proposed changes. As you can see coercion is the last resort.

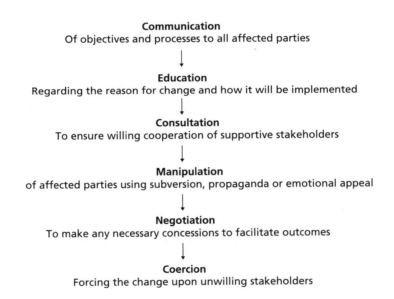

Communication
Of objectives and processes to all affected parties

↓

Education
Regarding the reason for change and how it will be implemented

↓

Consultation
To ensure willing cooperation of supportive stakeholders

↓

Manipulation
of affected parties using subversion, propaganda or emotional appeal

↓

Negotiation
To make any necessary concessions to facilitate outcomes

↓

Coercion
Forcing the change upon unwilling stakeholders

The management of change is never an easy process, and very rarely does the final outcome completely match the originally designed result. Remember there is no recipe for success, they simply do not exist.

Change is more likely to succeed if there is/are:
- clear understandable goals,
- realistic time frames and not looking for a 'quick fix',
- clear guidance as to how *individual behaviours* need to change, not just rewriting the mission statement,
- clear unified leadership with no conflict of management priorities,
- decentralisation/empowerment *preceding* integration and control,
- management do not cut back on training and other necessary investment.

9.10   Evaluating change programmes

Once a change programme is underway, or even when the management feel that it has been completed, some form of evaluation needs to be completed to determine if any lessons can be learnt from the process. Although there are no success formulae for change we can often learn from what has and has been done and the results that have been achieved.

Evaluating change programmes:

- Was there an appropriate problem diagnosis? Part of this will have involved a cultural analysis of the organisation and all of its aspects. Did the programme that was implemented deal with all aspects of the firm or only on one or two such as the structure and the control systems? Were a whole range of factors dealt with or just an isolated few? In medical terms, did the programme address the disease or only the symptoms?
- Were there realistic goals, time frame and resources? Was there a realistic assessment of how long the required patterns of behaviour would take to learn and embed? Was staff given the appropriate tools and training to be able to do what was required in the manner that was necessary? Was there a clear explanation of why the change was necessary and what the desired outcome, and patterns of behaviour, would look like to all of the people involved?
- Was there a holistic approach? Did the programme consider all of the organisation or was there a piecemeal implementation, leaving some staff in the dark, whilst others were fully informed? Did the programme address all of the issues that the organisation faced?
- Did the programme deliver the desired results? When the programme is finished, or when management believe it is finished, there needs to be a complete audit to determine if the desired results and patterns of behaviour have been achieved or if further change is necessary.

9.11   Change in perspective

 Exercise 9.7

Michael Jarrett cited in Stern (2005) identified what he called the 'seven myths of change management'. Based on your own experience and reading you have undertaken try to list arguments both for and against each of the seven items:

Organisational change management creates value	The truth is that organisational change is exceedingly difficult and expected benefits are rarely realised. Academic research suggests that 70% of change management programmes fail.
Resistance can be overcome	Fear and survival are at the roots of resistance. Resistance first needs to be understood and reinterpreted, and cannot be ignored or overcome.
Change is constant	There is a difference between transformational change which is rare and incremental change (or continuous improvement).
Change can be managed	Change agents might stimulate or even steer through change it, but that's not managing it.

The change agent knows best	Ultimately an organisation will find its own ways of responding to change.
Accepted wisdom is to follow the steps	A rational checklist approach is inflexibile, adjustments might be needed in the chaos of rapid change.
Big change require big changes	Small scale changes can build a critical mass, everything does not need to change at once, or on a big scale.

Now refer to the following website and make notes: http://www.beyondresistance.com

9.12 Summary

The successful management of change is the most crucial issue facing any manager or organisation. This chapter has dealt with certain aspects of this all-embracing and often complex subject. Specific attention has been paid to triggers for change both external and internal, the change process itself and ideas and approaches to change management by exploring the thinking of certain theorists. Finally, the importance of managing critical periods of change through the life cycle of an organisation has been highlighted.

References and further reading

Beer, M. and Nohria, N. (2000) Cracking the code of change. *Harvard Business Review*, May–June, pp. 133–141.

Cooper, N. (2007) How to . . . lead change from within. *Personnel Today*, Vol. 13th, p. 39.

Daft, R. (1998) *Organizational Theory and Design* (6th edn). New York: West Publishing.

Drucker, P. (1982) *The Changing World of the Executive*. London: Heinemann.

Goldratt, E. (1992) *Introduction to the Theory of Constraints – The Goal Approach Seminar*. Avraham Y Goldratt Institute.

Lynch, R. L. (ed.) (1972) *Corporate strategy* (4th edn). Harlow: FT Prentice Hall (2006).

Jarrett, M. and cited in Stern, S. (2005) Forever changing. *Management Today*, Vol. 7, p. 40.

Johnson, G., Scholes, K., and Whittington, R. (2005) *Exploring Corporate Strategy* (7th edn). Harlow: Financial Times Prentice Hall.

Kanter, R. M. (1983) *The Change Masters*. New York: Simon and Schuster.

Kotter, J. P. and Schlesinger, L. A. (1979) *Organization: Text, Cases, and Readings on the Management of Organizational Design and Change*. Homewood, Ill: R.D. Irwin.

Lewin, K. (1975) *Field Theory in Social Science: Selected Theoretical Papers*, Westport (Conn.): Greenwood Press A publication of the Research Center for Group Dynamics, University of Michigan Originally published, New York: Harper & Brothers, 1951.

Mullins, L. J. (2005) *Management and Organisational Behaviour* (7th edn). Harlow: Financial Times, Prentice Hall.

Paton, R. A. and McCalman, J. (2000) *Change Management: a guide to effective implementation* (3rd edn). London: Sage.

Peters, T. (1987) *Thriving on Chaos: A Handbook for a Managerial Revolution*. London: Pan.

Peters, T. and Waterman, R. (1982) *In Search of Excellence*. New York: Harper & Row.

Ridgeway, B. and Wallace, B. (1996) *Leadership for Strategic Change*. London: Institute of Personnel and Development.

Semler, R. (2001) *Maverick*. London: Random House Business Books.

Senge, P. (1992) *The Fifth Discipline: The Art and Practice of the Learning Organization*. London: Random House Business Books.

Senior, B. and Fleming, J. (2006) *Organisational Change* (3rd edn). Harlow: Financial Times, Prentice Hall.

Slatter, S. (1984) *Corporate Recovery: A Guide to Turnaround Management*. Penguin: Harmondsworth.

Thompson, J. L. and Martin, F. (2005) *Strategic Management Awareness and Change* (5th edn). London: Thomson Learning.

Torrington, D. and Weightman, J. (1994) *Effective Management: People and Organisation* (2nd edn). London, New York: Prentice Hall.

Worrall, L. and Campbell, F. (2000) 'Surviving Redundancy: the Perceptions of UK Managers'. *Journal of Managerial Psychology*, Vol. 15, No. 5, pp. 447–460.

Revision Questions

? Question 1

The country of Chapterland has a principle that healthcare should be free to its citizens at the point of access. Healthcare is funded from national taxation and organised through a series of large health units, one of which is known as 'Q2'. Q2 operates a huge, single-site hospital and offers a variety of community services (such as health visiting) that are taken to the local population. Q2 has a management structure consisting of eight clinical and administrative directors who report to Q2's Chief Executive Officer (CEO). The Q2 CEO is directly accountable to the national government through regular returns of information and year-end reporting.

Published 'quality league tables' of hospital performance against government targets suggest that Q2 has one of the worst records in the country. (Targets are for cleanliness of hospital wards, treatment waiting times and staff employed per patient cases dealt with). In addition, Q2 has in recent years been operating to a budget in excess of its funding, which is against government regulations. The current year budget again exceeds projected funding.

Last year Q2's previous CEO decided that certain changes were necessary including better cost control and improved performance measurement and management through benchmarking. He revealed this thinking for the first time in a global email he sent to Q2's staff. Later when conducting the annual performance appraisal of the Director of Human Resources (HR) he tasked her with implementing each and every form of benchmarking' within the next 4 months so that 'true' performance deficiencies could be addressed. However, the Director of HR left for a new job elsewhere within that period. The CEO then undertook to manage the change himself but was surprised to find directors unenthusiastic and even uncooperative. Under pressure from the government the CEO resigned 'for personal reasons' and no progress was made with his initiatives.

A new CEO has just been appointed. Her immediate concern is to reduce expenditure and improve performance. On her first day as CEO she spoke of a need to re-establish a culture of 'care through quality' within Q2. She wishes to discuss a number of ideas and issues with her clinical and administrative directors at a special 'away day' meeting to be arranged soon. You work in the CEO's central policy team and she has informed you that some ideas for initiatives include outsourcing, improved supply management and new performance management measures.

Requirement

You have been asked to provide the new CEO with briefing notes on a number of issues that will help prepare her for the 'away day' meeting

(a) Explain why the changes attempted by the previous CEO was unsuccessful.

(5 marks)

? Question 2

Great Value Foods (GVF) is one of Bigland's leading supermarket chains. Though fierce competitive activity had reduced the major players in the industry to half a dozen large chains in the years since 1970 the competitive pressures and large-scale capital investment required had not prevented all new entrants to the market. A few foreign competitors seeking new markets had managed to secure a foothold by offering unbranded goods at rock bottom prices. These companies kept costs low by displaying a limited range of grocery necessities on pallets in large warehouses and offering only minimal service. This development only served to increase the pressure on GVF since the new entrants nibbled away at what had been part of GVF's traditional customer base.

In the midst of all these difficulties, GVF was suddenly confronted with what seemed to be a golden opportunity. One of its competitors was experiencing trading difficulties and offered GVF the chance to purchase 60 of their stores in the south of the country. The opportunity was too much to resist and GVF borrowed £800 million and thereby doubled its outlets.

As GVF took over the management of their new clutch of southern superstores, however, it realised that considerable time and funds would be required to convert them to their own distinctive format and to the modern standards now expected by consumers. This not only delayed the expected revenue stream from the new outlets, it also required additional borrowing and raised gearing to an uncomfortable level. As if GVF did not have enough problems, the threat of inflation forced government to raise interest rates and so the burdens on GVF increased yet more.

During all this activity, GVF had been seeking to catch up on competitors in a number of ways. It had for instance managed to increase its number of own-label products significantly and had just developed a new central distribution system that experts agreed was among the best in the country. However, there were delays in distribution of supplies to some stores during the run up to the country's most important festive season. This resulted in a considerable loss for the company and three of the directors considered responsible for the problems were sacked.

These problems, together with an accompanying decline in profits, resulted in a fall in the share price GVF had paid too much for its 60 southern stores and that a rights issue would be necessary for the company to reduce its debt burden.

The first weeks of the new CEO were spent reviewing the company and its problems. She found that the company had too many layers of management, narrow functional attitudes and a controlling bureaucratic head office culture. Furthermore, the business was no longer effective and responding to customer needs.

Requirements

(a) Summarise the measures required to turn the company around. **(5 marks)**

(b) Describe:

   (i) the most likely sources of resistance to change;

   (ii) any model of organisational change and explain how it might be used to implement change in GVF. **(15 marks)**

(Total marks 20)

 # Question 3

Sparks company was until recently the high street market leader of the retail clothiers but last month it reported its worst sales fall in its 120-year history and end-of-year figures are predicted to show that its profits are a quarter of those of the previous year. Analysts have identified a number of problems they believe responsible for Sparks' present situation. These include:

- Lack of anticipation of changing consumer preferences, an over-reliance on the brand image of the company as the primary means of marketing its products, and a relative lack of efficiency in getting its new designs to its stores.
- An unwieldy management structure with many management levels presided over by a large board of directors and an expensive head office in which managers considerably outnumber other members of staff.
- An inefficient distribution system in which goods move via a series of regional warehouses instead of direct from the factory.
- A poor system of purchasing in which Sparks continues to rely on relatively expensive domestic suppliers rather than bring in alternative cheaper supplies that have become available from other countries.

Requirement

As a consultant, advise the board of directors of Sparks to help them to overcome their problems and to turn the company around. **(12 marks)**

 # Question 4

R&L is a large manufacturing firm that is well known as a 'good employer'. Over the past few years, R&L has experienced difficult times with reducing sales and mounting losses. In desperation it employed management consultants to analyse its situation. The consultants have concluded that the downturn in sales is permanent and that R&L needs to reduce its workforce by 50% over the next year in order to survive. Reluctantly, R&L's board of directors has accepted these findings, including the need to reduce the number of staff. The directors have also agreed to act as honestly and as fairly as possible, but realise that any changes they propose will be unpopular and may meet with resistance.

Requirement

Discuss the potential strategies available in order to overcome resistance to change, and identify those strategies that would be most suitable for R&L. **(10 marks)**

Solutions to Revision Questions

☑ Solution 1

(a) Why the changes attempted by the previous CEO were unsuccessful.

A number of mistakes were evident in the management of the change:

Lack of consultation
The CEO rightly decided that certain key changes were necessary. Although he may have been correct in identifying the areas he did there is no suggestion that he consulted on the required key changes. As a result there is no certainty that these initiatives alone would bring about the desired changes. The changes needed may have involved a need for cultural change, which appears to have been ignored.

Lack of two way communication and ownership
The CEO revealed his thinking for the first time in a global email sent to Q2's staff. It may have been advisable to use these thoughts as a basis for discussion and involve staff in order to:

- raise awareness of the issues.
- generate new thinking and ideas.
- take ownership of the change initiatives.

Taking responsibility for the change
The use of the annual performance appraisal process to delegate responsibility for the change was not advisable. Further it is debateable whether the Director of HR should be made responsible for it. It could be seen that the CEO abdicated responsibility rather than assuming a role of a visible driving force in the early stages. For such important developments, the CEO or perhaps some management consultant may have been more appropriate to lead the change programme. When the Director of Human Resources left for a new job elsewhere the CEO became the change agent himself. This meant that the impetus for change had been lost. The Chief Executive's subsequent resignation meant that two change agents had been unsuccessfully used.

Lack of involvement of clinical and managerial directors
Directors other than the Director of HR may have felt excluded from the process (hence their apparent lack of enthusiasm and cooperation). It would have been advisable to discuss matters with them initially before all staff were communicated with. They may have felt undervalued and also felt that their authority had been undermined.

Inappropriate communication method

Using email to inform staff of such important changes is inappropriate for communicating a change of this magnitude. Email is impersonal and it is unlikely that every member of staff would be able to access this medium. Email is in any case best for quick factual information sharing only.

Faulty planning

There is no evidence of

- how cost control might be improved
- specific plans for how changes were to be implemented
- allocations of extra time and resources
- sensitivity as to how the changes would affect staff.

✓ Solution 2

(a)   The inefficiency of GVF management appears to be related to the existing structure of the company. According to the CEO analysis there is a need to reduce the number of layers of management, to reduce controls from head office and to change attitudes from a narrow concern with departmental objectives to a broader concern with the demands of the business as a whole. The reduction in levels of management will help to reduce costs and to improve communications within the business. Store managers and others will welcome the reduction in bureaucratic head office controls, as the added autonomy will help motivate them.

The CEO's comment that the company 'was no longer effective and responding to vcustomer needs,' confirms what we already know from the case. What GVF needs to know more precisely, however, is exactly what the needs of customers are.

A useful framework for considering the causes of decline and the generic strategies required for turning a company around has been proposed by Slatter.

Reviewing the list of causes and proposed measures for action, it is apparent that many of the causes of decline listed by Slatter occur in the GVF case. Only in the instance of acquisitions is it necessary to note that, in GVF's case, the purchase of the 60 southern stores is probably a sound move. As to the recommendations for action, most of these have been accounted for in the proposals listed earlier.

(b) (i) Resistance to change in organisations can be considered according to whether the resistance comes from individuals, groups or the organisations themselves.

At the individual level the following reasons/causes have been noted as factors involved in resistance: fear of the unknown, well-formed habits, threat to economic interest/status and the threat of inconvenience. Given the present circumstances of GVF, it is likely that all of the above factors will be relevant to employees in the company. The press reports on the present position of the company will lead many of them fear for their job security and whether or not they will be able to continue with their present job or have to learn another one. Some will have few alternatives if they lose their present position and will be faced with the possible prospect of having to move to another part of the country to find another job or face the prospect of a less well-paid position or even to have to exist on state benefit payments.

Managers who have heard the new CEO statement about the company having too many levels of management will be the most fearful about the loss of a job. For those with much to lose and little to gain from any impending changes there will be an understandable reluctance to engage in the change process with any enthusiasm. There will of course be those who see the forthcoming changes as long overdue and perhaps as an opportunity to prove themselves and make headway in the organisation under a new regime.

At the group level there will be collections of individuals who see their position threatened and who will combine to resist any threats to their position. This will be particularly the case if the employees are unionised. In some countries it is common for shop workers to be members of a trade union and any changes that affect the union members may be, resisted by threats of some form of industrial action. Even where trade unions do not exist within the organisation, it is possible for groups of employees, including managers, to collude informally to resist changes in an organisation. This may be achieved by such measures as withholding information or not being wholly co-operative with those seeking to implement change. In the GVF case, directors, managers and employees who see their established positions threatened in whatever way are unlikely to give full co-operation unless they can see some long-term advantage for themselves.

At the level of the organisation, a number of factors will operate to make the change process difficult. These include the existing structure and culture of the organisation, the existing investment in resources and past contracts and agreements with various stakeholders within the organisation. The change to a flatter more decentralised structure at GVF, for instance, threatens the jobs and status of some layers of management.

(ii) The new CEO of GVF might use the force-field theory of change proposed by Lewin. Lewin's theory suggests that all behaviour is the result of equilibrium between two sets of opposing forces. One set he refers to as driving forces because they are the forces attempting to bring about change; the other set are referred to as restraining forces because they act in the opposite direction and seek to maintain the status quo.

In the case in question, the driving forces for change in GVF would be those to be implemented by the new CEO and her senior managers. It may be useful to regard the senior management team as an instrument of change because in many ways the team could be regarded as being driven by forces threatening the organisation's survival. Competitors in particular will take more and more of the market share of GVF unless the management team can improve the operational efficiency of the organisation and its effectiveness. As far as efficiency is concerned, better management control is required, especially in the management of the new central distribution system. There is also a need to be more responsive to changes in the market place and this is why the drive to a more decentralised flatter structure is required.

✅ Solution 3

In the case of Sparks, the analysis of the main causes of the company's decline has already been conducted for us and we have the results. It is thus only necessary to examine each of these and to decide on the appropriate action to be taken.

CHANGE MANAGEMENT

The first set of problems suggests the need for more thorough market research and of increased attention to marketing generally. In particular, Sparks needs to be better able to spot fashion trends and to be ready to cater for a range of customers. The company also needs to be able to get its new designs to its stores as fast or faster than competitors. This will be a difficult task but must be achieved if the company is to compete effectively with the best. Attention to the logistical problems of moving from the design stage to the store shelves will also be required. One way of achieving this, already practised by some competitors, is to have goods delivered directly to stores rather than to regional warehouses.

The expensive head office and tall hierarchical structure needs to be looked at and tackled by a series of linked measures. Sparks needs to look at the possibility of delayering The removal of layers of management has been common practice by a large number of organisations in recent years as a means of shortening reporting lines and thus enabling companies to be more responsive to competitive and other changes in the environment. This process of delayering will have the added advantage of reducing headcount and thus cutting costs – especially from the management-heavy headquarters.

The purchasing and distribution systems also appear to need a radical overhaul. The fact that Sparks takes so much longer to get its new designs into the stores than its major competitors underlines the need for this. The adoption of some overseas suppliers to replace some existing domestic suppliers could provide a jolt to existing suppliers and encourage them to work with Sparks into improving the efficiency of their supply chain. Care will be necessary in the selection of new suppliers. Though cost is a key consideration in the purchase of items of clothing, both quality and speed of delivery are also major considerations.

 Solution 4

Kotter and Schlesinger (1979) identify six main strategies for dealing with resistance. This might usefully serve as a framework for discussion:

- *Education and communication* is particularly useful when the basic problem is a lack of information about the need for, or the nature of, the planned change. The approach can be very time-consuming and will not work by itself if there are reasons other than misunderstanding leading to resistance to change. Such a strategy would seem to be appropriate in this case. As a good employer, R&L is honour bound to present all known facts on the plight of the company and discuss options openly and straightforwardly. A suitable strategy.
- *Participation and involvement* increases the chances of commitment to implementing the change particularly if their views are taken into account. This method is particularly appropriate when the people affected by the change have considerable power to resist it. This approach can be time-consuming. Such a strategy would seem to be appropriate in this case. Whatever positive measure is chosen, participation is vital to ensuring its success. The change is more acceptable if it is done by you rather than to you! A highly suitable strategy.
- *Facilitation and support* involves training, counselling and discussions, designed to reduce anxiety. This is particularly appropriate where the principal reason for resistance is based on insecurity and adjustment problems. Such a strategy would seem to be appropriate in this case; indeed the suggestion of outplacement is an embodiment of this strategy. A highly suitable strategy.

- *Negotiation and agreement* may be necessary to compensate those losing out because of the change. This may help avoid major problems, but it can be expensive in terms of, for example, redundancy packages. If there is little goodwill between the parties it may be protracted and bruising. Such a strategy would seem to be appropriate in this case, as R&L is a good employer there may be genuine goodwill between the management side and trade unions. A suitable strategy.

- *Manipulation and co-optation* involves presenting partial or misleading information to those resisting change and 'buying off' key players. This is a quick and relatively inexpensive approach, but normally results in future problems if the people involved realise they have been manipulated. Such a strategy would be inconsistent with R&L's philosophy of being a 'good employer'. An unsuitable strategy.

- *Explicit/implicit coercion* involves the use of force, or the threat of force, to enforce the implementation of change. It raises ethical (and potentially legal) problems as well as involving considerable risk of making a situation more difficult, especially if trade unions are in a position to provide opposition and protection. Such a strategy would be inconsistent with R&L's philosophy of being a 'good employer'. An unsuitable strategy.

Preparing for the
Examination

Preparing for the Examination

This chapter is intended for use when you are ready to start revising for your examination. It contains:

- details of the format of the examination;
- a summary of useful revision techniques;
- a bank of examination-standard revision questions and suggested solutions. These solutions are of a length and level of detail that a competent student might be expected to produce in an examination;
- a complete pilot paper. This should be attempted when you consider yourself to be ready for the examination, and you should emulate examination conditions when you sit it.

Format of the examination

The *E3 Enterprise Strategy* examination takes the form of a 3-hour written paper:

- Section A contains a compulsory question based on a scenario, and offering a maximum of 50 marks;
- Section B contains a choice of questions (two from three).

About the examination

Not every aspect of the syllabus will be covered in a single paper, instead the aim is to cover syllabus across a range of diets.

Numbers feature prominently as evaluation cannot realistically be done without making and appraising calculations. Throughout there will be a requirement to apply knowledge to various working contexts and situations.

The examiners require candidates to comply with the aims of the syllabus (see p. xix) when answering questions in the following ways:

- *Competency*: handling issues in scenarios and addressing the specific question set.
- *Adequacy of knowledge*: demonstrating knowledge levels with use of appropriate theories and models.

- *Understanding and mastery of knowledge and skills*: application of that knowledge sometimes in unfamiliar circumstances.
- *Complementary practical experience*: by providing realistic examples drawn from experience as well as study.

Revision technique

Planning

The first thing to say about revision is that it is an addition to your initial studies, not a substitute for them. In other words, don't coast along early in your course in the hope of catching up during the revision phase. On the contrary, you should be studying and revising concurrently from the outset. At the end of each week, and at the end of each month, get into the habit of summarising the material you have covered to refresh your memory of it.

As with your initial studies, planning is important to maximise the value of your revision work. You need to balance the demands for study, professional work, family life and other commitments. To make this work, you will need to think carefully about how to make best use of your time.

Begin as before by comparing the estimated hours you will need to devote to revision with the hours available to you in the weeks leading up to the examination. Prepare a written schedule setting out the areas you intend to cover during particular weeks, and break that down further into topics for each day's revision. To help focus on the key areas try to establish:

- which areas you are weakest on, so that you can concentrate on the topics where effort is particularly needed;
- which areas are especially significant for the examination – the topics that are tested frequently.

Don't forget the need for relaxation, and for family commitments. Sustained intellectual effort is only possible for limited periods, and must be broken up at intervals by lighter activities. And don't continue your revision timetable right up to the moment when you enter the exam hall: you should aim to stop work a day or even 2 days before the exam. Beyond this point the most you should attempt is an occasional brief look at your notes to refresh your memory.

Getting down to work

By the time you begin your revision you should already have settled into a fixed work pattern: a regular time of day for doing the work, a particular location where you sit, particular equipment that you assemble before you begin and so on. If this is not already a matter of routine for you, think carefully about it now in the last vital weeks before the exam.

You should have notes summarising the main points of each topic you have covered. Begin each session by reading through the relevant notes and trying to commit the important points to memory.

Usually this will be just your starting point. Unless the area is one where you already feel very confident, you will need to track back from your notes to the relevant chapter(s) in the *Study System*. This will refresh your memory on points not covered by your notes and fill in the detail that inevitably gets lost in the process of summarisation.

When you think you have understood and memorised the main principles and techniques, attempt an exam-standard question. At this stage of your studies you should normally be expecting to complete such questions in something close to the actual time allocation allowed in the exam. After completing your effort, check the solution provided and add to your notes any extra points it reveals.

Tips for the final revision phase

As the exam approaches, consider the following list of techniques and make use of those that work for you:

- Summarise your notes into more concise form, perhaps on index cards that you can carry with you for revision on the way into work.
- Go through your notes with a highlighter pen, marking key concepts and definitions.
- Summarise the main points in a key area by producing a wordlist, mind map or other mnemonic device.
- On areas that you find difficult, rework questions that you have already attempted, and compare your answers in detail with those provided in the *Study System*.
- Rework questions you attempted earlier in your studies with a view to producing more 'polished' answers (better layout and presentation earn marks in the exam) and to completing them within the time limits.
- You were advised earlier to read widely, stay alert for practical examples, incidents, situations and events that illustrate the material you are studying. If you can refer in the exam to real-life topical illustrations you will impress the examiner and earn extra marks.
- Make sure that you read as many of the articles from *Insider* and *Financial Management* that are relevant to the strategic level.

Revision Questions

Note that the published Examiner's Reports contain much useful detailed guidance on areas of difficulty experienced by candidates sitting examinations. You are strongly recommended to obtain the past examination papers and their associated Examiner's Reports, and read them after you have attempted your answer and before looking at the suggested solution.

The first part of this section contains questions which are typical of those that you will find in the second part of the examination. You should attempt those after you have studied the appropriate part of the manual. These are mapped in the table below. However, the first part of the *E3 Enterprise Strategy* exam is likely to combine syllabus topics within the scenario question. For this reason the second part of this revision section contains questions and scenarios requiring knowledge from throughout the syllabus. You are advised to leave this part until you have completed the first part of the revision section.

In the examination you will be presented with a compulsory scenario for 50 marks and a choice of further questions worth 25 marks each. Please bear this in mind when allocating your time during question practice.

Map of syllabus against questions

Syllabus topic	Question
E3 – A. Interacting with the Competitive Environment (20%)	
1. Evaluate the key external factors affecting an organisation's strategy.	1, 3, 4, 5, 7, 10, 12, 13, 14, 15, 16, 17, 18, 19, 20, 21, 2, 23, 26
2. Evaluate the impact of information systems on an organisation.	8, 12, 13, 16, 24, 25, 26
E3 – B. Change Management (20%)	
1. Advise on important elements in the change process.	27
2. Evaluate tools and methods for successfully implementing a change programme.	28, 29
3. Recommend change management processes in support of strategy implementation.	7, 19, 22
E3 – C. Evaluation of Strategic Position and Strategic Options (30%)	
1. Evaluate the process of strategy development.	4, 5, 9, 16, 18, 19, 20, 21
2. Evaluate tools and techniques used in strategy formulation.	2, 3, 5, 8, 11, 15, 16, 17, 18, 23, 24
E3 – D. Implementation of Strategic Plans and Performance Evaluation (30%)	
1. Evaluate the tools and processes of strategy implementation.	2, 6, 7, 11, 12, 13, 14, 16, 19, 22, 23, 24, 25, 26

Question 1

An increasing number of companies have expressed their willingness to consider their wider social responsibilities. This often involves them in voluntarily undertaking extra responsibilities and costs; for example:

- in order to reduce pollution, they may decide to treat waste products to a higher standard than required by legislation;
- they may decline to trade with countries whose governments they find objectionable;
- they may pay wages above national minimum levels.

Requirements

(a) Discuss:
   (i) whether the pursuit of a policy of social responsibility necessarily involves a conflict with the objective of shareholder wealth-maximisation;
   (ii) the extent to which the existence of a conflict between a company's objectives is acceptable.   **(9 marks)**
(b) Discuss the extent to which it is feasible for a company to 'operationalise' its social responsibility aspirations, that is whether it is possible to bring these considerations into strategic decision-making in a programmed or systematic way.   **(9 marks)**
(c) Discuss whether it is feasible for companies to include the requirements of their stakeholders when they seek to recognise their wider social responsibilities.

(7 marks)
(Total marks = 25)

 # Question 2

You have recently been appointed to lead the management accounting department of W Ltd, which is a small engineering company engaged in the manufacture of precision parts. The market in which the company sells its products is small and W Ltd faces severe competition. Due to the production facilities available, the company is able to undertake only small-scale engineering work. Large-scale engineering jobs are turned away as the company does not possess the manufacturing facilities to undertake them. At best, it can act only as agent for another contractor to do the work.

The board of W Ltd is aware that the volume of work which is being turned away is increasing. This is particularly frustrating as the company is unable to utilise its capacity to the fullest extent all the time. W Ltd has achieved a steady increase in profit over the last few years. Nevertheless, the board of the company believes that it could increase profitability still further by expanding and thus being able to carry out the larger scale work which is currently being turned away.

Budgetary control and standard costing information has, for many years, been provided as the sole output of the management accounting department. The previous management accountant prided himself on the punctuality and comprehensiveness of the reports produced. Each job is priced by adding a percentage to its total cost calculated in accordance with the company's standard costing procedures. The annual cost budget is split into monthly parts and flexed to take account of a particular period's actual production. Monthly cost variances, comprising those for direct materials, direct labour, variable and fixed production overheads, are produced and provided to the relevant manager. In addition, sales price and volume variances are produced by the management accounting department each period.

The company does not have a marketing department, although new customers are obtained from advertising within professional engineering journals and by attendance at trade shows. At one such recent trade show, the managing director was introduced to the concept of benchmarking. He believes that there may be advantages in W Ltd undertaking benchmarking.

Requirements

(a) In consideration of the need for the board of W Ltd to be provided with information which assists its strategic decision-making, comment critically on the management accounting reports currently provided. **(6 marks)**

(b) State and justify what changes you, as management accountant, would make in providing information which facilitates strategic planning in the company.

Within your answer, describe what financial and non-financial information you would supply which is different from that already provided. **(12 marks)**

(c) Explain the concept of benchmarking *and* suggest how it might be applied to information for strategic planning in W Ltd. **(7 marks)**

(Total marks = 25)

? Question 3

GC is a conglomerate which comprises five strategic business units (SBUs), all operating as subsidiary companies. Information relating to each SBU (and the market leader or nearest competitor) is given in the following table:

	Current market share			Market growth expected by GC
	GC	Market leader	Nearest competitor	
	%	%	%	
Building brick manufacturer (Declining profitability)	3	25		Small
Parcel carriage service (Long established, faces strong competition. Turnover and profitability over last 3 years have been stable but are expected to decline as competition strengthens)	1	6		Nil
Food manufacturer producing exclusively for household consumption (Long established with little new investment. High levels of turnover and profitability which are being sustained)	25		5	Slowly declining
Painting and decorating contracting company	0.025	0.5		Historically high but now forecast to slow down
(Established 3 years ago. Continuous capital injections from Group over that period. Currently not making any profit)				
Software development and supply company (Acquired 2 years ago. Market share expected to increase over next 2 years. Sustained investment from Group but profitability so far is low)	10		8	Rapid

Requirements

(a) Comment on GC's overall competitive position by defining and applying an appropriate model to its portfolio of SBUs. **(8 marks)**

(b) Discuss any limitations in the technique you have chosen to use. **(5 marks)**

(c) Discuss how GC should pursue the strategic development of its SBUs in order to add value to the overall conglomerate group. **(12 marks)**

(Total marks = 25)

? Question 4

In some situations, it is preferable to find another firm to acquire or to seek growth by merging with other firms.

Requirements

(a) Discuss where acquisitions or mergers would be the most suitable strategy to adopt. **(8 marks)**

(b) Explain how the shareholders of a company could benefit from a demerger. **(9 marks)**

(c) Draw Ansoff's product/market expansion grid and explain its usefulness in the development of corporate strategy. **(8 marks)**

(Total marks = 25)

? Question 5

Pharmia plc is a drugs manufacturing company. It is operating in an intensively competitive market and prices are being forced down all over the world.

To maintain its position, Pharmia plc utilises the concept of the product portfolio. Currently there are 34 new products in the portfolio, at various stages of development. Pharmia plc cannot predict if any of these will become a major product. However, its belief is that 'there are a number of runners in the race and the more you have the greater the chance of picking a winner'.

The company has also stated that it is a 'Research and Development (R&D) driven company'. Therefore Pharmia plc always tries to ensure that there is adequate investment in R&D. The other major aspect of its corporate strategy is a belief in aggressive marketing, occasioned by the circumstances of the global market. A product manager of Pharmia plc has been unexpectedly given £5m extra funding and has the following options available:

(i) Tyrix is a drug in the early stages of development. If £5m is invested now, it will reduce the time required before the drug is ready to be sold.

(ii) Medvac has been successfully introduced into the market. It is having to compete against two rival products. An investment of £5m would pay for an advertising campaign which it is thought would increase its market share.

(iii) Sonprex is a mature product and is probably going to be superseded in the near future. An investment of £5m would enable it to be repackaged and allow some promotional activities to be undertaken.

The following information has been provided by the marketing department:

Investment £m	Product	Outcome	Probability	Discounted payoff £m
5	Tyrix	Success	3%	150
		Failure	97%	–
5	Medvac	Market share		
		+30%	$\frac{1}{6}$	48
		+15%	$\frac{1}{3}$	27
		+10	$\frac{1}{2}$	(10)
5	Sonprex	Success	1	14

The options are mutually exclusive and must be undertaken completely or not at all. The payoffs are calculated before the cost of the investment.

Requirements

(a) Discuss the significance of the concepts of product portfolio and product life cycle for Pharmia plc. **(7 marks)**

(b) Present the expected values of the outcomes of the three options in the form of a decision tree. **(5 marks)**

(c) Evaluate the appropriateness of the use of expected values and subjective probabilities for the decision. **(4 marks)**

(d) Advise the product manager as to which drug should receive the investment.

(9 marks)

(Total marks = 25)

 **Question 6**

A tobacco company, Goulden plc, has diversified into several new industries and also into different countries. However, the financial results show that the whole company has declined steadily over the past 3 years. The decrease in return on capital employed is particularly noticeable in the tobacco sector, but this has been offset by improvements in the performance of companies in both the food and beverage industries. Recent financial reports show the following segmental information in the notes to the accounts:

Sector	Operating profit £m	Capital employed £m	Return on capital employed %
Tobacco	840	10,500	8
Agriculture	150	3,000	5
Food	100	500	20
Beverages	120	800	15

Requirements

(a) Discuss the problems of measuring performance in companies that operate in different industries and in different countries. **(8 marks)**

(b) Identify the advantages and disadvantages of the use of return on capital employed as a measure of performance in this diversified company. **(10 marks)**

(c) Explain an alternative method of measuring performance in a company with several different divisions. **(7 marks)**

(Total marks = 25)

Question 7

(a) Briefly explain how the measurement of divisional performance differs when assessing the achievement of strategic targets as distinct from operational targets. **(5 marks)**

J is a hospital which supplies a wide range of healthcare services. The government has created a competitive internal market for healthcare by separating the function of service delivery from purchasing. The government provides funds for local health organisations to identify healthcare needs and to purchase services from different organisations which actually supply the service. The service suppliers are mainly hospitals.

J is a service supplier and has established contracts with some purchasing organisations. The healthcare purchasing organisations are free to contract with any supplier for the provision of their healthcare requirements.

Previously, J was organised and controlled on the basis of functional responsibility. This meant that each specialist patient function, such as medical, nursing and pharmacy services, was led by a manager who held operational and financial responsibility for its activities throughout the hospital. J now operates a system of control based on devolved financial accountability. Divisions comprising different functions have been established and are responsible for particular categories of patient care such as general medical or general surgical services. Each division is managed by a senior medical officer.

J's board recognises that J exists in a competitive environment. It believes there is a need to introduce a system of divisional appraisal. This measures performance against strategic as well as operational targets, using both financial and non-financial criteria. The board is concerned to develop a system which improves the motivation of divisional managers. This will encourage them to accept responsibility for achieving strategic as well as operational organisational targets. In particular, the board wishes to encourage more contractual work to supply services to healthcare purchasing organisations from both within and outside its local geographical area. It is a clear aim of the board that a·cultural change in the management of the organisation will result from the implementation of such a system.

Requirements

(b) Discuss the issues which the board of J should take into consideration in establishing a system of performance measurement for divisional managers in order to ensure the attainment of its strategic targets. **(15 marks)**

(c) In the light of those issues identified in (b) explain how the directors might manage the change process. **(5 marks)**

(Total marks = 25)

 # Question 8

The WOWR organisation produces books and magazines. It employs 560 staff in 7 different locations. The organisation has been using IT in various departments as follows:

- *Production* – stock control including real-time stock and finished goods levels;
- *Sales* – historical record of books and magazines sold for the last 15 years;
- *Finance and administration* – maintenance of all ledgers, cash book and wages details;
- *Human resources* – factual information on employees, such as rate of pay, department, home address and date of birth.

In other words, most of the basic transaction systems within the organisation have been computerised. Additional investment in IT has been limited, partly as a result of the success of the organisation's core businesses, and partly from a lack of desire for change on the part of existing managers.

Recent changes in the senior management of the organisation now mean that additional appropriate IT investment is seen as being a key success criterion.

Requirements

(a) Explain a framework that can be used by managers to help assess the priority for investment in competing IT systems within the WOWR organisation.   **(10 marks)**

(b) (i) Explain the difference between process innovation and business process re-engineering.   **(5 marks)**

   (ii) Explain the reasons why process innovation and business process re-engineering are important in an organisation, making reference to the situation in the WOWR organisation where appropriate.   **(10 marks)**

(Total marks = 25)

Question 9

The Marketing Director of the company at which you work has stated that 'Products have life-cycles whereas brands do not'. Your Finance Director, recognising that you are studying for your final CIMA examinations, has asked you to prepare a briefing paper for the Board of Directors, addressing the following topics.

Requirements

(a) Discuss the validity of the above argument.   **(6 marks)**

(b) Explain the role of brands in the construction of barriers to entry.   **(8 marks)**

(c) Recommend some suitable financial criteria which could be used, at the different stages of the product life cycle, for the purposes of financial control.   **(5 marks)**

(d) Discuss, with reasons, the advantages and disadvantages of capitalising brands on the balance sheet.   **(6 marks)**

(Total marks = 25)

Question 10

Companies have an obligation to provide information to their stakeholders. The financial information provided tends to be of a historical nature. It has been argued that shareholders in particular should be entitled to receive forward-looking information. Some companies wishing to communicate selectively with a subgroup of shareholders are often prevented from doing so, as all shareholders should receive the same financial information.

Requirements

(a) Explain why a company may wish to disclose forward-looking information to its stakeholders and in particular to its shareholders.   **(10 marks)**

(b) Discuss the competitive issues a company must consider before disclosing forward-looking information to its shareholders.   **(10 marks)**

(c) Explain how they might convey this information to the stakeholders.   **(5 marks)**

(Total marks = 25)

Question 11

Within a diversified group, one division, which operates many similar branches in a service industry, has used internal benchmarking and regards it as very useful.

Group central management is now considering the wider use of benchmarking.

Requirements

(a) Explain the aims, operation and limitations of internal benchmarking, and explain how external benchmarking differs in these respects.   **(12 marks)**

(b) A multinational group wishes to internally benchmark the production of identical components made in several plants in different countries. Investments have been made in some plants in installing new advanced manufacturing technology (AMT) and supporting this with new manufacturing management systems such as just-in-time (JIT) and total quality management (TQM). Preliminary comparisons suggest that the standard cost in plants using new technology is no lower than that in plants using older technology.

You are required to explain possible reasons for the similar standard costs in plants with differing technology. Recommend appropriate benchmarking measures, recognising that total standard costs may not provide the most useful measurement of performance.   **(13 marks)**

(Total marks = 25)

 Question 12

Introduction

The 222 Organisation (222) is a large information systems consultancy, based in the southern African country of Jurania. 222 was founded in 1987 and has become very successful, both within Jurania and in neighbouring countries, due to growth in the economies of those countries and the highly developed technology sector of the Juranian economy. 222 advises organisations on the development of Intranet and knowledge sharing systems and has many clients among the top 100 companies in Jurania.

222 employs over 500 staff in its very impressive modern office building on a business park near the capital city of Jurania. Also based on the business park are several IT hardware and software companies, and the country's largest Internet service provider (ISP), JuraWeb. Many of 222's staff were trained at Jurania's university, which has an excellent reputation. Whenever 222 advertises for additional staff, it receives a large number of applications from suitably qualified applicants.

The Internet strategy

Recognising that the growth of 222 is limited by the size of the local market for its services, the directors of 222 are considering the further development of its rather basic website. At present, the 222.com website only contains a description of the organisation and contact details. The site was designed by employees of 222 and is hosted by JuraWeb. The directors hope that a better website will allow the organisation to develop new business in other parts of Africa, but have no desire to become a global business at this stage.

The directors are considering using the services of a local specialist web design company to develop a sophisticated website with case studies of previous 222 contracts, and detailed descriptions of staff and services. The directors also believe that 222 should be hosting the website itself, and are considering the purchase of a powerful web server. They also want to upgrade the telecommunications infrastructure of the organisation by investing in a new fibre-optic broadband service, which is available from a recently formed company that has just opened its office on the business park.

Requirements

(a) Evaluate whether the 222 Organisation might gain a competitive advantage as a result of being based in Jurania.   **(13 marks)**

(b) Evaluate the risks to 222 if it decides to pursue its Internet strategy as the directors have suggested.   **(12 marks)**

(Total for Question = 25 marks)

Question 13

C is a large multinational car manufacturer. It has factories in five countries and sells its products through networks of independent dealerships throughout the world. As part of its strategy of reducing unit costs and improving quality, C has entered into a number of 'sole supplier' agreements. This means that, on a worldwide basis, C buys all of its requirement for a specific material or component from a single supplier organisation. Such contracts are normally for a 5-year period.

S is a specialist manufacturer of safety equipment. It has recently been invited, by C, to submit a tender to supply all of the 'airbag' safety devices to be installed in C's cars. This will be the biggest order for which S has ever tendered and, if won, would require a 200% increase in production capacity (that is to three times its present scale) for S. In return for this large order, S would have to agree to deliver the required parts to each C factory twice a day. Any failure to deliver on time would lead to S being liable for the cost of lost production.

As part of the contract, C would allow S access to its extranet. This would mean that S was able to see C's forecast production schedules on a real-time basis. C maintains detailed forecasts of the number of each model of car being produced in each factory. This information is available on an hour-by-hour basis for the next month, on a day-by-day basis for the following 5 months, and a week-by-week basis for the subsequent 18 months. This means that S would be able to view detailed production forecasts for a 2-year period. The extranet also has a 'virtual trading room' where suppliers bid for new contracts. It also contains a lot of car industry information, some of which is not available to organisations that do not supply C.

Requirements

(a) Discuss the advantages and disadvantages, to S, of the sole supplier arrangement described.   **(15 marks)**

(b) Evaluate the benefits, to S, of access to the C extranet.   **(10 marks)**

(Total marks = 25)

Question 14

In the 'five forces model', one of the conclusions reached by Porter is that firms or strategic business units (SBUs) compete with their customers and suppliers.

The same model can be used to evaluate the competitive environment of the SBUs of large, complex organisations. In such organisations, some of the SBUs may be customer and supplier to one another. This leads to management accountants becoming involved in negotiations leading to the agreement of appropriate transfer prices between these SBUs.

Requirements

(a) Explain how the forces exerted in a customer–supplier relationship led Michael Porter to conclude that firms compete with their customers and suppliers.

Note: you are NOT required to explain the whole of Porter's model or draw the diagram

(10 marks)

(b) Discuss the issues to be considered when negotiating and agreeing transfer prices between SBU's within a large, complex organisation. You should make reference to Porter's model, and your arguments in part (a) where appropriate. **(15 marks)**

(Total marks = 25)

 ## Question 15

The MTM Group (MTM) is a major tobacco products manufacturer. As a global organisation, MTM has production facilities on every continent, and a highly sophisticated distribution network. MTM uses the 'rational planning model' to produce a strategic plan for each country in which it operates. The plan states any assumptions about the business environment in that country, then forecasts retail price levels, the market size and market share of MTM for each of the next 5 years. This plan is then used as a basis for next year's budget for that country. The budget is fixed at the beginning of the year, and used for control and reporting for the year. The directors of MTM are currently formulating the organisation's strategy relating to a small Asian country (referred to as the SAC) where the government is known to be considering the introduction of a ban on all tobacco advertising. At present, the probability of such legislation has been estimated at 40%, and the marketing department has estimated that the effect of the ban would be to reduce MTM's profits in the SAC by 20%. Such a reduction would be significant enough to threaten the viability of MTM's operations in the SAC. The marketing manager has therefore suggested that the strategic plan should assume an 8% reduction in profits from the SAC (40% × 20%)

Requirements

(a) Discuss the limitations of the use of the expected values technique in the context of a single strategic decision such as this. **(6 marks)**
(b) Recommend how the planning processes of MTM, for the SAC, should be modified to take account of the possible new legislation. **(12 marks)**
(c) Evaluate different methods that MTM might use to influence the government of the SAC. **(7 marks)**

(Total marks = 25)

Question 16

Background

Over 20 years ago, B plc was established to manufacture and sell naturally-based cosmetics and skin products. The first shop was opened in the UK in 1976. Since then, B plc has successfully expanded and now trades in over 40 countries worldwide through more than 1,000 retail outlets, 75 per cent of which are located outside the UK. The ecologically friendly aims of B plc have not changed since it was first established. The company campaigns against animal testing in the cosmetics industry and for human rights all over the world. It seeks to establish trade relations with overseas countries, and to integrate itself into the local communities in which it trades so that it can be more aware of the specific needs of its customers. B plc prides itself on its achievements in educating staff and customers through providing information on its products and methods of manufacture.

Corporate activities

B plc is intent on preserving the environment by promoting the efficient use of energy, keeping waste to a minimum and using only renewable resources whenever possible. These basic principles have been challenged by some observers who suggest that, in the aggressive corporate climate which currently prevails, B plc will need to abandon its environmentally friendly aims in order to compete. The company's chairman is determined that this shall not be the case and is proud of the fact that B plc was one of the first companies within the UK to publish environmental audit reports. Activities which B plc carries out include sourcing high-quality raw materials directly from producers throughout the world and extensive product research and development, both in the UK and Latin America. The results of successful research are converted into innovative products which are manufactured by B plc in its modern production facilities. The products are then transferred to its retail outlets. In addition, B plc is active in health education promotion throughout the world and, some years ago, initiated a newspaper designed to help the homeless, which sells throughout major cities in the UK.

Market share and financial review

The ecologically innovative approach adopted by the founders of B plc resulted in it initially attaining 100 per cent share of what was a niche market in the UK when the company first started. Since then, competition has developed to the extent that B plc now has 90 per cent of the naturally-based cosmetics and haircare market. In terms of profitability, B plc achieved in the last financial year an operating profit of £26m (previous year £29m) on a turnover of £175m (previous year £154m). The chairman of B plc attributed the reduction in profit to difficult trading conditions, particularly in the UK, and an increase in overheads due to the enlargement of its head office facilities. It is clear to B plc's directors that the increasing level of competition is now threatening its niche market domination.

Strategic development

The directors of B plc have considered a number of strategic options and have identified two possible courses of action. They could either invest more in quality improvement and further differentiate the company's products from its competitors, or increase the level of promotion and attract a higher market share. Capital constraints on the company prevent it from doing both in the next year.

Quality improvement

B plc's previous experience of improving quality has resulted in optimism about its potential success. The company estimates that it has obtained good results 70 per cent of the time by following the strategy of quality improvement. Unsatisfactory results have been experienced from the remaining 30 per cent of the time in which the strategy has been applied. The cost of carrying through the improvements in the next financial year would be £50m. Over a 4-year period it is estimated that, in present value terms, a net cash inflow of £100m would be made if the market response was strong, and £60m if it was weak. (Both of these values are before deduction of the capital cost of the improvements.) To assess the likelihood of a strong or weak market response, the directors have engaged a firm of consultants who have in the past been proved right on 80 per cent of occasions when they predicted a strong market response. The consultants have also been proved right on 90 per cent of occasions when they have predicted a weak market response.

The management accountant for B plc has carried out some decision analysis on this information and has concluded that the most likely outcome is a net cash inflow of £37.996m. The management accountant's workings to arrive at this value are as follows:

	Higher return £100m	Lower return £60m
Strong response	$0.8 \times 0.7 = 0.56$	$0.1 \times 0.3 = 0.03$
Weak response	$0.2 \times 0.7 = 0.14$	$0.9 \times 0.3 = 0.27$
Probability of a high return given a strong response is $0.56/0.59 = 0.95$		
Probability of a low return given a strong response is $0.03/0.59 = 0.05$		
Probability of a high return given a weak response is $0.14/0.41 = 0.34$		
Probability of a low return given a weak response is $0.27/0.41 = 0.66$		

The expected value of the proposal is:

Response	Return £m	Probability	Return £m	Expected value
Strong	Higher	0.95	100	95.0
	Lower	0.05	60	3.0
				98.0
Weak	Higher	0.34	100	34.0
	Lower	0.66	60	39.6
				73.6

However, there is a 59 per cent probability of a strong response and a 41 per cent probability of a weak response. The expected outcome of the investment is:

		£m
Strong	59% × £98.0m	57.820
Weak	41% × £73.6m	30.176
		87.996
Less: cost of quality improvement		50.000
Expected outcome		37.996

Increased promotion

The directors believe that by investing £10m in promotional activities in the next financial year, the net cash inflow, before deducting the cost of the initial investment, over a 4-year period in present value terms would be £40m.

Competitive reaction to proposed strategies

B plc's directors believe that the current competitors are likely to react to either of these strategies. The most likely reaction is to increase their own promotion activities; it is also likely that efforts will be made by competitors to identify and exploit areas where B plc is not able to maintain its high standards of ecological protection. It is very clear that improved information on its activities in order to counter this threat is an essential requirement for the directors to maintain customer confidence.

From the start, B plc has grown in size organically. The directors are keen to ensure that the company continues to develop and at the same time maintain its principles of ecological protection. They further recognise that organic growth is not the only route they could take and are seeking other potential forms of strategic development.

Requirements

(a) Present a corporate appraisal for B plc.   **(10 marks)**

(b) Comment on the two options evaluated. Your answer should:
  - include an assessment of the best and worst outcomes from the quality improvement option;
  - express any reservations you might have about the results; and
  - take into consideration the likely potential reaction of competitors if B plc implements either strategy.   **(18 marks)**

(c) Recommend what information the management accountant should provide to the directors of B plc to assist them in assessing the company's progress towards the achievement of its strategic environmental aims.   **(12 marks)**

(d) By reference to potential future market opportunities and threats, recommend a strategy which B plc may adopt in order to pursue its strategic environmental aims.

(10 marks)
(Total marks = 50)

？ Question 17

T plc is a well-established company providing telecommunications services both nationally and internationally. Its business has been concerned with telephone calls, the provision of telephone lines and equipment, and private telecommunication networks. T plc has supplemented these services recently by offering mobile phones, which is an expanding market worldwide.

The company maintains a diverse customer base, including residential users, multinational companies, government agencies and public-sector organisations. The company handles approximately 100 million calls each working day, and employs nearly 140,000 personnel.

Strategic development

The chairman of T plc stated within the latest annual report that there are three main areas in which the company aims to develop in order to remain a world leader in the telecommunications market. He believes that the three main growth areas reflect the evolving nature of the telecommunications market, and will provide scope for development.

The areas in which development is planned are:

1. Expansion of the telecommunications business in the national and overseas markets, both by the company acting on its own and through partnership arrangements with other suppliers.
2. Diversification into television and multi-media services, providing the hardware to permit telephone shopping from home and broadcasting services.
3. Extension of the joint ventures and strategic alliances which have already been established with companies in north America, Europe, India and the Far East.

The chairman explained that the company is intent on becoming a world leader in communications. This will be achieved through maintaining its focus on long-term development by improving its services to customers, developing high-quality, up-to-date products and being innovative, flexible and market-driven. His aim is to deliver a world-class service at competitive cost.

Financial information

Comparative statistics showing extracts from the company's financial performance in its national telecommunications market over the last 2 years are as follows:

	Last year £m	Previous year £m
Turnover	16,613	15,977
Profit before interest and tax	3,323	2,876
Capital employed	22,150	21,300

The company estimates its cost of capital to be approximately 11 per cent.

The chairman expressed satisfaction with the increase in turnover and stated that cost efficiencies were now being generated following completion of a staff reduction programme. This would assist the company in achieving a target return on capital employed (ROCE) in this market of 20 per cent over the next 3 years.

Business opportunities

The chief executive of T plc has stated that the major opportunities for the company lie in the following areas:

- encouraging greater use of the telephone;
- provision of advanced services, and research and development into new technology, including the internet and systems integration;
- the increasing freedom from government control of worldwide telecommunication services.

An extensive television and poster advertising campaign has been used by the company. This was in order to penetrate further the residential market by encouraging greater use of the telephone, with varying charging incentives being offered to residential customers.

To further the objective of increasing long-term shareholder value, the company is actively considering investment of £200m in each of the next 3 years in new technology and quality improvements in its national market. Because of its specialist technical nature, the investment is not expected to have any residual value at the end of the 3-year period.

Following the investment, the directors of T plc believe that its rate of profit before interest and tax to turnover in its national telecommunications market will remain constant. This rate will be at the same level as last year for each of the 3 years of the investment.

Markets and competition

The company is currently experiencing an erosion of its market share and faces increasingly strong competition in the mobile phone market. While T plc is the leader in its national market, with an 85 per cent share of the telecommunications business, it has experienced a reduced demand for the supply of residential lines in the last 5 years as competition has increased.

The market for the supply of equipment in the national telecommunications market is perceived to be static. The investment of £200m in each of the next 3 years is estimated to increase T plc's share of this market to a level of 95 per cent. The full improvement of 10 per cent is expected to be received by T plc next year, and its market share will then remain at this level for the full 3-year period. It is anticipated that unless further investment is made after the 3-year period, T plc's market share will revert to its current level as a consequence of the expected competitive response.

Industry regulation

The government has established an industry regulatory organisation to promote competition and deter anti-competitive behaviour.

As a result of the activities of the regulator and aggressive pricing strategies, it is anticipated that charges to customers will remain constant for the full 3-year period of the new investment.

All cash flows can be assumed to occur at the end of the year to which they relate. The cash flows and discount rate are in real terms.

Requirements

(a) Explain the nature of the political, economic, social, and technical forces which influence T plc in developing its business and increasing its market share. **(8 marks)**

(b) (i) Apply an appropriate analytical tool to assess the extent of the potential market development opportunities available to T plc. **(12 marks)**

(ii) Explain how the analysis you have conducted may be incorporated into the strategic planning process to determine the extent of the planning gap. **(5 marks)**

(c) Evaluate and comment on T plc's proposed investment in new technology and quality improvements in its national telecommunications market. Assume that variable costs are 80 per cent of the incremental revenue, and that fixed costs will not increase. Ignore working capital. **(12 marks)**

(d) (i) Assess to what extent the investment in new technology and quality improvements in T plc's national telecommunications market contributes towards the closure of the company's planning gap in respect of its target ROCE.
Note: You may assume that the entire capital investment is written off at the end of the 3-year period. **(5 marks)**

(ii) Recommend a strategy which T plc could employ to close the planning gap and achieve the strategic development aims identified by the chairman. Ignore taxation. **(8 marks)**

(Total marks = 50)

Question 18

Y-land FE
Introduction

The Y Corporation is based in the United States of America (USA). It was founded in the early part of the last century when Mr Y produced cartoon films. These soon proved very popular as a form of family entertainment and the characters in the films became household names.

The Corporation established a theme park (based around the film characters) in the southern USA, where there was a warm and mainly dry climate. The theme park, known as

Y-land, proved to be an immediate success, attracting millions of visitors each year. A whole range of family entertainment flourished, based on the original theme of the cartoon characters. These included shops, restaurants, hotels and amusement rides.

Following the success of Y-land in the USA, the directors of the Corporation established another Y theme park based in Northern Europe. The rationale behind this was that although many Europeans visited Y-land in the USA, the cost of travel made visiting the attraction very expensive. The directors believed that establishing a Y-land in Northern Europe would enable European people to visit the attraction without incurring high travel expenses. Y-land Europe was built in a highly-populated area of Northern Europe which is easily accessible. A factor which differentiates Y-land Europe from the theme park in the USA is that it is located in a region which is frequently affected by rain and it does not enjoy a guaranteed warm climate. Y-land Europe did not in fact attract the volume of visitors that were expected and almost went bankrupt before receiving a massive cash injection from a wealthy donor who took part shares in the theme park.

Further strategic development

The Y Corporation is now considering building another theme park, this time in a tropical area in the Far East. Y-land FE will be part-funded by the host government in the Far East, which will take a 60 per cent share in the park. The Y Corporation will fund the remaining 40 per cent. Profits and losses will be shared in direct proportion to the shareholding of each of the joint venture partners. It is believed that local tourism and related sectors of the entertainment industry will benefit from the development as the theme park will attract more visitors to the region. Similar to the other two Y-land theme parks, the development will include many facilities such as hotels, bars and restaurants as well as the entertainment attractions.

It will take 2 years to build Y-land FE before any paying visitors enter the park. The Y Corporation has based its estimates of visitors in the first year of operation (that is, after the 2 years of construction) on the following probabilities:

	Visitors	*Probability*
Optimistic	8 million	0.25
Most likely	3 million	0.50
Pessimistic	2 million	0.25

After the first year of operation, it is expected that the number of visitors will increase by 50 per cent in the next year. The Y Corporation directors consider that this number of visitors will be the maximum and after that the theme park will suffer a reduction in the number of visitors (marketing decay) of 5 per cent compound each year for the next 2 years. After 2 years, the directors expect the number of visitors each year to remain constant at this level.

The host government believes that the theme park will create about 15,000 new jobs in the area through servicing the facilities. It expects the construction of the park to create about 5,000 jobs in addition to the 8,000 who will be employed in land reclamation and other necessary infrastructural work associated with the project.

Cost and revenue estimates

It is expected that the overall capital cost of the theme park will be $2,200 million. This sum will be spread evenly over the construction period and, for the purposes of calculation, the actual cash outflow may be assumed to arise at the end of each of the 2 years. The Y Corporation will be responsible for raising 40% of this sum.

In any year, the visitors are expected to be in the proportion of 40% adults and 60% children or people who will obtain a concession (reduction) on their entrance fees. For simplicity, the entrance charges will be set at a flat rate of $50 for each adult and $30 for each child or concession. There will be no further fees for entertainment after the entrance charge has been made to the visitor.

Past experience has shown that running expenses of the theme park show a certain level of consistency. In terms of labour, the costs follow the pattern of a 90% learning curve which applies on average to every 1 million visitors. This lasts for the first 2 years, after which the labour costs for each visitor become constant. The cost of labour at the time the park will open is expected to be $3 for each visitor. The effects of this are that the cumulative average direct labour costs in the first year of operation (that is, year 3 of the project) are estimated to be $9.72 million (after being multiplied by the number of expected visitors in that year). The cumulative average labour costs for both the first and second years of operation (that is, years 3 and 4 of the project) are expected to be $21.14 million (after being multiplied by the total number of visitors for the first 2 years of operation). After this point the learning effect is expected to cease.

The other direct costs, which are not subject to learning, can be assumed to be incurred at the rate of $2 for each visitor. Attributable fixed running expenses are estimated to be $100 million each year in cash terms.

In addition, the Y Corporation expects that its joint venture with the host government will earn average net contribution of $10 from the sale of souvenirs and refreshments and $100 from accommodation charges for each adult, child or concessionary visitor each year.

The cost of capital for the whole project is expected to be 15%.

Shareholder value

The Y Corporation believes that its main objective is to increase the wealth of its owners. The Corporation requires a gross return on investment of 22% after 8 years of income generated from the venture. It has been recommended to the directors of the Y Corporation that the return is calculated by taking the net present value of the project after 8 years of operation and dividing this by the gross initial undiscounted capital outlay of $2,200 million.

Ignore taxation, inflation and variation due to exchange rates.

Requirements

(a) Evaluate the usefulness of Porter's Diamond Theory (the Competitive Advantage of Nations) in helping the directors of the Y Corporation to determine whether or not it should proceed with establishing Y-land FE.
It is not necessary to draw a diagram of the Diamond Theory. **(10 marks)**

(b) (i) Produce a discounted cash flow (DCF) calculation for Y-land FE from the start of building work in the first year until 8 years of cash inflows have been generated (that is, 10 years in total), and calculate the return on investment in accordance with the method recommended. **(15 marks)**

(ii) Analyse and critically appraise the DCF calculation and the resulting return on investment as defined by the method recommended to the directors of the Y Corporation, and advise the directors as to whether they should proceed with Y-land FE. You should consider financial and non-financial factors in providing your advice. **(15 marks)**

(c) Discuss how the directors of the Y Corporation can use Shareholder Value Analysis to determine the development of its portfolio of products and services. **(10 marks)**

(Total marks = 50)

Question 19

Company history

Myriad plc was founded in 1962 and its original business was as a manufacturer of metal castings. It became a listed company in 1977. Myriad plc has always traded profitably, but by 1987 the directors had become very concerned about the volatility of its earnings. Consequently, they commissioned a review from a firm of consultants which specialised in advising on corporate strategy. Following this review, Myriad plc announced that it would 'aggressively pursue a policy of conglomerate diversification, by external acquisition, to promote growth and reduce risk'.

By 1993 Myriad plc achieved the following structure: a group headquarters based in London and three divisions: Leisure, based in Oxford, Light Engineering in Coventry and Office Equipment in Birmingham. Each division has its own executive management team which has responsibility for earning a criterion rate of return on the funds invested in it by the group.

Group headquarters has the responsibility for raising capital and operates a group treasury function. The group headquarters has a staff of 25 which includes the main board of directors. The costs of running the group are charged out to the divisions by means of a management charge.

Divisions

- *Leisure.* This division operates fitness centres inside hotels; it developed from a personal interest in fitness of one of Myriad plc's directors. Profit growth has been 25 per cent per annum in the 2 years that the division has been in operation and it is forecast to continue at this rate following the recent signing of a 5-year contract with a national hotel chain. The division's managers believe that the prosperity of their business is dependent on growth in consumer spending which is forecast to grow by 5 per cent per annum for the next 5 years.
- *Light Engineering.* This activity formed the original basis of Myriad plc's business. The division's management has characterised its business as '. . . mature, stable and offering the prospect of modest but sustainable growth'.
- *Office Equipment.* This division was established immediately after the review in 1987. This was done by buying three separate companies which were then consolidated into one. Its managers regard it as operating in a mature market but the forecast target profit growth rate at 10 per cent per annum is higher than for Light Engineering. This division has a diverse customer base. Many of its customers are government agencies. This means that there is no chance of default and they also pay their bills promptly.

Financial characteristics

Myriad plc had the following earnings in 1993:

	£m	Stock market price/earnings ratios at 31.12.93*
Leisure	3	18.0
Light Engineering	5	6.0
Office Equipment	2	10.0
Group	10	8.6

* The divisions are not separately listed and they do not have p/e rations. However, p/c ratios are given above for sectors to which the divisions are most closely related. The group p/e ratio is the actual ratio at 31 December 1993.

The consortium's proposal

An informal consortium of institutional shareholders, who hold around 15 per cent of Myriad plc's equity, has been pressing the board for a review of strategy. Its members have indicated that if their wishes are not granted, they will raise the matter at the forthcoming AGM.

Their main concern is that Myriad plc has underperformed during the period 1987–93 and this is based on the fact the Myriad plc's share price increased by 16 per cent while share prices in Myriad's sector increased by 23 per cent. Other information relating to the period 1987–93 is given below. All the data are in real terms.

	Myriad's sector	Myriad plc
Average dividend yield	5%	3%
Average dividend cover	2	4
Average gearing*	60%	20%
Beta factor range	1.1–1.5	0.75–0.83

* Gearing: defined as total borrowings/total capital in issue plus reserves.

The consortium believes that Myriad plc should take the opportunity offered by current market conditions to rationalise its portfolio. Its members suggest disposing of the Leisure division, using half the proceeds to pay a 'once and for all' dividend to the shareholders and retaining the other half to strengthen Myriad plc's balance sheet.

The consortium has also suggested that after the Leisure division has been sold, Myriad plc could reduce its costs by closing its group headquarters and the treasury operation. After the consequent redundancies, the remaining staff could be relocated to either Coventry or Birmingham where labour costs and accommodation costs are significantly cheaper than in London.

Requirements

(a) Assess the implications for the strategic decision of 1987 on Myriad plc's shareholders and management. **(10 marks)**

(b) Assess the extent to which the diversification has been successful. **(4 marks)**

(c) Discuss the extent to which the board of Myriad plc should attempt to identify the wishes of the different interests affected by the forthcoming decision about Leisure. Explain how the board could implement a strategy for communication with the different interests. **(15 marks)**

(d) Describe the conflicts of interest which exist for Myriad plc in the 1993 situation. **(6 marks)**

(e) Advise the board on its response to the consortium. You should include in your advice any recommendations which you feel are appropriate and explain why you make them. **(15 marks)**

(Total marks = 50)

? Question 20

Background information

EuroFoods is a French–German consumer products group with a turnover of £8bn a year at 1992 retail prices. One of EuroFoods' activities is the manufacture of ice-cream.

Medley is an American company. It has worldwide sales of £5bn a year and these come mainly from chocolate products. Three years ago Medley started to diversify. It did this by selling a new product, ice-cream, in one of its existing markets, Europe. Although Medley has no prior experience of ice-cream, it believed that it could exploit its existing expertise in food products, marketing and distribution in this new area.

The European ice-cream industry turnover is £6bn at 1992 retail prices. The aggregate industry return on sales is estimated to be 10 per cent profit before tax.

Market share	%
EuroFoods	60
Medley	10
Local producers*	30
	100

* These are defined as manufacturers who sell within only one European country.

Distribution has always been a very important aspect of the food industry. However, it is particularly so in the ice-cream business. This is because the product must be kept refrigerated from factory to shop, and also while it is stored in the shop. Many of the shops which sell EuroFoods ice-cream are small businesses and the freezer which is required for storage is a costly item for them to buy. EuroFoods has therefore a scheme whereby it will install and maintain such a freezer in these shops. The shop owner does not have to pay for the freezer. The only condition which EuroFoods imposes is that the freezer must be used exclusively for the sales of its products.

EuroFoods believes that this arrangement has worked well for everybody in the past. EuroFoods' expenditure on the freezers have ensured that its products have reached the consumer in good condition and also enabled it to simplify stock control. It has also played a part in building its market dominance by enabling shops which otherwise would not be able to do so, to sell its products.

The European ice-cream business

The peak time of year for sales of ice-cream in Europe is mid-June to mid-August. These summer sales are deemed 'impulse' sales by the trade and are traditionally made from small retail outlets where EuroFoods tends to have its exclusive arrangements. The other sort of sale is the 'take-home', which are purchases made in larger quantities at supermarkets. These outlets do not have exclusive agreements with EuroFoods.

Analysis of European ice-cream sales in 1992

	Volume %	Value £bn	Return on sales: profit before tax £bn
Impulse	40	4	0.48
Take-home sales	60	2	0.12
Total	100	6	

Product development

Medley (see below) has been mainly responsible for the shift in recent years to higher-priced ice-cream. This trend is now being imitated by EuroFoods and some of the local producers.

Medley

Medley has transformed traditional ice-cream by combining it with its chocolate to make an ice-cream chocolate bar, which in 1992 retailed in the UK for about £0.60, which represented a premium of about £0.20 per bar.

Medley wishes to develop as follows. It has built an ice-cream factory in Europe, which cost £40m. To operate the factory economically it needs to work near the limit of its 50,000 tonne annual capacity. Consequently, it needs a correspondingly high sales throughput. Medley would like to obtain its future growth from the 'impulse' sector of the market. It owns 14,000 non-exclusive freezer cabinets mainly in the UK. However, it is costly to maintain these to sell the eight products which constitute its product range. Another problem is that in many cases small shops have room for only one freezer and this has often been supplied by EuroFoods. As Medley's UK managing director said: 'It means only big competitors with a full range of products can enter the market.'

Medley would like to be able to place its products in the freezers provided by EuroFoods. However, when it tried to do this 2 years ago in Spain, EuroFoods was successful in a legal action to prevent this.

Medley has now complained to the European Commission that EuroFoods' exclusive freezer arrangements restrict competition and are unfair.

Requirements

(a) Describe how McCarthy's marketing mix model could assist in the process of strategy formulation for both EuroFoods and Medley.   **(8 marks)**

(b) Explain, in general, how a firm may attain a competitive advantage.   **(9 marks)**

(c) Advise EuroFoods on its possible future competitive strategy and product and market development of ice-cream if the European Commission (EC) decides that exclusive freezer arrangements:

  (i) are anti-competitive and, in future, EuroFoods' freezers should be available to any manufacturer,

  (ii) are not anti-competitive and EuroFoods' freezers should not be available to any manufacturer.   **(16 marks)**

(d) Advise Medley on its future competitive strategy product and market development of ice-cream if the EC decides that exclusive freezer arrangements:

  (i) are anti-competitive and, in future, EuroFoods' freezers should be available to any manufacturer,

  (ii) are not anti-competitive and EuroFoods' freezers should not be available to any manufacturer.   **(17 marks)**

Note: A billion equals one thousand million.   **(Total marks = 50)**

 ## Question 21

Introduction

G plc is a long-established divisionalised company with its origins in shipping. The company has been in existence for nearly 160 years and has developed a reputation for reliability and quality of service. While the company obtains the majority of its turnover from various forms of shipping, its subsidiary interests extend into transport, construction and property.

The shipping activities in which G plc is engaged comprise four divisions – Cruise, Ferries, Containers and Bulk Shipping. The Cruise division is engaged entirely in the carriage of passengers and the Ferries division carries passengers and vehicles. The vehicles carried by the Ferries range from motor cars to articulated lorries and single-deck buses. The Containers and Bulk Shipping divisions are engaged in the carriage of freight only and do not carry any fare-paying passengers.

Organisational aims

The company has stated over recent years that it aims to achieve the following goals:

1. Increase its emphasis on international businesses to achieve long-term profitability.
2. Provide those businesses with the necessary capital investment to achieve their development.
3. Continued development and training of the company's employees to achieve the organisational objectives.

Environmental policy

The company has established an environmental policy which is monitored through an audit system in an effort to ensure that its policies are being achieved. It is the aim of the company to have operational standards which at least equate with the best industry practice. Training of management, staff and specialist auditors is seen as a priority within the organisation's environmental policy. This has become a major concern of the company which is aware of customer anxiety about travelling on roll-on roll-off (RORO) ferries following public debate about their safety.

Financial results

In the last financial year, earnings per share totalled £0.353 (35.3p) producing a dividend cover of 1.15. The dividend per share paid by G plc has remained at the same level for 5 years. Comparative values for divisional turnover and operating profit of each of the shipping divisions are as follows:

	Turnover			Operating profit		
	This year	This year adjusted for inflation	Last year	This year	This year adjusted for inflation	Last year
Divisions	£m	£m	£m	£m	£m	£m
Cruise	856	815	735	96	91	88
Ferries	667	635	626	90	86	80
Containers	1,262	1,201	1,051	42	40	40

During the year, general inflationary levels in the shipping industry were approximately 5 per cent per annum.

Chairman's statement for the financial year

In his statement, the chairman of G plc, commenting on turnover and profit before the inflation adjustment, said the company achieved encouraging results, particularly in the Cruise division. The company has taken delivery of a new cruise liner at a cost of £200m, and has two more on order. The chairman believes that this is an expanding market and considers the company to be in a good position to take advantage, as it is one of the world's largest cruise companies. With regard to the Ferries division, the chairman expects continued growth, although there is an expectation of a sharp decline in the number of routes across the English Channel due to the opening of the tunnel link between the UK and France. Economic recovery, a continual reduction in costs and increased cargo volumes were all cited by the chairman as reasons for the improved performance of this division. This contrasted with his view of the depressed containers and bulk shipping market which contributed to these divisions' continuing disappointing results.

Market information

G plc commissioned some marketing research into its passenger shipping activities. The results of this research indicate that in recent years within the cruise liner industry there has been a change in customer appeal. Traditionally, the main customer base has comprised wealthy retired people. In the last 5 years, the Cruise division has experienced an increase in younger customers. This stemmed from the late 1980s, when the world's largest cruise company shortened the length of some cruises to appeal to American passengers who have only a short vacation period. This resulted in more affordable prices: other cruise companies, including G plc, followed the market leader. This, in turn, resulted in even more affordable prices and the market expanded, with a younger age range of customer being identified.

By contrast, the research showed a 15 per cent increase in passengers crossing the English Channel, but G plc's market share actually reduced by 4 per cent. In its other ferry services, G plc has seen the market holding steady.

The report indicates that the probability of the cruise market continuing to grow for the next 5 years at the current rate is 0.6, and that a growth rate of half that which it currently enjoys, over the same period, has a probability of 0.3. There is no expectation of a decline in this market over the next 5 years, and the probability of the market remaining static is 0.1.

The report concludes that, in respect of the Ferries division, the passenger market across the English Channel is expected to reduce by a further 5 per cent over the next year and then remain at this level for the next 4 years. This is given a probability of 0.7, while there is a 0.1 probability that the market will remain at its current level, and a 0.2 probability that it will fall by a further 10 per cent next year and then remain static. The report concludes that the other ferry routes should maintain their current market levels.

Requirements

(a) With reference to the organisational aims set out in the scenario above, state what G plc's corporate objectives should address. **(5 marks)**

(b) It has been argued that an organisation which operates in a turbulent environment should include flexibility as an objective in order that it can be responsive to changing environmental conditions.

   Explain how G plc could achieve flexibility in its operations, and discuss potential areas of stakeholder conflict which may occur in satisfying its organisational objectives. **(15 marks)**

(c) Discuss the change in turnover and profit of the shipping divisions within G plc in the last financial year, and state, with reasons, whether you consider the chairman's statement reflects the divisional results achieved. **(10 marks)**

(d) With reference to the competitive forces in their industry, assess the nature of the cruise and ferry shipping market in which G plc is engaged, and discuss what opportunities and threats exist in respect of its market share. **(15 marks)**

(e) Discuss how monitoring through an audit system can be implemented to ensure that G plc's environmental policy is being achieved. **(5 marks)**

(Total marks = 50)

Question 22

The mission and objectives of the organisation are the starting point, but a discussion of performance measurement, the reports required to control the organisation, and the stakeholders, are other aspects of this question.

Background

Lindleys plc (the Bank) is a United Kingdom clearing bank. It has 2,000 retail branches. It categorises its business as retail and corporate. Each category currently accounts for half of the Bank's turnover.

The Bank defines retail business as 'banking for customers in their own right and small businesses where lending would not exceed £1m in any one year'.

Corporate business is defined as 'where lending would exceed £1m in any one year'. Corporate lending includes international lending.

Traditionally, corporate lending has been the most profitable business, yielding 70 per cent of profit before taxation. Corporate lending has been carried out by six regional offices and a department at head office in London. The London office is also responsible for international lending. There are 200 staff employed in corporate lending.

Retail banking has operated in the following way. The number of retail and small business customers at each branch has ranged from 1,000 to 10,000, although 5,000 is typical. The Bank has employed the following mission statement for its retail banking:

'Our mission is to deliver a high-quality service to customers based on our managers' personal knowledge of customers' affairs.'

The Bank recognised that retail banking was relatively unprofitable. It was willing to operate a policy of cross-subsidisation between corporate and retail as it hoped that some retail customers would become corporate ones. It saw its branch managers as assisting in this process because of their financing expertise and deep knowledge of their customers.

The Bank has operated each branch as a cost centre. Managers have been provided with a 3-monthly expenditure report which compared committed expenditure to budgeted expenditure. The Bank had not operated an accrual accounting system as regards branch expenditures for these 3-monthly reports. However, year-end adjustments reconciled committed, actual and budgeted expenditures. These accounting operations were carried out by management accounting staff based at head office.

The managers' remit was to operate within their expenditure budgets. In addition to this, they were set targets, for example, number of new accounts opened, amount of holiday insurance sold, level of bad debts.

The managers were not consulted about the size of their budgets or their targets. These were imposed by head office.

Proposals for change

The Bank is reappraising its corporate posture. Its corporate lending has declined in profitability because of problems with Third World debt and movements in foreign exchange rates. The Bank has also become concerned about the attitudes which it believes have become dominant in retail banking. Most of its managers have found their targets relatively easy to achieve. They have been criticised for a lack of entrepreneurial awareness and for being too inward-looking. The managers have retorted that 'as soon as a customer gets to be interesting we lose them to corporate, so why bother?' Because of these factors, the Bank has decided upon the following changes:

- Retail banking must, in future, earn 50 per cent of the Bank's profit before taxation.
- There will be a programme of branch rationalisation in which half the branches will close.
- New 'superbranches' will be established. These will be at the centre of a network of six to eight existing branches. The superbranch will contain the manager, who will make all the major decisions for the network of branches. He will be assisted in this by two assistant managers who will probably be drawn from the existing managers in the network.
- Each superbranch will be designated as an investment centre and must earn a return of 15 per cent. No target has been set for residual income, although the Bank intends to set such targets after it has gained some experience of the superbranches' operations. (Residual income should be taken as pre-tax profits less an imputed interest charge for net assets.)

  Each superbranch has been given an expenditure budget which equates to that of the cumulative total spent by its network branches in the previous year. No extra funds have been allocated for the establishment of the superbranches. The manager of the super-branch has discretion as to where the superbranch will be located. This could be inside an existing branch or in new premises.
- The manager of the superbranch will be responsible for the design and operation of all of the network's information systems. These will be capable of being interrogated by head office, which will continue to draw up the statutory accounts.
- The manager of the superbranch has discretion as to the number of employees working in the network. If there are to be any redundancies, head office will negotiate nationally to determine the terms for redundant staff. The superbranch will be charged with the costs, if any, of redundancies in its network.
- The managing director of the Bank has described the new philosophy for retail banking thus:

  'We are operating in a very competitive environment and in order to survive, we must change. We must never forget that we are a profit-seeking organisation. Retail banking has been subsidised in the past and had become inefficient. Our proposals will enable us to deliver an efficient, low-cost service. However, I am afraid the days of the bank manager being a personal friend and adviser are over.'

Requirements

(a) Explain the implications of the new philosophy for retail banking upon staff, customers and shareholders of the Bank. You should contrast the new philosophy with the old mission statement. **(12 marks)**

(b) Discuss the advantages and disadvantages of the proposal to make superbranches investment centres. **(8 marks)**

(c) (i) Describe the reports you believe will be necessary for the manager of a superbranch to manage successfully. Your answer should include the reasons for your suggestions. **(12 marks)**

  (ii) Suggest, and fully justify, three qualitative performance indicators you consider would be of assistance to a superbranch manager. **(12 marks)**

(d) State three stakeholders who should have been involved in the determination of proposals by the Bank to reorganise retail banking. Explain the reasons for each of your recommendations. **(6 marks)**

(Total marks = 50)

 Question 23

Introduction

C is a large civil engineering company which carries out various building contracts within both its home and overseas markets. Its main area of work, particularly overseas, is in road construction. The company has a strong financial track record and successfully survived a major recession within its home market about 10 years ago.

Economic circumstances in overseas markets

During the last 3 years, the overseas markets in which C has been carrying out building contracts have suffered a serious economic recession. Business confidence in these markets has been seriously weakened over this period. One country which has been affected by adverse economic circumstances is Eastlandia. C has been engaged in carrying out contract work in Eastlandia for several years. Government action in Eastlandia to protect its ailing economy has also had an adverse impact on foreign contractors such as C operating in this country.

The concern felt by C's directors regarding the economic situation in Eastlandia has been increased as a result of recent events involving a large development company (D) which C has worked with in the past. Company D, which is wholly owned by Eastlandian shareholders, had previously received Eastlandian government backing. However, it has recently been allowed to go into receivership without any further government support. The government announced that partial repayment of debts owed by the development company to local investors would take priority over those it owed to foreign investors. The result of this is that foreign investors are unlikely to see any recovery of their loans.

The serious economic situation developing in Eastlandia has threatened to result in an economic recession. There has been a consequent negative effect on related industries within the country, such as steel, building materials and transport. Another major concern for C's directors is the constant threat posed by currency fluctuations and the possibility of the Eastlandian government being forced into currency devaluation.

Work-in-progress

Currently, C is engaged in the construction of a major road linking two parts of a new Eastlandian city, bypassing the central congested area. C is engaged as a subcontractor to a major Eastlandian development company – a different company from D which went into receivership recently. The contract was accepted by C after estimating that it would provide a high positive net present value. At the time the investment appraisal calculation was made, the expected currency exchange rate between Eastlands (Eastlandia's currency) and £ sterling (C's home currency) was 7.26 to the £ in the current year and 7.54 to the £ next year. In fact, the current exchange rate is 7.74 to the £ and the forward rate in 12 months' time is quoted at 8.56 to the £.

As far as C's overall business is concerned, the contract represents about 10 per cent of total turnover for the company. The contract commenced 3 months ago and payment to C is to be in Eastlands. Progress payments for the work done so far have been delayed without any explanation. The contract is about 15 per cent complete and is expected to be finished in another 21 months, which is 3 months later than planned. This will result in penalty payments being incurred by C.

The directors of C have expressed to the contract manager for the road development in Eastlandia their concern regarding the need to undertake remedial work on what has been completed so far. This has resulted from the use of faulty materials obtained from an Eastlandian supplier. The remedial work has already consumed the total amount of the financial contingency which was allowed within the contract estimates.

Strategic information and market size

C uses external databases to establish the levels of its own share of the market and overall patterns of market growth and development. In addition, the management accounting department of the company provides internal information on market share and growth and internal capacity to meet its future contractual demands. Over the last 2 years, there has been a general decline in market opportunities, but C has in fact managed to increase its overall market share. This has been achieved because of its strong reputation for using good-quality materials and applying high standards of workmanship.

One of the major criticisms being made in Eastlandia is the poor quality of the civil engineering projects which have been completed quickly. There have been reports of numerous casualties among the site workers during the construction process. Some buildings have partially collapsed after completion and there have been instances where roads have begun to break up shortly after they have been opened. This has caused civilian casualities with some fatalities and resulted in noisy public protest in Eastlandia about the lack of attention to safety in civil engineering and building work.

C is well regarded by the Eastlandian government. It has taken a long time for the directors of C to build the company's reputation and gain recognition in Eastlandia for its workmanship.

Possible future development

The Eastlandian government has invited C's directors to tender for other civil engineering work. C has taken up the invitation and if the company is successful in all its tenders, the total commitment in Eastlandia would represent about 40 per cent of its order book.

In recognition of the importance of the Eastlandia market, and in order to reduce the potential losses from developers which engage their services becoming insolvent, the directors of C have proposed that a strategic alliance be formed. It is proposed that this alliance will be established with an Eastlandian civil engineering contractor who, it is expected, will have an insight into the financial integrity of potential customers. The alliance partner would be able to give clear advice as to which of these Eastlandian customers would be suitable for the establishment of contractual arrangements.

Requirements

(a) Prepare a corporate appraisal for C in respect of its strengths, weaknesses and opportunities. **(10 marks)**

(b) Discuss the threats posed to C by its involvement with the road-building project in Eastlandia and explain how it can reduce the impact of these threats on its own strategic position. **(20 marks)**

(c) Recommend appropriate sources of information which may be used by C's management accountants when evaluating the potential future demand for its services in its overseas markets. **(8 marks)**

(d) Discuss the strategic logic and practical considerations for C of entering into an alliance with an Eastlandian civil engineering contractor. **(12 marks)**

(Total marks = 50)

Question 24

Company background

The SF group is in the food processing and production business. The group comprises 42 companies, each of which specialises in a particular food. For example, some companies manufacture sweets and confectionery whereas others produce bread, drinks or other basic consumer foods.

One of the companies in the group, JTK Ltd, produces bread, cakes and similar products. It produces 3 million loaves of bread each day and supplies 15 per cent of the total bread demand for the country in which it operates. JTK Ltd's strategy is to sell as much bread as possible, making only a small margin on each loaf sold. This strategy has worked well in the past because most customers base their decision to purchase bread more on the price than the quality of the product.

Over the past 20 years, JTK Ltd has had two instances of adverse publicity about the quality of its bread. As a result of these, JTK Ltd ensured that the quality of the product was improved and quickly regained its market share.

Production process

The bread manufacturing system is based on the feedback model.

Average raw material stocks have shown a small but marked increase over the last 5 years, although suppliers have improved the efficiency of their delivery systems.

The production process is operating at full capacity.

Different staff work in the quality control department each day, on a rotation basis. Results from the day's quality control checks are pinned to a noticeboard along with summaries of changes to input mixes and any problems. This attempts to ensure that information concerning each day's quality control checks reaches the staff working on the next day.

Overview of production quality control system
Board opinions and market trends

Janice, a recently qualified and newly appointed management accountant, has obtained a copy of a market survey into the bread market. The survey predicts that:

- the demand for basic cheap bread will change in the next 3 years in line with the following information:

Probability		Demand
0.1	Increase by	10%
0.3	Decrease by	10%
0.3	Decrease by	15%
0.2	Decrease by	25%
0.1	Decrease by	35%

- over the same timescale, it is certain that demand will increase for breads containing fewer artificial additives and for speciality breads (such as bread with fruit or honey in it), although the extent of the increase in demand cannot be quantified.

JTK Ltd cannot make any of these breads with its current production system. To make these breads, JTK Ltd would need to invest in new capital equipment and computer-controlled monitoring systems for this equipment. This investment would replace the existing capital equipment and provide some additional production capacity.

Janice took this information to a board meeting and presented it in a fairly forceful manner in support of her recommendation for investment in new specialised capital equipment. The other board members were very sceptical of it. They are of the opinion that the company has made profits over the last 20 years and will continue to do so in the future. They consider that the market research information is incorrect and plan to invest a significant amount of money in new capital equipment to continue production in its present form. Janice believes that the capital investment must be directed towards new computer systems and specialised capital equipment that will enable JTK Ltd to produce the breads that are increasing in demand.

Requirements

(a) State and discuss the different sources of information that could be referred to by the management of JTK Ltd in order to monitor the quality of bread that is being supplied. Give examples of the information that each source might provide.

(10 marks)

(b) Explain the limitations of controlling the production process as a 'closed loop' system. Clearly explain any weaknesses that are inherent in JTK Ltd's system. **(15 marks)**

(c) Explain the limitations of using the information concerning future demand contained in the market research survey. **(5 marks)**

(d) Comment on the financial critical success factors and performance indicators that JTK Ltd can use to justify expenditure on its capital equipment as proposed by the new management accountant. Comment on any problems that might arise with using these CSFs and PIs. **(12 marks)**

(e) Comment on the problems that quality control staff may find with using a notice-board to display quality control information, and explain how a computerised bulletin board system could help to alleviate these problems. **(8 marks)**

(Total marks = 50)

 ## Question 25

Introduction

The criminal justice system in a country is based on a trial by jury. Defendants are examined before a judge and a 12-person jury in one of 42 Regional Courts, which are located in many of the major towns and cities of the country. Each Regional Court has up to six courtrooms, which are used to review individual cases. A larger Central Court in the country's capital city reviews appeals from people who believe that they have been wrongly convicted of a crime, and also makes judgements on cases that the Regional Courts cannot resolve.

Court Service information systems

Information systems are available within each court, providing details on:

- *Statute and case law.* These databases are updated each week as the country's government enacts new laws and the decisions in cases from all other courts are received.
- *Court organisation schedules.* These include lists of judges, jurors and court officials who will be present in court on any given day, along with details of the cases that will be heard in each courtroom.
- *Fixed asset register.* This contains details of the assets under the control and ownership of the court.
- *Salary information relating to court officials.* Note that the Central Court pays all judges.

Whereas the information systems in each Regional Court provide similar information, the actual method of processing is very different from court to court. Existing systems vary from complex manual systems to various types of database and management information systems. Any revisions to the system are likely to be expensive because the vast majority of courts do not have computers with a sufficiently high specification to run the latest software. The system is run by a Court Administrator in each Regional Court.

Government requirement for efficiency gains

Although there are no problems identified with the information systems in any court, recent political decisions require the Court Service as a whole to make some efficiency gains. The government has indicated that these gains may be achieved in various ways, ranging from the implementation of new information systems to the amalgamation of some Regional Courts. A management committee has been established to review what changes are feasible. Employees in the courts will welcome any review of the systems, because the implementation of common systems will enhance job mobility and sharing.

In an attempt to improve efficiency, two alternative information systems are actively being considered by the management committee of the Court Service. These two systems are:

Information System Alpha	*Information System Beta*
Decentralised configuration with all information required by each Regional Court being available from computer systems maintained within the court building.	Centralised configuration for common data required by all courts such as databases of case law, but each Regional Court maintaining its own information system regarding salaries and court scheduling.
Common information distributed via CD-ROM from the Central Court each week. Distribution will be by the standard postal service. A courier will transfer any urgent information from the Central Court between the weekly updates.	Information on common databases accessed via telephone lines from each Regional Court to a central server. Dial-in access is provided for each court.
The Court Administrator to remain in charge of running the information system in each court.	Responsibility for information systems split between the Head of Court Data Services for centralised information and the Court Administrator for local information. Court Administrators are likely to be averse to this move because of the reduction in their control over the databases.

Both systems will have a new management information system that will collate the operational information in each court and provide a summary of this information to the Court Administrator.

A further alternative information system (called Gamma) had been considered by the management committee. This system was to have held all information centrally. The data would have been accessed via a secure virtual private network (VPN) using spare capacity on the wide-area network of the national rail company. Each court would have been able to access the central database using a dedicated leased line to the nearest access point to the VPN. This alternative was dismissed as being too expensive.

A cost–benefit analysis is due to be carried out on systems Alpha and Beta to try to determine which system will be more cost-effective for the Court Service. It is hoped that this analysis will identify costs and benefits, both tangible and intangible, in areas like hardware and software requirements as well as systems development and usage within the Court Service.

Critical success factors (CSFs)

Efficiency in the Court Service is currently measured in terms of

- whether the annual budget has been spent (the Court Service receives a grant each year from the government that has to be accounted for on a cash basis – any cash not spent is deducted from next year's budget), and
- percentage utilisation of each courtroom.

The management committee of the courts has recognised that these measures may not be appropriate when the efficiency and economy of the Service is being investigated.

New CSFs have therefore been recently agreed:

- *Internal CSF.* To ensure efficient allocation and use of the public resources that the government commits to the courts.
- *External CSF.* To minimise the time for cases to be taken through the court system.

These new CSFs have met with broad approval from government, although not all court employees have yet accepted them.

Requirements

(a) Explain the likely costs and benefits (tangible and intangible) of each of information systems Alpha and Beta. **(20 marks)**

(b) (i) Explain the need for critical success factors (CSFs) and performance indicators (PIs) in a public service organisation such as a Court Service. **(8 marks)**

    (ii) Suggest PIs that can be used to support the new CSFs of the Court Service. Explain why the PIs that you have suggested are appropriate in this situation. **(10 marks)**

(c) Describe the data that will have to be input to the different sections of the new Court Service information system and explain why this data is needed in the information system. **(12 marks)**

(Note: Your answer to part (c) *should ignore case and statute law.)*

(Total marks = 50)

? Question 26

Current situation

KJ is a manufacturer of clothes, specialising in shirts, blouses, trousers and skirts. The company has an annual turnover of $450 million and manufactures its products in three factories. It employs 600 workers and 100 management and sales staff in the country in which it operates. Sales are predominantly to the local market, although there has been some growth in exports, particularly in the more specialist and expensive products.

All goods are currently sold through wholesalers, who then sell the clothes on to retail outlets such as supermarkets and dedicated fashion shops. This system proved very profitable for KJ because products were normally in demand and there was little effective competition. However, the last 5 years have produced falling profit levels resulting from:

- an increase in competition, particularly from cheap imports;
- a higher level of obsolete stock resulting from more frequent changes in preferences for different types of clothes;
- increased delivery time from raw material manufacturers, resulting partly from more complicated orders from KJ, but also as a result of poorer payment terms being imposed by KJ.

Staff are also becoming demotivated and staff turnover has increased substantially in the last 6 months.

Board response

The board of KJ has been considering the problems facing the company. Whereas there are various short-term actions that can be taken such as obtaining loans to pay suppliers more quickly, the general opinion is that the problems facing KJ require a more fundamental change in the method of selling. In consultation with some computer-aided design/ computer-aided manufacture (CAD/CAM) specialists, the following changes are being proposed to KJ's method of operation:

- *Method of selling.* All orders from customers to be taken on the telephone by the existing sales staff or via the company's new Internet site. The existing wholesale distribution system, including selling on to retail markets, will be disbanded and sales only made directly to customers.
- *Manufacturing of garments.* All garments will be made by the CAD/CAM system based on designs in the computer system. However, sufficient flexibility will be introduced into the system to allow customers to choose options such as fabric type, colour, size and other options like buttons or zips. The manufacturing workforce will be decreased by approximately one third as a result of the use of CAD/CAM systems.
- *Finished good stocks.* There will be no stocks of finished goods; all goods will be made to customer order only.
- *Raw material stocks.* Will be kept to a minimum with suppliers being asked to deliver stock on a daily basis. KJ seeks to make Electronic Data Interface (EDI) links with a few nominated suppliers so that customer order details are transferred directly to raw material suppliers as they are received at KJ. The materials to manufacture those garments will then be delivered to KJ on the next working day. In return for this quick response time, KJ will pay for all goods on receipt, via electronic funds transfer.
- *Delivery time.* Time from receipt of order to delivery of goods to the customer will be four working days.
- *Catalogue availability.* A detailed style catalogue will be available on the Internet. A paper version will be despatched to customers although a charge will be made for this service.

Internet site

Because of a lack of any in-house expertise on the establishment and maintenance of Internet sites, the board remains uncertain concerning:

- The writing of the software for the site itself. Many board members are keen to take advantage of the cost savings provided by generic Website production software, but recognise that this may not be the most appropriate course of action for the company.
- The physical location of the computer 'hosting' the Internet site. The main area of concern is not to lose control over the site, particularly as daily updates are necessary. However, 'hosting' the site at a third party does have distinct advantages of providing appropriate back-up and maintenance of the site, allowing KJ to concentrate on the core business of selling clothes.

Executive Information System (EIS)

To maintain control over the system, a new EIS will be installed in KJ. Ten of the existing sales staff will be promoted to tactical management and be given access to this system. These managers will then be responsible for the short- to medium-term operations and planning within the organisation. In particular, the tactical managers will be expected to monitor supplier relations, CAD/CAM usage, profitability levels and sales trends. They will be given authority to order repairs to equipment, amend selling prices, negotiate raw material prices and amend the number of operational staff as necessary. Strategic planning regarding the overall business aims of the organisation will remain with the board of KJ.

Requirements

(a) As far as the information allows, evaluate the board response (excluding the EIS), clearly explaining the tangible and intangible costs and benefits that will arise.

(22 marks)

(b) (i) In respect of set-up and maintenance of the Internet site, contrast the advantages of writing the entire software for the site with the advantages of purchasing a general website and tailoring this to the company's requirements. **(12 marks)**

(ii) Assuming that the site is hosted at a third-party Internet service provider (ISP) after it has been written, explain with reasons the critical aspects that should be included in the maintenance agreement to be signed with the ISP. **(7 marks)**

(c) Using relevant examples from KJ, comment on the impact on society of the ability to provide products to customer order on short delivery timescales through the Internet.

(9 marks)

(Total marks = 50)

? Question 27

S&C is a medium-sized firm that is experiencing rapid growth, thanks to increased turnover. It has been able to develop a range of new consultancy and specialist business advisory services that it offers to its growing customer base. To cope with these developments, several company-wide initiatives have been launched over the past 2 years.

The existing financial systems are struggling to cope with these developments. The replacement of the existing software is due to go ahead within the next 6 months. The new system was justified partly because it could reduce costs (although precise details have not been given). Although the application software does not fit existing business processes exactly, it has the clear advantage of giving S&C access to an industry best practice system and is identical to that used by all its main competitors and some of its clients. A three-person project steering group has recommended that a phased approach to introduction will be used and has undertaken most of the project planning. A programme of events for implementing the system has been agreed but is not yet fully operational. This group has not met for a while because the designated project manager has been absent from work with illness.

You are Head of S&C's Central Support Unit. You also serve on the project steering group.

A partners' meeting is due to take place soon. The firm's senior partner has asked you to prepare a PowerPoint presentation to other partners on implementation issues. You understand that partners are conscious that system implementation represents a form of further organisational change and are asking questions about the approach that will be taken to the introduction of the new system; likely changes to practices; critical areas for success, system testing, support after implementation and system effectiveness, and so on.

Requirements

You are required to produce *outline notes* that will support your eventual PowerPoint presentation. These notes should:

(a) Explain why a phased approach to introducing the system is, in this case, particularly more suitable than a more direct 'big bang' approach. **(4 marks)**

(b) Describe the options to overcome the fact that the software does not fit existing business processes exactly. **(4 marks)**

(c) Discuss the ways in which particular individuals and groups within S&C are important for implementation to succeed. **(4 marks)**

(d) Explain the aims of a post-implementation review. **(4 marks)**

(e) Describe the training that should be given in terms of topics, methods and targeted groups within S&C. **(4 marks)**

(f) Explain how users might be involved in testing the system during the implementation phase. **(4 marks)**

(Total marks = 24)

? Question 28

R&L is a large manufacturing firm that is well known as a 'good employer'. Over the past few years, R&L has experienced difficult times with reducing sales and mounting losses. In desperation, it employed management consultants to analyse their situation. The consultants have concluded that the down turn in sales is permanent and that R&L needs to reduce its workforce by 50% over the next year in order to survive. Reluctantly, R&L's board of directors have accepted these findings, including the need to shed staff. They have also agreed to act as honestly and fairly as possible but realised that any changes they propose will be unpopular and may meet with resistance.

Requirements

(a) Identify what positive initiatives R&L can take to achieve job losses needed.

(6 marks)

(b) Discuss the potential strategies available in order to overcome resistance to change, and identify those strategies that would be most suitable for R&L. **(13 marks)**

(c) Delayering, downsizing and outsourcing all normally have the effect of reducing staff numbers. Distinguish each of these terms, providing examples drawn from the scenario.
(**6 marks**)
(**Total marks = 25**)

Question 29

National Secure (NS) is a large insurance company. The company is structured into four Divisions and supported by a small headquarters that includes the personnel function (recently renamed the Human Resourcing (HR) Division). The post of Head of HR is vacant following the retirement of the long-serving post-holder, and the HR strategy is in urgent need of review and revision.

National Secure has recently announced a new corporate initiative of continuous improvement through the empowerment of its workforce. The Chief Executive explained: 'We value our people as our most prized asset. We will encourage them to think, challenge and innovate. Only through empowering them in this way can we achieve continuous improvement. Staff will no longer be expected just to obey orders; from now on they will make and implement decisions to bring about continuous improvement. We want to develop clear performance objectives and be more customer focused.'

Your line manager is one of the four Divisional directors and will soon form part of a panel that will interview candidates for the vacant role of HR director. She is particularly keen to ensure that the successful candidate would be able to shape the HR Division to the needs of the organisation. She is aware of your CIMA studies and has asked for your help in preparing for the interview.

Requirements

Produce outline notes for your Divisional director which discuss the main points you would expect candidates to highlight in response to the following two areas she intends to explore with candidates at the interview, specifically:

(a) The likely role that the HR function will perform in the light of the changing nature of the organisation.
(**8 marks**)

(b) The aspects of a revised HR strategy that will show significant change, given the nature of recent organisational developments.
(**9 marks**)

(c) Explain the concept of continuous improvement and its relationship to empowerment.
(**8 marks**)
(**Total marks = 25**)

Solutions to Revision Questions

☑ Solution 1

(a) (i) The adoption of socially responsible policies is likely to result in increased costs. This will reduce the profitability of the company, particularly in the short run, and will conflict with the objective of maximising the wealth of the shareholders. It is possible, however, that the adoption of the policies might increase the profit over a longer period of time and even result in the survival of the company.

   If a firm is seen as a 'good neighbour', it is likely that this image will be beneficial in terms of attracting customers. This means that expenditure on the social programmes can be regarded as a good investment of resources.

   (ii) It is possible that organisations which concentrate on the maximisation of profit in the short run will probably resist the adoption of social policies that involve incurring additional costs. However, by concentrating only on short-term goals, the total profitability of the organisation may be reduced over the life of the company or project. Adopting a long-term view can often be the best approach. This means that the adoption of social policies that increase costs may eventually lead to the maximisation of shareholders' wealth. This is the ultimate goal of many organisations.

(b) The company will need to appoint either an official or a committee to plan and implement policies which will improve the social responsibility of the organisation. It is also possible that the appointment of an outside consultant to monitor the position will be useful for implementing the social policies. Internal managers, who are under pressure to boost the results of the company, might neglect 'social responsibilities'. In this situation, there may be a temptation to reject policies that increase costs.

It may be difficult for the managers to identify the areas in which social responsibility issues arise. Training programmes and collaboration with other organisations may assist in the identification of the problems that need to be addressed. It is possible that the starting point should be a review of the present social policies and practices of the firm. In addition, it will be necessary to ensure that the social responsibility of the firm is monitored to ensure that this type of issue is considered before decisions are made. It is also important that social responsibility policy decisions should be widely publicised within the firm. This will ensure that managers incorporate environmental factors into all decisions.

(c) Although the shareholders will expect good financial returns from the company, they are also members of the general public who will be affected by the social policies of the company. In this context, they may be prepared to sacrifice short-term benefits for the long-run advantages. As discussed in part (a), sound social policies may even result in improved financial performance in the long run. The adoption of responsible social responsibility may, therefore, be the best policy for the company in the long run.

Employees are more likely to benefit from most of the social responsibility policies of the company. They are therefore likely to be in favour of the policies. However, if the policies threaten their jobs, this will not be the case.

The effect on the firm's other stakeholders, which include lenders, suppliers and the government, will depend on the particular situation. Their reaction to particular social responsibility issues will be determined by the way that the policy affects their interests. Lenders will be principally concerned with the settlement of the amounts owing to them and this involves the levels of liquidity and profitability. Suppliers will want to be sure that, in the short run, the amounts owed to them will be paid, but will be eager to retain links with a firm that is expanding. The government will be particularly interested in the levels of pollution in the country.

✓ Solution 2

(a) Management accounting is primarily concerned with providing information to managers to enable them to make decisions and to exercise control in order to eliminate wastage and inefficiencies.

There has been considerable discussion in the accountancy profession about the deficiencies of the accounting reports that are presented to managers. A particular area of concern is the fact that many of the reports concentrate on producing information which ignores the external environment. It has been suggested that the focus of most reports is on internal factors. Currently, the reports presented to the managers of W Ltd focus on the monthly cost variances in direct materials, direct labour and both the variable and fixed production overheads. As these reports highlight the differences in cost within the factory, they provide a useful means of directing the attention of the management to inefficiencies which have occurred. Although this is an important aspect of control for W Ltd, it is only one aspect of the information that is needed to manage the organisation efficiently and effectively.

W Ltd's current reporting system does not look forward, it ignores information needed to manage the strategic aspects of the company and appears to be inadequate for decision-making.

(b) In the initial stage of the strategic planning process, it is necessary both to review the external environment in which the company operates and to conduct a position audit of the firm. In order to be able to undertake these initial steps in the strategic planning process, it is essential that information is prepared regularly. This is so as to keep the managers informed about the firm's customers, suppliers and the availability of resources. In W Ltd, this type of information is not currently provided, but is essential if the company is to improve its strategic planning.

Regular reports should be prepared to provide both financial and non-financial information about a range of different factors, for example market share is important.

This refers to the position of the firm in relation to both its competitors and the size of the total market. Forecasts of future market trends would be helpful.

Reports about customers would provide details of the size of each organisation, the type of industry and their cost structure. It is particularly important to know about the profit generated by each group of customers. It is essential to know the reason why customers prefer to buy from W Ltd and what makes the company's technology and skills unique. These factors are what gives W Ltd its competitive advantage.

A specific issue in W Ltd is the amount of business that is turned down because of the lack of adequate facilities. Details should be recorded of the extent of the business that is rejected.

It is advisable to calculate the profit margin of the different products, jobs and customers. This will assist the managers to make correct decisions. This information should also include competitors' pricing policies.

The present system of budgetary control and standard costing should be retained to provide control within the organisation. The variance analysis provides information that highlights any deficiencies. The firm's current costing system should be reviewed as it is possible that the introduction of a system of activity-based costing (ABC) might improve the decisions made by the managers. ABC will focus attention on the cost drivers that generate the greatest cost for the company and this may provide better information for the strategic planning process.

In addition to the financial reports that are required in any company, details of the cash flows should also be reported. This will emphasise the importance of monitoring the cash flow of the business.

(c) Benchmarking is achieved by comparing the output of one organisation with that of another. It is usual to select an organisation which is reputed to offer a particularly high-quality product or service. Thus, W Ltd should try to co-operate with a firm which is in the same industry. In this instance, it is important that both firms manufacture precision parts using similar production methods. Major differences in the facilities would make the comparisons less meaningful.

It may be difficult to establish a link with another firm in the same industry as there is likely to be rivalry between the firms. There will be the possibility that sensitive information will be disclosed during the benchmarking process. However, if the areas are clearly defined, it will be possible for both organisations to benefit from comparing the performance of their organisations.

As it is possible to benchmark internal services of an organisation, W Ltd could benchmark its management information system with that developed by a firm in the same industry. This may be even more difficult to arrange because of the sensitivity of the information that may be disclosed in the benchmarking process. It is, therefore, necessary to be very specific about the nature of the information that will be provided by each firm.

It may be beneficial to benchmark with a firm which is not in direct competition with W Ltd. Although this may be more acceptable to the firms, it is likely that there will be significant differences between firms in different industries or with different situations. For example, a firm undertaking large-scale engineering jobs may not require the same management information as W Ltd which undertakes only small-scale engineering work.

It must be appreciated that the benchmarking of management information will be an initiative which will need to be developed over a number of years as considerable negotiation will be needed to ensure the mutual trust between the two organisations.

Solution 3

(a) An appropriate model would be the Boston Consulting Group matrix which classifies SBUs in terms of their market growth and relative market share. The categories are:

- *Stars* – high market growth and high market share: GC has the software development and supply company, which is experiencing a rapid market growth and has a market share of 10 per cent. Although the market share could be higher, it seems that this company should be considered to be a star.
- *Question marks (Problem children)* – high market growth and low market share: Although the market is slowing down, it seems appropriate to place the painting and decorating contracting company in this category. The position should be investigated to ascertain if the company could gain an increased share of this market. It is possible that this division could be moved into the star category.
- *Cash cows* – low market growth and high market share: The food manufacturer is in this section as it has 25 per cent of the market, but there is a slow decline in market growth.
- *Dogs* – low market growth and low market share: GC has both the building brick manufacturer and the parcel carrier service with relatively low market growth and market share.

    GC's situation is not good. At the present time there are two SBUs that are classified as dogs and the management should be considering the most appropriate action. The food manufacturer is a cash cow and steps should be taken to ensure that the software development and supply company receives resources that enable it to develop, as it seems that the future of the company depends on the proper handling of the company's only star. Finally the position of the painting and decorating contracting company should be reviewed in order to move it into the star sector.

(b) As the BCG matrix is based on the product life cycle, it suffers from the same limitations as that model. It is often very difficult to determine the position of a product in the life-cycle and products can remain in the mature stage for a long period of time.

    It is also possible that the financial return is not related directly to the two factors considered by the BCG matrix, rate of market growth and relative market share. Adopting a strategy to exploit a niche market is sometimes a profitable strategy for a firm. Factors which influence financial performance of an organisation are the relative competitive position of the business and especially the relative quality of the products, and the relative attractiveness of the market. The BCG matrix does include some of these aspects but ignores the investment intensity and also operational productivity of the industry. These can be crucial factors that are not included in the BCG matrix.

    Although the BCG matrix can be criticised, it provides a useful method of assessing the position of the products within a framework which is essential to consider at the beginning of the strategic planning process.

(c) In order to add value to the group, the management of GC must undertake a value chain analysis of its SBUs. At the outset, each activity must be analysed to determine where value is being added and also if value is being destroyed. When the individual value chains have been considered, then the position of the entire company must be analysed. The management must look for synergy within the various activities of the company and this will determine the appropriate strategy for the company. Links between the value chains of each activity would be important in determining the best course of action for GC.

The company should consider disposing of their interests in the building brick and parcel carriage service divisions. In addition, the future trends in the painting and decorating contracting service should be reassessed as this SBU is not contributing to the profitability of the group. There is a possibility that the building brick manufacturer and the painting and decorating contractor could be resuscitated. These alternatives should be investigated more fully before they are sold.

At the present time, the profitability of the building brick operation is declining and therefore the disposal of this part of the business would appear to be sensible. However, the parcel carriage service represents an activity in which GC has been involved for many years. The sales and profitability are stable and are not expected to improve. This is likely to be a difficult decision and it is important that the right buyer is obtained for this section of the company. This would ensure that a reasonable price was obtained for the business.

The resources that are obtained from the sale of dogs should be used to develop the software development and supply company that is classified as a star. This division is in a market that is expected to grow and although the profitability is low at present, it is likely to improve as the market develops. It is essential that GC focus attention on this division as it likely that the whole company will depend on the division for its survival in the future.

The food manufacturer is currently classified as a cash cow. Steps should be taken to explore the possibility of boosting the market growth by the introduction of new products. It should not be abandoned and allowed to run down, as it may be possible to revitalise this market to the advantage of GC.

It is vital for GC to plan its strategy to enable synergies to be developed between the different parts of the organisation. Presently, there would appear to be little possibility of the different parts of the business benefiting from being associated with GC. This is an area which should be considered in the decisions that are to be taken regarding the disposals of some of the divisions. It is important that the company undertake a complete review of its objectives, current position and the future prospects of its SBUs.

☑ Solution 4

(a) In order to either retain competitive advantage or achieve growth, it is sometimes necessary for a firm to acquire companies or merge with other firms. This strategy is particularly important if it is considered that the opportunities for organic growth are limited. It is possible that the existing products are not considered suitable for expansion in either the existing or new markets, and also that new products cannot be developed within the required timescale. In this situation, a firm will consider expanding by means of acquisitions and mergers.

Synergy is considered to be essential to any form of combination. The benefits of the enlarged organisation is expected to be greater than the benefits of the separate units and this provides an economic justification for the combination. It is often difficult to find practical examples of outstanding success in generating synergy, as the costs often equal or even outweigh the benefits.

However, especially in mature markets, it is possible to obtain advantages through economies of scale. Especially in the support functions, it is possible to reduce the total expenses of the combined organisation. It is possible to achieve rationalisation of administrative, sourcing and marketing functions. Offsetting these benefits, however, are the increased costs which arise from the increased size of the firm.

In general terms, the management need to consider the likely effect on the costs of both firms and also to assess the benefits arising from the acquisition and merger. Factors which are very important in assessing the viability of an acquisition or merger include the impact on the transfer of technology and distribution channels, the availability of finance and the ability to reduce costs through the bulk purchasing of resources.

(b) A demerger will result in the company being split into different segments which will operate as separate entities. If some parts of the firm are not expected to perform well in the future, it is sometimes better for these parts of the company to be isolated and sold. This would mean that the shareholders could dispose of their interests in the parts of the organisation which are expected to generate lower levels of profitability.

It is possible that a demerger will enable the company to:
- increase the dividends which might also affect the price of the share;
- reinvest the proceeds into different activities that are expected to result in the objectives of the company being achieved.

Both these results would be beneficial to the shareholders as they will benefit from the increased dividends, the higher share price and also the change to new areas.

It is sometimes possible that a demerger will act as a defence against hostile takeovers. This is likely to be of greater significance to the management of the company, but to some extent it will also affect the shareholders.

(c) The model in Figure 9.1 provides a useful starting point for considering the different methods by which a firm can expand its operations.

It is possible to choose market penetration, which means that more of the existing products would be sold in the existing markets. Alternatively, it is possible to introduce new products into the existing markets and this is market development. If new products were developed, then these could be sold in either the existing or new markets. Each of these alternative strategies involves the firm in different risks, and entering new markets with new products – diversification – is the most risky course of action.

Ansoff's matrix provides a framework which highlights the alternative courses of action that are available and, therefore, is useful in developing a strategic plan.

Figure 1

✅ Solution 5

The product manager has £5m to develop one of the following drugs:

- Tyrix which is in the early stages of development;
- Medvac – introduced recently, but threatened by two competitive products;
- Sonprex, a mature product which could be boosted by additional expenditure on repacking and promotion.

(a) The concept of product portfolio means that a firm has a comprehensive range of products which are in different stages of development. This enables the firm to meet competition within the market in which it operates. Changes in the environment are less likely to have a dramatic impact on the firm when different products are available to counter the changes. If a range of products are developed and marketed, the firm has a chance of minimising the risks.

The product life cycle is a valuable model for strategic planning. According to this theory, a product passes through four different stages – development, growth, maturity and decline.

At the present time, Pharmia has 34 different products 'at various stages of development'. This reinforces Pharmia's emphasis on research and development and shows the strategy adopted to retain its competitive advantage in the market.

(b) By estimating the probability of success and payoff for each product, it is possible to assess the most appropriate course of action. In this example, the investment of £5m will result in the following expected payoff from each product:

Product	Probability	Discounted payoff £m	Expected payoff £m	Initial outlay £m	Net payoff (discounted) £m
Tyrix	0.0300	150	4.5		
	0.9700	–	–		
			4.5	(5.0)	(0.5)
Medvac					
+30%	0.1667	48	8.0		
+15%	0.3333	27	9.0		
+10%	0.5000	10	(5.0)		
			12.0	(5.0)	7.0
Sonprex	1.0000	14	14.0	(5.0)	9.0

The options are mutually exclusive. On the basis of only these probabilities, Sonprex is the best investment, but it is possible that other non-financial factors should be considered before the decision is finally made.

The information can be summarised in a decision tree (Figure 9.2).

(c) To assess the possible alternative courses of action, the use of expected values is an excellent starting point. It is, however, very difficult to forecast accurately both the probability of success and the payoff of the proposed strategies. In this problem, the outcome for Tyrix is negative. However, there is a substantial difference in the two possible outcomes of Tyrix. There is a 3 per cent chance of a payoff of £150m which would clearly have a great effect on the firm. Even a small change in the probability of success of Tyrix would make a significant difference to the expected payoff and final decision.

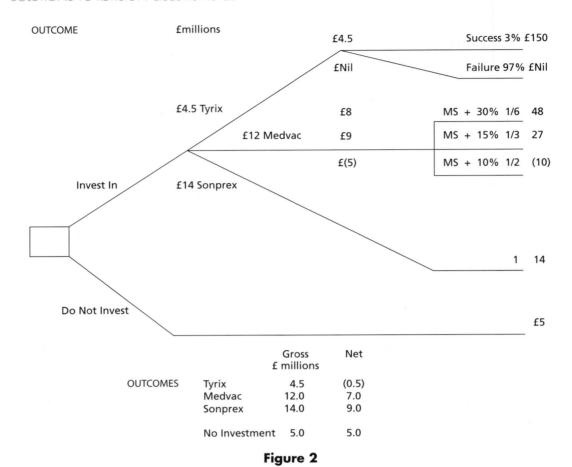

Figure 2

In addition, the concepts of product market portfolio and the product life cycle should be considered before reaching a decision. Placing too much emphasis on quantitative evaluation is unwise, as the investment in a new product provides payoffs over a long period and may even provide the firm with a significant future competitive advantage. Thus, an assessment of qualitative aspects must also be included in the decision process.

(d) On the basis of quantitative analysis, the decision would be to develop Sonprex. Although Sonprex provides a certain net payoff of £9m, it would be unwise to invest in a product which is declining and which will be superseded. In order to develop a major competitive advantage for the firm, it would be better to invest in a product with more potential.

The choice is therefore between either of the other two products. On the basis of the expected probabilities, Tyrix results in a negative outcome, but could bring considerable benefits if the product were a success. Although the probability of success is low, it might be worth while to improve the possibility of success of this product.

The other alternative is to increase the market share of Medvac by an advertising campaign. The expected outcome is only £2m less than the outcome from the investment in the mature product, Sonprex. To invest in Medvac appears to be the best solution, as it will provide the firm with a strong product in the long run. The final decision about the choice of products will be influenced by a number of factors. These include:

- *The attitude to risk.* If the product manager is risk-averse, investment of the additional funds in Sonprex will be favoured as this is certain to increase the profits. However, the long-term benefits will be relatively small as the product will be 'superseded in the near future'.

- *The concept of product portfolio.* Details are not available on the current products. It is necessary for the product manager to analyse the characteristics of the existing products to see which of the three new investment options should be adopted.

- *The product life cycle.* The product manager must determine the 'stages of development' of the existing 34 products. This will provide a useful basis for deciding between the three options. It may be necessary to increase the number of products in the development stage.

These are the factors which should be taken into account before the final decision is taken. It is possible that the product manager may prefer to consider other options before a final decision to invest the £5m is reached.

☑ Solution 6

(a) An effective system to measure performance must address the following issues. At the outset, it is important to select criteria which represent the goals and objectives of the organisation. It is possible that a range of different financial and non-financial variables will be needed to cover the different aspects of a firm's aims.

It is very important that the performance measures be defined appropriately to ensure that the correct messages are given to the management. In particular, the basis of calculating capital employed must be established, as there are a number of bases which can be used involving either historical cost or current values. It is also necessary to choose a benchmark of performance and the timescale that will be used within the organisation.

A system of performance measurement can be affected significantly if it is necessary to set transfer prices as goods pass from one division to another within the organisation. Even if market prices for the goods transferred exist, it is essential that the effect of the transfer pricing system be taken into consideration, especially when decisions are being made which involve the allocation of resources. It is possible that the transfer price can affect the entire performance evaluation process and so is an issue which must be resolved if a sound system is to be established.

It is intended that the management are motivated by a firm's performance measurement system. However, it is possible that sub-optimisation might occur, especially when managers take decisions which affect their division. Another aspect of this problem is 'short-termism' which might not be in the long-term interest of the whole organisation but show a better performance within one division immediately.

Finally, the performance reports must distinguish between the performance of the division and the manager of the division. It is likely that this distinction will be obtained through the non-financial indicators that are selected to show the level of success achieved.

(b) The advantage of ROCE as a measure of performance is that it is relatively simple to compute. As it relates the profit to the resources that are used to generate that profit, it can be understood by most managers. By using profit as part of this measure of performance, the level of sales, the selling prices and the level of expenses and costs will all influence the profit figure that is related to the capital employed.

The disadvantages, however, are that it is extremely difficult to be precise in defining both profit and capital employed. It is possible for there to be several different ways of determining the profit of an organisation and the general use of historical cost creates problems in establishing the amount of capital employed by an organisation. It is possible that this might be a problem in this company, as the investments in Agriculture appear to be performing particularly poorly.

Another difficulty arises if a division is not self-contained and independent. This is the problem of transfer pricing which can create problems in measuring the performance of a division. The transfers between the Agricultural and the Beverage divisions are likely to create performance measurement problems within Goulden plc.

The return on capital employed within the company ranges from 5 to 20 per cent. In fact, the overall ROCE is 8.2 per cent. Agriculture shows the lowest return and this may be a reflection of temporary problems in this industry. The relatively low return (8 per cent) in the tobacco industry reflects the decreased profits resulting from the declining markets. It is important, however, that the size of the investment in the tobacco industry in relation to the whole company is appreciated.

(c) As an alternative to ROCE, it is possible to use the concept of residual income. Under this system, a notional charge is calculated. The estimated cost of capital is determined and this is used to determine the amount of interest that would be incurred to finance both the fixed and working capital used by the division. The notional interest is then deducted from the profit and results in residual income which can then be used to assess the relative performance of the divisions within the firm.

It is also possible to compare the actual residual income with the budget and this will therefore provide a means of determining the level of success during the period under review.

Solution 7

(a) The broad overall aims of the organisation are identified in the mission statement and this is the starting point in the preparation of a strategic plan. Using the mission statement, it is possible to establish the objectives which are more specific and will incorporate criteria which will enable performances to be quantified and measured. When the objectives, as the long-term aims of the organisation, have been established, it is then necessary to identify and evaluate the alternative courses of action which can be adopted to achieve the goals.

The operational goals are short-term targets which are set in order to provide the basis on which the day-to-day performance can be monitored. The operational targets are the 'immediate steps' which will be taken and it is expected that they will eventually result in the long-term objectives being attained.

It is necessary that a system of performance measurement be introduced which enables the extent to which the organisation has moved towards its overall long-term objectives to be ascertained. The number of contracts gained, the quality of the service offered or the relative position of the organisation in relation to competitors would be appropriate non-financial measures to monitor the extent to which the long-term objectives of the organisation are being achieved.

Production levels as compared with the budget, the efficiency of the labour force, wastage rates of materials and levels of spending would be indicators of whether the operational targets of the organisation were being met and these would provide a means of monitoring the implementation of the short-term strategy.

(b) When establishing a system of performance measurement for divisional managers, it is important that a number of different aspects of the problem be addressed. These include the effects on the motivation of the management and staff and the establishing of measurable strategic and operational targets which are realistic and can be monitored effectively. Finally, consideration must be given to the manner in which the changes will be introduced and implemented within the organisation.

In a not-for-profit organisation, it is important that both financial and non-financial information be used. Within a hospital, divisional performance must be reported to focus on the crucial elements of performance in each area. This is likely to be difficult, as outputs are often hard to measure in non-profit organisations and imagination and creativity will be required in developing a useful system of performance measurement in the hospital.

- *Motivation.* The setting of performance targets will affect the morale and attitudes of the staff towards achieving the goals of the organisation. It is important that the management and staff identify with the goals and objectives that are set and are prepared to be assessed on the basis of these factors. It is likely that participation in establishing the goals, understanding the basis of the control system and appreciating the usefulness of the system will be important in ensuring that the system is accepted and will act as a motivating force, especially if the levels of delegated authority of each manager are made clear to all the senior staff. It is important that there is congruency between the goals and objectives of the organisation and the individual managers who are expected to act to ensure that these goals and objectives are attained.

- *Establishing measurable objectives.* Particularly in a non-profit organisation, profitability is not significant as the ultimate criterion of success. In addition, in organisations which provide services, there are problems in establishing meaningful objectives as the output is often difficult to measure precisely. It is, therefore, common to base the appraisal measurement on inputs to the departments. Although the inputs are a major factor, the outputs from the division are really more important and the performance appraisal system should be based on the outputs, both financial and non-financial, of the divisions within the hospital.

If inputs to the divisions are used, for example, the amount spent on wages or medicines, the implication is that additional costs represent improved services to the users. In fact, this may not be true as much of the additional resources could be wasted. It is, therefore, important that the economy, efficiency and effectiveness be used to evaluate the performance of each division:

- *economy* will measure the amount spent on the services that are provided by each division and it would be appropriate to compare the costs with similar divisions in other hospitals;

- *efficiency* focuses on the relationship between the input and output from each division. The cost of each type of treatment or process can be determined and compared with past performance, expected costs or the cost in other organisations;

- *effectiveness* measures the extent to which the organisation is achieving its objectives and is, therefore, an extremely important aspect of the performance appraisal system.

If the system of performance measurement is to be successful, it is important that the management negotiate the strategic and operational targets with the key personnel within the division. There will be a need to be sure that realistic targets are set and that elements chosen to be measured and reported upon reflect the objectives and aims of the division.

- *Cultural factors.* There is a need for the management to be aware of the cultural issues in the design of a performance evaluation system. In particular, the change from input to output measures should be handled carefully as there will be implications for the division and its staff in implementation procedures and system operation. It is important not to alienate staff if the system is to be successful.

(c) In order to bring about change in this particular project there are a number of strategies that the board can bring to bear:

- bring employees face to face with the external pressures to change. The point has been made that they are now operating in a competitive environment due to changes introduced by the Government. Staff are more likely to respond to the initiative if they have had a clear explanation of the new criteria under which J is now operating and the need for performance appraisal. A series of meetings at all levels, with an effective 'opening of the books' would go a long way to move staff from a culture in which performance, and particularly, cost are recognised as important.

- identify change agents who will 'own' the new system and drive the required change. Of these some will have influence because of their position in the organisation, others because of their charismatic power, they could be *early adopters* or *resistors to change*. It is important that the board identify those who are early adopters and co-opt them to the implementation process. Within any organisation there will be those staff who can be described *as found change agents* who are already demonstrating the required patterns of behaviour that a successful implementation will require.

- The board must take an empathetic view to the introduction of the new system remembering that there are a number of reasons why people will resist change.
  These can include;
  – fear of the new,
  – change fatigue,
  – different personal priorities,
  – annoyance at not being involved
  These are signs that should be watched for in the staff and addressed accordingly.

- The board need to support the change with new systems possibly offering incentives to the divisional managers with recognition for those divisions being most successful at the change programme. Any incentive programme will have to have it's negative side and, difficult though it may be, the board must make it clear that those that cannot change will have to move or leave the organisation.

☑ Solution 8

(a) One possible framework to help assess priority for IT investment was put forward by Davenport:
1. identifying business areas or processes that are suitable for innovation;
2. identifying 'change levers': those tools that can be used to innovate;
3. developing 'process visions': statements of purpose for the processes;
4. understanding existing processes:
5. designing and prototyping new processes.

Each of the stages of Davenport's framework is explained in more detail below.

1. As the essential Transaction Processing Systems (TPS) have already been implemented into the WOWR organisation, then it is unlikely that completely new systems would be needed in these areas. However, revisions to existing systems may be required as investment has been limited in recent years. The directors would need to check the business objectives of the WOWR organisation and then review the current IT systems to determine where amendments should take place.

   Areas for innovation may include direct linking of the production and sales systems, or providing customers with direct links into the production and sales systems to plan their purchases better.

2. This stage may involve looking at new technology or processes, or even current technology or processes, and checking whether these can be used in any of the business areas noted in stage 1. Again, given that the TPS appears to be implemented, opportunities for change could be found in providing better management information or Internet systems. Recent developments in MIS, including Artificial Intelligence and Expert Systems, may be investigated along with web design techniques.

3. The Board of the WOWR organisation needs to identify what the mission of the company is, and how the business areas and processes can be used to enhance that mission. For example, the sales system contains a lot of historical data. A mission could be to make more effective use of this data, perhaps by linking past sales trends with demographic information to try and determine sales potential for new books and publications.

4. Detail of the existing sales system will be required, including information on data held and how that database is updated. Having understood the existing system, then stage 5 can be undertaken.

5. Finally, new processes can be designed, using the change levers identified in stage 2 to amend the processes described in stage 4. In this situation, a sales database may be established using data mining techniques or intelligent agents to identify trends in that data to assist in forecasting future sales.

Examiner's note:
Other frameworks can be used as a basis for this answer.

(b) (i) Business process re-engineering (BPR) is the fundamental redesign of existing business processes to achieve improvement in critical areas of performance such as cost, quality, service and speed. BPR may be able to help in any given situation by:

- *Process identification.* Each task performed within the organisation or department being re-engineered is broken down into a series of processes. Each process is recorded and analysed to find whether it is necessary, either to add value directly or to support another value-adding process.
- *Process rationalisation.* Those processes which are not value-adding, or which are not essential to support a value-adding process, are discarded.
- *Process re-design.* The remaining processes are re-designed so they work in the most efficient way possible.
- *Process re-assembly.* The re-engineered processes are implemented, resulting in tasks, departments and an organisation that work in the most efficient manner.

   Process innovation is more radical than BPR, because it advocates the creation of new processes. It is likely to be a much more radical approach and may involve cultural changes within an organisation. Process innovation therefore has a greater chance of adding value to an organisation.

(ii) Process innovation and BPR are important within an organisation for various reasons:

- *Keep up with competitors.* Business processes, especially those enabled by IT, tend to change quickly. Competitors may attempt to use those new processes to their advantage. Companies which have chosen not to adopt that process will find themselves at a significant disadvantage. For example, customers may request that accounting information is transferred by EDI. If the WOWR organisation cannot provide this service, then customers may move to other suppliers.

  Investment in IT may be required to maintain competitive position, not necessarily to gain any significant advantage.

- *Competitive advantage.* Amending processes may provide an organisation with competitive advantage where competitors do not amend their systems as quickly or as effectively. For example, if the WOWR organisation provides an on-line ordering service before its competitors, then this may help provide some competitive advantage, especially if customers choose the WOWR organisation for this reason, rather than other similar suppliers.

  However, that competitive advantage will last only until other companies provide similar systems to the WOWR organisation. It will then either have to accept that the advantage has been lost, or find other ways of differentiating its service.

- *Cost savings.* Process changes will normally provide cost savings, especially where basic administrative functions are automated. The WOWR organisation has already implemented the administrative functions to achieve these savings. Further cost savings are likely to arise either from linking IT systems in the supply chain back to suppliers or forward to customers.

  Similarly, cost savings may arise from the provision of better information. In the case of a sales database, more reliable information may be available on proposed sales volumes. This will mean that more effective decisions can be made regarding the books or publications to produce. However, as these savings tend to be intangible, it may be difficult to justify expense based on this information.

- *Staff morale.* Morale may improve where an organisation is seen to be using the most recent technology and processes. Conversely, where technology and processes are out-of-date, staff morale may fall as they believe that appropriate expenditure is not being directed into these areas.

- *Technological change.* Technological change can also prompt process innovation. Because the technology is available, it may have to be used. This is particularly the case where competitors start using new technology. If the technology is not used (such as the Internet for ordering or selling of goods), the company may lose significant amounts of sales.

 Solution 9

Briefing paper
To: The Board of Directors
From: Management accountant
Subject: Products have life cycles whereas brands do not
Date: November 200X

As requested by the Finance Director in the memorandum of October 200X, I present information to clarify the issue expressed in the above quote.

This paper covers the following topics:

(a) the validity of the statement,

(b) the role of brands in the construction of barriers to entry,

(c) the financial control measures that might be used at the various stages of the product life cycle,

(d) the advantages and disadvantages of capitalising brands on the balance sheet.

(a) According to the product life cycle model, products move through different stages – development, growth, maturity and finally, decline. Although this model provides a useful insight into the phases through which a product passes, the timing of the changes and the extent of the growth or decline can vary significantly. This means that the model can only be used as an overall guide in the preparation of a strategic plan.

A particular issue is that individual brands often behave in a way that is different from their underlying products. By means of effective marketing, it is possible for a brand to exist, and even grow, for many years. Changes can be made to a brand's product, packaging and marketing effort. By incorporating changes into the marketing of a brand, it is possible to ensure that the brand is regarded as a separate entity from the product group in which it is classified. Marketing effort can often delay the decline of the brand and so modify the life cycle that affects products.

(b) If the competitive advantage of a brand is well established in the market, it is difficult for other products to compete. This means that potential entrants to the market, that is, new brands, will have to be clearly superior both in terms of quality and price. Even with these advantages, a promotional campaign will be needed to establish the new brand in the market. The initial launch of a product is often an expensive process and can only be undertaken by firms which have the necessary resources available.

The high cost of launching a new brand in terms of product development expenses, promotional expenses and necessary expertise acts as a barrier to entry. Only firms which have sufficient resources available can consider the launch of a new product which will compete with a well-established brand. In many situations, a firm will continue to advertise a brand even if there are no other products which are in direct competition. This is to make it more difficult for another firm to launch a similar product. In this way, the brand acts as a barrier to entry and safeguards the competitive advantage of the existing product.

(c) At the development stage, it is likely that large quantities of resources will need to be invested to ensure the continued growth of the product. It is therefore unlikely to have positive cash inflows from products in this stage of their development. The management reports should therefore provide information regarding the total outlays against the product. This will establish the extent of investment that takes place in the product.

- During the growth stage, the actual sales and market share are important. These statistics, together with the profit generated by the product, provide an insight into the success of the strategy adopted by the firm.

- The cash and profit generated during the maturity stage will be the most significant financial criterion when measuring the benefits generated from the past investment in the product.

- Finally, in the decline stage, the management will be concerned about the appropriate time to withdraw the product. The cash generated by the product will determine the exact time, and so information regarding the contribution from the product should be presented in the management reports.

(d) The capitalising of brands on the balance sheet means that the total assets of the company increase. In assessing capital structure, total debt is usually related to the firm's total assets. This means that capitalising brands will increase the asset base and will reduce the debt ratio. This is a statistic that is often used to monitor the financial position of the company and so the inclusion of the value of the brands in the balance sheet is likely to be advantageous to the firm by improving this statistic. The disadvantage is that there is an intangible asset in the balance sheet. This asset is difficult to value accurately, and in the event of a major change it may be necessary to adjust the value of the brands in the balance sheet. This could distort the financial performance of the company. In countries where it is usual to write off goodwill on acquisition, there is a greater incentive to value brands. The brands will be included as part of the assets that have been acquired. This means that the reserves will be reduced by a smaller amount as the whole of the goodwill need not be eliminated from the balance sheet. This is a matter on which there has been considerable discussion because it is difficult to justify the value placed on these intangible assets.

✓ Solution 10

(a) The management of a company is usually keen to show stakeholders that the company is being successful and, fundamentally, to publicise the fact that it is being managed efficiently and effectively. The published financial reports of the company are used by the directors and management of the company to disclose information to the stakeholders about the performance of the company. In particular, potential and existing shareholders, who own the company, would appreciate information about the future plans of the company to enable them to be aware of its strategic aims and objectives.

Although information is shown in respect of the company's past achievements, the management may wish to disclose strategically-sensitive management accounting information if they believe that this will maximise the long-term wealth of the owners to whom the management are ultimately responsible. It is likely that the stakeholders will be interested in receiving information which will enable them to form better opinions of the future performance of the company, especially regarding the future prospects of the company. In particular, the shareholders, creditors and lenders, employees and customers will be interested in receiving forward-looking information about the company.

- *Shareholders.* As the providers of the long-term finance to the company, the shareholders would be interested in being provided with information relating to the mission and objectives of the company. In particular, the expected changes in the share price and dividends would be of interest to the existing and potential shareholders. In addition, they would be concerned with the investment plans that the management are considering. It is possible that shareholders would be prepared to reduce the rate of return expected, as this additional information would reduce the risks faced by investors in the company.
- *Creditors and lenders.* This group would appreciate being provided with forward-looking information as they are interested in assessing the ability of the company

to repay the amounts owed to them. By having access to information which focuses on future rather than past performance, they would be able to judge the company's prospects of repayment more effectively. This would benefit the company if it leads to a reduction in the cost of borrowing.

- *Employees.* Providing forward-looking information to the employees would enable them to assess their long-term employment prospects which will be linked to the survival of the firm. Although this is difficult to assess, the provision of future-oriented strategic information would aid them and may act as a motivating factor which would benefit the company.
- *Customers.* This group of stakeholders would be interested in the forward-looking information as they are concerned with the long-term survival of the company. If they are convinced that the company was being managed effectively, it is possible that they would prefer to place orders with the company and this would represent a competitive advantage as a result of publishing the forward-looking information.

In general terms, the management would be motivated to disclose strategic, forward-looking management information, especially if it presents a favourable picture. However, it is not possible to direct the reports only to these interested parties because competitors, in particular, would be very interested in receiving the company's future strategy. This would clearly represent a major threat to the successful implementation of the strategic information plan, as it would enable the competitors to develop tactics and strategies which would counteract the company's plans. This means that the management accountant faces a dilemma in deciding the extent and nature of the strategic information to be disclosed by the company.

(b) The management must strike a balance between the benefits to be received by publishing forward-looking management information and the costs of the information being used to counteract the plans of the company. This is an area in which it is extremely difficult to assess the likely consequences of their decision. As previously discussed, it may be possible to reduce the cost of capital and borrowing, creating a climate within the company which motivates the workforce and attracts additional orders from customers, but it will place this information in the public domain which means that it could then be used by competitors to frustrate the company's strategy.

In order to cope with this situation, the management must carefully select the information to be published. The regulatory framework, which consists of the legislation, accounting standards and accounting practice, will prescribe the minimum disclosures in the published reports, but additional information can be provided in the chairman's report or in the reviews which are often included in the published statutory reports. It is also possible for the company to make known selected elements of its plans and strategy to the financial press which would be prepared to publish the information, if it was considered to be in the interests of the general public.

It is, therefore, for the management accountant to consider the type of information that would be beneficial to the company if made available to the public. At the same time, the possible use that could be made of the details by competitors would have to be assessed, and then the report prepared. It is likely that broad details of the strategy could be outlined in the reports, but the details of the plan and the tactics would not be disclosed. This would mean that the management accountant is reaching a considered compromise in terms of the costs and benefits of the disclosure of strategic management information.

(c) The means by which the board communicate with their stakeholders should be part of a broader stakeholder strategy. The four elements of such a strategy are:

- *Timing.* The board have already decided to inform in advance.
- *Techniques.* There are several direct and indirect approaches that the board can use. These may be communicative whereby the board speaks out on issues, via advocacy, corporate advertising, press releases and presentations to analysts and the media. They can also communicate by participative techniques whereby they will be seen to be lobbying, or make their point by association with particular groups such as business or industry associations.
- *Vehicles.* The communication medium that the organisation chooses to uses can either be internal to the company or external, that is, by using their own staff or an agency. Similarly they may choose to do this alone or in conjunction with other, well thought of, companies from the same industry.
- *Style.* This will depend upon the relationship which the board wish to maintain with the particular stakeholders or group of stakeholders. This could range from collaboration right through to defending. Much will depend upon what the board want to communicate, it may not always be good news.

 # Solution 11

(a) *Aims of internal benchmarking*

These are to establish best practices within an organisation with a view to improving effectiveness in activities (processes, products and services). This is achieved by comparing current operations with internal standards of performance or with other units in the organisation.

External benchmarking would differ in that current operations are compared against practices in other external organisations that are recognised as industry leaders. The external benchmark provides an independent assessment of what should be available with the aim of removing inefficiencies.

Operation

Activities are broken down into key stages, and inputs related to outputs and outcomes in order to diagnose areas of weakness. With internal benchmarking, activities, for example, the current level of customer complaints, could be compared with current standards (targets), past performance, or current performance in other units of the organisation.

External benchmarking differs in terms of the reference point used as a comparator. Current practices are compared against organisations perceived as being 'world class', for example, obtaining data from trade associations. It may be possible to compare data on cost levels and productivity with government-produced indices.

Limitations

The main problem with internal benchmarking is whether the reference point used is relevant. For example, if current performance is compared with historical data, the data may be distorted by changes in technology or in methods of working. Cost inflation would certainly make value comparisons more difficult. If current performance is compared with other units of the organisation, there is the danger of building in inefficiencies.

The main limitation with external benchmarking is likely to be the obtaining of current and reliable data. Competitors are likely to be secretive about any process that provides them with an advantage. Even if data is available, it will soon become out of date as external organisations move on.

(b) *Possible reasons for similar standard costs*

There are a number of possible reasons why standard costs may not have fallen as a result of investments in new technology and in new systems. Such investments may not have resulted in any immediate cost savings, although long-term benefits are anticipated. For example, there are likely to have been one-off costs incurred during the year in which new manufacturing technologies and manufacturing management systems have been introduced. Investments may also not have been made with short-term cost reductions as the target, but rather as a move towards long-term customer satisfaction through total quality management initiatives. The investment in technology may simply have substituted fixed costs, for example depreciation expense, for labour costs.

A further reason is that actual costs may be higher than planned because the new systems may be having unexpected implementation problems, possibly as a result of poor design in the planning stages. If significant, these extra costs may have been incorporated into revised standard costs.

New technologies often have a 'learning curve' effect and the standard costs in new technology plants may have been set above their expected long-run averages in order to prevent under-pricing of products in the short term.

It could be that if overhead costs are the most significant cost element, the standard costing systems may not have been reviewed in the plants with the new technologies. Revised overhead cost allocations may become necessary with the change in systems (ABC). Finally, although the standard costs may not differ between plants, the variances from standard may do so, and therefore a comparison should also be made of actual costs.

Appropriate benchmarking measures

Although standard costs can be benchmarked across plants, actual unit costs should also be compared. Such comparisons, however, need treating with care because of possible differing technologies in the plants, and the effect of different volumes on unit overhead costs.

Other benchmarking measures should review the effectiveness of management in each of the plants on important performance variables such as product quality, scrap rates and machine and labour productivity. Investment in new technologies and systems should be seeking improved production throughput times, faster responses to customers, lower stock holdings, and reductions in total quality costs: factors such as these should also be benchmarked between the plants.

 Solution 12

(a) Introduction

The 222 organisation can evaluate the potential for competitive advantage based on its location in Jurania by using Porter's Diamond. Michael Porter suggested that a firm can gain competitive advantage from its home nation by exploiting four aspects of that nation's business environment: factor conditions, demand conditions, firm strategy structure and rivalry and related and supporting industries.

Factor conditions

222 has access to its key strategic resource, qualified staff, in abundance. The local university has an excellent reputation, and job vacancies at 222 are over-subscribed. This may not be the case elswhere in Africa, so 222 should have a potential competitive advantage in countries where IT education is less well developed than in Jurania.

Demand conditions

Jurania has a growth economy and a highly developed technology sector. This suggests that the Juranian business of 222 will continue to provide it with cashflow to support international growth. This may put 222 at an advantage when competing with local rivals in target countries, who may lack the resources to defend their positions.

Firm strategy, structure and rivalry

222 has grown significantly in the 18 years since it was founded and now has a number of 'blue chip' clients. This means that 222 has experience in competing for (and winning) new business and may be better able to compete in new markets than established local rivals who lack this experience. 222 may therefore have a competitive advantage over local rivals who are not so commercially aware, or are competing in less mature markets.

Related and supporting industries

222 seems ideally placed to pursue international expansion. However, the directors will need to analyse each target country to see if competitive advantage is available. Its home nation may give a firm a potential for competitive advantage, but only if the aspects contained in Porter's Diamond are present to a greater degree 'at home' than in each specific target country.

(b) A number of risks related to the planned Internet strategy can be identified.

Lack of skills

For many organisations an e-commerce strategy is high risk because they have little knowledge or understanding of the technology involved. 222 is at a distinct advantage, as it operates in the IT sector and uses related technology in its products and services. This should mean that there is very little risk of 222 not understanding the implications of its new strategy.

Overtrading

There is a risk that the development of an upgraded website may lead 222 to receive a significant demand for its services from other countries. Whilst this is good in itself, 222 must ensure it has the capacity available to satisfy this demand as disappointed customers will not be good for 222's reputation. There is also a risk that financial resources may not be sufficient to finance rapid expansion, and this could even force 222 out of business. 222 also runs the risk of demand from non-target countries (that is outside Africa). The Internet is a global medium, and it is very difficult to exclude other continents from the marketing effect of the Internet.

Outsourcing

222 is proposing to outsource the development of its new website to a specialist organisation. While this may seem a sensible way to get a technologically advanced solution, there are a number of risks related to this option. It is possible that, by outsourcing, 222 may

find itself locked into a supply and maintenance contract that turns out to be restrictive and expensive. It is also questionable whether it is wise to outsource such a key element of 222's strategy, as there will be no incentive for the supplier to help 222 to gain a competitive advantage. 222 already has the experience of developing its current website and should have staff that are capable of the upgrade. The new website is only to be used for 'brochuring' services, not for e-retail, so should still be relatively unsophisticated, if much more extensive than at present.

Web hosting

It is unlikely that 222 has experience in web hosting, as it currently specialises in Intranet systems and uses JuraWeb to host its website. Web hosting is a specialised business that, it could be argued, is outside the range of 222's core competences. This would introduce significant cost and risk, as 222 would have to hire new staff or retrain existing staff. Web hosting also involves significant security risks, and it might be better to continue having the website professionally hosted.

Telecommunications

222 is proposing to develop its telecommunications infrastructure by using a start-up company supplier, and relatively new technology. This introduces significant risk into the strategy. A startup business may lack the financial resources to survive and this would leave 222 without support for vital equipment. The adoption of a new technology such as fibre-optic networking is also risky, as it may be unreliable or may become obsolete. It may be better for 222 to opt for a more conventional technology from a recognised supplier.

Conclusion

There are significant specific risks, both in the strategy proposed and the suggested implementation methods. 222 should perform a full risk analysis and consider avoiding the most serious risks and managing the remainder.

☑ Solution 13

(a) The main advantages of the sole supplier agreement to S are as follows:
  - Receiving such a contract from a major multinational customer would bring great prestige to S. This may allow it to use the publicity generated to its advantage and it should be able to generate still more business. Winning such a contract implies that S is a high quality, reliable supplier.
  - Such a significant contract will allow S to grow its business by two hundred per cent. Provided that the terms of the contract are favourable enough, this should lead to a significant improvement in S's profitability. S may also be able to improve margins on its existing business, as a result of economies of scale.
  - Having a large, long-term contract will allow S to plan for the future of its business with greater certainty. This will reduce the inherent risk in the business and may also reduce the cost of capital of S. This will further allow S to engage in other developmental strategies without worrying too much about its core business.
  - A secondary benefit of the contract to S will be that its employees feel more secure in their jobs. This should lead to improved motivation levels and a subsequent increase in productivity. This may further improve margins, as output increases and costs (such as sickness and absenteeism) reduce.

There are, however, a number of risks to S that may turn out to be disadvantages if not managed effectively:

- Such a significant growth in the business may lead to S 'overtrading'. The consequence of this may be that operational cashflows are insufficient to meet the needs of the business. This will be particularly true if the contract necessitates S undertaking large capital investments. S may need to build a new factory and will almost certainly need a large investment in working capital.
- There is also a credit risk inherent in any large contract. C may have a poor track record in the settlement of payables. It may also believe that S is a 'soft touch' when deciding on credit policies, as S relies on the large contract and is therefore unlikely to complain too much if payments are delayed.
- Having one customer representing a large proportion of turnover is a dangerous situation for S. If C were to become insolvent, the result might be that S also goes out of business. S should look for opportunities to secure other contracts that do not rely on C.
- The 'liquidated damages' payable to C, if S should fail to deliver on time, are likely to be many times higher than the cost of the airbags supplied. The price of a car will be much greater than the cost of an airbag. This may lead to S paying very large penalties for relatively minor delays in supply, so S may find that occasional delays in delivery lead to an erosion of the profit margin on the contract. This risk is much greater because C operates in five countries.
- Having a very large customer gives that customer significant bargaining power. S may find itself under continual pressure to improve quality and decrease price. The contract may also require a large amount of management and administration time, which would further decrease margins.
- There is also significant risk that C may not renew the contract when it expires in 5 years time. This would leave S with significant surplus capacity and may potentially lead to S becoming unprofitable.
- As C is a multinational, operating in five countries, it may require S to invoice in a currency (or currencies) other than S's own. This would introduce significant foreign exchange risk.

There are significant benefits to S, but it must manage the risks identified above if it is to make significant profit from the contract. A formal risk management strategy should be developed.

(b) The main benefits to S of being given access to the C Extranet are as follows:
- The detailed information of C's requirements for the next 2 years will allow S to plan its production schedules with certainty for a large proportion of its business. This significantly reduces the risk involved in recruiting and training staff and investing in capital equipment. S should try to integrate its production planning system with the information in the C Extranet, thus reducing costs and improving margins.
- The detailed information available for the next month's production will allow S to ensure that deliveries are made on time. This will reduce or eliminate the risk of penalty payments for failure to deliver. It is not clear whether these hour-by-hour requirements can change significantly, so efforts must be made to pursuade C to 'fix' the requirement for at least the first few days.
- S will be able to identify trends in the car industry and, for example, to predict the likely impact of any new technologies. This will further improve planning and may

also lead to a potential for competitive advantage (through differentiation) over those of its rivals who do not have access to the Extranet. This advantage would be gained if S was able to exploit trends earlier than its rivals.

- Access to the virtual trading room may give S a 'preferential bidder' status for any new contracts that C offers. This technology vastly reduces the costs of the bid process, so there may be a potential for S to quote lower prices or earn higher margins on future contracts. This, again, is a potential source of competitive advantage (this time through cost leadership).

Access to the C Extranet will provide S with significant benefits. It is difficult to see any disadvantage to S and there is a potential for competitive advantage that may outweigh the risks of the sole supplier agreement discussed above.

✅ Solution 14

(a) Michael Porter concluded that firms or SBUs compete with their customers and suppliers because they exert bargaining power over one another. The relative competitive advantage depends on the degree of bargaining power of each of the parties. As Porter views competition as activity that affects margins, he sees customers and suppliers as being involved in activity to 'steal' margin from one another.

The most obvious competitive force between customer and supplier is to affect prices and quality. A powerful customer will exert force by trying to persuade the supplier to improve quality, either of the product or service being provided, or of the service package supporting the product. Alternatively, a powerful customer might be willing to accept the standard product, but demands a discount, thus increasing its own margin at the expense of the supplier.

Bargaining power can also be determined by the relative size of the parties, or the extent to which they rely on one another. A large supplier or customer, for whom the other party represents a small or unimportant part of their business, will be more likely to exert power to get a 'good deal'. It is obvious that a small customer, for example, is in a much worse position to ask for a discount than one placing a very large order. Similarly, if a customer represents a significant proportion of turnover, a supplier will work hard to keep such a customer happy, thus increasing the service package and incurring cost.

A customer or supplier also has greater bargaining power if the other party would incur switching costs in doing business elswhere. This cost would, if incurred, reduce margins. This will lead to the party being less likely to break off the relationship.

Some element of bargaining power also depends on the availability of alternative suppliers or customers. A large supplier will give no concessions to a very small customer if it is confident that another customer will be available to replace it. Similarly, a customer looking for a very specialised supply may find that it has no alternative than to take the terms offered by a single supplier.

Thus, according to Porter, firms and SBUs 'compete' with their customers and suppliers. Whether you believe this depends on how broad is your definition of 'competition'. Porter starts from the premise of a very broad definition, so is able to prove his hypothesis.

(b) In a complex organisation SBUs may have been aquired or developed along a supply chain. This means that, within the organisation, there will be SBUs that are customer and supplier. The logic for this structure is that it cuts out supplier margins, reduces transaction costs and secures reliable supply of raw materials or components. In this situation, the organisation runs the risk of sacrificing any saving in transaction costs if these are replaced by management time spent negotiating transfer prices.

The SBUs concerned will, in effect, be competing with one another as customer and supplier during the negotiation, in the same way as described in part (a). The transfer price agreed will determine, to some extent, the profitability of each of the SBUs. If bonuses are paid to managers in line with SBU performance, the level of bonus paid will also depend on the transfer price. Thus, managers may have a vested interest in protracted negotiations that destroy value in the organisation.

The parent company must decide whether the transfer is in the best interests of the organisation. If it is, some authors suggest that the transfer price should simply be imposed. This eliminates 'competition' but may demotivate managers, particularly if divisional bonuses are paid. In most organisations, some degree of negotiation is permitted, but this may be unrealistic if there is a corporate strategy decision that the transfer is desirable. In this case, the bargaining power of the supplier SBU is vastly increased, thus distorting the balance of the negotiation.

The opposite is the case if the supplier SBU is not permitted to make external sales, or if there is no external market (for example, for a specialist component). In this situation, the bargaining power apparently lies with the customer SBU, as the supplier has no option but to make the transfer. However, if the specialist component or supply is not available from elsewhere, the bargaining power may shift to the supplier SBU as its product is differentiated.

The end result of any transfer price negotiation must be to result in a transfer at a 'fair' price. In this case, fair means that the price must be perceived as fair by the SBUs concerned. Any other outcome will result in a loss of motivation in one or both of the SBUs. A fair price is easier to determine if there is a free market in the Z product, component or service being transferred (in other words, it can be both sold and bought outside the organisation). If this is not the case, the range of transfer prices to be considered can be anywhere between marginal unit cost and full cost plus 'normal' margin.

The most important issue in transfer pricing is that, in corporate terms, the transfer price 'disappears' on consolidation of the accounts. When the supplier and customer SBU accounts are consolidated, the revenue from the transfer price cancels out the cost of purchase, so the net result is that the transfer 'disappears'. Value is destroyed by the negotiation, as any management time and effort is wasted, and simply increases internal transaction costs. Similarly, any 'competition' between the SBUs is dysfunctional. If the management accountant understands this, and the relative bargaining power of the SBUs concerned, it should be possible to conclude negotiations quickly, thus destroying as little value as possible.

☑ Solution 15

(a) Use of the expected values (EV) technique

Expected values is a technique that attempts to recognise the risk attached to a business decision. Because of that, it could be argued that using the EV technique gives a more meaningful result than if MTM simply ignored risk. However, the use of the EV technique in this situation is inappropriate for the following reasons:

- *The expected value is not an outcome.* This is a government decision that will either result in no effect on MTM's plans, or a decrease in profits of 20%. There are no circumstances in which profit is likely to fall by 8%.
- *This is a single, unique decision.* The EV technique is more suited to a series of similar decisions, where the EV is an 'average' of the impact of those decisions, viewed collectively.
- *The use of the EV technique does not truly recognise the nature of risk.* Assuming a certain outcome (an 8% fall in profit) ignores risk, and is therefore an inappropriate risk management response to this situation.

(b) Planning process

Like all organisations, MTM operates in a dynamic and uncertain business environment. The use of the rational planning model to generate a single scenario strategic plan ignores this. Carrying out the strategic planning process annually means that any changes in the business environment during the year, such as the enactment of new legislation, cannot be incorporated into the strategic plan. The use of a single, fixed budget for control purposes means that the organisation will continue to report variances from an increasingly meaningless budget.

There are a number of changes that could be made to MTM's planning process:

- MTM could introduce a system of scenario or contingency planning. This would mean generating a series of different scenarios, each based on different assumptions about the nature of the business environment. Each scenario would be used to develop a 'what if' strategy to be implemented if the actual business environment approximates to that scenario.
- The strategic planning process could be carried out more frequently, perhaps on a quarterly basis, with any changes in the business environment carried through to a revised strategic plan and new budget. MTM could even decide to carry out strategic planning on a continuous basis, updating its strategy to take account of any significant event.
- MTM could consider a change to flexible budgeting, where the budget would be updated to reflect any changes since the beginning of the year. Ideally the flexible budget should reflect any changes to MTM's strategy. This should improve the relevance of the budget and make variances more meaningful.

In the situation described, It is recommended that MTM should generate two different scenarios, one without the possible legislation and one with it. They should then develop an appropriate strategy for each scenario and an associated budget. MTM could then start the year using the more likely scenario, in this case without the legislation, and switch to 'plan B' either when it appears that the probability of the legislation has risen above 50% or when the legislation is actually announced.

(c) Influencing the government

MTM is in a difficult situation. While the possible legislation is likely to have a significant impact on its business, there are ethical and social responsibility issues to be considered in deciding upon an appropriate strategy to influence the government. It is recognised that tobacco products damage the health of smokers and others, and MTM must therefore bear in mind that it has a duty of care towards its customers and the population of the SAC. MTM must also ensure that any method of influencing the government is within the laws of the SAC.

MTM has a number of alternative approaches available to it:

- It could try to influence individual members of the government by lobbying. This involves the provision of information supporting MTM's position directly to the individual members of the government. While these individuals are easy to identify, it may be difficult to persuade them to meet with MTM or its representatives, or to read the information.
- MTM could engage in a public relations campaign, with a view to influencing the general public in the SAC to oppose the possible legislation. This could take the form of an advertising campaign, specifically aimed at raising opposition to any legislation, and could even be more general than just the tobacco industry. Encouraging the public to oppose controlling legislation in general might be perceived as more acceptable than a campaign aimed specifically at tobacco.

✓ Solution 16

(a) The identification of the strengths, weaknesses, opportunities and threats is an important part in the preparation of a long-term plan. By assessing both the internal and external environment, the corporate appraisal provides the basis on which these elements are incorporated into the strategic plan.

- *Strengths.* B plc has been operating for more than 20 years and this means that the management has considerable experience of operating in the UK and abroad. The quality of the products, service provided and the emphasis placed on ecological and human rights issues has resulted in the company having a market share of 90 per cent of the naturally-based cosmetics and skin products markets. This is a major strength and, at the present time, the company is generating an operating profit of £26m.
- *Weaknesses.* It has been suggested that the company's growth will be restricted if it continues to focus only on products which meet the environmental objectives of the company. This suggests that it may be necessary for the company to modify its objectives, if it is to continue to grow, as the conflicts in the company's objectives will restrict the number of new products available. However, the company's environmental policies are seen as strengths by some customers and so changing the strategy must be considered carefully by the management of B plc.
- *Opportunities.* The public is becoming more aware of the social responsibilities of companies and it is possible for B plc to benefit from its reputation. As a leader in the campaign against using animals to test cosmetics, the company has a reputation which it will be able to use in the development of its long-term plan. It will provide B plc with a significant competitive advantage with some customers. In addition, as 75 per cent of its retail outlets are outside the UK, it means that the management have experience of operating in many different countries and it is, therefore, possible to continue to expand overseas.
- *Threats.* Competitors are increasing and this has resulted in the market share in the niche market falling from 100 to 90 per cent. In addition, the operating profit has decreased as a result of difficult trading conditions and increased overheads. The objective of focusing attention on environmental issues may restrict the performance of the company by limiting the number of alternative courses of action available. It is also possible that the environmental policies may increase the operating costs of B plc.

(b) The company is considering two alternative investments. These are either improving quality or increasing the promotional activities of the company. It is necessary to consider the likely outcomes of both these courses of action.

- *Quality improvement.* This strategy is intended to differentiate the company's products from its competitors. The investment could result in a gross return of either £100m if the response is strong, or £60m if the response is weak. However, the expected outcome to the proposed course of action is a net return of £37,996,000.

- *Increased promotion.* It is proposed that the level of promotion should increase and an investment of £10m will increase B plc's market share and generate an overall return of £30m in present value terms over a period of 4 years after deducting the cost of the promotional campaign.

Comparing the net benefit over the 4 years, the company should invest in the increased promotional activities. This can be illustrated by relating the net benefit to the outlay required:

	Investment £m	Net benefit £m	Net benefit Index
Promotions	10	30.000	3.00
Quality	50	37.996	0.76

From these calculations, it appears that it would be more appropriate for the company to commit only £10m to the proposed strategy of increased promotion expenditure. In addition, it is important to consider that in the event of a weak market response to the investment in quality, the net benefit could be as low as £10m.

It is important to consider the maximum and minimum amount to be generated by the alternative strategies. Although the increased promotion alternative will provide a return of £30m for an outlay of £10m, it is less in absolute terms than the £37,997,000 which is the expected value to be generated by investing £50m in the quality improvement strategy. However, the outcome from the quality improvement strategy could vary between a maximum return of £50m (£100m less the initial investment of £50m) if the response is strong or £10m if the response is weak. The attitudes to risk of the managers of B plc will be an important factor in the final decision. If the managers are risk averse, then they will spend the funds on increased promotion. However, the possibility of generating a return of £50m could be very attractive to managers who are prepared to take risks.

In a dynamic environment, it is very difficult to predict the response to an adjustment in the quality of a product or an increase in promotional activities. The present position of the firm and the attitudes to risk of the management will be important factors in determining which alternative is considered to be most appropriate for the firm. The final decision, however, will depend on the confidence which can be placed on the forecasts that have been made regarding the outcomes of both investments and the attitudes of the managers to risk.

Other issues which might be considered to be important are the uniqueness of B plc's position regarding its image. Although the quality improvements must be appropriate to its ecological aims, it is possible that this approach may enhance the company's reputation and also increase its market share. This would be a major advantage to the company and it is therefore possible that the quality improvement strategy could also increase the sales of other products that are marketed by B plc.

The reaction of competitors will be an important issue. It may be difficult for competitors to react quickly to the quality improvement as there is often a considerable time lag in obtaining the improved raw materials or packaging materials, training the labour force or improving formulations of the products.

B plc's launch of the improved quality product may take the competitors by surprise and this may give the company a significant competitive advantage for a period of time. However, it is possible that the competitors could react more speedily to the increased expenditure on promotion and so the benefit may be relatively short term.

B plc must consider what action is required in terms of future product development and try to anticipate its competitors' reactions. It will be appropriate to produce an action plan based on the scenarios which might be implemented by the competitors. It would be sensible to establish probabilities for the optimistic, most likely and pessimistic outcomes of the response by competitors. This would enable B plc to develop plans to counter these reactions and to consider where the company is vulnerable to counter-attack as a result of adopting either the quality improvement or increased promotion strategy.

Other relevant factors are the availability of the financing necessary to undertake either of the proposed courses of action. In addition, the long-term effect of the quality improvement may be beneficial to the firm as a whole and may lead to improved sales of products in other divisions of the company.

(c) Environmental issues are an important part of the mission statement and objectives of B plc. It is therefore important that the management accountant provides information which highlights this aspect of the company's activities. The information should be provided in a clear and quantified manner to ensure that the managers are aware of the costs and benefits of B plc's environmental policy. Details should be provided of:

- energy usage and the costs incurred in each of the company's activities;
- the cost of waste and the expenses involved in disposing of the waste and reducing the effect of the waste products on the environment;
- legislation that regulates environmental issues and the costs incurred.

The management accountant must prepare regular reports which highlight the costs associated with the environmental policy being implemented by the management of B plc. In addition, reports must be prepared which assess the effectiveness of the policy and also comparisons should be made with the company's budget and plans.

Other information which should be provided by the management accountant is the effect of the firm's environmental policy on the pricing and investment decisions. Specific information should be provided on:

- *Energy costs.* The various energy costs should be identified and allocated directly to cost centres. This would highlight the amount of each energy source used and savings achieved against budget in both physical quantities and financial terms.
- *Waste.* The actual cost of waste should be reported and this expenditure should be related to the budget. Details of the potential savings should be assessed so that the effects of better waste management policies can be seen.
- *Legislation.* Information should be provided to show the extent to which B plc is meeting the existing legislation in respect of environmental issues. In addition, comparative data from other firms in the industry should be provided to enable the management of B plc to be aware of the position within the industry.

Although it is recommended that information regarding the environment is emphasised in the management accountant's reports, it is also important that the issues are always brought to the fore in all the activities of the company. Therefore, decision-making such as the investment appraisal of projects, the risks and potential liabilities resulting from the environmental factors should be highlighted. It is also important that information be provided about the costs over the entire life of the project, as it may be necessary to decide that the most profitable proposal may be unacceptable, if it does not meet the environmental objectives of the company. In addition, in the process of setting selling prices, the development of new products and the reporting of results should show that the firm's environmental policies have been taken into consideration.

It may be appropriate to introduce rewards for staff and management who are instrumental in introducing or implementing new and innovative approaches to achieving the company's environmental objectives.

(d) By emphasising its environmental policies and using these as a source of competitive advantage, B plc must assess the cost of this approach. This cost will not be easy to determine accurately, but it is important that the management are aware of the cost implications of the policy.

The company has adopted 'green policies' as a major objective and there is likely to be conflict between the different objectives of the company. In this instance, the non-financial objectives are likely to incur additional costs and also increase the capital invested in plant and equipment to reduce the effects on the environment. However, by being overtly concerned with the firm's social responsibility, it has provided the company with a major benefit as the methods of testing of cosmetics used by competitors may provide B plc with a favourable image within the industry. The additional costs can therefore be justified, as it will be possible to use this information to promote B plc's products.

As the company which initiated 'green policies', B plc will be able to use this to pursue its strategic aims and objectives. The management can focus on Ansoff's product/market growth strategies to improve its position and these include:
- market penetration by seeking increased sales in the existing markets with the existing products;
- market development which is a policy already adopted by the company as 75 per cent of its retail outlets are outside the UK;
- product development by seeking new products, sources of supply or production techniques through its development and research activities;
- diversification which could be achieved through takeovers, mergers or joint ventures, the result being that different products such as eco-friendly clothes or goods could be introduced to the existing and new markets.

The company has expanded overseas, but it may be necessary to develop products beyond its core interests if the expansion is to continue in the future. Retaining its eco-friendly image, the firm could diversify by means of strategic alliances or joint ventures to strengthen the likelihood of these new projects being successful.

Although the number of competitors is increasing, the turnover of B plc increased from £154m in the previous year to £175m in the current year. From the present position of B plc, the management must ensure that barriers to entry are established to minimise the effect of the competitors. At the same time, expansion opportunities and other niche markets must be investigated to ensure that the company maintains its current position and is also able to meet the growth objectives of the company.

Solution 17

(a) T plc operates in both the national and international environments as a provider of telecommunications services. The environmental forces which influence a company's business and especially its market share are the political, economic, social and technical elements within that environment.

- *Political.* As T plc has 85 per cent of the national telecommunications market, it will be a major target for scrutiny by the general public. This will mean that the activities of the company will be watched by politicians, pressure groups and individuals who are concerned with consumer and pollution issues. T plc is also subjected to scrutiny by the regulatory body that has been appointed to monitor the industry. This is an important aspect of the political environment in which T plc operates, as this regulatory body will be maintaining service levels and will also influence the level of price increases to be charged. This is likely to affect T plc significantly. These different groups are likely to be major forces within the environment in which T plc operates and the company must take into consideration the views of these stakeholders in developing its strategic plan.

- *Economic.* Increasing long-term shareholder value is stated as an objective of T plc. However, it is important that T plc balances this objective with the issues which arise from it having a high proportion of the market. As the telecommunications industry is significant in terms of a country's economic development, the conflict with a profit-maximisation objective will be particularly significant in countries that are developing economically. As T plc is aiming to expand overseas, the management should keep this in mind when developing a strategy in foreign countries. It is important in developing a strategic plan that the management are aware of the problems that could arise from the effects of regulators, technical advisers and other economic forces within the environment.

- *Social.* The pricing policy and the quality of service provided by T plc are factors which will be important in ensuring that the image of the company is acceptable within the community. As the company has such a high proportion of the total market, it must ensure that it projects a socially acceptable image to the public. The public relations department will be very important to ensure that the image projected is a good one.

- *Technical.* As a leader in communications, it is important for the continued success of the company that it retains this position. Many technological developments are taking place in the area of communications and so T plc will need to provide resources to the research and development departments to ensure that it does not fall behind in the technical area.

    As the dominant company in the industry, T plc faces a number of threats from the environment. Attention will need to be given to the political, economic, social and technical forces if the company is to retain its high market share. This is particularly important as the communications market has an impact on the daily life of most people and so this has implications both in its domestic and overseas markets. It will, therefore, be important for the management of T plc to project an image of an efficient company that provides a quality service at a reasonable cost.

(b) (i) An off's product/market growth vector matrix (Figure 3) provides management with a convenient method of assessing the strategic options that are available. When developing a strategic plan, a company must consider its existing and new products and also the existing and new markets.

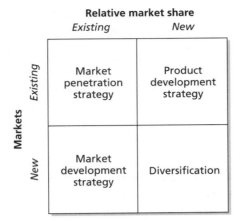

Figure 3

The model provides four courses of action:

- *Market penetration strategy.* At the present time, T plc has 85 per cent of the market. As it is acknowledged that the national market is static, it does not seem possible to increase the sales of existing products in the national market significantly, especially with the large number of other licensed operators. However, it is important that T plc should defend this large share of the market and the strategic plan must ensure that this advantage is not lost.

  In the international markets which T plc has already entered, there will be many opportunities to gain market share by offering the company's existing products. With the experience gained in the national market, this would appear to be a major competitive advantage of the company at the present time. This is confirmed by the objective of extending the strategic alliances in north America, Europe, India and the Far East.

- *Market development.* The experience and reputation of T plc will enable the company to offer the existing products in new markets. This is an area which was identified by the chairman in the annual report. The possibility of entering overseas markets by means of partnership agreements would seem to be extremely sensible as it will reduce the risks involved by collaborating with an organisation that is familiar with the market conditions.

- *Product development.* It is clear that T plc has considerable strength in this area as it has invested in research and development activities. It is therefore possible for the company to adopt a strategy which involves the introduction of new products into the existing markets. These are likely to be in both the national and overseas markets in which T plc is already operating. This strategy will use the technological knowledge that has already been acquired and T plc will therefore be in a position to introduce the new products into its existing markets. This will provide it with a method of expanding by exploiting the changes that are occurring in the telecommunications market.

- *Diversification.* The introduction of new products to new markets is a stated objective of T plc. This is recognised as being the most risky of the four alternative strategies and the management of the company are intending to form strategic alliances to minimise the risks.

  To summarise the position, T plc would be able to consider all four strategies. A strategy of market penetration is likely to be possible only in the international markets which the company has entered recently. However, there must be many international markets which would be receptive to the products offered by T plc. These opportunities need to be assessed by the management and the resources available will be a limiting factor. The strength of the company is its technological knowledge and so this provides it with a major strategic advantage. By offering new products in both the existing and new markets, it is possible that the company will be able to meet its aims and objectives included in the annual report.

(ii) When preparing a strategic plan, it is important to identify the difference between the extrapolation of the historical performance of the organisation, if no changes are introduced, and the results that are required to meet the organisation's objectives. Any shortfall reflects the extent of the new business that must be generated if the organisation is to reach the objectives. It is then necessary to consider the alternative courses of action that are available.

Ansoff's matrix provides the management with a convenient model to consider the different courses of action that could possibly be undertaken by the company (Figure 4).

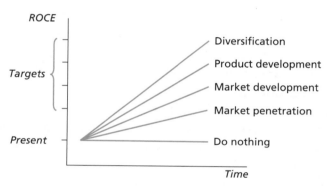

Figure 4

(c) It is expected that the annual expenditure of £200m will increase the company's market share by 10 per cent from next year for 3 years. At the present time, the sales of T plc are £16,613m and the company's market share is 85 per cent. This means that the total market is £19,545m. If the investment will result in an extra 10 per cent share of the market, the sales will be £18,567m. Last year, the profit before interest and tax was 20 per cent (£3,323m ÷ £16,613m). This should result in an increase in the cash flow of the company by 20 per cent. As the entire investment is written off over the 3-year period, this increase in cash flow may be regarded as an increase in profit.

The sales over the next 3 years will be (£16,613m ÷ 85% =) £19,545m × 95% = £18,567m, and the cash flow of T plc will increase by £391m (i.e. 20 per cent of £1,954m, which is obtained by deducting £16,613m from £18,567m). The net annual cash flow is:

Years	Cash in	Cash out	Net cash	Annuity factor	NPV
1, 2, 3	£391m	£200m	£191m	2.444	467

It would also be possible to evaluate this investment proposal using either the payback method, internal rate of return (IRR), or the accounting rate of return (ARR). The IRR is about 75 per cent and the ARR would be 96 per cent.

All the evaluation methods show that the investment should be undertaken. However, it is important that the management of T plc considers the likelihood of achieving the increased sales and also keeping the profit at the level of last year. There is clearly a need for a sensitivity analysis to be undertaken before the final decision is taken.

Management should also consider the longer-term effect of the investment. Will it adversely affect the long-term profitability of the company by forcing competitors to safeguard their positions by embarking on strategies, such as price-cutting, which could reduce the profit within the whole industry? The company would be wise to adopt a policy of conducting audits of the investments after 3 or 5 years to enable it to be aware of the changes that have occurred, especially in respect of the accuracy of forecasts and the reactions by competitors.

(d) (i) The company aims to produce a return on capital employed (ROCE) of 20 per cent over the next three years. If the capital employed remains at £22,150m, this means that the profit before interest and tax must be £4,430m. As the profit is currently £3,323m, it means that a further £1,107m profit before interest and tax must be made. Although the calculations in (c) above show that the investment should be undertaken, the return on this investment is insufficient on its own to achieve the chairman's objective.

(ii) The strategic aims that were identified by the chairman were to achieve growth through the development of new businesses in the national and overseas markets and to diversify into new services. The intention is to extend the strategic alliances that have already been established abroad by entering into partnerships with other organisations in the telecommunications industry. These areas of development were to be achieved by providing high-quality service and up-to-date products. The chairman is fundamentally concerned with ensuring that the company retains its position as a world leader in communications, increases its long-term shareholder value through the provision of quality products and services to its customers, and also maintains its competitive advantage in terms of its technological strength.

In order to close the planning gap, the company should develop a strategic plan which will incorporate strategies which cover all aspects of Ansoff's product/market growth vector expansion matrix. The following alternatives should be assessed.

- *Market penetration strategy.* As T plc has a large share of the static domestic market, it would be difficult to increase the sales of existing products in the national market significantly, especially with the large number of other licensed operators. However, it is important that T plc should defend this large share of the market by means of ensuring that the customers receive an excellent level of service, the introduction of new products and services, and ensuring that the competitive advantage is retained.

  The regulator will be very influential in determining the success of the operation. The management must co-operate with the regulator to ensure that the decisions do not have an adverse effect on the performance of T plc. The company has already established itself in some overseas markets. It is possible that a successful strategy of market penetration could be developed in these countries. With its UK experience, there are likely to be many opportunities to gain market share by offering the company's existing products.

- *Market development.* T plc's experience and reputation will enable it to offer the existing products in new markets. This is an area which is a stated aim of the chairman in the annual report. By using the policy of strategic alliances, it will be possible to reduce the risks as these people will have a better idea of local conditions. Resources must be allocated to developing the market development in these overseas countries.

- *Product development.* T plc must exploit its competitive advantage in terms of its research and development activities. It is acknowledged to have strengths in this area. It must therefore continue to allocate resources to maintain its position in an industry in which there will be major technological advances.

   At the present time, the company should adopt a strategy which introduces new products into the existing markets. This strategy will capitalise on the technological advantage that T plc has acquired.

- *Diversification.* T plc must recognise that the introduction of new products into new markets is a risky strategy. However, the company must be prepared to undertake some projects which fall into this category if it is to gain the dominant position in the world markets.

   In general terms, the number and competence of its competitors will affect the development of the company. It is essential that the quality of its products and services is made a high priority. In addition, the technology within the telecommunications industry has meant that there are alternative products which threaten the traditional telecommunication companies. Mobile telephones and advances in personal communication will decrease the demand for telecommunications. It is clear that T plc must keep abreast of the developments and it would appear to be essential that the company spends considerable amounts on research in order to retain its current position at the leading edge of the industry.

✓ Solution 18

(a) An appropriate model would be Porter's Diamond Theory which is concerned with national competitive advantage and aims to establish:

- why some nations have successful international firms;
- how these firms maintain high levels of performance in world markets;
- what impact this has on competitive strategy for an organisation and on government policy.

   It is not so much that nations themselves have particular competitive advantages, but more that specific industries within the nations can achieve high levels of profitability. Much of this is attributed to the way they exploit national attributes. Analysis of the four major elements of the theory may be undertaken by the directors of the Y Corporation (YC) to help determine whether or not the organisation should proceed with its Far Eastern development.

Demand conditions

High demand conditions in YC's home country (USA) have allowed it to obtain important experience in its delivery of entertainment. It has also enabled YC to obtain valuable information on its customer segments. However, there are important questions which need to be resolved in respect of its Far Eastern development.

1. Are its customer groups in its home environment representative of those it will encounter in the Far East?
2. YC has achieved excellence at home mainly because of the discerning attitude of its customers. Can it be assumed that such a discerning attitude will also prevail in the

Far East among its customers? Indeed, will its Far Eastern customers demand more services than its home customers?

3. Will the increasing demands of customers require continual development of innovation in all YC's market areas?

Related and supporting industries

This is a very important element of the Diamond Theory which the directors must carefully consider. An appropriate infrastructure in supporting service industries must exist in the Far Eastern location as it does in the USA and Europe. This is presumably why the directors have sought a partnership with the host government in the Far East, to ensure that such an infrastructure is in place.

Factor conditions

The directors of YC must be satisfied with the availability and calibre of labour in its Far Eastern location. There may be a need for considerable training to be undertaken.

Firm structure, strategy and rivalry

The directors of YC must consider how the joint venture should be structured and the attitudes of each partner. A further consideration will be the level of competing entertainment attractions in the Far Eastern location, and the opportunities which will be available for competitors to enter the market. Again, it will be important for the host government to provide some information to the directors on this and outline its policy on the development of other attractions, as well as further development of Y-land FE after its initial establishment.

Allied to this last point is the role of government in terms of possible subsidies and regulation. It is clearly going to be useful for the directors of YC to have the host government as a partner, with a majority holding in the venture.

The directors will also need to take account of uncontrollable unforeseen events, which being unpredictable by nature will leave the eventual outcome open to chance.

The whole of the diamond theory is based on a sample of countries surveyed by Porter. It really relates to helping an organisation select countries for development of production, rather than service facilities. It does provide information on the nature of customers and competitors in certain countries and this is valuable. The theory also emphasises that it is an understanding of the characteristics of the market which is crucial to the success of the Y-land FE development, particularly following the experience of Y-land Europe.

(b) (i) The expected number of visitors in the first year of operation (year 3) will be 4 million.

Workings

Optimistic	8 million $\times$ 0.25	= 2.0 million
Most likely	3 million $\times$ 0.50	= 1.5 million
Pessimistic	2 million $\times$ 0.25	= 0.5 million
Total		4.0 million

Visitors (millions)

		Adults	*Children and concessions*	*Total*
Year 3		1.60	2.40	4.00
Year 4	+50%	2.40	3.60	6.00
Year 5	−5%	2.28	3.42	5.70
Years 6–10	−5%	2.17	3.25	5.42

Author's Note:

These italicised workings were not required in the answer. They are printed here for information purposes only.

Labour: $y = ax^b$

$b = log\,0.9/log\,2 = -\,0.152$

Therefore in year 3: a = \$3 * 1m = \$3m
x = 4m/1m = 4
y = \$3m · 4^{-0.152}
y = \$2.43m cumulative average cost per million visitors.
Therefore the third year labour costs are: \$2.43m * 4 = \$9.72m.
The year 3 labour cost per visitor is estimated to be: \$9.72m/4m = \$2.43.
In year 4: y = \$3m·10^{-0.152} y = \$2.114m cumulative average cost per million visitors.
Costs
Year 3 Labour costs are therefore:

$$\frac{\$9.72m}{4m} = \$2.43 \text{ per visitor.}$$

	$
Year 4 Labour costs	
Total labour costs for years 3 and 4 = \$2.114m * 10	= 21.14m
Less: Year 3 labour costs	= 9.72m
Resultant year 4 costs:	= 11.42m

The year 4 labour cost per visit or is estimated to be: \$11.42m/6m = <u>\$1.90</u>.

Contribution	*Adults*		*Children and concessions*	
	$	$	$	$
Year 3:				
Revenue per visitor		50.00		30.00
Less: Labour	2.43		2.43	
Other	<u>2.00</u>	<u>4.43</u>	<u>2.00</u>	<u>4.43</u>
		45.57		25.57
Plus: Additional contribution		<u>110.00</u>		<u>110.00</u>
Total contribution		<u>155.57</u>		<u>135.57</u>
Contribution	*Adults*		*Children and concessions*	
	$	$	$	$
Year 4:				
Revenue per visitor		50.00		30.00
Less: Labour	1.90		1.90	
Other	<u>2.00</u>	<u>3.90</u>	<u>2.00</u>	<u>3.90</u>
		46.10		26.10
Plus: Additional contribution		<u>110.00</u>		<u>110.00</u>
Total contribution		<u>156.10</u>		<u>136.10</u>

The Year 4 level of contribution per visitor will apply until year 10.

DCF calculation

	Adults	*Children and concessions*	*Total*	
Year 3	1.6m	2.4m	$m	$m
	<u>\$155.57</u>	<u>\$135.57</u>		
	\$248.91m	\$325.37m	574.28	
Less: Fixed costs			100.00	
Net cash flow			474.28	
15% cost of capital at year 3			<u>0.658</u>	
				312.07

DCF calculation

	Adults	Children and concessions	Total
Year 4	2.4m	3.6m	$m
	$156.10	$136.10	
	$374.64m	$489.96m	864.60
Less: Fixed costs			100.00
Net cash flow			764.60
15% cost of capital at year 4			0.572
			437.35
Year 5	2.28m	3.42m	$m
	$156.10	$136.10	
	$355.91m	$465.46m	821.37
Less: Fixed costs			100.00
Net cash flow			721.37
15% cost of capital at year 5			0.497
			358.52
Years 6–10	2.17m	3.25m	$m
	$156.10	$136.10	
	$338.74m	$442.32m	781.06
Less: Fixed costs			100.00
Net cash flow			681.06
15% cost of capital at years 6–10			1.667
			1,135.33
Total cash inflow			2,243.27
Less: Capital costs of			
$2,200m/2 = $1,100m × 1.626			1,788.60
NPV(CPV 15% for 2 years)			454.67

The return on investment per the formula applied by YC is:

$$\frac{\$454.67m}{\$2,200.00m} = \underline{20.7\%}$$

(ii) *Commentary.* It is advisable that the expected value of 4 million visitors in the first year of operation should be questioned. None of the probabilities given in the case include this number of visitors in the first year. The most pessimistic value of visitors indicates there will be only 2 million visitors in the first year. If the pessimistic view is taken, then the forecast for the number of visitors over the first 8 year period of operation becomes 2m + 3m + 2.85m + 13.54m = 21.39 million. This compares with 42.8m included in the estimate giving rise to the positive NPV of $454.67m. In other words, it is just half the expected number of visitors over the whole period and there is a 25% probability of this occurring. The directors are further advised that it would be wise to carry out some sensitivity analysis on the variables to determine which are most sensitive to change.

If the variables turn out as expected, the return on investment makes just under the 22% which is required by YC's directors. However, the method of calculating the return on investment is questionable. It would be more accurate to relate the NPV to the present values of the capital cost. This would result in a return of $454.67m/$1,788.6m = 25.4%, higher than the required return. However, it should also be stated that the definition applied by YC is prudent. (This concept now has less prominence in the UK following the adoption of FRS 18.)

Should the project be assessed purely on financial grounds? This is clearly important, but the directors should review what other issues should be considered.

There should be some consideration given to the issues relating to the balanced scorecard. In addition to the financial perspective, which is the most important issue, consideration needs to be given to the customer perspective, the internal business processes and the learning and growth perspectives.

There are many assumptions made in respect of the expected costs and revenues. For example, what happens if the learning curve effects do not occur? This may address, in some part, the internal process perspective. Can the directors be so confident about the popularity of the YC brand and image in the Far East? This addresses the customer perspective. Is there some way that the marketing decay of 5% after the first 2 years can be addressed? This requires appropriate marketing research to be undertaken with regard to YC brand's popularity in the area. It may be necessary for YC to carry out some extensive promotion in advance of the opening of the park. If so, how much will this cost and has it been built into the cost estimates?

Where may the park draw its visitors from? Is it situated in an area that is densely populated? Will it be served by appropriate infrastructure in terms of transport links?

There are no details given about how the theme park may need to be improved and changed over its life. This kind of popular attraction is highly volatile and dependent on public response. The directors are advised to consider from where will the funds be generated to develop the park. How many more visitors will be required to justify this development? Competition in the area in terms of other attractions should be considered carefully by the directors. What other attractions already exist and what has been their success rate?

There is no information about competition in the area. This is an important factor for the development of the theme park and is likely to have a major effect as the park matures. The host government's view on this is crucial.

It is recommended that the directors of YC need to be very mindful of the lessons which have been learned from the theme park established in Europe. This is concerned with the learning and growth perspective. Is the climate in the Far East satisfactory? Is it in fact too hot? If so, will most of the attractions be located in air-conditioned buildings? Is there likely to be any seasonal fluctuation in demand?

It is further recommended that the directors should be mindful that the local community will place much reliance on the joint venture for employment. The reputation of the YC will suffer serious damage if the venture fails and this is likely to impact on its other businesses. The directors must be fully committed to the theme park and regard it as a long-term strategic development. However, they are advised to carefully consider the risks which it poses.

(c) The main objective of developing corporate strategy is to add value to the inputs of an organisation. The overall objective of the YC is to increase the wealth of its owners. Consequently, strategy must firstly concentrate on sound business principles irrespective of any other benefits which may accrue to the organisation or stakeholders.

Rappaport (1986) stated that all activities of business need to be managed in such a way as to increase shareholder value. Shareholder value is concerned with the economic value of an investment by discounting forecast cash flows by an appropriate cost of capital. The theoretical logic behind this is straightforward. It is cash flows which provide dividends and expectations about future cash inflows and give rise to market action which affects the share price. The YC could use of DCF approach similar to the one contained in requirement (b). If the assumptions made are valid, then the return on investment will almost achieve the required level of 22%. However, this is not the sole criterion on which the directors should judge the organsiation's portfolio development.

Shareholder Value Analysis (SVA) is purported to be concerned only with increasing shareholder wealth. This may be a simple philosophy, but it is also often a short-termist view. The directors cannot ignore the impact of the development in the Far East on the local community. They need to consider the service to the local community as well as the customers. Neither of these can be dismissed by the directors on the grounds that to enhance these services would not increase shareholder wealth in the short term. Given the nature of YC's business and its heavy reliance on customer satisfaction, it is necessary for the directors to take a long-term perspective on their business strategy and development.

The directors must, therefore, consider other stakeholders besides the shareholders. YC's employees are one of its main assets as they directly add value to the customer which in turn leads to income generation, resulting in future cash flows giving rise to added shareholder value. The directors are clear that increasing shareholder wealth is important. They must also be clear about how that wealth is generated and how it adds value.

The directors may aim to calculate the level of shareholder value which is added. Crudely, this is the difference between the return on investment and the cost of capital multiplied by the investment made by the shareholders. This simple formula will need to be refined to determine the economic value added. Such refinements will take account of the level of marketing research which is essential to the YC. The results of the marketing research significantly contribute to the achievement of future shareholder value as they indicate the strategic direction of future developments.

Determining YC's economic value and raises interesting questions such as over what period should the marketing investment in the YC brand be depreciated? The directors must also consider the risks associated with their portfolio developments. The calculation of shareholder value added is more difficult to estimate in conditions of uncertainty. Other problems which would need to be addressed by the directors in undertaking SVA include the following:

- SVA uses accounting data which was not intended to be used for this purpose. This results in such data being manipulated, which, in turn, may make the results questionable.
- SVA does not take account of the effects of intangible assets, for example the skills and personality of the employees. Such skills and customer rapport is a crucial element of the success for the YC.
- How accurately can the cost of capital actually be measured over a 10-year period, which is the timescale being applied within the case?
- SVA has often been regarded as being judgmental, using may estimates which may have questionable accuracy.
- The basic danger for the directors of the YC is that SVA is a short-term approach, when by necessity they need to take a longer term view of their portfolio development.

Solution 19

Background information

From 1962 to 1977, Myriad plc operated in the light engineering industry, manufacturing metal castings. The company traded profitably, but the earnings were volatile. On the advice of a firm of consultants, a decision was made to 'aggressively pursue a policy of conglomerate diversification, by external acquisition, to promote growth and reduce risk'.

In 1987, a number of companies in the office equipment industry were acquired and, in 1991, Myriad entered the leisure industry by purchasing fitness centres in hotels. Since these acquisitions in 1987, the share price has increased by 16 per cent and the dividend yield has averaged 3 per cent. This performance is below the level in the sector in which Myriad operates. This can be attributed to the fact that Myriad had adopted a relatively conservative strategy. This is evident from the gearing being only 20 per cent, against an industry average of 60 per cent, and the dividend cover being double the level of the industry as a whole.

(a) The strategic decision of 1987 resulted in Myriad plc becoming a conglomerate. This was because of the acquisition of the Office Equipment and Leisure divisions which were quite different from the original activity of the company. The decision to diversify aimed to promote growth and reduce risk. The reduction of the volatility of the total profits of the group was another benefit expected from the diversification. It is important to consider each of these objectives from the viewpoint of the shareholders.

The acquisition of the new firms would certainly achieve growth in terms of the assets owned. This, however, is not necessarily beneficial to the interests of the shareholders, as increased size does not necessarily improve the shareholder's financial position. By acquiring firms in different industries, it is likely that the group's unsystematic risk will be reduced. However, it is possible for the individual investors to achieve this benefit more cheaply by purchasing shares in forms operating in different industries. The volatility of Myriad's earnings is unlikely to be a major problem to the shareholders, unless the magnitude of the differences is extremely large, so that the dividends paid are affected.

Although the strategic decision of 1987 was likely to have been of limited benefit to Myriad's shareholders, the management of the company would have gained from the growth of the company. If the company increased in size and also operated in a number of industries, the management's jobs would increase and it would be likely that their personal remuneration would have increased. Their personal position would have also been improved by the reduction in the unsystematic risk of the firm and a 'smoothing' of the earnings of the company. Thus the personal risks of the managers would have decreased.

The diversification decision highlights the conflict between the best interest of the shareholders and those of the management. However, as the directors take the strategic and operational decisions, it is sometimes possible for the directors to take decisions which will meet their personal objectives rather than those of the shareholders. It is possible that shareholders who were opposed to the strategic decisions of the directors would dispose of their interest in the company.

(b) The current market capitalisation of the divisions can be identified as follows:

	1993 earnings		Market capitalisation
	£m	p/e ratio	£m
Leisure	3	18	54
Light Engineering	5	6	30
Office Equipment	2	10	20
			104
Group	10	8.6	86

It is clear that, at the present time, the original Light Engineering division represents only about 30 per cent of market capitalisation of the group. Thus, acquisitions now constitute over 70 per cent of the market capitalisation value of Myriad. In addition, the profit of the Leisure division is expected to grow at 10 per cent. The p/e ratios confirm that the market expects the Light Engineering division to perform at a lower level than either the Leisure or Office Equipment divisions.

The diversification policy adopted in 1987 has resulted in the firm acquiring two businesses which have demonstrated a higher growth rate than the original business. It is expected that this trend will continue for at least the next 5 years. Although the share price has increased at a slower rate than the total sector, this is expected from the differences in the beta factors. The significantly lower gearing in Myriad and the higher dividend cover also show that the management of Myriad is adopting a conservative approach and this is likely to result in a share price which is lower than the total sector.

The performance of the Leisure and Office Equipment divisions has introduced growth into Myriad. This will have influenced the share price and, consequently, the shareholders' wealth. The return earned by the Light Engineering division appears to be relatively stable and with a p/e ratio of 6 is clearly not expected to generate increased levels of earnings in the future. The diversification has, therefore, improved the prospects for Myriad and appears to have been sound financial policy.

(c) There are a number of different interest groups which will be affected by the proposed investment of the Leisure division of Myriad. It is important that the directors take into account the wishes of the different groups.

The shareholders

The institutional investors represent only 15 per cent of the shareholders of Myriad. This means that individual investors hold 85 per cent of the shares. (It is possible that the directors' own shares are included in this group.) The directors of Myriad should be aware of the wishes of both the institutional and individual investors. In particular, it is important that the directors consider the likely reaction to the sale of the Leisure division by the individual shareholders, as the proposed change in strategy will influence the position of all shareholders significantly.

It is difficult for the directors to be able to communicate directly with the shareholders. The AGM does provide an opportunity, but the prescribed nature of the agenda and the low level of attendance does not usually provide an opportunity to discuss the wishes of the shareholders in relation to the future strategy of the firm. 'Open days' are another possibility, but the response of the shareholders may not be sufficient to assess the opinions of this group of stakeholder.

The appointment of independent directors to the board, however, would be a method of assessing the preferred course of action of the shareholders. There are difficulties in selecting representatives of the small investors, but it is possible to provide an opportunity for their appointment by encouraging the small investors to nominate candidates for election to the board of directors. The published annual report provides the directors with no opportunity to inform the shareholders of their strategy, but it is not possible to ascertain shareholders' reaction to the policy decisions, except in cases where there is a significant reaction to the policies. In addition, this published information will usually be published only after the decisions have been finalised. The use of the annual report as a means of communication is clearly limited.

The employees

Although all Myriad's staff will be affected by the divestment decision, those who work in the Leisure division and the redundant head office staff will be most affected. The extent to which the directors will respond to this group will depend on the importance placed by them on the interests of the employees.

It is becoming more usual for companies to hold 'information sessions'. The staff can be given details of the past results, future prospects and any major decisions which are likely to affect them. These can be useful in ascertaining the reactions of the employees to the major issues facing the business. However, they are usually very formal occasions and the possibility to discuss matters that arise is often relatively limited. The use of works committees might be a more effective way of encouraging interaction between representatives of the management and staff.

Other interested groups

The directors will need to ascertain the opinions of Myriad's customers and suppliers. It is possible that these people might be against the divestment of the Leisure division and it is important for the directors to be aware of the implications for the strategic decision. This could really be done only on an individual basis as there is unlikely to be an opportunity to meet these groups together at one time.

The directors must assess the benefits to be obtained from identifying the interests of these different groups. The cost, in terms of time and resources, must be taken into account. It will, however, provide the directors with an insight into the possible reactions to strategic decisions, such as the one under consideration at the present time. Another difficulty is that it is often not possible to make public the intentions of the board as this might prejudice the outcome of the decision.

(d) The institutional investors are keen for the company to dispose of the successful Leisure division and to declare a 'once-and-for-all' cash dividend and to 'strengthen Myriad's balance sheet.' This is unlikely to be the opinion of either the directors and management of the company or the individual shareholders, who own 85 per cent of the shares in the company. There will, therefore, be a conflict of interest between these groups.

The directors and management of Myriad will not be to keen to reduce the size of the business by selling the Leisure division. Their interests are better served by the business being large and the disposal of the high-performing division is not likely to be a popular strategy with the management. In addition, the sale of the Leisure division might result in an increase in the risks and volatility of earnings. These were both reasons for the conglomerate diversification policy in 1987.

Because of the tax implications, many of the individual investors will not be keen to receive the large dividend. If they do not wish to reduce their investment in equities, it would be necessary for them to reinvest the cash received. The institutional investors would not be affected by the personal tax implications and they have, therefore, suggested the 'one-off dividend'. Their cash resources will be increased by the 'once-and-for-all' dividend and these funds can be invested in the course of their regular business.

The proposal suggests that the remainder of the receipt from the sale of the Leisure division should be kept to 'strengthen the balance sheet'. At the present time, the gearing of Myriad is 20 per cent, compared with 60 per cent in the sector as a whole. As the company has already adopted conservative financial policies, it seems unnecessary to strengthen this position further.

As it is usual for the professional institutional investors to be more visible and vocal, it is important that the directors are aware of the wishes of all parties and especially those of the group which holds a substantial portion of the equity. In addition, the effect of any major decision on the employees should be considered. It is possible that the proposed sale of the Leisure division will be seen as increasing the likelihood of redundancies. The decrease in the size of the business may create concern among employees, which might be detrimental to the decisions as it is possible that their concerns could affect performance throughout the company.

(e) There are a number of different responses that the board can adopt in order to deal with the issues raised by the institutional investors:

- Do nothing until the issue is discussed at the AGM. It is possible that a small minority who attend this meeting could reach a decision which might be against the interests of the other stakeholders, including the directors.

- Try to convince the institutional investors that the divestment is not a sound proposal.

- Pay a larger dividend. As an alternative to selling the Leisure division, the board could increase the dividend payout ratio of the company. At the present time, Myriad's dividend cover is four-times. This is double the sector average. This means that the shareholders will receive additional cash and the directors could inform the shareholders of the change in dividend policy. If the company does not have sufficient cash resources, it would be possible to borrow funds as the gearing, at the present time, is well below the sector average. Alternatively, the directors could increase the gearing and provide the shareholder with a large 'one-off' dividend. The public could be informed that this resulted from the success of the diversification policy and that large dividends could not be expected each year.

- Make a rights issue. The company could make a rights issue to the existing shareholders. This would enable the present shareholders to invest additional funds in Myriad. However, if an individual shareholder did not wish to invest additional funds in the company, it would be possible to sell the rights. In this way, funds could be obtained. This would not cause problems to the individual investors who would not be required to pay tax on the money received from a rights issue. The company would, however, have to find projects to utilise the additional funds received from a rights issue.

- Repurchase part of the issued share capital. The company could offer to repurchase the shares at the current value and this would enable the institutional investors to reduce their investment.

Fundamentally, the opinion of the majority of the shareholders should influence the final decision about the proposal. The directors must ascertain the views of all the stakeholders in the company and base their decision on the wishes of the majority.

✔ Solution 20

(a) McCarthy has developed a model which focuses attention on the variables which are important in formulating a competitive strategy for an organisation. The four main parts of the marketing mix model are product, place, promotion and price.

The management of EuroFoods and Medley need to pay attention to these factors when developing a strategic plan. To achieve the objectives of each company, the planners need to identify the present position of their products and plan a strategy which co-ordinates the four aspects of the marketing mix model. In addition, they must also consider the effect of competitors on their strategic plan.

- *Product.* Quality, brand name, packaging, warranty and the service level offered are all parts of product. The resources allocated to this aspect of the marketing mix is often crucial in the development of a strategic plan. Quality can be affected in a number of ways and involves both the individual product features as well as the firm's range of products. To achieve the best possible competitive advantage for the firm, the management must decide on the most appropriate policies for branding, packaging and level of service.

- *Place.* Distribution coverage and channels, as well as the sales territories and the outlet locations, are the main aspects of place. Alternative strategies must be considered in the preparation of a plan. The stock level of finished goods is another factor which can contribute to competitive advantage but which can result in increased costs for the firm. All these issues are particularly important in the sale and distribution of products such as ice-cream.

- *Promotion.* The management need to decide the nature and extent of the firm. Promotion is an important part of the strategy of many firms, especially in the marketing of a consumer product.

- *Price.* The price level, payment terms and discounts are also factors which are important in formulating a strategic plan for an organisation.

The use of McCarthy's marketing mix model will ensure that the management of EuroFoods and Medley consider the different aspects of each of the four P's. This should result in a co-ordinated and therefore more effective strategic plan for each firm.

(b) There are a number of strategies which result in a competitive advantage for the firm. Porter has identified three different strategies which can be used:

- *High volume/low cost.* The firm reduces the cost of production. This means that the products can be sold more cheaply and this increases the volume of sales and results in better returns than those of the competition.

- *Differentiation.* Significant differences between the firm's products and those of the competitors are developed. This can be based on product quality, special product features which are often based on technological advantages, and superior after-sales service. A product which will be preferred by the consumers will allow the firm to charge higher prices and this should lead to increased profitability.

- *Focus.* The firm concentrates on a relatively small consumer groups or market segment. This means that the firm can specialise and is able to gain a competitive advantage over firms which adopt either high volume/low cost or differentiation strategies.

  By identifying the strategy to achieve competitive advantage, the firm can ensure that resources are channelled appropriately and used efficiently and effectively.

(c) The future competitive strategy of EuroFoods will be based on a co-ordinated plan of product, place, promotion and price. These elements of the marketing mix, however, must be placed within the 'generic strategies' of high volume/low cost, differentiation and focus. Porter's 'fundamental competitive forces' should also be considered. In particular, the 'threat of entry' and the 'threat of substitutes' are particularly relevant to the situation of both EuroFoods and Medley.

The present position in the European ice-cream industry is that EuroFoods has gained a dominant position in the market (60 per cent). The provision of in-store refrigeration has provided EuroFoods with an important 'barrier to entry' in the 'impulse' sector of the ice-cream market. The 'impulse' sector is very important as it represents 40 per cent by volume, 67 per cent of the market value (£4bn in a total market of £6bn) and, most importantly, 80 per cent of the profit of the European market. Thus, the provision of the in-store refrigeration provides EuroFoods with an important competitive advantage.

Although the provision of refrigerators has involved considerable capital expenditure for EuroFoods, it has resulted in the product being sold in good condition. In addition, the sole use of the cabinets represents a significant entry barrier to competitors. The advantage obtained from the supply of the refrigeration, however, will be lost if the European Commission (EC) deems that the exclusive freezer arrangements are anti-competitive. It will then be possible for competitors to enter the market more easily. This presents a major threat to EuroFoods.

(i) *Strategy if freezers are available to EuroFoods' competitors.* To ensure that customers continue to purchase their products, when other products are available in the freezers, EuroFoods will need to adopt a strategy of differentiation.

- *Product.* Since the competitor, Medley, has successfully introduced a new product to the market, EuroFoods should also try to develop new products. This will help to retain market share. Products with sales spread throughout the year would be a major advantage.

- *Place.* The freezer decision has affected this aspect of the marketing policy of EuroFoods. It will be necessary to reconsider the implications of the change and develop tactics to ensure that the previous advantage is not lost.

- *Promotion.* EuroFoods will need to retain its market share through the provision of a good merchandising service to the small retail shops. In addition, sales promotion and increased advertising are necessary in order to compensate for the loss of competitive advantage resulting from the EC decision. It might be possible to charge the shops for any new freezers and the revenue could be offset against the additional promotional and advertising expenditure.

- *Price.* As the product introduced by Medley is selling at a premium, EuroFoods will be able to take advantage of the price differential between its own existing products and those marketed by Medley. EuroFoods should aim at introducing higher-priced products. It may be possible to start a price-cutting strategy which will reduce margin. This, however, is a high-risk strategy as Medley is unlikely to be forced out of the market and the price-cutting could damage EuroFoods.

There are many alternative strategies which could be adopted by EuroFoods to defend its market position. As an example, it may be able to acquire some of the local producers (30 per cent of the market). This might lead to considerable competitive advantage in the individual countries.

(ii) *Strategy if exclusive freezer arrangements are possible.* The immediate threat will be removed. However, EuroFoods must ensure that every effort is made to prevent Medley from providing freezers to retailers. All new outlets should be approached at an early stage to be certain that a EuroFoods freezer is installed. This will provide EuroFoods with a major competitive advantage.

It is important that the management of EuroFoods recognise that Medley has gained 10 per cent of the European market in 3 years. This should be a warning to EuroFoods, which must develop competitive advantages for its long-term survival. In order to gain market share, EuroFoods' competitors may adopt a policy of price-cutting. For this reason, it would be wise for EuroFoods to control costs. If EuroFoods is to maintain its dominant position within the market, it will need to ensure that all aspects of the marketing mix are efficiently managed.

(d) (i) *Strategy if EuroFoods' freezers are available to Medley.* It is possible that Medley may take advantage of this substantial benefit resulting from the decision of the EC. It is likely that EuroFoods will respond by increasing and improving the quality of its products. Medley should develop a strategic plan which maximises the advantages conferred by the EC decision.

- *Product.* Medley must introduce new and improved products and establish a range of its products in the market.
- *Place.* The availability of EuroFoods' freezers will enable Medley to expand, especially by introducing new products. Clearly, EuroFoods will try to minimise the benefits accruing to Medley. It will be necessary for Medley to enter into negotiations with EuroFoods to agree on the sharing of the cost of using the freezers. This will increase Medley's costs, but it provides a major marketing opportunity to Medley.
- *Promotion.* It is likely that EuroFoods will increase promotional expenditure and this must also be counteracted by Medley.
- *Price.* In order to retain its market share, EuroFoods may resort to price competition. Medley may have to use resources to obtain market share under new conditions. It will be necessary for Medley to introduce new low-priced products to counter EuroFoods' competition.

(ii) *Strategy if EuroFoods' freezers are not available to Medley.* Medley must adopt a strategy of 'focus' in order to establish its product in a market niche. By using special promotions, it should be possible to introduce products which do not compete directly with those of EuroFoods. It will be necessary to devise a distribution system to ensure that the product is delivered to customers efficiently and that product quality is maintained. To make the public aware of the product, advertising and promotional activities can be used.

As an alternative, Medley could concentrate on the 'take-home' market which would not be affected to any great extent by the EC's decision. The danger of this strategy is that EuroFoods may focus on this market after it has secured the dominance in the 'impulse' market.

It might be possible for Medley to introduce freezers into the retail outlets. However, this would involve a considerable capital outlay and could result in a major confrontation between the two firms. The overall objectives and resources of Medley would need to be carefully considered before adopting this aggressive strategy.

✅ Solution 21

(a) Mission statements contain the broad aims of a company and this is the starting point when defining the goals and objectives of an organisation. One of the aims of G plc is to improve its long-term profitability through increased international business. This will require the provision of capital so that these additional overseas investments can be undertaken. Another aim involves the training and development of employees. This is in order to implement the company's environmental policy.

The objectives of a company are usually more specific than the overall aims. Quantifiable financial objectives for G plc should be prepared to cover the following areas:

- the rate of return on the capital employed and the rate of growth both for the company as a whole and for each division;
- the extent to which the international business activities are to be increased within a given period of time.

In addition, G plc should establish non-financial objectives to cover the staff training and development activity. The number of training opportunities and the areas of training within a period of time should be identified. It would be advisable for the company to include an objective in respect of the safety of the RORO ferries, as this is a major concern of the company. In addition, the other aspects of the environmental policy of G plc should also be included in the objectives.

Quantifiable objectives provide a benchmark against which the actual performance of the company can be measured. It is also important to include a time-scale in the statement of objectives, so that the success of the achievements can be assessed.

(b) It is important that a company's managers identify any significant changes in the environment and this should be included in the strategic planning process. Particularly in a turbulent environment, the company must be able to respond to any potential threats and opportunities that are expected. In order to be in a position to respond appropriately to changing situations, the company needs to be aware of the importance of flexibility when establishing the objectives and also when devising the company's strategy. By ensuring that the company has access to cash and specialised inputs such as skilled labour, it is possible for it to have some flexibility. This will enable the company to respond to both threats and opportunities and it will therefore have a degree of flexibility.

It is, however, not always possible for a company to respond to every threat or opportunity as the company may be already committed to a particular course of action. Nevertheless, flexibility objectives should be given a high priority by companies which operate in a turbulent environment.

As G plc has interests in a number of areas of shipping as well as in transport, construction and property, it is essential that the management information system monitors all these industries, especially the activities of competitors, and particularly new entrants. This will assist the management of G plc to respond appropriately to changes within the environment. This response will depend on the availability of resources, but will provide the management with flexibility within G plc. It is usual to find conflicts between the interests of the firm's stakeholders, which include shareholders, management, customers, suppliers and the general public. For example, if some of the aims and objectives of the company reduce the profitability of the company in the short run, this may benefit customers and employees but may not be acceptable to the shareholders. This type of conflict could arise if G plc adopted its training objectives, which will reduce profitability in the short run but will be beneficial in the long term.

Similarly, resources allocated to achieve the objectives of the company's environmental policy are likely to increase costs immediately, but may not have any noticeable effect on the immediate performance of the company. The benefits arising from improved safety might be vital to the continuing success, or even survival, of the company. However, it is often difficult to assess the effect of investments of this kind because of the subjective nature of the benefits.

The development of the international markets of G plc will require capital investment. If the capital is obtained through retained profits, this is likely to affect the company's dividend policy and will mean a reduction in the dividends paid to the shareholders in the short term. However, the expansion of the company may lead to increased job opportunities for the management and staff. In the longer run, however, successful investments will mean that the shareholders' wealth will improve and this is the fundamental objective of profit-seeking firms.

In summary, it is important that a firm should have flexibility in order to respond to important threats and opportunities. Especially in a turbulent environment, it is important for a business to be able to adapt to changes in the environment.

(c) The total turnover of G plc increased from £2,524m to £2,910m during the year. This represents an annual increase of 15.3 per cent. At the same time, the operating profit increased from £205m to £223m which represents an improvement of 8.8 per cent. This does not, however, take into account the effect of inflation during the period. The adjustment for inflation shows that the real growth in turnover is reduced to 9.7 per cent and the increase in operating profit is only 3.4 per cent.

When comparing the growth in turnover and operating profit of the individual activities, it is clear that there are significant divisional differences. The growth rates, after adjustments for inflation, are as follows:

Division	Turnover %	Operating profit %
Cruise	10.9	3.4
Ferries	1.4	7.5
Containers	14.3	–
Bulk Shipping	6.3	–

From the information provided, it is possible to calculate the return on sales. Although this is limited as a measure of performance, it does provide a means of comparing the relationship between revenue, costs and expenses and so provides a starting point for measuring the profitability of the company. During the year, the return on sales for the whole company decreased from 8.1 to 7.7 per cent. After adjusting for inflation, however, the return is 7.6 per cent for the 2 years.

The return on sales for each division is as follows:

	This year actual	Return on sales This year adjusted	Last year actual
Divisions	%	%	%
Cruise	11	11	12
Ferries	14	14	13
Containers	3	3	4
Bulk Shipping	–	–	–

Cruise division

Although the turnover has increased by 10.9 per cent, the profitability of this division decreased from 12 to 11 per cent during the year. It is, therefore, strange that the chairman has referred to 'encouraging results' in this division. The decision to increase the investment in this division should be reconsidered. Although it is possible that this division is yielding a satisfactory return on capital invested, this cannot be judged from the available information.

Ferries division

The only improvement in the adjusted return on sales is in this division. However, this division is likely to face greater competition in the future. Although the growth in turnover was modest, the operating profit did improve by 7.5 per cent.

Containers and Bulk Shipping divisions

The turnover for both these divisions increased. However, the results were poor and there was no improvement in performance in these divisions. In fact, Containers remained static and Bulk Shipping continued to make a small loss.

It appears that the chairman should reconsider his statement, especially when the effect of inflation is taken into account. However, if another measure of performance was used, such as return on capital employed, it might support the chairman's view of the company's performance.

(d) Porter's model identifies the competitive forces as the threat of entrants to the industry, the extent and character of the present competition within the industry, the bargaining power of buyers, the bargaining power of suppliers and the availability of substitute products or services. Within the Cruise and Ferries divisions, it is possible to identify the effect of these different forces and it would be necessary for the management of G plc to consider these possible outcomes in respect of each of the five forces.

- *The threat of new entrants.* Before another organisation can commence operating in either the Cruise or Ferries divisions, it is necessary to purchase vessels and this usually represents a major investment. Thus, the amount of capital required is likely to act as a barrier to entry and will reduce the threat of new entrants in both these divisions. It is possible, however, that the cruise ships and ferries could be rented and so the amount of capital required reduced. As this would increase the likelihood of new entrants to the industry, this is an area which should be monitored by the management. However, with the current levels of profitability, it would not appear to be a major threat at the present time.

- *The degree and character of the present competition.* Competitors will have large investments in their businesses if they own the ships and ferries that they operate. In addition, it is likely that the fixed costs of the cruise and ferry operators are relatively high. It is therefore important that the vessels are relatively full on each journey. This will mean that the existing operators will compete vigorously to obtain the maximum number of passengers. It is possible that in this situation the competition will be intense and the existing operators, especially ferries across the English Channel, will resort to price competition with the opening of the Channel Tunnel.

- *The bargaining strength of buyers.* The passengers will be concerned with safety and comfort in their use of the ships and ferries. As there are a number of alternatives, the buyers are in a relatively strong position and G plc must consider this in the strategic planning process.
- *The bargaining strength of suppliers.* This does not appear to be of particular significance to G plc, as there will be many suppliers available for the fuel, supplies and repair facilities required by the ships. Landing rights and fees could be an issue, but it is possible that there are alternatives available. However, the company is dependent on the labour force, especially for the cruises and ferries, as the staff will be dealing with the public. It is essential that they are courteous and attentive to the needs of the passengers if G plc is to be successful in these areas.
- *The availability of substitute products or services.* The customers have other forms of transport available to them and a major threat will be the airlines. Air travel will reduce the travelling time. This is likely to be less of a threat to the Cruise division, as people choose to cruise as a part of their holiday. It is possible, however, that they may prefer to get to their destination quickly and reduce the travelling time to a minimum. The time will be much more significant to the Ferries division, as airlines will offer a quicker service to passengers without cars. The issue of safety will also be very important and so the company should be concerned about the safety record of the RORO ferries in assessing its competitive advantage.

When considering the five forces, it seems that G plc faces a number of different threats at the present time. There are issues which are specific to each division and these may be extremely important in developing the company's strategic plan.

Cruises

The growth in this market is an opportunity for G plc. The ordering of a new cruise liner shows that it has already responded to this expected increase in the market. It is important that the change to younger cruise passengers is recognised and that the nature of the service offered and the marketing of the cruises reflects the different customer profile.

It is expected that the cruise market will grow over the next 5 years. The probability of the growth being at the current rate is 0.6, half the current rate is 0.3, while the expectation of a static market is only 0.1. It is clear that the company should plan for increases in the turnover of this division. However, it is important that the marketing management recognise that the cruise customers are changing from wealthy retired people to younger customers. This has resulted from shorter and less expensive cruises being offered. As there is no information available on the number of existing suppliers, it is not possible to assess the alternatives available to the buyers.

Ferries

Although the cross-Channel traffic has increased by 15 per cent, the company's market share has decreased by 4 per cent, which is presumably as a result of the opening of the

Channel Tunnel. This represents a major problem for the management of G plc and it is likely to erode the Ferry market in the future. The probabilities are:

% Reduction	Probability
no change	0.1
5%	0.7
10%	0.2

The expected value of this market information is that there will be a reduction in Channel crossings by 5.5 per cent. Although the other routes are expected to remain static, this is a major threat to the profitability of the Ferries division, as it is unlikely that the costs of the ferry operations can be reduced significantly. The issue of the safety of the RORO ferries is a matter which must be considered carefully by G plc.

From the information available, it is clear that the management of G plc must consider the implications of Porter's model in the development of a strategy that will enable the company to maintain and even improve its current competitive advantage.

(e) The company has already established an environmental policy and it is important that the aims and objectives of the policy are quantified so that it is possible to measure the effectiveness of the means adopted to implement the policy. The main thrust of the company concerns are in the area of safety in the Cruise and Ferries divisions.

In the design of the ships, it is important that the staff are aware of the safety factors. It is possible, however, that the design of these major projects will be undertaken by naval architects and designers who are not employees of G plc. The outside consultants should be made aware of the company's concern regarding the environmental factors, and details should be included in all specifications issued by the company. It is possible that additional costs may be an issue, but this must be included in the feasibility studies if the projects are to meet the environmental aims of the company. The environmental issues must be overseen by appropriately qualified staff of G plc.

The environmental factors, and especially safety, will be extremely important in the operating procedures of the ships and ferries. It is essential that the staff are given training to ensure that they are aware of the issues involved and knowledgeable about the procedures that will minimise the possibility of a safety crisis.

To ensure that the environmental issues are carried out within the company, a committee should be established to consider the different aspects of the company's policy on a continuing basis. It will be necessary to introduce training courses for all staff to ensure that they are aware of the importance that the company places on this aspect of the business.

Finally, a system of monitoring the implementation of the policy will need to be introduced to ensure that the operating staff adhere to the rules that have been established, especially in respect of the safety practices aboard the ships and ferries. This may be achieved by regular surveys and also by placing employees on board as passengers to provide a regular monitoring of the safety procedures.

☑ Solution 22

(a) In the past, retail banking was based on providing a high-quality service to customers, by means of a close relationship between the bank managers and their customers.

The new philosophy which emphasises profitability through 'an efficient, low-cost service' will result in a significant change in approach. The proposed change in the philosophy of retail banking will have an impact on the Bank's staff, customers and shareholders.

The closure of about 1,000 retail branches will result in the redundancies of employees in this section of the Bank. This will be offset, however, by some additional management posts created within the superbranches. As about 130 superbranches will be formed, this will create employment opportunities for about 400 of the existing managers. It is likely, therefore, that about 50 per cent of the existing staff and 600 managers will be declared redundant. Although the redundant staff will be compensated, it is inevitable that the uncertainty will create a considerable amount of anxiety and will reduce staff morale within the whole organisation. This is a situation which may have a significant impact on the efficiency and motivation of the employees, especially during the transitional period.

In addition, the creation of the superbranches will alter the nature of the jobs for many of the staff. It is likely that fewer jobs within the branches will require professional skills. This could lead to decreased job satisfaction and fewer opportunities for staff development.

Adopting a policy of performance measurement based on profitability will affect the management's behaviour. Factors such as customer satisfaction, or expansion through the opening of new accounts, will be considered less important with the adoption of this new method of assessing performance. It is also possible that the superbranch managers will consider only the short-term implications when making decisions. Although this will result in a better current result, performance over a longer period of time will be affected.

Many customers will have established a close relationship with their bank manager and it is likely that they will value the manager's advice and assistance in the management of their businesses. It is, therefore, important that research is undertaken to establish the importance of the close relationship between a bank manager and the customers. Basically, it is essential for the Bank to estimate the effect of the changed philosophy on the customers. This may be particularly significant if the Bank's competitors are still providing this type of service. In addition, the attitude of the customers to the 'efficient, but low-cost service' must be predicted, as the loss of a large number of existing customers will be detrimental to the Bank. It is possible that the superbranches will not be so conveniently located for many of the customers, and they may decide to move their accounts to a bank that has a branch that is more convenient. It is also possible that customers, who use many of the services offered by the Bank, will find that their total bank charges increase as a result of the changes at Lindleys plc.

The shareholders will be primarily interested in the profits generated by the changed policy. If costs are reduced and profitable customers are not lost, it is likely that the profits will increase. However, the additional cost of the superbranches will reduce the profits. In addition, the one-off payments in respect of redundancies must be included in an economic assessment of the impact of the change in policy.

Finally, the effect of the changes in the branches may have an impact on the corporate banking business. This is an aspect of the proposed changes which will be difficult to predict, but could be important when evaluating the consequences of the decision to increase the bank's efficiency through reducing costs.

(b) Changing the superbranches to investment centres will focus attention on both the profitability and capital employed in each superbranch. This contrasts with the previous situation, in which the branches were treated as cost centres. The new approach to performance measurement means that the management of each unit will be able to take decisions which commit resources, knowing that the performance of the unit will be measured in terms of profitability.

Managers will have a greater degree of freedom and authority to undertake projects which are expected to meet the organisation's performance criteria. This autonomy is likely to increase the motivation and experience of the managers, as it will be possible to operate with a degree of independence. In addition, it will enable the senior management to compare the performance of each superbranch and this may encourage improved performance through generating interbranch competition. In the longer term, it may be possible to 'float off ' parts of the Bank into specialist sections. It is even possible that independent sections might be sub-contracted to other organisations.

A possible disadvantage of using profitability to measure performance is that the managers may concentrate on activities which will show improved performance only in the short run. This will mean that the targets for the current year may be achieved at the expense of the longer term growth and progress of the organisation. An example of this problem is the reduction in advertising expenditure in order to improve the profit in a particular accounting period. However, this will have a detrimental effect on future business. In addition, concentrating only on projects which do not use large amounts of capital may result in the rejection of capital-intensive projects, because they do not meet the immediate criterion of profitability targets.

Another possible problem area is the lack of experience within the Bank of the use of profitability as a measure of performance. Inappropriate targets may be set and this may affect the managers' motivation and behaviour.

(c) (i) In order to assess the performance of each branch, reports will be required by the branch managers, the superbranch managers and the senior management of Lindleys plc. To supply the relevant information, both annual and monthly reports will be needed.

Although it is possible that residual income will eventually be used, it is proposed initially to introduce return on capital employed. With either of these performance measures, the managers should be provided with regular reports to provide information about the profit generated by each branch, the amount invested by each branch and details of other important factors. These might include the number of new accounts opened. The reports should provide information to both the superbranch managers and the senior management within the Bank. This will enable appropriate action to be taken and allow for comparison of the performance of the different superbranches.

The annual budget should include both details of the expected revenue from the different activities of the Bank and a forecast of the total expenses. The staff costs will represent a high proportion of the total costs and so details of both staffing numbers and costs will need to be made explicit in the report. The capital investment budget will be the other aspect of profitability that will need to be included in the annual budget reports.

The monthly reports will contain details of the revenues, expenses and details of staffing for the current month and also for the year to date. Finally, both the profit of the superbranch and the return on investment will be shown to ensure that each manager is aware of the performance of each superbranch.

Details of the level of sales of holiday insurance and similar financial products will be needed regularly, possibly weekly. However, as a high proportion of the expenses of each branch will be relatively 'fixed', a monthly report is likely to be adequate for the purpose of controlling these expenses. Since travel costs, advertising and entertainment are likely to be substantial, the management will need to monitor the monthly details of these expenses.

Details of new accounts opened, existing accounts closed and complaints about the service offered in a branch will need to be presented to the management regularly. It is possible that bi-monthly reports will be sufficient to monitor these aspects of each branch's performance.

Finally, the managers will need ad hoc reports to provide information about the profitability of different categories of customer, services or products offered by the bank.

(ii) There are a number of non-financial areas which should be monitored continuously by the managers of the superbranches. These include the qualitative performance indicators for:

- staffing levels;
- the number of new customer accounts opened;
- the quality of service offered to customers, especially in comparison with the service provided by the bank's competitors.

Since the number of staff employed is a major expense of a bank, it is essential that this is monitored. However, length of service, experience, and training are qualitative indicators that should be available to the management in respect of individual staff members. In particular, the level of staff competence in information technology is an area which should be monitored, as the retail bank's operations use computers extensively.

In order to monitor the Bank's growth, details should be provided of the number of new customers. This information, if provided on a regular basis, will reflect the growth of the business. Details of the different types of customer will be an important aspect in monitoring the success of the activities to attract new customers and in assessing the needs of the public.

As the Bank aims to offer an 'efficient, but low-cost service', it is vital that the management is aware of the customers' opinions regarding the quality of service offered to them. This information may be difficult to measure accurately, but some possible qualitative measures are queuing and waiting times in branches, the number of mistakes in customers' accounts and the number of complaints lodged by the public. In addition, surveys could be organised regularly to measure the reactions of the Bank's customers. A matter that should be of major concern to the management of the Bank is the nature and frequency of complaints that are received from the public. This information should be recorded to indicate the areas which need to be improved. This type of indicator will be crucial in a period of cost-cutting to ensure that the customers are not dissatisfied with the changes.

Another area which should be considered by the management of each superbranch is the activities of competitors. Within the Bank it will be possible to compare the performance of each superbranch. This information will be relatively easy to obtain and will allow the performances of the superbranches to be compared. However, it will be necessary to take into account differences between superbranches in terms of the profile of their customers and the nature of their services. Although the performance of other banks is difficult to measure, appropriate measures should be devised in order to assess the relative performance of Lindleys plc.

This qualitative information will be important in the planning and management of both the individual branches and the superbranch. In fact, qualitative data will provide information regarding the staff, the growth of the business and the levels of customer satisfaction. This is essential information for monitoring performance and for developing strategic plans.

(d) Since the stakeholders will be affected by the changes, it is advisable to obtain their views. The opinions of employees, customers and shareholders should be considered in order to assess their likely reactions to the proposed changes in the Bank's organisation.

The participation of the staff will be extremely helpful in the reorganisation. It is clear that there will be redundancies as a result of the changed structure. The arrangements for reducing the number of staff will be a problem and it is advisable that the changes should be undertaken with the participation of the staff representatives.

The customers should not be inconvenienced by the change. However, it seems likely that there will be less personal contact with the bank manager. Emphasis should be placed on the improvements to customer service that will result from the change. It is essential that the Bank provides the service and advice that is required by the customers and this information should be obtained in order to ensure that the requirements of the customers are not forgotten in the search for increased profitability.

If the profitability increases, it is the shareholders who will benefit most from the reorganisation. Although it does not seem appropriate to increase their expectations until the success of the new arrangement is known, it would be advisable to obtain their opinions about the changed character of the Bank.

☑ Solution 23

(a) In preparing a corporate appraisal of the company, the strengths, weaknesses, opportunities and threats of the company should be analysed so that both the internal and external factors are taken into account in the development of C's strategic plan.

Strengths

C is an established company that has a strong financial track record. It is, therefore, likely that it has an experienced team of managers and also resources that will enable it to grow. C has successfully survived a major recession and this should give its stakeholders greater confidence. It is likely that C's success has resulted from the resources that it has developed and retained. Also, C has a strong reputation as a company that has undertaken major contracts and it is acknowledged to be a company that produces work of a high quality.

Weaknesses

C has specialised in only one activity, namely building roads. The company has been engaged as a sub-contractor to construct a road on behalf of an Eastlandian development company. However, another development company, D, has gone into receivership recently. If this were to happen to the company that is using C as a sub-contractor, it would create major problems for C. It is therefore essential that C monitor the financial position of any businesses with which it is associated.

At the present time, there is the possibility that C will lose significant amounts on the current contract to construct a major road in Eastlandia. The losses could arise through either the foreign exchange position or possible penalty payments being incurred as a result of the later completion of the project. The failure of the supplier to provide high-quality materials will have damaged C's reputation in Eastlandia. As 40 per cent of C's order book could relate to Eastlandia, the problems in that country could have a significant impact on C.

Opportunities

The lack of confidence in civil engineering contractors benefits C, which has a good reputation in Eastlandia. This means that C has a competitive advantage as it is reputed to produce work that is of a high quality of workmanship. This is particularly important, as some of the other contractors have been responsible for constructions that have collapsed. The invitation to tender received by C is a confirmation of the good reputation that C has established in Eastlandia. C could use its good reputation to diversify into other related areas of civil engineering.

(b) *Threats.* C, as a sub-contractor to the Eastlandian development company, faces a number of different threats as a result of its involvement in the road-building project in Eastlandia. The economic recession, particularly in Eastlandia, may pose serious problems for C.

The government is likely to reduce the levels of spending on the country's infrastructure and so the number of building contracts available will be reduced. This will probably result in the postponement of civil engineering projects in Eastlandia. However, as Eastlandia could represent 40 per cent of C's order book, the effect of the recession could be a major setback for C. The problem is compounded by the decline in economic activity in C's overseas markets and this is likely to reduce the company's growth and profitability. Although C is established as a high-quality contractor in Eastlandia, it is important that other markets be developed in order to diversify the risks of recession in any one country.

As a foreign contractor, C may face a problem if preference is given to local companies. This situation could be remedied by entering into a strategic alliance that would ensure that C was not excluded on the basis of being a foreign contractor. There would, however, be other problems in the management of strategic alliances.

At the present time, C is a sub-contractor to an Eastlandian development company. It is possible that this organisation could get into financial trouble and this could have serious repercussions for C. Another company has already failed and so it is important that C's management take steps to safeguard its position in the event of the development company experiencing difficulties. In future, C must ensure the viability of all companies with which it becomes associated. The delay in the progress payments should be investigated immediately. It is possible that the development company is in difficulties already and assistance should be offered to ensure that the contract does not continue if the position is already impossible to save. At a relatively early stage, it may be possible to reschedule the payments and institute a plan that can be managed effectively. It is imperative that action be taken immediately to make sure that the position is not allowed to drift until it is beyond rescue.

The contract work in Eastlandia represents 10 per cent of C's turnover, which is a high proportion of its total business. Any difficulties there could create problems for C worldwide. It is, therefore, important that C takes steps to ensure that it is not associated with problem companies as this could create financial difficulties for C and also affect its reputation worldwide. It is important that C's management review the other contracts that they have in the region to ensure that the problems experienced with this contract are not repeated.

As it is now expected the contract will be completed 3 months late, it is likely that C will be liable to pay penalties. It is essential that C's management undertake a thorough investigation of the causes of the delays and take steps to ensure that the project is completed as soon as possible. It would seem to be sensible to inform the other parties involved in the contract that it could be completed 3 months late. Once this information is disclosed to the public, it is possible that the share price will be affected as a result of the increased possibility of losses on the Eastlandia contract.

The weaknesses of the Eastlandian currency will adversely affect the financial performance of the companies working there. Also, as C is a sub-contractor to an Eastlandian development company, this could cause major problems if the development company were to 'get into difficulties'. The expected fall in the value of Eastlands will have an impact on C's profitability. It was expected that the rate of exchange would be 7.26 to the £ in the current year and 7.54 to the £ next year. However, the rate of exchange is now 7.74 to the £ and the forward rate being quoted is 8.56 to the £. This represents a decrease of 6.6 per cent in the current year and 13.5 per cent next year. These reductions in the value of local currency represent a threat to C's future profitability. A detailed investigation into C's foreign currency exposures should be prepared and hedging techniques used to minimise the effects of devaluation of Eastlands.

The growing importance of Eastlandia as an area in which C has major contracts must be taken into consideration in developing its strategic plan. The country is facing an economic downturn and it may be wise for C's management to identify other markets that may offer better opportunities. The most important strategic decision is the extent to which C should commit itself to working in Eastlandia. It is possible that more business should be obtained in other countries. This may ensure C's long-term survival even if it reduces its profitability in the immediate future.

(c) The demand for C's services will depend on many factors. Both external and internal sources of information should be used to assist in predicting future demand.

External information

The external forces should provide indicators of the general economic climate and particularly the amount to be spent by the government on infrastructure projects. This information should be monitored and data could be obtained from a variety of different sources. These include the publications of trade associations and professional bodies that publish economic surveys to help businesses that operate overseas. In addition, many banks and the International Monetary Fund publish reports that provide information about the economic conditions in different countries. These reports may provide the management of C with useful information about the likely level of investment in capital projects in different countries. Also, there are external databases and local and national government statistics that may include relevant information. Finally, it is possible that benchmarking with competitors may be a useful method of obtaining external information.

Particular areas that should be monitored are:

- The monetary policies to be adopted by the government, particularly in respect of interest rates, will have an effect on the number of civil engineering projects that will be undertaken especially by C's non-government customers. It is likely that government statistics will be published so that it will be possible to forecast the level of economic activity within Eastlandia. In particular, the budgeted spending by the government on capital projects would be very significant.
- The building plans passed would enable C's management to assess their success in gaining contracts against the competitors. This information could be used to predict the number of contracts that C might obtain in the future. This information may be available in economic surveys that are produced for both trade and economic journals.
- The political stability of the countries should be considered before any decision is made regarding an expansion into a foreign country. The political risk faced by a company that is involved in business overseas can range from excessive bureaucracy to the extreme situation of confiscated assets in the country. This is a matter that is very difficult to assess but information should be obtained to include an assessment of the political risks into the decision.
- It is important that C monitors the activities of its competitors both in Eastlandia and in other parts of the world. This will indicate their success and also give an indication of the overall demand for the type of work in which they specialise.

Internal information

The internal sources of information that could be used are the previous histories of clients, including customer account profitability, the past records of their preferences and also their record of payment. The trends in terms of the order book, size of orders and sales volume is another area that would provide useful information. Also, the analysis of the competitors' turnover and profitability especially in respect of their activities in foreign environments would be a useful area to investigate. The experiences of suppliers overseas is another area that should be investigated as it may provide an insight into the problems that are faced in foreign countries. Finally the effectiveness of the tender process and procedures should be researched and the success rate in the foreign environment reviewed.

The information regarding both clients and trends within the industry should be studied continuously. This will provide information regarding the trends of the market and the competition that C is facing, particularly in Eastlandia, one of C's major markets.

At a different level, it is important that information is gathered regarding the payment of records of organisations that are likely to place orders with C. In future, it is essential that C exercises good credit control. Also, the reputation and performance of major suppliers should be monitored to ensure that C can be certain that only quality suppliers are used.

(d) By entering into a strategic alliance with an Eastlandian civil engineering contractor, C will acquire local knowledge and experience. The strategic alliance will enable C to obtain benefits relatively quickly and this will place the expanded company in a position to benefit when the economy improves. It is possible that the benefits arising from the strategic alliance will be obtained at a lower cost than if either company had to obtain the knowledge and experience alone.

It is important that C choose its partner carefully. Ideally the local company should have a good reputation especially in respect to quality. Also, the management should understand the customs and protocols of operating in Eastlandia. A sound knowledge of current developments in Eastlandia and local legislation especially in respect of civil engineering would be a major benefit to C. Also a good relationship with the government would be useful as many of the contracts will be initiated by government agencies.

As a result of the depressed economic conditions in Eastlandia, some of the existing developers have failed to survive. However, if C establishes a strategic alliance at the present time, it would be in a better position when the economy recovers. By combining with a local company, both parties will benefit from the arrangement.

By obtaining local knowledge, it is possible that C will be able to reduce the risks of default by a developer. The failure of a developer could cause considerable financial losses to C and so any means of preventing this could be very worthwhile. Alternatively, the local company could gain from being able to obtain advice and technology from C. This might be in a number of areas, but C's reputation as a quality contractor might be in an area that would prove very useful to the local developers. There are currently problems with accidents as a result of poor-quality construction and this could be an area where the advice from C's management might benefit the local developer.

In seeking a strategic alliance, C's management must be creative and find a partner that will complement C's strengths or reduce its weaknesses. However, it is important that the arrangements of the alliance are studied carefully. C's management must consider some practical issues. These include the financing arrangements to be used to ensure that the resources needed by the alliance are available. It is also necessary to discuss how the alliance will be managed, especially in terms of the decisions and controls of the alliance. In particular, the procedures should be agreed to deal with the problems that would arise if the local company experiences financial difficulties. These are all issues that must be discussed and agreed before the strategic alliance is finalised.

✅ Solution 24

(a) The different sources of information that will be required to monitor the quality of bread are:

1. *Customers*. The perception of customers is the most important aspect in assessing the quality of any product. JTK Ltd has had adverse publicity twice within the last 20 years and therefore needs to monitor this aspect continually. Customers tend to have long memories and it can take a great deal of time and effort to rebuild perceptions of a quality image.

   Information should be obtained direct from customers by way of questionnaires or surveys, and this should be done on a regular and continuous basis. This will enable the quality satisfaction of customers to be assessed.

2. *Competitors*. Quality is really one aspect of the information assessed from competitors. If formal benchmarking techniques were in place, then quality would be one of several attributes assessed in comparing JTK Ltd with the rest of the market.

Having 15 per cent of the total bread demand, JTK Ltd should be something of a market leader and so it should be able to exercise some influence regarding standards within the market. It may well be in a position to instigate benchmarking with other firms. The information this would provide would enable an independent comparison to be made about JTK Ltd's quality performance and JTK Ltd would therefore be able to use this information to improve quality.

3. *Suppliers*. The final quality of any product is very heavily dependent on the components or raw materials that are used in production. The standards used by JTK Ltd are all based on internal measures and more information is therefore required on the quality of inputs from suppliers.

    Raw materials appear to be purchased on a casual basis when the economic order quantity indicates. There is no evidence of alternative suppliers, and information regarding quality of inputs, for example, in respect of the various types of flour, will be essential if quality is to be maintained.

4. *The quality control department (QCD)*. There are a number of problems with the operation of the QCD including hours of work, number of loaves sampled and the timing of the samples. Information from this department is therefore not as good as it could be.

    However, the QCD will be able to provide variance analysis that can be used to compare against the quality standards that JTK Ltd uses. The variances will tend to concentrate on output rather than input and reports will therefore be restricted to comments on the look and texture of the product. The QCD will also need to give assurances that legal requirements have been met in respect of the allowed additives. They will therefore need to be aware of the sources of current legislation.

5. *Information from production*. The QCD can also monitor production runs, that is, the amounts of materials used and overall control of batches of bread baked. This will be more in keeping with ensuring that overall costs of production can be measured, so that profitability as well as quality is maintained.

    Samples should be taken throughout the production run so that information is available for the whole production period. One of the most important aspects of quality is consistency, and it may well be that throughout this period standards could fall at different points if production is not consistently monitored. It should also be pointed out that having the information about quality is one thing, but JTK Ltd also needs to be able to take corrective action, that is, vary the input mix; the present production process would tend to indicate that this is not possible because all raw materials are combined in a set formula.

(b) *Introduction*. There are benefits that can be associated with closed systems, such as monitoring of inputs and evaluating outputs, and this can be important in respect of ensuring that legal requirements are met. JTK Ltd's system also provides for the purchasing of raw materials on a regular basis. Therefore, there is an element of control over the production process.

However, the system, like all closed systems, suffers from entropy, that is, through time the system has become less effective. It demonstrates a lack of flexibility, and the information emanating from it tends not to change rather than responding to dynamic or innovative requirements.

The major weaknesses are:

1. *Inflexibility*. JTK Ltd seems unwilling to change and the fact that the board members wish to continue as they have done for the last 20 years does not help.

The overall process seems old-fashioned as the flexibility to produce a variety of different types of bread in response to customer demand is missing. The system is certainly not responsive enough for today's economic conditions, which involve greater consumer awareness and discernment. If JTK Ltd cannot satisfy the very demanding requirements of today's consumer (and the current system does not appear able to do this), then its market share will fall and it will lose customers.

The system acts as a closed-loop feedback system and there are inherent weaknesses with such systems, including time delays before corrective action can be taken. The production process itself is also inflexible, and the ability to control it seems limited as inputs are combined in a set formula and the old machinery makes the quantity of input difficult to manage on a consistent basis.

The information coming to and from the system is extremely limited because the control loaves are taken from the start of a process, which suffers from entropy, and variances therefore will not show the full details of the complete production process.

2. *Internally focused.* The production process resembles a closed-loop system because it is almost totally internally focused. Organisations cannot operate in isolation of their environment, and therefore external information, for example, from customers, suppliers and competitors, is essential if meaningful quality control standards are to be applied.

3. *Supply – chain management (SCM).* JTK Ltd's procurement processes appear to be very casual. The EOQs have been unchanged for 15 years, there is no evidence of competitive tendering and stock levels are rising. There appears to be no control over ordering, and the consequences of increased stock are increases in wastage and deterioration. A proper SCM system, perhaps incorporating the just-in-time (JIT) philosophy, should be employed to ensure that the best-quality and value-for-money raw materials are available when required, rather than automatically purchasing the same materials for stockpiling in accordance with out-of-date measures.

4. *Production process.* The main inputs are transferred to production and then combined in a set formula to produce the bread. As the machinery is old it makes the inputs difficult to manage towards the end of the production run. The major weakness here is that no advanced production techniques are in place. This will result in variable quality and means that JTK Ltd will be unable to respond to any changes required. The management accountant wishes to invest in new systems and equipment to alleviate this weakness.

5. *Quality control.* Production will be in batches as it is not possible to bake 3 million loaves at a time. Therefore, each batch should be subject to quality inspection prior to the batch being placed in finished goods stock. Following on from acceptable quality inspection, the batch can be placed in finished goods ready for despatch.

This obviously has implications for the QCD as their hours of work are 12 noon to 10 p.m. The QCD must work the same hours as production so that quality checks can be carried out in parallel with the production runs.

Quality control should also be extended to include the testing of the quality of supplies, so that supplier quality performance can be monitored.

6. *Feedback.* The feedback from the QCD needs to be compared with JTK Ltd's company standards, but more importantly with external information, particularly customer satisfaction questionnaires. The overall isolation of the system from external information means that the company can become completely out of step

with market requirements. Comparisons should also be made with competitors' products, perhaps by an independent panel.

7. *Conclusion.* The current system is not suitable for today's needs and will be unable to cope with future demands. The need to be continually aware of environmental factors and the ability to respond in a dynamic way is of paramount importance to all businesses.

(c) Predicting future demand is always uncertain and care needs to be taken that future forecasts are not spuriously accurate just because they have probabilities assigned to various outcomes. The basic problem is making decisions under conditions of uncertainty, for example, the basic premise is that demand for cheap bread will decline while the demand for more natural and speciality breads will increase. The latter will invariably attract a price premium and the overall economic background needs to be considered in conjunction with these forecasts.

It is also difficult to use the forecast information that is available. The demand profile for cheap bread is inconsistent. There is a 10 per cent chance that demand may actually increase over the period although, with a 90 per cent chance of a decrease, it seems more likely that demand will decline, but by how much is almost anybody's guess.

The demand forecasts are for a 3-year period, which makes it difficult to see how probabilities can be assigned. A 1-year forecast can be reasonably accurate as it is relatively short term. However, if the product is dependent on weather conditions, for example, then this can add a further element of unpredictability.

Risk is the measure of the degree of uncertainty or the degree of probability of any particular outcome occurring. It is clear that the information provided by the market survey alone is insufficient for the decision now facing JTK Ltd and that, although risk is an inherent part of decision-making, it can be reduced by appropriate access to relevant information. This information should include: demographics, gross domestic product, socio-economic groupings of consumers, etc.

(d) Justification of expenditure on new equipment and computer systems would normally be subject to the standard management accounting investment appraisal techniques such as DCF, IRR and payback. These techniques depend on a number of critical success factors (CSFs) and the major ones are as follows:

1. *Return on investment.* The return on investment CSF needs to be controlled in order to ensure that wise investment decisions are made. Problems that may arise are in respect of isolating the effects of the investment decision from the return achieved from normal day-to-day operations. Performance indicators (PIs) that can be used are as follows, although in some situations these may also be CSFs in their own right:

- *Return on capital employed (ROCE).* At the group level, SF may be able to use ROCE as a PI, although this ratio can also be subject to other factors that go to make up the calculation. However, the success of JTK Ltd would be measured over the long-term achievement of ROCE, which is dependent on appropriate investments being made at the right time.
- *Internal rate of return (IRR).* At the subsidiary company level, JTK Ltd would be looking for projects of this nature to pass a hurdle rate of return based on the DCF of the project. Problems with this PI are in respect of estimating benefits. However, this type of evaluation gives a good indication of the success of the investment.

- *Cash flow.* Using the cash flow generated, for both group and subsidiary, is another PI for such an investment, and timescales, which are linked very closely with the pattern of costs and benefits, can also be considered here.

2. *Profitability and cash flows.* The overall objective will be to generate cash and profits from such investments, and these are measures that can be used to justify expenditure. The PIs are as follows:

   - *Annual profits and cash inflows.* At group level, overall annual profits and cash inflows of JTK Ltd will be some of the main PIs in achieving this CSF. The PIs will indicate whether the business is being run efficiently and whether correct investment decisions are being made. However, the problem here is that overall profits can be in respect of earlier decisions and cannot always be easily ascribed to a particular investment.

   - *Sales volumes and values.* Sales volumes and sales values are also PIs that can be used here to support the profitability CSF, although these are dependent on other factors, such as general market conditions, as well as decisions to invest, and so cannot be relied on exclusively. There are underlying assumptions about all investments at the time they are made, including the prospective behaviour of customers and competitors.

(e) Various messages may be displayed and staff may not take much notice of handwritten notes pinned to a board. It is uncertain and inconsistent and it cannot be determined with any certainty who exactly has seen the information. A noticeboard does not convey a professional image and will not, for example, instil the necessary discipline for staff to look at it at the start of each day.

- The nature of the note may be variable as it is difficult to enforce standards, that is some staff may take a great deal of time and show headings for categories of input, etc., whereas others may simply write down numbers in what they perceive to be a logical order, but which may not be readily apparent to others.

- During the course of a working period, there may be various emergency situations where staff are required to take immediate action and therefore they may not be able to spend time looking for the latest note among other material on a noticeboard. Similarly, they may not have time to produce updates for subsequent QCD staff who will need the information the following day.

- Another problem with manually prepared notes is that they may be illegible. Even if the note predominantly consists of numbers, these can be misinterpreted if not clearly written.

Computerised bulletin boards

- When QCD staff log on to their terminals, the system can send a prompt to remind them to look at the bulletin board for the latest update. The system could actually display this as the first screen following log on. This would be particularly apt if all QCD staff were required to input to a time-recording system, so that they had to log on and off at the beginning and end of each day worked.

- A computerised bulletin board can facilitate standardisation as screen-based 'forms' can be completed so that information is always presented in a straightforward way.

- The bulletin board system can be linked to any other systems that the QCD staff may need to use so that, following input to one system, they are again prompted to go to the bulletin board and update it. Alternatively, the systems can be automatically linked so that the inputs are taken directly into the standard 'forms' within the bulletin board.

- As the information is displayed on a terminal, not only will it be legible, but it is also ergonomically better as it will be presented in a standard way and the whole production situation can be assimilated much more quickly, especially if computer graphics are used.

 Solution 25

Part (a) Information System Alpha
Costs – Tangible

- *Hardware and software in Regional Court.* A full review of the hardware and software currently in use at each court will have to be undertaken (although some of the information should be available from the asset register). Hardware and software listing will then need comparing against the new system hardware and software specification. The difference between the existing system and the required system will provide the actual hardware and software spend in each court. Some courts will have a significantly higher spend than others because they are using manual as compared with computer-based processing.

- *Remainder of Systems Development Life Cycle (SDLC) for new system including implementation of new system and system changeover and training.* Finding the hardware and software to be purchased is only one part of the overall systems change that will be necessary in each court. Additional costs will also be incurred from planning for the actual systems change, including transfer of files, training of users and actual implementation of the new system. Given the size of the project, the Court Service may wish to involve a consulting company to review the change and present a generic solution that can be applied to any court location. This will be a cheaper option than each court planning for implementation separately and therefore duplicating many of the transition costs.

- *New MIS.* Both options assume that a new MIS will be required in the court. Implementing the new MIS will involve the cost of a full analysis of what it is supposed to do, and then the programming, implementation and training to ensure that staff know how to use the system.

Costs – Intangible

- *Information out of date by up to one week.* Using System Alpha, the court information systems will only be updated each week via CDROM. This means that information will always be out of date by anything from a few hours to one week. Although this may not be an issue, there may still be situations where information is needed urgently, for example, the decision in a recent court case, and this information will not be on the computer. There is a tangible cost involved in sending that information separately to the regional court. There is also an intangible cost in that an incorrect decision may be made on a case. At the extreme, this will result in a trial being started again, with a consequent loss of funds to the Court Service.

- *Possible delays in receiving new information via the postal service.* Placing the CDs in the post may provide a relatively quick transfer medium. However, CDs may still be lost or delayed in the post, so it will be appropriate to use some form of registered post to confirm delivery. Then intangible costs of losing a CD include the delay in having accurate information at the individual court and the possibility that sensitive data is obtained by unauthorised individuals. Disclosure of the information could be embarrassing for the government and Court Service.

- *CD damaged in post.* A CD may also be damaged in the postal system. Although the CD will be safely received at the court, there will be an additional delay while a replacement is obtained. Information at the individual court will therefore become even more out of date.

Benefits

- *Introduction of common systems across Court Service.* At present, each court has its own individual system; although this does not appear to have been a problem, it does mean that common training programmes cannot be implemented and that staff cannot work in different courts without having to learn a new system. Implementing a common system will allow for common training and staff transferability, which will in turn decrease the overall costs of running the Court Service.
- *Decision congruence.* The present IT configuration means that courts are using different IT systems, so they will have different information systems with different standards and timeliness of information on each system. Implementing a common system will help to ensure the same information in a common format in all courts. This will help to ensure that decisions made in each court are based on the same information; the decisions themselves should therefore be the same.
- *Better information from the new MIS.* In most courts, the new MIS will provide enhanced decision-making abilities. This will help staff in all courts make better decisions.
- *Future system updates easier.* As all courts are now working from the same system, future upgrades to the entire system will be easier. There will be no need to worry about having to plan for a separate upgrade in each court.

   Individual courts retain some independence in decision-making, and they are therefore more likely to accept new systems. Staff tend to work better when they can have some control of the data that they are using or have input into the system. Information System Alpha helps provide that autonomy by having most systems controlled from the local court.

Information System Beta
Costs – Tangible

- *Hardware and software.* A review of hardware and software will be needed in a similar way to System Alpha. However, additional costs will be involved in System Beta of the networking hardware and software and dial-in access to the main server at the court's head office.

   Additional hardware will also be needed at head office to provide for the central file server and communication links to the individual courts.
- *Remainder of the SDLC, as for System Alpha.* The SDLC will also need completing, as for System Alpha. An additional cost will be establishing a central data processing and distribution department at the head office. This may involve additional hardware and software costs, as noted above, as well as staffing costs for new programmers, IT support and information specialists to input the court data into the system.
- *New MIS, as for System Alpha.* A new MIS will also be required, as for System Alpha. There will be an additional complication in that some of the information for the MIS will be held centrally. This may involve an additional cost of having the MIS online to

the head office, at least during office hours. Additional software may also be needed to manage the split location of the data.

Costs – Intangible

- *Split of responsibility for data.* Data for each court will now be stored in two different locations: the local court and the head office main server. This may lead to friction and conflict between the head office and individual courts because there will be no overall responsibility for the data. The result will be a lack of goal congruence as each location maintains the data that it requires rather than meeting the overall data requirement of the company.
- *Possible breach of security using telephone lines to transfer information.* Transferring information over the standard telephone system does not necessarily provide a secure transmission medium. It is possible that the data can be intercepted and copied without the knowledge of the Court Service. Publishing sensitive data may result in bad publicity for the Court Service as well as prejudicing the outcome of cases in progress.

Benefits

- *Quicker update of material than System Alpha.* This system provides for a quicker update of information than System Alpha or the current system. This means that decisions can always be made on the most recent information, which minimises the risk of incorrect decisions being made.
- *Share common database between all courts.* A common database will be shared between all the courts. This will help all courts make similar decisions because the information they are using is the same.

Part (b)

(i) Critical Success Factors (CSFs) and Performance Indicators (PIs) provide an important method of monitoring an organisation, no matter what activity or funding method the organisation uses.

Income and expenditure must still be monitored in absolute money terms, therefore some method of ensuring that income and expenditure are within acceptable limits is needed. CSFs and PIs may be used initially to set the budgets for income and expenditure; determining what the organisation wants to achieve in terms of CSFs and PIs in turn identifies the level of income required and the expenditure necessary to meet those CSFs. Although monitoring of income and expenditure is a normal budgetary activity, additional CSFs and PIs may be linked to this monitoring, such as the need to obtain roughly equal amounts of income each month or propose only a given quality of equipment or service.

There is a need to check the quality of service being offered by the court. Although the Court Service, in common with many government-funded organisations, receives income in the form of grants rather than direct sales, this does not mean that the Service is not accountable for that income. Setting appropriate CSFs and PIs is a key method of showing that an appropriate service has been provided by the non-profit-making organisation. This in turn justifies the actual funding given to that organisation. This monitoring will be further enhanced if comparative information from similar organisations is also available. In this case, an individual court could show how efficient it was compared with other courts in the same country or in different countries.

The Court Service is still accountable to government, and people either using or paying for that service must therefore see that a good service or 'value for money' is being provided. The provision of appropriate CSFs and PIs will provide that assurance.

Any non-profit-making organisation, including the Court Service, must be seen to be giving good value for money to other third parties or government organisations, which may otherwise complain of unfair treatment. Setting appropriate CSFs will help to show that government funding has been appropriately spent and so provide justification both for the existing level of expenditure and the continued funding of the organisation.

(ii) CSF 1: To ensure efficient distribution and use of public resources that the government commits to courts. This CSF is focused on trying to ensure that the Court Service is making efficient use of government funds. PIs will therefore be looking to the use of those funds in both absolute and relative terms.

- *Amount of money devolved to each court compared with population served, number of cases heard or successful prosecutions.* PIs can be calculated on a per capita basis and then compared year on year within the same court and between different courts to show how well each court is performing.

- *Amount spent per head on lighting, heating, etc. compared with similar institutions and offices.* The amount spent on utilities such as heating and lighting will vary according to the type of building. However, an indication of whether this expenditure is roughly correct can be obtained by comparing per capita figures between courts and between other office-based jobs.

- *Percentage of funding spent on salaries, administration, etc. compared with other courts, both in this country and in other countries.* Comparing the percentage of funding spent on different expenditure headings will enable areas of unusual expenditure to be identified for each court. Comparison in percentage terms will help remove the problem of comparing actual amounts when total funds for each court will differ. Unusual differences can be investigated and appropriate reasons obtained for any significant variances.

- *Absolute expenditure on court service compared with other countries.* It is likely that other countries have a similar court system. An overall idea of the efficiency of the system can therefore be obtained by comparing absolute and per capita expenditure with other countries.

CSF 2: To minimise the time for cases to be taken through the court system. From the point of view of the consumer, the main success factor will be how efficient the court service is regarding the length of time for a case to be resolved.

- *Average time for case to be taken through court system compared with other courts in the same county and courts in other countries.* This PI provides a comparative to show not only where the individual court is within the country's league table but also performance compared with other countries. If individual courts are taking a significantly longer time to process cases than other courts in the country then the reason for this can be investigated. Similarly, if all the courts in the country are taking longer than other countries to process cases then reasons for this can be obtained.

- *Mix of court cases by category and average time taken for each type of case.* One of the main reasons why the average time to process a case will be different is that one court may have a relatively high proportion of cases that always take a long time to resolve. Comparison of this information with similar times for other courts in this country and other countries will help to highlight these differences and may explain why an individual court appears to be less efficient. Similarly, differences in the type of case may be referred back to the police or other authorities to identify whether there is any particular bias in bringing these cases to a particular court.

- *Average time taken compared with expenditure per capita on each court.* Check for correlation between higher-expenditure courts and decrease in time taken for cases; there may be some correlation between the provision of more funding and a decrease in the time taken for cases to be resolved. If this is the case, then it provides a strong argument for increasing the funding to all courts.

Part (c)

Various data will have to be input to the revised Court Service information system (CSIF); this data will be used to provide the relevant output from the CSIF. The aim of the CSIF under either new system is to collate operational information for each court and provide summary information to each administrator. The outputs therefore depend on the requirements of the Court Administrator, which can be split into three main areas:

Court organisation schedules

- Staff availability, including judges and other court officials. This information will be required to ensure that the court has an appropriate number of staff to manage the caseload on each day.
- Availability of jurors. As each case is heard before a panel of jurors, the Court Administrator will need to ensure that a sufficient number of jurors are available to meet the caseload for each day. Information input to the CSIF may be the confirmed availability of jurors, as well as initial requests being sent to potential jurors to ask them to attend court on specific days.
- Trends in cases regarding time actually taken in court and court usage. This data is essential to track trends in the overall workload of the court. This strategic information will be used to provide a rough forecast of the number of judges, court officials and jurors required in the future.
- Detailed information from the police and other sources confirming cases that need to be heard on specific days. This information will be matched with detailed availability of judges, court officials and jurors to check that sufficient staff are available to meet the caseload.

  Other data that may be useful in determining trends in the number of cases to be heard in the longer term will include:

- Trends in population at national and regional level.
- Trends in crime from the police, again at a national and regional level.
- Scheduled closure of any courtroom for essential maintenance.

Fixed asset register

The administrator has to monitor the fixed assets owned by the court. Data required to provide effective monitoring will include:

- A list of all fixed assets owned by the court. This list will be used for audit purposes to ensure that all assets are still in the court. It will also be used to monitor the age of the assets and provide input into the budget for repair and replacement of those assets.
- Budgets for replacement of fixed assets and actual expenditure to date. This information will be used to establish the annual budget for fixed asset expenditure, and then to monitor the actual expenditure against budget for the year.

Salary information

Salary information is required because court staff are paid locally from each court from either information system.

- List of staff currently employed at the court, including amendments to the list as they arise. This information is needed to ensure that there is an accurate staff listing. If this information is not available then salaries may be paid to staff who no longer work for the court, and it will be difficult to determine which staff are available to run the court on specific days.

  Details of grade and salary rate for each member of staff. This information is required to ensure that staff are paid the correct amount each week or month. Amendments to grades and salaries will also be required to ensure that salaries change as required.

 Solution 26

(a) The board response is likely to have the following costs and benefits:

Tangible

Costs

New CAD/CAM system will have to be purchased, so there will be hardware and software budgets to agree and specifications to check. The latter will have to be reviewed to ensure that they meet the company requirements.

Bank loan and interest to pay for new hardware, software and working capital to pay suppliers on delivery of raw materials.

Redundancy costs will arise where the new CAD/CAM system results in fewer workers being employed. Alternatively, there may also be some retraining costs so that existing employees can use the new systems.

Producing and maintenance of Internet site. Even if this site is hosted outside KJ, there will be payments due to the Internet service provider. After initial set-up, the costs will focus on the running and updating of the site, and then the transfer of orders to KJ so that these can be included in the manufacturing system.

Benefits

Savings in staff costs (reduced workforce) will occur in the longer run; in the short term there will be some redundancy costs.

Savings on working capital costs (no finished good stocks to store) will result as long as garments can be made to order.

Savings on obsolete stock because all stock made to order. Stocks of unwanted garments should be limited to returns where the customer does not like the garment. Setting up some form of second-hand selling system for these garments could be appropriate.

Savings in raw material stock because all stocks made to order so no obsolete raw materials stock.

Increased contribution from sales because no wholesalers involved in selling goods.

Possible one-off income from equipment sales although this is unlikely to be significant given relative rapid technological change that can occur.

Intangible

Costs

More difficult to obtain customer feedback on goods. As goods are made to order then presumably customers will like those items. Feedback is likely to be negative and focus on features like production quality and delivery time.

Possibility of returns that cannot be sold (already bespoke order for customer's preference). The cost here is the manufacturing cost that cannot be covered as part of a sale. However, there will be other intangible costs if repeat orders are lost because customers were unhappy with the purchasing experience from KJ.

Sales staff may not like loss of direct contact with wholesalers/customers and this may result in loss of sales due to lack of personal contact.

Similarly, charging for a paper version of the catalogue may result in lost sales where customers do not want to pay for the catalogue.

Benefits

Improved service to customers because customers are receiving exactly the garments that they required. Furthermore, those garments are made for each customer individually rather than have to purchase a mass-produced item – the customer should be more 'proud' of the garment and want to keep it.

Competitive advantage will result if no other competitor is using this system. Any advantage is unlikely to be long term, because if the system works then other firms will establish similar systems; if the system doesn't work then KJ may not be in business very much longer. Either option will lose the competitive advantage!

More effective and efficient decision-making from new tier of management because they have better and more up-to-date information.

The implementation of the new system should have a positive effect on morale because staff will be learning how to use more up-to-date technology and be happy to work for a more forward-looking company.

Better and more up-to-date management information on actual sales.

(b) (i)

Advantages of in-house writing

Meeting system requirements – because Internet site written with company requirements in mind. Off-the-shelf systems start from the abilities of the software as written, not the requirements of the company.

Updated easily for the company's specific information and requirements. Off-the-shelf systems may not be able to accommodate changes so easily.

Advantages of third-party writing

Cheaper to purchase and produce. Bespoke system will require additional programming effort.

More experience available regarding programmers to write the site. Supplier may be able to recommend appropriate programmers. Although some knowledge will be available from similar systems (e.g. AMAZON), use of the site in this way may still be unique and provide challenging programming activities.

Staff training and manuals available from supplier. By definition a new site, hence no manuals – must write from scratch.

May be easier to maintain – less reliance on original programming staff. Writing own system means that good system manuals must be produced and that ongoing support and upgrade for new Internet features may be more difficult to incorporate into the system.

(ii) Items to include in the maintenance agreement with the ISP include:

- Guarantees on how quickly the Internet site will become available again should hardware or software at the ISP fail. As KJ will be receiving most of its orders over the Internet, having the site unavailable will result in lost sales.
- The cost of providing the service compared with the service level provided. There is likely to be a trade-off between cost and the level of service, and KJ may need to choose a comparatively expensive ISP to obtain an acceptable level of service.
- Ease of update and transfer of information to KJ regarding sales orders received. Orders will need to be transferred on a regular basis to ensure that they are included in the production planning at KJ as soon as possible.
- Guarantee site and software availability for x number of years. Having chosen the ISP, it is unlikely that KJ would want to move again in the short term. Although the Internet domain name could be moved to a different ISP, this would involve more time and effort for KJ and so would not be cost-effective in the short term.
- Back-up and maintenance arrangements are essential; KJ would need assurances that appropriate back-up is taken and that preventative maintenance is used to ensure that the ISP service is maintained at a high level.

(c) Impacts on society will include:

- Customers increasingly design their own products rather than taking what is available in the shop. This may decrease demand for retail shops and increase demand for Internet access and use.
- More personalised goods, a trend away from standard designs. If this does become a fashion trend, then manufacturers of standard designs will find demand falling for their products. Additional investment in CAD/CAM systems may therefore be necessary to maintain market share.
- Increased need to learn about new products and technology for customers to order via the Internet and sales staff to understand how CAD/CAM works and what is available.
- Increased reliance on the Internet and non-personal communication systems decreases social interaction. People will not need to go out so frequently to shop, and so social interaction at this level will fall. However, an increase in leisure time may result in more sport being played, so offsetting this trend.

☑ Solution 27

(a) A phased approach: more suitable than a 'big bang' approach.
The more direct 'big bang' approach generally represents the highest risk, as at a pre-determined point in time the old system ceases to operate completely. Using this approach, there is no opportunity to validate the new system's output with the old, so management must have complete confidence in the new system. As the software in question appears to be something of an industry standard, there is likely to be some general confidence in it. However, there appears to be something of a mismatch between the system and corresponding processes, which could prove a difficulty.

The phased approach involves gradual implementation possibly involving one sub-system at a time. This might involve implementing the system by first converting the customer accounts subsystem then the reporting subsystem and so on. This offers distinct advantages in this particular case:

- Staff are likely to be suffering 'change fatigue' from previous initiatives and can only endure so much upheaval while continuing to function effectively.
- The continued support of the partners as project sponsors is important and they are likely to see 'deliverables' sooner with a phased roll-out.
- The phased approach is less risky given that the project manager could be unavailable to oversee the change.
- The project management risk (heightened by the absence of the project manager) will be reduced as issues found in small-scale use of the new system can be remedied in time for wider software roll-out.

(b) Options to overcome the software not fitting the existing business process exactly. Change will be required as a result of the mismatch between the software and the existing business process. There appear to be two distinct options:

Option 1, Change the software or
Option 2, Change the business process.

The choice should be made taking account of all relevant costs and benefits and might be made using suitable evaluation criteria such as suitability, acceptability and feasibility (or similar).

The applications software is designed to perform specific financial functions of the business. It is essentially an 'off the shelf rather than a bespoke solution but could conceivably be adapted. Such an adaptation could be financially costly. There is also a need to identify the necessary expertise to carry out this software development and the company may need to employ outside source for the purpose.

Changing the business process represents yet another change initiative that staff may respond to negatively. As competitors and peers are using the software already, it is reasonable to assume that it will encapsulate industry best practice. These organisations apparently operate in that way that is consistent with the software. This implies that S&C may operate in an inconsistent and possibly inefficient fashion.

(c) The ways in which particular individuals and groups within S&C are important for implementation to succeed.

- *Partners*. Support from the top is crucial. They must visibly support the implementation.
- *Users*. Successful user acceptance and must buy-in is also key, as they are the main recipients of the change. Meaningful communication is necessary, also participation to get commitment through joint analysis of issues to engender feelings of 'ownership'.
- *The users' managers*. These managers will be called upon to help ensure that disruptions are kept to a minimum during and immediately after changeover. Communication and involvement again is necessary (albeit to a different degree to users).
- *Project manager*. Effective project management is crucial which ensures that S&C's corporate performance does not fail. The project manager has been absent with illness and matters cannot be allowed to 'drift'. If the illness is long term, a replacement project manager needs to be appointed swiftly.
- *HR department*. If system success depends on people behaving in certain ways (e.g. sharing information across departments and taking greater responsibility), reward

systems may need to be adjusted possibly including new incentives, metrics and evaluation criteria. Effective training programmes will also be needed. Formal policies and structures may also need adjustment.

- *Project steering group.* Need to address the real sources of resistance to change and means of overcoming them. Proposals are also needed in order to successfully align financial systems and business processes (it is important that some members of the group are available in the weeks after going live to answer questions and give support to users).

(d) Aims of a post-implementation review.

Post-implementation review should be carried out as soon as the system is fully operational, in order to assess the effectiveness of the system, adjustments that may be required and lessons that can be learnt for the future. This should take place possibly between 1 month and no longer than 1 year after changeover is completed. The findings and recommendations from the post-implementation review should be formally reported on.

The specific aims of the review will include:

- Whether the system satisfies user needs.
- How the actual costs and benefit of the system compare with what was anticipated.
- Making recommendations for improvement (if necessary).
- Determining the quality of systems of change and project management.
- Making recommendations that will help shape future management of implementation and change initiatives where necessary.

(e) The training topics to targeted groups within S&C.

The nature and content of training will inevitably need to be tailored to the needs of the relevant groups, for example:

- *Partners.* General overview of the system and its benefits possibly through executive training seminars.
- *Users.* Instilling detailed user knowledge on how to operate the new system. Specific detailed applications training (including procedures, commands and data-entry requirements).
- *Users' managers.* Giving an understanding of the elements of the system for which they are responsible, including particular business issues and security and control features related to a particular system. Possibly general training in basic computer literacy and user skills.

The sort of training provision might include:

- Seminars and workshops and so on.
- User manuals, 'help lines' and dedicated support teams.
- Online computer-based support.
- On-the-job training while staff are actively using the new system.
- Quality circles and discussion forums for users to address problem areas.
- Short demonstrations and the use of DVD/ Video media support.
- Updates as users become familiar with the system and require further knowledge and skills development or consolidation of existing knowledge and skills.

This can be provided:

- in-house;
- outsourced to specialists; or
- some combination.

(f) Users involvement in testing the system during the implementation phase.

As mentioned earlier, user acceptance is vital. It is also important to test the system during the implementation phase. It is a good idea to combine these two requirements.

Users might be usefully involved in a number of ways and could be used to:

- Act as guinea pigs for any system developments through testing in association with the new procedures and processes.
- Contribute to quality circles and discussion forums.
- Assess the effectiveness of training programmes, and so on and provide feedback.
- Provide mutual mentoring/assistance 'buddying' to other new users of the system.
- Collect data on the costs and benefits of the overall business change, not just the software application.
- Be involved and act as advocates of change to colleagues.

✔ Solution 28

(a) Positive initiatives

A number of positive initiatives could be adopted by R&L. In the first instance, R&L should review staff turnover rates that presently exist and determine how much of the 50% can be achieved through natural wastage. They should also be able to project from HR records those who will reach retirement age within the next year.

As a next step, R&L should then put an embargo on further employment and seek to fill vital posts short term through inter-company transfers of staff. They should also stop any overtime and seek to spread excess work to other underutilised employees.

R&L will need to consider and discuss possible alternatives with the relevant trade unions or staff representatives such as:

- Contracting out non-core functions (e.g. IT) and try to negotiate a transfer of staff to the outsourcing firm.
- Encouraging those over retirement age to leave.
- Job-sharing (between two or more people?).
- A shorter working week.

The important thing is that any initiative is adopted in conjunction with employee groups (e.g. trade unions) rather than being imposed.

(b) Kotter and Schlesinger (1979) identify six main strategies for dealing with resistance. This might usefully serve as a framework for discussion:

1. Education and communication is particularly useful when the basic problem is lack of information about the need for, or the nature of, the planned change. The approach can be very time-consuming and will not work by itself, if there are other reasons than misunderstanding leading to resistance to change. Such a strategy would seem to be appropriate in this case. As a good employer, R&L is honour bound to present all known facts on the plight of the company and discuss options openly and straightforwardly. A suitable strategy.

2. Participation and involvement increases the chances of commitment to implementing the change particularly if their views are taken into account. This method is particularly appropriate when the people affected by the change have considerable power to resist it. This approach can be time-consuming, but such a strategy would

seem to be appropriate in this case. Whatever positive measure is chosen, participation is vital to ensuring its success. The change is more acceptable, if it is done by you rather than to you! A highly suitable strategy.

3. Facilitation and support involves training, counselling and discussions, designed to reduce anxiety. This is particularly appropriate where the principal reason for resistance is based on insecurity and adjustment problems. Such a strategy would seem to be appropriate in this case; indeed the suggestion of outplacement is an embodiment of this strategy. A highly suitable strategy.

4. Negotiation and agreement may be necessary to compensate those losing out because of the change. This may help avoid major problems, but it can be expensive in terms of, for example, redundancy packages. If there is little goodwill between the parties it may be protracted and bruising. Such a strategy would seem to be appropriate in this case, as R&L is a good employer there may be genuine goodwill between the management side and the trade unions. A suitable strategy.

5. Manipulation and co-optation involves presenting partial or misleading information to those resisting change and 'buying off' key players. This is a quick and relatively inexpensive approach, but normally results in future problems if the people involved realise they have been manipulated. Such a strategy would be inconsistent with R&L's philosophy of being a 'good employer'. An unsuitable strategy.

6. Explicit/implicit coercion involves the use of force, or the threat of force, to enforce the implementation of change. It raises ethical (and potentially legal) problems as well as involving considerable risk of making a situation more difficult, especially if trade unions are in a position to provide opposition and protection. Such a strategy would be inconsistent with R&L's philosophy of being a 'good employer'. An unsuitable strategy.

(c) Delayering, downsizing and outsourcing all normally have the effect of reducing staff numbers:

'Delayering' is a term used when an organisation removes layers of the workforce from the structure. If an organisation has a hierarchical way of operating with lots of management layers, then there is ample scope to reduce staff numbers in this way. The effect would probably be to get rid of middle management posts, which would leave the structure flatter and significantly closer in touch with customers and their needs.

Downsizing normally occurs when an organisation decides that it can operate with fewer staff numbers overall. This might be a decision unforced by a takeover and unlike delaying may not have the effect of flattening the organisational hierarchy.

Outsourcing by comparison occurs when an organisation decides that instead of providing central ancillary or central services for themselves it is cheaper or makes more sense to get outside contractors to perform that service for them. It follows, therefore, that outsourcing might contribute to downsizing.

R&L is well known as a 'good employer' but is faced with the dilemma that the downturn in sales is permanent and that it needs to reduce its workforce by 50 % over the next year in order to survive. It is likely that each of the three alternative staff reduction strategies might be considered.

1. *Delayering*. R&L might decide the structure and staff mix that it needs in the future and this may involve removal of surplus layers of workers, possibly middle managers.

2. *Outsourcing*. Contracting out non-manufacturing activities (e.g. finance, information management facilities, catering and, cleaning) will certainly reduce its workforce nearer the target of 50%. The effects, however, may not be to reduce cost by the same proportion, and replacement consultant provided services will still have costs attached. In practice, outsourcing might be transfer costs from R&L's payroll to consultancy fees.

3. *Downsizing*. This will be the dominant action with a likely shedding of staff in all areas: including production. The reason is that the downturn is permanent and R&L now have overcapacity for the potential demand.

☑ Solution 29

(a) Likely role HR will perform in the light of the changing nature of the organisation.

- *Company background*. The company appears to be 'traditionally' structured with four divisions and a small HQ staff. The signals for change include a re-branding of personnel to human resources. The retirement of the long-serving head of this function is also of significance. This implies that a traditional well-established way of operating in the past is not required in the future. The fact the HR strategy is in 'urgent need' of review and revision underlines this point.

- *An HR rather than personnel role*. Personnel management is seen as focusing on day-to-day 'people-related' issues. In the past, NS's small specialist personnel support function would undoubtedly have attempted to ensure consistency and fairness of treatment throughout the organisation. Personnel management is seen as ensuring compliance with organisational procedures as well as reacting and responding to external environmental changes (including employment legislation and labour market conditions). The changes taking place at NS mean that the function will have different objectives more easily identified as human resource management (HRM).

- *A strategic role*. The new function would be expected to view employees in a different, more strategic way. A reasonable revised focus would be upon the long-term development of human resources in such a way as to deliver the strategic aspirations of the company (i.e. to achieve continuous improvement). The specialist HR Division should provide support to Divisional Directors and other managers in order to meet detailed organisational objectives.

  The new HR function would be expected to have key inputs into the strategic deliberations that are apparently underway including the setting of clear objectives. The HR Division will now be expected to shape and deliver strategies.

- *A training needs role*. NS's new corporate initiative of continuous improvement through empowerment is of major significance for the HR Division. Under the initiative, people are seen as crucial, exercising skills of thinking, challenging, innovating and implementing. The function will need to ensure that the workforce have these skills.

  Empowerment involves passing power downwards for staff 'closer to the action' to be responsible for making decisions and initiating actions. This involves a high degree of trust in the workforce and less directive, authoritarian control from management. This new management style means that Departmental Directors and managers will need to be encouraged by the function to make this change.

- *A role in cultural shaping*. NS's initiative of an empowered workforce normally involves a major organisational cultural change. There is no evidence from the scenario as to how this is to be brought about other than an apparent rethink of the role of specialist personnel function. The HR function will be crucial in affecting the necessary cultural change and the new Head might be expected to perform a change agent's role.

- *A role in championing corporate initiatives*. In an empowered organisation, people are active in solving problems, looking for better ways of working, and co-operating freely with others in and across teams. Continuous improvement is a collective approach towards improving performance throughout the organisation. Clearly, the HR function will need to champion and support these developments.

(b) Aspects of HR strategy showing significant change, given the nature of recent developments.

Given the changing nature of the organisation and the initiatives being progressed, attention should be given to the following aspects of the HR strategy:

- *Structure and job roles*. The overall structure should be configured in order that individuals are developed to their full potential and encouraged to do 'things right' (what needs to be done in organisational terms), not merely 'the right things' (what job descriptions require of them). The strategy will need to articulate the structure, control and functioning of the organisation. Layers of management that add no value or that damage empowerment should be eliminated as part of a systematic review.

- *Job content*. Job content will also need to be reviewed and then be articulated in overall terms in the strategy. This review could conveniently follow on from the structural review identified earlier and might feature broader spans of managerial control. This should in turn encourage managers to delegate and trust subordinates to exercise their increased autonomy and power effectively.

- *Education and training*. Education and training in empowerment and continuous improvement will be vital components of the strategy. This might be achieved by facilitating workshops and ongoing support mechanisms such as mentors, buddying systems and/or counsellors. Changes to role requires training at all levels, particularly senior management, where individuals will need to be persuaded to relinquish power. For 'front line' staff, mechanisms for training and building self-confidence are vital. This will undoubtedly involve enhancing existing skills and the identification of new skill requirements.

  It is good practice to undertake a training needs analysis of the workforce and shape the strategy accordingly. Specific likely skills will include problem-solving, data-gathering techniques, teambuilding, listening and customer care. Teams of people will need to be built that co-operate and support one another in continuously improving customer service and improving efficiency.

  Senior managers may need training in facilitation and leadership skills. It is vital that senior managers (whose role should include setting the 'right' examples) provide consistent messages and behaviour.

  The strategy will need to articulate how this is delivered (whether in-house by trainers, externally, or by the use of existing managers). Systems for monitoring the effectiveness of these 'interventions' will also need to be articulated in the strategy.

- *Reward systems*. These systems represent the ways in which staff are recognised and rewarded for their endeavours. A revised strategy must ensure that such systems are consistent with, and encourage, the identified concepts of empowerment and continuous improvement. The HR function in conjunction with senior managers will need to agree behaviour patterns required in the future and ways of measuring outcomes. Those who actively support and embrace the twin concepts identified (of empowerment and continuous improvement) should be rewarded appropriately. Typical organisational rewards usually include pay, promotion and other rewards. Other rewards need not have financial implications and might, for instance, include still greater empowerment. It is a good idea to communicate these points widely and reward publicly, making role models and heroes of those who achieve. In this way, positive performance standards might be signaled.

This thinking should be embodied in the HR strategy.

- *Target setting and appraisals.* A mechanism for review and target setting will need to be considered in the strategy. Although this might already exist, major revisions to these targets will be needed in the light of organisational initiatives. New personal plans/targets/key performance indicators (KPIs) will need to be created for every manager and then cascaded down through subordinates and work groups so that the whole organisation's performance is assessed having regards to the twin initiatives. Reviews of performance after a few months by using small groups should highlight progress, problems and areas for adjustment. Once overall review mechanisms are established, annual appraisal and monthly target setting might reasonably be employed. Upward and 360 degree appraisal schemes might be considered in order to strengthen reflective practice.

- *Review mechanisms.* Revised review mechanisms should concentrate on monitoring progress on the initiatives and taking corrective action where necessary. This should be at the expense of previous forms of control, direction and reporting in order to drive decision-making down to the lowest level.

- *Communication systems.* Channels of official communication should be articulated in the strategy. The existing strategy may already do this, but the focus may need to be reorientated in the light of new corporate initiatives. A new emphasis should be placed upon encouraging open communication, sharing of information and honesty.

(c) Empowerment is a management technique whereby power and authority is delegated downwards within an organisation. The effect is that subordinates are trusted to work towards their managers' goals. This is obviously an enlightened and wholly sensible strategy to pursue so long as there is mutual trust, sufficient training and a supportive culture.

The fact that NS has recently announced a new corporate initiative based on empowerment underlines their commitment to it. There is clear evidence that the Chief Executive trusts the workforce and provides sufficient encouragement, specifically:

- People are apparently valued and regarded as NS's most prized asset.
- Staff are encouraged for them to think, challenge and innovate.
- Clear individual performance objectives are to be determined.
- Staff are no longer expected just to obey orders, instead they will make and implement decisions.

The fact that the Chief Executive sees this as bringing about continuous improvement is of relevance. He/She states quite clearly: 'Only through empowering them in this way can we achieve continuous improvement.' The process is meant to enable NS to become more customer focused.

Continuous improvement is closely linked with the process of TQM: Total Quality management. It is a philosophy to continually improve the quality of goods or services (in this case services), and hence performance and quality. TQM as a philosophy encourages and fosters continuous improvement throughout the whole organisation:

Total	Everyone linked to the organisation (staff, customers and suppliers) is involved in the process. The concept of viewing every business activity as process that can be improved is shared.
Quality	The requirements of customers are achieved.
Management	Senior managers must be fully committed to continuous improvement if all other parties are to help achieve it.

This all-inclusive approach including the consideration of quality from a customer perspective is entirely consistent with empowerment. (Some would go further and argue it is dependent upon it.) TQM encourages the full involvement of all people, at all levels, working within multidisciplinary teams to suggest and implement improvements from within the business. This corresponds with NS's philosophy on its workforce and their value.

The Chief Executive's standpoint that empowerment is the only route to continuous improvement appears well founded.

Exam Q & As

At the time of publication there are no exam Q & As available for the 2010 syllabus. However, the latest specimen exam papers are available on the CIMA website. Actual exam Q & As will be available free of charge to CIMA students on the CIMA website from summer 2010 onwards.

Index

Index